AN ARCHAEOLOGY OF NORTHERN IRELAND 1600–1650

ROWAN McLAUGHLIN & JAMES LYTTLETON

EDITORIAL CONSULTANT
BRIAN G. SCOTT

ACADEMIC ADVISOR
NICK BRANNON

PRODUCTION EDITOR
CHRISTINA O'REGAN

Published 2017 by Department for Communities

First Edition
First Impression

A catalogue record for this book is available from the British Library.

Design and Layout by April Sky Design / Colourpoint Books
an imprint of Colourpoint Creative Ltd
Colourpoint House, Jubilee Business Park
21 Jubilee Road, Newtownards, BT23 4YH
Tel: 028 9182 6339
Fax: 028 9182 1900
E-mail: info@colourpoint.co.uk
Web: www.colourpoint.co.uk

Printed by W&G Baird Ltd, Antrim

ISBN 978-1-5262-0612-1

Table of Contents

Foreword

Echoes of the Plantation period run deeply within the physical, political and cultural landscape we inhabit today. A more detailed understanding of this period will help to foster an inclusive, wider understanding of the Ulster-Scots language, heritage and culture in a way which will contribute towards building a strong and shared community. The events of the plantation period in the early 17th Century, whether in terms of the settlement of Scots in Antrim and Down from 1606 onwards by James Hamilton, Hugh Montgomery and later Randall MacDonnell; or the official government plantation from 1609 which encompassed the six counties of Armagh, Fermanagh, Tyrone, Cavan, Donegal and Coleraine, changed the face of Ulster.

The people who came from other parts of the British Isles, mostly from Scotland, gave Ulster an identity which is unique in these islands. The three strands of Ulster-Scots, Ulster-English and Ulster-Irish can be seen in terms of the language, heritage, traditions and even the names of people here.

It is important for everyone in Northern Ireland to have greater knowledge of the events and the legacy of this period, so that we can move forward in a way which respects the identity of everyone here, whether they are from established communities or those that are new to Northern Ireland.

This publication is the culmination of a project, commissioned by my Department, to research the local archaeology of the Plantation period. It brings together the results of a comprehensive survey of approximately 600 sites from that period and presents detailed descriptions of six exemplar sites, including three set piece research excavations at Monea Castle, Co. Fermanagh, Derrywoone Castle, Co. Tyrone, and Servants Hill outside Bangor, Co. Down. Through those excavations, along with open days and outreach events, the project gave school children and local communities the opportunity to experience archaeology hands-on. This book continues that theme of enabling public access to heritage.

It documents the period in an accessible style and is designed to be a resource both for the general reader and also for academics, researchers, policy makers and our education sector. I would encourage anyone with an interest in our shared history to make use of it.

This work compliments the other initiatives which my Department continues to develop in increasing the understanding and awareness of the Ulster-Scots identity across the entire community. It will help contribute to our sense of place and give us a better understanding of who we are and where we came from.

I thank all those who have played a part in bringing the project to fruition.

Paul Givan MLA
Minister for Communities

Acknowledgements

The authors are grateful for the assistance of the many individuals and organisations who contributed to the production of this volume. Foremost among them is Neil Macnab (AECOM), who co-ordinated the Ulster-Scots Archaeological Project and made many helpful comments on the text of this book. The field survey of some 600 sites was led by Andrew Copp (AECOM), assisted by David McIlreavy, Paul Duffy and Siobhán Ruddy (IAC Archaeology Ltd), while much of the initial literature research was undertaken by Thom Kerr. The field surveys were conducted across several weeks and the team are grateful to Conor Gormley and Colette Rynhart (IAC Archaeology Ltd) who were involved in the co-ordination of the surveys and organised accommodation for the team. Thanks are also due to Rob Lynch (IAC Archaeology Ltd) who has been involved in the delivery of this publication from the outset.

There are several individuals within the Department for Communities: Historic Environment Division (DfC:HED) without whose assistance and advice this book would not have been possible. They are: Paul Logue, John O'Keeffe, Terence Reeves-Smyth, John Murphy, Ken Neill, Gail Russell, Liam McQuillan and Emma McBride. We are especially grateful to Tony Corey and Gail Pollock (DfC:HED) for preparing the many Crown copyright plans and photographs used throughout the volume. We are also grateful to the individuals within DfC (formerly Department for Culture, Arts and Leisure) for their assistance throughout the project: Brian McTeggart, Arthur Scott, Anne Tohill, Richard Sproule, Stephanie Brotherston, Lucy Geddes, Ciara Shevlin and Gerry Kelly.

We are indebted to the following people for their advice and assistance with sources and illustrations: Colm Donnelly, Audrey Horning and Ivan Herbison (Queen's University Belfast), Audrey Gahan (Gahan and Long Ltd), Lianne Heaney (Northern Archaeological Consultancy Ltd), Brett Irwin (Public Records Office of Northern Ireland), Gary McCormick (Ards and North Down District Council), Isabel Bennett, Gavin Donaghy, Emma Hannah, and Eóin Parkinson.

Our editorial consultant, Brian G. Scott, undertook a herculean copy-editing task, which improved the manuscript immensely, we are also grateful for the many helpful suggestions he made throughout the process. Production of this volume was managed by Christina O'Regan (IAC Archaeology Ltd), to whom we extend our warmest thanks.

Special thanks are due to Nick Brannon. The layout of this book, which aims to retrace Pynnar's survey of 1619, was conceived by Nick. His expertise, assistance, good humour and encyclopaedic knowledge of the Plantation period have ensured the successful delivery of this publication.

Project Acknowledgements

This book is the culmination of four years' work collating all known data relating to the archaeology of the Plantation period in Northern Ireland. It has involved field surveys, excavations, community projects and extensive research. The project was a collaborative effort undertaken by AECOM, IAC Archaeology Ltd (IAC) and Northlight Heritage. Thanks are due to Annette Roe (AECOM) and Conor Gormley and Rob Lynch (IAC), who have been actively involved in the development of the project from the beginning and have provided unwavering support to their respective project team members.

Community engagement was an important aspect to the project and thanks are due to Heather James, Katy Firth, Aoife Gould and Ingrid Shearer (Northlight Heritage) for organising school visits and open days at the excavations, and to Maeve Tobin (IAC) for maintaining the dedicated blog, http://ulsterscotsarchaeologicalproject.blogspot.co.uk/.

Special thanks are due to Fintan Walsh (IAC) who directed and organised the three research excavations, as well as tirelessly leading troops of children and teachers on tours of the sites on a regular basis. He was assisted throughout by Christina O'Regan, Camilla Brännström, Stephen McLeod, Marie-Therese Barrett, Rowan McLaughlin, Tony Wilkinson, Lucy Chapman, Timo Wegner and Agnieszka Dulkiewicz. We are also grateful to the landowners for permitting the excavations: The Bell family (Servants Hill), The Baronscourt Estate (Derrywoone Castle) and Arthur and Liz Cadden (Monea Castle). Several individuals volunteered their time on the excavations: Ken Pullin, Sandra Millsopp, Conor Murphy, Eirnin Lindsay, Joanne Jones, Kate Whalen, Michéal Murphy and Gordon Allard. Thanks are due to members of the Clogher Historical Society who volunteered their time at Monea Castle: Deborah Flack, Ann-Marie Rice, George Knight, Michael Watters, Plunket Mone, Laurence McKenna and Lulu Wojnar. Thanks are also due to members of the Cavanaleck Community Association who volunteered their time at Monea Castle.

The results of the excavations have been disseminated in the form of a General Reader text and thanks are due to Fintan Walsh and Christina O'Regan for compiling this document. An Education Pack, aimed at Key Stages 2 & 3, was also produced as part of the project. This was developed by Heather James, Fintan Walsh and Christina O'Regan and is used as a valuable teaching aid when discussing the history of the Ulster Scots. Special thanks are due to Gerry Kelly for his helpful comments throughout the evolution of the Education Pack.

In recognition of its success in cross-community engagement, the project received a high commendation at the 2016 British Archaeology Awards.

Neil Macnab (AECOM), Project Co-ordinator

List of Abbreviations

DfC	Department for Communities, formed in May 2016 from parts of the Department of Environment, Department of Culture, Arts and Leisure and Department for Social Development
DfC:HED	Department for Communities: Historic Environment Division
NA	National Archives
NISMR	Northern Ireland Sites and Monuments Record
NLI	National Library of Ireland
PRONI	Public Records Office of Northern Ireland
TCD	Trinity College Dublin
OS	Ordnance Survey

Chapter 1
Introduction

Background to the Project

This volume was commissioned by the former Department of Culture, Arts and Leisure in response to a need identified by the Ministerial Advisory Group for the Ulster Scots Academy (MAGUS). As part of its remit, MAGUS and the Department of Culture, Arts and Leisure funded the preparation and publication of this archaeological survey of plantation-period sites across the Province which date to between *c*. 1600 and 1650. The principle aims of the project have been to identify the contribution that the Scots made to the process of plantation, and the collation of archaeological sites and monuments related to their daily lives, settlements, traditions and culture. Sites associated with the Gaelic Irish and English populations are also included, as all three groups interacted with each other.

Research was carried out, using the Sites and Monuments Record held by the Department for Communities along with various historical, archaeological and literary sources, to identify early 17th-century sites. This was followed by visits to assess the current state and condition of sites, and to seek to clarify any issues outstanding over their interpretation. This facilitated the creation of the gazetteer which records some 600 sites across Northern Ireland.

In previously published county surveys, like those for Co. Armagh in 2009 and Co. Fermanagh in 2014, sites were arranged in chapters dealing with specific archaeological monuments such as megaliths, raths, mottes and castles. These in turn were listed in alphabetical order by the townland in which they were found. A different approach was taken to the compilation of this gazetteer, with the sites grouped according to the respective proportions or estates in which they lie, using the various government surveys that were carried out following the implementation of the Ulster Plantation, drawing on Nicholas Pynnar's detailed survey of 1618/19 in particular. The following chapters on Cos Antrim, Down, Fermanagh, Tyrone, Armagh and Londonderry contain an introduction to the nature of early 17th-century settlement in their respective counties, followed by the different proportions or estates that were granted out to the new landlords of Scottish, English or Irish origin in the various baronies. On some estates (as in the instance of the estate of Ocarragan in the barony of Mountjoy, or Roe in the barony of Dungannon in Co. Tyrone) there are no known archaeological sites that date to the plantation period. Also listed are 'other sites' that fell outside of the scope of Pynnar's survey, namely sites that were not situated on the plantation proportions or were situated on church lands, but which were still an integral part of the built environment of the time.

Fig. 1.1 Andrew Copp surveying Strangford Tower, Co. Down.

Background to the Ulster Plantation

The Elizabethan plantation schemes in east Ulster

While the Ulster Plantation scheme of 1610 saw the large scale appropriation of native lands and their planting with English and Scottish settlers, it was not the first attempt by the Crown to establish colonies there. As early as the 1570s English colonists were settled in present day Cos Antrim and Down in an effort to block the spread of the O'Neills, along with Scots from across the North Channel, into areas of eastern Ulster. There were concerns that Scotland, in league with the Gaelic Irish nobility and Continental powers, might use Ireland as a springboard from which to attack England. The death in 1567 of Shane O'Neill, head of the Tyrone lordship, provided an opportunity to deal with these undesirables but the Crown, not wanting to invest significant resources, called on private adventurers with their armed retinues to carve out territories for themselves, and in the process remove interloping Scots and undermine native landowners at the same time (Loeber 1991, 31).

This policy of colonisation by proxy was put into practice in 1571, when Sir Thomas Smith was granted the territory of the Clandeboye O'Neills on the Ards Peninsula. Despite two expeditions sent there in 1572 and 1574, the scheme petered out due to lack of support and because of the strong resistance encountered both from the native Irish and Old English (descendants of the original Anglo-Norman colonists) in the area. Permanent settlements did not materialise and it is unlikely that fortifications were constructed (Ellis 1985, 266–267; Loeber 1991, 31–32). Walter Devereux, the 1st earl of Essex, launched his own colonial expedition into eastern Ulster in August 1573 with the intention of conquering and colonising most of southern Co. Antrim (Ellis 1985, 267). Essex arrived in 1573 and commenced a military campaign aimed at dislodging the Scots already living there and thwarting further Scottish immigration. This culminated in 1575 in the slaughter of almost the entire population of some six hundred people on Rathlin Island, off the coast of Co. Antrim. A garrison was put in place there, as well as at Dunluce Castle on the mainland, while another was established on the Co. Armagh bank of the River Blackwater in 1573, to protect his western flank from attack by the O'Neill lordship.

Further to the south, Essex had also been granted extensive lands on the Lecale Peninsula in Co. Down, formerly in the hands of the earl of Kildare, who had failed to plant them (Ellis 1985, 267–268; Loeber 1991, 32–33). In 1575, the then Lord Deputy, Sir Henry Sidney, observed (Loeber 1991, 33) that these lands were waste,

> …but nowe on the mendinge Hand, and far the better since the Earl of Essex had it, and that by his Plantinge of Tenauntes, and Placinge of Soldiours; so that it doth verye well defende it selfe.

However, this was Essex' only success, as the garrisons on Rathlin Island and Dunluce had to be recalled through problems of supply, while the fort on the Blackwater river was attacked and overrun. The scheme failed to establish English farming communities supported by a network of towns and fortifications and, as a result, only Newry and Carrickfergus remained as English outposts in Gaelic Ulster (*ibid.* 33–34).

Since the dissolution in 1550–52 of the Cistercian monastery, the town of Newry in Co. Down was under the control of the Bagenal family, who maintained it as an important outpost. It was at the centre of a large estate that included Greencastle in the same county, and Carlingford in Co. Louth (*ibid.* 29). As early as 1575, the estate was described in glowing terms by Lord Deputy Sidney, with 'the towns so well planted with inhabitants, and increased in beauty and building' (*ibid.*). In the years following 1603, Newry was redeveloped and became a focal point for British settlers just like Belfast and Carrickfergus (Bardon 2012, 65). Carrickfergus itself was the centre of the Anglo-Norman earldom of Ulster, which had declined in the face of the Gaelic Resurgence in the 14th century. However, the town with its large castle remained in English hands throughout the Middle Ages and was to become a focal point for renewed colonial activity in the late 16th century.

Informal plantations in Ulster after the Nine Years' War

The conclusion of the Nine Years' War, following the Treaty of Mellifont in March 1603, created further opportunities for private plantations like that of Sir Thomas Smith in eastern Ulster. One of the most active colonisers was Sir Arthur Chichester, an army officer who had fought in the recent war. He went on to become a leading figure in the Dublin administration, eventually becoming the Lord Deputy, the king's chief representative in Ireland. In 1603 Chichester was granted the governorship of Carrickfergus, along with the lands in southern Co. Antrim originally granted to the earl of Essex in the 1570s, and his intention was to settle the region with army officers who had previously served with him. One of these was John Dalway who was granted an estate near Carrickfergus in 1608 (Loeber 1991, 63–64; Robinson 1984, 54) on the condition that he would build, within seven years,

> a castle or house of stone or brick, thirty feet long, and twenty broad at least, with a court or bawne about the same...

By 1611 he had erected a bawn with flankers (Inv. 35), the wall of the bawn being 15ft high, and inside it 'a pritie house of tymber after the English manner...' (Loeber 1991, 64). Another officer was Moses Hill, a former lieutenant in Chichester's horse troop who was leased Malone outside Belfast in 1611. Here he built a fort near the present Shaw's Bridge and a fortified house (Inv. 11) at Stranmillis (Bardon 2012, 64).

Belfast itself was just a small village at the time, a cluster of houses surrounding a ruined Clandeboye O'Neill castle on the banks of the Farset River where it entered the Lagan estuary. Its strategic location at the mouth of the Lagan, where a number of land routes met, was recognised by Chichester, who set about building a new town there. In 1605 he ordered the firing of a million bricks, and on the site of the ruined castle he erected a fine Jacobean mansion (*ibid.* 63). A survey of Belfast in 1611 reported that Chichester had settled the town with people from England, Scotland and the Isle of Man, who had built 'good tymber houses w(i)th chimneys after the fashion of the English palle…' (Loeber 1991, 63). Chichester also developed Carrickfergus, attracting immigrants from his native Devon to settle there. Their houses were to be built in the English fashion of 'brick and lime, or stone and lime, or of cage-work, well tiled or slated, with handsome lights well glazed' (*ibid.* 63). Between 1609 and 1615 Chichester oversaw the walling of Carrickfergus, enclosing an area about twice the size of the original medieval town, and in 1610 built a second mansion for himself within the new walls, naming it 'Joymount'.

In 1605 a significant proportion of the lands originally granted to Sir Thomas Smith, namely the Great Ards territory of north-eastern Co. Down, was parcelled out by James I/VI (king of England and Scotland) to two Scottish gentlemen from Ayrshire – Sir Hugh Montgomery and Sir James Hamilton. Both encouraged Scottish and English immigrants to settle on their estates. Montgomery's lands were located around Comber, Newtownards and Greyabbey at the head of Strangford Lough, while the Hamilton estate was situated along the southern shore of Belfast Lough, from Holywood to Bangor and Groomsport (Robinson 1984, 52–53). The results of this informal plantation were impressive, with towns developing at Holywood, Bangor and Newtownards. By 1611 Hamilton had built a 'fayre stone house' in Bangor, with the new town containing eighty houses with Scottish and English occupants (Loeber 1991, 65). Even though this area remained outside the scope of the Ulster Plantation, it was to become the most intensively settled during the first half of the 17th century (Robinson 1984, 53).

In north Co. Antrim Sir Randal MacDonnell, a younger son of Sorley Boy MacDonnell, was granted the territory of Route and the Glens in 1603, which included lands that he had taken from the MacQuillans of the Route (Bardon 2012, 80). In the following year, a renewal of the same grant contained a clause stipulating that his large estate (totalling almost 340,000 acres) was to be divided into precincts or manors, each containing 2000 acres at least, with 500 acres set aside for demesne lands surrounding a castle or strong house. These new residences were to be built within seven years in places where local courts administered by seneschals could be held. While no mention was made specifically of settling British tenants, this clause served as a template for the allocation of estates in the Ulster Plantation a few years later (Robinson 1984, 52; Bardon 2012, 81). Sir Randal leased land to native farmers, as well as invited Lowland Scots to settle on his vast estate, and attempted also to introduce modern agricultural practices keeping in line with the contemporary notion of the improving landlord. One of the MacDonnell strongholds, Dunluce Castle, was also restored and a new town was established beside it (Loeber 1991, 64).

Elsewhere in Ulster there was some pre-plantation activity: by the end of the war Sir Henry Docwra, the governor of Loughfoyle, had established a new settlement at Derry, building a house for himself, as well as a timber church and buildings for his tenants. However, no land was assigned to support the fledgling town, which was burnt down during the revolt of Cahir O'Doherty in 1608. It was only later under the ownership of the London Companies that its future became more firmly secured (Moody 1939, 123–132; Loeber 1991, 60). Another settlement was founded in 1604–05 by Sir Thomas Phillips at Coleraine Abbey, where an earlier fort had been built in 1584 by Christopher Carleill. By 1609 Phillips claimed that he had spent £1,000 on the settlement, as well as an additional £400 on fortifications and £150 on building a water mill (*ibid.* 45 and 61).

The Ulster Plantation

The defeat of the Gaelic political and social order, and the conclusion of the Nine Years' War in 1603, followed by the flight of the earls of Tyrone and Tyrconnell in 1607 and the rebellion of Sir Cahir O'Doherty in 1608, cleared the way for plantation across Ulster. Excluding Cos Down, Antrim and Monaghan, where arrangements were already advanced with planters and natives, the scheme finally agreed allowed for the division of the six remaining Ulster counties into precincts or baronies. The baronies, in turn, were divided into 'proportions' of 1,000, 1,500 and 2,000 acres of profitable land, each allocation to the new owners also having a proportionate assignment of wasteland and bog. These new owners were to be divided into three categories, undertakers, servitors and loyal native grantees (Curl 1986, 23). The scheme in Ulster, the most extensive of all plantation schemes in Ireland, was innovative on two counts. First, servitors (army officers or officials who had a record of service to the Crown) were now allowed to play a major role, such as had been denied to them in the previous Munster Plantation. The second innovation was designed to overcome financial difficulties faced in establishing model settlements by 'persuading' London merchant companies to assume responsibility for planting one whole county and to erect fortified towns at both Coleraine and Derry (Curl 1986, 29–30 and 2015, 24; Canny 2001, 199).

The first category of landowners were the undertakers (either English or Scottish). These were landed gentlemen of considerable means, who promised to undertake the construction of defensible buildings on their estates, to remove native occupants from their properties by a designated date, and to resettle their lands only with English and Scottish tenants. Unlike the earlier plantations, serious consideration was given to the defences of the new colony. Undertakers would be responsible for constructing stone or brick houses

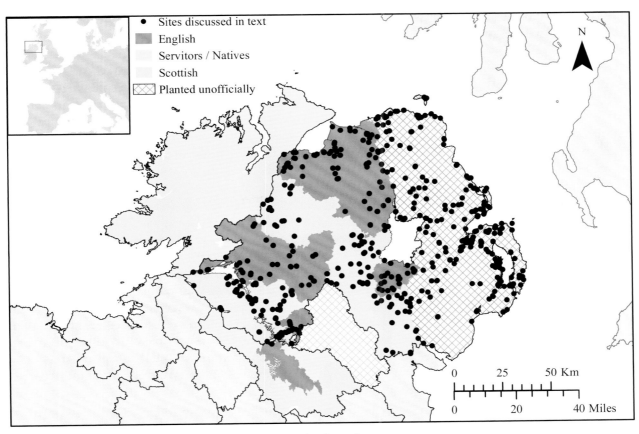

Fig. 1.2 Map showing lands granted to English, Scottish and Irish servitors.

surrounded by bawns (Canny 1987, 164 and 2001, 200–201), and for maintaining suitable stores of arms for local defence, while their tenants were to build houses near the bawn for security, and for the establishment of nucleated settlements. No land was to be leased to any natives or anyone who had not taken the Oath of Supremacy. All of the obligations concerning building, planting and residence were to be fulfilled within five years on pain of forfeiting £200 per 1,000 acres granted, though as the scheme slowly progressed, this stringent timetable for completion had to be relaxed (Robinson 1984, 64–65).

The second category of planter consisted of servitors, mostly of English origin, who had served the Crown in a civil or military role. They were also obliged to build defensive buildings on their new estates and were encouraged – but unlike the undertakers, not obliged – to settle English and Scottish tenants on their properties. However, depending on the nationality of their tenants, after two years the servitors were to pay a yearly rent of £8 per 1,000 acres if their tenants were Irish, or £5 6s 8d per 1,000 acres if British. It was assumed that most of these servitors would be former army officers and that many of their tenants would be former soldiers. They were therefore to be assigned lands in key strategic areas (Robinson 1984, 64; Canny 1987, 164–165 and 2001, 201).

The third category comprised native landowners who could lay claim to previous landowner or freehold status in Ulster, and who were considered deserving either by the Crown or the Dublin administration. They also faced the same building obligations, and were to assign their property by lease to tenants who were expected to be natives as well. They were also to promote 'tillage and husbandry after the manner of the English Pale' (Canny 1987, 165 and 2001, 201). These native grantees were to be removed from the lands that they had traditionally occupied, and assigned estates elsewhere in the Province where they would be separated from their traditional support. In addition, these properties were to be close either to the garrisons that were to be retained in Ulster for the foreseeable future, or to the proportions of those servitors whose special function in the Plantation was to fulfil the role of a garrison without pay (Canny 2001, 203).

All grantees in the Ulster Plantation were to pay stipulated annual rents to the Crown, and undertakers and servitors were obliged to take the Oath of Supremacy, to take up residence by a certain date, and were permitted to dispose of their lands solely to other Protestants. There were no such religious stipulations binding native grantees, but they were required to hold their lands by knight-service tenure, rather than by free and common socage, as was the case with the undertakers and the servitors. This implied that the heirs of the initial grantees would have to take the Oath of Supremacy before the Crown would pass their title of inheritance. The final element of the Plantation was put in place when the entire county of Coleraine, along with a Tyrone barony and nine Antrim townlands in the vicinity of the town of Coleraine, were placed in the possession of the London Companies, creating the new 'County of Londonderry'. The Companies agreed to plant the entire area according to the obligations of undertakers, and also to establish fortified port towns at Derry and Coleraine (Moody 1939, 122–123; Canny 1987, 165–67 and 2001, 201).

An important consideration for the planners was that provision was also to be made for the Anglican Church, so that the propagation of religious reform, which had been neglected up to that point, would have a fresh start. Those lands and ecclesiastical rights which had traditionally belonged to the Church in Ulster were identified before any settlers took up occupancy of their lands. It was stipulated that each proportion should become a parish, and that every such parish should receive 60 acres for every 1,000 acres of plantation land to provide glebe land for its rector, who would also benefit from tithes derived from agricultural produce. Further property was identified for the support of a grammar school in each of the six counties, and of Trinity College, Dublin, which was expected to supply the necessary clergy. It was believed that this would provide a solid basis for the reformation of the native population once the proclamations against the Catholic clergy were enforced, and the native grantees were compelled to attend Protestant service (Robinson 1984, 64; Curl 1986, 24; Canny 2001, 202–203).

Four official surveys were undertaken in the years immediately after the establishment of the Plantation. Lord Carew conducted the first in 1611, followed by Sir Josias Bodley in 1613 and 1616 (though of the latter, only some fragments remain), by Captain Nicholas Pynnar in 1618–19, and finally by a government commission in 1622. These were designed to record not only colonist numbers, but also the level of building taking place on the newly planted estates. By 1619 Pynnar was able to report the construction of

> 107 castles with bawns, 19 castles without bawns, 42 bawns without castles or houses, 1,897 dwelling houses of stone and timber, after the English manner (Robinson 1984, 129).

A pictorial survey of the Londonderry settlement by Thomas Raven, working alongside the 1622 commissioners, depicted in great detail the nature and layout of the new plantation villages in that county. English-style timber-framed and stone houses, along with Irish-style cabins, were situated in the environs of fortified manor houses, the latter protected by bawns with corner flankers. Older medieval churches were also re-used on a number of estates. As with the earlier Munster Plantation, the Ulster scheme saw problems with many of the original undertakers failing to endure as planters. Only twenty-nine out of the fifty-one original assignments to English undertakers remained in the hands of original grantees or their heirs by 1619, and only twenty-six out of the fifty-nine Scottish undertaker families were still on the ground in Ulster by the same date. There was also a failure on the part of those remaining to attract the requisite numbers

Fig. 1.3 Raven's map of Bangor.

of British settlers to their estates, and a tendency to retain native tenants in defiance of government policy (Curl 1986, 25; Canny 2001, 210). This reality was recognised in 1621 when undertakers were allowed to apportion one-quarter of their estates to natives, preserving the required number of British settlers in the remaining three-quarters. Settlers, like those a generation previously in Munster, had minds of their own, and were not prepared to move to poor-quality farmland, or to be persuaded to remain in locations far from ports or navigable rivers (Canny 2001, 210).

The Commissioners of 1622, who were responsible for reporting on all Irish plantations, while able to praise aspects of the work in Ulster, arrived at negative conclusions. They complained repeatedly of the extent to which the counties remained under native cultural and economic influences, and were also critical of many planters who failed to fulfil even minimal building and tenanting obligations. They despaired greatly of the general failure to proceed towards the reform of the native population in religion and civility, which was the ultimate justification of the scheme in the first place. According to them, despite careful planning and a high level of expenditure, the plantation that emerged in Ulster was not qualitatively different from what had been accomplished through more casual efforts in eastern Ulster or in other parts of Ireland. To this extent the Commissioners concluded that the ideological justification, to reform the native population to cultivation and civility, had been compromised (Canny 2001, 240–241).

However, despite the negative tone of their conclusions, the notion that the policy of plantation was wrong was never countenanced, and the quest to remedy what had proven insufficient continued to preoccupy officials who remained committed to the general strategy of making Ireland conform to accepted English norms (*ibid.* 242). Indeed, it has been estimated that a total adult British population of 12,079 had taken up residence in Ulster before 1622. Spread over a decade, this was substantial by the standards of most European migrations to colonial destinations in the early modern period, and becomes even more so when consideration is taken of the more than 7,000 Scottish adults who moved into Cos Antrim and Down during the same period (*ibid.* 211). Across Ulster there was now established a network of towns and villages surrounded by farms, all populated by people of Scottish, English and Gaelic Irish origins. The sweeping away of the old Gaelic political order had brought about significant changes in the material environment with new styles of houses, more diverse consumer goods, and the adoption of English-style clothes. More fundamentally, there was a re-ordering of the countryside with fields now beginning to be surrounded by permanent hedgerows. This process of field enclosure began to create a landscape different to that depicted by Elizabethan map-makers. The new political order was beginning to establish a degree of permanency, with one of the architects of the Ulster Plantation, Sir John Davies, hoping that the Gaelic Irish population in 'the next generation would in tongue and heart and every way else become English so as there will be no difference or distinction but the Irish sea between us' (Canny 1988, 38). However, a generation later, a combination of economic hardship, religious dissension and political instability created circumstances under which the whole scheme nearly came to nought with a major rising led by a number of Gaelic Irish landowners in Ulster that broke out in the late autumn of 1641.

The Ulster Rebellion of 1641

Many of the native landowners had not coped well with the new market-based economy that emerged in the aftermath of the Ulster Plantation. Much of their land was mortgaged off to maintain solvency, with the result that English and Scottish landlords still continued to acquire land through the 1620s and 1630s at the expense of the Gaelic aristocracy. For example, in Co. Armagh, the amount of land held by Gaelic Irish landlords fell from 25% in 1610 to around 19% in 1640 (Gillespie 2006, 140). Poor harvests in 1638 and 1639 created immediate hardship for the bulk of the population and exacerbated local tensions between natives and newcomers. Political and religious dissension was also stoked by developments in Britain. The Bishops' Wars in Scotland in the late 1630s demonstrated the value of extra-parliamentary activity in forcing concessions, while the rise of a parliament in London dominated by Puritans aroused Catholic fears of religious repression.

Matters came to a head when there was a rising of the Ulster Irish on 23 October 1641. Following an abortive attempt to seize Dublin Castle, a number of prominent Gaelic Irish landlords in Ulster, led by Sir Phelim O'Neill, attacked and took over a number of forts and castles in Ulster. O'Neill took Charlemont Fort in Co. Armagh, while the O'Hanlons took Tandragee in the same county, the O'Quinns seized Mountjoy Castle in Co. Tyrone, and the Magenisses and MacCartans occupied Newry (Gillespie 2006, 142). This signalled a more widespread rising that saw most of the plantation settlements attacked with settler families being stripped of their properties and their goods. In symbolic fashion many were stripped of their clothes and forced out into the cold weather of winter. By the end of November 1641, the Rebellion had spread westwards into Connaught and southwards into the Pale and Leinster, and early the following year it reached Munster, causing widespread disruption in the country.

While many settlers died during the course of these attacks, events like the massacre of Protestants in

Portadown gave rise to exaggerated accounts of the mass slaughter of settlers. Estimates at the time varied between 150,000 and 300,000, numbers which were used as propaganda to attract support from Scotland and England. A more realistic figure was given by Sir William Petty in 1672 who reckoned that 37,000 had died (Gillespie 2006, 144). The Scots responded with the mustering of an army under the command of General Monro which was dispatched to Ulster in the spring of 1642. One consequence of the arrival of this army was that Presbyterianism became established on a more formal footing in Ulster with the foundation of the first presbytery in Carrickfergus by his soldiers (Gillespie 2006, 164). At the same time, the English Parliament passed the Adventurers' Act that allowed for funding to be raised from London merchants who would be repaid grants of Irish land following the cessation of hostilities (*ibid.* 154 and 159). A meeting on the Hill of Tara in Co. Meath in December 1641 saw the Old English of the Pale join in with the Gaelic Irish of Ulster. The Catholic gentry in Ireland, both Gaelic Irish and Old English, were becoming concerned that events were spinning out of control, with the commoner sort indulging in looting and violence, and that there was a need to reassert their control. A Catholic Confederation was established in October 1642, with a Supreme Council and General Assembly based in Kilkenny City.

By the end of 1642, the conflicts had evolved into a civil war which was to continue for another ten years. Low-level warfare was marked periodically by significant engagements such as battles at Kilrush, Co. Kildare and Liscarroll, Co. Cork in 1642, and Clones, Co. Monaghan in 1643, although these did little to alter the status quo. Much of what was happening in Ireland was taking place against the background of the Civil War in England and political instability in Scotland. Consequently a number of different factions arose, each vying for military superiority, but constrained by limited financial and logistical resources. There were Catholics under the leadership of the Papal Nuncio Giovanni Battista Rinuccini and supported by the military leader General Owen Roe O'Neill, who wanted a complete restoration of Catholic rights and all lands lost previously. Other Catholics came largely under the leadership of the Old English gentry who sought a rapprochement with the Crown in return for the maintenance of current rights. The Scottish settlers wanted not only to protect and restore the Plantation and punish the rebels, but also to advance the cause of Presbyterianism in Ireland. The Solemn League and Covenant, an agreement reached between the English parliament and the Scots in September 1643, was exported to Ulster where taking the Covenant or oath became one of the hallmarks of identifying oneself with Scottish Presbyterianism (Gillespie 2006, 163–164). Then there was the New English population, who followed developments in the English Civil War, but largely remained royalist in sentiment under the leadership of the earl of Ormond, the king's chief representative in Ireland. On occasion, figures within this community approached the English parliament for support in putting down the Irish insurrection.

While there was a cessation of hostilities in September 1643, and later the first Ormond peace agreement in March 1646, and second Ormond truce in January 1649, warfare continued between the different factions. There were significant battles at Benburb, Co. Tyrone in June 1646, and in the following year at Dungan's Hill, Co. Meath in August, and Knocknanuss, Co. Cork in November, along with the sacking of Cashel, Co. Tipperary in September (Gillespie 2006, 174). It was only with the conclusion of the Civil War in England and the subsequent execution of Charles I that the Parliament in London felt able to deal decisively with Ireland. In August 1649, Oliver Cromwell arrived with 12,000 troops, augmenting the existing 8,000 forces already in Ireland (Gillespie 2006, 177). Following a campaign that saw the surrender of a number of cities and towns to the Cromwellian army, most notably Drogheda and Wexford which were sacked following their capture, the Confederation collapsed and along with it hopes for the survival of a Catholic political order. Cromwell left Ireland in May 1650, leaving the rest of the campaign to his subordinate officers, while in December 1650 Ormond, along with other royalist leaders, departed from Ireland to join the royal court of Charles II in exile in France. The last Catholic positions, including Clough Oughter Castle in Co. Cavan, held out until 1653.

Contemporary sources tell of the damage wrought upon the English and Scottish settlements in the province. One of these is the Civil Survey of 1654–56, which detailed on a county-by-county, barony-by-barony basis, a list of estates confiscated and their owners. It contains information on the owners of properties in 1641 and at the time of the survey, the amount of land profitable and unprofitable, and whether a castle, a house, garden or a mill was present and in what condition. Of the six counties in present-day Northern Ireland, only the volumes for Cos Londonderry and Tyrone survive, revealing that many prominent buildings were in a ruinous condition having fallen victim to the troubles. However, they show also that the renewed confiscation of lands under the Cromwellian administration had increased the amount of land held by Scottish and English landowners at the expense of the Gaelic Irish gentry, consolidating the achievements of the Ulster Plantation and paving the way for further migration into Ulster.

Historical, architectural and archaeological sources on the Ulster Plantation

Introduction

Ireland experienced a series of colonial adventures through the Tudor period and into the reign of James I, part of which involved surveying and mapping lands of interest to government administrators, especially the Gaelic Irish lordships of Ulster that were hitherto relatively unknown. Special attention was paid to the territorial boundaries of these lordships and the smaller subdivisions within, as knowledge of such was prerequisite for the allocation of lands to undertakers when conquest and confiscation made the same available. Note was made of the quality of farmland, with the acreages for profitable and unprofitable land calculated, as well as proximity to natural resources such as woodlands and rivers. Some of the previous plantation projects in Ireland, such as the 1584 scheme in Munster, have been reasonably well documented, though that in Ulster stands out in particular due to the survival of a series of surveys or progress reports carried out on behalf of the Crown in the period 1611 to 1622. These also include a series of pictorial maps produced by Thomas Raven as part of the survey undertaken in 1622, depicting the appearance and layout of the various new towns and villages established by the London Companies in the newly created county of Londonderry. Thirty years later, following the Cromwellian Reconquest, the Province was the subject of two major surveys, the Civil Survey between 1654 and 1656, and the Down Survey between 1656 and 1658, each of which provided a detailed picture of landholding patterns in both planted and unplanted areas of Ulster. Such sources proved to be a boon for historical research with the publication of *An historical account of the plantation in Ulster* by Rev. George Hill in 1877 and *The Londonderry Plantation 1609-41* by Theodore William Moody in 1939. They were followed in later decades by scholars such as M. Perceval-Maxwell, Philip Robinson, James Stevens Curl, Raymond Gillespie and R.J. Hunter.

The surveys of the Ulster Plantation

Much of the work carried out on the gazetteer of archaeological sites drew on the government surveys compiled between 1611 and 1622 to review progress in the implementation of the Ulster scheme. The first was conducted in the summer of 1611, when Sir George Carew was dispatched by London. He had previously spent a number of years in Ireland as a soldier and administrator, and consequently was familiar with the country. At the end of July, he and his fellow commissioners left Dublin, travelling through Cos Down and Antrim which lay outside the Plantation. They then visited the port town of Derry, followed by Cos Donegal, Fermanagh, Tyrone and Armagh. By 5 September they had returned to Dublin. Given that the trip only lasted a month not every proportion could be covered, and its brevity meant that they did not have the opportunity to visit Co. Cavan. While Carew viewed some of the settlements personally, most of the information was derived from interviewing local officials (Perceval-Maxwell 1973, 124). This survey is presently kept in the Carew manuscripts now held by the Lambeth Palace Library in London, and a summary was published by the Rev. George Hill in 1877. The second survey was carried out in the spring of 1613 by Sir Josias Bodley, at the time Director General of Fortifications in Ireland. Compared to the twenty-one days spent by the 1611 commission in the escheated counties, Bodley accrued seventy-nine days personally inspecting the various settlements and estates. Given his official work, he took particular interest in the castles, bawns and other buildings erected by the planters (Perceval-Maxwell 1973, 140). His survey was later included in the fourth volume of the *Hastings Manuscripts*, a collection which was published by the Historical Manuscripts Commission in 1947 (*Hist. MSS Comm.* 1947).

The next survey, by Captain Nicholas Pynnar, began in November 1618, and he spent the next 119 days surveying the various proportions in the escheated counties. The length of time spent in Ulster allowed him to report in far more detail than had been possible with the previous two surveys. He visited individual proportions personally, describing the various buildings as well as the type of farming carried out on the estates. He also noted the numbers of freeholders, leaseholders and the total number of armed men and families, as well as the number of those who had taken the Oath of Supremacy (Hill 1877; Perceval-Maxwell 1973, 165).

In April 1622 a government Commission of Enquiry consisting of twenty-one people (of whom only seven visited Ulster) arrived in Dublin to look into how Ireland was governed. Matters of concern included the workings of both the civil and ecclesiastical administrations, as well as the operation of the legal system, the regulation of trade, the maintenance of the standing army and the progress of the plantations (and not just that in Ulster). Information was gathered on how the proportions were being settled, what buildings were being constructed and which landowners had performed well in fulfilling their obligations. Unlike the previous surveys, the Commissioners had to come up with solutions for any shortcomings that they encountered (Perceval-Maxwell 1973, 191). The seven who visited Ulster were divided into two teams of two and one of three, each being allocated two of the six escheated counties. Lord Caulfield, Sir Dudley Digges and Sir Nathaniel Rich surveyed Cos Tyrone and Armagh, Sir Thomas Phillips and Richard Hadsor reported on Cos Donegal and Londonderry, while Sir Francis Annesley and Sir James Perrott covered Cos Cavan and Fermanagh (*ibid.* 191). In late July or early August they commenced work in Ulster, with most returning to Dublin by 18 September (*ibid.* 191). Because different teams were involved, the information gathered differed from county to county, and even between different parts of the same county (*ibid.* 192). Also, much of the supporting material for this survey has not survived except that for Cos Tyrone and Armagh (*ibid.*). The survey of Armagh was published by Victor Treadwell in the 1960 volume of the *Ulster Journal of Archaeology*, while the survey of Tyrone was published by Treadwell in the 1964 volume.

Another product of the 1622 Commission was Thomas Raven's coloured pictorial maps, which were produced at the behest of Sir Thomas Phillips, one of the Commissioners surveying the Londonderry plantation. Raven produced small-scale maps illustrating the proportions granted to individual London companies, along with large-scale maps of the various towns and villages in Co. Londonderry. English-style manor houses and bawns in a variety of forms are depicted, either finished or incomplete, and in the immediate vicinity, villages are shown with mixtures of building types adopted – mud-walled and thatched cabins, timber-framed and stone-built houses. Houses could be placed along a regular street pattern as with the crossroads at Limavady, or lining a single, long street as at Bellaghy. In some cases, a company was not concerned with establishing a formally designed village, resulting in a more dispersed pattern of houses, as was the case at Movanagher. Two copies of these maps exist, both drawn by Thomas Raven, one being held in the Lambeth Palace Library (MS 634) in London, while the other is in the archives of the Drapers' Company, a 19th-century copy of which is now held in the Public Records Office of Northern Ireland (D446/A/4/15). It has been suggested that the Drapers' version is the more accurate of the two sets and may in fact be a corrected version (Curl 1986, 75). In 2009, the Ulster Scots Agency released a double CD ROM set of Raven's maps, along with an e-book version of Hill's book on the Ulster Plantation in a CD entitled *The dawn of the Ulster Scots: the plantation of Ulster*.

Outside the area of formal plantation, Raven was contracted by Sir James Hamilton to map his estate in northern Co. Down in 1625. Like the Londonderry maps, this survey recorded in minute detail the form and layout of settlements, property boundaries and economic resources, providing important information on a part of the county where the process of settlement was not as well documented. These maps can be seen in the North Down Museum, in Bangor, Co. Down, where they are on public display, and where a digitised version is also available for viewing.

Surveys of Ulster in the 1640s and 50s

Following the outbreak of the 1641 Rebellion, many Protestant refugees made their way towards Dublin, providing accounts of the robberies and violence that they had witnessed or heard of. To document this evidence, the government established a 'Commission for the Despoiled Subject', its membership consisting of eight Church of Ireland clergymen headed by Henry Jones, Dean of Kilmore and later bishop of Meath. As its remit was to interview witnesses or deponents to provide written evidence of what happened, their records came to be known as the '1641 Depositions'. Jones presented the preliminary findings to the English Parliament which was subsequently published in 1642 as *A remonstrance of divers remarkeable passages concerning the church and kingdome of Ireland*. The 1641 Depositions were used in one of the more noteworthy accounts of the Rebellion, Sir John Temple's *The Irish Rebellion* which was published in 1646. Depositions continued to be collected for much of the 1640s, along with further evidence gathered by the Cromwellian administration in 1652, all of which was used in the trials of Irish leaders. In 1741 on the centenary of the Rebellion, the Depositions were sold to Trinity College Dublin where they are still held today (MSS 809–841), and images of the documents with transcripts are available on a searchable database online at http://www.1641.tcd.ie. These eyewitness accounts provide information to archaeologists and historians interested in plantation-period settlement. Sometimes houses and villages are mentioned, along with the sorts of goods taken from settler households by rebels. It is planned that all will be published in hardcopy by the Irish Manuscripts Commission. Of these, the volumes covering six of the nine Ulster counties were published in 2014; Co. Armagh (Volume 1), Co. Fermanagh (Volume 2), and Cos Antrim, Down, Londonderry, and Tyrone (Volume 3).

In the aftermath of the Cromwellian reconquest there was a major confiscation of Catholic land, which was redistributed to Protestant landowners. To aid in this, a survey was instigated by the civil authorities to record the ownership and extent of forfeited properties, as well as lands owned by the Crown and church, and lands claimed by English proprietors. Coming to be known as the 'Civil Survey', it covered the period between 1654 and 1656. Of the nine counties of Ulster, only the volumes for Cos Londonderry and Tyrone survive, and these were published by R.C. Simington for the Irish Manuscripts Commission in 1937. Recording in tabular form the various estates and their owners, it contains information on who owned properties in 1641 and who was the owner at the time of the survey, the amount of land profitable and unprofitable, and what buildings stood on the properties. The acreages quoted in the Civil Survey were disputed, as the information was derived orally from local juries, and it was argued that there was more confiscated land available than had been estimated in the survey.

To remedy this, the Cromwellian authorities authorised the creation of maps that would depict the forfeited properties in a more accurate manner. This survey, which came to be known as the 'Down Survey', was directed by the physician-general of the army, Dr William Petty. Between 1656 and 1658, Petty and his surveyors recorded the physical and territorial boundaries of most counties, baronies and parishes in the country. Twenty-nine counties were surveyed in whole or part, with only Cos Galway, Roscommon and most of Mayo not visited as they had previously being mapped in the Strafford Survey of Connaught in the 1630s (though they were included in the final published survey). The Down Survey has been described as Ireland's 'Domesday Book', the maps of the baronies and parishes not only recording estate boundaries, but also depicting nucleated and dispersed settlement including manor houses, castles, churches, homesteads, mills, bridges and mines (Smyth 2006, 174). Accompanying each baronial map is an index of Irish Catholic landowners, townlands, glebe land and other church lands, along with crown lands and woodland. These maps are available through the website http://www.downsurvey.tcd.ie which is hosted by the Dept. of History in Trinity College Dublin.

Published secondary sources on the Ulster Plantation

This wealth of documentary and cartographic sources has encouraged much research on the plantation in Ulster, going back as far as the late 19th century. In 1877 the Rev. George Hill published *An historical account of the plantation in Ulster at the commencement of the seventeenth century, 1608–1620*. This book is a compilation of official papers relating to the planning and establishment of the plantation scheme. Of particular interest is a chapter on the grants and grantees which lists the various proportions or estates that were passed to undertakers, servitors and natives, including the names of the townlands concerned. This information is of particular interest to settlement historians and archaeologists as it can allow for the reconstruction of early 17th-century estate boundaries. The chapter on Pynnar's survey is even more important for reconstructing the archaeological landscape. Listing on a county-by-county, precinct-by-precinct basis the proportions or estates granted, this survey included details on whether the new landlords were fulfilling their building obligations. Pynnar recorded the types of buildings that he saw newly occupied or in the process of being built, a significant source of information that allows for the dating of fortified houses and bawns that survive to this day.

T.W. Moody's *The Londonderry Plantation 1609–41* is a thorough treatment of the scheme in the west of Ulster, examining the establishment of the city of Londonderry and the other villages and towns by the various London companies. The Company archives preserve much documentation, including maps and plans such as those by Thomas Raven, although many of the records relating to the Plantation were destroyed in a fire in 1786. Nonetheless, the survivals provided the base for two further major works on the Londonderry Plantation by James Stevens Curl, in his *Londonderry Plantation 1609–1914* published in 1986 and *The Honourable The Irish Society and the Plantation of Ulster 1608–2000* published in 2000. The first sets the historical background before moving onto examine in detail the histories of the estates of the Twelve Great Companies, as well as those of The Honourable The Irish Society and Sir Thomas Phillips. Important and unique house plans are included, particularly examples held by the Drapers' Company of their buildings at Moneymore, as well as detailed maps by Thomas Raven, both for the 1622 Commissioners and for individual companies such as the Merchant Taylors and the Goldsmiths. Curl's second book focuses on the work of The Irish Society which was responsible for the settlements of Londonderry and Coleraine.

R.J Hunter's *The Ulster Plantation in the Counties of Armagh and Cavan 1608–41*, published posthumously in 2012, is a comprehensive account of the political, social and economic consequences of plantation in these two counties. The chapter on towns covers the settlements in Co. Armagh, principally Charlemont,

Mountnorris, Tandragee, Lurgan, Markethill, as well as Armagh itself. Philip Robinson, in his book *The Plantation of Ulster* (1984), delves into the geography and history of settlement in the scheme, looking at the demographics, settlement patterns and built environment. Chapter six covers bawns, castles, manor houses, vernacular dwellings, churches, mills and other buildings, while the following chapter covers towns, villages and dispersed rural settlement.

As colonial settlement was already gathering apace in Cos Antrim and Down during the first decade of the 17th century, they were not included in the Plantation of Ulster. Consequently, settlement in eastern Ulster in this period is not as well documented as elsewhere in the province. Raymond Gillespie's book *Colonial Ulster, the settlement of east Ulster 1600–1641* redresses this imbalance by providing an in-depth account of the demographic, economic and social structures of the English and Scottish settlers who arrived into this region. M. Perceval-Maxwell focuses solely on Scottish planters in his book *The Scottish Migration to Ulster in the Reign of James I*, discussing the involvement of the Scottish landowners as documented through the different surveys, including the Scots who settled in Cos Antrim and Down.

Besides Curl, others have taken an interest in 17th-century architecture in Ulster, with Alistair Rowan having written a book entitled *North West Ulster: the counties of Londonderry, Donegal, Fermanagh and Tyrone* in 1979, one of the volumes in the Buildings of Ireland series. He discusses in his introduction the various Jacobean mansion houses, castles and bawns to be found in that part of the province, along with 17th-century churches and their monuments. These sites across Cos Londonderry, Tyrone, Fermanagh and Donegal are listed in alphabetical order. Hugh Dixon's *An Introduction to Ulster Architecture* (1975) includes a chapter on plantation and Renaissance architecture, illustrating some of Ulster's more impressive 17th-century buildings including fortified houses, mansions, churches and farmhouses. A second edition of the same, revised and provided with more up-to-date images of buildings, was published in 2008. The journal *Ulster Folklife* includes a number of articles written on aspects of vernacular architecture from the period, including Mike Baillie (1974) who wrote on dendrodating post-medieval buildings, and Philip Robinson (1979 and 1985) who delved into the development of vernacular architecture of the time.

Since the 1950s a number of archaeologists have taken an interest in the Ulster Plantation. Martyn Jope published research on a number of 17th-century fortified houses in the *Ulster Journal of Archaeology*, as well as articles focusing on the evolution of formal architecture and Scottish architectural influences in the province (1951, 1954, 1958a, 1958b and 1960). Dudley Waterman also published articles on individual sites in the same journal, as well as writing a more general study on the architectural ancestry of 17th-century Irish houses (1959a, 1959b, 1959c, 1960, 1961). A summary of all archaeological excavations carried out across Ireland from 1970 to 2015 is available on http://www.excavations.ie. It was compiled mostly from the *Excavation Bulletin* edited by Isabel Bennett, which appeared in print annually until 2010, when summaries were henceforth only made available online. Over the years a number of these excavations have focused on urban and rural sites of the plantation period in Ulster. The unearthing of buried building structures and the recovery of numerous artefacts has increased our understanding of how people lived their lives at the time. Such insights are provided in a number of recent books by Ruairí Ó Baoill looking at the archaeology and history of Carrickfergus (2008), Belfast (2011b), and Derry~Londonderry (2013). Colin Breen (2012) has published a book on the architectural history of Dunluce Castle, along with the archaeology of the adjacent, well-preserved early 17th-century town founded by Sir Randal MacDonnell, 1st earl of Antrim. Looking at the broader picture, Audrey Horning's *Ireland in the Virginian Sea* (2013a) investigates the process of colonisation and its impact on both settlers and natives in both Ulster and Virginia, situating both regions within an emerging English global empire.

The above primary and secondary sources are readily accessible in public libraries as well as on the internet, and can provide useful information on many of the 17th-century sites listed in the gazetteer. Research on the period has not been exhaustive and the use of these sources may reveal previously unknown sites in the localities, allowing a better appreciation of the archaeological landscape bequeathed by early 17th-century society in Ulster. Such work is to be encouraged.

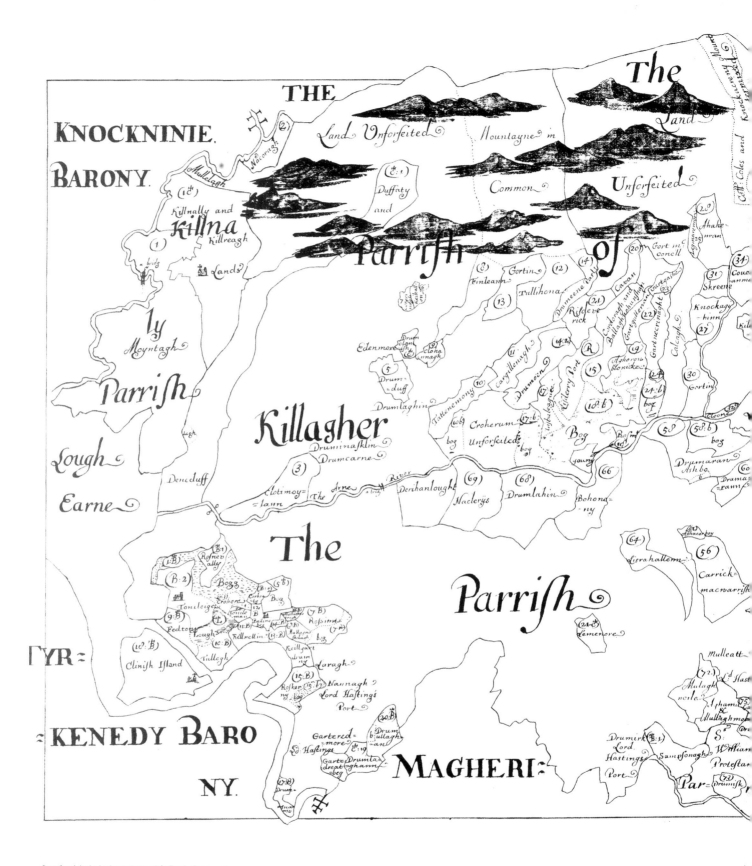

THE

KNOCKNINIE.

BARONY.

The *Land*

Land Unforfeited *Mountayne* *in*

Common *Unforfeited*

Mulleagh

Killnally and
KILLNA *Killreagh*

Lands

Duffaity
and

Parrish

Ahahenran

Gort mC
conell

Finleam *Gortin*
Tullihona

Skreene
Coue
anmeu

Knockagu
hinn

ly

Moyntagh

Parrish

Edenmore
Clona nagh

Drum=
duff

Drumlaghin

Killagher

Drumcarne

Derihanloughs
River
Arne *The*

Nacleryis

Drumlahin

Bohong=
ny

Lough

Earne

Bog

Drumaran
Ashbo

Druma
=ramm

Lisrahallem

Carrick=
macuarrish

The

Parrish

Mulleatt

TYR=

=KENEDY BARO

Clinish Island

NY.

MAGHERI=

Drumirk
Lord
Hastings
Port

Sampsonagh

Williams
Protesta=
Par=

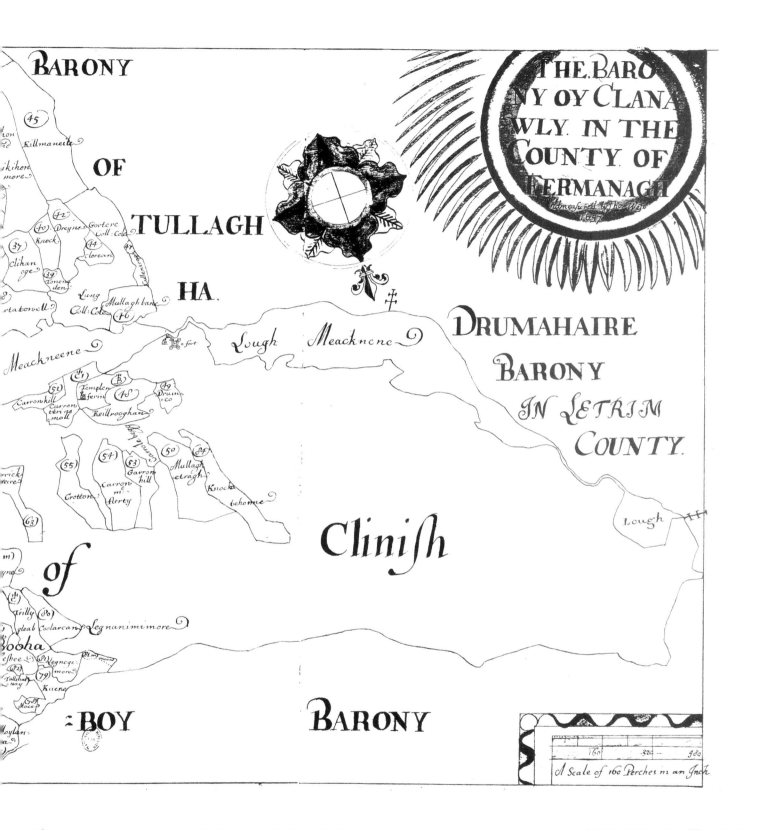

BARONY

OF

TULLAGH

HA.

THE.BARO
NY OY CLANA
WLY. IN THE
COUNTY. OF
FERMANAGH
Admeasured by Tho: Raven
1657

(45)

Killmaneih

ikihon
more

(42) Dreynes Gortere
Coll: Col:

(37) (44)
Knock Clorean
(40)
(39) Clihan (47)
oge Tonena
den

rtatorvell Lung Mullaghbane (46)
Coll: Cole:

Meackneene

a fort Lough Meacknene

DRUMAHAIRE

BARONY

IN LETRIM

COUNTY.

(51) (41)
Carronkill Templen
ferini (48)
Carron Drum
terina =co
mall Reillrooghan

(55) (54) (50) (54)
(53) Mullagh
Crotton Carron Garron etragh
mc hill Knocks
flerty bchorne

(63)

rrick
eire

Clinish

Lough

of

rilly (80)
gleab Coolarcan Legnanimimore

booha

eshee (81) Legnega (81) mc mound
more
(82)
Tullihad (79)
hay Kuena

(84)
Mace

oylan
a

BOY BARONY

160 320 980
A Scale of 160 Perches in an Inch

Published at the Ordnance Survey Office Southampton,
Colonel R.C.Hellard C.B.,R.E.,Director General, 1908.

1/
s colored 2

on reserved.

17

Chapter 2
County Antrim

Introduction

Unlike most of modern Northern Ireland, Co. Antrim was not subject to formal plantation, as lands there were already being settled with English and Scottish tenants, a process that had greatly accelerated since the conclusion of the Nine Years' War in 1603. Prior to this migration, the region was dominated by a number of Gaelic Irish families such as the O'Neills of Clandeboye, who controlled lands along Belfast Lough and in the Lagan Valley, and the MacQuillans of 'The Route' in north Antrim. During the Middle Ages, the chief Anglo-Norman settlement in the region was Carrickfergus, a town founded in the late 12th century by one of most prominent participants in the Anglo-Norman conquest of Ireland, John de Courcy. This port town, with its substantial castle, was to become the centre of English governance in Ulster throughout the Middle Ages, up to the mid- to late 16th century. By then, the county was attracting the attention of the MacDonnells, lords of the Scottish Isles, who began establishing castles and villages along the coastline and further inland, building on pre-existing links between Gaelic communities on both sides of the North Channel.

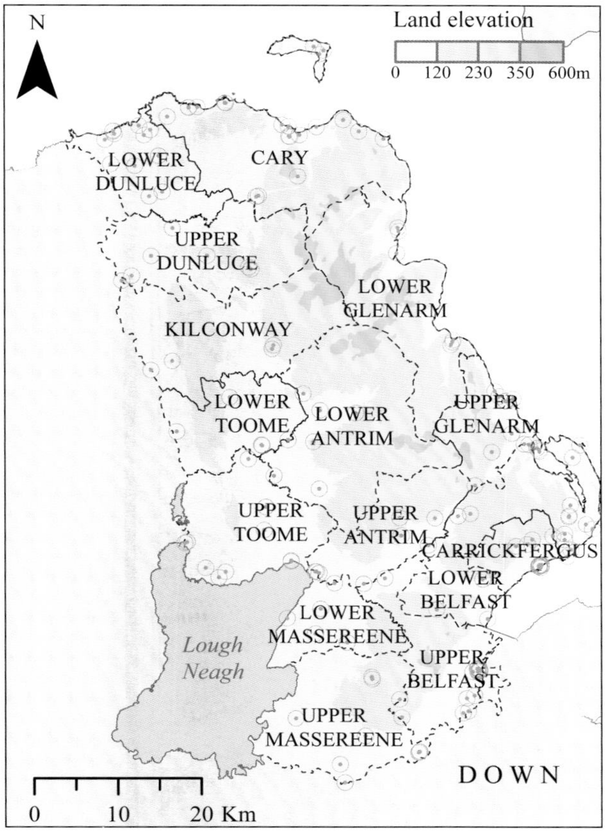

Despite attempts by the English government to forestall this unregulated movement of people, it was eventually given official recognition by King James I in 1603, with the grant of the lordship of 'The Route and Glens' to Sir Randall MacDonnell, subsequently the 1st earl of Antrim. The following year saw the O'Neill lordship of Clandeboye in southern Antrim, along with Carrickfergus, being granted to Sir Arthur Chichester, just before he was made Lord Deputy of Ireland. Other major landowners who began making their mark on the county included Sir Fulke Conway, whose estate was centred on Lisburn; John Dalway in Ballyhill outside Carrickfergus; and William Adair in Ballymena. Proximity to Scottish and northern English ports, the availability of good farmland and other natural resources such as fisheries and timber, ensured that a British population would become established in the Lagan and Bann river valleys, around Lough Neagh, as well as along the coastline.

Many of the castles and houses established by these landlords have disappeared from view, although some still can be found in the landscape, including MacDonnell's Dunluce Castle, John Dalway's bawn in Ballyhill, James Shaw's Ballygalley

Fig. 2.1 Map of Co. Antrim showing sites and baronies.

Castle and Sir Faithful Fortescue's Galgorm Castle. Many others have not survived the rigours of time, such as Sir Arthur Chichester's Joymount House in Carrickfergus, which was a fashionable mansion, described as 'very stately...or rather like a prince's palace'. Such residences became the focus for civic and commercial life as villages and towns developed around their environs such as Belfast, Larne, Glenarm, Dunluce, Ballymena, Antrim and Lisburn. On the new estates, family homes were being built by tenants borrowing from different architectural traditions – mud-walled thatched cabins, timber-framed houses and stone-built houses. Deeply held spiritual beliefs, whether in the guise of Anglicanism, Presbyterianism or Catholicism meant that parish churches and graveyards continued to exert an influence on the development of local communities in both urban and rural areas. The estate structure in Co. Antrim is not as well documented compared to other counties as it was not included under the official scheme. Consequently, the sites here are listed on a geographical basis, rather than on the basis of which estates they were located in. The chapter starts with sites in the barony of Upper Belfast, and then follows northwards to include the baronies of Lower Belfast, Carrickfergus, Upper Glenarm, Lower Glenarm and Cary; and then turning southwards, the baronies of Dunluce, Kilconway, Toome, Antrim, and Massereene.

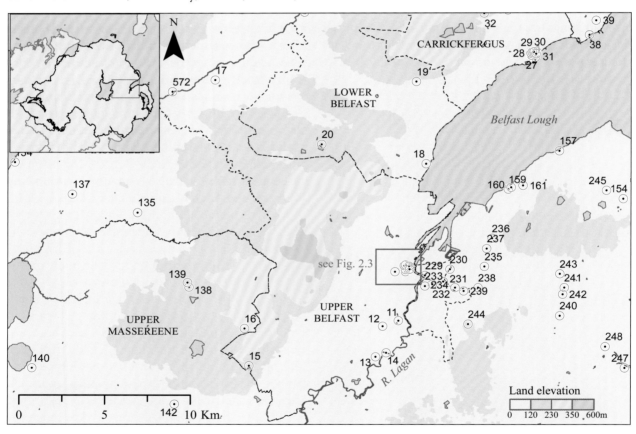

Fig. 2.2 Barony map of Belfast Upper showing the site locations discussed in text.

Barony of Belfast Upper

Belfast City Centre

Belfast and its environs today constitute by far the largest and most densely populated settlement in Ulster. The city surrounds the site of a medieval castle, itself probably associated with a small settlement of similar date, although the origins of urbanism proper in Belfast can be traced to the Plantation. Prior to this, in the 16th century the lands were held by the O'Neills of Clandeboye, who suffered various incursions by the earl of Kildare, and others. They were eventually granted to Sir Arthur Chichester (see also Carrickfergus and Dungannon) in 1604, the year before he was appointed Lord Deputy of Ireland. Sir Arthur built a castle on the site of the older structure in 1610–11 and, between 1604 and 1613, encouraged settlers from England and Scotland to

Belfast, Carrickfergus and Malone (Vinycomb 1892). Sir Arthur was made Baron Chichester of Belfast in 1612, and in 1613 the fledgling town was incorporated by royal charter, becoming Belfast city. Growth accelerated in 1637 when the 'Carrickfergus privilege' – an ancient entitlement of that town to one-third of the customs duties payable to the Belfast port – was abolished. When Carrickfergus stopped profiting from its customs revenue, some merchants relocated to Belfast, hastening the decline of Carrickfergus while helping Belfast to develop further (Benn 1877, 62–63). In 1642, amid the turbulence of the Rebellion, funds were granted to the city by Charles I to enclose it within defences (Young 1895, 22–28). These took the form of an earthen bank with an external water-filled ditch (see Invs 6, 7 and 8). The city was accessed through three gates — Mill Gate (see Inv. 2), North Gate (in North Street), and Strand Gate (see Inv. 7), as well as by the River Lagan. The earliest known map

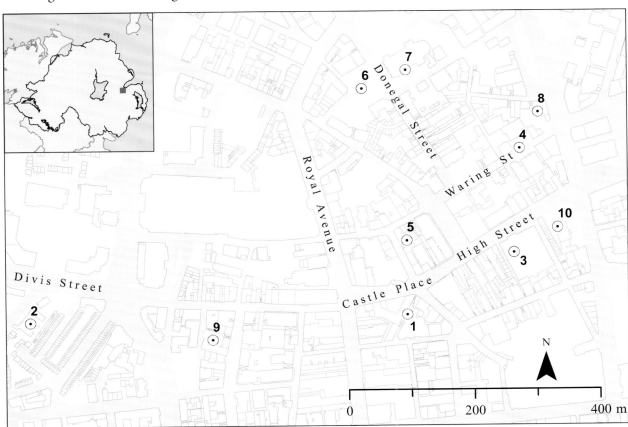

Fig. 2.3 Map of Belfast showing the individual site locations discussed in text.

of the plantation city was made by Thomas Phillips in 1685 (NLI MS 3137/41) and shows a street layout still recognisable within the larger modern city of today.

The initial success of Belfast was perhaps not only due to its own inhabitants, but also to its central geographical location in relation to the settlements of Hamilton and Montgomery in Cos Down and Antrim, those of Sir Moses Hill in Malone, Sir Fulke Conway in Lisburn, and Chichester's well-established town in Carrickfergus. Belfast grew rapidly over much of the 17th and 18th centuries (Benn 1877; Vinycomb 1892), and the expansion that occurred during the Industrial Revolution removed much of its 17th-century built environment. There are, however, many places where the 17th-century layout has influenced how the modern city is currently configured. Archaeological mitigation of development projects continues to unearth new data on how the city has developed and helps to tell the story of life in Belfast during its formative years.

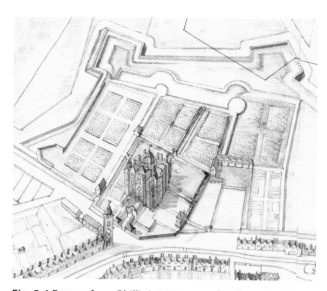

Fig. 2.4 Extract from Phillip's 1685 map of Belfast, showing a close-up of Belfast Castle, built by Sir Arthur Chichester in 1610–11. At the time this would have been one of the finest residences erected in Ireland.

1   CASTLE PLACE, BELFAST: 333900 374280
   CASTLE, SITE OF

This is the reputed site of Belfast Castle, where Sir Arthur Chichester built on the site of an earlier, late medieval structure. There are numerous historical references to a castle at Belfast during the 16th century and the Nine Years' War, it being likely that a tower house stood here when Chichester took possession. Nothing survives above ground, although its memory is preserved in the various place- and street-names in the immediate locality. Chichester's castle was situated between Castle Place and Castle Lane, and was — according to pictorial evidence — originally a square, three-storey building with projections flanking each side, and surrounded by formal gardens. In 1611, Carew described the new building then under construction as a brick-built house, 50ft by 20ft, surrounded by a bawn with flanking towers and a ditch. An English visitor in 1635, Sir William Brereton, described it as

> ...a dainty stately palace, which is indeed the glory and beauty of that town, where he is mostly resident.

It was burnt in 1708, with the last vestiges disappearing over the course of the 18th century.

During the Victorian era, the sewage system in the area was upgraded, affording antiquarians an opportunity to study features and artefacts from earlier phases of the history of Belfast. Among the unstratified finds in Castle Place were human remains of unknown date, numerous coins and 17th-century tokens, and other objects of stone, bone, ceramic, metal, wood and leather. A walkway, perhaps a former street, was also uncovered. Excavations in 1983 revealed evidence of an enclosing wall of the castle. Although none of the structure survived, it was identified as a 'robber trench', one from which all of the stone had been robbed out for use on other buildings. More recent excavations have revealed various wall foundations and drainage features, none of which have been associated unequivocally with Chichester's castle.

ANT 061:005

Report of the Plantation Commissioners, 1611 (PRONI T811/3); G.B. 1857; Grainger 1862, 113–121; Benn 1877, 22; Jope 1960, 97–123; Brannon 1980–4; Bowen 2005; Gahan 2007

**2   BARRACK STREET, BELFAST: 333300 374270
MILITARY INSTALLATION**

Various historic accounts of Belfast indicate a garrison, fort or other military installation at this site, which was located at a 'Mill Gate' where the original road to Dublin entered Belfast through its earthwork defences. It is not clear what form the 17th-century fort originally took as it was replaced by a barracks in the 18th century.

ANT 061:012

G.B. 1857; Bigger 1911a

**3   POTTINGER'S ENTRY,   334070 374380
BELFAST: SETTLEMENT**

At this site, excavations uncovered a large, 17th-century rubbish pit containing animal bones and various artefacts: pottery sherds, clay tobacco pipes, painted window glass and animal bones.

ANT 061:015

Brannon 1988c

**4   WARING STREET, BELFAST: 334080 374550
HOUSE STRUCTURES**

Excavations at the former site of Benny's Bar in Waring Street in 1999 revealed the remains of a brick-built, 17th-century structure, possibly one of the houses shown on Phillips' 1685 map. It had the same orientation as the modern buildings, indicating that the alignment of the street had not changed

Fig. 2.5 Archaeological excavations in 2002 of 17th-century terraced housing on Waring Street, Belfast.

substantially. Evidence of floor joisting was found, as was a doorway, and there were numerous finds including sherds of tin-glazed earthenware. The building was probably part of a terrace of houses, further evidence of which was uncovered in 2002 near the corner of Hill Street and Waring Street. Drainage features and pits containing butchered cattle horn — a by-product of the tanning process — were also discovered during the 2002 excavations. The buildings here were known in the 18th century as the Potthouse tenements, perhaps associated with a nearby (but now unlocated) late-17th century Belfast pottery.

ANT 061:020

Ó Baoill and Logue 2005

**5   ANNE STREET/CORN   333900 374400
MARKET, BELFAST: SETTLEMENT**

The former Woolworth's Building bounded by High Street, Corn Market and Ann Street is at the centre of the plantation town of Belfast. Excavations in 2003 revealed, among many indications of previous building phases, a structural timber dated dendrochronologically to AD 1619±9.

ANT 061:017

MacDonald 2006

**6   BELFAST, WRITER'S SQUARE: 333830 374650
TOWN DITCH**

Excavations revealed the truncated lower part of the 17th-century defensive town ditch around Belfast. The ditch, which was 3m wide and 1m deep, had been cut into waterlogged subsoil, with excavated material cast onto an earthen bank supported by boulders laid along the inner edge of the ditch (see also Inv. 7 and 8). Much of the feature in this area is now preserved, *in situ*, under Writer's Square.

ANT 061:018

Brannon 1990a; Ó Baoill 2011b, 104–105

**7   BELFAST, TALBOT STREET: 333900 374680
TOWN DITCH**

Excavations revealed two linear features, drainage

gullies orientated north-south lying below various other archaeological features, and surfaces of 18th-century date. Both gullies were filled with fine-grained organic sediment, and it is possible that they were open in the early 17th century and drained water from the town ditch.

ANT 061:025

Dunlop 2005b

8   BELFAST, GORDON STREET: 333590 374240 SETTLEMENT

Excavations on the corner of Gordon Street, close to where part of the original earthwork defences of Belfast were breached by Strand Gate, revealed numerous 17th-century pottery sherds and clay pipes, but no structural remains earlier than the 18th century. In 2001, a length of the town ditch was excavated and found to be 2m–3m wide and almost 1m deep, and filled by deposits containing 17th- and 18th-century pottery and animal bones.

ANT 061:019

Ó Baoill 1999b and 2011b 104–105; McConway 2001

9   BELFAST, QUEEN STREET: 333597 397424 TOWN DITCH

The most substantial remains of the Belfast town ditch yet located were discovered in 2005 during excavations in Queen Street. Here it was 7.5m wide and 90cm deep with preserved, layered deposits and wooden stakes *in situ*. It was filled in and built over in the 18th century.

ANT 061:022

Dunlop 2005a; Ó Baoill 2011b, 104–105

10   BELFAST, HIGH STREET: 334140 374420 ST GEORGE'S PARISH CHURCH

St George's Church was built in 1813-6 on the site of the 'Chapel of the Ford', where formerly a small chapel (possibly of 13th-century origin) was situated, at the point where the Farset and Lagan rivers meet. The chapel was rebuilt early in the 17th century and became Belfast Corporation Church. According to Benn, it was fortified and used for military purposes during the 1650s, although it was never actually attacked. In 1657 the building was rebuilt as a cruciform church with a central tower, the form that subsequently appeared in an illustration of 1685. There are no apparent remains of the 17th-century church, and the area today attests to considerable changes in the townscape over the intervening centuries. For example, the River Farset, now culverted beneath High Street, originally flowed a short distance from the front of the church.

ANT 061:004

Reeves 1847, 6–7; G.B. 1857; Grainger 1862; Benn 1877, 141

Malone

In 1606, Sir Arthur Chichester leased Stranmillis and Malone to Sir Moses Hill, who built two houses: at Stranmillis, overlooking the Lagan at the upper reaches of its tidal limit (see Inv. 11), and at 'Hilsborowe', now Upper Malone (see Inv. 13: not Hillsborough, Co. Down, to where the Hill family moved after being attacked in 1641). The under-tenants of Malone in the 17th century were English settlers who held long strip farms spanning the land between the modern Malone Road and the Blackstaff River, almost constituting a linear village (Carleton 1976, 65). There were several 'gentleman's residences' to be found along the Malone Road (*ibid.*).

Fig. 2.6 Archaeological excavations on Queen Street of a 17th-century defensive ditch that originally surrounded Belfast.

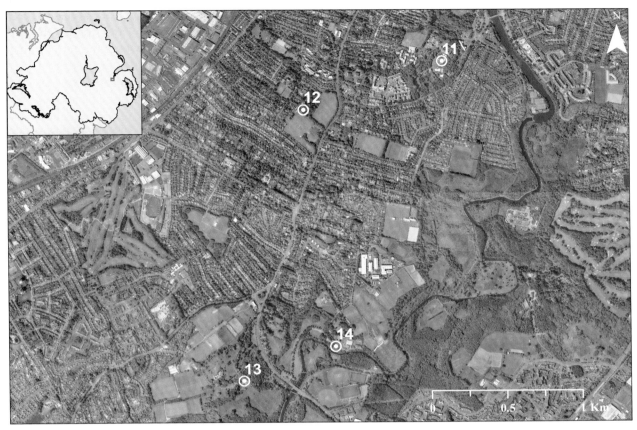

Fig. 2.7 Aerial photomosaic of Malone showing sites discussed in the text.

The remains of one of these survive at Cranmore (Inv. 12), indicating that such small estates could include impressive and comfortable residences.

11 BELFAST, STRANMILLIS 333500 371300
HOUSE: HOUSE AND BAWN

This is the approximate site of Sir Moses Hill's house and bawn, which was described by Carew in 1611 as being in the process of construction

> ...by the river of Lagan where the sea ebbes and flowes in a place called Strandmellis we found the said Moyses Hill in hand with building of a strong house of stone 56 foot longe, and entendes to make it two stories and a halfe high.

Carew also mentioned plans to build a bawn. The house is shown on the Down Survey map of Belfast barony c. 1657. Although its exact location is not known, the most likely site is the summit of the hill at Stranmillis House, now in the grounds of

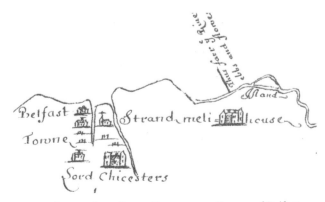

Fig. 2.8 Extract from Down Survey map, Barony of Belfast (c.1656–58) showing Stranmillis House.

Stranmillis College. Local accounts indicate that the cellars of an old building were found during work here in the 19th century.

ANT 061:016

Report of the Plantation Commissioners, 1611 (PRONI T811/3) and Barony map of Belfast (PRONI D597/2); Reeves 1847, 185; Benn 1880, 86; Carleton 1976, 63–65

**12   MALONE: CRANMORE   332579 370970
        HOUSE**

Cranmore House is the ruined shell of a 17th-century house, located close to the modern Malone Road, and is the earliest identified upstanding domestic structure in Belfast. Its walls were originally of stone rubble, but very little of this survives, having been greatly modified with significant insertions of hand-made brick. The brick chimney breasts, which protrude from the gables, may be original.

According to pictorial evidence, the five-bay façade was originally asymmetric, and the gables were slightly curved, supposedly a Dutch influence that is a characteristic feature of English-style Renaissance architecture.

ANT 064:093

Carleton 1976, 65–66

Fig. 2.9 View of Cranmore House with its front façade heavily repaired with brick.

**13   MALONE UPPER: FORTIFIED   332170 369110
        HOUSE, BAWN**
'Hilsborowe', Malone House

A house and bawn built at this location by Sir Moses Hill were described by Carew in 1611 as a fortified house of brick and timber, enclosed by a palisade with a drawbridge, and situated near a ford on the Lagan – a crossing now spanned by Shaw's Bridge. Known as 'Hilsborowe', it was attacked and destroyed by insurgents in 1641. When the original Malone House was built in the late-17th century, the vestiges of Hill's fort were used as a gazebo within formal gardens. Nothing now survives above ground, the site having been levelled and partially built over in the 19th century by the present Malone House. Nearby Shaw's Bridge is named after Captain John Shaw, a Parliamentarian officer who is said to have built a timber bridge spanning the ford in the 1650s to allow cannon to cross the Lagan easily.

ANT 064:091

Report of the Plantation Commissioners, 1611 (PRONI T811/3); Anon 1855, 83; Carleton 1976, 62–63; Ó Baoill 2011a, 129–130

**14   MALONE UPPER: 332780 369350
        IRONWORKS**

This is the approximate site of an ironworks that, according to McCracken, was established on the banks of the Lagan around 1630, probably by the earl of Wilmot. It is approximately 600m downstream from Hill's property by Shaw's Bridge, and was also destroyed in 1641. The Lagan allowed for transport of raw materials to the works, while the heavily wooded Lagan Valley in the early 17th century was the source of the wood for the charcoal to fuel the smelting process. Recent research in nearby Belvoir Park Forest has revealed that an ancient oak still standing was planted in 1642. This implies, perhaps, that there was some forest regrowth during the troubled times of the later 17th century, with the regeneration incorporated into the designed landscape at Belvoir.

ANT 064:092

McCracken 1957, 127; Carleton 1976, 66; Simon 2009

Other Sites in the Barony of Belfast Upper

15 MULLAGHGLASS: FORTIFIED HOUSE
324790 368570
Castle Robin

The remains of a fortified 17th-century rectangular house of three storeys is located close to the site of an Anglo-Norman motte and bailey, with commanding views of the Lagan Valley. According to the *OS Memoirs*, the building stands on land granted to one Robert Norton, and was constructed in 1611, and subsequently ruined in 1641. It seems possible, however, that it was constructed earlier, since the land grant was made in 1579. The house was originally 12.2m by 6.4m externally, with walls 1m thick, and only the northern gable wall and the south-western corner of building now survive. Elsewhere, the walls stand to no more than four or five courses high, or as low embankments of stone. At the time of writing, the entire structure was enveloped by vegetation, making further survey difficult.

ANT 064:014

O'Laverty 1878–1887, II, 335–336; Belshaw 1896; *PSAMNI* 59; McNeill 1975, 52; Day and McWilliams 1991b, 92–94, 101, 107, 120

16 SLIEVENACLOY: ENCLOSURE 324530 370830

The remains of a possible earthwork, perhaps a 17th-century enclosure, are mentioned in the *OS Memoirs*, but its history is otherwise obscure. The site, located on the baronial border of Massereene, has panoramic views, especially to the west and toward the distant lowlands of central Co. Antrim. It consists of a large trapezoidal area, approximately 1 ha, enclosed by a flat-topped bank, averaging 4m in width and 1.25m in height, with an outer ditch 4m to 6m wide, and a small outer bank 30cm high. A large earthen platform 1.2m high is positioned to the south of the main enclosure, and two outlying earthen banks, also 1.2m high, are positioned to the south-west.

ANT 064:087

Williams 1985; Day and McWilliams 1991b, 97

17 TEMPLEPATRICK: CASTLE 322800 385900
Castle Upton

A castle (still a private residence) was built here in the early 17th century on the site of an earlier monastery, a house of the Order of St. John of Jerusalem. The lands were held by Sir Arthur Chichester, and leased to Sir Humphrey Norton, a member of an English military family that had risen to prominence in Ulster (see Inv. 15). Carew reported *c.* 1610 that Norton had already built two towers and had materials on hand to construct a bawn of lime and stone. It seems the building was completed in 1611, as this date appears on a plaque preserved at the site. The castle was sold to Captain Henry Upton in 1625. It was greatly extended in 1783 and renovated in 1837, the surviving early 17th-century features being the substantial round towers, originally positioned at the diagonals of the building, the walls of which contain gun loops.

ANT 051:059

Reeves 1847, 65 and 194; Anon 1855, 83; O'Laverty 1878–1887, III, 335–337; PSAMNI 46; Gwynn and Hadcock, 1970, 107, 342, 368; Day et al. 1996b, 25–27, 37, 71 and 74

Fig. 2.10 View of Castle Upton.

Carrickfergus and the Barony of Belfast Lower

Sites in the Newtownabbey Area

Although not strictly a focus of settlement during plantation times, the lands between Belfast and Carrickfergus were under the control of Sir Arthur Chichester throughout the period. The area would presumably have seen much activity, with people, animals and goods constantly on the move between those two important towns.

Fig. 2.12 Front façade of the White House in Newtownabbey with large, circular flanking towers at either end of its eastern wall.

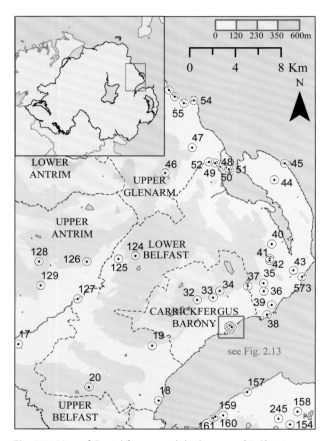

Fig. 2.11 Map of Carrickfergus and the barony of Belfast Lower.

| 18 | WHITE HOUSE: HOUSE | 335100 380820 |
| | AND BAWN | |

The White House

The remains of the 'White House' lie on the original shoreline of Belfast Lough. The *OS Memoirs* state that the vestiges of a 'pleasure garden' and a fish pond were once visible to the west of the house, implying that the grounds were quite extensive. According to O'Laverty, the earliest written reference to a house at this location is in 1574, when it was inhabited by a soldier named Brounker. The property is also mentioned in grants of land to Sir Arthur Chichester in 1604. More recently, the building has been used variously as a Gospel Hall and a community centre. It was extensively restored between 2008 and 2010, with a new roof added, and is currently an exhibition and meeting centre.

The remains comprise a two-storey rectangular house, with large circular flanking towers at either end of its eastern wall. Gun loops are visible in the flankers and in the gable walls. The walls are built of basalt rubble and lime mortar, with non-original brick relief arches above the windows and doors. A timber lintel from the structure has been dated by dendrochronology to between 1599 and 1624, supporting an early 17th-century construction date. Excavations at the site in 1996 uncovered 17th-century (and later) pottery, and further archaeological work in 2009 revealed ephemeral evidence for an earlier timber building, which could be the structure referred to in 16th-century sources.

ANT 057:008

Anon. 1855, 83; O'Laverty 1878–1887, III, 2–4; Jope 1960, 97–123; Day and McWilliams 1990b, 68–69; Ó Baoill 2011b, 130–131

19	**MONKSTOWN: CHURCH AND GRAVEYARD**	**334530 385790**

Monkstown Church

The fragmentary remains of Monkstown Church stand on a terrace next to Pound Burn. This is a medieval church first referred to in 1306, but mentioned also in various 17th-century sources. It survives as traces of a simple, rectangular building, measuring 19.2m by 6.1m internally and aligned east to west, with walls 90cm thick. Only the western gable survives to any significant height. The building lies within a rectangular graveyard that was used for burial until 1780.

ANT 052:054

Reeves 1847, 69; O'Laverty 1878–1887, III, 9–11; Day and McWilliams 1990b, 104–105

20	**MALLUSK: FORTIFIED HOUSE AND EARTHWORK**	**329000 382000**

Grange of Mallusk

This is the approximate site of a house and earthen bawn, the history of which is obscure and which is without any known archaeological traces. It was described by the Plantation Commissioners in 1611 as

> …a large house with chimneys, which is enclosed by a rampart of earth sods & flankered.

A nearby copse of trees within a rectangular earthen enclosure is another possible location (grid ref. 328840, 382150).

ANT 056:050

Report of the Plantation Commissioners, 1611 (PRONI T811/3); O'Laverty 1878–1887, II, 458

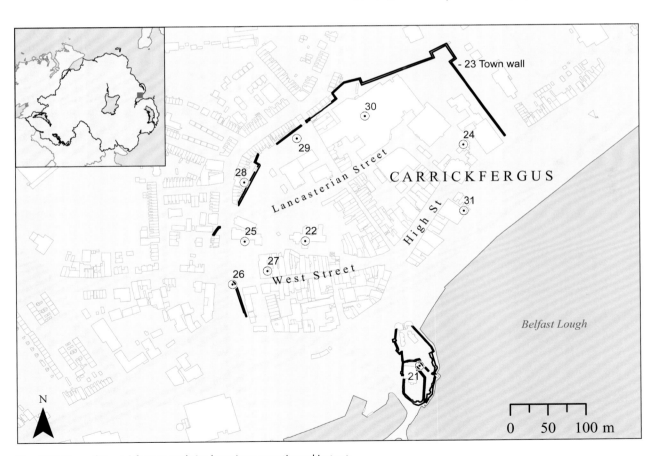

Fig. 2.13 Map of Carrickfergus and site locations mentioned in text.

Carrickfergus Town

Carrickfergus was founded in the 12th century by John de Courcy, an ambitious Anglo-Norman knight who planned to use the town as his base for further conquest in Ulster. It quickly became established as the most economically important population centre in the province, only surrendering that status to Belfast in the 18th century (for an overview, see Ó Baoill 2008). Throughout its early history, the town was under the control of the English Crown, and during late medieval times its castle was the only substantial Crown-held fortification in the region. As such it was frequently attacked by both Irish and Scots (*ibid.* 24). Thus, when Thomas Smith's Elizabethan plantation in Co. Down failed (see Inv. 177), the O'Neills, whose lands had been targeted by the effort, burned Carrickfergus in revenge (Ó Baoill 2008). In 1597, Sir John Chichester was appointed as its governor, and he led his troops into a disastrous battle with the MacDonnells soon after, an encounter that cost him his life. Sir Arthur Chichester, his brother, was appointed governor in 1599; the acumen and ruthlessness that he displayed during the closing years of the Nine Years' War saw him rise in prominence as a central figure in Ulster during the early 17th century.

Fig. 2.14 Plan of Carrickfergus Castle showing the development of the castle over time, including alterations made in the mid-16th century. These included the construction of storehouses, the insertion of canon emplacements, and the refurbishment of the gatehouse.

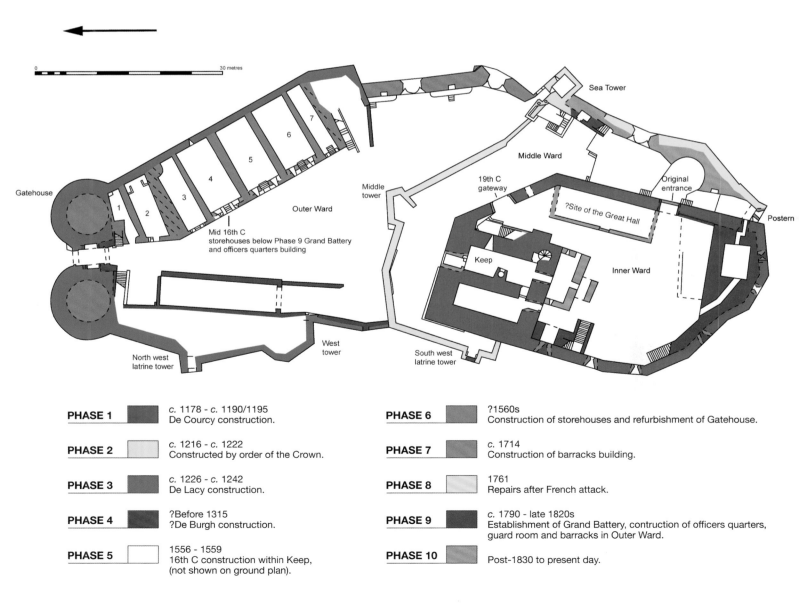

PHASE 1		*c.* 1178 - *c.* 1190/1195 De Courcy construction.
PHASE 2		*c.* 1216 - *c.* 1222 Constructed by order of the Crown.
PHASE 3		*c.* 1226 - *c.* 1242 De Lacy construction.
PHASE 4		?Before 1315 ?De Burgh construction.
PHASE 5		1556 - 1559 16th C construction within Keep, (not shown on ground plan).
PHASE 6		?1560s Construction of storehouses and refurbishment of Gatehouse.
PHASE 7		*c.* 1714 Construction of barracks building.
PHASE 8		1761 Repairs after French attack.
PHASE 9		*c.* 1790 - late 1820s Establishment of Grand Battery, contruction of officers quarters, guard room and barracks in Outer Ward.
PHASE 10		Post-1830 to present day.

21   CARRICKFERGUS: CASTLE   341430 387250
Carrickfergus Castle

The impressive medieval Carrickfergus Castle stands on a rocky peninsula on the shoreline of Belfast Lough. The complex consists of a square keep, surrounded by three curtain walls, the middle one now being reduced to foundation level, and the outer incorporating two circular gatehouse towers facing the town. Originally built in the late 12th century, and greatly expanded in the 13th, the castle was under continuous military occupation until 1929. In the later 16th and early 17th centuries, it was altered to accommodate cannon. The castle walls facing the harbour were given widened embrasures, and the courtyard side of the gatehouse towers were removed, thereby providing additional barrack accommodation for the garrison. The inner courtyard of the castle was also modified to add more accommodation space.

ANT 052:059

Shirley 1855, 276–291; Bigger and Fennell 1908, 183–189; Lawlor 1939b; Waterman 1952; McNeill 1981; Reeves-Smyth 1995, 6–8; Ó Baoill 2008

Fig. 2.15 View of Carrickfergus Castle. Note the brick-lined gun emplacements of 16th-century date in the circuit wall of the castle.

22   CARRICKFERGUS: CHURCH, 341280 387420
GRAVEYARD
St Nicholas' Church

St Nicholas' Church contains elements from several different building phases, among the most prominent of which are those carried out by Sir Arthur Chichester in 1614. It is a medieval foundation, the oldest portions of the extant structure being the nave arcades that date to around 1200, while parts of the eastern end of the chancel date to the late 13th century. Pictorial evidence suggests that the building temporarily lost its roof during the wars of the 16th century. Chichester subsequently commissioned a master mason named Thomas Paps to enlarge and strengthen the medieval building – the aisles and much of the nave date to this phase of work. The northern aisle was screened by ornately carved wooden panels – still visible – and the floor was raised to accommodate a burial vault in which are interred the remains of Sir Arthur, his wife Letitia and his brother Sir John, and many other members of the Chichester family. A spectacular memorial to the Chichesters situated in the northern aisle comprises a marble and alabaster carving, with effigies of Sir John, and Sir Arthur and Letitia and, poignantly, a representation of their only child, also called Arthur, who died in infancy.

The tower at the western end of the church was built in 1778, and other episodes of renovation

Fig. 2.16 St Nicholas' Church in Carrickfergus from the south-east.

Fig. 2.17 A marble and alabaster memorial to the Chichesters in the northern aisle of St Nicholas' Church, with the effigies of Sir Arthur and his wife Letitia facing each other in prayer. Poignantly, situated between the couple is a representation of their only child, also called Arthur, who died in infancy. Below the family is a smaller effigy of Sir Arthur's brother Sir John, one-time governor of Carrickfergus, who was killed during a military campaign against the Gaelic Irish. The decorative style of the memorial with its round arches, columns and entablatures is one of the finest examples of early classical design to be found in Ulster.

ANT 052:060

Reeves 1847, 61–62; Drew 1872; *PSAMNI* 48–49; McConnell 1999; Ó Baoill 2008, 42–57; Murray 2010

23 CARRICKFERGUS: TOWN WALL 341500 387610

Carrickfergus was enclosed within a town wall in the 17th century. Approximately half of the circuit survives, mainly on the northern side of the old town. This is the earliest extant town wall in Ulster – pre-dating that of the City of Londonderry by at least two years. As the Commissioners reported in 1611, their construction must have been an expensive undertaking, and requiring an enormous physical effort. They wrote that

> …we found many masons and labourers at work about the erection and building of the walls of that town and sundry quarry men and labourers at work about a quarter of a mile from the town in breaking of rough stones for the works…4 lime kilns on fire employed in burning of limestone…a boat of 8 tons…and a barge of 15 tons which was purposely made for that work…and continually employed in bringing limestone, freestone and other materials.

and repair occurred in the 1870s and in 1932. Surrounding the church is a rectangular graveyard, with excellent views of the town due to its elevation. On the early town maps, the graveyard of the 17th and 18th centuries appears to have encompassed a larger area than today; indeed archaeological excavations in 1972 and 2010 have revealed burials outside the current boundary.

Fig. 2.18 North-west bastion of Carrickfergus town wall.

Fig. 2.19 The best-preserved of the gates in the town wall of Carrickfergus is the North Gate.

the entire circuit can be traced, the best-preserved being the northern corner bastion, which is a diamond-shaped, crenellated structure that would have allowed for flanking fire along the town walls. Abutting the bastion here, and extending eastwards, is a section of 17th-century brickwork that originally formed part of the boundary of the gardens or orchards of nearby Joymount House.

ANT 052:061

Report of the Plantation Commissioners, 1611 (PRONI T811/3); Shirley 1855, 276–291; Benn 1877; *PSAMNI* 49; Jope 1950; Simpson and Dickson 1981; Day and McWilliams 1996, 86–92; Ó Baoill 2008, 71–77

24   CARRICKFERGUS: 341490 387550
FORTIFIED HOUSE
Joymount

Joymount House was built between 1610 and 1618 by Sir Arthur Chichester on the site of a 13th-century Franciscan friary. It stood until 1779, when the county gaol and court house, which became the town hall in 1934, were erected in its place. What form Joymont took can only be gleaned from pictorial evidence, particularly the Phillips map of 1685 (NLI MS3137), which indicates that it was a fine example of Jacobean architecture, consisting of a tall rectangular building, at least three storeys in height.

The wall was built of basalt boulders in regular courses, with the largest stones near the base. It ran from the castle along the shoreline and around the town, and had angle bastions at the corners and at several points in between. Excavations at several of the bastions have revealed that they were never filled in with earth, and thus were probably too weak to have withstood assault with cannon, or to have allowed for the deployment of defensive ordnance. The walls were pierced by four gates: Quay Gate, to the west of the castle and probably the main entrance to the town from the harbour; Water Gate, to the north-east; North Gate, on the northern limb of the town; and Irish Gate, on the western flank, the main approach from Belfast. The best-preserved of these is North Gate, which was heavily modified in the 19th and 20th centuries.

Over half of the town wall still survives and

Fig. 2.20 The base of a circular stone tower attached to the town hall in Carrickfergus is probably a surviving element of a barbican and is the only upstanding structure associated with Chichester's 'Joymount'.

The north-western side of the house was flanked by a pair of projecting wings, while the south-eastern, overlooking the sea, was wholly dominated by three curving bay windows set side-by-side, running the full height of the building. There were chimney stacks peering above a balustraded roofline, while wide and tall windows lit the interior. Each floor of the residence was marked externally by string-coursing. The house was described by the English traveller Sir William Brereton (who also praised Chichester's castle in Belfast) as a

> …verye statelye house, or rather like a princes palace…in this house you may observe the inconvenience of great buildings, which require an unreasonable charge to keep them in repair, soe they are a burden to the owners of them.

Nothing of the house survives, although archaeological excavations in the area revealed ephemeral traces in the form of a wall foundation, timber elements (dated dendrochronologically to the early 17th century) and dressed stones. A barbican gate was located immediately to the south of the house. The base of a circular stone tower attached to the eastern wall of the current town hall is probably a surviving element of the barbican and, indeed, is the only upstanding structure associated with the Joymount complex.

ANT 052:062

Shirley 1855; Pinkerton 1859; Waterman 1960, 95; Day and McWilliams 1990b, 5–10; Ó Baoill 2008, 61–63.

Excavations in Carrickfergus

Carrickfergus is perhaps the most archaeologically excavated town in Ulster, and the resulting archaeological material makes an invaluable contribution towards our understanding of how the town evolved and of the daily lives of the inhabitants that would otherwise be unavailable. Listed below (Table 2.1) are the sites of excavations

No.	Site	Grid Ref.	SMR	Description
25	Corke Hill	341200 387420	ANT 052:147	Medieval features and features from the late-17th to the 20th centuries
26	Town ditches	341184 387362	ANT 052:148	Medieval town ditch, traces of the town wall; an early 17th-century extra-mural ditch which encompassed the wall
27	West Street	341230 387380	ANT 052:149	Medieval and 17th-century occupation layers, 17th-century structural features
28	Queen Street	341200 387500	ANT 052:150	Town wall
29	North Street	341270 387560	ANT 052:151	A 17th-century building, probably a malting kiln (mentioned in corporation documents), in association with occupation levels
30	St. Nicholas Parish Hall	341360 387590	ANT 052:153	The point of the 17th-century bastion here contained no structural remains
31	Joymount	341490 387460	ANT 052:155	Town wall

Table 2.1: Sites of archaeological excavations in Carrickfergus.

in the town that have revealed plantation-period features and/or artefacts; a more detailed summary of these can be found in the review by Simpson and Dickson (1981), and publications by Ó Baoill (1993, 1998, 2003 and 2008).

There are no visible remains of the excavated features at any of these locations, although most are comparable in date to the upstanding sites in the town discussed above (Dunlop 2010; Ó Baoill 1993, 1998, 2003, 2008 and 2011c).

Sites Outside Carrickfergus Town

**32   DUNROCK, MIDDLE   338480 389920
        DIVISION: RECTANGULAR ENCLOSURE**

These are the remains of a rectangular earthwork enclosure defined by a ditch, and divided by a modern field boundary. The enclosure measures approximately 55m by 40m internally and is roughly orientated east-west; the ditch is 3m wide. The *OS Memoirs* record that the 'foundations of an ancient castle surrounded by a moat' were visible at the site in the 19th century. It is located immediately to the west of the medieval motte known as 'Duncrue Fort' and, although it is possible that the earthwork is connected with the motte, it is generally considered on grounds of morphology to be of 17th-century date. O'Laverty identified this site with the castle of 'Dunrock', marked according to O'Laverty, on Speede's map of 1610 at a wrong location approximately 10km to the north.

ANT 052:015

O'Laverty 1878–1887, III, 78–79; Day and McWilliams 1996, 182

**33   MIDDLE DIVISION: 339850 390120
        CHURCH, GRAVEYARD AND ENCLOSURE**

A church on this site, referred to in the Terrier map of 1615 and which still stood in ruins in 1829, has now vanished completely. A burial vault dates to the 18th century, and is the only visible indication that there was ever a church at this location.

ANT 052:019

Reeves 1847, 276; O'Laverty 1878–1887, III, 72; Day and McWilliams 1996, 89–92

**34   MIDDLE DIVISION: 340450 390740
        FEATURE**

Various subsoil features of post-medieval date were discovered during archaeological investigations in advance of the Phoenix Gas Belfast Transmission Pipeline. None could be dated directly, and so their relationship with the nearby town of Carrickfergus and its complex post-medieval history could not be established. However, the site does at least illustrate the potential for archaeological traces of post-medieval agricultural practices to be found in the countryside surrounding Carrickfergus.

ANT 052:145

Crothers 1996

**35   BALLYHILL: BAWN   344270 391430
        Dalway's Bawn**

Dalway's Bawn was built by John Dalway, who came to Ireland from England in the late 16th century as a soldier under the earl of Essex, and subsequently married into the family of Shane mac Bryan O'Neill. Presumably he received the lands hereabouts as part of the marriage contract. Following the Nine Years' War, in 1603 he was re-granted the lands by James I, and received a second re-grant in 1609, under the express condition that he build a castle or house and bawn within the townland of Ballynowne, the house (according to the terms to the grant) to be at least 30ft by 20ft (*c.* 9m by 6m). The bawn must have been

Fig. 2.21 View of Dalway's Bawn with its two eastern flankers visible from the roadside.

built soon after, as Carew mentions it as standing in 1611, along with

> …a pritie house of tymber after the English manner thatched for the pr'sent, but entended to be slated.

Following Dalway's death in 1619, his brother Giles inherited the estate, and his descendants continued to live in the house within the bawn until the late 18th century. In 1636, two of the bawn flankers were furnished with wooden staircases, while the bawn was modified in the 19th century for use as a farmyard. Its northern wall was demolished in the mid-20th century, although two of the flankers continued to be inhabited into the 20th century. Various phases of restoration work have been undertaken at the site since the 1970s, but despite the long and complex history of the buildings, the site remains one of the best-preserved examples of a plantation-period bawn in Co. Antrim.

The house has disappeared, and its remains are probably buried under a shed at the northern end of the site. The remains of the bawn consist of a rectangular enclosure of split basalt boulder walls, the eastern wall of which was heightened in the 19th century, while the northern wall was demolished in 1948. The ground level in the interior is lower than that of the exterior, as the southern and western walls are set against an external hill slope. Originally there was a very large drum flanking tower at each corner. That on the south-west disappeared long ago, but its presence is suggested by a gap in the bawn, although some scholars dispute its existence.

The two eastern flankers, which are visible from the roadside, have been much modified and restored, the north-eastern structure having been rebuilt completely in 1972. Both incorporate rectangular projections at their inner edges, facing the centre of the bawn and housing the entrances and stairs. Interestingly, these projections incorporate crow-stepped gables and turreted stairways, details from the Scottish masonry tradition. The north-western flanker is remarkably well preserved, and displays gun loops in the ground floor and a pair of mullioned windows on each of the upper two floors.

ANT 047:015
Report of the Plantation Commissioners, 1611 (PRONI T811/3); O'Laverty 1878–1887, III, 89–90; *PSAMNI* 40; Jope 1960, 108; McGranaghan 2007

36   DOBBSLAND: CASTLE   344302 390723
Castle Dobbs

In his *Brief Description of the County of Antrim* (1683), Richard Dobbs mentioned a castle as having been built by his grandfather, which is now in ruins. The Carew survey records that

> One John Dabb buylte a fayre Castle w'thin to myle of Knockfargus called Dabbs Castle aboute w'h he entend to buylde a bawne of stone. Some Irish people of civill behavio'r are planted there who made good houses after the manner of the Palle. This castle is buylte upon p'te of Ensigne Dallawayes lands.

Built of stone rubble and incorporating timber lintels, the remains consist of the walls of a small, square castle. The end wall stands approximately 11m high, and is joined by two lower side walls.

ANT 053:001
Report of the Plantation Commissioners, 1611 (PRONI T811/3); O'Laverty 1878–1887, III, 90; Dobbs 1683 quoted in Hill 1873, 378; *PSAMNI* 51; Day *et al.* 1994c, 58–59 and 67–79

37   CROSSMARY: SETTLEMENT   342890 391170
AND BAWN

This rectangular enclosure is defined by a broad, low earthen bank running north-south on the eastern side of a field. This could constitute the remains of a bawn, the history of which is unknown.

ANT 047:054
Unpublished notes in the SMR file

38   KILROOT: MILL   344600 388600

The approximate site of a water mill is marked near the mouth of the Kilroot River on the Down Survey barony map, and a mill dam and mills were recorded here in the mid-19th century at the time of the first Ordnance Survey. No visible remains survive, as the area is now occupied by Kilroot Power Station.

ANT 053:016

Down Survey Barony map of Belfast (PRONI D597/2)

39   KILROOT: HOUSE AND   345000 389480
         BAWN
         The Bishop's House

The ruins of a house and 17th-century bawn survive at the site of Kilroot Church. Although the extant ruined house probably dates to the 18th century, it is possible that an earlier building phase might be found within its fabric. It seems a house was built on the site around 1604, incorporating part of the graveyard of the former church in its bawn. The Carew survey reported that the construction of the bawn was due to

> …Mr Homstone the late Bishop of Downe at a place by the sea called Kilroote and a stone walle aboute it 10 foote high repaired by the now Bishop.

The incumbent bishop was Robert Echlin, who was also resident for a time at The Abbacy on the Ards peninsula (see Inv. 174). Homstone's house, however, is not the current 'Bishops House' – the early 17th-century structure was an apsidal building, and appeared on early edition OS maps of the site. The site is also associated with the Brice family. Presumably it was demolished at some point between the 1857 and 1933 revisions of the OS six-inch map. The surviving 18th-century building is a three-storey structure similar to a tower house, but unusually narrow, measuring 18m by 7m, and obscured by dense vegetation. Occupation of the site during the 17th-century is represented by two circular flanking towers, one of which contains

Fig. 2.22 View of the Bishop's House in Kilroot. Although the extant ruined house probably dates to the 18th century, it is possible that earlier building phases can be found within its fabric.

the remains of a dovecote, and part of a bawn wall. Excavations at the site in 2003 revealed burials of likely medieval date and 18th-century garden features.

ANT 053:004

Report of the Plantation Commissioners, 1611 (PRONI T811/3); O'Laverty 1878–1887, III, 85

Island Magee and Templecorran

The parish of Broadisland or Templecorran lies on land originally held by John Dalway (see Inv. 35). In 1609 he granted much of the property to William Edmonstone, one of the tenants of Sir Hugh Montgomery on the Ards Peninsula (Hill 1869, 57–58). Edmonstone rebuilt and occupied a castle at Red Hall (Inv. 40), and may have been involved in the construction of the bawn-like site discovered recently on land he rented at Ballycarry (Inv. 42). In 1611, he invited a minister from his home county of Stirlingshire, the Rev. Edward Brice, to settle in Ballycarry. Two years later, the Scottish minister officially began his duties in the old church there, establishing one of the oldest Presbyterian congregations in Ireland (Anon. 1982, 57). Also in the area is Whitehead, a port with close links to Scotland, and a settlement during plantation times, situated on the southern shore of the Island

Magee peninsula, close to both Templecorran and Carrickfergus. In Whitehead, aside from a small tower house (Inv. 43) and its continued existence as a coastal village, nothing remains of the port and associated settlement referred to in various sources (O'Laverty 1884, III; *PSAMNI* 40). Island Magee is mentioned by Carew as the landing place of Andrew Stewart, through which cattle and horses for his huge estate in Co. Tyrone were brought to Ireland from Scotland (Hill 1877, 546).

40   RED HALL: HOUSE   344990 394970

This country house, continuously occupied since perhaps the 16th century and incorporating 17th-century structural elements, remains a private residence. The earliest historical reference is the grant to William Edmonstone in 1609, although the thickness and batter of some walls suggest that he re-edified an existing tower house of 16th-century or earlier date. The Edmonstone family owned the house and estate until the late 18th century, enlarging and aggrandising the house. The estate has changed ownership several times since then, with yet more phases of rebuilding.

What survives from the 17th century are the walls of the core of the house, which originally was a three-storey, three-bay structure, perhaps not dissimilar to

Joymount in Carrickfergus. The building contains a 17th-century oak staircase and the house also displays wooden wall panelling dating possibly to the later 17th century and many other architectural details accumulated in its long history.

HB06/05/013B

PSAMNI 38–39; Bence-Jones 1978, 241; Brett 1996, 76–77

41   FORTHILL: CHURCH AND   344831 393693
GRAVEYARD
Templecorran Church

The ruins of Templecorran Church are located at the southern end of Main Street, Ballycarry, at the site of the current parish church, which was built in 1848. The building dates from the early 17th century, and was described in the Visitation Book of 1622 as 'Temple-i-corran the walls newly erected but not roofed yet'. It seems to have been in use for a relatively short time, as sources imply that it was ruined by 1679. The *OS Memoirs* recall that it was in the parish of Edward Brice, often identified as the first Presbyterian minister in Ireland, from 1613 until his death in 1636.

The church was built close to the summit of a ridge of high ground overlooking Larne Lough. The roofless building is of cruciform plan, and is largely intact. The

Fig. 2.23 Red Hall, a country house in continuous occupation, perhaps since the 16th century, incorporates 17th-century structural elements, and remains a private residence.

Fig. 2.24 Elevated view of Templecorran Church.

walls are built from stone rubble, with some dressed stone used in the door jambs and window surrounds. A number of gun loops are visible at ground level within the western gable and southern wall of the church, a feature not normally associated with churches, but nonetheless illustrating their occasional use as defensive holdouts during the plantation-period. There are a number of 17th-century memorial stones in the graveyard, near to the church building, and the graveyard is still in use, although later interments have been made in extended areas, away from the church. It has been suggested that a wall on the southern side of the ruin represents the remains of a session house erected by the Presbyterian congregation during the 17th century.

ANT 047:010

Reeves 1847, 58; O'Laverty 1878–1887, III, 90 and 92; *PSAMNI* 39–40; Anon. 1944; Day *et al.* 1994c, 108–113; Crothers *et al.* 2000; Roulston 2004

42 BALLYCARRY: ENCLOSURE 344800 393510

A large quadrangular enclosure of unknown date, 54m^2 in area, but only faintly visible on the ground, is associated with Templecorran Church (Inv. 41). Geophysical survey of part of the interior of the enclosure in 2008, and subsequent excavations in 2009–2010 revealed another, smaller square enclosure, of sides *c*. 35m in length, with two angle bastions at opposing corners. The enclosure was delineated by a rock-cut ditch, *c*. 1.3m in depth and around 2.7m wide.

The bastions are of a form typical of defences in Ireland from the mid-16th century, while the size and shape of the enclosure suggests a bawn, perhaps that of the Edmonstone family, who owned this land in the early 17th century.

ANT 047:068

Murray 2011

43 WHITE HEAD: CASTLE 347651 392022
Castle Chichester

The remains of Castle Chichester are situated near the shore of Belfast Lough, on the southern edge of

Fig. 2.25 View of Castle Chichester.

the Island Magee peninsula. The site was described by Carew in 1611 as

> …latlie buylte by Moses Hill, sometime lyvtent of the hourse troope of Sr. Arthur Chichester and now Provost Marshall of the government and tenant of the said Sr. Arthur Chichester, a pritie Castle nowe called Castle Chichester. That Iland is well inhabited by English and Scotish men and by civill Irish men, such as for the most p'te can speake English.

Its origins are thus usually attributed to Hill, although there is also the possibility that the castle (rather than that at Mahee Island in Strangford Lough) is associated with Captain Browne's failed colonial project of around 1570. Irrespective of its origins, it was certainly at the centre of a successful British settlement in the early 17th century. The *OS Memoirs* suggest that there was an associated quay used in frequent trade with Scotland, the vestiges of which could still be seen in the mid-19th century. It is likely that the castle functioned as a customs house for the port here.

The structure consists of a small square tower with sides measuring *c*. 8m and standing 11m high.

The walls, which are over 3m thick, are built mainly of sea-washed basalt boulders. The entrance, now blocked, is in the south-eastern wall, in which a stone staircase led to the two upper floors. Each side of the castle contains several small, square-headed windows, splayed on the inside, and a number of gun loops. The remains of two chimneys can be seen in the north-western and north-eastern walls. The walls have been stabilised in recent decades, with some repairs made to the upper levels.

ANT 047:025

Report of the Plantation Commissioners, 1611 (PRONI T811/3); O'Laverty 1878–1887, III, 126–127; Shirley 1855, 83; *PSAMNI* 40; Day and McWilliams 1991d, 27–29, 47–50, 98–104; O'Dowd 2000; MacDonald 2002

44 BALLYPRIOR MORE: CHURCH 345230 400860

This is the site of a church referred to as the 'Church of Ranseeyn' in some 17th-century documents, 'Ranseeyn' being an old name for the Island Magee peninsula. There are no visible remains and, although in the past the site has been used for burials, the earliest memorial stones date to the 18th century.

ANT 041:005

Reeves 1847, 59; O'Laverty 1878–1887, III, 140–141; Day and McWilliams 1991d, 43

Fig. 2.26 The ruins of Portmuck Castle consist of the heavily-robbed stump of a small tower-house.

45 PORTMUCK: CASTLE 346125 402371

The ruins of Portmuck Castle consist of the heavily robbed stump of a small tower house, with walls of large split boulders supporting a barrel vault. It is likely that the castle was built in the 16th century and was associated with maritime trade at Portmuck. Its appearance on the Down Survey county and barony maps suggests that it was still occupied in the early 17th century, but its history is otherwise obscure.

ANT 041:003

Down Survey Barony map of Belfast (PRONI D597/2); O'Laverty 1878–1887, III, 139–140; *PSAMNI* 35

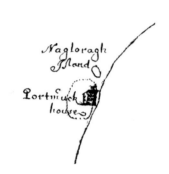

Fig. 2.27 Portmuck Castle, as depicted on the Down Survey barony map of Belfast, c. 1656–1658.

Barony of Glenarm Upper

Larne

Since the mid-19th century, Larne has become a key seaport, catering for a significant proportion of the trade between Britain and Ireland (McKillop 2000, 2–4). In the 16th and 17th centuries its harbour was known as 'Olderfleet Haven', and although not as important as Belfast, Carrickfergus, Donaghadee or arguably Whitehead, it was nonetheless a convenient crossing point to Scotland. According to Speede's map of 1610, it was defended at that time by three small castles (see Inv. 48). The area was also the seat of the Agnew family (Inv. 46).

46 DEMENSE: CASTLE AND BAWN 335650 401500
Kilwaughter Castle

The remains of a 17th-century castle, and part of

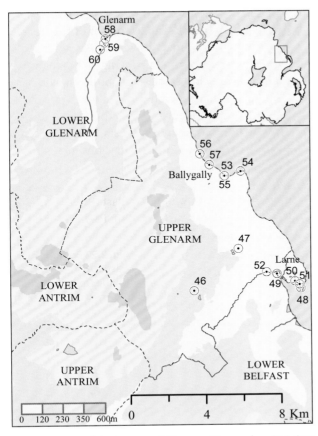

Fig. 2.28 Map of the barony of Glenarm Upper showing sites discussed within text.

a bawn, are incorporated into an 1807 mansion house that is now also ruinous. This was the seat of descendants of Philip d'Agneaux, a Norman knight who came to Ulster with de Courcy, and the building was the residence of the Agnew family until World War II. During the early 17th century, the Squire was Captain John Agnew, who married Eleanor Shaw, a daughter of Scottish settlers in Ballygally (see Inv. 53).

The early 17th-century building consists of a T-plan, gabled structure of four storeys, 15.2m by 8.5m externally, orientated north-west to south-east, with a large rectangular projection on the north-eastern side containing the entrance and stair. The walls are of white limestone blocks and strongly built, up to 1.8m thick. In Scottish style, turrets project from each corner of the main block at second-floor

level (although it is not certain that these are original features), and there are traces of chimney stacks in each gable. The chambers on the lower three floors were lit only by narrow slits, while the upper floor contains small rectangular windows immediately under the eaves. The castle is positioned projecting outwards from the south-western wall of a bawn. Only fragments of this wall and the north-western return survive, although it is possible to suggest that if the castle was centred on the south-western wall, the bawn wall would have sides some 40–50m long.

ANT 040:008

Hill 1873, 304; Dickson 1901; Jope 1956 and 1960, 97–123

47   BALLYBOLEY: HOUSE   338000 403800
Ballyboley townland

This is the approximate site of a house marked on the Down Survey barony map of Glenarm, but no trace of the structure has been located.

ANT 035:085

Down Survey Barony map of Glenarm (PRONI D597/2)

48   CURRAN AND DRUMALISS: 341300 401600
TOWER HOUSE
Olderfleet Castle

Olderfleet Haven is the name given to Larne Harbour on maps of the 16th and 17th centuries. On Speede's Map of 1610, three castles ('Coraine', 'Tchevet' and 'Olderfleet') are shown (perhaps erroneously) surrounding the harbour. Of these, Coraine is the only one that survives and, somewhat confusingly, this castle is now known as Olderfleet, with the name 'Coraine' surviving as 'Curran Point', the land upon which the castle stands. It is likely to have been constructed in the 16th century to guard the harbour, and perhaps also operated as a defended warehouse throughout the 17th century.

The remains consist of a square, three- or four-storey tower, now ruined, the southern side and much of the western side having been almost completely robbed. The walls are of split basalt rubble, with occasional limestone blocks and roughly hewn basalt quoins. The basement level includes an inner dividing wall and several double-splayed gun loops. The upper levels have window openings and sockets for floor joists at irregular intervals and levels.

ANT 040:040

Bound volume – Irish Historical Atlas (PRONI T2543/1); *PSAMNI* 33; Jope 1960, 100

49   INVER: TOWER HOUSE   340050 402400

Perhaps now under the Harbour Highway in Larne, this is the approximate site of a tower house shown on Speede's map of 1610 as 'Olderfleete Castle', although different to the castle currently known

by that name at the mouth of the Larne River (see Inv. 48).

ANT 040:034

Bound volume – Irish Historical Atlas (PRONI T2543/1); *PSAMNI* 33

50   CURRAN AND DRUMALISS: 341000 402000 TOWER HOUSE

The precise location of a tower house shown on Speede's map of 1610 as 'Tchevet Castle' is unknown and there are no visible remains, the approximate area now being an industrial estate.

ANT 040:038

Bound volume – Irish Historical Atlas (PRONI T2543/1); *PSAMNI* 33

Fig. 2.29 Ballygally Castle built by James Shaw in 1625 is a fine example of a Scottish-style fortified residence on the Antrim coast.

**51   CURRAN AND DRUMALISS: 341240 401820
        EARTHWORK**

According to O'Laverty, this was the site of earthworks erected in 1640 by an army of Irish soldiers under Sir William St Leger. No trace remains due to development at the site.

ANT 040:039

O'Laverty 1878–1887, III, 160

**52   TOWN PARKS OF LARNE: 339500 402500
        HOUSES**

There are no visible remains of a group of houses marked at this approximate location on the 1656–58 Down Survey map of the parish.

ANT 040:103

Down Survey parish map of Larne (PRONI D597)

Ballygally

Ballygally, also spelled 'Ballygalley', is a village on the Antrim coast near the southernmost part of what once was the estate of the earls of Antrim. In the early 17th century the freeholder there was James Shaw of Greenock, who was also the brother-in-law of Sir Hugh Montgomery. Shaw built a castle (Inv. 53), and the surrounding land was probably relatively well populated during the plantation period, as the Down Survey barony map of Glenarm, drawn 1656–58, indicates numerous structures in the area.

**53   BALLYGALLY: CASTLE   337250 407810
        AND BAWN**

This coastal castle was built in 1625 by James Shaw,

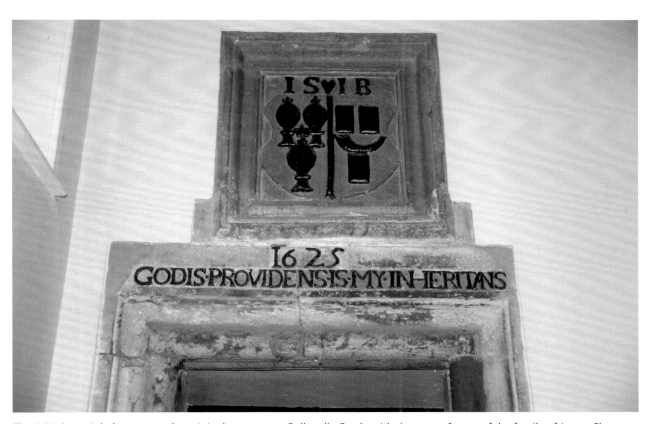

Fig. 2.30 Armorial plaque over the original entrance to Ballygally Castle with the coat-of-arms of the family of James Shaw alongside that of the family of his wife, the Montgomerys of Braidestane. Above the armorial device are the initials I.S. and I.B. for Shaw and Elizabeth Braidestane respectively. Carved into the door lintel is the year 1625 and the following inscription: 1625 GODIS.PROVIDENS.IS.MY.INHERITANS.

and became a place of refuge during the 1641 Rebellion when it was attacked, though not severely damaged. Indeed, there are accounts of a member of the Shaw family, with Captain Agnew of Kilwaughter, riding out to inflict vigilante retaliation upon any Irish persons that they encountered. The castle was modified and extended during the 18th and 20th centuries, including its subsequent development as a hotel, its current use.

The original 17th-century elements are the walls – approximately 1.5m thick and perforated with gun loops – of a three- to four-storey tower house, rectangular in plan, with a square projection at its north-eastern corner, containing the entrance and stone spiral stairs. A turret is corbelled out of this projection at upper levels, with a further two on the southern side of the main block. Over the doorway is the patrons' armorial plaque, bearing an inscription with the date 1625.

The tower is surrounded by a bawn, originally with circular flanking towers with conical roofs at each corner, although the side of the bawn nearest the sea was removed when the Antrim Coast Road was built in the 1840s, and the current wall and flankers are reconstructions.

Excavations in 1996 in the western corner of the bawn revealed a cobbled courtyard, with no sign of any buildings. The north-western bawn wall appears to have stood on the line currently occupied by a boundary between gardens and a tennis court.

ANT 035:015

Porter 1901; Marshall 1905; *PSAMNI* 16 and 20–30; Jope 1951; Hurl 1996a

54   CARNCASTLE: CASTLE   338150 408050

The remains of a small stone tower that lends its name to the local parish, and possibly the foundations of a castle built of basalt boulders, are located on a rock stack and tidal island on the northern side of Ballygalley Head. The walls, which are 1.0m thick and measure 9.0m by 7.4m internally, are orientated north-east to south-west, and rise to 1.8m at the south-western corner. The history of the site is obscure, but given the significant number of

Fig. 2.31 View of Carncastle.

plantation-period sites in the immediate area, an early 17th-century association seems plausible.

ANT 035:016

PSAMNI 30; Johnston 2003

55   BALLYGALLY: MILL   337300 407800
Balligolly Mill

The site of a mill is marked at this approximate location on the Down Survey map of the barony of Glenarm, and a mill was also shown here on the 1st edition OS six-inch map. The locality is still known as 'Old Mill', although nothing survives of any building.

ANT 035:086

Down Survey Barony map of Glenarm (PRONI D597)

56   BALLYRUTHER: HOUSE   336000 409000
AND WATER MILLS

No remains are known to survive of a house marked on the Down Survey map of the barony of Glenarm, or of two water mills mentioned in Inquisitions.

ANT 035:087

Down Survey Barony map of Glenarm (PRONI D597); *Inq. Ulst.* Antrim Car. I (40)

57   CORKERMAIN: HOUSE   336500 408400

No archaeological traces are known of what may have been a stone tower house marked on the

Down Survey map of the barony of Glenarm at this approximate location.

ANT 035:088

Down Survey Barony map of Glenarm (PRONI D597)

Barony of Glenarm Lower

Glenarm Village

'The Route', the lordship formerly held by the McQuillans and comprising the baronies of Glenarm, Cary, Dunluce and Kilconway (333,907 acres), was granted to Sir Randall MacDonnell in 1603 (Hill 1873, 196–198). One of the conditions of the grant was that he maintain a castle in each barony —a stipulation already met by his possession of Dunluce Castle (see Inv. 87), Clare Park (see Inv.

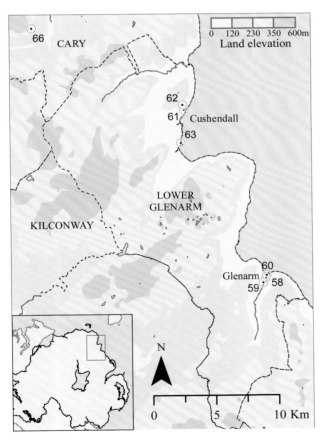

Fig. 2.32 Sites in the barony of Glenarm Lower.

73 and 74, although it is likely that building work was needed here), and Clough Castle (see Inv. 102), but Glenarm lacked a suitable seat (*ibid.*). A medieval castle, built by the Bissets, once stood in Glenarm, although this was abandoned in the late 16th century (Hill 1873, 188), while the castle (Inv. 58) was built between the time of the grant and the death of the 1st earl in 1636. In the early 17th century the village was also the site of an old friary (Inv. 60) and presumably a small population centre, although nothing visible of this phase of its history survives.

58   GLENARM: CASTLE   330960 415090

Glenarm Castle, the seat of the MacDonnell earls of Antrim, is still occupied by the family as a private residence. The current building is an 1825 remodelling of the 1756 mansion, but displays elements of the original castle, built between 1603 and 1636 by Sir Randal MacDonnell, the 1st earl.

The castle became the family seat in 1639, following a partial collapse at Dunluce Castle (see Inv. 87). It was burned by an invading Scots army in 1642, but was probably repaired and re-inhabited soon after, although until the 18th century the family had their main residence at Ballymagarry, near Dunluce (see Inv. 90). The core of the castle probably contains many 17th-century elements, but it is impossible to identify original fabric in a building so heavily rebuilt over several successive phases, especially given that most of the internal walls are either rendered or plastered. The kitchen of the house is said to be an original room, and a 17th-century coat of arms, probably originally attached to the castle, is now incorporated into the barbican of the complex.

HB06/02/001

Hill 1873, 188; Brett 1971, 11–43; McNeill 1983, 125

59   GLENARM DEMESNE: 330750 414730
       CHURCH, GRAVEYARD
       AND FINDSPOT

A small and relatively modern building, roofless and missing its south-western corner, stands on

Ballygally Castle (Inv. 53)

Standing within the village of Ballygally is Ballygally Castle, one of the finest examples of early modern Scottish architecture to be found in Ireland. It was built by the planter James Shaw, who came from Greenock, a coastal town overlooking the Firth of Clyde in Renfrewshire, an area from which many settlers arrived in search of a new life in Ulster (Porter 1901, 65–67). According to a date stone found over the main entrance into the castle, it was built in 1625. Shaw was well connected in east Ulster, being the brother-in-law of Sir Hugh Montgomery, a prominent landowner in the Ards area of Co. Down. But rather than establishing himself in that county, Shaw acquired lands around Ballygally from the 1st earl of Antrim as a gentleman freeholder. The location of the estate on the eastern coastline of Co. Antrim, relatively close to Scottish ports, was an important consideration no doubt for this aspiring Scottish landowner. Ease of communication with the homeland made it easier and more economical to develop the estate, allowing the necessary numbers of tenants and tradesmen to be brought in, since one of the major issues facing new landowners was the difficulty in attracting settlers, especially to the more remote parts of the province. This was particularly problematic for those who did not already have holdings in England or Scotland from which they could draw tenants.

1 Ballygally Castle on the east coastline of Co. Antrim is one of the finest examples of early modern Scottish architecture to be found in Ireland. It was built in 1625 by James Shaw who originally hailed from Greenock in Renfrewshire.

Indeed, Shaw himself might not have had significant resources to invest initially in his new property. He was living in Ballygally as early as 1613, when he was recorded as being a member of the Co. Antrim jury in that year (*ibid*. 66), but the castle itself was not built until some twelve years later. Such a building would not have taken that length of time to build, and one can only surmise that Shaw lived in an earlier building on the site, focusing on developing his lands before building a residence befitting himself and his family as members of the local gentry.

Ballygally Castle is in an excellent state of preservation, having been occupied continually for almost four hundred years. It is a rather tall building with a high dormered roof, while against one corner is a smaller tower, creating an L-shaped plan. Unlike the later Georgian country houses, the main entrance is not placed centrally in the main façade, but is located on the northern side, in the re-entrant angle between the tower and main block. Large windows on the southern side provide lighting for the rooms, and face into the relative security of where the bawn would have been located, while much smaller windows on the other sides of the building face outwards. The grounds of the house would have been enclosed by a bawn, which no longer survives, though the present boundary walls may preserve its original extent. The circular flanker at the south-eastern corner of the property is a late

2 The original entrance into Ballygally Castle with armorial plaque and date stone above. Inside is a stairwell that is significantly wider than those within Irish tower houses, providing a more grandiose, spacious approach to the upper floors.

Victorian garden folly, along with the perimeter wall that runs northwards from it; this side of the original bawn was removed when the Coast Road was built through the village in the mid-19th century. During the course of the 18th century, a larger residence was built abutting onto the western side of the house, creating a larger residential complex that is now the Ballygally Hotel.

The castle has been fully integrated into the later house, and the entrance is now located off the main foyer of the hotel. It is a flat-headed doorway with an attractive moulded sandstone surround. Above the doorway is a date stone carrying the inscription:

1625 GODIS.PROVIDENS.IS.MY.INHERITANS.

Above this is a square-moulded frame, within which is an armorial plaque displaying the Shaw family coat-of-arms impaled with those of Shaw's wife, the Montgomerys of Braidestane. Above the armorial device are the initials I.S. and I.B. for James Shaw and Elizabeth Braidestane respectively. This communicated to everyone coming and going through the entrance that the lineage of the household was of respectable origins, and that faith in God had granted them success in Ireland. At a time when Shaw's ownership of lands was contingent on the continuing success of the Plantation, the use of such carvings was important in reaffirming the status of the family and their entitlement to the lands surrounding Ballygally. During the 1641 Rebellion, James Shaw, a son of the founder, managed to hold out against Irish Confederate forces. With Captain Agnew of nearby Kilwaughter Castle, he rode out to inflict vigilante retaliations upon any Irish that they encountered. Despite such turbulence, the castle continued in the ownership of the Shaw family for the remainder of the century and beyond, until it was eventually sold by them in 1820 (*ibid.* 68–69 and 74).

Ballygally Castle is rather unusual – a Scottish castle in the Irish countryside (Jope 1951, 36 and 44). The overall appearance of the building, with the main floors contained within a tall, oblong block joined to one side by a tower of equal height containing the stairwell, is paralleled by contemporary fortified houses in Scotland. The walls are quite substantial, being around 1.5m thick. The relatively plain façades of Ballygally, with the limited number of plain windows, and the contrast with the more elaborate roofline is also characteristic of Scottish élite architecture in the early 17th century. The high, steeply pitched roof has no battlements, but defensive concerns are still expressed through the addition of the conical turrets or bartizans at the south-eastern and south-western corners of the roof, as well as on the north-eastern corner of the stairwell tower. According to architectural plans made of the castle *c.* 1900, these turrets were provided with gun loops that allowed the surrounding grounds to be covered by musket fire in case of attack (Porter 1901, 75). A pair of loops is still visible at basement level, flanking the approach to the main entrance (one of these forms part of an exhibit on the castle by the hotel owners).

Inside the entrance, a stone spiral staircase allows access to the upper floors. Such staircases are commonly found in contemporary tower houses and fortified houses in Ireland, but the Ballygally example is different, probably reflecting the work of Lowland Scottish masons employed by Shaw. It is significantly wider than those within Irish tower houses, and provides a more grandiose, spacious approach to the main chambers on the floors above. The basement contained the kitchen with its massive fireplace, along with a pair of smaller rooms – the buttery and scullery. The first floor is divided into two chambers, larger and smaller, probably reflecting their original use as great chamber and withdrawing room respectively. The original layout has been altered somewhat to accommodate the addition of a modern entrance and accompanying hallway. Judging by the placement of the windows, the second and third floors were also divided into two rooms. The third-floor attic is lit by a pair of dormer windows, the stone surrounds of which are still evident. These are rather attractive in appearance, being crowned with decorative pediments. The

3 The turreted roofline is the most striking aspect of Ballygally Castle. The conical turrets are supported by moulded corbels, a feature that is very much Scottish in inspiration and which reflects the Renfrewshire background of its builder.

semicircular pediment on top of the western dormer window is decorated with a fanlight motif, while the triangular pediment on the eastern window contains a triangle, inside of which are three circles.

The turreted roofline is the most striking aspect of Ballygally Castle. Even in the early 17th century it must have provided a clear architectural expression of the Scottish identity of the Shaws. The conical turrets are supported by moulded corbels, a feature that is very much Scottish in inspiration and which reflects the Renfrewshire background of its builder. The use of conical roof turrets supported by moulded corbels is commonplace across the western Lowlands of Scotland, but is limited in number in Ireland. Nine other survivals are known in Ulster (Jope 1951, 41-44): Dunluce Castle in Co. Antrim (Inv. 87), Old Customs House in Bangor, Co. Down (Inv. 149), Enniskillen Castle, Monea Castle, and Castle Balfour in Co. Fermanagh (Invs 342, 326 and 249) and Aughentaine Castle, Mountcastle, Derrywoone Castle and Roughan Castle in Co. Tyrone (Invs 391, 347, 353 and 402). A further six, no longer standing, are known from antiquarian records and drawings, and 17th-century pictorial maps to have had such features (*ibid*. 44–45). A variant of this Scottish architectural embellishment can be found in Parke's Castle, Co. Leitrim and Rathlee, Co. Sligo, where the turrets are supported with smoothed, rather than moulded corbels (Donnelly 2012, 45). The presence of these conical turrets on a building was usually as a result of a Scottish landlord, such as Shaw, bringing masons over from the homeland, and indeed none of these buildings were Irish owned.

the former site of a medieval church and graveyard that has now disappeared. Noted in the Papal Taxation of Pope Nicholas of 1306 as the Church of St Mary of Glenarm, the Ulster Visitation Book of 1622 recorded the church as already ruined, so it is possible that it fell out of use before the plantation period. While there are no graves visible at the site, which is much obscured by vegetation, a quantity of bone and a hoard of six Philip and Mary coins (1554–1558) were once found here.

ANT 029:007

Reeves 1847, 299; O'Laverty 1878–1887, IV, 570–571

60   GLENARM DEMESNE: 331032 415333
GRAVEYARD
St Patrick's Church, Glenarm

St Patrick's Church was built directly on the foundations of a Franciscan friary, some of the walls of which can be traced in the surrounding graveyard. Although the friary was abandoned in 1584, and building on the current church did not begin until 1768, the site was used as a cemetery from the early 17th century onwards. Excavations in the graveyard in 2005, in advance of refurbishment of the church, revealed several complete burials and the fragmentary remains of many others. It is likely that some of these individuals (whose remains were reinterred at the site) were buried in the early 17th century, although dating of the graves was not possible.

ANT 029:006

Reeves 1847, 299; O'Laverty 1878–1887, IV, 271–272; Gwynn and Hadcock 1970, 271; Dunlop and Dunlop 2005

Sites in the Cushendall area

Cushendall is a village of 19th-century origins on the Antrim coast, and is situated at a natural focal point in the landscape, at the foot of three of the Antrim glens.

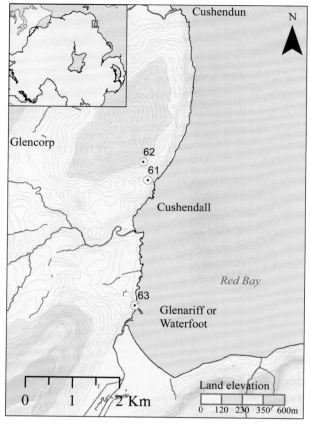

Fig. 2.33 Sites in Cushendall area.

61   MONEYVART: CHURCH   324539 428930
AND GRAVEYARD
Layd Church

Layd Church, now in ruins, was a parish church of early 14th-century date that continued in use until 1790. Its history is obscure, and the somewhat enigmatic remains consist of a rectangular, roofless building showing numerous phases of remodelling. The masonry suggests that the eastern end of the building is more recent than the western, although none of the building phases are dated. The eastern wall is gabled, and the western end consists of a two-storey tower, with the upper floor carried on a massive barrel vault. The church was built in at least two phases, and on stylistic grounds, a date in the late 16th century or early 17th centuries can be suggested for it. The remains stand within a graveyard, in a steep-sided valley, and close to

Fig. 2.34 View of Layd Church with the remains of the belfry tower at its western end. Access into the church was gained via the round-arched doorway of 17th-century date in the southern wall.

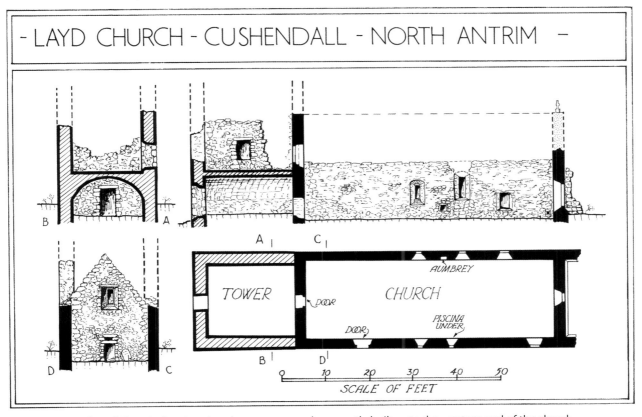

- LAYD CHURCH - CUSHENDALL - NORTH ANTRIM -

Fig. 2.35 Plan of Layd Church showing that the tower was subsequently built onto the western end of the church.

the stretch of coast where Ireland and Scotland are closest. The graveyard contains several memorials to prominent 18th-century MacDonnell family members, linking the site with the earls of Antrim.

ANT 015:001

Fennell 1900; D'Arcy 1930; Smyth 1939, 50; *PSAMNI* 17–18; Hamlin 2008, 213–214

62   LAYD: HOUSE   324438 429331
The Old Castle

The ruins of this dwelling comprise of a chimney stack that once belonged to a larger three-storey building, the foundations and lower levels of which can be traced from other ruinous walls on the site. From these, it seems that the ground floor was divided into three rooms. The *OS Memoirs* recorded that the house was old but still roofed in the late 18th century. The history of the building is otherwise obscure, and although it may date to the plantation period on architectural grounds, McNeill suggested that the building is probably of late 17th century date.

ANT 015:047

O'Laverty 1878–1887, IV, 557; McNeill 1983 126; Day and McWilliams 1992a, 40

Fig. 2.36 Aerial view of The Old Castle in Layd.

63   RED BAY: TOWER HOUSE   324290 426170
AND BAWN
Red Bay Castle

The ruins of Red Bay Castle, which is of 16th-century origin, stand on earthworks suggestive of an Iron Age promontory fort and an Anglo-Norman motte, although this appearance may instead be due to a combination of natural features and the collapse of the castle itself. It is situated on a rocky precipice above the sea, and its remains consist of the south-eastern corner and the eastern wall of a rectangular tower house, originally *c.* 12m by 8m externally, of three storeys, and built of red sandstone rubble. A corbelled string course runs along the eastern wall at second floor level. Vestiges of a roughly rectangular bawn extend from the tower, enclosing the ground to the south.

The castle was built by James McDonald for Captain Piers of Carrickfergus in 1561, and taken by Shane O'Neill (along with the old castle in Glenarm) in 1565, and there are numerous late 16th- and early 17th-century accounts of skirmishes at the site between English, Scottish and Irish protagonists. Carew noted that the castle was restored in the 1600s by the 1st earl of Antrim, and was still habitable when leased to John Stewart by the 2nd earl in 1637, although it perhaps became ruinous

Fig. 2.37 Aerial view of Red Bay Castle overlooking the Antrim coastline.

soon after. In 1683, Dobbs said that the site '…had been a handsome pile of red sandstone'.

ANT 020:010

O'Laverty 1878–1887, IV, 545–548; *PSAMNI* 21; McNeill 1983, 123–124

Barony of Cary

Sites in the Armoy Area

The Armoy area contains fertile farmland overlooked by Knocklayd Mountain and other higher land to the east. It was probably a small freehold estate during plantation times, and the uplands in the surrounding area display numerous features that may constitute a preserved post-medieval landscape (Inv. 66).

64 TURNAROBERT: HOUSE 307510 433140

This is the possible site of a house built by Anthony Kennedy, who was granted the townland of Turnarobert by the 1st earl of Antrim in 1606. A 'gentleman's residence' was built on the site in the late 18th century, replacing any earlier structure, although a small stone-built, two-storey building in the grounds of the present house may be a remnant of the original dwelling.

HB05/05/009

Unpublished notes in listed buildings database (currently available via *http://www.doeni.gov.uk/ services/buildings-database*)

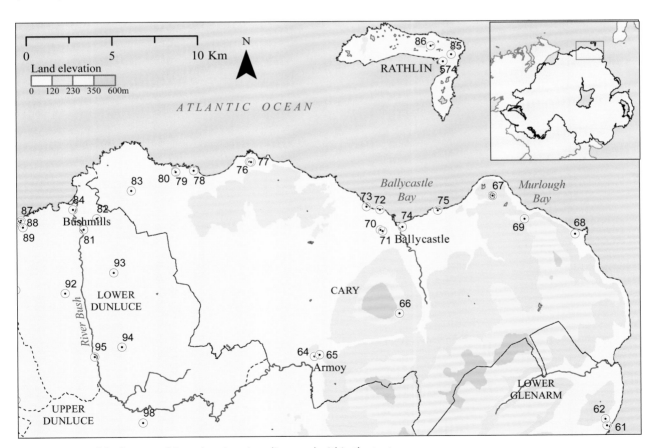

Fig. 2.38 Map of the barony of Cary showing sites discussed within the text.

Fig. 2.39 Possible 17th-century building at Turnarobert.

**65   DRUMSONNUS: CHURCH   307806 433246
AND GRAVEYARD
St Patrick's Church, Armoy**

A church built in 1820 on the site of an earlier structure that was described as a roofless ruin in the Ulster Visitation Book of 1622. The stump of an early medieval, ecclesiastical round tower stands at the site, although there are no surface remains of the earlier church. Excavations here in the 1990s revealed traces of the medieval building and human remains, including those of an individual with leprosy, radiocarbon dated to between AD 1444 and 1636.

ANT 013:010

Reeves 1847, 80 and 243–245; O'Laverty 1878–1887, IV, 443–450; *PSAMNI* 15; Murphy and Manchester 2002

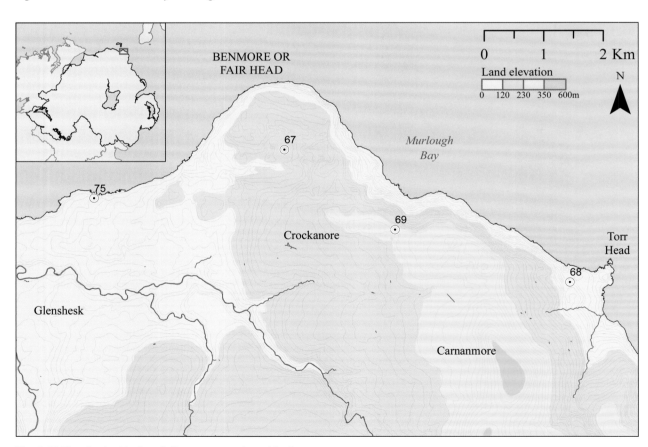

Fig. 2.40 Sites in the Murlough Bay area mentioned in the text.

66 AGHALECK AND CORVALLY: 312470 435700
SETTLEMENT AND FIELD SYSTEM

These townlands include the remains of earthworks, twelve possible stone structures (of which some may be domestic houses), field banks and an enclosure that together cover a large area. The features, constituting a remarkably preserved agricultural landscape, are undated but are probably post-medieval. Excavation would be required to ascertain if these features were part of the plantation-period landscape.

> ANT 009:170
> O'Laverty 1878–1887, IV, 427; Evans 1945, 29–30

Murlough Bay Area

Murlough Bay is a rugged length of coastline between Fair Head and Torr Head on the north-eastern extremity of Ireland, and overlooks the 20km of sea that separates Co. Antrim from the Mull of Kintyre.

67 CROSS: FORTIFICATION 317950 442700
Crannagh Island

Crannagh Island is an artificial island, or *crannóg* which, like many similar sites, is presumably of early medieval date. It is situated at the centre of Lough na Crannagh, standing *c.* 1.5m above the shallow lake bed and is faced with stone. The *crannóg* is the presumed site of Loughdisnard Fort, which is marked on the Down Survey parish map of Kilfaghtrim. There are no visible remains of the fortification, although the centre of the *crannóg* is overgrown making detailed survey difficult.

> ANT 005:011
> Down Survey parish map of Kilfaghtrim, *c.* 1656 (PRONI D597/1)

68 TORR WEST: SETTLEMENT 322750 440400

The approximate location of the historic town of Tore, as marked on the Down Survey map of the parish, lies approximately 300m to the north of the modern settlement of Torr, but there are no

Fig. 2.41 View of Crannagh Island juxtaposed with an extract from the Down Survey parish map of Kilfaghtrim.

visible remains.

ANT 009:211

Down Survey parish map of Kilfaghtrim, *c.* 1656 (PRONI D597/1)

69   GOODLAND: SETTLEMENT   319810 441300

The earthwork remains of 129 domestic rectangular huts of likely post-medieval date cover a hillside, and excavation has produced evidence of unstratified occupation horizons of Neolithic, Bronze Age and early medieval date, as well as material from the 15th to 17th centuries. The landscape here is particularly rich in archaeological sites of all periods, likely due to the unusual existence of rich pasture at high altitude, something that has protected the remains from the destructive effects of modern intensive agriculture. The site has commanding views over

Rathlin Island, the Mull of Kintyre and Islay, where similar post-medieval structures have been found. It is possible that the post-medieval settlement equates to the town of 'Ballycron' that is marked on Down Survey maps. Jobson's map of 1598 includes at or near Goodland, the legend 'Ye Scottes warning fyer'; Norden's map of 1610 includes at a similar location 'at this marke the Scottes used to make their warning-fires'.

The rectangular huts probably date to the 17th century, and constitute a Highland Scots village, although definitive material evidence of this has yet to be found. The site is almost certainly related to the tradition of seasonal transhumance practised by the Highland Scots and the Irish, a mode of pastoral economy that, ironically enough, the official Plantation of Ulster aimed to extinguish. Excavations of one hut in 2007 revealed that it was

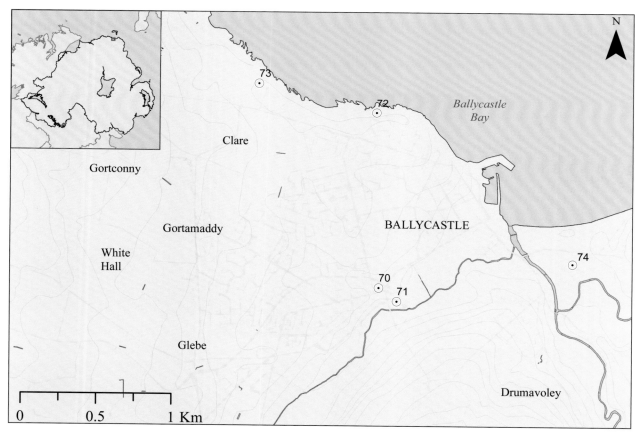

Fig. 2.42 Sites in the Ballycastle area.

constructed of sods, interleaved with loose gravel, and that the entrance was lined with large stones.

ANT 009:043

'Ulster', by Francis Jobson, *c.* 1590/1591 (TCD 1209/17); Evans 1945, 30; Sidebotham 1950; Case 1953; Horning 2004; Horning and Brannon 2007

Ballycastle

Ballycastle is at the centre of an estate leased in 1611 by Sir Randal MacDonnell to Hugh McNeil, the constable of both Bally Castle (Inv. 71) and Dunineany Castle (Inv. 72). Clare Park, just outside the town, is also notable as a seat of the MacDonnell family (Inv. 73).

| 70 | TOWN PARKS, | 311400 440700 |
| | BALLYCASTLE: SETTLEMENT | |

Although Ballycastle was a settlement at the centre of the McNeil estate, there are no visible 17th-century structures or features in the town. Excavations have revealed various post-medieval features, and one wall in particular predates 1740, although more precise dating proved not possible.

ANT 008:135

Lewis 1837, I, 127–128; O'Laverty 1878–1887, IV, 109–119; Bigger 1904, 56–66, 104–112; McNeill 1983, 101–128

71	TOWN PARKS,	311520 440610
	BALLYCASTLE: CASTLE AND BAWN	
	Bally Castle	

The castle after which the town of Ballycastle is named, was demolished completely in the 1850s, but was still standing in ruins at the time of the first Ordnance Survey. It was apparently a tower house built in a Scottish style, having at least two corbelled-out turrets, and was surrounded by a bawn. The *OS Memoirs* recorded a stone inscribed 'WRKGS, 1625' which, together with the various surviving descriptions of architectural details, would date the structure to the early 17th century.

ANT 008:028

Hill 1865, 28; Bigger 1901, 7–9; Jope 1951, 31–47; McNeill 1983, 114; Day *et al.* 1994a, 88–98, 125

72	TOWN PARKS,	311380 441900
	BALLYCASTLE: CASTLE	
	Dunineny Castle	

The ruins of a small castle stand on the site of a late prehistoric promontory fort, on cliffs that jut out into the western end of Ballycastle Bay. It was probably rebuilt by Sir Randall MacDonnell as his official seat in the barony of Cary. Much of the history of the site concerns its role during the 16th century when it was a military base, and until excavated in 2000, the upstanding remains were thought to date to the 16th or even 15th centuries. The remaining castle consists of an early 17th-century gatehouse standing up to 2m in height, along with traces of curtain walls, which appear not to have been strongly built.

ANT 004:001

G.H. 1859; *PSAMNI* 6–7; Proudfoot *et al.* 1962, 112; McNeill 2004

Fig. 2.43 View of Dunineny Castle.

| 73 | CLARE: HOUSE | 310600 442100 |
| | **Clare Park** | |

This country house, founded in the late 17th century and now demolished, is often identified as the seat of the MacDonnells in the barony of Cary, although there is no clear consensus. McNeill's work at Dunineany Castle (Inv. 72) has demonstrated that it was more likely to be the administrative centre of the barony, and although an early 17th century MacDonnell presence at Clare Park cannot be ruled out, archaeological traces of it have not yet been discovered.

The possible site of a bawn was discovered in the townland on an aerial photograph taken in 1983 (grid ref. 310650 411560). This appears to show traces of a rectangular enclosure measuring *c.* 60m × 40m, with projections similar to flankers, and an apparent rectangular building at its centre. Some roughly hewn stones have also been found in the locality, suggesting the former presence of a masonry structure, but there are no visible remains on the ground.

ANT 004:123

Hill 1873, 188; McNeill 2004; unpublished notes in the SMR file

74 BONAMARGY: FRIARY 312685 440867

Rory McQuillan founded a friary around 1500 or slightly earlier, built near the *'Mairgie'* where the Cary and Glenshesk rivers converge and discharge out to the Atlantic. This was one of a number of Third Order Franciscan friaries established in Ireland around that time, and it continued to function after the dissolution, albeit embroiled in the troubles of the late 16th century – the friary's church was burnt in 1584 when a combined force of Irish and Scots attacked English troops who were resident there. The church was repaired, and although historical accounts are incomplete, the site was probably used by other Franciscans until at least 1642. By that point, the friary was under the patronage of the MacDonnell earls of Antrim, who extended or adapted the buildings to include a chapel and a burial vault.

The ruins of the friary consist of a simple rectangular stone-built church (30m by 24.5m internally), with a range of domestic buildings to its north. The southern wall of the church contains a monument to the founder of the McNaughten

family, dated 1630. The MacDonnell alterations comprise of a square projection, with sides 5m long internally and walls 2.5m thick. This contains a burial vault, with a now-roofless chapel above; the vault is accessed through a doorway on the southern wall of the church. This structure is dated 1621, although most scholars agree that this building probably took its current from around 1666, perhaps through the enlargement of an earlier vault.

A small, perforated gravestone by the entrance to the church marks, according to local tradition, the burial site of the 'black nun' Julia McQuillan, an early 17th-century recluse and reputed seer.

ANT 009:003

Biggar and Fennell 1898; Reeves 1847, 282; O'Laverty 1878–1887, IV, 468–478; *PSAMNI* 11–12; Anon. 2009

75 TORNAROAN: SETTLEMENT 314750 441850 AND SALT PANS

The Down Survey parish map of Kilfaghtrim and the barony map of Cary indicate that the town of Tournaghroaghan was close to, or within, the modern hamlet of Tornaroan. The map of Killfaightrim parish depicts the settlement nearer to the eastern edge of the townland (approximate grid ref. 315400 442000). There are no visible remains, although the site is currently the focus of a research project in the University of Ulster Centre for Maritime Archaeology. Two salt pans are shown on the barony map, at either end of the coastal edge of the townland (approximate grid refs 315380 442030 and 315840 442200).

ANT 005:040

Down Survey barony map of Cary and parish map of Kilfaghtrim (PRONI D597/1); *Archaeology of Salt Production in Ireland* website (www.saltarch.wordpress.com)

White Park Bay

There are two clusters of 17th-century sites at White Park Bay, one situated near the village of Ballintoy, and another at the opposite, western end of the

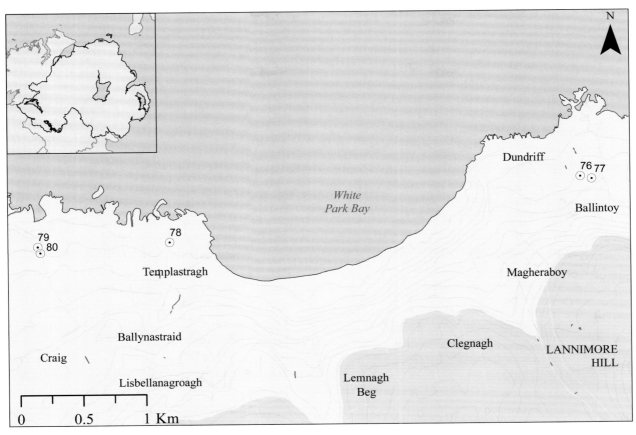

Fig. 2.44 Sites in and near White Park Bay.

bay. Ballintoy and the White Park Bay area, today a well-known beauty spot, formed a small freehold estate, granted to Archibald Stewart by Randal MacDonnell in 1625 (Hill 1865).

76   BALLINTOY: SETTLEMENT   303800 444800
Ballintoy, a linear village near Ballintoy Harbour, was a small settlement in the early 17th century. There are no longer any remaining features or structures from that period, and a church was replaced by the current parish church in 1813. The church and castle (see Inv. 77) were attacked and besieged by Irish insurgents in the winter of 1641–2, until finally driven off by the forces of General Monro.

ANT 004:122
Hill 1865; O'Laverty 1878–1887, IV, 335–337

**77   BALLINTOY DEMENSE: 303890 444780
HOUSE**
Ballintoy Castle
A fortified house that stood on the western outskirts of Ballintoy village is depicted at this approximate location as 'Stewards House' on the Down Survey map for the parish of Billy. The building was removed in the 19th century, with nothing visible surviving above-ground.

ANT 004:007
Down Survey parish map of Billy (PRONI D597/1); Hill 1865, 7; O'Laverty 1878–1887, IV, 335–337; McNeill 1983, 109

78 TEMPLASTRAGH: CHURCH AND GRAVEYARD 300530 444280

Teampull Lastrac

The ruins of a post-medieval church built on an early church site, two graveyards (one attached to the church, and another 60m to the north) and a well, none of which are well dated, are located on an elevated site at the western end of White Park Bay. The post-medieval ruins consist of the side walls and eastern gable of a roofless, rectangular building. There is a window in the southern wall in a ruinous condition, and a narrow, splayed opening (of which only the lower half survives) in the eastern gable. The graveyard attached to the church is enclosed by a stone and mortar wall. The outlying graveyard was known as 'The Scotch Kirkyard', and according to the *OS Memoirs* the site was chosen as a burial ground by Scottish settlers. The precise location of the spring

Fig. 2.45 Aerial view of the church and two graveyards at Templastragh. The outlying graveyard is known as 'The Scotch Kirkyard'.

well known locally as the 'Priests' Well', is now lost, but was some 200–300m to the south of the church.

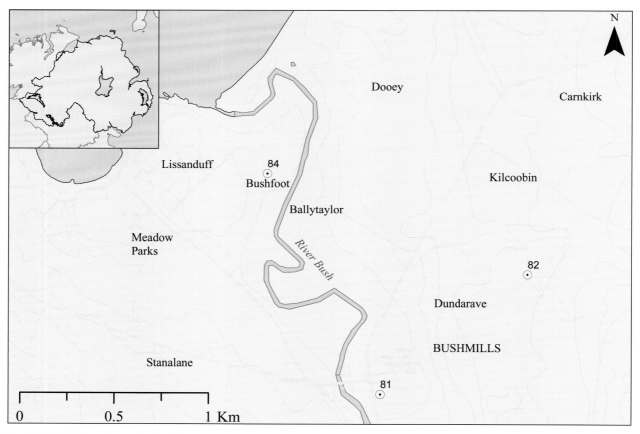

Fig. 2.46 Sites in and near Bushmills.

ANT 003:012

Reeves 1847, 285–286; O'Laverty 1878–1887, IV, 316–318; Bigger and Fennel 1899; Crookshank 1899; Crawford 1912; Cordner 1942, 92; Day *et al.* 1994a, 12; Hamlin 2008, 218–220

79 CURRYSHESKIN: MILL   299480 444250

The approximate site of a mill is marked on the Down Survey map of the parish, at a location now known as Milltown, but there are no visible remains.

ANT 003:116

Down Survey parish map of Billy (PRONI D597/1)

80 CURRYSHESKIN: SETTLEMENT   299500 444200

The approximate site of the village of Dunseverick is marked on the Down Survey map of the parish, but there are no visible remains.

ANT 003:117

Down Survey parish map of Billy (PRONI D597/1)

Bushmills

Bushmills is reputedly the location where Sir Thomas Phillips was granted a licence to distil *aqua vitae* on 20 April, 1608, although this is more likely to have been on his lands at Limavady, Co. Londonderry (Hill 1877, 393). The old distillery in Bushmills itself dates from the 18th century, and archaeological remains from even that time are ephemeral.

81 CLOGHER NORTH: WATER MILL   294100 440800

Three water mills at this approximate location were described in the 1633 Inquisitions as

> ... lyeing upon the river of the Boish, under the church of Portcamon, with 5 acres of land bordering upon.

No traces of them, or of any related features, are known, although the mills are, of course, remembered in the name 'Bushmills'.

ANT 003:118

O'Laverty 1878–1887, IV, 288

82 CLOGHER NORTH: FORT   294880 441450

A small fortress was built around the time of the 1641 Rebellion at this approximate location by a Mr McNaughten 'to preserve himself and followers from outrages.' The site presumably correlates with the existing McNaughten house at Dundarave (built 1846), although there are no obvious visible remains.

HB05/08/005

Gilbert Coll. Ms. 101; O'Laverty 1878–1887, IV, 269

83 BALLYMOY: CASTLE   296900 443100

The *OS Memoirs* describe the approximate site of a structure as that of

> ...an ancient castle or other extensive building, now better known by the 'Burnt House' and which building about the 1641 war was inhabited by a late Ringan Stewart Esquire ... there is nothing now to denote its existence ... but tradition ... and some crumbles of old mortar and broken rubbish appearing on the site.

Today, not even these traces of the building are visible. A rath to the east known as 'Ballymoy Castle' is a possible alternative location (grid ref. 297052 443129), and although there are no obvious remains there, some stones are strewn upon the ground. A second alternative position is suggested by place-name evidence in neighbouring Castlenagree townland where a hamlet, also called 'Castlenagree', appears on the 2nd edition OS six-inch map (grid ref. 295800 441800).

ANT 003:078

O'Laverty 1878–1887, IV, 296; Day and McWilliams 1992d, 52 and 64–65

84   BUSHFOOT OR   **293500 442000**
LISSANDUFF: HOUSE

There are no visible remains at the approximate site of a house depicted on the Down Survey barony map in Lissanduff townland near Bushmills, on the western bank of the River Bush in the barony of Dunluce.

Down Survey barony map of Dunluce (PRONI D597)

Rathlin Island Sites

Rathlin Island lies 8km off the north coast of Co. Antrim, but only 20km from Kintyre. As such, its ownership was contested by the various propertied families of both Ireland and Scotland over the centuries. From the late 15th century, the island was part of the MacDonnell estates (the Irish branch

of the Clan Donald of Argyll and the Western Isles), although never unequivocally so until after the Nine Years' War (Forsythe and McConkey 2012, 166–169). In the 17th century, amid so much other upheaval and unrest, the island was drawn into a long standing clan feud between the MacDonnells and the Campbells of Argyll, and then into the Confederate Wars when the 2nd earl of Antrim sided with the Cromwellians, leading to the temporary forfeiture of the island to the earl of Argyll. Rathlin was garrisoned by Argyll, although it is not known where (*ibid.*). The medieval Bruce's Castle was re-occupied in the 16th century, but fell out of use following the Nine Years' War. It was depicted as ruinous on the Down Survey maps and recent excavations have failed to find 17th-century material (Donnelly *et al.* 2012). As an island so rich in archaeological sites, and one so centrally placed

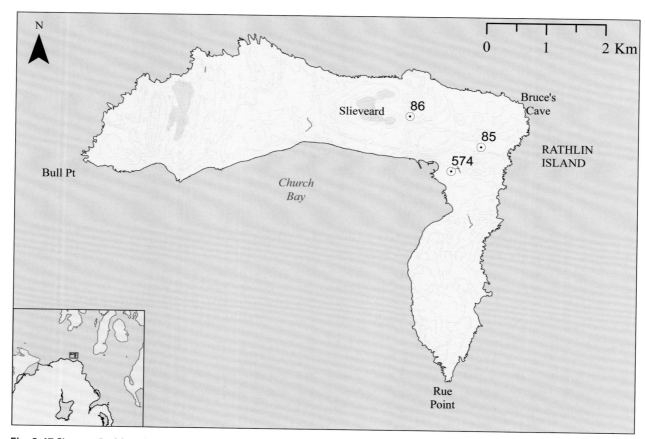

Fig. 2.47 Sites on Rathlin Island.

between Ulster and Scotland, it is perhaps surprising that archaeological traces from the plantation period are so few and so slight.

85   BALLYCARRY: 315600 451280
FOLKLORE SITE
Cnoc na Scriodlaine

A hill named Cnoc na Scriodlaine, 'the hill of the screaming', overlooks the battle site of 1642 (see Inv. 574). Folklore suggests that the hill is where the local men camped before meeting their fate at the battle, and from where women and children watched, with horror, at events unfolding upon the lands below. No traces remain, and the hill is covered with bracken and gorse. Local accounts do not agree on the location of the site, with some maintaining that it is at a convergence of earthworks and natural features known as 'The Castle' (ANT 001:052, grid ref. 315320 451250).

ANT 001:051

O'Laverty 1878–1887, IV, 377; Morris 1911; Forsythe and McConkey 2012, 433 and 451

86   BALLYCONAGHAN: 314400 451800
COIN HOARD

A hoard of silver coins was discovered in 1931 following its upcast and scatter by rabbits. Totalling £4 9s 1d, it consisted of two Irish James I shillings and 99 English coins from the reigns of Mary, Elizabeth I, James I and Charles I, ranging in date from 1553 to 1641. They were probably deposited during the troubled times of the 1640s; we can only speculate as to the circumstances that led to their original owner being unable to recover them. The hoard was displayed in Carrickfergus Castle soon after its discovery, from where several coins were stolen, and the remainder are now held in the collections of National Museums Northern Ireland.

ANT 001:064

Heslip 2012

Barony of Dunluce Lower

Dunluce

Dunluce on the Atlantic coast is central to North Antrim, and lies roughly between the Bann and Bush rivers with their valuable salmon runs. The area has seen almost constant population movements between Ulster and the Western Isles of Scotland throughout recorded history and beyond; indeed it is likely that Ireland's first human settlers arrived in the area from northern Britain, not long after the end of the last Ice Age. As a result, the region has strong cross-channel ties; in the early medieval period, people known as the *Dál Riada*, came to share similar Gaelic culture, language and religion on both sides of the North Channel. When,

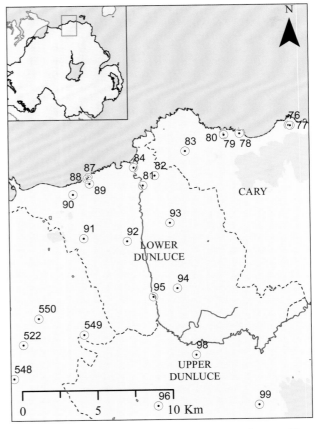

Fig. 2.48 Sites in the barony of Dunluce Lower discussed in the text.

in 1399, the powerful Clan Donald was joined through marriage to the Bisset family's inheritance of Antrim, the scene was set for much migration to the area from the Hebrides, the residents of which faced continual persecution from various Edinburgh administrations (for an overview, see Breen 2012, 19–62). By this time, the MacQuillan family (whose origins are debated and largely unknown) had emerged as the most powerful family in North Antrim, but were constantly engaged in struggles with neighbouring groups (*ibid.*). A MacDonnell-MacQuillan struggle for control of the region reached its climax in the mid-16th century, with political manoeuvring and a series of military encounters on land and sea, with the MacDonnells ultimately emerging victorious (Hill 1873, 50). In 1603, following the Nine Years' War, the MacQuillan lordship of the Route was granted to Sir Randall

MacDonnell, who was made 1st earl of Antrim in 1620. Dunluce Castle (Inv. 87) became his seat for the barony of Dunluce, and the permanent residence of his family until their move to Glenarm in 1639. A village (Inv. 88) adjoined the castle, one of several privately planted settlements that the 1st earl established on his lands. The traditional burial site of the MacDonnells was at Bonamargy friary, a 3rd Order Franciscan foundation near Ballycastle (Inv. 74), a place where Roman Catholic clergy were trained during the Counter-Reformation.

87   DUNLUCE: CASTLE   290460 441370

Dunluce Castle is one of the foremost visitor attractions in Northern Ireland. Its ruins stand on a spectacular rocky precipice on the north coast, with views of the Atlantic from Inishowen to Islay

Fig. 2.49 Aerial view of Dunluce Castle overlooking the North Antrim coastline. The early 17th century formal gardens of the MacDonnells are visible in the foreground.

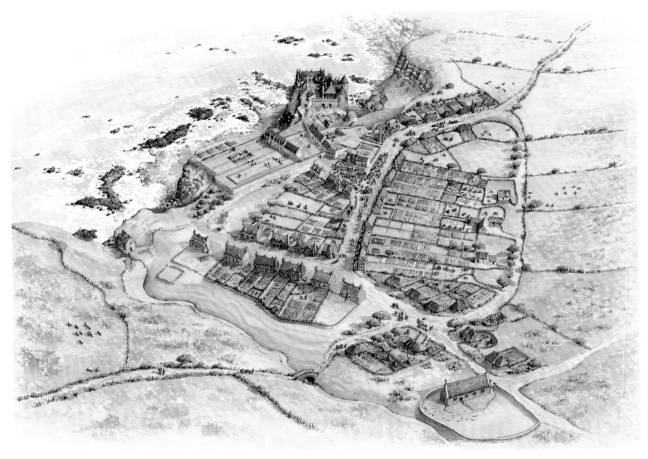

Fig. 2.50 Reconstruction drawing of Dunluce Castle and its associated town as it would have appeared in its heyday in the early 17th century.

(see pp 70-73 below). It was built around 1500 by the MacQuillan family and had passed to the MacDonnells by the mid-16th century, the castle being very much central to the interests of the MacDonnells in Antrim and the Western Isles of Scotland. A detailed overview of its early history and architecture is given by Breen (2012), but in summary, the core of the castle was built by the MacQuillans, with the MacDonnells adding the Scottish-style gatehouse, and various other parts of the castle, in the 16th century. Extensive 17th-century additions are discussed below, although soon after these were made the castle entered a phase of decline, subsequently falling into increasing levels of disrepair during the 1640s and 1650s. It was re-occupied briefly as the residence of the 3rd earl of Antrim in the 1670s, but was abandoned completely by the end of the century.

Seventeenth-century remains at Dunluce exist in two main groupings, those upon the cliff-top spur where the main castle was already situated, where a new manor house was built by 1611, and those on the 'mainland' adjacent to the castle, where an enclosure wall and stable block were built initially, followed by a brew house, a large lodgings building, and formal gardens. The manor house is a two-storey L-shaped building, 20.5m × 6.7m internally, with gable ends and attics, built against pre-existing buildings in the castle enclosure. The walls are of basalt rock, with hewn sandstone quoins, approximately 1m thick, and were originally rendered. Impressive examples of Renaissance masonry and architecture abound, with fireplaces and elaborate windows. The entrance is crowned with decorative carvings, and three large bay windows originally dominated the western façade. The original window surrounds have not survived, but one of the bay windows has been reconstructed. Internally the building would have contained much timberwork, such as the stairs and internal divisions, some of which can still be traced in the stone sockets and plaster impressions.

An inventory dating to 1645 lists the wealth of furnishings that the manor house contained. These included thirty-seven cushions, at least seventeen bed mattresses and a vast quantity of bed hangings, bedlinen and towels, twelve armchairs, sixty-three chairs and stools, and more than two-thirds of a mile of tapestries. There were also more than thirty oriental carpets, as well as paintings in gilded frames, a library of books, and even two globes, one terrestrial, the other celestial.

A kitchen building, partly timber-framed, was added to the complex to serve the manor house. The remains of this structure include a stone-built chimney stack housing an oven and a fireplace, and it was modified or upgraded at some point after its initial construction, probably in the 1620s.

The 'mainland' saw much construction in the opening decades of the 17th century. A wall was built enclosing a courtyard in which a stable block was constructed at its western edge. This is a simple, rectangular gabled building, 20m × 6.5m, with a first floor or attic. Recent excavations have revealed that the ground floor was probably of packed clay, drained via a stone-lined gully, and finds included butchered horse bone and a horseshoe. At some later date, a brewhouse was added to the eastern side of the courtyard. This was a two-storey building that included, amongst other internal features, a vat

Fig. 2.51 View of the manor house in Dunluce Castle built by Sir Randal MacDonnell (later 1st earl of Antrim) by 1611.

for brewing or mashing large quantities of beer, supported by a keyhole-shaped masonry platform, the foundations of which have been purposely heightened in recent times to enhance their visibility to visitors.

Probably in the 1620s, a large 'lodgings' was added to the northern end of the stables. This two-storey building range measures 36m × 5.8m internally, and was divided into southern and northern blocks with separate entrances, adjoined by a smaller apartment building overlooking the cliffs at the northern corner of the building. This range contained a series of rooms, many with fireplaces and windows, providing accommodation for guests. The northern block, the larger of the two, supported a wooden balcony with views of the gardens and the vast ocean beyond. Around the same time, further walls were added to the courtyard, including a compound

to the east, and the 'funnel' walls to the north that run towards the gatehouse of the castle.

The castle gardens, three broad terraces that survive as a series of low earthwork features, are immediately to the west of the castle, and were accessed through the lodgings.

ANT 002:003

O'Laverty 1878–1887, IV, 274–286; Bigger 1905, 154–162 and 1906, 22–35; Lynn 1905; Jope 1951 and 1960; MacDonnell 1992; Breen 2012

88 DUNLUCE: SETTLEMENT   290410 441260
Dunluce Village

The earthwork remains of a village or small town lie immediately to the south-west of Dunluce Castle. It was founded by Sir Randal MacDonnell around 1608 on an unusual choice of site, with exposed

Fig. 2.52 A defensive feature of the gatehouse that allowed access into the 'Upper-Yard' of Dunluce Castle – a corner bartizan supported by Scottish-style corbelling.

Fig. 2.53 View of archaeological excavation of the early 17th-century town established by Sir Randall MacDonnell beside Dunluce Castle.

north-facing slopes and lack of access to the sea. Nevertheless, at least forty houses were built, together with infrastructure such as roadways, a counting house, and probably a courthouse and jail. The village was attacked and burned in 1641 and was gradually abandoned thereafter. The site was never redeveloped and hence it is of almost unrivalled archaeological potential in the context of plantation-period towns in Ulster.

Excavations at the site since 2009 have revealed the foundations of several rectangular buildings with stone-built walls (although timber framed structures were also found), and finds indicate that they were rendered and had glazed windows. The buildings ranged from 30–85m^2 in size, and were at least one-and-a-half storeys high, similar in scale to modern houses. Two main streets ran though the village, and at their junction was a smithy, a small stone building containing a compacted clay floor with much evidence for burning. Finds from the settlement include early 17th-century coins and a great variety of pottery. It has been interpreted as a mercantile settlement, with a mixture of Scottish and Irish inhabitants, who perhaps gradually turned towards subsistence agriculture when the geographic constraints of the town limited its prosperity.

Excavations in 2014 uncovered late 15th- and 16th-century settlement remains associated with the earlier MacQuillan lordship. The remains of a stone building, an enclosing ditch and a sod-built structure were found at different locations outside of the castle.

ANT 002:008

Breen 2012, 130–163; McAlister and Gault 2015

89   DUNLUCE: CHURCH AND   290559 440959
GRAVEYARD
Dunluce Church

The ruins of a post-medieval church stand on the original site of a medieval parish church. A church at Dunluce was mentioned in the 1306 Taxation, and a church building there was described as ruinous in 1622. It was reconstructed by Sir Randall to serve the needs of the Scottish

Fig. 2.54 View of the church and graveyard at Dunluce.

Fig. 2.55 View of the 1630 grave memorial to Walter Kid, a merchant originally from Irvine in Scotland.

Protestants who inhabited his village. The precise date of this work is unknown, but presumably took place shortly after 1622. The ruins consist of a large and rectangular gable-ended building, measuring 23m by 7m internally. The entrance porch at the western end is an 18th-century addition. The entrances originally were two doors (later converted to windows) in the southern wall, which also contains three other windows in a ruinous condition. In addition, there is a very large window in the eastern gable, now denuded of any decorative stonework, which would have ensured that morning services were brightly illuminated. The graveyard contains many burials, with the earliest memorial stone dated 1630 and reading

'Here lyeth the children of Walter Kid, marchnat Dunluce, burges if Irvvin'.

ANT 002:005

Reeves 1847, 76–77; O'Laverty 1878–1887, IV, 273; Bigger and Fennell 1900; *PSAMNI* 3

90   BALLYMAGARRY: CASTLE   289450 440240

A castle noted in the *OS Memoirs* as built by the MacDonnells sometime after 1641 and destroyed by fire in 1746, was replaced by a two-storey house but has left no visible remains. Ballymagarry was the temporary residence of the 2nd earl of Antrim, between the period when the family lived at Dunluce Castle, and their permanent move to Glenarm in 1639.

ANT 006:035

O'Laverty 1878–1887, IV, 273; Day and McWilliams 1992d, 120

Revallagh Sites

Revallagh is a small, dispersed hamlet in the Co. Antrim countryside approximately half way between Coleraine and Bushmills.

91   BEARDIVILLE: HOUSE   290120 437230

A 17th-century house on property passed from the MacDonnells to the McNaughtens in the early 18th century was replaced by the current building, Beardiville House, shortly thereafter (*c.* 1713), obliterating any earlier features.

HB03/05/014

Girvan 1972

92   BALLYCLOGH: CASTLE   293000 437000

This is the approximate site of a castle mentioned in the *OS Memoirs,* the exact location of which is unknown, and indeed is no longer remembered locally.

ANT 007:124

Day and McWilliams 1992d, 106, 119

93   BILLY: SETTLEMENT   295840 438240

There are no visible 17th-century remains at the approximate site of a settlement, still a small hamlet, marked at Cregballynabanagh on the Down Survey map of the barony.

Down Survey barony map of Dunluce (PRONI D597)

Derrykeighan Sites

Two sites, listed below, are located within the environs of Derrykeighan and Ballybogy, which lie on the road from Coleraine to Ballycastle.

94   GLEBE: CHURCH AND   296295 433762
GRAVEYARD
Derrykeighan Old Church

The ruins of a post-medieval church, which stand on a notable early church site, occupy a raised area within the graveyard. The remains consist of a roofless, rectangular gabled building, with a large arched window in the eastern gable and three smaller, flat-headed windows along the southern wall. The western gable has a flat-headed doorway positioned centrally, while the northern wall is featureless. Although the building itself is undated, there are several 17th-century memorial stones along the inside of the southern wall, and

Fig. 2.56 View of Derrykeighan Church.

Dunluce Castle (Inv. 87)

One of the finest and best-known monuments in Ulster is Dunluce Castle, a multi-phase fortification that stands on a rocky headland jutting out into the Atlantic Ocean. The placename element 'Dún', meaning 'fort', suggests that there was a fortification here on this spot from the early medieval period, and a souterrain (an underground passage typically associated with settlement of the period) found underneath the castle, was likely associated with it. Much of north-eastern Antrim and a large part of western Scotland in the early medieval period encompassed a single kingdom known as Dál Riada. Dunluce would have lain outside this territory, but nonetheless would have been influenced culturally and politically by the strong links that existed between Scotland and Ireland at this time (Breen 2012, 19).

In the late medieval period, the MacQuillans, who possibly came from Scotland as mercenaries, built a castle at Dunluce in the late 15th or early 16th centuries. In 1544, they invited the MacDonnells from across the North Channel to fight for them, and this family settled in the area. The MacDonnells were related to the Clan MacDonald, Lords of the Isles, whose power base lay at Finlaggan and Dunyvaig Castles on the Scottish island of Islay. This ambitious family, led by Colla MacDonnell, soon ousted the MacQuillans from Dunluce Castle in the mid-1550s, and established themselves there, controlling territory along the northern coastline and the Glens of Antrim. Colla died in 1558 and was replaced by his famous younger brother,

4 Dunluce Castle rises from a basalt stack dominating this stretch of the Co. Antrim coastline.

Sorley Boy. The MacDonnells were in a continual power struggle with the MacQuillans, who were now pushed southwards towards Lough Neagh, as well as with the O'Cahans and O'Donnells, who all sought political primacy in the region. At the same time, the Crown government in Dublin sought to control these Gaelic lords lest they conspire with overseas powers such as Scotland, France or Spain. Military campaigning against the MacDonnells included the attack by forces under Lord Essex on Rathlin Island in 1575, and Sir John Perrot's successful siege of Dunluce Castle in 1584. In 1586, Sorley Boy was given back the castle on the promise of remaining loyal to Queen Elizabeth, though the family continued to be viewed with suspicion. In 1589, Sorley Boy was succeeded as head of the MacDonnell family by his son James who, in turn, was replaced by his brother, Randal. Following the coronation in 1603 of James VI of Scotland as James I of England, Randal was granted the territories of the Route and the Glen in northern Co. Antrim, allowing the MacDonnell family position to be consolidated in this part of Ulster (*ibid.* 63–96).

Randall invited large numbers of Scottish settlers to settle on his lands, and established a number of settlements across the area, including a town in the immediate environs of Dunluce Castle (*ibid.* 99–102). Following the latest fashion in cultivating gentility and civility, he was among that breed of landlord who sought to improve estates, developing agriculture, industry and trade in their localities. While he invested much in the town of Dunluce, its potential for economic success was compromised by its location on a cliff without any suitable access to the sea below. Archaeological excavations in recent years have discovered extensive remains of this town, revealing cobbled streets, and evidence for stone-built and timber-framed houses lining their sides. The buildings included a merchant's house and a smithy, and the many artefacts found bear testimony to the daily lives of the townsfolk (*ibid.* 130–163).

In 1620 Randal became the 1st earl of Antrim, giving formal recognition of his position as one of the pre-eminent landlords in Ulster. In 1636 he died and was replaced by his son, also called Randal, as the 2nd earl of Antrim. He was married to Catherine Manners, widow of the Duke of Buckingham who, before his assassination, was the most powerful courtier at the London court. In 1638 the newlyweds moved to Dunluce, and furnished the main residence with the most fashionable of goods, including oriental carpets, expensive furniture and elaborate tapestries. Chairs were upholstered in valuable fabrics such as

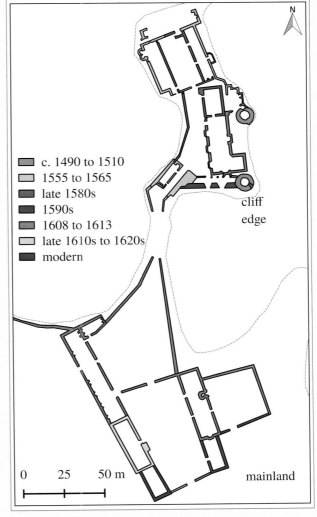

c. 1490 to 1510
1555 to 1565
late 1580s
1590s
1608 to 1613
late 1610s to 1620s
modern

cliff edge

mainland

0   25   50 m

5 Plan of Dunluce Castle. The castle was originally built by the MacQuillans in the late 15th or early 16th century, with the MacDonnells rebuilding other parts of the castle later in the 16th and early 17th-centuries including the gatehouse and manor house (after Breen 2012, Figs. 9.2 & 9.3).

silk, damask, velvet and satin. Fitting in with the image of a learned and genteel household, well-versed in classical writing, there was a library, along with a telescope and a number of globes, reminders that they were now living in a global world where new connections were being forged through exploration, trade and migration (MacDonnell 1992, 111–112; Breen 2012, 164).

Troubled times arose with the outbreak of the 1641 Rebellion. The town was attacked and burnt by Scottish soldiers forcing many of its occupants to flee. During the course of the subsequent wars, Randal was arrested on suspicion of involvement, but escaped and fled into exile in England. Catherine gathered many of their possessions and shipped them to Chester in England, where they were kept until Cromwellian officials seized them and sold them off. The castle was left to fall into dereliction, but following the Restoration of Charles II to the throne in 1660, the castle and estate were granted back to the 2nd earl. Attempts were made to revitalise the town, but these were unsuccessful, and the castle and settlement gradually fell into complete ruin. Unhappy with the location and condition of Dunluce Castle, the family moved to another residence in nearby Ballymagarry, before making their permanent home at Glenarm on the eastern coast of Co. Antrim later in the 17th century (*ibid.* 164–177).

The core of the castle complex at Dunluce was built by the MacQuillans in the late 15th or early 16th centuries, with the MacDonnells rebuilding the gatehouse in Scottish style and other parts of the castle later in the 16th century, including the erection of a loggia, or covered walkway, an architectural innovation more commonly known in southern Europe. This is the only known example of its kind in Ireland, and illustrates the influence of the Renaissance on the thinking of the MacDonnells. Extensive alterations and additions were made in the following century, with the erection of a fashionable manor house in the centre of the castle complex, along with the addition of an outer ward across 'The Gap' on the mainland proper. Called the 'Mainland Court', it included a stable block, a brew house, as well as an impressive range of lodgings.

Beyond the southern walls of the ward a pleasure garden with three broad terraces was created. Hedges, flowers and trees, all arranged in symmetrical plots called parterres, were planted beside the lodgings so that guests of the earl could enjoy a view of the ornate garden, with its unusual and delicate plantings, placed against the backdrop of the wild Atlantic – a suitable metaphor for 'civility' (i.e. English order) being wrestled from the power of unbridled nature (i.e. Gaelic Irish order). In early modern élite society, gardens were more than just about providing pleasing views; they were seen as complex metaphors that expressed class, religious and cultural identities. In the case of Dunluce Castle, here was a garden placed in full view of esteemed guests, reinforcing the standing of the earl in the new political dispensation.

6 The MacDonnells also erected a loggia or covered walkway in Dunluce Castle, an architectural innovation more usually associated with buildings and gardens in Italy to provide a grandiose shelter from oppressive heat. While not a consideration on the north Antrim coastline, the presence of the loggia does point to the influence of cultural trends inspired by the Renaissance.

But it was not just the gardens that expressed his social standing. Dunluce Castle is situated on a rocky headland, an architectural achievement that could also act as a metaphor for the triumph of civility and order over unruly nature. The very appearance of the castle, with its high battlemented walls, gabled building ranges and fine manor house, was contrived to provide the ideal image of a great lord, an aristocrat whose familial and political connections spanned the three kingdoms of James I. The Irish-built mural towers, the gatehouse with its Scottish appearance and the English-style manor house reflected this reality in a very physical, material manner. The form and style of the architecture in the castle complex was chosen with deliberation – it was more than just creating a defensive stronghold for the embattled MacDonnells – it was about creating an arena through which the social standing of the family was displayed and reinforced.

To walk towards the castle today is to follow a route dictated by its layout – a spatial ordering that in the past underpinned early modern understandings of social etiquette and class. The rituals of the élite household governed how far one could progress through the castle: where one could stop, where one could turn, and where (and indeed when) one could

7 Artistic reconstruction of the manor house in Dunluce Castle.

proceed deeper. The entrance into the 'Mainland Court' originally faced onto the marketplace, acting as a constant reminder to the townsfolk, traders and visitors that the town was under the patronage of the MacDonnells. Proceeding through the front entrance into this court, visitors were met by the stables to the left, and a large brewhouse to the right. It was clear that any horsemen would have to dismount once inside the entrance. In the early modern period, the typical horseman belonged to the upper echelons of society, and as such there was a certain symbolism involved in dismounting from one's horse on entering the castle complex – friend or foe, you were now under the protection of the earl. Further into the courtyard, and again on the left, is a long building range containing a series of small rooms, each with a fireplace and large window. This level of provision for guest accommodation was unusual, and certainly advertised to any visitors the generosity and munificence of the earl.

Beyond the accommodation range, the courtyard walls converge, creating what is known as 'the Funnel', leading down to 'the Gap', a rocky breach in the headland that separates the core of the castle from the mainland. An arched bridge leads to the gatehouse, a substantial edifice, largely plain in appearance except for two corner bartizans supported by Scottish-style corbel mouldings. The gatehouse represented the last defence before the core of the castle was reached. Along the adjacent curtain wall are embrasures which originally housed cannon. Any horseman, who failed to dismount beforehand, would now have to do so and proceed on foot through a narrow and dark passageway, before re-emerging into the 'Upper Yard'. At this point everyone would have their first view of one of the finest residences in early 17th-century Ulster – the family home of the earl of Antrim.

The English-style manor house originally had its front façade embellished with three large bay windows, advertising well-lit, well-furnished rooms within. Entry was via a large door with elaborate carvings overhead leading into a dark passage that emerged into the hall, where on certain times of the year the earl would hold court. Beyond this was the parlour, where family members and senior servants would congregate, and from this a large staircase led to a landing on the first floor that acted as a sort of antechamber. Here, people would wait before being called into the most important room in the residence – the Great Chamber – where the earl would host more formal dinners and entertain the most important guests. The castle would gradually unfold itself to the visitor, the depth to which they could penetrate very much depending on their social standing and relationship with the earl. This spatial grammar, which underpinned the social organisation within a household, was commonplace in early modern society, and can be traced at other sites where preservation allows.

Fig. 2.57 17th-century grave memorial at Derrykeighan Church.

outside near the eastern gable, the earliest of which dates to 1625.

ANT 012:003

Reeves, 1847, 78–79; O'Laverty 1878–1887, IV, 127–130; *PSAMNI* 15; Hamlin 2008, 204

95   BENVARDIN: HOUSE   294710 433190

The earl of Antrim leased lands here in May 1636 to Daniel McNaughten, whose own estate at Ballymagarry was later occupied by the earl and his household (see Inv. 90). There are no known 17th-century features on the estate, which was bought by a branch of the Montgomery family in the late 18th century, and the present house and gardens, which date from the 18th century, are later features.

HB04/02/002; ANT 002:005

Girvan 1972

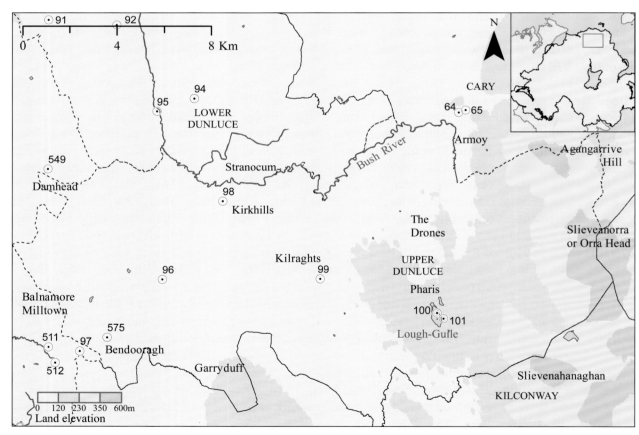

Fig. 2.58 Map of the barony of Dunluce Upper showing sites discussed in the text.

Barony of Dunluce Upper

Ballymoney and environs

The town of Ballymoney formed part of a land grant acquired by the MacDonnells in the late 16th century (Breen 2012, 85), and became established at its present location during the early 17th century. Pre-17th century settlement in the surrounding area was focussed on a ford on the River Bann near Bendooragh, and nearby Cross townland (Inv. 97) was the seat of a branch of the MacDonnells throughout the plantation period (Hill 1873, 64). A castle once stood near the town, to the south on the approach to the ford. The *OS Memoirs* recorded its approximate location but no other details (Day and McWilliams 1992d, 20), although it is remembered in the modern street names Castle Street and Gate End. It is likely that this castle pre-dated the plantation-period town, and Bell (1897) suggested that it was a 16th-century MacQuillan structure, later held by Archibald Stewart around the time of the outbreak of the 1641 Rebellion.

A brick kiln near Ballymoney was reported by an agent of the London companies, whose estates were situated on the other side of the Bann, but the bricks apparently were of dubious quality (Hill 1877, 442). Nevertheless, it is likely that they were used in the parish church tower (Inv. 96), now ruined, which is the only surviving early 17th-century structure in Ballymoney. No archaeological traces of the old town have been discovered during recent developments.

| 96 | GLEBE: CHURCH AND GRAVEYARD | 294940 425806 |

Ballymoney Old Church

This parish church, now in ruins, was completed in 1637, probably on the site of its medieval predecessor. It has a somewhat ecumenical history, as the construction was funded by the earl of Antrim, a Roman Catholic, while the early congregation was drawn from the largely Presbyterian settlers in the town, whose origins were in Lowland Scotland. It was burned in 1642 following the Battle of Bendooragh, but was rebuilt and functioned as a parish church, albeit with non-conformist leanings: a Presbyterian meeting-house was later built in 1690 to serve that congregation. The remains consist of traces of the western gable end of a stone building, adjoined by a later, brick-built square tower. Although the exact date for these structures has not been established, it seems feasible that the stone church is an early 17th-century structure, and that the brick tower is an addition made following the destruction of 1642. The graveyard contains several 17th-century memorial stones (*contra* the *OS Memoirs*), the earliest of which is dated 1610.

ANT 017:003

Reeves 1847, 80–81; O'Laverty 1878–1887, IV, 119–120; Day and McWilliams 1992d, 2, 6, 19; Arthur 2009; Beattie undated

Fig. 2.59 View of Ballymoney Church.

AN ARCHAEOLOGY OF NORTHERN IRELAND, 1600–1650

97 CROSS: FORTIFIED HOUSE 291450 422700
Cross Castle

No visible archaeological remains survive at the approximate site of Cross Castle. Originally a MacQuillan stronghold, it became the residence of a branch of the MacDonnell family, notably Alexander MacDonnell, nephew to the 1st earl of Antrim, and James, a commander on the Irish side during the Great Rebellion that broke out in 1641. The foundations of the castle could still be seen at the time of the first Ordnance Survey, and the *OS Memoirs* recorded that the site was besieged at some point during the troubles of the 1640s, resulting in earthworks being dug around the castle. They also mentioned the discovery of some forty human skeletons (many of which were said to show signs of healed injuries, thus implying that they were perhaps experienced soldiers), a sword, lead fragments, a brass weight and various other items on the site.

ANT 016:001

Hill 1873, 64; Day and McWilliams 1992d, 4, 20 and 23

98 KIRKHILL: COIN HOARD 297500 429240

A hoard of twenty-two 17th-century silver coins was discovered by workers digging a pit for a cattle grid. It comprised nineteen Belgian patagons of Maximilian Henry of Bavaria (1597–1651), two Spanish eight-real coins (*i.e.* pieces-of-eight) of Philip IV of Spain (1621–65), and a thaler of Vladislaus IV of Poland (1632–48), and was found in association with a fragment of leather, presumably the remains of a purse.

ANT 012:062

Fourth Annual Report to Parliament on the Operation of the Treasure Act 1996, 2001, 102 (currently available via *http://finds.org.uk/documents/treasurereports/2001.pdf*)

99 KILRAGHTS: CHURCH AND 301640 425830
GRAVEYARD

The ruins of a post-medieval church and graveyard stand on the site of a medieval church. A church

here is referred to in 17th-century taxations and terriers, which also indicate that the glebe land was possessed by Sir Randal MacDonnell. It is not known whether these ruins date from the time of Sir Randal's possession, although it is possible. The remains consist of the lower levels of the western gable and southern wall of a rectangular building. Stones projecting from the ground surface at the north-western corner could be the remains of the northern wall. The graveyard is enclosed by a modern wall, with the earliest memorial stones being of 18th-century date.

ANT 017:013

O'Laverty 1878–1887, IV, 107; Hamlin 2008, 212

Loughguile Sites

Loughguile is a village on the lower slopes of Slievenahanaghan, to the east of Lough-Guile, where the O'Hara family had an estate from the 14th through to the 18th centuries (McNeill 1983, 121–123).

100 CASTLEQUARTER: CASTLE 306600 424370
Lissanoure Castle

Lissanoure Castle is a private residence that sits on a hilltop in a large estate surrounded by woodland. The site was originally a seat of the O'Hara family, who were prominent within the medieval Lordship of the Route (before it was amalgamated by the MacDonnells into the Lordship of the Route and the Glens). The Speede map of 1610 shows a castle (indicated as 'Castle Balan') near this location, on the northern shore of Lough Guile. The O'Hara family owned the land until 1733, when it was sold and much development has ensued since. The existing buildings date to the 18th and 19th centuries, and no earlier structures are known at the site.

ANT 018:011

O' Laverty 1878–1887, IV, 100–106; *PSAMNI* 18–19; McNeill 1983, 121–123

**101   CASTLEQUARTER: CHURCH   306870 424130
AND GRAVEYARD**

Lissanoure Castle church

A graveyard and the ruins of an 18th-century church are located on the site of a medieval church or friary. Although there are no visible remains from the 17th century, it is likely that there was continuity of worship here since the 14th century, with the post-medieval congregation drawn from the O'Hara estate.

ANT 018:013

Reeves 1847; O'Laverty 1878–1887, IV, 93–94

Barony of Kilconway

Clogh

The small village of Clogh or Clough was important during medieval times, being the site of a castle (Inv. 102) and a church (Inv. 103). During the plantation period, it became the MacDonnell seat for Kilconway.

**102   CLOGHGALDANAGH: 309540 414700
CASTLE**

Clough Castle

The ruined gatehouse of a castle, built on a basalt outcrop, stands on what is thought to be the site of an Anglo-Norman motte and bailey. Much of the site has been lost to quarrying and road-works, and more extensive remains than those seen now were reported in the 19th century. What survives comprises the southern wall, entrance, and part of the northern wall of a C-shaped gatehouse, approximately 10m × 6m externally, with a 4.2m wide opening and walls 1.4m to 1.9m thick.

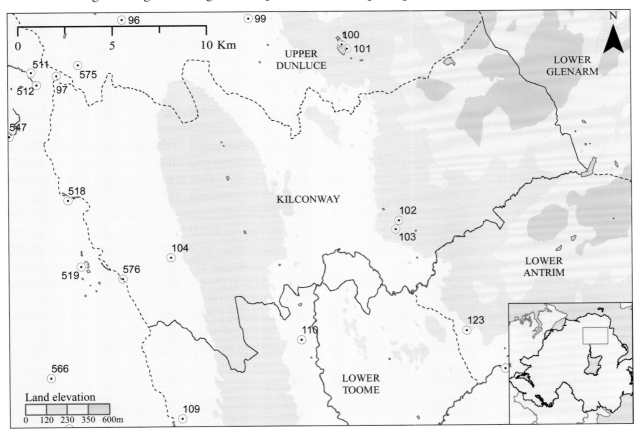

Fig. 2.60 Map of the barony of Kilconway showing sites discussed in the text.

While its origins are somewhat obscure, it is known to have been held by the MacQuillans, and when granted to Sir Randall MacDonnell as part of the Route and Glens grant in 1603, it was already known as 'Oldstone Castle'. The castle became the MacDonnell baronial seat for Kilconway, and Sir Randall probably carried out alterations or repairs at the site. The castle was seized by Crown forces during the 1641 Rebellion, but bloodshed was subsequently avoided by the Crown commander, whose negotiations under the terms of a MacDonnell-O'Neill alliance cut short the insurgents' attempts to retake it. The castle was ruined in the 1650s by Cromwellian forces.

ANT 027:016

O'Laverty 1878–1887, IV, 49–50; *PSAMNI* 23; McNeill 1983, 124

Circuit of Muircheartach mac Néill. The ruins consist of the walls of a simple rectangular building, surrounded by a large graveyard enclosed by a modern wall. The church was abandoned in the 19th century when a replacement was built in a different location, although the graveyard is still in use. Several authorities have suggested that the building dates from the 17th century, although it is possible that the structure is earlier. There are few architectural features; three windows in the southern wall have roughly hewn surrounds, and there is an entrance door and bell-cote in the western gable.

ANT 027:015

Reeves 1847, 71–72; *PSAMNI* 24; Smyth 1939

Church Site Near Rasharkin

103 GLEBE: CHURCH, GRAVEYARD
309380 414230
Dunaghy Old Church

A post-medieval church, now in ruins, and a graveyard were built on the summit of a hill on the site of a medieval church. Although its history is obscure, the site, *Dun Eachdach*, was clearly important in medieval times. It is positioned at a crossroads on an ancient road network, and is mentioned as a stopping place in the 10th-century

104 GLEBE: CHURCH AND GRAVEYARD
297470 412760
Rasharkin Old Church

A post-medieval church in ruins and its graveyard are located on the site of a medieval church that is mentioned in the 1306 Papal taxation. The medieval church was described as ruinous by the 1622 Visitation and, according to the *OS Memoirs*, it was rebuilt around 1650. In the 1860s, the current St. Andrew's Parish Church was built immediately to the north. The remains comprise a simple, rectangular gabled building, now roofless, the walls of which survive almost fully intact, albeit obscured by vegetation, and there are no visible traces of earlier features. There are a number of burials in the interior of the church, and in the graveyard (which is still in use), the earliest memorial stone bearing the year 1723.

ANT 026:011

Lewis 1837, II, 486; Reeves 1847, 89–90; O'Laverty 1878–1887, IV, 68–71; *PSAMNI* 23; Day *et al.* 1993, 130, 136; Hamlin 2008, 216

Fig. 2.61 View of Dunaghy Church.

Barony of Toome Lower

Ballymena and its Environs

Ballymena was part of a land grant given to Rory Óg MacQuillan in 1607. He had lost his estates to Sir Faithful Fortescue by 1618, who in turn sold part of the land holding to William Adair (Hill 1869, 113). Adair was responsible for the early development of Ballymena and built a castle there (Inv. 105). Other parts of the estate were sold in 1630 to Alexander Colville, a Scottish Professor of Divinity and famed alchemist, who was a relative of Bishop Robert Echlin, the then Protestant Bishop of Down and Connor (see Inv. 39; Hill 1869, 140).

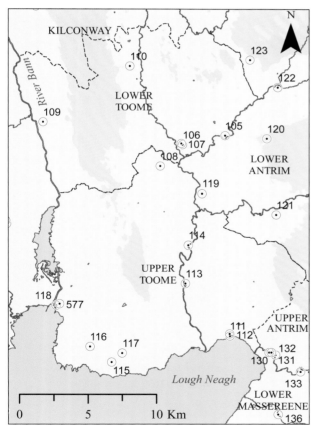

Fig. 2.62 Map of the baronies of Toome Upper and Lower showing sites discussed in the text.

| 105 | TOWNPARKS OF | 311270 402980 |
| | BALLYMENA: CASTLE | |

Ballymena Castle

The Adair family built a castle in the early 17th century at this location to control a fording point on the Braid River. It burned down in 1740, and a replacement was built in the Scottish baronial style in the 19th century. This in turn was demolished in 1950 following arson, something which presumably erased any earlier features.

Girvan *et al.* 1969

| 106 | GALGORM: HOUSE | 308180 402280 |
| | AND BAWN | |

Galgorm Castle

These are the substantial remains of a 17th-century bawn, built by Sir Faithful Fortescue in 1618–9, and of a house renovated in 1832, but originally built by Dr Alexander Colville sometime after he purchased the estate in 1630. The bawn is a rectangular stone-built structure, 77m by 22m, orientated north-west to south-east, with a rectangular flanker at each corner. Eastern and western walls, which survive to a height of 3.5m, are capped with modern crenellation. The northern side has been replaced by a modern wall, while only fragments of the southern wall survive, adjoining the flankers. The northern flankers are

Fig. 2.63 18th-century drawing of Galgorm Castle published in the Dublin Penny Journal in 1834.

Fig. 2.64 Galgorm Castle is an unusual example of a double-piled building from the mid-17th century. Also noteworthy are the elaborate crenellations at parapet level, with the central rounded merlons. The gables of the roofs are similarly decorated with concave and convex profiles.

unroofed and have been reduced from their original height, while the two southern flankers have been refurbished and re-roofed in recent times.

The house spans the full width of the bawn, and is of three storeys. The interior consists of rooms on either side of an oak stair, which spans the ground and upper floors and is similar to the example at Red Hall (Inv. 40), and which is likely to be original. Nineteenth-century restoration of the structure has rendered original features invisible, but it is likely that much of the core of the building still survives.

ANT 037:014; HB/07/15/001/A

PSAMNI 30; Girvan *et al.* 1969

107   GALGORM: CHURCH AND   308090 402380
GRAVEYARD

On level ground just north-east of Galgorm Castle and bawn there are the remains of a church, apparently built or repaired by Alexander Colville. The east and west gables of the church still stand to full height, with the walls built of roughly coursed

Fig. 2.65 View of Galgorm Church.

stone rubble. While the building is mostly covered with ivy, there are a number of architectural features which suggest an early 17th-century date for construction – the round arched doorway in the south wall with its moulding (at some stage re-constructed), and the twin-light round-headed window placed high in the west gable. A large pointed window with no dressed surround is in the east gable, while less preserved are large window openings in the north and south walls. The floor of the east end of the church has been raised to facilitate the insertion of a burial vault. The entrance into this subterranean space is now open, with a series of steps leading down into the vault, but there appear to be no burials inside. The immediate area around the church was probably used for burials, though

there are no visible headstones.

ANT 037:013

O'Laverty 1878–1887, III, 384

108 BALLYMINSTRA: COTTAGE 306550 400650

This stone-built vernacular cottage, situated near Gracehill and just beyond the baronial boundary with Toome Upper, is a long building of one and a half storeys, and has clearly been subject to several phases of refurbishment. The style of cruck used to support the cottage's roof indicates that it may have a relatively early construction date, perhaps in the early 17th century.

HB07/08/016

Gailey 1984, 74-80

Fig. 2.67 The style of cruck used to support the roof of a cottage at Ballyminstra indicates that it may have been built in the early 17th century.

Miscellaneous Sites in Toome Lower

109 PORTGLENONE: 298000 404000 SETTLEMENT

Portglenone is a village straddling the border with Co. Londonderry where, during the early 17th century, the local freeholder and garrison commander was Sir Edmond Stafford. Later in the century, a wooden bridge over the Bann was described by Dobbs as among the best '…of the three kingdoms; there are seats upon it to rest and view the Pleasures of the Band water.' (Hill 1873, 381). There are, however, no

Fig. 2.66 Round-headed doorway, with decorated surround, giving access into Galgorm Church.

remaining features or structures of early 17th-century origin in the village, and it is not clear whether the village was a settlement during that time.

ANT 031:051

Graham 1841, 299; Hill 1873, 381

110 CRAIGS: CASTLE 304340 408240
Craigdun Castle

Craigdun Castle was one of three castles erected by Edmund O'Neill under a grant from James I. It was replaced by a country house in the mid-19th century, although there are possible fragmentary remnants of the castle within a farm building on the site, which has incorporated a wall that includes hand-made bricks and possible gun loops.

HB07/02/009

Girvan and Rowan 1970

Barony of Toome Upper

Randalstown or Feevah Estate

Sir Brian MacPhelim O'Neill of Clandeboye was a dominant figure in Ulster in the 16th century, his estates covering much of south Co. Antrim, north Co. Down and the Ards. The Clandeboye O'Neills were resistant to English attempts to colonise Ulster, which eventually led to the capture of Sir Brian by the earl of Essex, and his subsequent execution. The Clandeboye estate was subdivided and re-granted to a nephew and two sons of Sir Brian, his son Shane MacBrian O'Neill taking possession of an estate around Randalstown (O'Laverty 1878–1887, III, 299–303). The descendants of Shane MacBrian managed to consolidate the estate into one property, known as the Feevah estate (Reeves 1847, 300). Today, the family seat remains at Shane's Castle (Inv. 111), to the south of Randalstown. Very little is known of the form that the town took in the early 17th century. It was named after Randall MacDonnell, the 2nd earl of Antrim, who married Rose O'Neill, the town being part of her inheritance (O'Laverty 1878–1887, III, 302–303).

111 SHANE'S CASTLE PARK: 311624 387979
TOWER HOUSE
Shane's Castle

Shane's Castle is a ruined tower house named after Shane MacBrian O'Neill, with his residence built on the site of an earlier structure located here, originally named Edendowcarrick. Indeed, this had long been a military stronghold, as there is a motte and bailey nearby. The 17th-century tower house was greatly extended and altered through the late 17th and 18th centuries, before suffering a fire during major rebuilding in 1816, from which it never recovered.

Fig. 2.68 View of Shane's Castle. Note the 17th-century tower house in mid-ground that was subsequently incorporated into the later country house.

Seventeenth-century fabric at the site includes the walls of a rectangular, three-storey tower house, 7.5m × 6.6m externally, with walls approximately 1m thick, which partly incorporate fragments of a 16th-century structure. Much of the 17th-century walls have been rebuilt, although the northern, southern and eastern angles are original. The southern wall has a batter at its base, and is considerably thicker than the others. The walls are of split stone rubble, with roughly dressed basalt quoins, with some sandstone quoins that may have been robbed from the earlier structure. One basalt quoin is carved with a rather striking human head, known as 'The Black Head'. It is undated, but on stylistic grounds the 16th or early 17th-centuries seem plausible.

ANT 049:029

O'Laverty 1878–1887, III, 299–312; Smyth 1939, 11; *PSAMNI* 41; Abraham 1997

**112   SHANE'S CASTLE PARK: 311610 388120
           GRAVEYARD**

The private 17th- and 18th-century graveyard of the O'Neill family, located on the Shane's Castle estate, is enclosed by a modern stone wall, and contains several burials. The oldest legible memorial stone is dated 1620.

ANT 049:054

O'Laverty 1878–1887, III, 300–301; Day and McWilliams 1993b, 62–63.

Fig. 2.69 17th-century grave memorial in graveyard on the estate of Shane's Castle.

113   BALLYGROOBY: MILL   308400 391900

There are no visible remains at the site of iron mills marked on the Down Survey barony map on an island in the River Main, although the area is heavily overgrown.

ANT 043:051

Down Survey barony map of Toome (PRONI D597)

114   CADDY: MILL   308600 394750

A water mill is marked on the Down Survey map of the parish of Drumaule and Magherochill, on a bend of the Maine River. There are no visible remains, although a level platform of ground to the south-west indicates that there was probably a building here in the past.

ANT 043:052

Down Survey parish map of Drumaule and Magherochill (PRONI D597)

Duneane

Duneane is a parish on the northern shore of Lough Neagh, between the 17th-century settlements of Randalstown and Toome. Various references in the *OS Memoirs* for the parish (Day and McWilliams 1993b, 70–71), suggest that the land owner or freeholder in the area in the early 17th century was Edmond Stafford (see also Portglenone, Inv. 109), the name of the village hereabouts being Staffordstown. There were substantial See lands in the parish (Reeves 1847, 300–301), which were presumably leased by Stafford.

115   PORTLEE: CASTLE   303000 386000

This is the approximate site of a castle mentioned in the *OS Memoirs*, possibly Stafford's castle, the precise location of which is not known.

ANT 049:071

Day and McWilliams 1993b, 53

116 CARLANE: HOUSE 301420 387180

Carlane House was a possible 17th-century gentleman's residence. It was photographed still standing in the early 20th century, but was demolished in the 1960s or 1970s. The photograph shows a two-storey house with a thatched roof and two chimney stacks. The last occupants of the house believed its construction date to be 1603. The site is now within a farm complex.

ANT 048:027

Unpublished photograph in SMR file

117 STAFFORDSTOWN: CASTLE 303780 386690

A fortification or castle was mentioned in the *OS Memoirs* as once standing on this site, but its location is not marked on any Ordnance Survey map. According to tradition, the site was destroyed by Irish insurgents during the 1641 Rebellion, and human remains and troopers' horse-spurs are said to have been found in a nearby orchard. These events have left no visible traces above-ground, nor are there any upstanding structures.

ANT 049:070

O'Laverty 1878–1887, III, 336–337; Day and McWilliams 1993b, 120

118 TOOME: CASTLE 298945 390271

The site of Toome Castle, a tower house, was historically documented but its whereabouts was unknown until it was rediscovered in 1991 during development. It was described by Carew in 1611 as a castle enclosed by an earthen rampart, built during the Nine Years' War, and garrisoned by Sir Thomas Phillips. Demolished around 1783, the castle was the eastern one of two fortifications in Toome, one on either side of the Bann, depicted on a 1622 map. One of these Toome forts was repaired in 1641 by James Clotworthy, as a defence against insurgents. Excavations in 1991 revealed part of the eastern wall of a bawn, with a flanker or five-sided bastion at the north-eastern corner of the site, all surviving to a height of 1.5m. Cobbled surfaces were discovered within the bawn, as was part of a roadway that led

Fig. 2.70 Excavation of the bastion wall associated with Toome Castle.

from it. Medieval layers were also uncovered, but these were reburied and preserved *in situ*.

ANT 042:012

O'Laverty 1878–1887, III, 257, 342–348; Ó Baoill 1991; Day and McWilliams 1993b, 99, 107 and 11

Barony of Antrim

Miscellaneous Sites

119 SLAGHT: CASTLE 309600 398600

This is the approximate site of a castle of the O'Hara family destroyed and abandoned in 1641. The O'Haras were in possession of the lands of Slaght and Crebilly, as well as their large estate at Loughguile (see Inv. 100) and other holdings at Dunaghy.

ANT 037:061

O'Laverty 1878–1887, III, 423–428

120 CREBILLY: CASTLE, 314330 402740
ARMORIAL STONE

The O'Hara family built a castle here following the destruction of Slaght (Inv. 119) in 1641. It was replaced in the 18th century with Crebilly House, which itself was subject to various phases of rebuilding. Vestiges of the original castle were still visible at the time of the first Ordnance Survey, but these were demolished during further building

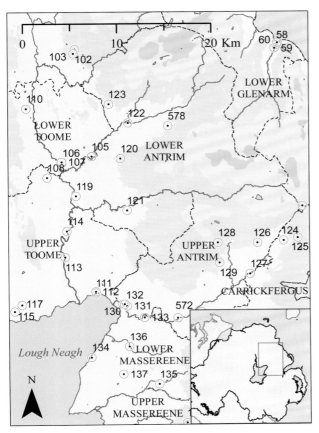

Fig. 2.71 Map of the baronies of Antrim Upper and Lower showing sites discussed within the text.

Fig. 2.72 View of armorial stone at Crebilly.

works in the 1960s. All that survives is a weathered and damaged armorial stone, mounted in the wall of the modern house. Excavations at the site in 2008 revealed extensive remains of the 18th-century building, but no traces of the 17th-century castle.

ANT 038:039

O'Laverty 1878–1887, III, 423–428; Day *et al.* 1993, 52–57; Kilner and Bailie 2008

121 CONNOR: CATHEDRAL   315000 397000

The site of the Cathedral Church of St Saviour in Connor is the location of a succession of important ecclesiastical sites dating from the early medieval period onwards. The medieval cathedral in the village was a diocesan centre in the 17th century. The Down Survey parish map shows the Cathedral and, adjacent to it, the Bishop's house. No traces of the house survive, but it is presumably in the vicinity of the present rectory.

ANT 038:030

Down Survey parish map of Connor (PRONI D597/2); Hamlin 2008, 202–203

Fig. 2.73 Extract from Down Survey parish map of Connor (*c.* 1656-58) showing Connor Cathedral.

122 BROUGHSHANE: CASTLE   315130 406630

A castle and bawn, or 'fortified yard', are mentioned in the *OS Memoirs*, and by O'Laverty, as once standing on the northern side of the village of Broughshane. These structures were, however, demolished during development in the village in the 19th century. Broughshane is so-named after Shane McBrian O'Neill (see Inv. 111), but what form the village took in the early 17th century is unknown.

ANT 033:004

O'Laverty 1878–1887, III, 428; Day and McWilliams 1992a, 101

123   EGLISH: SETTLEMENT   313100 408700

A village, now lost, was mentioned by O'Laverty as associated with a well or holy well, and near a church. The place is named 'Ballieglislane' in the 1606 Patent Rolls of James I, but no settlement is marked on any OS map, nor are there any remains visible above ground.

ANT 033:096

O'Laverty 1878–1887, III, 456

Ballynure

Originally, Ballynure was part of the estate conferred on John Dalway by the O'Neills (see Inv. 35). His daughter Margaret married John Dobbs, but was disinherited by her father. A lawsuit ensued between the Dobbs and Dalways, which eventually resulted in the award of Ballynure to Hercules Dobbs, son of John and Margaret (O'Laverty 1878–1887, III, 89–90). Their grandson, Richard Dobbs, was the author of the *Brief Description of the County of Antrim* (1683).

124   TOBERDOWNEY: CHURCH   331580 393620

The history of the site, with its fragmentary remains of a post-medieval church and graveyard, is obscure. Reeves identified it with the 'Church of the Ywes' in the 1306 Papal Taxation. The church remains consist of a bell-tower, the eastern wall of which contains an arched window opening. The earliest memorial stone in the graveyard is dated 1628. Dobbs mentions that a holy well was also once present on the site, but this is now unlocated.

ANT 045:016

Dobbs 1683; Reeves 1847, 68; Hamlin 2008, 394

Fig. 2.74 Memorial of Ellinor Clements, 1628, at Toberdowney Church.

125   CASTLETOWN: BAWN   333070 393920

The Dobbs family built a bawn at this approximate location, near a road which led to Carrickfergus, and a bridge erected in 1590. The area is now a farmyard with no visible remains of any antiquity.

ANT 046:007

O'Laverty 1878–1887, III, 177; Day and McWilliams 1995c, 63, 67–69

Ballyclare

In the early 17th century, the lands surrounding Ballyclare, a town situated between Antrim town and Carrickfergus, were a patchwork of properties held by the church, Sir Arthur Chichester, and the Dalway and Dobbs families (Reeves 1847, 165–205).

126 BALLYEASTON: CHURCH AND GRAVEYARD   328810 393380

Ballyeaston Old Church

The ruins of a post-medieval church probably stand on the site of the medieval church of Austins-town, itself perhaps an Augustinian foundation. The remains consist of a rectangular, unroofed gable-ended building with a tower at its western end. The tower is built from smaller stones and may be earlier than the rest of the building. There is a west-facing entrance in the tower through a tall, arched doorway. The southern wall of the tower contains a narrow, dressed pointed-arch window. Near the top of the tower are three pointed-arch windows; a fourth window at a higher level is now blocked. A large opening connects the tower to the church, which has lost much of its northern wall and some of the eastern gable.

ANT 045:020

Reeves 1847, 69; O'Laverty 1878–1887, III, 195–196

Fig. 2.75 View of Ballyeaston Church.

127 BALLYCLARE: DEERPARK   328000 390000

There are no visible remains at this approximate location of part of the boundary of an extensive deerpark created by Sir Arthur Chichester, and mentioned in the *OS Memoirs* for the parish of Doagh. The village of Parkgate, some 6km to the south-east is so-named after the deerpark, and it seems the boundary once enclosed perhaps 30 sq. km, encompassing the village of Doagh.

ANT 045:072

O'Laverty 1878–1887, III, 186–187; Day and McWilliams 1995a, 80

128 DRUMADARRAGH: HOUSE   324600 393400

This 19th-century house is in a vernacular Georgian style, built around the core of a house erected in 1742, itself a rebuilding of an earlier structure. According to the *OS Memoirs*, the original house dated to 1641, although it is unlikely that fabric from the earlier building survives.

HB20/06/012

Day and McWilliams 1995a, 138 and 150

129 KILBRIDE: SETTLEMENT   324760 391210

According to O'Laverty, this is the approximate site of a small village destroyed during the 1641 Rebellion, and also of house foundations that were dug up in the 19th century. No visible traces of the settlement remain.

ANT 045:060

O'Laverty 1878–1887, III, 187

Antrim Town

Antrim town straddles the baronial boundary between Antrim Upper and Massereene Lower. It was an Anglo-Norman manor that was granted in 1605 to Sir Hugh Clotworthy, who had previously served in a military capacity to both the earl of Essex in 1573, and Sir Arthur Chichester in 1603 (O'Laverty 1878–1887, III, 254–246). Sir Hugh, and his son Sir John, both served as Captain of Boats of

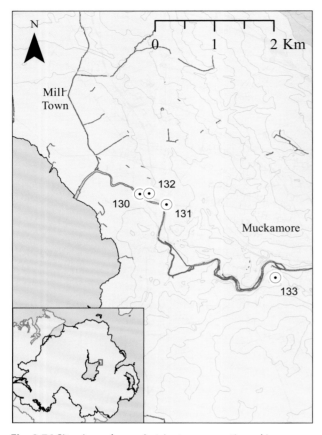

Fig. 2.76 Sites in and near Antrim town mentioned in the text.

Fig. 2.77 Excavation at Antrim bastion in 1998.

of gravel paths. Archaeological features relating to the 17th-century castle were recovered during excavations in 2007, when the stone foundations of the southern and western curtain walls, and a square flanking tower to the south-west of the site, were discovered approximately 1m below the current ground surface, although the demolition of the building was so thorough that the surviving traces were slight, and finds were scarce.

ANT 050:174

O'Laverty 1878–1887, III, 254–259; Reeves-Smyth 1991; Conway 1994; McMullen 2007

Lough Sidney (i.e. Lough Neagh), while Sir John and his brother James were very active during the 1641 Rebellion in actions to suppress the insurgents (*ibid.* 246–249).

**130   TOWNPARKS OF ANTRIM   314500 386730
        AND BALLOO: CASTLE
        Antrim Castle**

Antrim Castle was destroyed by fire in 1922, and demolished in the 1970s, with the site extensively landscaped. It was built around 1613 by Sir Hugh Clotworthy and substantially extended in 1662. A formal garden was added between 1680 and 1715, parts of which can still be traced on certain aerial photographs, with excavations at the site in 1991 and 1994 revealing evidence for the garden in the form

**131   TOWNPARKS OF ANTRIM: 314950 386550
        CHURCH AND GRAVEYARD
        All Saint's Church**

In the centre of the northern wall of the late 16th-century parish church, rebuilt in the early 19th century, there is a small limestone slab inscribed with the year 1596, which probably marks the initial phase of building at the site. The church and its graveyard would have served the town throughout the 17th century. However, virtually all of the fabric visible is likely to date to various 19th-century rebuilds and extensions, while the earliest memorial stone in the adjoining graveyard is dated to 1734.

ANT 050:180

Reeves 1847, 62–64 and 277–281; Collis 1896, 30–39 and 1897, 90–98

132 TOWNPARKS OF ANTRIM: 314660 386740
FORTIFICATION
Antrim bastion

The remains of a stone-built bastion presumably of early 17th-century date stand on the northern edge of Market Square in Antrim town. Excavation and survey at the site in 1998 revealed, amongst other features, blocked gun loops. The bastion, located near the site of Antrim Castle, was perhaps part of a 17th-century artillery fort, the remains of which have been incorporated into the town walls of Antrim.

ANT 050:183

Logue 1998

133 MUCKAMORE: CHURCH 316780 385280
AND GRAVEYARD

A church was constructed in post-medieval times at Muckamore, on the site of an early medieval monastic foundation. Post-dissolution, the lands were subject to a bewildering number of grants to different individuals, including James Hamilton, Arthur Chichester, various clergymen and church groups. The site, which overlooks the Six Mile Water, is identifiable as a level area cut into the natural topography, but the church has been demolished, and all that remains is the graveyard, with memorial stones dating to the 19th century and later.

ANT 050:078

O'Laverty 1878–1887, III, 224–249

Barony of Massereene

Miscellaneous Sites: Massereene Lower

134 BALLYGINNIFF: 311130 380920
FORTIFICATION

The remains of three deserted stone buildings are known locally as 'Sir Niall O'Neill's Castle' or 'The Lodge'. Although thought to be once the site of a castle subsequently used as a hunting lodge, the structures appear to be of 19th-century date.

ANT 054:023

Day *et al.* 1996b, 50

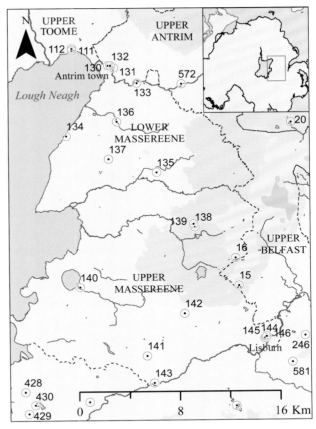

Fig. 2.78 Map of the baronies of Massereene Upper and Lower showing sites discussed in text.

135 DUNDESERT: CHURCH 318300 377880
AND GRAVEYARD

A church and graveyard, once enclosed by an earth-and-stone enclosure, were removed completely in the late 18th century, and there are no visible remains. The church is recorded as having been ruined by insurgents in 1641.

ANT 055:103

Reeves 1847, 4–5 and 181–183; O'Laverty 1878–1887, II, 312–314; Hamlin 2008, 209

136 CROOKEDSTONE: MILL 315150 382100

There is now nothing visible of a mill that is marked at this approximate location on the Down Survey barony map of Massereene, on the east bank of the Dunore River at the boundary with the townland of

Dungonnell. The 1st edition of the OS six-inch map shows a 'Corn Mill' at this location, and a mill race immediately to the south, which may be correlated with the position of the 17th-century mill.

ANT 055:275

Down Survey barony map of Massereene (PRONI D597)

137 SEACASH: FORTIFICATION 314500 379000

This is the approximate site of a fort that is marked in the corner of Seacash, Ballyquillin and Ballynadrentagh townlands on the Down Survey barony map of Massereene. It now lies within the grounds of Belfast International Airport, and there are no visible remains.

ANT 055:276

Down Survey barony map of Massereene (PRONI D597)

The Estate of Sir Fulke Conway

Lisburn, or 'Lisnagarvey' as it was known before 1641, was the centre of a large estate, consisting of much of the Lagan valley between Ballinderry and Lambeg, and the entire barony of Massereene Upper. It was granted by James I to Sir Fulke Conway in 1609, who later consolidated his landholding with the purchase of further lands in Co. Down from Con O'Neill (O'Laverty 1878–1887, II, 252–253). Conway established a private plantation, bringing tenants from his own ancestral lands in the Cotswolds. The Plantation Commissioners in 1611 described his house at Ballyellough (Inv. 142) and fortifications at Inisloughlin (Inv. 143), and also mentioned a timber bridge. An early map of Lisburn depicts the core of the town in a configuration similar to that of the present day, then including a castle which Sir Fulke also built, and fifty-three other buildings (O'Laverty 1878–1887, II, 254–255).

138 TULLYRUSK: CHURCH 321290 373350
AND GRAVEYARD

The remains of a church mentioned in the 1306

Taxation can be traced in a series of faint earthen banks and hollows extending over an area measuring 22m by 9m. It was reputed to have been destroyed by Cromwell during his campaign in Ireland, although there are no records of him actually visiting Ulster, and the tradition probably refers to forces siding with the parliamentarian cause. The site is now a burial ground, with mainly 18th- and 19th-century memorial stones.

ANT 059:041

Reeves 1847, 6; O'Laverty 1878–1887, II, 334; Cordner 1942, 94; Day and McWilliams 1993d, 132–133

139 TULLYRUSK: FORT 321200 373620

According to the *OS Memoirs*, this early medieval raised rath once contained the traces of an 'ancient castle', possibly a plantation-period structure. Aside from the earthwork remains, there are no other visible structures.

ANT 059:042

Day and McWilliams 1993d, 132–133, 139

140 PORTMORE: CASTLE 312150 368450

There are no longer any visible remains of a castle built in 1664 by Lord Conway, on the site of what was, according to O'Laverty, an earlier fortification. It is not known if the earlier structure was associated with the events of the early 17th century, as the site was cleared in the 18th or 19th centuries when an orchard on the site was enclosed.

ANT 062:007

O'Laverty 1878–1887, II, 285–287

141 TRUMMERY: COTTAGE 317439 362769

This cottage may possibly be dated to the early 17th-century on the basis of its full-cruck roof construction, although there have been several episodes of alteration and addition to the building since then. The style of cruck-framing, where continuous, large oak members sweep from the ground to the ridge of the roof, and are tied at the height of the walls, exemplifies an English vernacular method of roof construction. The earliest recorded valuation of the property was made in 1834, when it was clear that the building was already of some considerable antiquity. Fragments of a date stone suggest construction in 1629.

The cottage is a single-storey structure with a thatched roof now covered in corrugated iron. The walls are of roughcast stone, and there is a central hearth served by a corbelled-topped chimney-stack. The entrance faces south, and is flanked by a pair of windows on each side. If the early 17th-century date is accurate, then the cottage represents a highly unusual survival of vernacular architecture from the period, the significance of which is heightened by the imported style of cruck-framing.

HB19/03/048

Robinson 1982; Gailey 1984

142   BALLYELLOUGH: HOUSE AND BAWN   320450 366260

A house and bawn built by Sir Fulke Conway was described by the Plantation Commissioners in 1611 as a

> ...house of Cadgeworke at Moynargedell with a stone bawne about it, which shall be buylded 15 foote high.

The site is named 'Brookhill' after a subterranean stream that flows under the hill upon which the house and bawn were built. Conway later moved to Lisburn Castle (Inv. 146), which was built in 1622. In 1641 Brookhill was the residence of Captain George Rawdon, and was seized by insurgents, who then burnt it following their defeat at Lisburn (see Inv. 144). The farm on the site is still known by that name, but more recent buildings have enveloped the area, and it is not known what elements, if any, of the bawn survive. A portion of wall orientated north-south, delimiting *c.* 40m of the western side of the farmyard, is a possible candidate. It is of stone, brick and mortar and stands 3.4m high, but has no datable features.

ANT 063:059

Report of the Plantation Commissioners, 1611 (PRONI T811/3); O'Laverty 1878–1887, II, 266–267; Day and McWilliams 1993d, 48–49

143   INISLOUGHLIN: BAWN   318000 360500

Inisloughlin is the site of a 16th-century Gaelic fort located between Antrim and Carrickfergus, and was of considerable strategic importance. It was captured in 1602 by Sir Arthur Chichester, and when the Nine Years' War had drawn to a close, was granted to Sir Fulke Conway. A pictorial map

Fig. 2.79 Extract from Bartlett map depicting Inishloughlin Fort *c.* 1600 provides a rare view of a contemporary Gaelic Irish fortification. Note the presence of the English military encampments illustrated at the bottom of the image.

of the fort was drawn by Richard Bartlett *c.* 1600, providing a rare view of a contemporary Gaelic fortification, which consisted of a large, rectilinear bawn with a pair of flankers on opposite corners, further defended by water-filled fosses and timber palisades around its exterior.

In 1611 the Plantation Commissioners wrote that

> Sir Foulke hath buylt a fayre gate at the forte of Enishelaghlin, in Killultagh, where he entends to buyld a good house; he hath already at the place 150,000 of brickes burnte, with other materials.

There are no upstanding remains either of the fort or of Conway's buildings. Indeed the site was lost until its rediscovery through geophysical survey in 2008. Subsequent excavations revealed earthworks and a possible timber palisade related to the fort, but no clear evidence for Conway's subsequent activities.

ANT 067:029

Report of the Plantation Commissioners, 1611 (PRONI T811/3); O'Laverty 1878–1887, II, 270; Hayes-McCoy 1964, 11, pl. VI; MacDonald 2008

144   LISNAGARVY: SETTLEMENT 326800 364200
Lisburn

Lisburn was founded in the early 17th century by Sir Fulke Conway, who established an English colony in the town and in the surrounding countryside. The town was attacked by a major force of Irish insurgents on 27 November, 1641, under the command of Sir Phelim O'Neill and Sir Conn Magennis, although the garrison managed to fend them off. In 1649, the garrison was attacked by the royalist army under George Munroe. The town suffered a catastrophic fire in 1707, after which it was rebuilt and, aside from the Cathedral and Castle Gardens, nothing remains from the early 17th-century phase of the town's history.

ANT 068:011

Lewis 1837, II, 278–279; Burns 1984

145   LISNAGARVY: CHURCH,   326875 364310
TOWER AND GRAVEYARD
Christ Church Cathedral

Christ Church Cathedral, Lisburn, is the site of a church dedicated to St Thomas, which was built in 1623, probably as a private chapel, and which was destroyed in 1641. The church was rebuilt, with works commencing in 1642 and lasting twenty-three years. In 1662 it was elevated to cathedral status. Disaster befell the building when it burned down in a fire in 1707, although parts of the tower survived and these still stand today, albeit with more recent repairs and modifications. The rest of the cathedral was entirely rebuilt in the early 18th century; new foundations were laid in 1708 and the work took many years to complete; in 1724 the vestry was added. Between 1804 and 1807, the cathedral was crowned with a spire, which has been a prominent landmark in the Lagan Valley ever since. The graveyard contains a number of later 17th-century memorial stones, but nothing earlier than 1642 survives.

HB19/16/001A

O'Laverty 1878–1887, II, 262–263; Brett 1996

Fig. 2.80 Most of Lisburn Cathedral dates to the 18th century and later, though the belfry tower is partly mid-17th-century in date.

146 LISNAGARVY: CASTLE,   326940 364330
      ARTILLERY FORT
      AND GATE
      Lisburn Castle

Lisburn Castle was built in 1622 as the residence of Sir Fulke Conway, perhaps at the site of an artillery fort used during the Nine Years' War. The building was depicted on the early 17th-century 'Ground Plotte' map of the town as an E-shaped structure. Sir William Brereton (who also described Chichester's houses at Belfast and Carrickfergus: see Inv. 1 and 24) wrote about it thus:

> Linsley Garven is well seated, butt neither the towne nor the countrie thereabouts well planted. This Town belongs to my L. Conoway, who hath there a handsome House, but far short of both my L. Chic. Houses. And this House is seated uppon an Hill, upon the site whereof is planted a Garden and Orchard, and att the bottome of wh. Hill runnes a pleasant River, which abounds with Salmon. Hereaboutes, my L. Conoway is endeavoureing a Plantation; though the land hereaboutes be the poorest and barrenest I have yett seen, yett may itt bee made good land with labour and chardge.

The castle was burnt in 1707, abandoned and never rebuilt. All that remains above ground is a gateway, largely reconstructed, with a 1677 date-stone, although the garden terraces survive. The gardens have recently been restored, and archaeological excavations in 2001–2003 revealed that the terraces originally encompassed a larger area. Excavation also uncovered the foundations of a gazebo or pleasure-house, which contained an oven in its masonry walls. Seventeeth-century artefacts from the site included English, German and Dutch pottery, decorated tin-glazed earthenware tiles, clay tobacco pipes, window glass, personal jewellery, cut sandstone and a glazed roof tile, perhaps from the castle itself.

ANT 068:002

PSAMNI 60; Burns 1984; Ó Baoill 2006

Fig. 2.81 Excavation of the 17th-century garden at Lisburn Castle.

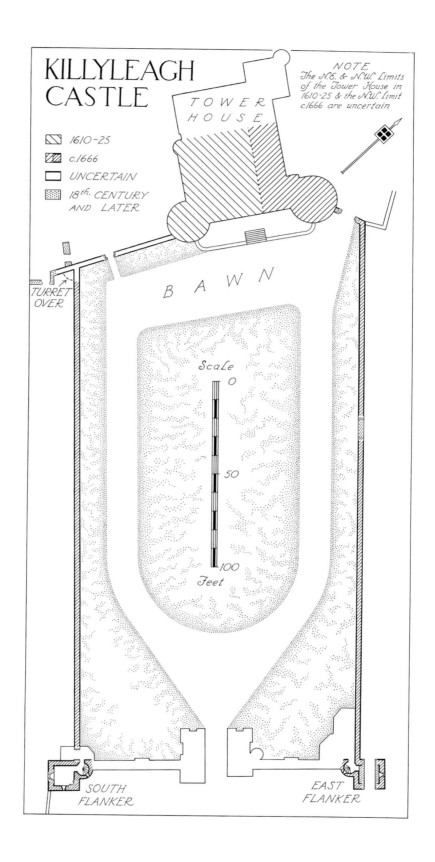

KILLYLEAGH
CASTLE

1610~25
c.1666
UNCERTAIN
18th. CENTURY
AND LATER

NOTE
The N.E. & N.W. Limits
of the Tower House in
1610-25 & the N.W. limit
c.1666 are uncertain

TOWER
HOUSE

TURRET
OVER

B A W N

Scale
0

50

100
Feet

SOUTH
FLANKER

EAST
FLANKER

Chapter 3
County Down

Introduction

Like neighbouring Co. Antrim, Co. Down experienced Anglo-Norman settlement in the late 12th century under John de Courcy, though this was largely confined to the area around Strangford Lough where certain families, such as the Savages, held lands throughout the Middle Ages. Many of their tower houses are still to be found, including at Kirkistown, Portaferry and Quintin. The Gaelic Irish lords remained pre-eminent elsewhere in the region; the O'Neills of Clandeboye continued to control lands along Belfast Lough, while the Magennises held significant territory to the south and west of the county.

Given its rich farmland and advantageous location on the eastern seaboard of Ireland, Co. Down attracted the attention of Elizabethan adventurers well before the Ulster Plantation. A prominent courtier, Sir Thomas Smith, attempted to establish an English colony on the Ards Peninsula as early as 1573, but was thwarted by Sir Brian O'Neill, lord of Clandeboye. In the 1570s also, Sir Nicholas Bagenal was more successful in gaining a permanent foothold at Newry, which lay on an important route between Ulster and the Dublin Pale, the

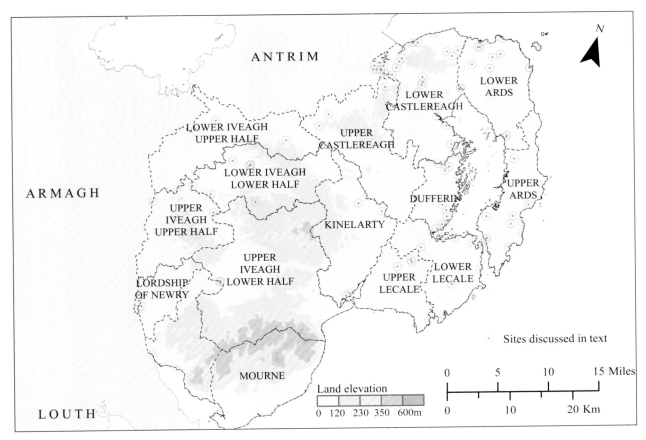

Fig. 3.1 Map of County Down.

'Gap of the North'. And Sir Marmaduke Whitechurch built a castle and settlement at a former Magennis stronghold in Loughbrickland in 1585.

Following the conclusion of the Nine Years' War, there was a more substantial and sustained movement, this time of Scottish settlers into the county. Under the auspices of two Scottish landowners – Sir James Hamilton and Sir Hugh Montgomery – the north and east of the county, including the Ards Peninsula, saw the establishment of new country estates that superseded those of the old Gaelic Irish and Anglo-Norman orders. Hamilton initially established his main residence in Bangor in 1611, before moving on to Killyleagh and erecting a substantial castle there. Montgomery chose Newtownards as the centre of his estate, where he refurbished the medieval priory; a doorway in the old priory wall which once led to his lavish dwelling still survives. The importance of investment by landlords in settlements such as Newtownards can be illustrated by a small, but fine octagonal structure in the town – the market cross.

While Thomas Raven is famous for his maps of the Londonderry settlements, he also drew a detailed estate map of lands in the barony of Castlereagh, on the eastern outskirts of present-day Belfast. This depicted numerous settlements along with dispersed houses, mills, bridges and churches, the majority of which have not survived, though archaeological investigations in the future may find their remains. Other buildings are still upstanding, such as the fortified houses at Dundrum, Ringhaddy, and Whitehouse, along with the Old Customs House in Bangor and an artillery fort at Hillsborough. A possible survival of an ordinary domestic residence is a thatched cottage in Groomsport. Religious buildings were integral to the built environment at the time, and St. Patrick's Church in Newry is one of the oldest Protestant churches in the province. It was built in 1578, and there are 17th-century parish churches to be found at Magheralin, Tullynakill, Donaghadee and Greyabbey, the last two patronised by the Montgomery family.

As with the Co. Antrim chapter, the sites here are listed on a geographical basis, starting with the Hamilton and Montgomery estates in the baronies of Lower and Upper Ards, Dufferin and Kinelarty, then continuing southwards to include the baronies of Lecale, Upper Iveagh, and Newry, before turning northwards again to include Lower Iveagh and Castlereagh.

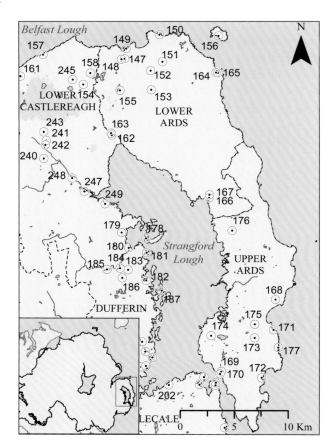

Fig. 3.2 The baronies of Upper and Lower Ards with sites discussed in the text.

Barony of Ards Lower

Hamilton's estate in Bangor and North Down

Sir James Hamilton's portion of the Upper Clandeboye estate consisted of a large part of what is now known as North Down – Bangor and Holywood, spanning large parts of the Ards and the neighbouring barony of Castlereagh (Perceval-Maxwell 1973, 371). Bangor, originally a monastic settlement of key importance, was substantially redeveloped by Hamilton, with eighty new houses constructed between the time of his land grant in 1605 and the Plantation Commissioners' survey in 1611 (PRONI T/811/3). Under Hamilton, former monastic churches at Bangor (Inv. 148) and Holywood (Inv. 160) were repaired and used for worship by the new settlers. In 1610, he acquired additional lands in the Barony of Dufferin, and eventually moved

his household there in 1625 (see Inv. 188), although ties with Bangor remained. Hamilton died in 1644 (by then ennobled as Viscount Clandeboye) and was buried at Bangor Abbey (Hunter 2004).

**147   BANGOR: HOUSE   350450 381190
         AND GARDEN
         Bangor Castle**

Bangor Castle was built in 1852 on the former site of the house and gardens of Sir James Hamilton, who built his residence here in 1611 on lands to the east of Bangor Abbey. The Plantation Commissioners reported in 1611 that:

> Sir James Hamilton, Knight, hath buylded a fayre stone house at the towne of Bangor … about 60 foote

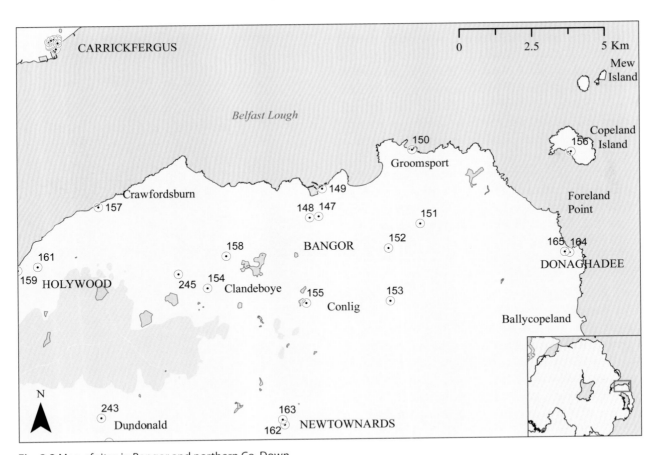

Fig. 3.3 Map of sites in Bangor and northern Co. Down.

Fig. 3.4 Extract from one of Thomas Raven's 1625 maps of the Clandeboye estate depicting Bangor Castle.

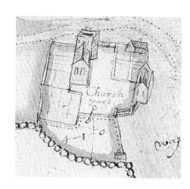

Fig. 3.5 Bangor Abbey as depicted on one of Raven's 1625 maps of the Clandeboye estate.

longe and 22 foote broade; the towne consistes of 80 newe houses, all inhabited with Scotyshmen and Englishmen. And hath brought out of England 20 artificers, who are makinge materialles of tymber, bricke, and stone, for another house there.

It seems that Hamilton was not satisfied with the dwelling and was planning another; indeed the Commissioners also mention planned building at Holywood (see Inv. 159). Ultimately, he moved his main residence in Ulster from Bangor to Killyleagh around 1625. That year, the only visual record of the house that exists was made by Thomas Raven, whose map depicts a two-storey, three-bay house with attics and gable ends, set in formal gardens. There are no visible remains dating to the 17th century at the site.

HB23/07/001A

Map of Clandeboye estate by Thomas Raven, 1625 (PRONI T870/1)

148   BANGOR: CHURCH   350141 381146
Bangor Abbey

Bangor Abbey, a celebrated centre of early medieval learning was, according to tradition, founded in the 550s AD by St. Comgall. It was subject to many episodes of building, pillage, ruin and repair over the span of its long history. The current church building consists of a 15th-century stone tower attached to a church built in 1830 to replace a church built or re-built by Hamilton in 1617–23, the building depicted

on Raven's map of Bangor. Raven's map also shows a former 13th-century abbey building standing complete to the north-east of the church; the highly fragmentary ruins of this structure can still be traced.

Fig. 3.6 Bangor's Old Customs House is a rectangular tower-house with a circular tower at its north-western corner. The corbelled stairwell and the crow-stepping on the gable end are Scottish architectural features.

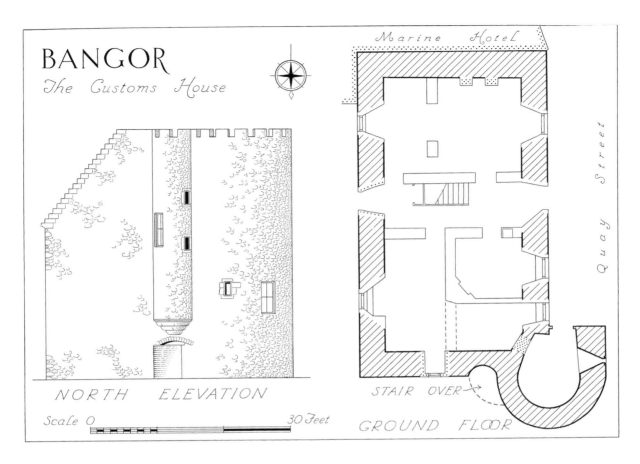

Fig. 3.7 Plan of Bangor's Old Customs House (after *ASCD*, 228).

The former site of a house with dovecote can be located approximately 300m to the east of Bangor Abbey, as it is shown in this position on Raven's map, but it is now a farmyard on the castle estate; no remains survive.

DOW 002:002

Map of Clandeboye estate by Thomas Raven, 1625 (PRONI T870/1); Harris 1744, 61; Reeves 1847, 99–201; *PSAMNI* 81–82; *ASCD* 265–256; Hamlin 2008, 285–286

149 BANGOR: TOWER HOUSE   350577 382170
Old Custom House

The building currently occupied by Bangor Tourist Office is, in fact, an altered but well-preserved tower house, originally built in the early 17th century as a customs house for the port of Bangor. Built by Hamilton around 1637, it was located upon the quay front until the construction of Bangor Marina in the 1990s moved the shoreline westwards. Although modified during recent centuries, a number of original details are still visible, and the general format of the building is relatively intact. Constructed using split-stone rubble with sandstone dressings, it is a rectangular tower house of two storeys with a four-storey circular tower at its north-western corner, as well as a corbelled stairwell, suggesting a Scottish influence or perhaps the direct involvement of Scottish masons. It measures 13.0m by 6.25m internally, with walls 1.2m thick; the circular tower has an internal diameter of 2.75m. The overall height of the structure is 13m. The original opening on the ground floor does not survive, and the tower is entered from the southern side by a door with decorative jambs. Most of the original windows are now blocked, and replacements inserted, although three original, square-headed windows are present in the eastern wall at first-floor level. The northern gable is crow-stepped; the southern gable is incorporated into the adjoining modern hotel building. Any surviving internal features have been obscured by plaster or other recent modifications.

DOW 002:003

PSAMNI 81; *ASCD* 227–228

150   GROOMSPORT: 353684 383524
SETTLEMENT

The village of Groomsport rises from the shoreline of a small bay at the mouth of Belfast Lough, situated on lands that were granted to Hamilton in 1605. It was an important port during the 17th century – in 1637, for example, a group of Co. Down Presbyterians set sail from here in an ill-fated attempt to establish a colony in Massachusetts. On Raven's 1625 map of the area, a harbour and several rows of buildings are depicted. Today, Cockle Row, which runs at 90° to Main Street and close to the shoreline, includes a terraced pair of fisherman's cottages; the building at the southern end is possibly 17th-century in date, given that its position correlates with structures shown on Raven's map. As such, it is perhaps the only surviving element of the 17th-century settlement.

Fig. 3.8 The harbour and settlement of Groomsport as depicted on one of Raven's 1625 maps of the Clandeboye estate.

Fig. 3.9 Cottage on the left, possibly of 17th-century date, now used as part of the tourist office in Groomsport.

The building, now used as a tourist office, is a single-storey cottage (with an attached outbuilding), with whitewashed stone walls and a thatched roof. It has a simple rectangular plan, with a central doorway, a central hearth, and windows on each side.

DOW 002:040

Map of Clandeboye estate by Thomas Raven, 1625 (PRONI T870/1); Boston 1910, 7–11

151   BALLYMACONNELL: MILL   353950 380900

A mill was marked on or near this site on Raven's map of Bangor, but nothing visible now survives. An alternative location is approximately 250m to the north-west, where the six-inch OS maps depict a water course and at least two small ponds (grid ref. 353753 381094).

DOW 002:041

Map of Clandeboye estate by Thomas Raven, 1625 (PRONI T870/1)

Fig. 3.10 Raven's 1625 map of Bangor in the Clandeboye estate also depicts a mill at Ballymaconnell.

152   BALLYCROGHAN: HOUSE   352850 380050
  Camel's House

A house marked as 'Camel's House' is shown on Raven's map, surrounded by a small, square bawn-like enclosure. The former site of the house is now enveloped by a substantial modern residential development, with no remains known to exist. A second, unenclosed house is also depicted on Raven's map; the location (approximate grid ref. 354000, 380350) is now a modern farmyard with no known remains.

DOW 002:042

Map of Clandeboye estate by Thomas Raven, 1625 (PRONI T870/1)

153   GRANSHA: SETTLEMENT   352900 378200
  Servants Hill

The approximate site of the settlement 'The Servants Hill', depicted on Raven's map as four houses and a mill race, is located to the south-east of Bangor, and lying immediately outside of Hamilton's demesne boundary. Three of the houses are depicted in an Irish style – single-storey, oval cottages with thatched roofs; the fourth is a rectangular English-style masonry building. There are no visible remains, and excavations in 2012 (see pp 120-122) did not locate any remains of the houses.

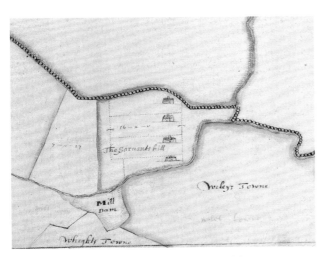

Fig. 3.11 Raven's map of Bangor in the Clandeboye estate also depicts a number of houses at Servants Hill.

DOW 002:043

Map of Clandeboye estate by Thomas Raven, 1625 (PRONI T870/1); Walsh 2014

154   BALLYSALLAGH MINOR: 346600 378700
  HOUSE

'Sander Cunningham's house' is depicted on the Raven maps in the immediate vicinity of the modern Ballysallagh House. Nothing of this 17th-century structure is known to survive.

DOW 001:046

Map of Clandeboye estate by Thomas Raven, 1625 (PRONI T870/1)

155   CONLIG: HOUSE   350000 378150

This is the approximate site of the house of James Oge, as marked on the Raven map to the north of the ford on the Bangor road entering Conlig. This area is now completely built over, and no 17th-century archaeological remains are known.

DOW 002:044

Map of Clandeboye estate by Thomas Raven, 1625 (PRONI T870/1)

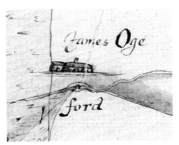

Fig. 3.12 Extract from Raven's 1625 map of the Clandeboye estate depicting a house at Conlig.

156   COPELAND ISLAND: 359160 383400
  SETTLEMENT

The largest of the three Copeland Islands (located just off shore between Bangor and Donaghadee) is the former site of a post-medieval settlement, shown on Raven's map as several cabins and a rectangular building. The islands were the property of Bangor Abbey at the time of its dissolution. There are no surviving features on the island that are datable to the 17th century; a graveyard on a terrace above the shore contains a few 18th-century memorial stones, and a few small gravestones of unknown date. Various field boundaries and cultivation ridges exist, but these could have their origins in more recent times.

> DOW 003:007
>
> Map of Clandeboye estate by Thomas Raven, 1625 (PRONI T870/1)

157 CRAIGAVAD: CHURCH AND GRAVEYARD   342860 381590
Cragger church

Overlooking Belfast Lough is the former site of a church, on lands originally possessed by the abbot of Bangor Abbey, and subsequently part of Hamilton's estate. Although the building was reported as ruinous in 1622, burial probably continued throughout the 17th century, as a memorial stone dated 1714 was once visible at the site. The church and graveyard are no longer visible, being in an area that has been landscaped as a golf course.

> DOW 001:009
>
> Reeves 1847, 13; O'Laverty 1878–1887, II, 188–191; *PSAMNI* 1940

158 BALLYLEIDY: MILL   347250 379820

A mill and mill-race are depicted on Raven's map at a location now within the Clandeboye Demesne. However, the site is probably now under the waters of an artificial lake.

> DOW 001:047
>
> Map of Clandeboye estate by Thomas Raven, 1625 (PRONI T870/1)

159 HOLYWOOD: SETTLEMENT   339883 379263

The Plantation Commissioners reported that in 1611 Holywood contained 20 houses inhabited by English and Scots settlers. Raven's map of 1625 depicts at least 52 houses of various architectural styles, arranged around a cross-roads, with a maypole at the centre

Fig. 3.13 Raven's 1625 map of Holywood on the Clandeboye estate centred on a cross-roads.

of the town. Today, although nothing from the early 17th century survives, the arrangement of roads at the town centre still conforms to this pattern, and a maypole – the only one in Ireland – is still present at the crossroads of Main Street and Shore Road.

> DOW 001:043
>
> Report of the Plantation Commissioners, 1611 (PRONI T811/3); O'Laverty 1878–1887, II, 216

160 HOLYWOOD: CHURCH   340060 379380
Holywood Old Priory

Sanctum Boscus, meaning Holy Wood, was the 13th-century name for an ancient church founded near the shore of Belfast Lough, perhaps as early as the 7th century; during the 14th or 15th centuries the church became a Franciscan priory. In the early 17th century, in pace with development of the nearby village of Holywood, Hamilton converted the old priory for use as a parish church. The building consists of a rectangular ashlar stone structure, 22.5m by 6m internally, which dates to the early 13th century, although its western end was rebuilt in the 15th century, and a tower was added in the 18th century. The surviving early 17th-century modifications to the site are a cornice that crowns the southern wall, and four window openings (now blocked-up) in it. Only the central two are preserved with their stone surroundings, and these have semicircular heads and chamfered jambs.

DOW 001:002

O'Laverty 1878–1887, II, 190–199; *PSAMNI* 81; *ASCD* 282–283

161   BALLYMENAGH: HOUSE   340750 379500

A large house and associated gardens are shown on the Raven maps near Bangor. This is likely to have been the structure that the Plantation Commissioners had reported in 1611 as the one that Hamilton had intended to build near Holywood. They wrote:

> The said Sr. James Hamilton is pr'paringe to buyld another house at hollywoods three mylles from Bangor and two hundred thowsand of bricks w'th other materials ready at the place.

The whereabouts of the house possibly correlates with Ballymenoch (also known as Ballymenagh) House which, although present on the 1st edition six-inch OS map, has also vanished. The grounds of the house are now a public park.

DOW 001:048

Map of Clandeboye estate by Thomas Raven, 1625 (PRONI T870/1)

The Estate of Hugh Montgomery in the Ards

Newtownards was the principal focus of efforts by Sir Hugh Montgomery to build a town in Co. Down. The prefix 'Newtown', however, does not date to the Plantation; the settlement is referred to as 'Newtown of Blaethwyc' as early as the 14th century, Blaethwyc

Fig. 3.14 Circular arched doorway at Newtownards Priory, framed on either side by pilasters and with an entablature above, richly decorated with an array of strapwork, vegetal decoration and other motifs.

being the local deanery within the wider Anglo-Norman *bailiwick* or county of the Ards (O'Keeffe 2008, 98). Immediately before Montgomery's Plantation, the area was desolate, following the ravages of war in the late 16th century (*ASCD* 431). Montgomery's settlement flourished, and in 1611 the Plantation Commissioners found a town of some 100 houses, inhabited by Scots. The town was incorporated in 1613, sold to Robert Colville in 1675, and later passed to the Stewart family whose descendants were the Marquises of Londonderry (*ibid.*). The town was centred upon the market cross (Inv. 163), with Montgomery's residence (Inv. 162) being within 200m of it and therefore very much within the core of the settlement.

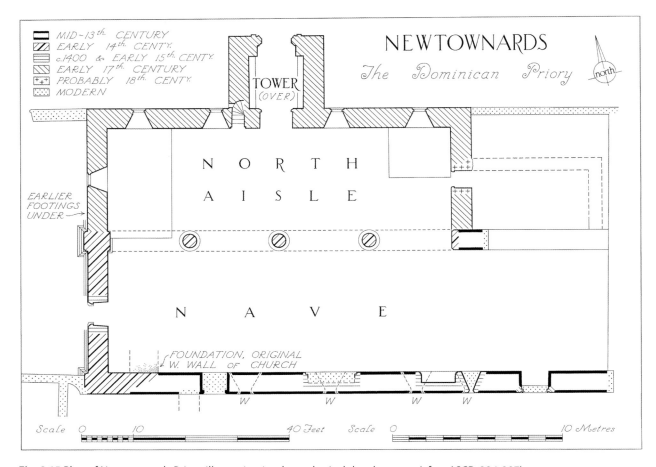

Fig. 3.15 Plan of Newtownards Priory illustrating its chronological development (after *ASCD*, 284-287).

162 NEWTOWNARDS: HOUSE AND GARDENS   349230 373850
Newtownards Priory

The Priory in Newtownards was founded by the Dominicans in 1244. The site was re-used from 1618 as one of the main private residences of Sir Hugh Montgomery. Historical descriptions of the house indicate a lavish dwelling incorporating many exotic materials; it was slated with Scottish tiles, had glazed windows throughout, and floors of Norwegian softwood. It was destroyed by fire in 1664, and the site was sold in 1675 to Robert Colville (son of Dr Alexander Colville – see Inv. 106), who built another house on the site.

Although there are significant remains of the Dominican Priory, traces of Montgomery's house are ephemeral. Sections of the Priory may have been remodelled for it (especially the northern aisle), although this is difficult to determine with any certainty. The only obvious feature is the northern door of the Priory tower, which is a highly elaborate, circular arch, framed on either side by pilasters and with an entablature above, richly decorated with an array of strapwork, vegetal decoration and other motifs. Carried upon this is a panel containing, among other decoration, a semicircular pediment emblazoned with Montgomery's coat of arms. His initials are also carried upon a central projection over the arch. The features on the doorway have weathered over the centuries, but a reconstruction, together with most of its masonry features, was made in 1988 and can be seen in a reconstructed wall immediately to the east of the original.

Colville's late 17th-century house was surrounded by walled gardens, including a kitchen garden, a 'bog garden' and a water feature, as shown on the early six-inch OS maps. Harris, in 1774, wrote that the gardens were 'inclosed [sic] with a high and firm wall, with flankers at each corner'. The walls of this very large, bawn-like enclosure (measuring 219m by 158m), which later became incorporated into various other buildings and businesses in the town, can be traced at various locations. In places they stand close to the original full height of *c*.2m, although with many episodes of repair and rebuilding evident. It is likely they were constructed on or after 1675, the year in which Colville's house was built. The wall footings of a masonry structure are present between the northern side of this walled enclosure and the Priory buildings. This includes a fragment of a splayed arrow loop, suggesting that it is the remains of an 'old castle' that according to the *Montgomery Manuscripts* was occupied by Montgomery whilst the Priory was prepared for his domestic use.

> DOW 006:018 and DOW 006:019
> Harris 1744, 58; Hill 1869, 61 and 87; O'Laverty 1880, II, 1; *PSAMNI* 84–85; Cordner *et al.* 1947, 70 and pl. iii; *ASCD* 260 and 284

163   NEWTOWNARDS: MARKET   349159 374031
CROSS

A market cross was erected at the eastern end of Newtownards High Street in 1636. Uniquely for a plantation-period cross in an Irish context, it survives in the modern townscape of which it is a prominent feature, located on a small road island at the junction of Castle Street, Castle Place and High Street. Built as a small octagonal structure from local Scrabo sandstone, it has a blocked doorway at its north-eastern side and a pyramidal stone roof, encompassed by a cornice with animal gargoyles placed at the angles. Each side is 1.6m in length. It was originally painted and gilded. The structure was restored in the 19th century, when a replacement stone roof was installed, and again in 1979, when some of the

Fig. 3.16 View of the Market Cross in Newtownards today.

highly degraded original carved stones (including the gargoyles) were replaced with modern copies.

> DOW 006:020
> Harris 1744, 58; *PSAMNI* 84; *ASCD* 260–261 and pl.67

Donaghadee

Adding to the lands granted to him in Co. Down, Montgomery purchased an estate in Galloway from William Adair; some sources suggest erroneously that lands in Ballymena, Co. Antrim, were swapped with the Adairs, who did settle in that region (see Hill 1869, 113). Montgomery thereby became the laird of lands on either side of the relatively short (34km) crossing of the North Channel. Donaghadee and Portpatrick, temporarily renamed Portmontgomery, became important international ports, with a legally regulated ferry operating between them from 1616, for which Montgomery built a stone quay at Donaghadee (MacHaffie 1975, 1–2). An additional quay was built in the 18th century to accommodate the mail trade; indeed Portpatrick–Donaghadee became the main route between Scotland and Ireland for mail, passengers and livestock between 1770 and 1830 (*ibid.*). Montgomery's quay disappeared in the 19th century, but a church (Inv. 165) and an inn (Inv. 164) in the town still contain fragments from the early 17th century.

164   DONAGHADEE: INN   359089 379843
Grace Neill's Bar

This is a small, two-storey inn, said to have been constructed in 1611, but heavily modified since that time. A pictorial map of Donaghadee drawn around 1700 indicates that the structure was originally a single-storey building. The façade is 19th-century, although portions of the building suggest an earlier construction date. A surviving blocked-up central chimney stack is of a form typical of 16th- and 17th-century vernacular building styles.

HB24/07/059

Pollock 1975; Dixon 1977, 15

165   DONAGHADEE: CHURCH   358920 379870
AND GRAVEYARD

Donaghadee Parish Church

This 17th-century church was rebuilt by Sir Hugh Montgomery on an earlier church site and is in active use today as the parish church of Donaghadee. It exhibits various phases of construction – the earliest, possibly re-using medieval fabric, consists of the lowest part of the church tower at the northern end of the nave, while the main core dates to the 1620s, and is cruciform in plan. The pictorial map of Donaghadee that dates to 1700, perhaps rather fancifully, depicts a church with a spire. The most detailed depiction occurs in *The Compleat*

Fig. 3.17 View of Donaghadee parish church.

Irish Traveller (1788), where it is described as an old building but in good condition, with narrow pointed arched windows. The tower was rebuilt in 1833, while significant additions were made to the nave and transepts in the late 19th century. Conservation of the building has been carried out in recent years.

The graveyard contains a memorial stone dated 1671; opposite this is a tall stone with an inscription dated 1660. Elsewhere, the graveyard is heavily populated by a large number of later memorial stones and enclosed, and in places revetted, by a stone wall of irregular plan.

DOW 003:006

Luckombe 1788, 235; Reeves 1847, 17 and 179; Dixon 1977, 9–12; Hamlin 2008, 291

Greyabbey and Sir James Montgomery's Estate

In 1629, Hugh Montgomery granted his second son, Sir James Montgomery, an estate in Greyabbey, a village on the Ards Peninsula that had formerly been an ecclesiastical centre (Hill 1869, 1–2; see also Inv. 167).

166   ROSEMOUNT: HOUSE   358260 367850

The manor house was built by Sir James Montgomery around 1634, accidentally burned down in 1695, and replaced twice in the 18th century. The original manor probably stood on the site of the modern stable block in the grounds of Rosemount House, a private residence still belonging to the Montgomery family. Although no 17th-century buildings survive, according to local tradition, a stone set into the lawn marks an alternative location for the 1630s house.

HB24/04/017A

Hill 1869, 1–2 and 28; Day and McWilliams 1991a, 67–72

167   GREYABBEY: CHURCH   358300 368140

The Cistercian abbey founded in 1193 by Affreca, the wife of John de Courcy, was burned down in 1572 by Sir Brian O'Neill. This was an act designed to

Fig. 3.18 View of the western gable and southern wall of the monastic church at Greyabbey.

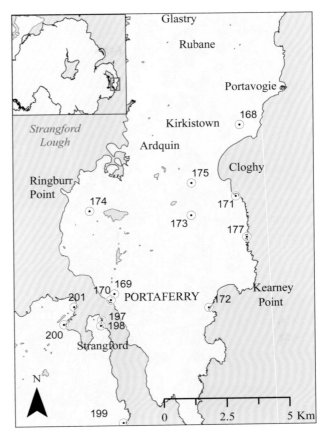

Fig. 3.19 Map of the barony of Ards Upper depicting sites mentioned in the text.

prevent the English colonists who were attempting to occupy the Ards Peninsula under the failed Smith plantation from sheltering there. Under the rule of James I, the abbey passed into the ownership of Sir Hugh Montgomery before being granted to Sir Hugh's son, James, in 1629. It remained under the ownership of the Montgomerys until 1652, when it was granted as a forfeited estate to Colonel Robert Barrow, commander of Cromwell's northern forces. The church was re-roofed some time during the 17th century and used as the parish church until 1778.

The substantial ruins consist of a complex of buildings, most significantly a church, containing a nave, chancel and two transepts, in each of which were two chapels. The western gable of the nave is surmounted by a bell-tower which was constructed during the 17th century. Other 17th-century alterations include the blocking of two original doorways along the southern wall of the nave, and the opening of a replacement doorway. A memorial to Sir James Montgomery on the north wall bears an inscription 'Sir James by pirates shot, and thereof dead / By them [in the] sea solemnly buried'.

DOW 011:010

Harris 1744; Campbell and F.J.B. 1910, 96; *PSAMNI* 89–90; Waterman 1958; *ASCD* 275–279; Hamlin 1983, 156–158

Barony of Ards Upper

Portaferry and the Savage estate

In the early 17th century, two strands of the Savage family – the Ardquin and Portaferry Savages – dominated the southern part of the Ards Peninsula (Hill 1869, 407). Although part of the established Anglo-Norman order in Ireland, the Savages were quick to form new allegiances with the wave of Scottish settlers, joining with the Montgomery family by marriage (see Inv. 170).

168   KIRKISTOWN: 364454 358010
TOWER HOUSE
Kirkistown Castle

A well-preserved, 17th-century tower house and bawn were reputedly built at Kirkistown by Roland Savage in the 1620s. However, given that the building shares architectural details with 15th-century tower houses, and Lythe's map of 1567/8 shows a castle in the area, it seems reasonable that only the bawn and its flankers were built by Savage, with the tower house being an earlier structure. Original elements survive on all three storeys, with the extant roof crenellation being an 18th-century addition. Three buttresses against the eastern wall, and two metal braces around the tower at first-floor level, were added in the 20th century to stabilise the structure.

Fig. 3.20 Kirkistown Castle, a tower house that was restored in the 18th century with new battlements, and stabilised in the 20th century with substantial buttresses and metal braces.

Indeed, a small-scale excavation in 1984 indicated that the building lacked deep foundations.

The tower house is square, each side measuring 8.5m externally, with walls approximately 1.5m thick and standing to a height of 15m. The floors are reached via a spiral stairwell in the southern corner, and each floor consists of a single room, with ancillary spaces on the south-eastern side. The south-eastern side of the second floor is split into a lower chamber with a mezzanine above. The tower house appears to be placed off-centre towards the northern side of the bawn, which was originally a roughly square enclosure, with each side approximately 45m in length.

The bawn only survives in part, and consists of the south-western and south-eastern walls, both approximately 3m high, along with two large, circular flankers of two storeys, furnished with gun loops. The south-western wall has a series of gun loops at either side of a central entranceway.

DOW 025:007

PSAMNI 100–101; *ASCD* 238–241; O'Keeffe 2008, 173–176

169   TEMPLECRANEY: CHURCH   359410 351100
AND GRAVEYARD
Portaferry Old Church

The ruins of a stone-built, post-medieval church and belfry, currently heavily overgrown with ivy, and a graveyard stand near Portaferry. It is likely that the church was built on the site of a medieval building; the church of 'Felipton' or Ballyphillip – an old name for Portaferry – was mentioned in various medieval documents, according to O'Laverty. The precise date of the ruined church, and the overall significance of the site during the early 17th century is unknown, but there was a continuity of worship and burial here throughout the plantation period, as the graveyard contains a memorial stone likely dated 1692, and there are several others with indecipherable inscriptions.

DOW 032:004

Harris 1744, 46; Reeves 1847, 25; O'Laverty 1878–1887, I, 396–399; *PSAMNI* 109; Anon. 1941, 42; *ASCD* 309

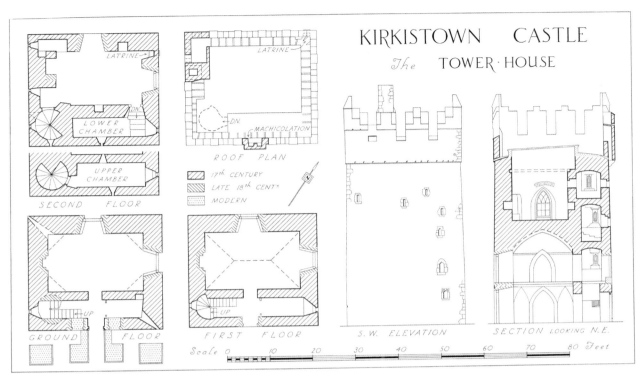

Fig. 3.21 Plans of the tower house at Kirkistown (after *ASCD*, 238–241).

170   PORTAFERRY: TOWER   359269 350850
         HOUSE
         Portaferry Castle

The tower house in Portaferry overlooks the 'narrows', the highly strategic waters at the mouth of Strangford Lough. It was probably originally built by the Savage family in the 16th century, although there are no contemporary historic accounts until 1635, when Sir James Montgomery of Greyabbey (whose sister Jean married Patrick Savage) repaired the castle, re-roofing and re-flooring the structure, and enlarging the windows. At this time, a slated stone house – of which no remains survive – was built adjoining the castle. The tower house, however, is in excellent condition, and consists of a rectangular three-storey building, 10.3m by 9.7m externally, with stone walls 1.5m to 2m thick, comprised of split-stone rubble, quoined and dressed with carved stones. A four-storey, square turret is joined to the structure at its southern corner, which contains the original entrance, stairs to the first floor (including a murder-hole), along with additional second and third floor chambers accessed separately from the main tower. The second floor and roof level of the main tower are reached by a spiral staircase in the western corner of the building. There are large chambers at each level, with various windows lighting the space within; however the original vaulting has collapsed and the structure has been subject to various phases of rebuilding and repair over the years.

The tower house is now enveloped by a complex of modern buildings including, on the southern side, a tourist information and visitor centre. Archaeological monitoring of the construction of the lifeboat station between the castle and quayside did not reveal any features or finds of interest.

DOW 032:003
Hill 1869, 280; *ASCD* 245–246; Sloan 2007

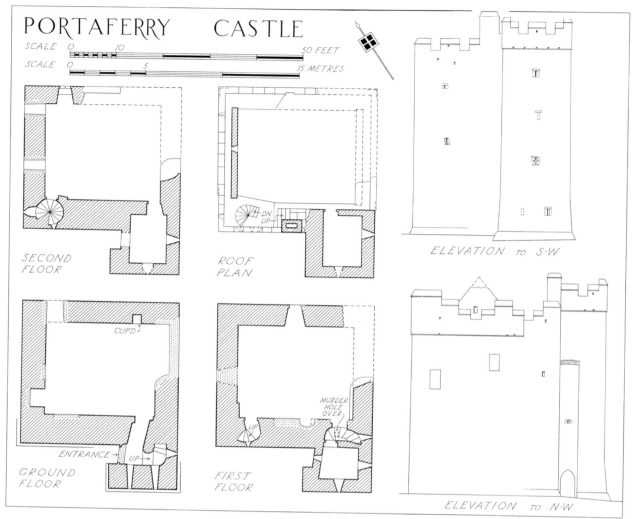

Fig. 3.22 Elevations and floor plans of the tower house at Portaferry (after *ASCD*, 245–246).

171 BALLYSPURGE: FORTIFIED 364277 355062
HOUSE AND BAWN
The White House

According to some accounts, a strong house and bawn at Ballyspurge, the ruins of which still stand, were built by Patrick Savage in the 1640s. Sources for the history of the structure are, however, scant and it is possible that the structure was originally built as part of the failed Smith plantation in the 16th century (see Inv. 177). The remains consist of a house that is aligned north-west/south-east, and two storeys in height. There are large fireplaces in each gable end at ground-floor level. The north-eastern and south-western walls, which are *c.* 80cm–1m thick, survive to a height of *c.* 3m and contain various plain flat-headed windows; those in the north-eastern wall are complete. A pair of doorways are placed off-centre along the north-eastern and south-western walls, slightly offset from each other. There are three deeply splayed gun loops along each of the north-eastern and south-western walls. Outside, and to the south-west, are the remains of a bawn wall and entranceway. The wall stands to a height of *c.* 2m at this location, although it does not

Fig. 3.23 View of the White House, a fortified house and bawn at Ballyspurge.

survive elsewhere. Archaeological investigations in 1996 within the interior of the house and bawn in advance of conservation works revealed considerable disturbance, though the floor level at the north-western end of the house did survive.

DOW 025:019

PSAMNI 102; Jope 1960, 107–110; *ASCD* 256–257; Hurl 1996b

172   BALLYMARTER: TOWER 363170 350500
HOUSE AND BAWN
Quintin Castle

A tower house probably dating originally to the 16th century, and with 17th- and 19th-century phases of rebuilding, stands overlooking a rocky foreshore and a small bay beyond. Its origins are obscure, but it is marked as 'Smith's Castel' on the 1567/68 map attributed to Lythe. In William Montgomery's description of the Ards (1683) it is stated that:

> Quintin Bay Castle, which commands ye Bay, that is capable to receive a bark of forty tunns burthen. Sir James Montgomery of Rosemount purchased the same, and lands adjoining therunto, from Dualtagh Smith, a depender on ye Savages of

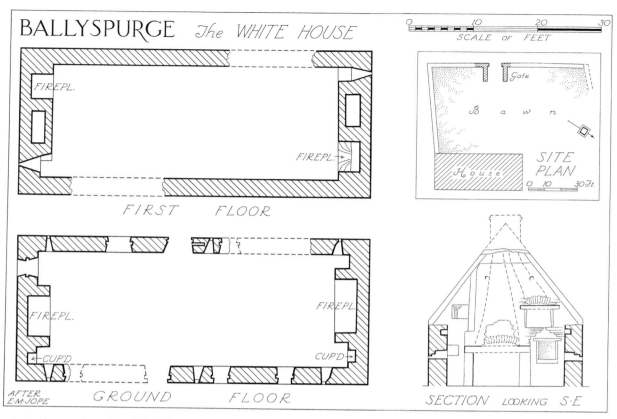

Fig. 3.24 Plans and section of the White House, a fortified house and bawn at Ballyspurge (after *ASCD*, Fig. 169, 257).

Portneferry, in whose manner it is: and ye said sir James roofed and floored ye castle, and made free-stone window cases, andc., therin : and built ye baron, and flankers, and kitchen walls contiguous ; all which, W. Montgomery, Esq., and his son James (joyning in ye sale) sold unto Mr. George Ross, who lives at Carney, part of ye premises.

The castle was therefore, in all likelihood, built by the Savages, who then leased or granted it to a local family named 'Smith' (who probably bore no relation to Thomas Smith, whose attempt at plantation is discussed below). At some point between 1625 and 1650, the castle and its lands were sold to Sir James Montgomery, who performed the building works and alterations referred to.

The core of the castle is a stone tower and it is possible that many original details and 17th-century features survive. However, the 19th-century building phase added large and ornate crenellation to the roof, and the walls were rendered, thus obscuring architectural details and the distinction between earlier and later elements.

DOW 032:019

Hill 1869, 221–222; *PSAMNI* 110; *ASCD* 246; O'Keeffe 2008, 176–177 and 185–188

173 BALLYGALGET: FORTIFICATION 362500 354290
Knockdoo

A castle was built by Roland Savage in the early 17th century, and local tradition states that a prominent hill, Knockdoo, which has excellent views and defensive capabilities, is where it was sited.

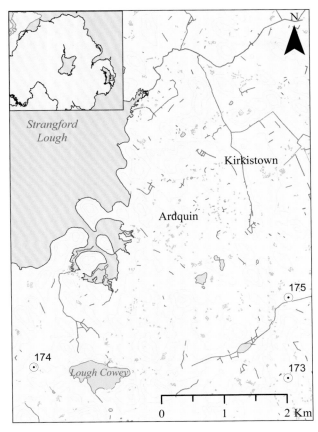

Fig. 3.25 Map of church lands in Little Ards.

Fig. 3.26 One of the gable ends of the Abbacy, a manor house built by Robert Echlin, Bishop of Down, in the early 17th century.

However, there are no visible remains of a castle at this location; the ground is uneven and obscured by vegetation, and what archaeological traces of the castle survive are currently unknown.

> DOW 025:023
>
> Hill 1869, 276 and 286; Savage-Armstrong 1888; *ASCD* 261

Church Lands in the Little Ards

The 'Little Ards' is situated at the southern end of the Ards Peninsula, divided from the 'Great Ards' by the River Blackwater. Much of the area was owned by the church in the early 17th century.

174   ARDQUIN: MANOR HOUSE   358455 354500
The Abbacy

A manor house was built within a medieval abbey complex for Robert Echlin, Bishop of Down, in the early 17th century. The fragmentary remains, which surround a modern two-storey, red-brick dwelling, consist of the stone-built gable-ends of a building aligned north-south, joined at 90° to a second building. Possible bawn walls could be traced to the east of the house at the time of the Archaeological Survey of County Down, although these are no longer visible. Ardquin Church and graveyard (DOW 024:032), a 19th-century building, lie immediately to the south of the house, and it seems that the Abbacy buildings were once a significant part of a larger ecclesiastical site. It is also possible that the upstanding remains were originally part of the abbey, and may therefore date from medieval times. However, details of what modifications or repairs were made by Echlin are unclear.

> DOW 024:032
>
> Harris 1744, 47; Reeves 1847, 21–22; *PSAMNI* 98; *ASCD* 255–256; O'Keeffe 2008, 181

175   CASTLEBOY: TOWER   362520 355620
HOUSE

A tower house, now highly ruinous, was built in Castleboy in the 15th century, and geophysical

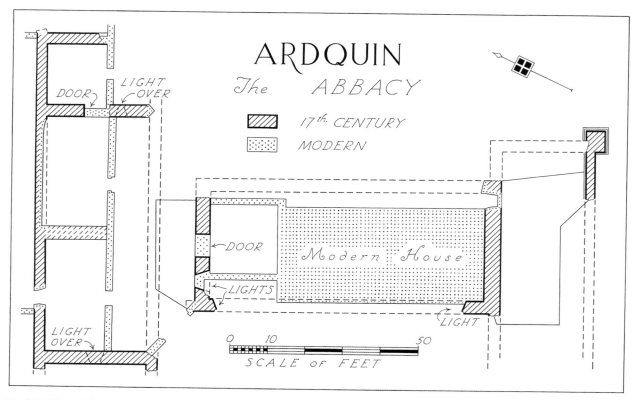

Fig. 3.27 Plan of the Abbacy, a 17th-century manor house (after ASCD, 255–256).

survey of the surrounding land has revealed that it stood at the edge of a large, polygonal enclosure. The site was originally a preceptory or house of the Knights Hospitallers, who were resident here from the 13th century. In the 15th century, the preceptory and its lands were leased to various individuals, one of whom probably built the tower house. Following the Reformation, the lands were granted in 1571 to Sir Thomas Smith on the condition that an English plantation be established (see below). When this was unsuccessful, there were re-grants to George Alexander in 1584, and finally to Hugh Montgomery in 1605, but it is unclear who, if anyone, was in residence during this period. A memorial stone at the old church in Ardkeen reads 'Robert Echline, of Castel Boye, esqr., who died the 25 day of April, 1657, in the 29 year of his age', suggesting that the tower house may have been occupied by a relative (or, perhaps, younger son) of Bishop Echlin (see Inv. 174). The remains consist of a three-storey turret

Fig. 3.28 The remains of Castleboy tower-house.

that once formed the south-eastern corner of a substantial tower house; the approximate shape and dimensions of the remainder of the tower house is marked out by low, highly ruinous, walls. The tower house was rectangular, with sides measuring 11m by 8m externally and walls 1.2m thick.

DOW 025:016

Hill 1869, 251; *PSAMNI* 102; *ASCD* 230; O'Keeffe 2008, 236–237 and 245

176   INISHARGY: HOUSE AND   360408 364724
**   BAWN**
**   Bailie's House**

This is the site of a house and bawn continuously inhabited since the early 17th century, and now occupied by a modern house and farmyard. Various phases of modification and rebuilding have resulted in a building of great complexity, yet with the outward appearance of a relatively modern dwelling. The house was built by the Bailie family around 1620, adjacent to the site of a medieval church (DOW 018:001).

Renovations to the building in 2013 afforded the opportunity to survey its fabric in detail. The two-storey building measures 23.0m by 10.0m externally, and was originally U-shaped in plan, with the south-eastern wing demolished in the 20th century. It is built of random rubble stone with dressed stone quoins and a projecting stone plinth at ground level. The walls contain large areas of red brick, suggesting extensive 18th/19th-century alterations. Many of the original openings and windows do not survive, but the entrance probably faced south-west, and consisted of a central doorway with flanking windows. A stone jamb survives in the north-western corner at first-floor level, and the details of a number of walls are obscured beneath cement render. A range of outbuildings adjoins the house, and at the western end of these is a semicircular flanking tower – all that remains of the bawn that once surrounded the dwelling.

DOW 018:020

Oram and Robinson 1986, 26–28; O'Keeffe 2008, 413–418

Smith's Plantation

Pre-dating the formal Plantation of Ulster, and any private enterprise by Montgomery or Hamilton, was a venture undertaken by Sir Thomas Smith and his son, also called Thomas, in 1572–74. This was ultimately an unsuccessful attempt to gain physical possession of lands granted to Sir Thomas by Elizabeth I. His plan was to divide the landscape into smaller units among his followers, and build infrastructure and defences for the colony, thereby providing local stability and a base for the furtherance of English interests in Ulster. This model was to become widely adopted in Ulster in the early 17th century. However, the venture was undertaken amid a complex web of hostility and diplomatic tension between the Crown, the Dublin

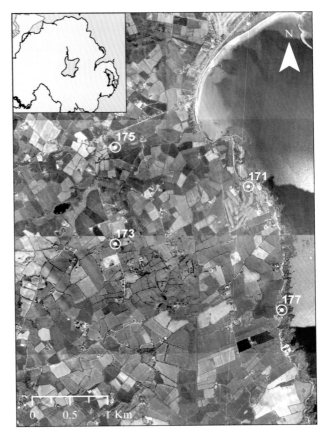

Fig. 3.29 Aerial photomosaic of the southern Ards peninsula, showing sites mentioned in the text.

administration, and the Gaelic landlords. Tensions quickly boiled over into violence following the younger Smith's arrival, leading to his assassination after only fourteen months in Ulster (Lowry 1867, 25–28; Hill 1869, 405–415). The only lands occupied by Smith were on the eastern coast of the Little Ards, in a townland and small village still known as 'Newcastle'.

177 NEWCASTLE: CASTLE AND FIELD SYSTEM   364702 353377

Local tradition identifies the site of Thomas Smith's castle as New Quay, on the shoreline of the North Channel, but nothing visible survives at the site. According to historical accounts, the castle was built very quickly, suggesting that Smith restored or otherwise adapted an existing structure. The layout of the fields in this townland forms a co-axial pattern, differing from that which is usually encountered in the region, and it is possible, therefore, that the system of land subdivision imported by Smith is fossilised in the field boundaries of the current landscape.

DOW 025:003

Hill 1869, 405–415; O'Keeffe 2008, 224–229

The Baronies of Dufferin and Kinelarty

Ardmillan and Killinchy

The barony of Dufferin, on the western shore of Strangford Lough, was awarded to the White family in Elizabethan times, and a large number of townlands in the barony were leased to Sir James Hamilton in 1610 and granted to him in the following year (Lowry 1867, 58). These included the lands surrounding Ardmillan and Killinchy, where a number of archaeological sites dating to the early 17th century exist. Hamilton's estates here border with Montgomery property, as the lands between Killinchy and Kilmood were (along with Greyabbey on the opposite shore of Strangford Lough) part of Sir James Montgomery's inheritance; he named the estate here 'Florida' (Hill 1869, 1–2).

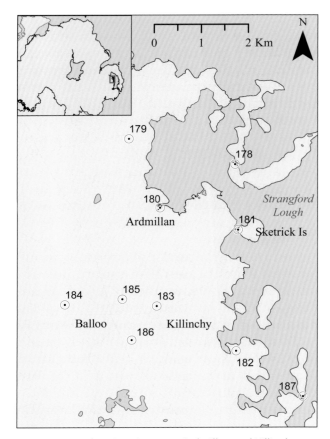

Fig. 3.30 Map showing sites near Ardmillan and Killinchy.

178 MAHEE ISLAND: TOWER HOUSE 352363951 AND BAWN
Mahee Castle

The ruins of a tower house, which is generally thought by historians to have been built in the 16th century on church land associated with the nearby early medieval monastery of Nendrum, stand on Mahee Island, the largest island in Strangford Lough. It is adjacent to a fording point – now a causeway – that connects with Reagh Island to the north, a siting with strong parallels to the locations of Sketrick and Ringhaddy Castles (see Inv. 181 and 187). A castle was built on lands leased from the Bishop of Down by Captain Thomas Browne in 1570, who was planning an English colony in Ulster – a venture that ultimately proved unsuccessful. However, there is some ambiguity over whether the historical documentation refers to this site, or to Chichester

Fig. 3.31 View of the ruins of Mahee Castle.

Castle in Island Magee, Co. Antrim. By extension, it is possible that Mahee Castle is unrelated to any 16th- or 17th-century event, and may therefore date to the 15th century. Ownership of the church estate here passed to the Montgomerys in 1606; two castles (presumably Mahee and Sketrick) were explicitly mentioned in the grant, suggesting that Mahee Castle was still occupied at that stage.

The remains consist of the heavily-ruined stump of a rectangular tower house, originally three storeys high, but now only represented by the ground floor and the southern and northern corners of the upper floor levels. A bawn wall tightly encloses the site. South-eastwards from the castle, on the foreshore, is a concentration of boulders, constituting the remains of a pier that may be associated with the tower house. The remains of the tower house were consolidated in the 1920s, when a buttress was added to the northern corner, and again in the 2000s when the surviving walls were stabilised. Excavations in 2001 and 2002 revealed 15th- and 16th-century pottery, supporting an early date for construction of the site. A cobbled surface and drainage system were discovered, and the abandonment of the site could be dated to the 17th century at the latest.

DOW 017:004

PSAMNI 94; *ASCD* 244–245; MacDonald 2002; McErlean *et al.* 2002, 112–115

179 TULLYNAKILL: CHURCH AND GRAVEYARD 350136 364516

The parish church for Nendrum during the 15th century was renovated in the 17th century, and abandoned in 1825 when a replacement was constructed. The ruins of the old church consist of the gable ends and side walls of a simple rectangular building at a prominent location on the eastern slope of a low hill. The southern windows and door, with round heads and dressed stone labels and jambs, date to a 17th-century phase of building; other windows were enlarged at this time but are less well-preserved. The graveyard is enclosed by a series of stone walls and terraces, forming an irregular polygonal plan, and containing numerous memorial

Fig. 3.32 View of altar window at Tullynakill Church.

stones, including one dated 1612, inscribed on both sides, and others dated 1669, 1695 and 1697.

DOW 017:003

OS Field Report no. 119; *PSAMNI* 93; *ASCD* 311–312 and fig. 211

**180 BALLYMARTIN: 350800 363000
      SETTLEMENT
      Ardmillan**

The village of Ardmillan is shown on the Raven map of Hamilton's estates, drawn in 1625. Although still a small village today, there are no features or structures in Ardmillan of obvious 17th-century date. A fortified house is shown on the Raven Map on the southern edge of the village, though there are no visible remains of this either, a location which lies within the townland of Craigaruskey (approximate grid ref. 350750 363000).

DOW 017:052

Map of Clandeboye estate by Thomas Raven, 1625 (PRONI T870/1)

Fig. 3.34 The ruins of Sketrick Castle in Ballydorn.

Fig. 3.33 Extract from Raven's 1625 map of a settlement at Ardmillan.

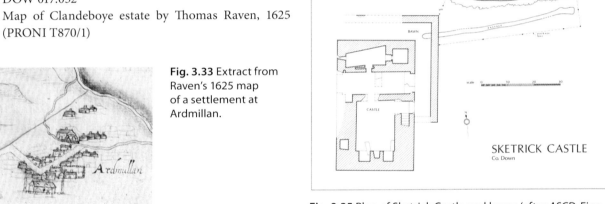

Fig. 3.35 Plan of Sketrick Castle and bawn (after *ASCD*, Figs. 165a and b).

**181 BALLYDORN: CASTLE   352458 362520
      Sketrick Castle**

The remains of a substantial late-medieval tower house and bawn stand immediately to the south of Mahee Island on Sketrick Island, which is now joined to the mainland at Ballydorn via a causeway. It was first recorded in historical sources in 1470, and last mentioned in 1536 when it was captured

and occupied by John Prowse. Ownership of the lands passed to the Montgomerys in 1606, although the role of the tower house during the 17th century, if it had one, is unknown. Inquisitions in 1617 stated that Ballydrain (a neighbouring townland) and the three islands about Mahee Island were leased to Henry Savage by Sir Hugh Montgomery, and had been leased to Savage before 1606 by the Bishop of Down. The island was also mentioned in the grant of Dufferin to Sir William Parsons in 1624.

The remains comprise a rectangular tower, contained within a small bawn, through which a culvert leads to a freshwater spring. Only the north-eastern corner of the building survives close to its original height of four storeys – a major collapse having occurred in the late 19th century. The tower house measures 15.0m by 10.0m externally, with walls up to 2.5m thick. The ground floor consists of a guard room on the northern side of the castle and a kitchen occupying the southern side. The upper floors, now highly ruinous, were originally divided into two chambers, and reached by stairs in the eastern and southern walls, with a spiral stair connecting the second and third floors in the north-eastern angle.

DOW 017:008

Quinn 1933, 133–4; *PSAMNI* 94–95; *ASCD* 250–252 and Fig. 165a and b; Salter 1993, 158

182   BALLYMORRAN: 352620 360030
SETTLEMENT   **and 352420 359860**

Two sets of houses are shown on Raven's 1625 map in the area overlooking Ballymorran Bay. There are now no visible remains of this settlement at this location.

DOW 017:025 and DOW 017:026

Map of Clandeboye estate by Thomas Raven, 1625 (PRONI T870/1)

183   KILLINCHY: CHURCH   350730 360850

The parish church in Killinchy was built upon an earlier site on a commanding position overlooking the surrounding countryside. Although there are no obvious remains that pre-date the current structure, there are numerous historical references to a church being located here since medieval times. In all likelihood, 'St. Brides' church, shown on Speede's 1610 map of Down and Antrim, correlates with this building. It was mentioned by Harris in 1744 as 'seated on a high hill, and therefore by some called in jest, the Visible Church'. The Parish of Killinchy has significance as an early site of Presbyterianism in Ireland; in the 1630s the minister there, Rev.

Livingstone, who was called from Stirlingshire by Viscount Clandeboye, was suspended for non-conformity.

DOW 017:018

Harris 1744, 76; Reeves 1847, 10–11 and 381; Gwynn and Hadcock 1970, 393; Hamlin 2008, 303

184   BALLOO: MILL   348780 360880

The approximate site of a plantation-period mill, shown on Raven's 1625 map on or close to the site of 18th- and 19th-century mills. The remains of the later works are still extant as a brick chimney stack, a water-wheel and a number of mill races remain, although nothing is known to survive from the 17th century.

IHR 02931:000:00

Map of Clandeboye estate by Thomas Raven, 1625 (PRONI T870/1)

185   KILLINCHY: HOUSE   350000 361000

The house of Robert Savage is shown on the Raven map near a road running east from Lissupp Fort (DOW 017:013). There are no visible remains of the house at this location.

DOW 017:053

Map of Clandeboye estate by Thomas Raven, 1625 (PRONI T870/1)

186   CARRIGULLIAN: 350200 360100
SETTLEMENT

A number of Irish-style houses are shown on the Raven map in an area called 'Ballygwillan', south of Lissupp Fort (DOW 017:013). There are no visible remains at this location.

Fig. 3.36 Extract from Raven's 1625 map of a settlement called 'Ballygwillan' at Carrigullian.

Servants Hill (Inv. 153)

There does not appear to be anything of note today in this field, on a low hill to the south of the A2 South Circular Road, and surrounded by suburban development on the outskirts of the town of Bangor. However, what attracted archaeologists to the site was a map drawn in 1625 by Thomas Raven on behalf of Sir James Hamilton, whose extensive estate covered much of northern Co. Down. Hamilton had been encouraging the migration of settlers from Scotland, and the map depicts a group of four houses at Servants Hill that probably housed some of these settlers. Since modern development had not encroached on the site, it seemed that there was a reasonable chance of finding the remains of the structures. Unlike the fortified houses and castles occupied by wealthy landlords, little or no evidence survives today of the homes erected by their tenants. The rigours of the Irish climate, combined with the instabilities and destruction experienced periodically in the 17th century, has meant the loss of virtually all of the houses and cabins that would have housed the bulk of the population in Ireland. Even with excavation, most have proved elusive – building techniques such as mud walling, the use of portable cruck timbers to support roofs, and timber frame construction all leave only ephemeral traces in the ground, which makes it more difficult for archaeologists to locate such buildings.

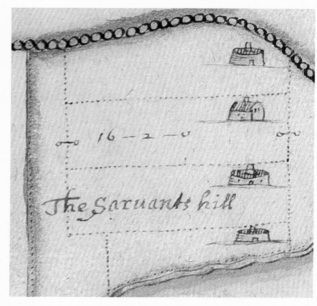

8 Extract from one of a series of maps drawn by Thomas Raven in 1625 of the estate of Sir James Hamilton estate in northern Co. Down. This Scottish landlord encouraged the settlement of fellow countrymen on his estate, and the map depicts a group of four houses at Servants Hill that probably housed some of these settlers.

The four houses depicted on the Raven map of 1625 were on linear properties lying parallel to each other. All were thatched, and appear to have been stone- or mud-walled with a lobby-entry plan. At a glance, the houses seem largely uniform, but on closer inspection of the map, differences in the depictions of the houses become evident. Two were small, windowless cabins with rounded corners, while a third, also with rounded corners, had a window on either side of the central doorway. The fourth house appears to have been more substantial, with gable ends defining a pitched roof. There is a window on either side of the doorway, as well as a pair of windows in the visible gable end. Why these variations occur is not clear, but they may have reflected social ranking within the local community.

Similar variations in house design are seen elsewhere in early 17th-century Ulster. On another set of maps compiled a little earlier in 1622 by Thomas Raven, the appearance and layout of the villages that were established by the London Companies in Co. Londonderry, and of the manor houses and bawns, and houses of the tenants, are recorded in detail. Thatched, stone- and mud-walled cabins and houses, similar to those depicted at Servants Hill, with centrally placed chimneys and doorways are common, but other house types are also evident. Timber-framed houses with diagonal braces and horizontal ties are depicted as having central chimneys, along with two dormer windows in the front elevation, while most of the roofs are shown as slated or tiled. Raven included a number of modest stone houses one-storey and one-and-a-half storeys high with dormer windows and slate or tile roofs, although several were thatched.

9 Archaeological excavation on Servants Hill uncovered Bronze Age houses, with the only evidence for early modern activity consisting of late 17th-century pottery recovered from a pit. The result highlights the difficulties faced by archaeologists in identifying ordinary domestic settlement associated with the Ulster Plantation.

10 A television crew recording the proceedings of the archaeological fieldwork at Servants Hill.

Few houses were equipped with gable hearths, with most having central chimneys and central doorways. They were gabled, with windows at a raised level indicating the presence of lofts (Robinson 1979, 17–19). Comparison of these drawings with other documents and proposed plans in the archives of the London Companies, suggests that Raven represented actual buildings on the ground with moderate accuracy (Jope 1960, 105). This made the attempted identification of the early 17th-century houses at Servants Hill all the more important.

Geophysical survey was carried out at the site and initial results were encouraging, when a number of sub-surface anomalies were found, possibly representing traces of the houses, along with former field boundaries. However, such survey can only indicate that a buried feature is present; it cannot identify or date it, so it was necessary to follow up with archaeological excavation. Five cuttings were opened to see if the anomalies did indeed represent the remains of the four houses recorded on Raven's map (Walsh 2014, 2–3).

Cutting 1 was opened to investigate a large, rectangular anomaly which was thought to represent the remains of one of the four houses, but no archaeological traces were found. The only feature found was a small ditch at the western end of the cutting, likely the remains of a late-18th century field system. Cutting 2 revealed a possible foundation trench which produced a radiocarbon date of 1397–1133 BC, suggesting that it was dug in the Middle–Late Bronze Age. In the same cutting also was a metalled surface of compacted gravel of unknown date, which may represent traces of a yard. In Cutting 3 six pits were uncovered which corresponded to numerous anomalies found throughout this area, with the fill of one yielding late 17th-century pottery. A ditch at the eastern end of this cutting (aligned north-south, measuring 2.5m in width and up to 64cm in depth) was undated but appears to have corresponded with a large linear anomaly identified during the geophysical survey. In Cutting 4 an Iron Age ditch dating to AD 245–397, and measuring at least 3.54m wide and up to 60cm deep was revealed. An early medieval bone pin was recovered from the topsoil of this cutting (*ibid.* 5–11).

Cutting 5 produced the most unexpected results, with at least two phases of Bronze Age house construction found. First was a roughly circular structure *c.* 4m in diameter and defined by a combination of post- and stake-holes, along with associated pits, one of which produced Middle Bronze Age pottery. Radiocarbon dating of material from one of the postholes confirmed that it dated to 1874–1627 BC (Early–Middle Bronze Age). This appeared to have been truncated by another building, now only represented by a single slot trench for a timber wall of upright planks set in between vertical posts. Its plan could not be deduced as it ran into the edge of the cutting, but packing material in the trench yielded a date of 1412–1135 BC (Middle-Late Bronze Age) (*ibid.* 11–20).

A series of pits was also found in Cutting 5, the largest of which lay within the earlier structure, and was caused by the wearing away of the internal floor during occupation. Its fill yielded grain of late medieval date (AD 1411–1449), but this was considered intrusive as it could easily have filtered down through the porous and sandy ploughsoil, or have been introduced by a process known as bioturbation – the reworking of soil by animals or plants. A similarly intrusive find was a sherd of early medieval Souterrain Ware found in another pit nearby. An analysis of lithic artefacts found in this cutting suggests that domestic activities such as food- and hide-processing were being carried out, and represented general prehistoric household and knapping waste (*ibid.* 11–20).

The discovery of Bronze Age settlement at Servants Hill is not surprising, as there is evidence for contemporary activity in the surrounding area. At nearby Ballycroghan there was a complex of burnt mounds and a hut site with associated Bronze Age finds (*ibid.* 21–22). The Souterrain Ware also points to settlement during the early medieval period. This is also not to be unexpected given that Servants Hill is surrounded by numerous raths, and that a monastery was established at Bangor as early as the 6th century AD (*ibid.* 22). The only evidence for activity in the post-medieval era was the late 17th-century pottery recovered from one of the pits in Cutting 3 (*ibid.* 7 and 9). While excavation failed to identify houses occupied by tenants on the Hamilton estate in the early 17th century, the fieldwork did highlight the difficulties faced by archaeologists in locating ordinary domestic settlement associated with the Ulster Plantation. Despite the challenges, such houses have been found elsewhere in Ireland, most notably at Movanagher, Co. Londonderry. Here, one of the thatched cabins depicted on Thomas Raven's 1622 map of the Mercers' Company village was located. Excavation revealed that the mud walls, containing a wattle core supported by small stakes, were strengthened by more substantial posts, providing a valuable insight into the use of native vernacular building practices among the newly arrived planters (Horning 2001).

11 Children from a local school visiting the archaeological excavation at Servants Hill.

DOW 017:054

Map of Clandeboye estate by Thomas Raven, 1625 (PRONI T870/1)

187 RINGHADDY: TOWER 353840 358860
HOUSE

Ringhaddy Castle

The remains of a 15th-century tower house built, in all likelihood, by the MacQuillans, then rebuilt in the early 17th century, are situated on Castle Island in Strangford Lough at a causeway where the island is separated from the mainland at high tide. The ground

Fig. 3.37 Ringhaddy Castle was originally a tower house with the upper two floors rebuilt in the early 17th century.

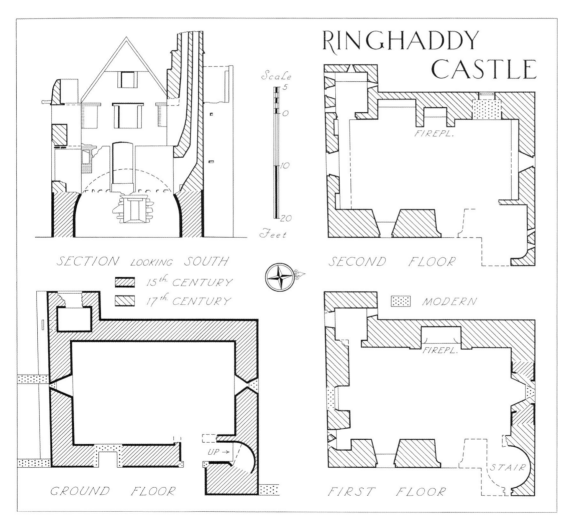

Fig. 3.38 Plans and section of Ringhaddy Castle (after *ASCD*, Fig. 164).

floor and parts of the first-floor levels are original. From the mid-16th century, the castle was part of the large Dufferin estate held by the White family of Dublin; the tower house, however, was situated beyond the bounds of the estate, and was occupied – and perhaps destroyed by – Bryan McArt O'Neill during the Nine Years' War. In 1601–2, it was rebuilt by Sir Ralph Lane and became a site of significance throughout the plantation period. The Dufferin estate was leased to Sir James Hamilton in 1610, and then granted to him in 1611. In Hamilton's will, it was stated that his widow (Sir James's third wife, Jane) should have the choice between Ringhaddy and Killyleagh for her residence, although it is not known whether she ever took up residence at Ringhaddy – she died in 1661. The Hamilton Manuscripts record repairs to the tower house being financed in 1683, but it is not known when the site was finally abandoned.

The remains consist of a rectangular tower house, 11.7m by 8.5m externally, built of split-stone rubble, with wrought quoins added in the 17th century. The ground floor is original, whereas the upper two floors were re-built by Lane. Rectangular windows and gable walls also date to Lane's rebuilding, giving the outward appearance of a structure designed for domestic rather than military purposes. The western wall incorporates two large fireplaces, while the north-eastern and south-western corners contain angled turrets, the former with a circular staircase, the latter a latrine. The first floor was originally carried on a semicircular barrel vault, traces of which survive, although this was replaced by timber flooring in the 17th century.

DOW 024:012

Cal. SPI 1601–3, 391 and 502; *PSAMNI* 100; *ASCD* 249–250, Fig.164 and pls 61 and 62

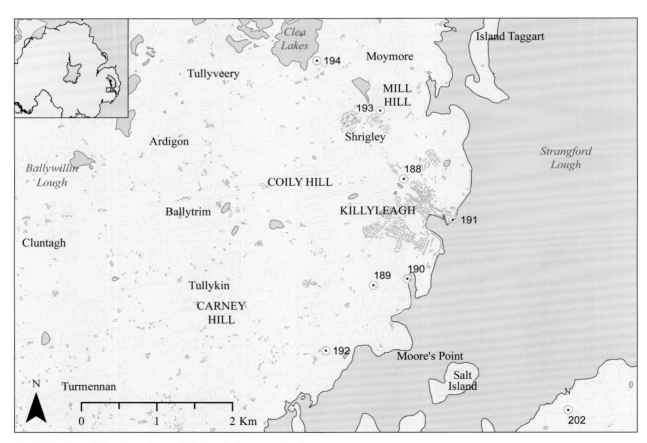

Fig. 3.39 Map of sites in and near Killyleagh discussed in the text.

Killyleagh

Killyleagh and the surrounding lands were also part of the grant to Hamilton in 1611, and this was the area to which he chose to move from Bangor around 1625 (see also Inv. 147).

188   KILLYLEAGH: CASTLE   352350 352960

A castle was built here by Sir James Hamilton in the 1610s, and this remains the private residence of the descendants of the Hamilton family, a building which was re-edified in the 19th century. The site was probably originally an Anglo-Norman motte and bailey. In the 13th century, a stone castle was built on the site by the Mandevilles, and was later held by the O'Neills; it is now incorporated into the south-western tower of the current building. Extant 17th-century features include the entrance to the present house and its machicolation, along with the bawn wall. The castle was damaged in 1648, and restored and heavily modified in 1666. It was restored again in 1850–62, following a period of dereliction, resulting in the Rhineland-style *Schloss* (castle) standing today.

DOW 024:030

Map of Clandeboye estate by Thomas Raven, 1625 (PRONI T870/1); Reeves 1847, 185; Stevenson 1920; Lawlor 1939a; *PSAMNI* 98–99; Jope 1951; *ASCD* 236–238; Salter 1993, 153

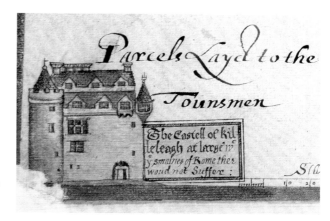

Fig. 3.41 Extract from Raven map of Killyleagh showing the castle.

189   KILLYLEAGH: HOUSE   351950 351510
Castlewilliam

A house is shown on the 1625 Raven map at a position marked 'Site of Castlewilliam' on the 2nd edition OS six-inch map of 1862–3. The site is close to two platform raths, although there are no visible remains of a castle or any other building at this location.

DOW 031:043

Map of Clandeboye estate by Thomas Raven, 1625 (PRONI T870/1)

190   CORPORATION: FORGE   352400 351600

A smithy is shown on the Raven map to the east of Castlewilliam House. There are no visible remains of a smithy at this location.

DOW 031:074

Map of Clandeboye estate by Thomas Raven, 1625 (PRONI T870/1)

191   CORPORATION: MILL   353000 352400

A mill and mill dam are shown on the Raven map in the vicinity of the forge and house noted above. This is also the location of a 'Bath House' on the 2nd edition OS six-inch map. There are no visible remains of the mill, or of the bath house at this location.

DOW 031:075

Map of Clandeboye estate by Thomas Raven, 1625 (PRONI T870/1)

Fig. 3.40 The front façade of Killyleagh Castle. First built in the 1610s, it has seen substantial rebuilding in the centuries since.

192   MULLAGH: HOUSE   351320 350620
      Delamont House

A house is shown in the Raven map on what appears to be also the site of a rath. The site is Delamont House, now a public park, and although the rath can still be traced, there are no known features of 17th-century origin visible at this location.

   DOW 031:027

   Map of Clandeboye estate by Thomas Raven, 1625 (PRONI T870/1)

193   TULLYVEERY: MILL   352039 353907
      Shrigley Mill

A mill is shown on the Raven map to the north of Killyleagh, on the banks of a stream running into the town. Presumably, it was destroyed by the Shrigley cotton factory that was built here in the 19th century, and itself replaced by the construction of a later tannery (recently closed) at the site. A large mill pond still exists between the Clay Lakes and the Dibney River in Shrigley, and a prominent drumlin in this location is called Mill Hill.

   DOW 024:500

   Map of Clandeboye estate by Thomas Raven, 1625 (PRONI T870/1)

194   TULLYMACNOUS: MILL   351200 354600

A mill is shown on the Raven map immediately south of South Clay Lake. However, no visible 17th-century remains can be found in the vicinity.

   DOW 024:052

   Map of Clandeboye estate by Thomas Raven, 1625 (PRONI T870/1)

Other Sites in Dufferin and Kinelarty

The barony of Dufferin also contains a 17th-century estate that stands remote from any known plantation period land estate (Inv. 195). The archaeological record of Kinelarty – the central part of Co. Down – is not well understood for the period, and contains only one possible site (Inv. 196).

Fig. 3.42 The remains of a 17th-century house known as 'The Ha' or 'The Haw' in Drumaghlis.

195   DRUMAGHLIS: HOUSE   342166 351183
      The Ha'

The remains of a 17th-century house known locally as 'The Ha', or 'The Haw', stand on a boundary between two different farmyards. The 1659 census records 'James Whatope [sic.] gent' as resident in Drumaghlish; Wauchope was probably a descendant of James Wauchope, a Scottish leaseholder on the Hamilton lands, and was awarded the lands surrounding this site following military service in the 1640s or 1650s. The remains consist of the poorly preserved walls of a rectangular, two-storey house with an attic and a steeply-pitched roof. The gable walls contain fireplaces, and the side walls contain windows with oak lintels and a door with massive oak posts. The interior of the house is obscured by thick vegetation.

   DOW 030:041

   Wauchope 1929

196   BALLYLONE BIG: HOUSE   338200 351500

A house was shown on the Down Survey map of the parish located within the 'half town of Ballimaglagh'. At the site, which is near to the Ballynahinch River, there are no visible remains.

   DOW 029:054

   Down Survey parish map of Magheredril (PRONI D597/4)

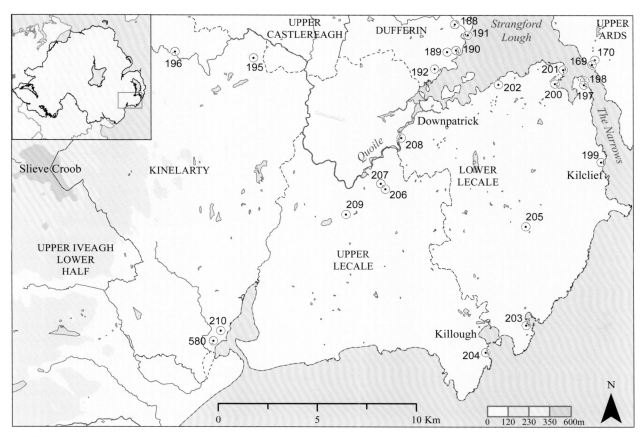

Fig. 3.43 Map of sites on the Lecale Peninsula discussed in the text.

The Lecale Peninsula

Sites in Lecale Lower

Lecale Lower – the shore of Strangford Lough opposite to the Little Ards – is a region of much historical and archaeological interest. However, despite a series of prominent and well-preserved 15th- and 16th-century coastal tower houses (Strangford Castle, Audleystown Castle and Kilclief Castle), archaeological traces of the plantation period are slight. Not one of the tower house sites has any history that directly associates it with the 17th century, although given that they were standing throughout the period, it seems likely that they were places of local importance.

197 STRANGFORD: STONE   **358906 350023**
TOWER AND BAWN
Old Court

The remains of a small stone tower to the north of Strangford village, with views over the Narrows of Strangford Lough, and Portaferry beyond, is located within the private lawned garden of an adjacent house that dates from the 1970s. The tower was originally three-quarter-round in plan, with two storeys and a battlemented parapet, and was perhaps the south-eastern flanking tower of a stone-built bawn, giving the site a tentative typological association with other defensive settlements from the plantation period. Other flankers have, presumably, been demolished but their former presence was documented on the 2nd edition OS six-inch map, which indicated 'Towers' at this site. A watercolour painting of a second tower exists in a

Fig. 3.44 A stone tower outside Strangford.

local private collection, but the history of the site is otherwise unknown.

DOW 032:002
ASCD 253, pl. 62

**198   STRANGFORD: TOWER   358862 349795
HOUSE
Strangford Castle**

A small, well-preserved three storeyed tower house stands in the centre of Strangford Village, visible from Portaferry Castle (Inv. 170) on the opposite side of the lough. Its history is rather obscure. Some sources suggest that perhaps it was the residence of a local merchant during the late 16th and early 17th centuries. It is probably a 15th-century building, although heavily modified in the late 16th century

Fig. 3.45 View of Strangford Castle.

following the report of its ruinous state in 1540. It is square in plan and, uniquely in a Co. Down context, was originally entered at first-floor level.

DOW 032:001
Harris 1744, 71; *ASCD* 252–253; Waterman 1967a

**199   KILCLIEF: TOWER HOUSE   359720 345750
Kilclief Castle**

This is a 15th-century tower house standing near to the entrance to Strangford Lough, and situated on its western shore, reputed to have been built as the residence of the Bishop of Down. It is a four-storey structure with an arched machicolation – similar to that at Audley's Castle (Inv. 201). From around 1441, when the bishop was deprived of the tower house for the crime of co-habiting with a married woman, until the early 17th century, the tower house and its surrounding lands were leased from the church by the Fitzsimon family, who eventually were able to claim a freehold of the estate. In 1601–2 the tower house was garrisoned with ten men on behalf of the crown by Nicholas Fitzsimon, but there are no

Fig. 3.46 View of Kilclief Castle.

128

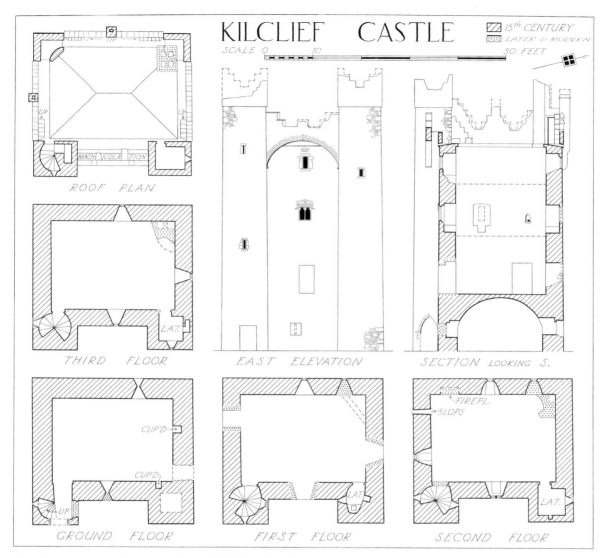

Fig. 3.47 Plans, elevation and section of Kilclief Castle (after *ASCD*, 233–235).

known modifications to its fabric that were made during that time.

DOW 039:002

Harris 1744, 24; Reeves 1847, 218-9; *PSAMNI* 122; *ASCD* 233–235

**200   CASTLEWARD: TOWER   357392 349850
        HOUSE**
       Old Castle Ward

A small, well-preserved tower house stands approximately 60m from the shore of Strangford Lough in the farmyard of the Castle Ward estate. The Ward family, originally from Cheshire (who, in the early 18th century, were joined by marriage to the Hamiltons of Bangor) purchased the lands here from the Earl of Kildare around 1570. The tower house was built after this purchase – in 1610 according to some accounts – and stands 900m to the south of a larger and rather more prominent 15th-century tower house, Audley's Castle (Inv. 201). The building, three storeys high plus an attic, measures 8.5m by

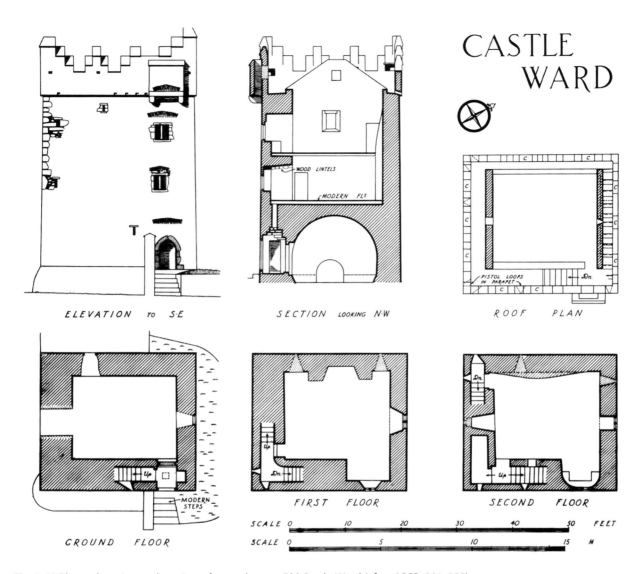

Fig. 3.48 Plans, elevation and section of tower house, Old Castle Ward (after *ASCD*, 231–233).

7.7m externally, approximately 5m square internally, and is built of split-stone rubble with sandstone dressings. The ground floor entrance allows access into a lobby area, which is protected from above by a murder-hole. The first floor is carried on a barrel vault, and both it and the second floor are reached by a mural staircase which runs through the thickness of the south-eastern and south-western walls. A machicolation box and battlemented parapet defended the structure at roof level.

DOW 031:005
The Ward Papers, 1691–*c.* 1745

**201 CASTLEWARD: TOWER   357810 350580
HOUSE AND BAWN**
Audley's Castle
Probably inspired by the design of nearby Kilclief Castle (Inv. 199), this tower house was built in the 15th century, perhaps by the Audley family, who

Fig. 3.49 Audley's Castle is another tower house in Castleward, the residence of the Audleys till 1646 when it was sold to the neighbouring Wards.

Fig. 3.50 The tower house and bawn at Walshestown.

were resident in the area since the 13th century and were certainly owners of the tower house by the 16th century. The building was occupied by the Audleys until 1646, when it was sold to the neighbouring Wards (Inv. 200). The tower house is a three-storeyed square structure, with sides 9m in length, 1.25m in thickness and standing to a height of over 14m. The tower is at the northern angle of a roughly-rectangular bawn, measuring 31m by 22.5m.

DOW 031:006
PSAMNI 104; *ASCD* 121, 126, 225–227

**202   WALSHESTOWN: TOWER   354529 349816
          HOUSE AND BAWN**

A tower house and bawn are located in the abandoned walled garden of Myra Castle, a short distance from the southern shore of Strangford Lough. The earliest reference is its inclusion in the Smith map of *c.* 1580, while one Christopher Walsh was recorded as its owner in 1613. It is probably late 16th century in date and measures 8.8m by 8m externally. It consists of a near-square, four-storey tower, with square turrets rising from the northern and southern corners. The staircase is within the north-eastern wall, each floor opening to a large chamber, with the first floor

carried upon barrel vaulting. The tower house is enclosed by a bawn wall with double-splayed gun loops that survives only to the south-west of the main building. The masonry here is coursed differently to the rubble walls of the castle, and therefore may date to a different building phase.

DOW 031:008
PSAMNI 103; *ASCD* 253–255, Fig.167 and pls 61 and 65

203   ARDGLASS: SETTLEMENT   355900 337220

A settlement comprising houses and a castle appears on the shore at Ardglass on the Down Survey maps of Lecale, but nothing visible remains of these structures.

DOW 045:030
Down Survey barony map of Lecale (TCD)

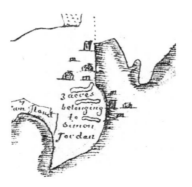

Fig. 3.51 Extract from the Down Survey map of the barony of Lecale (*c.* 1656–58) showing settlement at Ardglass.

204 KILLOUGH: SETTLEMENT 353850 335800 to 354034 336311

The Down Survey map of Lecale shows two houses on the western shore of Killough Bay, marked as 'Killaugh' and 'Kilbride'. Today, both locations lie within the village of Killough, but there are no surviving structures or features there that date to the 17th century. A small, square-sided stone structure with castellated walls in the village is, in fact, an unusual limekiln of 19th-century origin. The harbour at Killough was built in the 18th century at a place favoured for landing ships in the 17th century, but no material evidence for this earlier activity survives.

DOW 045:500
Down Survey barony map of Lecale (TCD)

Fig. 3.52 Extract from the Down Survey map of the barony of Lecale (*c.* 1656–58) depicting settlement at Killough.

205 BISHOPS COURT: BAWN 355900 342400

A bawn was constructed in 1601 at 'Lismolyn', on the orders of Lord Mountjoy, Lord Deputy of Ireland, whose army was active in Lecale at that time. The site has not been located, but although it was mentioned as a 'castle' in a parliamentary report from 1833, it does not appear on the 1st edition OS map. The hill to the south-east of the Bishops Court crossroads is called 'Mountjoy Hill', and two fields nearby are known locally as 'Green Bawn' and 'Cool Bawn', but there are no upstanding archaeological remains.

DOW 038:022
Reeves 1847, 165; O'Laverty 1878–1887, I, 178–179; *ASCD* 261

Downpatrick

Downpatrick and its surrounding lands have a rich and complex history, the town having been an important ecclesiastical centre since the early medieval period. Following the dissolution of the monasteries in the mid-16th century, the extensive church lands hereabouts were subject to several successive land grants, including a purchase by Charles Blount, Baron Mountjoy, shortly after 1603 (Parkinson 1927, 33–35). The Mountjoy family sold to, or exchanged lands with, Edward Cromwell of Devonshire, a grandson of the Earl of Essex and a very distant relation to Oliver Cromwell (*ibid.*). Cromwell, or his son Thomas, was said to have built a castle in the town, and lived there for part of the year (Inv. 206). He also built a bridge across the Quoile near the site of an old mill, and the town and his castle were military centres, both for Cromwell's own militia, and for British forces during the 1640s (*ibid.* 36–38). A port on the Quoile Estuary, the town was certainly a hive of activity in the 17th century, and the street layout of the time does not differ significantly from the pattern seen today. That said, none of the buildings in the town are definitively 17th-century in origin (although see Inv. 207).

206 DOWNPATRICK: CASTLE 348820 344350 Irish Street

A castle was built by the Cromwell family in Downpatrick at the corner of Folly Lane and Irish Street. There have been local accounts of thick walls and ruined arches, perhaps vaulting, found underneath more recent buildings at this location, but there are no visible remains of the castle above ground.

DOW 037:110
Parkinson 1927, 33–46, 152; Wilson 1991; Day and McWilliams 1992e, 42

207 DOWNPATRICK: HOUSE 348586 344631 English Street

Historical sources indicate that Denvir's Hotel

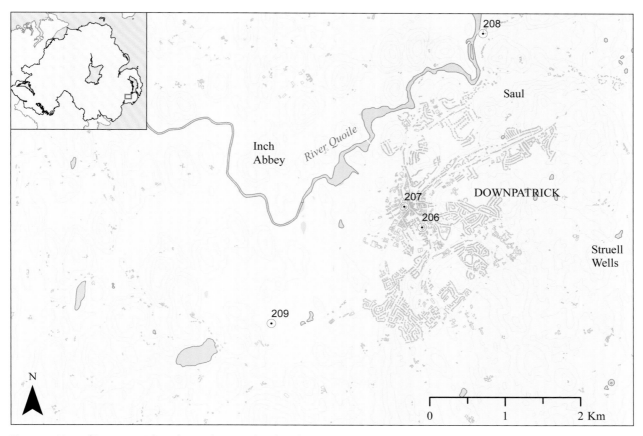

Fig. 3.53 Map of Downpatrick and sites discussed within the text.

in English Street was built in 1642, although a date stone of 1667 could be seen on its exterior, until weathering and over-painting rendered it invisible. Much of the fabric of the building dates from the 18th century or later, although the core of the structure may be mid-17th-century in origin. Archaeological fieldwork in the 1980s in one of the hotel rooms found medieval deposits and two large well-preserved 17th-century fireplaces.

DOW 037:109

Dunleath *et al.* 1970; Brannon 1988a; Day and McWilliams 1992e, 41

208   QUOILE: TOWER HOUSE   349630 347010
      Quoile Castle
The remains of a tower house are located on the southern bank of the River Quoile, on the north-

eastern fringes of Downpatrick. Its origins are somewhat obscure, but it is likely that it was constructed *c.* 1600 by Captain Richard West, whose

Fig. 3.54 The remains of Quoile Castle.

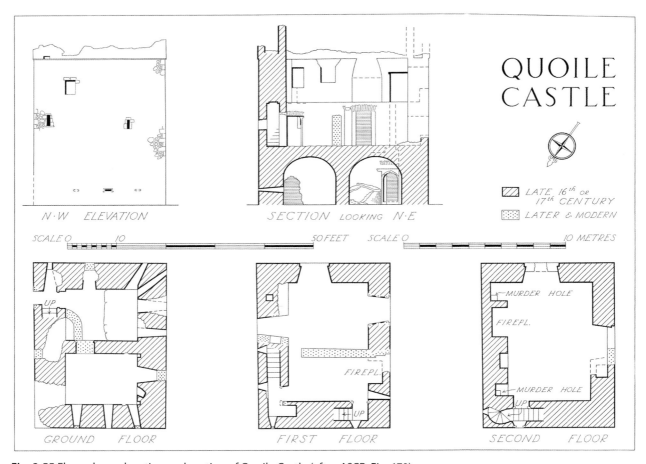

Fig. 3.55 Floor plans, elevation and section of Quoile Castle (after *ASCD*, Fig. 170).

descendants remained in residence until the 18th century. A hoard of seven silver Elizabethan coins was found during conservation works in the 1980s. The tower house is rectangular in plan and consists of three storeys and an attic, with walls 10.0m by 8.5m externally and 1.5m thick, constructed of split-stone rubble with sandstone dressings. There are two chambers at ground-floor level, each with a stone vault where evidence for wicker centring is visible. Several gun loops are also visible. A straight staircase in the north-eastern wall leads to the first floor, which has a fireplace. At this level, a second set of stairs in the north-western wall leads to the second floor and continues to the wall-walk at roof level.

In 2011, the southern first floor chamber was excavated to facilitate drainage works, uncovering the roof of one of the ground floor vaults.

DOW 031:009

ASCD 247–248; Ó Baoill 2011a

Other Sites in Lecale Upper

Beyond Downpatrick, Lecale Upper consists of rolling countryside between the River Quoile and the sandy beaches on the coast between Minerstown and Dundrum.

209   BALLYDUGAN: BAWN   346820 343030

A bawn, originally measuring 38m by 25m and

Fig. 3.56 L-shaped house built by Sir Francis Blundell at Dundrum Castle in 1636.

oriented north-west to south-east, was built in the early 17th century on a prominence near the shore of Ballydugan Lake, but by whom is unknown. The landscape in this locality has changed considerably since the 17th century; when originally occupied this site would have been isolated by the extensive saltmarshes of the Quoile estuary, and could only have been approached from higher ground to the west. Harris stated that there was a large, strong house on the site, with a bawn and a drawbridge, which was attacked and damaged in the 1641 Rebellion. The surviving remains consist of the poorly-preserved south-eastern and south-western walls of the bawn, and part of a circular flanker at the western corner. A number of gun loops are preserved in the south-western wall, although these are now filled with concrete. A lane runs through the interior as the bawn is now part of a farm estate.

DOW 037:022

Harris 1744, 39; *ASCD* 257–259, Fig.170 and pl.68

Fig. 3.57 The triangular panels on the southern gable of the east wing of Blundell's house in Dundrum Castle.

210   DUNDRUM: HOUSE   340475 336930
Blundell's House,
Dundrum Castle

The remains of an early 17th-century house stand in the lower ward of Dundrum Castle, an important Anglo-Norman site dating from the late 12th century, and occupied by the Castlewellan branch of the Magennis family from the 14th century until the Nine Years' War. The castle and surrounding lands were granted to Edward Cromwell (see Downpatrick above), who sold the estate to Sir Francis Blundell in 1636, and it was he who was probably responsible for building the house, although Cromwell may have contributed an earlier phase. The castle and house were garrisoned during the 1640s, and were slighted by Parliamentarian forces in 1652, at which point Blundell's house may have been abandoned. However, the surviving remains suggest a complex

history, with more episodes of modification than would be expected of a house that had been occupied for only a relatively short period of time.

The remains consist of the random-rubble walls of an L-shaped house, two- to three-storeys high, which interrupts the curtain wall of the lower ward of the castle at its south-western corner. It is likely that the eastern and western wings were built in different phases – the western wall of the eastern wing butts against the western wing, suggesting that the eastern wing is later. The house bears evidence for changing floor levels, and the eastern wing originally had a low basement under a main ground-level floor, with an attic above. There are many architectural details visible, such as fireplaces, cupboards, recesses, windows, joist sockets and gun loops. Two triangular panels, one containing seven courses of brick, on the southern gable of the

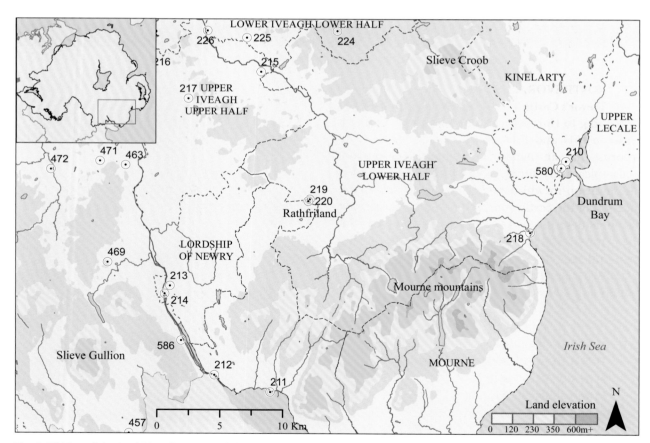

Fig. 3.58 Map of the lordship of Newry and the barony of Iveagh Upper showing sites mentioned in the text.

east wing, have parallels with a house of 1631 in Nithsdale, Dumfries.

Excavations in 2009 discovered locally manufactured stone roofing slates, presumably used to cover the roof of the eastern wing of the house, as well as landscaping features that post-date it.

DOW 044:006

PSAMNI 126; Waterman and Morton 1958; Waterman 1951 and 1964; *ASCD* 207; Day and McWilliams 1990c, 58–59; Salter 1993, 146; MacDonald 2009 and 2011

Lordship of Newry and the Barony of Iveagh Upper, Upper Half

Carlingford Lough Sites

Carlingford Lough is a shallow *fjord* at the mouth of the Newry River, between the Mourne and Cooley mountains. The lough is a natural frontier, forming part of the border with Co. Louth.

211   ROSTREVOR: CASTLE   317000 318000
      Trevor's Castle

According to Harris, a castle was built in Rostrevor between 1611 and 1612. Another source from 1752 records that an Alderman Ross had a '...small house pleasantly situated under the hills ...near an old mansion in which his father liv'd'. The precise location of the castle is unknown, but 19th-century accounts describe it as being near the waterfront in the centre of the town. The 1st edition OS six-inch map indicates an 'old hall' in this area.

DOW 054:020

Harris 1744, 87; Pococke 1752, 8; *ASCD* 263

212   NARROW WATER: TOWER   312560 319390
      HOUSE AND BAWN
      Narrow Water Castle

This tower house, which was defended against parliamentary forces in 1644, controls the Clanrye River as it enters Carlingford Lough, and is thought to have been built by the English around 1560 on

Fig. 3.59 View of Narrow Water Castle, a tower house and bawn which overlooks the Clanrye River as it enters Carlingford Lough.

an earlier Anglo-Norman site. Throughout much of the 17th century, it was occupied by the Mourne Magennises, who were granted it on the condition that their allegiance to the English crown would be maintained. In the late 17th century it was sold to the Hall family, who retained possession of it until 1956 when it was given into State Care.

The tower house measures 11.2m by 10.1m and is comprised of a square tower of three storeys plus attic, with a crenellation at roof level, set within a roughly square bawn. The entrance faces north-west and each floor contains a large chamber, with stairs in the north-western and north-eastern walls. The tower house is located towards the southern side of the bawn, and was constructed on level ground, with its foundations built directly on natural rock

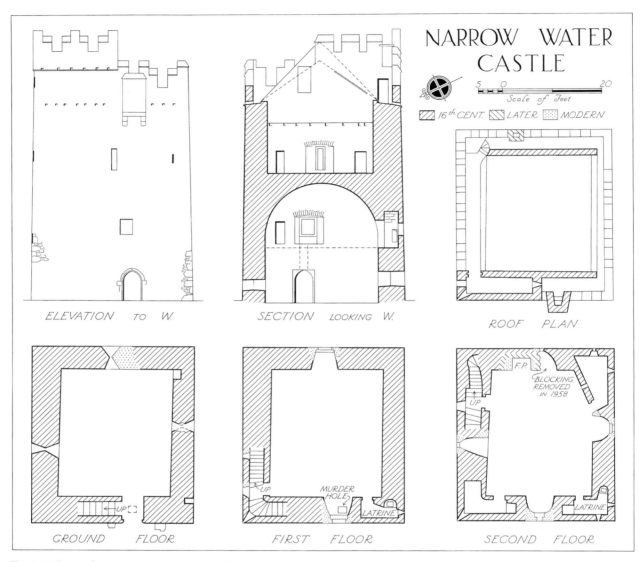

Fig. 3.60 Front elevation, cross-section and floor plans of the tower house at Narrow Water Castle (after *ASCD*, Fig 158).

outcrops. The bawn wall survives to a height of 3–3.5m, and has a curved south-eastern corner, where openings in the wall provide views across the strategically important waters of Carlingford Lough.

DOW 051:044

PSAMNI 136–137 and pl.35; Waterman 1962; *ASCD* 241–243, Fig.158, pls 60, 61, 64 and 65; Day and McWilliams 1990c, 116, 119 and 124; Salter 1993, 155

Sites in the Lordship of Newry

Newry is situated at a point in the landscape known as 'the gap of the North', a natural routeway between north and south that has been important since prehistoric times. The area was a focus of monastic settlement in the medieval period, but its development as an urban centre largely began in the mid-16th century, initially as a garrison town along the eastern bank of the Newry River. It was occupied throughout the 17th century, although archaeological traces of this phase of its history are slight.

213 NEWRY: CHURCH AND GRAVEYARD 309020 326640
Saint Patrick's Church

A church overlooking the historical centre of Newry was built in 1578 by Sir Nicholas Bagenal – making it one of the oldest Protestant churches built *ab initio* in Ireland. It was ruined before 1641 and subsequently repaired between 1720 and 1729, and has undergone phases of extensive rebuilding since. There is an original moulded window label in the southern wall of the southern transept, while within the tower, but originally mounted on the exterior of the building, is Sir Nicholas' coat of arms carved in stone and dated 1578.

DOW 046:039
ASCD 308–309

214 NEWRY: SETTLEMENT 308600 326000

There are no surviving structures or upstanding features of 17th-century date in Newry, although excavations in and around the city have revealed traces of plantation-period settlement. At Bagenal's Castle, which was built in the mid-16th century by Sir Nicholas Bagenal, excavations revealed a cemetery of 16th- or 17th-century date. Excavations at Carnbane in 2011 also revealed a rath that had been re-used, perhaps as a military encampment, around this time. Evidence for a cobbled surface and associated wells was uncovered. Based on ceramics and clay pipe fragments, the surface was dated to the early part of the 17th century.

DOW 046:042
Harris 1744, 88–94; Lewis 1837, II, 430–434; Knox 1875, 326–340; Camblin 1951, 33–34 and 47–49; *ASCD* 418–420; Day and McWilliams 1990c, 61–66; Walsh 2013

Loughbrickland and the Surrounding Area

The western fringes of Co. Down to the south of Banbridge had been a centre of English settlement since Elizabethan times, when Sir Marmaduke Whitechurch established a colony near Loughbrickland (Inv. 217). The area is also crossed by the main route from Belfast to Dublin and therefore military encampments from multiple periods abound in the area.

215 TULLYCONNAUGHT: ARTILLERY FORT 316230 344310
Fort Charles

What appears to be a 17th-century artillery fort survives as an earthen bank at this location, topped by a hawthorn hedge, which joins with other modern field boundaries to form a trapezoidal enclosure with somewhat angular corners measuring 28m by 21m. A level, round-edged platform, some 7m in diameter, in the south-eastern corner of the site may be a gun platform. The history of the site is not known.

DOW 034:114

216 SCARVA: CASTLE 306470 343660

The site of a castle, erected by General Monk in 1647, levelled in 1847, overlooks the village of Scarva and a nearby river crossing. The castle was surrounded by earthen ramparts, but the site is now occupied by St. Matthew's Church, built in 1850, and a graveyard. Local accounts indicate that stones from the castle were used for the foundations of the church.

DOW 033:047
Harris 1744, 85; Lewis 1837, II, 546; Knox 1875, 354–355; *ASCD* 263–264

217 LOUGHBRICKLAND: SETTLEMENT 310448 342084

The village of Loughbrickland was founded by Sir Marmaduke Whitechurch, who purchased the surrounding lands from the Magennis family in

Elizabethan times and built a castle and a church, and encouraged English settlement there. A castle was reputed to have been built in 1585 to the south of the village, on the shore of Lough Brickland, on the site of a Magennis stronghold (approximate grid ref. 311200 341400). Castle, church and village were destroyed in 1641, but the village was rebuilt soon afterwards, as shown by the 1659 census, which indicated that the area had a relatively large number of occupants. No 17th-century structures or features survive in the village.

DOW 034:127

ASCD 262

Barony of Iveagh Upper, Lower Half

Newcastle

Prior to the 17th century, the western half of Co. Down, Iveagh, was dominated by various septs of the Magennis family, native Irish who had been allies of the Anglo-Normans for centuries (Quinn 1933). Among their various bases of power was Newcastle, the seaside town at the foot of the Mourne Mountains, not to be confused with the townland of Newcastle on the Ards.

218   MURLOUGH UPPER: TOWER   337630 331050
        HOUSE

Nothing remains of the late-medieval Magennis tower house in Newcastle, which was demolished in 1830. Harris recorded a date stone above the door inscribed with the year 1588. The tower house was occupied by the Magennisses throughout the 17th century; several 19th-century paintings and drawings of the tower house exist, which depict a two- or three-storey structure with corbelled turrets. This led Jope to include the site in his list of 'castles' in Ulster with Scottish architectural influences.

DOW 049:004

Harris 1744, 80; Jope 1951, 44–45; *ASCD* 262

Rathfriland

Before its destruction during the 1641 Rebellion, Rathfriland, a hilltop settlement occupied since early medieval times (Inv. 220), was the seat of a branch of the Magennis family. The town had 53 residents in 1659, according to the Co. Down census held that year (Rankin 1979).

219   RATHFRILAND: TOWER   320127 333741
        HOUSE
Rathfriland Castle

The ruins of a tower house built, in all likelihood, by the Magennis family in the late 16th century, stand on the summit of a prominent hill, surrounded by the town of Rathfriland. The remains consist of fragments of the eastern, southern and western walls, located within a private garden. It was square in plan, with sides 8m long and walls at least 1m thick. In 1586 it was occupied by Hugh Magennis, who was said to have lived there 'very cylville and Englishe-like'. The tower house was seized and destroyed by English forces, first under Alderman Hawkins, then General Ireton, during the wars of the 1640s, though it was still standing (albeit in a ruinous condition) when described by Harris in 1744.

DOW 041:051

Harris 1744, 87; Bagenal *et al.* 1854, 152; *PSAMNI* 123–124; *ASCD* 248; Day and McWilliams 1990c, 12, 14 and 16

Fig. 3.61 Ivy-covered remains of Rathfriland Castle.

220   RATHFRILAND: 320003 303360
SETTLEMENT

The historic centre of the town is located around Church Square, and the roads that converge upon the square at the top of the hill. No early 17th-century structures survive, but those buildings at the junction of Church Square and Newry Street apparently date from 1682.

DOW 041:092

Rankin 1979

Dromore

Dromore was an early monastic centre, which from the 12th century onwards acted as the administrative centre of the diocese of the same name (see Inv. 222). William Hawkins, an alderman of the city of London who was instrumental in the destruction of Rathfriland Castle (Inv. 219), was awarded an estate near Dromore around 1650, as a reward for military service during the wars (Lewis 1837, I, 507–508).

221   DROMORE: TOWER HOUSE   320093 353237
Dromore Castle

This castle was reputedly built *c.* 1610 by William Worsely for his father-in-law John Todd, the first Protestant Bishop of Dromore. Worsely also leased a portion of See lands from the bishop. The ruins consist of a square, three-storey tower house, located within Dromore close to a crossing point on the River Lagan. Much of the north-eastern corner of the building has been lost. It is square in plan, *c.* 7m by 7m internally with walls approximately 85cm thick, and a square projection, now damaged, on its eastern side presumably containing the original entrance. The walls are of random split-stone rubble, with no dressed or moulded stones present. At first-floor level there is a flat-headed central window opening in the northern wall; a similar opening may have once existed in the southern wall at second floor level, but this is no longer clear, due to a substantial breach. In addition to these windows, there are narrow slits on each level.

DOW 021:051

Reeves 1847, 309–311; *Cal. Pat. Rolls Jas I*, 190–191, 309 and 394–396; Atkinson 1925, 34; *PSAMNI* 97; *ASCD* 233 and Fig.152

222   DROMORE: CATHEDRAL   320040 353350

This site, which overlooks the northern bank of the River Lagan in the town of Dromore, was the location of an Early Christian monastery, traditionally founded by St. Colman in the 6th century. The church associated with the monastic settlement became a cathedral in the 12th century, although nothing of the medieval building survives, as it was ruined in the late 16th century. John Todd was appointed to the vacant bishopric in 1607; two years later James I issued letters patent conferring upon it a new title, 'The Cathedral Church of Christ the Redeemer, Dromore', and issued funds for the building's repair. Nothing from this phase of the church's history survives; it was rebuilt in 1661, following destruction that most sources suggest occurred in 1641, and again rebuilt in the 19th century.

DOW 021:050

Reeves 1847, 303–306; *ASCD* 275; Hamlin 2008, 296–297

223   GRENNAN: BAWN   317140 353190
Gill Hall Castle

The possible site of a bawn lies within the Gill Hall estate near Dromore, granted during the reign of Charles II to William Hawkins. Its identification here was seemingly based on local information available at the time of the first Ordnance Survey. There are no visible remains.

DOW 020:059

OS Field Report no. 146; *PSAMNI* 95; *ASCD* 171

224   FEDANY: CHURCH   322290 347660
Garvaghy Parish Church

The small parish church is recorded in local tradition as being of 17th-century date, and built upon an older site; indeed there are 11th- and 15th-century references to the parish. A simple, rectangular building, it has rendered walls, with annexes at the western gable end, and the eastern side of the northern wall. It is set within a graveyard enclosed by hedging, stone walls and revetments, and both church and graveyard are still in active use.

DOW 028:067

Harris 1744, 83; Reeves 1847, 309–311, 316 and 318

225   TULLYRAIN: CASTLE   315100 347100

The Down Survey map of Iveagh shows a castle or structure in this area. However, much of the land hereabouts has been quarried in recent decades, removing any archaeological traces.

DOW 027:115

Down Survey barony map of Iveagh (PRONI D597/2)

Fig. 3.62 Garvaghy parish church in Fedany.

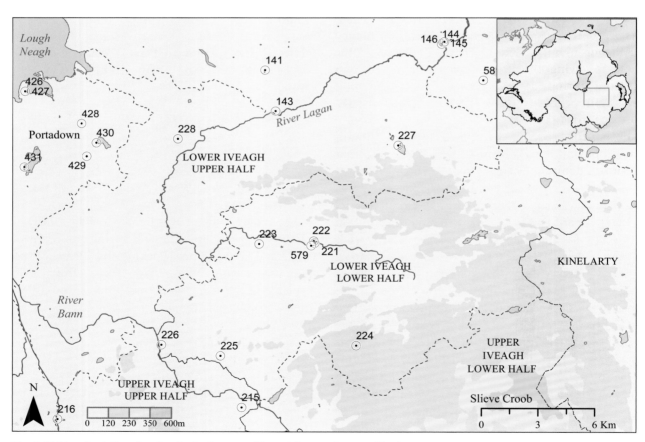

Fig. 3.63 Map depicting the sites in the barony of Iveagh Lower discussed in the text.

226 KILPIKE: CHURCH 311970 347690
   Seapatrick Church

A church was erected in 1698 on the former site of one destroyed in 1641, and Reeves identified it with the medieval parish church of 'Disertunde'. Only a single gable wall survives, standing on a ridge of high ground, with a small, flat-headed window opening visible in its upper part. The former interior of the church now contains numerous burials, and the ruin is surrounded by a graveyard in which the earliest memorial stones have 18th-century dates.

   DOW 027:071

   Reeves 1847, 106–107; *ASCD* 309

Barony of Iveagh Lower

Hillsborough

The village of Hillsborough was originally known as 'Cromlyn' or 'Crumlin', but was renamed 'Hillsborough' when the Hill family moved to the area following the destruction of their house at Malone during the 1641 Rebellion (Anon. 1860). It was an important place in the 17th century, situated on the road between Belfast and Dublin, with another road leading to Carrickfergus. Subsequent development in the village has erased all 17th-century domestic structures, although there has

been continuous occupation since the 17th century at the fort near Hillsborough Castle, which is now government buildings and the official royal residence in Northern Ireland. The current parish church building was founded in 1667; an earlier church was situated on ground now within the castle park, but this was in ruins long before 1622 (O'Laverty 1878–1887, II, 247–248).

227 HILLSBOROUGH: 324500 358600
   ARTILLERY FORT

An artillery fort was constructed by Col. Arthur Hill around 1650 on the site of an early medieval rath. It consists of a square, earthen enclosure of sides 82m in length, faced on the outside with a wall of roughly dressed boulders with sandstone quoins. This rises above the level of the earthen rampart to

Fig. 3.64 The gatehouse of Hillsborough Fort, first constructed in the 17th century and subsequently remodelled in the mid-18th century.

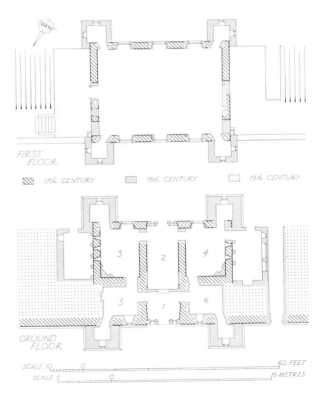

Fig. 3.65 Ground and first-floor plans of the gatehouse of Hillsborough Fort, showing its different phases of construction (after *ASCD*, 114–116).

form a parapet wall – now largely reconstructed. The north-western rampart has a gatehouse at its centre, the core of which is an original, rectangular 17th-century building. This was remodelled in the mid-18th century with corner towers, battlements, along with pointed doors and windows in a gothic revivalist fashion. Other buildings along the ramparts also date to this time, as do the entrances on the southern sides of the enclosure.

DOW 014:012

PSAMNI 92; Jope 1960, 114–116; *ASCD* 409–411; Gaskell-Brown and Brannon 1978

Other Sites

228   BALLYMAKEONAN: 312830 358950
CHURCH AND GRAVEYARD
Magheralin Old Church

The church of 'Lin' is referred to in the 1306 taxation, although nothing of this medieval building remains. The church was described as ruinous in the 1657 Inquisitions, but was rebuilt shortly after. The present-day ruins of Magheralin Church consist of the eastern, western and northern stone-rubble walls of a rectangular nave, which measures 23.1m by 11.2m and is of early 15th-century date, along with the western tower and traces of a northern transept, with its double arch, all of which are likely to be 17th-century additions. The windows of the nave were altered or rebuilt during the 17th century, and are relatively simple openings with semicircular heads. The tower is four storeys high, although the upper level may be a more recent addition. The church is located within an extensive graveyard, enclosed by stone walls, with an earthen bank on the eastern side. There are local reports of human bones having been found in adjacent fields, but in 2006 archaeologically supervised test-trenching nearby failed to reveal anything of interest.

DOW 013:030

Reeves 1847, 110–111; Atkinson 1925, 210-11; *PSAMNI* 91; *ASCD* 307–308, Fig. 206; Hamlin 2008, 309; MacManus 2006b

Fig. 3.66 View of Magheralin Church.

Barony of Castlereagh

Castlereagh Hills, Dundonald and East Belfast

Castlereagh was the seat of Con O'Neill (Inv. 244), whose large estate was dispersed to Hamilton and Montgomery. Although he retained one third of his original holding, the rich agricultural lands surrounding what is now Dundonald and East Belfast (Bally-Dunkilmuck, Balle-Tullegoan and Ballecrossan) were leased to Viscount Montgomery, then passed to Sir Robert McClelland who married Montgomery's daughter Mary. After she died, the lands were sold to Peter Hill, son of Sir Moses Hill who had held lands in Kilwarlin townland since 1611 (*ASCD*, 259 and refs therein). Raven's map of 1625 (PRONI T870/1) depicts a number of potential archaeological sites in this area, listed in Table 3.1.

244   CASTLEREAGH: TOWER   337550 371090
HOUSE AND BAWN
Castle Reagh

Con O'Neill's tower house and bawn of Castle Reagh were situated in the Castlereagh Hills overlooking Belfast. According to the Carew papers, it was built in the early 16th century, and was captured by Chichester in 1601 during the Nine Years' War. Con O'Neill rebelled subsequently, which led to his arrest

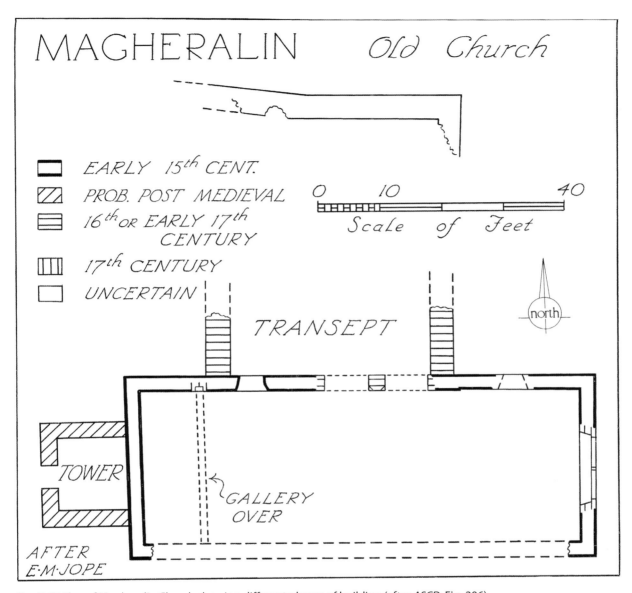

Fig. 3.67 Plan of Magheralin Church showing different phases of building (after *ASCD*, Fig. 206).

and detention in Carrickfergus and, ultimately, the surrender of much of his estate to Hamilton and Montgomery. In 1616, Sir Moses Hill purchased a large proportion of the lands still held by O'Neill, including Castle Reagh which, according to Carew, had already been occupied since at least 1611 by Sir Moses, who had built a bawn with flankers around the tower house. Archaeological evidence for the castle itself is scant. The site can be identified with

accuracy however, as a castle was recorded here on the Downshire estate map of 1803, and the *OS Memoirs* recorded a square building, with turrets, at this location. The building disappeared when robbed for its stone in the early 19th century.

DOW 009:006

Harris 1744, 73; *DEP*; O'Laverty 1878–1887, II, 254; *PSAMNI* 1940; *ASCD* 262; Day and McWilliams 1992e, 120; McNeill 1987.

Inv.	Site	Grid ref.	Description	SMR
229	Thompson Street	335040 374050	Settlement.	DOW 004:006
230	Ballymacarret	336490 374430	Mill, near the Conns Water.	DOW 004:007
231	Flora Street	336110 373690	Settlement.	DOW 004:008
232	Willowfield	335480 373520	Settlement. An archaeological evaluation carried out just south of here in 2007 revealed nothing of archaeological significance (Kovacik and Bowen 2007).	DOW 004:009
233	Park Parade	335050 373410	Settlement.	DOW 004:010
234	Ballyhackamore	336800 373300	Settlement.	DOW 004:011
235	Belmont Road	338510 374590	A bridge was noted by Raven, but all water courses in the immediate area have been culverted.	DOW 004:014
236	Knocknagoney	338950 376300	A mill was shown on the Raven map, and although nothing remains, a stream that flows through a deep, narrow gully could indicate the location of the site.	DOW 005:057
237	Finchley Park	338640 375680	A house located near a motte.	DOW 005:091
238	Sandown Road	338140 373300	A bridge, presumably over the stream adjacent to this location.	DOW 004:013
239	Orangefield Park	337300 373100	Mill.	DOW 004:012
240	Hillhead, Ballyrussell	342900 371600	A cluster of houses.	DOW 005:092
241	Ballyoran	343160 373300	A group of Irish-style houses (wattle walls and thatched roofs).	DOW 005:066
242	Ballylisbredan	343070 372890	A mill, and although the site has been lost, it probably correlates with a later mill, marked as Milltown on the 1948 OS six-inch map.	DOW 005:067
243	Carrowreagh	342900 374150	Mill.	DOW 005:093

Table 3.1: Potential archaeological sites in the vicinity of Dundonald and East Belfast, indicated on Thomas Raven's maps of the Clandeboye estate, 1625 (PRONI T870/1)

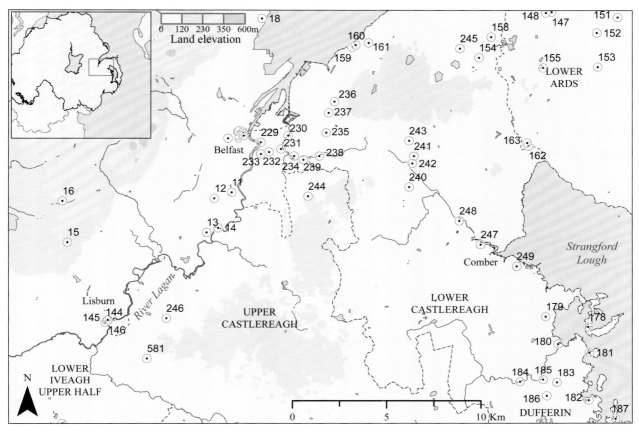

Fig. 3.68 Map of the sites in the barony of Castlereagh discussed in the text.

**245 BALLYSALLAGH MAJOR: 345600 379200
      HOUSE**

A house is depicted on Raven's 1625 map on the summit of a drumlin, and seems to match the location of Silver Tongue Hill, destroyed in the construction of a covered reservoir.

> DOW 001:049
> Map of Clandeboye estate by Thomas Raven, 1625 (PRONI T870/1)

**246 HILLHALL: HOUSE   330031 364420
      AND BAWN
      The Court**

A house and bawn were built shortly before 1637 by Peter Hill (son of Sir Moses Hill) on the summit of a drumlin, with panoramic views in all directions. The bawn walls have been incorporated into a more recent house, garden and farmyard, but nothing remains of the original 17th-century house itself. Measuring 61m by 43m, the walls survive on all sides and are oriented north-east to south-west, reaching a height of 3.5m in places, except along the north-eastern side; along the north-western return it is topped with crenellation. In 1744, Harris described four flankers, only one of which still exists, a circular structure standing at the western corner.

> DOW 015:001
> Harris 1744, 72; *OS Field Report* no. 108; O'Laverty 1878–1887, II, 183 and 243; *Cal. SPI* 1633–47, 145; Bigger 1911b; *PSAMNI* 92; Green 1949, 25; *ASCD* 259–260, Fig.171

Comber

Comber was the seat of the younger Hugh Montgomery, the second Viscount. A new town (Inv. 247) was built on the periphery of an older settlement originally associated with the Cistercian abbey, but the new urban foundation has since disappeared, with all subsequent growth of the village stemming from the original, 'old' Comber (Hill 1869, 93).

247   CATTOGS: SETTLEMENT   346690 368450
New Comber

The Raven map of 1625 shows 'Old Comber', with its abbey in ruins but no houses, and 'New Comber', containing houses and a market cross centred upon the place still known as 'New Comber Bridge'. At this location, however, there are no structures or features of 17th-century origin. It is interesting that the development of the town since the 17th century has concentrated on the old town rather than the new.

> DOW 010:061
> Map of Clandeboye estate by Thomas Raven, 1625 (PRONI T870/1)

248   COMBER: HOUSE   345560 369740
Mount Alexander

Still known as 'Mount Alexander', this is the site of the house built for the younger Hugh Montgomery (before his succession as 2nd Viscount Montgomery) on the occasion of his marriage in 1623 to Jean Alexander. The family probably moved to Newtownards, following the death of the 1st viscount, but returned to Mount Alexander. He died in 1642, and his widow married Major-General Robert Munro, who took up residence there. The later history of the house is not known, nor is it clear what form and layout it took, as no archaeological traces survive.

> DOW 010:028
> Hill 1869, 93, 174–175; O'Laverty 1878–1887, II, 137; *PSAMNI* 87; *ASCD* 262

249   CASTLE ESPIE: BAWN   348600 367270

Castle Espie is traditionally associated with a bawn at this location, although there are no clear historical references to such a structure. 'Castle Ruins' are marked here on the 1st edition OS six-inch map, and in 1878 O'Laverty noted ruins of a castle within a large rath at this location, on lands that belonged to the church during the 17th century. There is a large rath nearby (DOW 010:032), but this does not enclose any upstanding structure.

> DOW 011:001
> *OS Field Report* no. 87; O'Laverty 1878–1887, I, 369; *PSAMNI* 88; *ASCD* 262

150

Chapter 4
County Fermanagh

Introduction

Following Plantation in 1609, the lordship of the Maguires was transformed into the County of Fermanagh. Among the incoming English and Scottish landowners were Sir James Balfour, Sir William Cole and Sir John Dunbar, who were granted estates around the shores of Lough Erne. Some of the native landholders were included in the scheme, including Conor Roe Maguire who was granted the entire barony of Magherastephana. A consequence of English, Scottish and Irish landowners living in close proximity was an intermingling of architectural influences in the design of fortified houses. Castle Balfour, for example, is a building embellished with English-style bay windows, along with Scottish-style turrets corbelled out from the building. Castle Archdale exhibits a T-plan, an arrangement common to English houses, but its bawn gateway is decorated with a moulded surround of Scottish origin. More explicitly Scottish in appearance is Enniskillen Castle, where the Watergate Tower is flanked by two circular, corbelled turrets with conical stone roofs. Intriguingly, a number of planter landlords built in the Gaelic

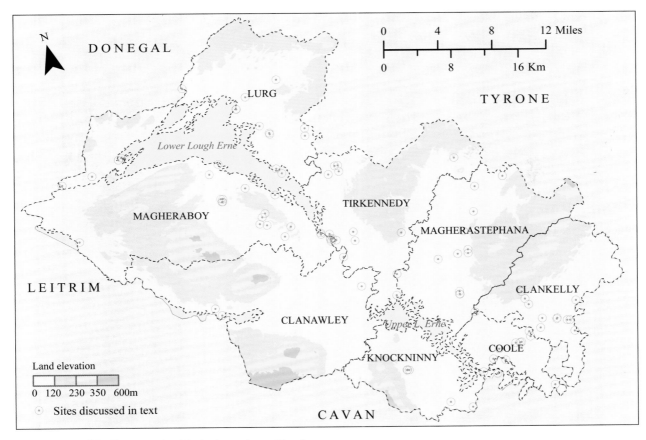

Fig 4.1 Map of Co. Fermanagh with the baronies outlined

Irish architectural idiom, including Captain Rodger Atkinson who built an Irish-style timber house on the Coole estate. Tully Castle, a T-plan fortified house, with Scottish style corner turrets, possesses vaulting clearly built by Irish masons.

Perhaps the finest fortified house in the county is Monea Castle, which was built by Malcolm Hamilton in 1618. It is an oblong building, the front façade of which is flanked by two circular towers, each carrying square upper floors, placed diagonally in relation to the rest of the towers below. Such an arrangement, along with the crow-stepped rooflines, corbelling, stone mouldings and internal layout of rooms, points to it having been built by Scottish masons. The castle was excavated as part of the Ulster Scots Archaeological Project, revealing terracing to the south of the castle, and evidence for quarrying to the north. Other buildings in the county were also built to unusual plans. Tullykelter Castle is a Y-plan house, the front façade of which is flanked by two wings, along with another wing projecting from the rear. Castle Irvine (also known as Necarne Castle), no longer survives, but an old print depicts it as cruciform. Other residences were more prosaic in design, including Portora Castle and Castle Caldwell where a rectangular building occupied one side of a bawn in both places.

Towns and villages, including Belleek, Enniskillen and Newtownbutler, were established to create markets and to encourage the diversification of trade. Subsequent development has erased any traces of the homes and other buildings erected in these settlements, though the original layout may be preserved in the modern street patterns. In Pynnar's survey, a village of six timber-framed houses was mentioned as being on the Lisfrisk estate in the townland of Shannock, while four other similar houses, along with six more under construction, were noted on the Cloncarn estate in Magheraveely. Such houses, whether built of timber, mud or stone, typically did not survive the passage of time. There is a rare survival of a mid- to late 17th-century vernacular cottage in the townland of Corry, a three-room, mud-walled dwelling, the thatched roof of which is supported by cruck trusses.

Religious buildings were also to be found in this plantation-era landscape. Enniskillen Church was rebuilt as St. Macartin's Cathedral in the mid-19th century, but its belfry tower dating from 1637 still stands, albeit modified. Another example, Callowhill Church, was built around 1610 by the Maguires, the ruined building preserving in its walls 17th- and 18th-century gravestones. Most notable is Derrygonnelly Church, with its round-arched doorway embellished with moulded and facetted blocks, a design inspired by the Renaissance. Above the doorway is a fine armorial plaque bearing the year 1627.

Current Barony	17th-century 'Precinct'
Knockninny	Knockniny
Coole	none, part of Knockniny
Clankelly	Clankelly
Magherastephana	granted entirely to Connor Roe Maguire
Tirkennedy	Coole and Tircanada
Lurg	Lurg and Coolemackernan
Magheraboy	Magheriboy
Clanawley	Clinawly

Table 4.1: Modern Baronies and their equivalent 17th-century territories, then also known as 'Precincts'

Keeping to the sequence in which the plantation estates were described in Pynnar's survey of 1618/19, this chapter takes each barony in turn. However, modern baronies in the county, for the most part, do not correspond exactly with those of the 17th century (Table 4.1). A source of particular confusion is the placename 'Coole'. This modern barony in the southernmost part of Co. Fermanagh, was part of Knockninny in the 17th century. The Coole estate, including Castle Coole on the outskirts of Enniskillen, is situated in the barony of Tirkennedy. Coolemackernan is yet another distinct place, situated in Lurg at the northernmost part of the county (see also Muhr 2014, 17–54).

Barony of Knockninny (Scottish undertakers)

Legan and Carrowshee estate

The lands comprising this estate are situated near Lisnaskea, in what is now the modern barony of Magherastephana, but were considered part of the precinct of Knockninny during the Plantation. This estate comprised two grants totalling 3,000 acres granted to the Balfour family (Hill 1877, 475). At the time of Pynnar's survey, it was in the possession of Sir James Balfour, and a bawn and castle (Inv. 250) 'both strong and beautiful', a church (Inv. 252), and a school, 64ft by 24ft and of two storeys, were all described as under construction. Completed buildings were a dwelling house for the Balfour family, and a town of 40 houses (Inv. 251).

250   CASTLE BALFOUR DEMESNE: 236214 333670 CASTLE

Castle Balfour or Lisnaskea Castle

The remains at Castle Balfour are among the best-preserved of any plantation castle in Ulster, exemplifying the traditions of Scottish masonry building. It was under construction when visited by Pynnar in 1619, who also described the construction of a bawn (which has not survived) extending from a large, defensive, three-storeyed house. The castle was modified in the 18th century, when most of the windows were enlarged; it later became ruinous and was rendered uninhabitable by fire in 1803.

Castle Balfour sits in a prominent position overlooking the western approach to Lisnaskea. The ruins consist of a rectangular block, 24m by 7.3m in extent, orientated north-south, with projections east and west, with all of the walls of local limestone

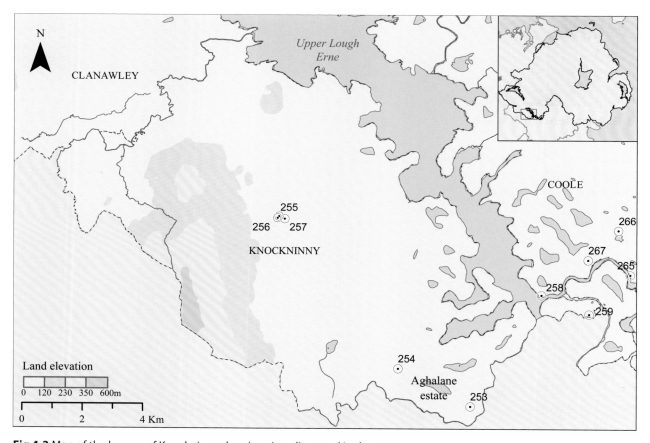

Fig 4.2 Map of the barony of Knockninny showing sites discussed in the text.

Fig 4.3 Front elevation of Castle Balfour, also known as Lisnaskea Castle, looking from east.

and sandstone. In the north-western and south-eastern re-entrant corners there are corbelled stair turrets at first-floor level, and the western side of the main block and the northern side of the west wing have corbelled parapets. The northern end of the main block contained a stairwell; otherwise the ground floor consists of a series of barrel-vaulted passages and chambers leading to a large apartment in the south of the building, which is largely a 20th-century reconstruction. The first floor of the castle was dominated by a large hall, with fireplaces at both eastern and western ends, while the second floor contained a large apartment above the hall. There was also an attic lit by windows. A vault was discovered during restoration works at the site, immediately to the north of the main building, although it was necessary to dismantle it. The eastern wall of the main block, at upper levels, contains

Fig. 4.4 Rear elevation of Castle Balfour from the north-west.

Fig. 4.5 Rear elevation of Castle Balfour from the south-west.

several pieces of dressed masonry that have been re-used, perhaps from an earlier Maguire tower house on the site, or may constitute evidence that Castle Balfour was refurbished early in its history, possibly in the mid-17th century.

> FER 246:057
>
> Hill 1877, 300 and 475–477; Erne 1896, 79–85; *PSAMNI* 180; Jope 1951; Ó Gallachair 1958, 294–295; Waterman 1968, 74–75; Johnston 1976, 152–154 and 1980a; Day and McWilliams 1990d, 9; Reeves-Smyth 2014, 332–333

251   LISNASKEA: SETTLEMENT   236280 333990

Aside from Castle Balfour itself and the general configuration of the street pattern of Lisnaskea with respect to the castle, nothing remains of Balfour's town. The Royal School – the free school for Fermanagh – was founded in the town in 1618 and remained there until its move to Portora in 1662.

> FER 246:063
>
> Lewis 1837, II, 286–287; Hill 1877, 108–109; Camblin 1951, 34; Robinson 1984, 141

252   LISNASKEA: CHRUCH   236250 333650
Holy Trinity Church

During the Plantation, a church, mentioned by Pynnar, was built on this site by Sir James Balfour, but it has vanished without trace, having been replaced by a 19th-century building. Archaeological monitoring of groundworks at the site has not revealed any remains of the earlier structure.

> FER 246:065
>
> Hill 1877, 477; Ó Gallachair 1958, 293; Johnston 1976, 143; Kilner and McClorey 2009

Aghalane estate

1,000 acres were granted in 1610 to Thomas Moneypenny, Laird Kinkell, who sold his proportion to Thomas Creighton in 1613. Creighton died in 1618 or 1619 and his widow married George Adwick who was the landlord of Aghalane at the time of Pynnar's survey, which described a bawn of clay and stone on the estate. The estate later passed back to the Creighton line and was held by various other individuals and generations of the family, whose property eventually became merged with the landholdings of the earl of Erne (Hill 1877, 477).

253   KILLYCLOGHAN: 234100 320000
CASTLE AND BAWN
Aghalane Castle

The ruins of a castle, built by the Creightons between 1614 and 1619, stand at the summit of a broad drumlin, near the border with Co. Cavan. The castle was described by Pynnar as 50ft square, roughcast with lime, with two flankers, and containing a 'poor thatched house'. A similar description was given in 1622, while Inquisitions held during the reign of Charles I described a bawn with four flankers. The castle was captured and held by Irish forces during the 1641 Rebellion, and was eventually destroyed by a fire in the 19th century.

The upstanding remains consist of a square curtain wall with three small, circular flanking drum towers some 4m in height. These are located on the south-western, south-eastern and north-eastern corners of the bawn respectively. On the northern side of the bawn are the remains of two small square towers, although these only survive as low walls or foundations, and are covered with grass. There is an entrance in the southern bawn wall, with windows at either side. The drum towers each have two gun loops, covering the curtain walls. These towers also have various rectangular and cruciform opes opening to the north-east, south-east, south-west and north-west. The square towers have no visible architectural features. Features in the bawn interior are impossible to discern.

FER 271:002

Hill 1877, 447; *Inq. Ulst.* Fermanagh, Car. I (3 & 9); Erne 1896, 73–79; Trimble 1919, 148–150; *PSAMNI* 184; Ó Gallachair 1958, 295; Johnston 1976, 147–149 and 1980a, 79–89

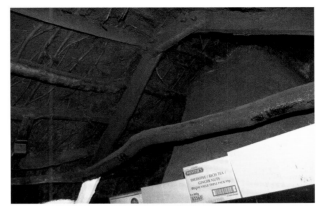

Fig. 4.7 The roof of the early modern cottage in Corry supported by cruck trusses.

254   CORRY: COTTAGE   231702 321280

The history of this early to mid-17th century vernacular thatched cottage in Corry or 'Corre' townland, which was situated in the plantation estate of Aghalane, is unknown, but it represents the rare survival of a structure that typifies a building style that once must have been very widespread in the region. It has three rooms, mud walls, and a roof supported by cruck trusses. Like the houses depicted on Raven's maps, for example, the roof is hipped at both ends, with deep thatching extending below door height. The front door, on the north side of the cottage, opens into the eastern end of the central room. Two chimneys on the roof ridge align with the internal partition walls that separate the rooms. The cruck trusses and hipped roof are consistent with an early 17th-century date, although this is not definite, as vernacular cottages with hipped roofs from later periods – although unusual in Ireland – are known elsewhere in Co. Fermanagh and parts of neighbouring Co. Cavan.

HB12/08/013

Gailey 1984, 88

Dristernan estate

An estate of 1,000 acres was granted in 1610 to James Traile (Hill 1877, 302). Carew reported that Traile sent four freeholders and six horses and mares from Scotland, and had cut down trees in the locality to prepare timbers for building; Bodley noted the presence of fifty cattle, but little other activity. The estate changed ownership several times, Pynnar noting that it was in the possession of a Mr Adwick, a tenant of Sir Stephen Butler (who purchased the estate in 1615) and describing a bawn under construction (Inv. 255). At some point after 1615, the estate came into the possession of Sir James Balfour, Lord Glenawley, followed by Sir William Balfour (Hill 1877, 478).

Fig. 4.6 View of the early to mid-17th-century cottage in Corry.

**255 CALLOW HILL: HOUSE 227750 326460
AND BAWN**

This is the former site of a bawn, recorded by Pynnar as being 60ft square, with two flankers, but no visible traces of any plantation-period buildings survive. Inquisitions held in 1629 mention a bawn 68ft square, built by Sir Stephen Butler at 'Callaghill', enclosing two mansions of stone and lime. In 1641, the house and bawn were destroyed by Irish insurgents, but the site was reoccupied by the family subsequently. The house was replaced in the 18th century, and the bawn demolished in the 19th century. A sculpted stone head and torso mounted on a stone plinth in the gardens may be contemporary with the bawn, or else a more ancient artefact found nearby and perhaps used as an ornament by the 17th-century builders.

FER 260:035

Hill 1877, 302 and 478; *Hist. MSS Comm.* 1947, 166; Johnston 1976, 149–150

Fig. 4.8 A sculpted stone head and torso mounted on a stone plinth on the site of a bawn in Callow Hill.

**256 CALLOW HILL: 227700 326400
SETTLEMENT**

The 1629 Inquisitions recommended a weekly market and a thrice-yearly fair to be held at Callowhill. It is not known whether this plan was ever put into action, but the pasture here may contain archaeological traces of an associated settlement.

FER 260:036

Hill 1877, 302, 478

**257 CALLOW HILL: CHURCH 227940 326370
AND GRAVEYARD**

The ruins of a small, early 17th-century church stand within a wooded graveyard. As with many others of the period, it was likely built in or around 1610 on the site of a medieval parish church, perhaps even on the foundations of the earlier building itself. It was extensively repaired in the 19th century, and largely demolished in 1967. Built of stone rubble with hammer-dressed quoins, it measures 12.4m × 5.6m internally and survives to a height of *c.* 2m at its eastern end. Inset into the western, northern and eastern exterior walls are 17th- and

Fig. 4.9 The ruins of a small, early 17th-century church at Callow Hill.

18th-century gravestones. The inscriptions are now illegible, but the *OS Memoirs* records one dated 1669 and inscribed 'Here lyeth the body of Hugh Rosse, son to William Rosse of Derrikeenan, gentleman'.

FER 260:013

PSAMNI 182; Ó Gallachair 1958, 291; Rogers 1967b, 161; Waterman 1969, 113; Johnston 1976, 140 and 142; Day and McWilliams 1990d, 111 and 116

Kilspenan (Crom) estate

This estate was formed from a grant of 1,500 acres to Michael Balfour, Laird Mountwhany. Carew and Bodley reported that Balfour had appeared personally with a number of men, servants, and horses, and was in the process of providing timber and lime – presumably for the construction of the castle described below (Inv. 258). By 1619 it was owned by Sir Stephen Butler, and Pynnar described the finished bawn and castle, but no other works on the estate. The 1622 survey revealed that although occupied by three English families, two of the husbands were gone and the bawn was 'seated in a remoate place amongst woods, and the land for the most part left to Irish'. The estate, however, had a complicated later history. It was leased around 1624 to James Spottiswoode, Bishop of Clogher, whose daughter married into the Creighton (or Crichton) family, later the earls of Erne, whose family seat remains at Crom (Johnston 1976, 83).

258   CROM: HOUSE, BAWN   236450 323800
AND GARDENS
Crom Old Castle

These ruins of a bawn overlooking Upper Lough Erne have been incorporated within the gardens of a later mansion, and therefore also include fake ruins added in the 19th century for romantic effect. The 'castle' was described by Pynnar as a bawn and two flankers, containing a stone-built house. In 1622, one flanker was described as square, whereas the other was round and filled with sod. The bawn was attacked, damaged, captured and repaired by

Fig. 4.10 View of the remains of Crom Old Castle.

Irish forces in 1641. The site came under siege twice in 1689, and was destroyed by fire in 1764, an event that renders it difficult to reconstruct details of the early history of the building.

The remains of the 'old castle' consist of two northern gables and towers built of stone rubble at the north-eastern and south-eastern corners of the building, as well as various foundations and low walls. Surviving architectural detail includes extensive use of brickwork around the windows and in the fireplaces and gun loops in the walls. The adjoining gardens were laid out in the 19th century, but historical sources document the presence of formal gardens here in the early 18th century, hinting that the gardens were perhaps a plantation-period feature. Two yew trees, which would have been ancient even then, still stand on the northern side of the gardens next to the ruins.

FER 261:020

Hill 1877, 300–301; Erne 1896, 7–9; Trimble 1919, 147–148; *PSAMNI* 183; Ó Gallachair 1958, 285; Johnston 1976, 156–158; *idem* 1978, 369–370 and *idem* 1980a, 79–89; Day and McWilliams 1990d, 98–102

259   INISHFENDRA: CASTLE   238034 323156

A small L-shaped length of stone walling on the causewayed island of Inishfendra in Upper Lough Erne, overlooking the lough to the south, constitutes the possible remains of a castle, perhaps originally associated with Crom. Little remains above the ground apart from a wall, approximately 4–5m high, containing a chimney breast with a small opening located at its centre, and a chimney flue at a height of *c*. 3m. The causeway that leads to Inishfendra, which also crosses the border with Co. Cavan, is named the 'Bloody Path', a reference to one of the numerous violent encounters that occurred on the estate during the 17th century, when Jacobite fugitives from the battle of Newtownbutler (1689) were killed.

FER 261:029

PSAMNI 183; Day and McWilliams 1990d, 87–95; Reeves-Smyth 2014, 334

Leitrim estate

A grant of 1,500 acres was made to Sir John Wishart for lands now situated in the barony of Coole, but considered part of Knockninny during the Plantation. Carew reported that no building works had begun, but that fifteen men had appeared, presumably from Scotland, with two ploughs and the ambition to sow wheat and begin building. The estate was sold to Sir Stephen Butler in 1615 (Hill 1877, 489), with Wishart building a house elsewhere in Co. Fermanagh, in Clankelly barony (see Inv. 282). Pynnar documented a bawn, noting that a stone house was also under construction (Inv. 262), and recording the lessees living in the town of Newtownbutler adjoining the bawn. The estate was well populated, with sixty-six men in Pynnar's time, but no identifiable sites from the estate are known, other than the town.

260   NEWTOWNBUTLER: 241780 326100
**   SETTLEMENT**

Continual development over the last 400 years in Sir Stephen Butler's town has obliterated any original 17th-century structures, and archaeological evaluations on Main Street in 2004 did not find any traces of the plantation town. That said, the original configuration of the town is probably still reflected in the road layout.

FER 261:050

Hill 1877, 479–80; Dempsey 2004

261   AGHAGAY: CASTLE   241600 326100

The former site of a 'castle' marked on the 1st edition OS six-inch map is now a rough field with a quarry at its centre. It is likely, however, that this was where the original Butler Castle stood, briefly described by Pynnar as being built in 1619, but of which no archaeological traces survive. The stone wall that separates this field from Newtownbutler may have been constructed of stones robbed from the castle.

FER 261:042

Day and McWilliams 1990d, 89 and 95

262   SHEENY: HOUSE   241100 326200
**   AND BAWN**

This is the possible site of a bawn described by Pynnar as constructed of lime and stone, 70ft square, and with two three-storey flankers. At the time of the 1622 survey, the bawn was still unfinished, but the house was 'the length of the Bawne & 22ft broad'. The site cannot now be located.

FER 261:047

Hill 1877, 301, 479–480; Johnston 1976, 169–70

Derriany estate

An estate of 1,000 acres was granted in 1613 to George Smelhome, on lands situated near the north-eastern shore of Upper Lough Erne. This is the parish of Galloon, which today lies within the barony of Coole, but the estate was considered the most northern part of the Scottish plantation of Knockninny in all relevant historical sources. The earliest account of progress on the estate was provided by Pynnar, written after it was sold to Sir Stephen Butler in 1618. Pynnar described a bawn and house (Inv. 263), which the 1622 survey recorded as an almost token structure, only one foot high. A second house adjoining the bawn was occupied by a Scottish gentleman. In 1629, Butler sold the estate to Charles Waterhouse, a former lessee who had married Butler's sister, and who was formally granted the Manor of Castlewaterhouse in 1630 (Trimble 1919, 150–151). Aside from the townland name 'Manor Water House', no sites of the period are known to survive on this estate.

263 MANOR WATER HOUSE: 237400 331100
HOUSE AND BAWN

Pynnar described a bawn of clay and stone with two flankers, 60ft square, enclosing a small house built from the same materials at this probable location. The 1622 survey recorded a bawn, 53ft square, 1ft high and 2½ft thick, the house at that time being unoccupied. Some 17th-century occupation did eventually occur however, as a house on the estate was burnt in 1689 by the Jacobite army during its retreat from Lisnaskea before the Battle of Newtownbutler. A new manor house was built in the early 18th century, but was demolished before the 20th century. Among the modern farm buildings that stand on the site are a number of old stone structures and garden enclosures that are probably associated with the 18th-century manor, with nothing that is clearly 17th-century in date apparent.

> FER 246:027
>
> Hill 1877, 302–303 and 480; Trimble, 1919, 150–153; *Hist. MSS Comm.* 1947, 166; Ó Gallachair 1958, 296; Johnston 1976, 177–178

Other sites in the modern barony of Coole

264 DRUMMULLY: CHURCH   244270 320060

At this site, which is located on the summit of a prominent drumlin, an early church or monastery was depicted in the 1609 Bodley map as a roofed building with a tower, but the 1622 survey described it as ruinous. The foundations and eastern gable wall of a church building however still survive, contained

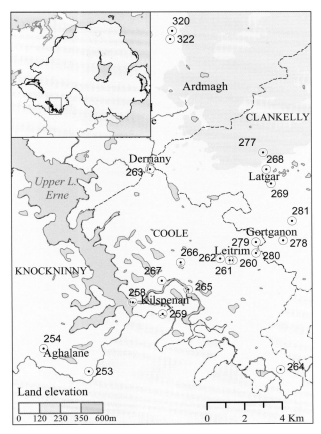

Fig. 4.11 Map of the barony of Coole showing sites discussed in the text.

within a polygonal graveyard, which contains a scatter of gravestones of 18th-century date and later.

> FER 272:009
>
> McKenna 1920, 115–116; *PSAMNI* 185; Rogers 1967a, 396; Johnston 1976, 140 and 141; Day and McWilliams 1990d, 36; Hamlin 2008, 343

265 DRUMBRUGHAS EAST: 239400 324500
CASTLE

According to the 1629 Inquisitions, there was a stone house on this site on the shores of Quivvy Lough in Upper Lough Erne. This may have been a tower house not documented elsewhere, possibly one that pre-dated the Plantation. The site consists of a low bank with traces of ashlar walling and other loose fragments of masonry. Immediately to the west of the site, and above the shoreline of the lough, is another retaining wall that could be associated with the structure, although it also clearly functions as a field boundary.

FER 261:021

PSAMNI 183; Day and McWilliams 1990d, 105

266   DERRYCORBY: CASTLE   239000 326000

This is the approximate site of a post-medieval castle that was recorded in the *OS Memoirs*. It was destroyed in the late 18th century and cannot now be precisely located.

FER 261:035

Day and McWilliams 1990d, 105

267   DOOHAT: HOUSE   238000 325000

This is the approximate site of a stone-built 'castle', 22ft square and 20ft tall built by Sir Stephen Butler, according to the 1629 Inquisitions. Although the *OS Memoirs* state that there were no remains at the time of the first survey in the 1830s, Jope recorded the fragment of a gable wall with gun loops still standing in 1960, and described the structure as a 'Yeoman's defended house'. It was a one-and-a-half storey building once covered by a thatched roof, similar in many ways to The White House on the Ards Peninsula in Co. Down (Inv. 171). However, no remains can be located today.

FER 261:039

Inq. Ulst. Fermanagh, Car I (3 & 12); Jope 1960, 107; Johnston 1976, 150; Day and McWilliams 1990d, 105

Barony of Clankelly (English undertakers)

Latgar estate

1,000 acres were granted in 1610 to John Sedborough, and in 1611 Carew reported that the grantee had arrived with his family and various under-tenants and was in the process of building. An oven and a wattled chimney were made for his three-roomed Irish house, and timber and stone were prepared

for other structures, including a bawn, and there were mares, garrons and twenty cows, as well as a plough. Later historical accounts differ from this description of rather lively activity. Pynnar described a poor round bawn of sods in a derelict state, although he mentioned a cattle pound. In the 1622 survey, a thatched, mud wall house was recorded in a 'most poor round Bawne of sodds', but nothing else. Sedborough was absent, and his freeholders were rather disgruntled. It seems that he lost interest in the estate and following his death in 1629, it was regranted to Lord Dillon and Lord Mountnorris in 1630 (Hill 1877, 482). Pynnar's account and the 1622 survey seem to describe the re-use of an early medieval rath for the bawn, but precisely which site in the area corresponds to it is not certain, although there are two possibilities, Rathmoran and Golan (Invs 268 and 269). The 1629 Inquisitions measure the bawn as 240 feet in circumference (*ibid.*), equivalent to a diameter of approximately 23m – smaller than either enclosure in the locality.

268   RATHMORAN: CASTLE   243570 331070

Earthworks on the summit of a prominent drumlin in Rathmoran mark the site of a 17th-century castle, and ruins are marked here on each edition of the OS six-inch map. It was the residence of the Galbraith family, descendants of Hugh Galbraith, land agent to James Spottiswoode, the Bishop of Clogher, although it is not known precisely when the Galbraiths lived here. The remains consist of a series of stone and earth banks and walls that together form a D-shaped enclosure 39m in diameter. The best-defined of these is a 4m length of stone and earthen walling, *c.* 1.20m in height and L-shaped, perhaps the remains of the castle, but its outward similarity to the walls of 18th and 19th century farm buildings in the immediate area suggests that the wall is more recent than the 17th century.

FER 246:037

PSAMNI 182

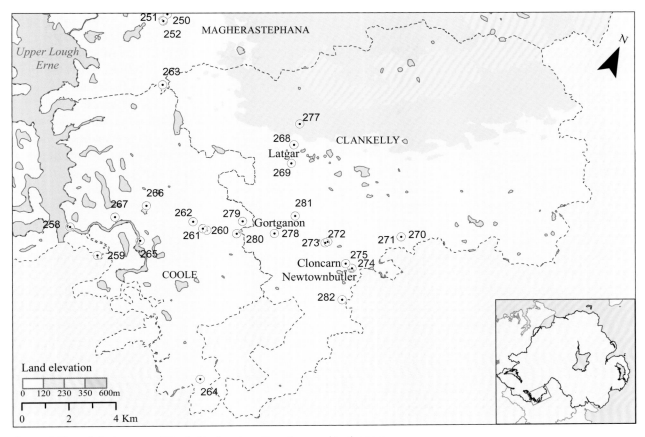

Fig. 4.12 Map of the barony of Clankelly showing sites discussed in the text.

269   GOLAN: ENCLOSURE   243810 330290

This is the site of a rath within the Latgar estate, and it is possible that the initial focus of settlement on the estate was here, rather than Rathmoran. However, it is very large (*c.* 60m in diameter) and so well-preserved that any modifications in the 17th century are likely to have been very slight.

FER 246:049

Hill 1877, 482; Foley and McHugh 2014, I.2, 481–482

Lisfrisk

1,000 acres were granted in 1610 to Thomas Flowerdew and, similar to the estate at Latgar, it appears that the initial focus for works at Lisfrisk was at an early medieval rath. Carew reported that building on the estate involved entrenching an 'old

rath' (Inv. 270). Pynnar also mentioned a village adjoining the rath (Inv. 271). In 1629 the estate, along with Roseguire in Lurg, which was also in the possession of Thomas Flowerdew, was re-granted to Edward Flowerdew (presumably his son), and became known as 'Shanocke' (Hill 1877, 482). This places the settlement in Shannock or Shannock Green townlands, although the only known rath in these townlands (Foley and McHugh 2014, I.2, 560) seems far too well-preserved (besides the addition of a tree-ring around it) to be a candidate for Flowerdew's bawn.

270   SHANNOCK: TOWER   249400 329300
HOUSE AND BAWN

A note appended to the report by Carew stated that Thomas Flowerdew

…built an Irish house with a chimney at the end, made of wattles, contrived in two rooms, and a frame for a timber house of birch, most part to be set up in a Dane's fort.

The whereabouts of the site is unknown, though one possible location lies just to the east of the co-ordinates cited above, where an old L-shaped boundary wall is incorporated into later farm buildings. On each return there are three openings in the style of gun loops, although these could be for the ventilation of farm buildings and do not help date the structure.

The house was still under construction in 1613 when visited by Bodley, who also mentioned plans to palisade the entire enclosure, and build a gatehouse. Pynnar described a large round bawn of lime and stone enclosing a small house. The 1622 survey confirmed that the gatehouse had been built, as was a small castle.

FER 247:012

Hill 1877, 481–482; Day and McWilliams 1990d, 133

271   SHANNOCK: SETTLEMENT   249400 329300

There are no visible remains of the village on the Lisfrisk estate, which Pynnar described as six houses of cage-work, next to the bawn.

FER 247:030

Hill 1877, 481–482

Cloncarn

1,000 acres were granted in 1611 to Robert Boges, who in 1614 sold his proportion to Edward Hatton, the Archdeacon of Ardagh (Hill 1877, 274, 483). No development was documented before Pynnar's survey in 1619, when he described a village (Inv. 272), a bawn and strong house, and a water mill for corn adjacent to the same house. In the 1622 survey, the bawn was described as being seventy feet square, and the house being seventy feet long (thus taking up the full width of the bawn) and a remarkable five storeys high.

272   UTTONY: SETTLEMENT   246660 327800
Magheraveely

Magheraveely was originally a plantation village in Cloncarn, built at some point between 1614 and 1619 by Edward Hatton within half a mile of his bawn. Pynnar described four timber houses, with six more under construction, standing on the 'common road'. Archaeological evaluations carried out in the village have not located any features or artefacts of the time.

FER 262:027

Hill 1877, 483; Ó Gallachair 1958, 297–298; Sloan 2010

273   MAGHERAVEELY: CHURCH   246580 327710
AND GRAVEYARD

This is the site of a chapel of which nothing visible survives, and was shown roofless on the Bodley map of 1609–10. Ruins were still standing in 1786, perhaps implying that it was restored during the Plantation, as it stands within the bounds of Edward Hatton's estate. The graveyard consists of a platform enclosed by the faint traces of a low bank and an outer ditch. Within the graveyard are gravestones dating to the 18th century and later.

FER 262:006

Lowry-Corry 1919, 40; Day and McWilliams 1990d, 91; Hamlin 2008, 357

274   LISLEA: HOUSE   248080 327170

There are no visible remains of a strong house and bawn described by Pynnar as 'well seated for the King's service and strength of the country'. The 17th-century building was, presumably, replaced by the mid-18th-century house 'Knockballymore' which currently stands at this location.

HB12/01/001A

Hill 1877, 483

275   DRUMRAINY: WATER MILL   247750 327250

This is the approximate site of a water mill mentioned in Pynnar's survey. Although no upstanding remains are visible, the meadow at this location is bordered to the south and west by two streams, the confluence of which at the south-western corner of the field drains into the nearby Knockballymore Lough. It is possible that one of these watercourses was adapted and used for the mill in the 17th century.

FER 262:030

Hill 1877, 483

276   AGHAVEA: HOUSE AND CHURCH   237300 338500

The townland of Aghavea, now in the neighbouring modern barony of Magherastephana and some 15km from other sites in this estate, was mentioned in the grant of Cloncarn. The townland, or perhaps the wider parish of Aghavea, is the approximate site of a house described as '86ft long, 20ft wide & 14ft high in Aghavea townland in the Manor of Knockballymore' in the Inquisitions of 1629. The site cannot now be located. The medieval parish church nearby, set within an oval enclosure (FER 231:036, grid ref. 237060 338830), is notable for its later-17th-century decorative headstones.

FER 231:041

Inq. Ulst. Fermanagh, Car. I (6); Johnston 1976, 181

Ardmagh

An estate of 1,000 acres was originally granted to Thomas Plumstead who, in 1610, immediately sold it to Sir Hugh Wirrall (Hill 1877, 274, 484). No building work was documented before 1619, when Pynnar described a bawn (Inv. 277), which was still unfinished at the time of the 1622 survey. But by that time, although some fifteen free farmers were resident, much of the land was still occupied by Irish workers. According to the Inquisitions (cited in Hill 1877, 484), Sir Hugh defaulted in 1629, unable to keep to the terms, and so the lands were regranted to Sir Thomas Rotherham, Stephen Allen, and Martyn Baxter.

277   TATTYCAM: TOWER HOUSE AND BAWN   243400 332000

This is the approximate site of a tower house and bawn recorded by Pynnar and the 1622 survey. Both sources described a 60-feet-square bawn, with two small flankers covering the walls and a tower house in one corner. The area has been extensively planted with forestry in recent decades, further reducing the probability that archaeological remains survive.

FER 246:064

Hill 1877, 274 and 484; Ó Gallachair 1958, 298–299

Gortganon

This estate of 1,000 acres was granted to Robert Calvert. Carew mentioned that a house 'after the English manner' had been built, and that the process of plantation had begun. In 1613, Bodley recorded that a lime kiln had been provided, stone excavated and timber felled. However, Calvert sold the lands at some point after 1613, and although Pynnar recorded George Ridgeway as owner in 1619, the 1629 Inquisitions (Hill 1877, 484) recorded that James Highgate, Archdeacon of Clogher, was the purchaser. A bawn (Inv. 278) was documented in Pynnar's survey and the 1622 survey, while in 1629, a second bawn was recorded at Agharowskye (Inv. 281), and the Inquisitions also noted houses at Lisnashillida (Inv. 279) and Mullynagowan (Inv. 280). Highgate was appointed Bishop of Kilfenora, and in 1637 he granted at least some of the lands in Gortganon to James Spottiswoode, the Bishop of Clogher (*ibid.* 485). Spottiswoode was also a tenant of the Kilspenan estate, which adjoins Gorganon along the border of the barony. The population of the estate remained relatively small, and indeed declined from 41 adult males in 1622 to 22 by 1630 (Robinson 1984, 218).

278   FARGRIM: HOUSE AND BAWN   244450 327180
Manor Highgate

This is the site of the residence of James Heygate

or Highgate, Bishop of Kilfenora. The castle was described by Pynnar as a bawn of lime and stone sixty feet square; the 1622 survey described a bawn, sixty feet square with two thatched flankers, containing a small, unfinished house. It seems to have been damaged or destroyed in 1641, but re-built at some point after, eventually becoming Manor Highgate, which was demolished in 1971.

> FER 261:049
>
> Hill 1877, 275, 481 and 484–485; *Hist. MSS Comm.* 1947, 166; Ó Gallachair 1958, 298–299; Johnston 1976, 176–177

279   LISNASHILLIDA: HOUSE   243000 327100
AND BAWN

This is the approximate site of a 17th-century house, perhaps the structure described as built 'after the English manner' by Carew. A house was documented in this townland in the Inquisitions, but its exact location is unknown.

> FER 261:048
>
> *Inq. Ulst.* Fermanagh Car. I (6); Hill 1877, 484

280   MULLYNAGOWAN: HOUSE   243000 326500

No upstanding remains survive at the approximate site of a house mentioned in the Inquisitions.

> FER 261:082
>
> *Inq. Ulst.* Fermanagh Car. I (6)

281   AGHERAROOSKY EAST: 244920 328250
CASTLE AND BAWN
Lord Highgate's Castle

Known as 'Lord Highgate's Castle', this is the site of the residence of a tenant on the Gortganon estate. A house, sixty feet square and eleven feet high, surrounded by a wall, was recorded in this townland in 1629. The remains were depicted on the 1st and 2nd editions of the OS six-inch map, but were largely levelled in the 20th century, and nothing upstanding remains, although a level platform with indications of terracing on a slope below, may indicate the presence of archaeological remains.

> FER 261:004
>
> Johnston 1976, 181

Other sites in the barony of Clankelly

282   CLONTIVRIN: HOUSE   248281 325751

Records of Bishop Spottiswoode indicate that Sir John Wishart, who sold his proportion of Leitrim (barony of Knockninny) in 1615, built a house at Clontivrin. According to the Census conducted in 1659, there were fifty-one Irish and five British living in the townland. The location of Wishart's house probably coincides with the present Clontivrin House, although there are no obvious surviving 17th-century features at the site.

> FER 262:026
>
> Johnston 1976, 172–173

Barony of Clanawley (allotted to servitors and Irish)

Lisgoole

In 1610 Sir Henry Bruncker was granted 1,500 acres of picturesque countryside on the banks of the Erne. Due to its physical beauty, the estate was considered for the site of the proposed county town of Enniskillen. Sir John Davies, Attorney-General of Ireland, was also attracted to the area, and he arranged to purchase the estate in January 1611 (Hill 1877, 330; Trimble 1919, 8–12). By 1619, Davies had built a house on the site of a ruined Franciscan monastery (Inv. 283), much to the consternation of the monks, who continued to reside elsewhere on the estate throughout the period. Davies probably, however, never took residence, having returned to England to further his political career.

283   LISGOOLE: HOUSE   224070 341730

Building and settlement at Lisgoole has a long and complex history. It is the site of an Augustinian Abbey, founded in the 12th century, perhaps on the site of an older, pre-Norman monastery. The Augustinians

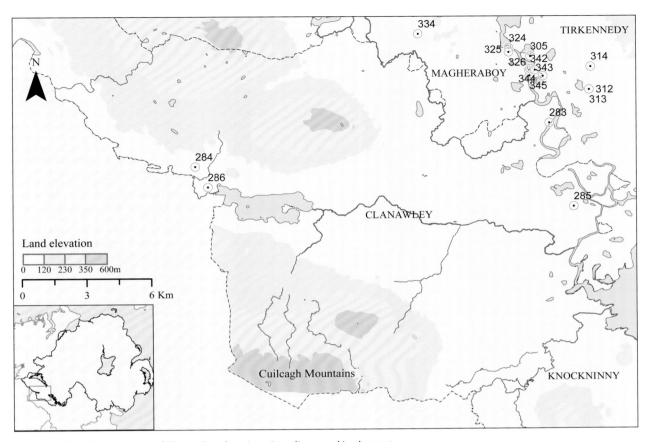

Fig. 4.13 Map of the barony of Clanawley showing sites discussed in the text.

were succeeded by the Franciscans, who occupied the site until 1598. Bodley's baronial map of 1609–10 depicts a roofless monastery and a ruined church. Pynnar noted that Sir John Davies built a 'fair stone house' upon the abbey lands at Lisgoole, but no other structures. The house was probably destroyed in 1641 by the Maguires, and was eventually replaced in the 18th century by the house that still stands on the site.

Lisgoole House is located on a river terrace on the lower slopes of a small drumlin and is enclosed by mature landscaped gardens. It is not known whether any parts of the 17th-century building were incorporated into the 18th-century house. The northern wing of the house consists of three sides of a large square tower, with thick walls and a batter. Unfortunately, roughcast render and ivy make it impossible to discern whether the walls are part of an earlier phase of building, and if they are earlier,

it is possible that they may be associated with the abbey buildings rather than with Davies' house.

FER 211:043

Hill 1877, 330 and 485; McKenna 1896; Lowry-Corry 1919, 40; *PSAMNI* 148; Ó Gallachair 1958, 299; Rogers 1967b, 173–4; Gwynn and Hadcock 1970, 185; Johnston 1976, 160–2; Hickey 1985, 84 and 87; Day and McWilliams 1992b, 20–21; Hamlin 2008, 355; Foley and McHugh 2014, I.2, 779–781

Gortin

A small estate of 500 acres was granted to Mrs Harrison, widow to Captain Harrison. There are no historical accounts of any activity, and Pynnar recorded that Mrs Harrison 'hath built nothing at all' (Hill 1877, 485).

Moycrane

This was a small estate of 300 acres granted to Peter Mostin, but there are no accounts of any activity occurring, and indeed Pynnar reported that Mostin, originally from Wales, was living in Connaught (Hill 1877, 485).

Irish estates in Clanawley

Forty-nine small estates in Clanawley were allotted to native Irish, mainly the marginal, less productive lands, distant from the low-lying meadows that were granted to the servitors in this barony. The Maguires and the McHughs feature prominently in the list of grantees (Hill 1877, 331–334). Archaeological traces of any activity on these estates is generally lacking, aside from a possible market cross (Inv. 284).

284   CAVANCARRAGH: CROSS   207640 339670
A large boulder, located in lands that were probably allotted to a member of the Maguire family, carries a small stone cross of post-medieval date. It has

Fig. 4.14 Possible market cross at Cavancarragh.

no ecclesiastical associations and was used, in all likelihood, as a landmark for convening a market.
FER 228:073
Hill 1877, 331; *PSAMNI* 171; Hamlin 2008, 346

Other sites in Clanawley

285   TONYTEIGE: CASTLE   225200 337700
What appears to be a castle is marked at this location on the 1650s Down Survey county map. However, no other record or archaeological remains of the castle are known to exist.
FER 229:063
Down Survey county map of Fermanagh (TCD)

286   BELCOO WEST: 208220 338680
**   FORTIFICATION**
The 1650s Down Survey map of the barony of Clanawley depicts a fort between the upper and lower stretches of Lough Macnean, in what is now the border village of Belcoo. The outline of this fort seems to have been traced, in part, by the townland boundaries on the 1st edition OS six-inch map. A disused railway line, which may have destroyed any archaeological remains, runs through the area.
FER 228:102
Down Survey barony map of Clanawley (TCD)

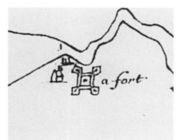

Fig. 4.15 Extract from the Down Survey map of the barony of Clanawley (1656–58) depicting a bastioned fort at Belcoo.

Barony of Lurg (English undertakers)

Drumunshin estate

This estate of 1,000 acres lies partly in Lurg and partly in the barony of Coole, and was granted to Thomas Barton in 1611 (Hill 1877, 279). Bodley described a bawn in construction, but aside from one tenant and two or three masons, Barton was 'alone upon the place, without servant or follower' (*ibid.* 468). Barton sold this estate, and the adjoining Necarne proportion, to Sir Gerrard Lowther in 1615, except for 100 acres of land called Inishclare, upon which the bawn of Rossclare was built (Inv. 288). Initially, he kept this property for himself, but sold it to Henry Flower in 1616 (*ibid.*). The 1622 survey implied that Flower did not reside in the bawn, but that the wider estate was populated with English settlers.

287   HORSE ISLAND: BAWN   219700 353600

The approximate site of a bawn that Rogers suggests was built by Thomas Barton on 'Horse Island', identified with Inishclare, before 1618. There are no visible remains nor known local traditions concerning a bawn.

FER 192:046

Rogers 1967b, 61

288   ROSSCLARE: BAWN   219200 354300

Bodley recorded that a bawn was being built somewhere near this location in 1613. Writing six years later, Pynnar described 'a good bawne of Clay and Stone, rough cast over with Lime, 60 feet square, with two Flankers, but no House in it'. The 1622 survey revealed that the bawn had been abandoned, and today its exact whereabouts are

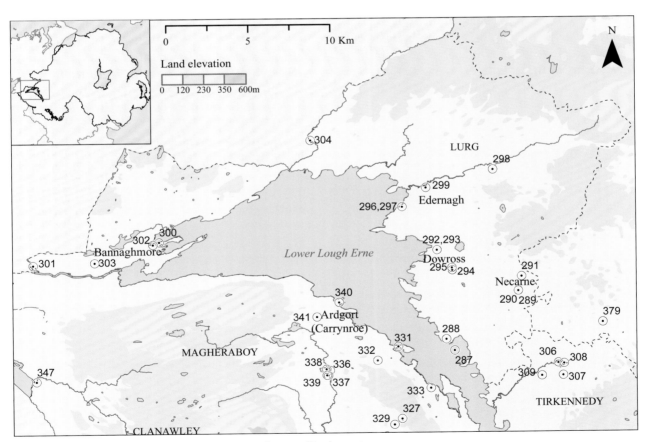

Fig. 4.16 Map of the barony of Lurg showing sites discussed in the text.

not known. A likely location would be the current Rossclare House, which replaced an earlier building in the mid-19th century.

FER 192:057

Hill 1877, 279, 485–486; Ó Gallachair 1958, 300; Johnston 1976, 179

Necarne

In 1611, the initial grant of this estate of 1,000 acres was made to Edward Ward but it changed hands rapidly. Ward soon sold to Harrington Sutton who, in turn, sold to Thomas Barton, who then sold to Sir Gerrard Lowther, seemingly the first landlord to actually undertake any development (Hill 1877, 486). Pynnar described a bawn and house (Inv. 289), and a village (Inv. 291), and the population of the estate rose steadily throughout the 1620s (Robinson 1984, 218). In 1622 much activity was reported, including the establishment of clothworking businesses (Johnston 1976, 178). Sir Gerrard, who had a flourishing legal career, sold the estate in 1630 to Sir William Parsons (the Surveyor-General) and Sir Adam Loftus (Hill 1877, 486).

289   CASTLE IRVINE DEMESNE: 223600 357300
HOUSE or CASTLE AND BAWN
Necarne Castle

Necarne Castle, which is also known as 'Castle Irvine', was built between 1613 and 1619 by Sir Gerrard Lowther. Pynnar described a 'strong bawn' enclosing a house, along with an adjoining village. The 1622 survey described the bawn as 87ft by 66ft and 14ft high, including two flankers, and curiously described the village as 'Within the Bawne'. Adding to this confusion, in 1630, its measurements were given as being slightly larger at 17ft high and with a perimeter of 324ft. An old castle, without any bawn, still stood on the site at the time of the first Ordnance Survey, and was described as having round towers. This is clearly not the building depicted in a privately-owned undated watercolour of the old castle, published by Trimble in 1919, which shows a four-storey, cruciform building, similar to Castleraw, Co. Armagh (Inv. 436). It is not clear what plantation-period structures survived the 17th century, but any that did were likely demolished in the 19th century when a mansion house was built on the site.

FER 173:066

Inq. Ulst. Fermanagh, Car. I (15); Hill 1877, 279, 486–487; Trimble 1919, 130–131; Ó Gallachair 1958, 300; Johnston 1976, 178–179 and 1980a, 79–89; Day and McWilliams 1992b, 33

290   CASTLE IRVINE DEMESNE: 223600 357300
WATER MILL

Nothing remains of the water mill or market house that, according to Pynnar, once stood near this location. A stream, culverted in places, flowing through the field in front of the 19th-century mansion is the most likely source of water for the mill.

FER 173:066

Hill 1877, 279, 486–487

291   TOWNHILL: SETTLEMENT   223800 358200
Irvinestown

Pynnar mentioned a village of ten houses in 1619, which developed into Irvinestown. Although it is possible that remains survive below ground, there is nothing visible in the village that dates from the 17th-century.

FER 173:097

Hill 1877, 279, 486–487

Tullana

1,000 acres were granted to John Archdale in 1612. The earliest account of progress on this estate was provided by Pynnar, who described a bawn and house built in 1615 (Inv. 292), a water mill (Inv. 293), and two villages, each with eight houses, which today cannot be located. Similar descriptions were given in 1622. Initial population increases on the estate were marked – twenty-four adult males in 1618 and around fifty-four by 1622 (Robinson 1984, 218).

292   BUNANINVER: HOUSE AND BAWN   218660 359890
Old Castle Archdale

According to an inscribed stone at the site, Castle Archdale was built in 1615. Pynnar described an impressive bawn with three slated flankers each containing lodgings, enclosing a three-storey house 80ft in length, although that measurement was clearly exaggerated as the 1622 survey stated that the bawn measured 66ft by 64ft, which is the approximate extent of the archaeological remains. In 1641, the bawn was captured by Rory Maguire and the house damaged. It was repaired in 1665, reinhabited thereafter, but burnt again in 1689.

The present Castle Archdale house was built in the 18th century, while the old house and bawn fell into decay and had collapsed by 1883.

The 17th-century buildings survive in a highly fragmented state, consisting of part of a two-storey house, with a three-storey tower projecting from its northern side, and part of the southern bawn wall, including the entrance. The remains have been partially rebuilt in places, although other elements of the structure are now missing – for example, the square flankers at the southern end of the bawn. The house plan consists of a hall and cross-passage, with stairs in the northern projection, which also served as a bawn flanker and contains gun loops. Four window openings survive, three in the upper floors of the northern projection and one in the eastern gable. The windows were designed to hold glass, thus emphasising the domestic character of the building.

Fig. 4.17 Front elevation of Old Castle Archdale. The eastern gable and a rear wing that once would have contained a stairwell still stand.

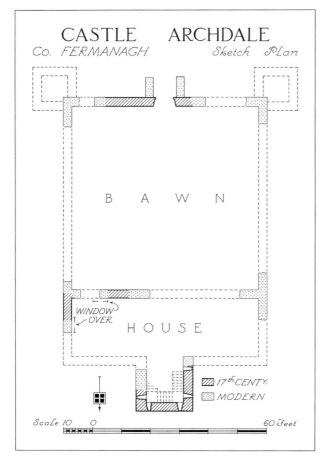

Fig. 4.18 Plan of Old Castle Archdale depicting the remains of house and bawn (after Waterman 1959a, Fig. 1).

Although an English estate, the moulding around the bawn gateway is typical of the Scottish masonry tradition, which (if the 1615 date is applicable to this feature) constitutes the earliest manifestation of Scottish building methods in plantation-period Fermanagh.

> FER 173:032
> Hill 1877, 278, 481, 487–8; Trimble 1919, 121–127; *PSAMNI* 148; Ó Gallachair 1958; Waterman 1959a; Jope 1960, 104; Johnston 1976, 151; 1978, 370; 1980a, 70–89; Day and McWilliams 1992b, 34

293   BUNANINVER: WATER MILL   218660 359890
This is the approximate site of a water mill mentioned

by Pynnar, the nearest watercourse lying just to the north of the co-ordinates above. An alternative location is in the townland of Shallany (grid ref. 219194 359655), where a vernacular mill cottage still stands near a mill-race.

> FER 173:032
> Hill 1877, 487–488

Roseguire

This estate of 1,000 acres was granted originally in 1610 to Thomas Flowerdew, although no progress had been made by the time of Pynnar's survey, apparently due to incoming English settlers mistaking glebe land in the parish of Derryvallane for this estate (Hill 1877, 488). The lands were eventually purchased by a neighbouring landlord, Sir Gerrard Lowther (see Inv. 289). No archaeological sites dating to the period are known within the bounds of Roseguire.

Dowross

1,000 acres were granted in 1612 to Henry Hunings. The next year, Bodley described the preparation of building materials on the estate, with limestone having been excavated, timber felled, squared and seasoned, and stones delivered to where a bawn was due to be constructed. In 1619 Pynnar reported that the bawn was built (but used as a cattle pound), and that nearby was a village of fourteen houses (Hill 1877, 488), which later grew into the village of Lisnarrick. By Pynnar's time, the estate was jointly held by Edward Sibthorp and Thomas Flower, with Flower's descendants later taking exclusive ownership (*ibid.*).

The scale of settlement at Dowross is debatable. The 1622 survey noted 120 English families resident, which seems like a transcription error, and analysis by Robinson (1984, 218) suggests a much more modest population, not exceeding 30 adult males. The 1622 survey also mentioned a market and fair associated with the manor, although it is unclear whether any building or other works were associated with these events.

294   LISNARRICK: BAWN   219580 358610

Pynnar documented a bawn sixty feet square with two flankers, but lying waste and used as a cattle pound, and a similar description was given in 1622. The bawn seems to have disappeared early in its history, perhaps to supply stone for other projects, and as a result its location is not known with any certainty. Johnston suggested that the large open space in the centre of Lisnarrick or a cattle pound depicted in the area on the 1st edition OS six-inch map are possible locations, as are various farmsteads near the village in the townland of Drumshane.

> FER 173:095
>
> Hill 1877, 279–280 and 488–9; *Hist. MSS Comm.* 1947, 167; Ó Gallachair 1958, 301; Johnston 1976, 183–184

295   LISNARICK: SETTLEMENT   219570 358760

The village of Lisnarick was originally a plantation settlement which, according to Pynnar, contained fourteen houses in 1619. No traces of any 17th-century buildings can be located today, and an archaeological evaluation in 2009 found nothing of significance.

> FER 173:096
>
> Hill 1877, 279–280 and 488–489; *Hist. MSS Comm.* 1947, 167; Ó Gallachair 1958, 301; Johnston 1976, 183–184; Bailie and Ward 2009

Edernagh

This estate was formed from a grant of 1,500 acres made in 1610 to Thomas Blennerhassett. Gatisfeth reported that in 1611, a joiner, a carpenter, three other workmen and one tenant were at work there (Hill 1877, 489). A boat had been constructed, lime manufactured, timber prepared and a large Irish-style house had been constructed with 'windows and rooms after the English manner'. A similar account of building materials was given by Bodley. Pynnar recorded a bawn and house (Inv. 296), a church under construction (Inv. 297) and a village of six houses (Inv. 298), built of cagework. The 1622 survey revealed that the church was nearly complete, and

that a second house was under construction, and several 17th-century accounts mention a water mill on the estate (Trimble 1919, 128–129).

The same survey also noted a degree of discord among Blennerhassett's lessees and freeholders, and suggested that the estate was a 'dangerous place' due to the numbers of Irish under-tenants. By 1640, the estate was under the control of Rory Maguire, who had married Blennerhassett's widowed daughter-in-law Deborah, the sister of Sir Audley Mervyn of Trillick. Whilst initially appearing to fit well into the new order, Maguire became one of the leaders of the 1641 Rebellion, unsuccessfully attempting a massacre of prominent persons he was entertaining at Crevinish Castle (Wakeman 1884). After the wars, the estate passed through various generations and branches of the Blennerhassett family, until it was sold piecemeal in the 18th century to the Vaughan and Irwin families (Trimble 1919, 313).

296   CREVINISH: HOUSE   216548 362623
AND BAWN
Crevinish Castle

The remains of Crevinish Castle are located close to the eastern shore of Lower Lough Erne, on a spur of slightly higher ground above the water's edge. A house and bawn built here by Thomas Blennerhasset, were described by Pynnar as a bawn

Fig. 4.19 View of Crevinish Castle.

Monea Castle (Inv. 327)

One of the finest examples of an early 17th-century fortified house in Ulster is to be found at Monea, Co. Fermanagh, in the townland of Castletown Monea. Consisting of a single-piled, four-bay oblong block, three storeys high, it is a somewhat forbidding building, its grey walls rising skywards to dominate the local landscape. The walls are of local carboniferous limestone, with sandstone door and window dressings. Projecting from the corners of the front façade are two circular towers, three storeys high and, quite

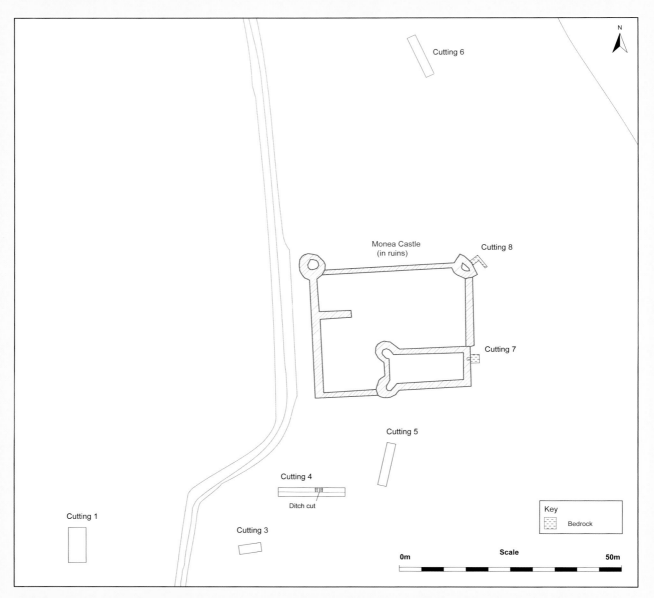

12 Plan of Monea Castle showing the location of the excavation cuttings. The fortified house stands in the south-eastern corner of a rectangular bawn, protected by a D-shaped flanker at the north-eastern corner and a circular flanker at the north-western corner.

unusually, each crowned with a square, gabled attic storey. The castle stands in the south-eastern corner of a rectangular bawn, and is protected by a D-shaped flanker at the north-eastern corner and a circular flanker at the north-western corner that was also used as dovecote.

Construction of the house was finished in 1618 by the Scottish undertaker and clergyman, Malcolm Hamilton, who was granted 1,500 acres in the proportion known as 'Derrinefogher' in 1615 (Belmore 1895a, 195, 205; Jope 1951, 42). In 1619, the house was described by Pynnar (Belmore 1895a, 196) as

> …a strong Castle of Lime and stone, being fifty-four feet long, and twenty feet broad; but hath no Bawne unto it, nor any other defence for the succouring or relieving his Tenants.

This apparent lack of defence was remedied in 1622 or 1623 when a bawn, consisting of 'a wall 9 feet in height and 300 feet in circuit', was constructed (Belmore 1895a, 196).

In 1622, Hamilton was appointed rector of Devenish, and in the following year he became the archbishop of Cashel (*ibid.* 196–197). Following his death in 1628 or 1629 (the year is disputed), all of his lands in Fermanagh were granted to his fourth son, Malcom Hamilton, including the lease of church lands in 'Moyneagh' (Monea) (*ibid.* 197–199). He also allocated half of all the rooms in his 'castel of Casselton' (Monea Castle) to his wife, Jane née Crawford (*ibid.* 199). Malcolm junior does not seem to have produced a male heir, and the lands appear to have passed on to his younger brother, Lewis (Ludovic) Hamilton. Lewis married a Swedish lady, Anna Catherina Grubbe Stjernfelt, and they produced two sons, Gustavus and Malcolm, along with a daughter (whose name is not recorded) (Belmore 1898, 140–141). The castle was attacked by forces under Captain Rory Maguire during the 1641 Rebellion (Belmore 1895b, 256–257), but does not appear to have been badly damaged, as Gustavus Hamilton was still in residence in 1688, and by then Governor of Enniskillen (*ibid.* 260–261). Gustavus died around 1691, and after 1704, his eldest son, William, appears to have sold the estate. The house was eventually abandoned following a fire in the mid-18th century (*ibid.* 263).

Like Derrywoone, the fortified house was located in close juxtaposition to a pre-existing Gaelic Irish élite site, a *crannóg* on the adjoining lake that was occupied by the Maguires of Co. Fermanagh until the advent of the Plantation. The plan, while unusual and probably based on the personal choice of Malcolm Hamilton, is not atypical in an age when fortified houses came in many different shapes and sizes. This was a time of architectural experimentation, when owners sought to create living spaces inspired by Renaissance concepts of genteel living and polite disposition, while still respecting older traditions of authority. The roof turrets and gun loops were integral to the principles of castle architecture, both in defensive and symbolic senses. The metaphorical importance of the parapet can be clearly illustrated in the advice of a Scottish laird to his son not to build his house without battlements, as the resulting edifice would be construed as demeaning to the family's heritage, undermining their standing in society (McKean 2001, 57). To some extent there are parallels with England, where the most striking

13 The attractive moulded corbelling on the front towers of Monea Castle are used to mark the transition from the circular lower floors to the square attic space. This architectural elaboration may perhaps be derived from Claypotts Castle in Dundee, Scotland.

aspects of the majority of 16th- and early 17th-century English architecture are their elaborate rooflines. However, with Scottish architecture there was a sharper contrast between the rooflines and the lower elevations of the houses, which were more simple and mundane, as can be seen at Monea Castle.

Scottish architectural features including crow-stepped gables, conical-roofed turrets – commonly supported on moulded corbel courses, and rounded stair-turrets containing a newel stairwell (often corbelled out from the face of the building at high level) can be found on a number of fortified houses in Ulster including Monea Castle. Many of the Scottish settlers came from the western areas of Lowland Scotland, where a large number of early

14 Excavations were carried out within the environs of Monea Castle as part of the Ulster Scots Archaeological Project.

modern castles possess these features. At Monea Castle, the attractive moulded corbelling that is used to mark the transition from the circular lower floors to the square attic space of the towers in the front façade may perhaps be derived from Claypotts Castle in Dundee, Scotland. This is not the only aspect of Monea Castle that specifically illustrates the use of Scottish masons by Malcolm Hamilton – the wrought stone surrounds of the surviving doorways and windows are quite different from the carved stonework that can be seen in tower houses and fortified houses built elsewhere in Ireland.

The layout of the house consisted of vaulted chambers at ground floor, containing the kitchen and other working spaces. There was a large hall and great chamber at first-floor level, and a number of smaller chambers at second floor level. Such an arrangement has clear parallels with contemporary Scottish castles, where the first floor, the *piano nobile*, contained the most important chambers, with each successive floor above less exalted than the one below. This also parallels the layout of tower houses in the Pale, though the positioning of the hall differs in southern and western Ireland where, in contrast, tower houses usually have their halls at the highest floor level with the other chambers graded in decreasing importance from top to bottom.

As part of the Ulster Scots Archaeological Project, archaeologists attempted to locate the dwellings of the tenants of the estate in the neighbourhood of the castle utilising geophysical prospection and excavation. A number of underground anomalies were detected, possibly representative of features such as pits, a wall, a linear ditch, and a roadway or path. Six cuttings were opened to see whether these results represented real archaeology on the ground. Cuttings 1 and 3 did not reveal the structural evidence suggested by the geophysical results, the anomalies turning out to be areas of loose rock surrounded by peat deposits. The possible walling in Cutting 3 was a single course of loosely scattered stones that may have served as stepping stones along the nearby lakeshore. Cutting 4 revealed an area of compacted stone one course deep, with peat deposits to the east and west. This overlay a ditch that had been filled in with large rocks, and which measured 3.4m wide and 1.23m deep, but produced no dateable artefacts. In contrast, Cutting 5 produced many artefacts, with the upper peaty deposits containing numerous fragments of window glass, slag, clay tobacco pipes, pottery, iron nails, animal bone and a single lead musket ball. This cutting appeared to yield evidence of landscaping around the southern extent of Monea Castle. Cutting 6 to the north of Monea Castle revealed that the bedrock there had been subject to quarrying. Several artefacts were recovered including two musket balls, clay tobacco pipe fragments and sherds of glazed earthenware (Walsh 2016b, 14–16).

At the castle itself, excavation focused at the base of the latrine in the eastern wall (Cutting 7), to gauge if the eastern area of the castle was of earlier construction. No archaeological features were uncovered, with only natural bedrock found underneath the sod layer (*ibid*. 9–10). Lastly, Cutting 8 was opened adjacent to the north-eastern flanker of the bawn in an effort to see if this angular flanker had originally been circular as suggested by an earlier plan published by Jope (1951, 37, Fig. 3). This cutting again only revealed bedrock underneath the topsoil, there being no evidence for an earlier flanker foundation, countering the suggestion that the extant flanker had originally been circular (Walsh 2016b, 17).

15 A local school group visiting Monea Castle during the course of archaeological excavations at the site.

of lime and stone with four flankers, enclosing a house that took up approximately half its area. A similar description was given in 1622. The fate of the bawn during the 1641 Rebellion is not known, despite historical associations with the war (see entry on estate above). Rory Maguire, who was in control in 1641, probably abandoned it, heralding a period of decline for the building and its associated grounds. It is not clear precisely when the buildings became ruinous, but it was probably in the 18th century. The site had long been in ruins by the time of the first Ordnance Survey, though the *OS Memoirs* erroneously identified Sir Phelim O'Neill as the former owner.

The castle consists of a two- to three-storey house, with a spear-shaped, three-storey corner turret on the north-eastern corner. The south-western corner of the building has collapsed, although remnants of a bawn wall can be traced on the ground, forming the boundary between an adjoining graveyard (Inv. 297) and 18th-century farm buildings at the site. Other features remain hidden beneath large heaps of rubble and spoil.

FER 153:020

Inq. Ulst. Fermanagh Car. I (2); Hill 1877, 277, 489; Trimble 1919, 127–129; *PSAMNI* 145; Ó Gallachair 1958, 302; Johnston 1976, 154–156; 1980a; 1980b, 204; Day and McWilliams 1992b, 106

297   CREVINISH: CHURCH   216555 362607
AND GRAVEYARD

The fragmentary remains of a churchyard and possible church are located within a narrow rectangular walled enclosure on the eastern side of Crevinish Castle. The western wall of the graveyard may have originally been part of the adjoining bawn. There are only two memorial stones surviving within the graveyard; one against the eastern wall of the castle bears the coat of arms of the O'Neills, another with no inscription or markings lies at the northern end. The entrance to the graveyard is along the eastern wall and is flanked by the stone jambs of a doorway. These may originally have been used for a church which

was mentioned by Pynnar and the 1622 survey.

FER 153:038

Hill 1877, 277, 489; *PSAMNI* 145; Ó Gallachair 1958, 302

298   EDERNEY: SETTLEMENT   222100 364900

The crossroads village of Ederney, although not mentioned in the various surveys, was probably founded in the 17th century, given that Inquisitions held in 1639 recorded that a large number of leases had been taken out by English settlers in the area over the period 1624 to 1636. There are, however, no known archaeological traces of this early phase of the history of the village, which was likely abandoned after 1641.

FER 154:098

Inq. Ulst. Fermanagh, Car. I (48); Johnston 1976, 125–126

299   KESH: SETTLEMENT   218000 363800

The village of Kesh began as a plantation settlement, and was described by Pynnar as 'six Houses built of Cagework'. However, there are no visible remains of any 17th-century structures.

FER 154:099

Hill 1877, 489; Johnston 1976, 123

Bannaghmore

A grant of 1,500 acres was made in 1610 to Sir Edward Blennerhassett, whose son Francis was responsible for establishing the estate. No progress was documented until Pynnar's 1619 survey described a bawn and house (Inv. 300) and a village (Inv. 301). In 1611, Gatisfeth (Hill 1877, 490) recorded that the English settlers had horses and had brought a dozen cattle with them, while the 1622 survey noted the presence of a water mill. Francis Blennerhassett inherited the estate around 1630 and resided there until his death. Thereafter it passed through other members of the family until it was sold to James Caldwell in 1670 (Johnston 1976, 170).

300 ROSSBEG: HOUSE AND BAWN   201730 360480
Castle Caldwell or Belleek Castle

The ruined remains of a house and bawn stand in woodland on a peninsula at the northern end of Lower Lough Erne. This 'castle' was built by Francis Blennerhassett, although its precise date of construction is unknown, as the accounts made by Carew and Gatisfeth (both in 1611) are not clear. The site was certainly well under construction at the time of Pynnar's survey in 1619, when a strong bawn and three-storey house were described. Inquisitions in 1629 documented a stone house 67ft by 26ft, and a bawn 316ft in 'circumference' which approximately matches the 30m by 30m enclosure that can be traced at the site today. Much of the original building still survives in ruins, although substantial remodelling and enlargement of the house took place in the late 1780s.

The walls of the ruins are covered with dense vegetation, particularly ivy, and although the remains are quite extensive they are in poor condition. Many of the walls show evidence for plaster and lime render although this may date from later remodelling of the building.

FER 171:003

Inq. Ulster, Fermanagh, Car I (3); Hill 1877, 277–278 and 490–491; Belmore 1903b, 20; Ó Gallachair 1958, 302; Johnston 1976, 170–171 and 1980a; Day and McWilliams 1992b, 3–4

301 BELLEEK: SETTLEMENT   194044 359070

The village of Belleek was founded during the Plantation but nothing survives from the 17th century, aside from the general street layout. A small, single-storey, white-washed thatched building in the village, now a café, is claimed to be the oldest surviving property in the area. Although this certainly dates to the 19th century or earlier, its precise date of construction is unknown.

FER 170:037; HB12/13/034

Hill 1877, 490

Fig. 4.20 At Castle Caldwell much of the early 17th-century building still survives, although substantial remodelling and enlargement of the house in the late 1780s has obscured this.

Fig. 4.21 Church and graveyard used by the Caldwell family at Rossbeg.

302 ROSSBEG: CHURCH AND   201340 360320
GRAVEYARD

Begun in 1630 but abandoned during the 1641 Rebellion, the church at Castle Caldwell was not completed until the mid-18th century when it was rebuilt for use as a chapel and burial ground by the Caldwell family. The church stands on a slight rise within a woodland setting. The building measures 15.6m by 6.4m internally, and is orientated east–west with its entrance facing to the south. The eastern and western walls have large arched windows, while those in the northern and southern walls do not survive to their full heights. The burial vaults of the Caldwells are located at the eastern end of the building.

> FER 171:019
>
> *PSAMNI* 147; Johnston 1976, 139 and 141–143; Day and McWilliams 1992b, 4

Other sites in Lurg

303   MAGHERAMEENAGH: 197790 359210
CASTLE

The site of a castle built by James Johnston in the early 1700s. It is speculated that the castle may have replaced a 17th-century house or castle destroyed during the Jacobite war, although no traces of an earlier structure are known to survive.

> FER 171:046
>
> Rogers 1967b, 164; Johnston 1976, 176

304   PETTIGOE: SETTLEMENT   211000 366800

The village of Pettigoe straddles the border with Co. Donegal. During the Plantation, the lands surrounding the village were under the control of Miler Magrath, Archbishop of Cashel, who built Pettigoe Castle *c.* 3km to the south, on the Co. Donegal side of the border. Although not strictly a plantation village, the Inquisitions of 1629 mention a few Irish tenants. At the northern end of High Street, the road layout of The Diamond may reflect how the original settlement was configured.

> FER 153:043
>
> *Inq. Ulst.* Fermanagh, Car. I (3); Johnston 1976, 134

Barony of Tirkennedy (or Coole and Tircanada, allotted to servitors and Irish)

Cornagrade

1,000 acres were granted in 1611 to Sir William Cole, encompassing the town of Enniskillen and straddling the River Erne, thus lying partly in

the barony of Clanawley (Hill 1877, 335). Bodley reported that Cole had built a water mill and had prepared 150 tons of timber, and quantities of lime, stone and sand for a bawn. This structure (Inv. 305) was recorded by Pynnar and the 1622 survey, but no other buildings were reported.

305   CORNAGRADE: HOUSE   223200 344900
AND BAWN

This is the former site of a plantation house built by Cole around 1614, which by 1619 was defended by a bawn with two flankers. According to the 1622 survey, the house was 'English style', and thatched. A plan of Enniskillen in 1688 shows a square structure, with four corner towers. The plantation building, known as 'Cornagrade House', was still extant at the time of the first Ordnance Survey, when it was shown as T-shaped in plan on the 1st edition of the six-inch map. The building was demolished in the late 19th century, and the site later became a farmstead, before being enveloped by modern housing on the outskirts of Enniskillen. No traces of the building or structures survive.

> FER 211:080
>
> Hill 1877, 491; Ó Gallachair 1958, 304; Johnston 1976, 174

Newporton

Also known as 'Dromchine', the estate comprised 1,500 acres and was granted in 1610 to Sir Henry Folliott. Bodley stated that 'Foliot hath caused a great Irish house to be framed upon his proportion, for present succour of his workmen', but this is not mentioned in later sources. Bodley also described the gathering and preparation of materials for the bawn (Inv. 306 or 307), which Pynnar found finished, along with a corn mill (Inv. 309) and a village (Inv. 308). Folliott was later involved in various exchanges of lands and property, with Newporton coming under the control of Sir William Cole and Sir Robert Kinge (Hill 1877, 492). According to the *OS Memoirs*, the estate later came into the possession of the Murray

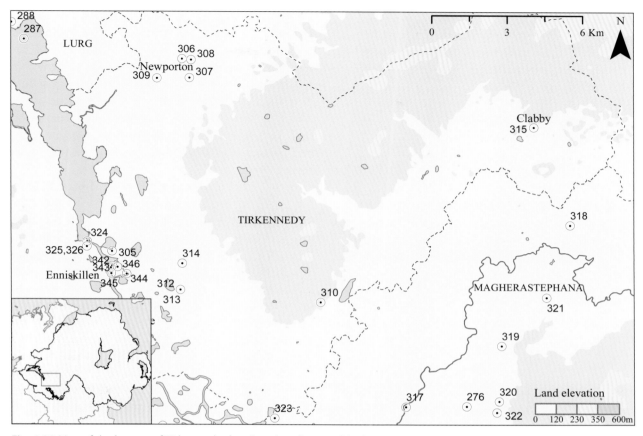

Fig. 4.22 Map of the barony of Tirkennedy showing sites discussed in the text.

family, but the circumstances of this sale or transfer are unknown (Day and McWillams 1992b, 93).

306   DRUMMURRAY: HOUSE   226000 352800
AND BAWN
Castle Murray

This is the approximate site of a castle built by Sir Henry Folliott, which was under construction in 1613, and described by Pynnar as a bawn with three flankers measuring 120ft by 150ft and enclosing a strong house. The 1622 survey stated that there were two large flankers at the corners of the bawn opposite the house, each 25ft square and containing lodgings. The 1622 survey also described the house as of three-storeys, and measuring 68ft by 25ft with a projection at its rear, presumably a stairwell that also functioned as a flanker. Such a house plan is

typical of the English-style plantation houses such as Old Castle Archdale (Inv. 292). It was possibly sited at a fording point across a stream to the south of Ballinamallard, and although the *OS Memoirs* record the structure as still standing in this townland in the early 19th century, its exact location is unknown, although another potential location is nearby Drumkeen House (see Inv. 307 below).

> FER 192:036
>
> Hill 1877, 334–345; Ó Gallachair 1958, 303–304; Johnston 1976, 181–182; Day and McWilliams 1992b, 93

307   DRUMKEEN: CASTLE   226300 352020
Drumkeen House

A castle was shown at this approximate location on a 1777 map of the road between Omagh and

Enniskillen, annotated as 'castle ruins'. The likely site for this castle is at Drumkeen House, which may have replaced an earlier structure. This house was recently demolished and no 17th–century building fabric or features are visible.

FER 192:041

Taylor and Skinner 1778, 254

308   BALLINAMALLARD: 226360 352760
SETTLEMENT

Ballinamallard was established during the Plantation, with Pynnar describing the settlement as a 'town' of 11 houses, situated near the bawn of the Newporton estate. Nothing from the early 17th century survives in the village.

FER 192:056

Hill 1877, 491–492; Ó Gallachair 1958, 303–304; Johnston 1976, 119–120; Day and McWilliams 1992b, 92–94

309   SALRY: MILL   226230 352730

The 1st edition OS map marks a 'corn mill' at this location, but it is not known if this is also the site of a 17th-century mill mentioned by Pynnar. The area has been subsequently redeveloped, and no trace of any mill or mill race survives.

FER 192:095

Hill 1877, 491–2

Carrick

A grant of 1,000 acres of lands to the south and east of Topped Mountain, and an additional 348 acres comprising of Belle Isle, at the northern end of Upper Lough Erne, was made in the winter of 1610–11 to Captain Paul Gore. Belle Isle was also known as 'MacManus Island', traditionally the place where the Annals of Ulster were compiled, and where the MacManus family remained until 1636 (Rogers 1967b, 95–96). Historical accounts are vague. Bodley reported that Gore had employed persons in the preparation of timber and Pynnar mentioned a bawn and house, but does not indicate whether this was on Belle Isle (i.e. Inv. 311) or on the mainland (i.e. Inv. 310). It seems from the 1622 survey that Gore took up residence on an estate in Co. Donegal, and leased the Carrick estate to a nameless individual described in the survey as 'a kinsman of his owne' (Ó Gallachair 1958, 305). The same survey reported that the bawn on Belle Isle was under construction, and present were a 'good stock of very fair English cattle'.

310   COOLBUCK: BAWN   231500 342800

The various editions of the OS six-inch maps mark 'Tharlegh Bawn' at this location. However, as there are no visible remains, nor any local tradition nor remembrance of such a structure, it is impossible to say whether this is the bawn at Carrick mentioned by Pynnar.

FER 212:091

Hill 1877, 335–336 and 492

311   BELLE ISLE: CASTLE   228940 335530
AND BAWN

Belle Isle Castle is a 19th-century country house that incorporates fragments of a late 17th-century building in its northern end. The site was mentioned in the 1622 survey as a bawn 60ft square with two flankers, although not finished. Indeed, it is not known if the bawn was ever finished, but when the 19th-century house was built on the site, the old bawn was completely destroyed, and no traces of it are known to survive. It has been suggested that a tower house was built on the site during the 15th century by Cathal Óg MacManus, Vicar General of Clogher and compiler of the *Annals of Ulster*.

FER 230:097; HB12/05/032

Hill 1877, 335–336 and 492; *Hist. MSS Comm.* 1947, 168; Ó Gallachair 1958, 305; Johnston 1976, 169; Reeves-Smyth 2014, 334–335

Coole

1,000 acres were granted in 1610 to Captain Rodger Atkinson. In a pattern matching that of progress at Newporton, Bodley reported that Atkinson had built an 'Irish' house 'strongly timbered and very large, and hedged in a garden plot', and was preparing to build a bawn (Inv. 312), which Pynnar recorded, along with two water mills – one for corn, the other a tucking mill. These structures were all documented by the 1622 survey, which also added that the estate had 'orchards and gardens fair, better than we expected to see in so remoat (sic) a place' (Ó Gallachair 1958, 304). Also documented in 1622 were seven lessees and eight cottagers, each with a house and garden allotment. The estate changed ownership several times in the 17th century, and was badly damaged during the 1641 Rebellion. Coole was sold in 1656 to John Corry, a Belfast merchant and ancestor of the earls of Belmore, whose family seat was subsequently established on the estate (Trimble 1919, 181).

312   CASTLE COOLE: HOUSE   225924 343310
AND BAWN
The site of a bawn and house mentioned in the 1622 survey was described as a bawn of lime and stone, 60ft square, with two slate-roofed flankers, 12ft square, each containing rooms. The house that it enclosed was described as measuring 59ft by 24ft of three storeys, and with a rear stair projection that doubled as a third bawn flanker – similar to other contemporary houses of English design. The house was attacked during the 1641 Rebellion, and burnt in 1688 to avoid capture by the Jacobite army. Castle Coole was rebuilt at a new site *c*. 1km away, and nothing remains of the original site. The gardens adjoining the house, praised in the 1622 survey, were substantially enlarged and remodelled in the early 18th century, and now survive as a series of landscaped features and earthworks, some of which may have their origin in the plantation period.

    FER 211:082

    Hill 1877, 492; Ó Gallachair 1958, 304–305; Johnston 1976, 171–172; McErlean 1984, 23–26

313   CASTLE COOLE: WATER   225924 343310
MILL
Two water mills located near the bawn at Castle Coole were noted by Pynnar, but no visible remains survive of either structure. On an estate map of Castle Coole there is a 17th-century canal depicted to the north-east of the 18th-century Queen Anne House, but no traces of it are visible today. This presumably was a mill-race associated with the corn mill or the tucking mill recorded by Pynnar and the 1622 survey.

    FER 211:122

    Hill 1877, 492; Ó Gallachair 1958, 304–305

314   AGHARAINEY: HOUSE   226000 344400
The townland of Agharainey was leased in 1639 to Zachary Rampagne, who built a stone house on the summit of a prominent drumlin at this location. The house was still visible in 1881, although no remains of it survive today.

    FER 211:081

    McErlean 1984, 23–26

Clabby

The grant of 1,500 acres to Con McShane O'Neill in the winter of 1610–11 was one of the larger grants to an Irish landowner in Co. Fermanagh during the Plantation, the other major grantees being members of the Maguire family. The estate was regranted to John Connelly, a Dublin merchant, in 1632, and the bawn was attacked and damaged during the 1641 Rebellion (Trimble 1919, 324; Johnston 1976, 173).

315   CAMGART: HOUSE   240000 350000
AND BAWN
Carew reported that Con McShane O'Neill had begun construction of an earthen bawn, which was found complete by Pynnar, and contained a 'strong house' of lime and stone, but its whereabouts are unknown. Possible locations include the higher ground to the north of the co-ordinates above, the village of Clabby itself to the east of this location,

and an earthwork thought to be a rath on the eastern limb of the village in the adjoining townland of Ramaley (FER 194:017, grid ref. 241150 350590).

FER 194:027

Hill 1877, 336 and 492; Trimble 1919, 324; *Hist. MSS Comm.* 1947, 168; Ó Gallachair 1958, 305–306; Johnston 1976, 173; Foley and McHugh 2014, I.2, 548

Other Irish estates in Coole and Tircanada

Pynnar reported that lands in the grant to Brian Maguire of 1,500 acres forming the estate of Tempodessell (also known as 'Inseyloughygeasse'), and 500 acres to his late brother (whose name was given as 'Tirlagh' in the 1610–11 land grants), contained 'a large Bawne of Sodds, and a good House of Lime and Stone', now unlocated (Hill

1877, 493). Other Irish grants included 120 acres to John Maguire at 'Clough', 'Creena', 'Kilbrissill' and 'Dromloe', and 120 acres to Richard Maguire, at 'Agharynah' (*ibid*. 337). 'Agharynah' may correspond to the modern townland of Agharainey, part of Castle Coole, or perhaps Aghavoory in the modern barony of Magherastephana, where the remains of a castle stood until the 1960s (Inv. 316).

Barony of Magherastephana (granted to Conor Roe Maguire)

The entire barony of Magherastephana, 6000 acres, was granted in 1610 to Conor Roe Maguire, whose own lands around Lisnaskea were confiscated and granted to the Scottish Balfour family. 'Aghalun', the original name for Brookeborough, was the location

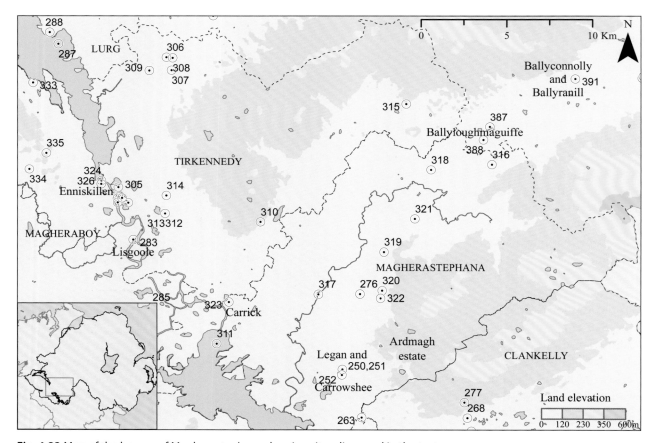

Fig. 4.23 Map of the barony of Magherastephana showing sites discussed in the text.

for the castle of Conor Roe Maguire (Inv. 319), and it and the adjoining village were at the centre of his new extensive estate. There were other Maguire castles at Agheeghter (Inv. 316) and at Stranafeley (Inv. 320), but these and associated lands were not well documented during the 17th century. Following the 1641 Rebellion and the various upheavals in the latter part of the 17th century, much of these lands were regranted to the Brooke family, descendants of a servitor who was granted land in Co. Donegal during the Plantation (Trimble 1919, 263).

316   AGHAVOORY: 244990 346320
TOWER HOUSE
Agheeghter Castle

This tower house was excavated in 1964–65 in advance of its destruction as part of a road widening scheme. Prior to the excavation, the upstanding remains consisted of the stair projection of a 16th- or 17th-century tower house, which already had been significantly damaged when the road between Fivemiletown and Cooneen was built. The castle is not mentioned by primary historical sources, but the *OS Memoirs* stated that that old castle here was 'said to have been the residence of one of the Maguires'. When excavated, what remained of the tower house foundations could be traced in the ground, indicating a square or rectangular tower house. Since the site was already heavily disturbed, no further archaeological remains were uncovered.

FER 213:007
PSAMNI 168; Waterman 1967b; Day and McWilliams 1990d, 9; Reeves-Smyth 2014, 331–332

317   MAGUIRESBRIDGE: 234880 338480
SETTLEMENT

Maguiresbridge was established as a nucleated settlement before 1630, when a licence to hold a weekly market and an annual fair in the town was awarded to Sir Brian Maguire, son of Conor Roe Maguire. However, the Down Survey map of the barony, drawn in 1657, shows no sign of any village, nor is one mentioned in a 1659 census, making

it likely that it was destroyed in 1641, and not reoccupied until the 1660s. No visible remains of the 17th-century settlement exist.

FER 230:098
Johnston 1976, 133–134

318   RAFINTAN: 241440 345990
FORTIFICATION

This is the site of an early medieval rath, and possibly also a 'fort' marked on the Down Survey map of the 1650s, indicating that this rath may have been re-used as a military site in the 17th century. The enclosure is not marked as a rath or fort on early OS six-inch maps (until the 3rd edition); instead it is shown as a rounded, tree-lined enclosure with an angled corner at its north-western edge. Such a feature would be typical of a 16th- or 17th-century fortification, although the angled corner has since vanished, and the extant earthworks are typical of a rath. A second rath (FER 213:004), now ploughed-out, lies 170m to the north-west of this location and is another possible location for the fortification shown on the Down Survey map.

FER 213:005
Down Survey barony map of Magherastephana (PRONI D597); Foley and McHugh 2014, I.2, 545–546

319   BROOKEBOROUGH: 238700 341000
CASTLE
Aghalun Castle

This is the approximate site of Conor Roe Maguire's plantation-period castle. The structure was shown on the Down Survey barony map (1650s) and mentioned in Lewis' *Topographical Dictionary* (1837), although it was not shown on the 1st edition OS six-inch map. Building work and test trenching at and near this site in the 1970s and 2000s did not reveal any archaeological traces of the castle or any other 17th-century structure.

FER 231:006
Down Survey barony map of Magherastephana (PRONI D597); Lewis 1837, I, 16–17; MacManus 2006a; Reeves-Smyth 2014, 334

320   STRANAFELEY: CASTLE   238600 338700
Deer Park Castle

The former site of a castle marked on a Down Survey map is located on a prominent, flat-topped ridge. Although there are a number of derelict farm buildings here, none include any castle fabric, although the various buildings and walls here could contain stone robbed from earlier structures. The northern slope of the ridge exhibits several possible small-scale stone quarries, some of which have been infilled with modern farm debris.

> FER 231:020
> Down Survey barony map of Magherastephana (PRONI D597); Lewis 1837, I, 17

321   DRUMHOY: CASTLE   240500 343000

Nothing survives of the castle marked on or near this location on the Down Survey map of the barony. Any archaeological remains that may have existed are likely to have been destroyed by modern development; the location is next to the old alignment of the A5 trunk road, in the grounds of Stonepark Baptist Church.

> FER 213:097
> Down Survey barony map of Magherastephana (PRONI D597)

322   STRANAFELEY: MILL   238500 338250

This is the approximate site of a mill shown on the 1657 Down Survey map of the barony, to the east of Aghavea Church. Locally, the placename Mill Hill attests to the memory of a mill nearby. According to the 1610 Patent Rolls, the neighbouring townland of Aghavea was granted as part of the Cloncarn estate (barony of Clankelly), where Pynnar recorded the presence of a mill, although this was described as being located near the bawn in Lislea rather than in Aghavea itself (see Inv. 274).

> FER 231:049
> Down Survey barony map of Magherastephana (PRONI D597); Hill 1877, 274–275 and 483

323   GOLA: ABBEY   229650 338020

Some sources indicate that an abbey was founded here in the 14th century, originally under Dominican rule and later Franciscan. Gola is not, however, mentioned in any of the inquisitions and surveys of the early 17th century, so it is not known whether it was continuously occupied until then. The abbey and surrounding lands were formally granted by the Maguires to the Dominicans shortly before 1641, with no building occurring until the 1660s. The Dominican and Franciscan orders subsequently became embroiled in a dispute over possession, with the Dominicans gaining full control in 1678. No traces of the abbey survive, and the *OS Memoirs* recorded that the last remnants were demolished in 1801.

> FER 230:048
> McKenna 1900, 136–141; Lowry-Corry 1919, Tables 3 and 4, 44; Rogers 1967b, 178–179; Gwynn and Hadcock 1970, 233; Day and McWilliams 1990d; Hamlin 2008, 400; Foley and McHugh 2014, I.2, 758–759

Barony of Magheraboy (Scottish undertakers)

Drumskeagh

This estate, measuring 1,000 acres, was granted to Jerome Lindsey and sold thereafter to Sir William Cole in 1612 (Hill 1877, 304). There was apparently little progress made in its development before Pynnar carried out his survey there, recording a castle and bawn (Inv. 324) and fourteen British families. He added 'He hath also an excellent Wind Mill' (Hill 1877, 494). The 1622 survey also documented the bawn, which by that time was leased to the Bishop of Clogher, and enclosed two three-storey timber houses. Fifty-three families were mentioned in the 1622 survey, and it seems that Drumskeagh was a model plantation proportion for the surveyors, who wrote (Ó Gallachair 1958, 307):

> he [Cole] hath let his land at easie rents, and for long tearms, which is the

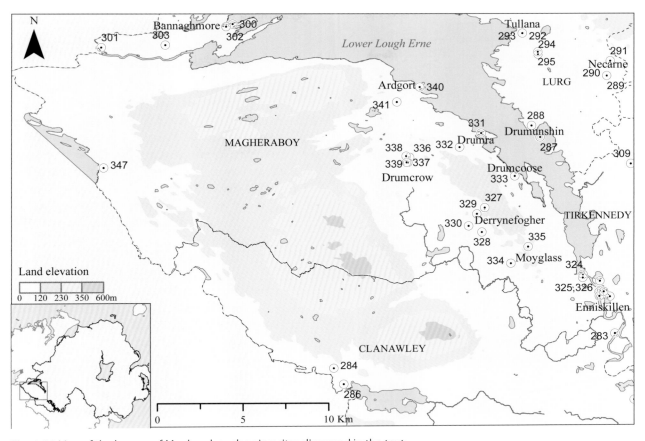

Fig. 4.24 Map of the barony of Magheraboy showing sites discussed in the text.

cause it is so well planted, we haveing seen none like it, for which the Gent deserves high comendacions.

324   PORTORA: CASTLE   222210 345300

The ruined remains of a castle built in 1614 by Sir William Cole stand on the western bank of the River Erne, at a highly strategic location close to where it enters the Lower Lough Erne. Pynnar described a bawn 68ft square with four flankers, containing a three-storeyed stone castle. The 1622 survey added that the castle and two of the flankers contained 'many good rooms'. From approximately 1621 to 1628, it was leased to James Spottiswoode, Bishop of Clogher, who used it as his family residence. The castle survived the 1641 Rebellion, and was also besieged by Jacobite forces in 1689,

Fig. 4.25 The remains of a house span the north-western end of the bawn at Portora Castle.

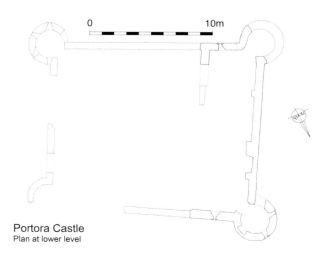

Portora Castle
Plan at lower level

Fig. 4.26 Plan of Portora Castle illustrating that both the house and bawn were provided with circular corner flankers.

but remained undamaged. The castle finally fell in the 19th century, partly as a result of storms, partly through schoolboys experimenting with homemade gunpowder.

The ruins are still substantial and consist of bawn walls built from local limestone rubble, which survive to a height of 3m, with round flankers at each corner containing numerous gun loops, although parts of the eastern flanker and south-eastern wall do not survive. The remains of a house span the north-western end of the bawn. A number of features are evident in the rear wall of the house, including a fireplace at ground-floor level, and a window and two other fireplaces at first-floor level. There are also windows in the western and northern flankers. In 1997 the house and bawn were excavated in advance of conservation works, revealing that the interior of the house was divided by timber partitioning into two or three rooms, the room at the south-western end probably containing the kitchen. No structures were found within the bawn, suggesting that the site had undergone considerable clearances and tidying in the past.

FER 211:019

Hill 1877, 304–305 and 494–495; Trimble 1919, 153–160; *PSAMNI* 162; Ó Gallachair 1958, 306–307; Jope 1958b and 1960; Johnston 1976, 164–165 and

1980a; Day and McWilliams 1992b, 117; Brannon and McSparron 1997

325   PORTORA: SETTLEMENT   222200 345100
Nothing remains of the plantation settlement associated with Portora, and much of the area is now under sports fields, with much potential for archaeological deposits to survive. However, testing in 2007, in advance of development, did not reveal anything of significance.

FER 211:084

Hill 1877, 304–305 and 494–495; Ó Gallachair 1958, 306–307; Bowen 2007a

326   PORTORA: WINDMILL   222200 345100
This is the approximate site of a windmill noted by Pynnar, but no archaeological remains have yet been located.

FER 211:084

Hill 1877, 494

Derrynefogher

A grant of 1,000 acres was made to Sir Robert Hamilton in 1610, and in the following year Carew and Gatisfeth (Hill 1877, 304, 494) both reported that he had arrived with tenants, cattle and horses, and was busy preparing building materials. Bodley later reported that a water mill had been built on the estate. Pynnar documented the presence of a castle (Inv. 327), but no other defensive structures, and a population of seventy-seven 'British' men and their families. By this time, the estate was owned by Malcolm Hamilton, rector at Devenish and Chancellor of Down, and from 1623, Archbishop of Cashel. The Inquisitions held in 1630 (Belmore 1895a, 207) described a bawn in addition to the castle, and noted a village on the estate that held a weekly market (Inv. 329) and a church, the glebe lands of which were encompassed by the estate. There were three major freeholders, and the house of one of these survives, albeit in ruins (Inv. 330).

Fig. 4.27 Aerial view of Monea Castle.

327 CASTLETOWN: CASTLE AND BAWN

216470 349370

Monea Castle

Monea Castle was built in 1618 for Malcolm Hamilton, with a bawn added at around the time of the 1622 survey. The castle was seized – but not damaged – by Irish forces in 1641, and later retaken. By 1688, it was the residence of Gustavus Hamilton, the Governor of Enniskillen. It was abandoned following a fire in the mid-18th century.

The castle stands on a rocky ridge, overlooking marsh and low-lying ground. In fact, the ground to the east was once open water and is now undergoing the slow, natural process of transforming from lake to bog. Built of local carboniferous limestone, with sandstone dressings, the structure exemplifies various aspects of Scottish architecture.

Fig. 4.28 Two circular towers flank the front façade of Monea Castle, each of which supports square upper stages with crow-stepped gables, diagonally placed in relation to the floors below.

Fig. 4.29 Reconstruction drawing of Monea Castle as it would have appeared in the early 17th century.

It is oblong in plan, of three storeys, and consists of a rectangular building, orientated east-west. There are two circular towers at its western front, which support square upper stages with crow-stepped gables, diagonally placed in relation to the towers below. The hall was probably on the first floor, with barrel-vaulted chambers below and further living space above (see also pp 174–177).

The castle stands at the south-eastern corner of a bawn, with flankers on the north-western and north-eastern corners, while the foundations of a later building occupy the south-western corner. The north-eastern flanker has an unusual D-shaped plan. The north-western flanker was re-used as a dove cote at an unknown date. The bawn was moated on three sides until the early 1900s when the River Erne was drained, while the castle garden once stood on a ridge at the northern edge of the site, beyond the bawn.

Excavations in 2014 revealed evidence for terracing to the south of the bawn, and bedrock quarrying to the north. Musket balls were discovered in the ground at two locations, possibly from when the castle was seized in 1641. Seventeenth-century clay pipes were also found. Curiously, a Neolithic polished stone axe was discovered in a post-medieval context at the site.

FER 191:061

Hill 1877, 303–304 and 494–496; Belmore 1895a and 1895b; Trimble 1919, 137–142; *PSAMNI* 40; Jope 1951; Ó Gallachair 1958, 307 and 1979, 371; Johnston 1976, 162–4 and 1980a; Day and McWilliams 1992b, 54–55; F. Walsh *pers. comm.* 2014

328 TULLYMARGY: CASTLE   216300 347900

There are local accounts of a castle built some distance to the south-west of Monea Church. Although it no longer exists, it is thought that some stones had been removed from it for farm buildings, now also demolished.

FER 210:009

PSAMNI 160

Fig. 4.30 Internal view of gun ope in southern wall of Tullykelter Castle.

329 CASTLETOWN: SETTLEMENT   216000 349000

This is the approximate site of the 17th-century plantation village at Castletown, Monea. Aside from the castle itself (Inv. 327) nothing remains above ground of the village.

> FER 191:106
>
> Hill 1877, 303–304, 494 and 495–496; Belmore 1895a

330 TULLYKELTER: CASTLE   215520 348270

A small fortified house or castle was built by James Somerville, a freeholder on lands granted to him by Hamilton in 1616. It was abandoned in the mid-18th century, and the remains are now incorporated into a later farm complex, which is much overgrown with vegetation.

The castle is a rectangular building, 17m by 8m, orientated approximately north-south, with stairs in a rear projection, and also two projecting blocks on either side of the east-facing front façade. Large windows on the ground floor suggest a dwelling built for comfort, though there are also several gun loops for defence. Unlike neighbouring Monea Castle, Tullykelter exemplifies English rather than Scottish architectural traditions, although the decoration on the remains of a carved stone door surround in the front entrance suggests the work of Scottish masons.

> FER 191:066
>
> *Inq. Ulst.* Fermanagh, Car. I (24); *PSAMNI* 159; Waterman 1959c and 1961; Jope 1960, 104; Johnston 1976, 167–168 and 1980a; Day and McWilliams 1992b, 55

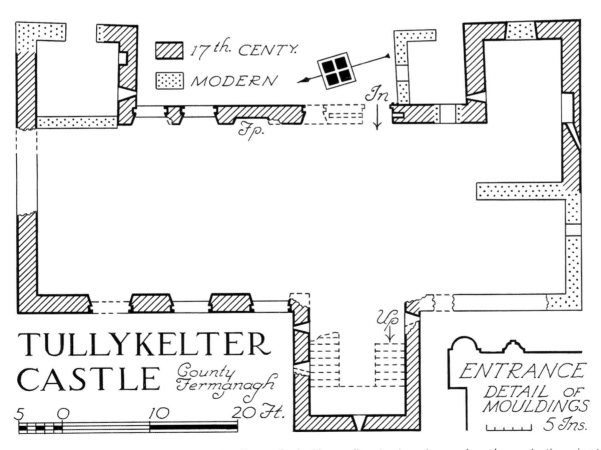

Fig. 4.31 Plan of Tullykelter Castle with front side of house flanked by small projecting wings and another projecting wing to the rear that once would have contained a stairwell (after Waterman 1959c, Fig. 1).

Drumra

1,000 acres were granted to James Gibb in 1610, who sold his estate to James Hamilton of Keckton, who in turn, sold or otherwise regranted the estate in 1617 to John Archdale (Hill 1877, 496), who was already the undertaker of the estate of Tullana, in the barony of Lurg. There was no progress documented on the estate until Pynnar reported that a house was being built and a bawn was finished (Inv. 332).

331   ROSSPOINT OR   216260 353850
COSBYSTOWN EAST: FORTIFICATION

A stone wall spanning a peninsula in Lough Erne was mentioned in a survey of Archdale's estate in 1720. It is not remembered locally and nothing remains, the narrowest part of the peninsula now being traversed by a road, leading to a slipway.

FER 191:089

A Survey of Col. Mervyne Archdal's Estate, 1720 (PRONI D605/1)

332   CLARAGH: HOUSE   215000 353000
AND BAWN

Pynnar described a bawn of lime and stone, 60ft square, with two flankers, and a one-storey house. By 1622, the bawn was derelict, and the house was still unfinished. No traces of these structures are known to survive.

FER 191:102

Hill 1877, 304, 496–497; Trimble 1919, 122–124; *Hist. MSS Comm.* 1947, 169; Ó Gallachair 1958, 307–308; Johnston, 1976, 182

Drumcoose

Alexander Hume's estate of 1,000 acres, granted in 1611, was immediately transferred to his brother Sir John Hume, whose son George later inherited the land (Hill 1877, 305, 497). The Humes consolidated their various holdings in Fermanagh, which became centred in Drumcoose after the 1641 Rebellion (see

Invs 333 and 340). Eventually, in the 18th century, the estate was merged with that of the earl of Ely, which included Ely Lodge.

333   ROSSNAFARSAN: HOUSE   218220 351270
AND BAWN

Pynnar described this site as a bawn measuring 80ft square. The 1622 surveyors reported 'a stone house half the breadth of the Bawne, one storie thatched'. This house became the main residence of the Humes, after the destruction of Tully Castle in 1641 (see Inv. 340). The current Castle Hume is built on the site of this earlier bawn, and later building has presumably obliterated any original structures.

FER 192:037

Hill 1877, 305, 494 and 497; Steele 1937, 46–47; Ó Gallachair 1958, 308; Rogers 1967b, 165

Moyglass

William Fowler was granted 1,500 acres in 1611, which he sold to Sir John Hume in 1615 (Hill 1877, 498). No progress at this estate was noted until 1622, when the government survey of that year described a scene typical of the progress of the Plantation in the early 1620s:

> …there is built a Bawne of stone and some lyme, 69 foot square and 4 open flankers, 9 foot high, the wall 2 foot and a half thick, noe howse within it, noe gate to it, but lies waste. There are 12 yeomen of British upon the land, but noe freeholders made nor Leaseholders but by promises and they are afrayd to be put out of their holdings (Ó Gallachair 1958, 310).

334   DINNYDOON: BAWN   218000 346000

A bawn near this site, first recorded in the 1622 survey, was probably destroyed before 1641, and is not mentioned thereafter. Nothing remains today and its precise location is unknown.

FER 211:078

Ó Gallachair 1958, 310

335   KILNALOO: HOUSE   219000 347000

A small stone house built on this site in the 17th century, and occupied by Thomas Creighton, was demolished during the Great Famine in the 1840s.

FER 211:079

Johnston 1976, 188

Drumcrow

1,000 acres were granted in 1610 or 1611 (the original grant does not survive) to John Dunbar, who was later knighted and appointed High Sheriff of Fermanagh (Waterman 1971). Progress on this estate was contrasted with the decline observed on so many other properties. Carew noted that although absent in person, Dunbar's freeholders, lessees and under tenants had been provided with money, materials and eight horses, and that building works were underway. Bodley reported '…a dwelling house of indifferent strength, for the time, of stone and clay, with a preface of lime, the roof thatched', and that stones for the bawn were gathered, and a water mill was constructed (*Hist. MSS Comm.* 1947, 169). Pynnar found a bawn (Inv. 338), and a second water mill (see Inv. 339). The 1622 survey also described the bawn, adding that it enclosed two English-style houses, and stated also that

> …the undertaker himself lives within the country which is a great comfort to his owne and his neighbouring tenants & he complains that his neighbours doe not the like (Ó Gallachair 1958, 310).

Later in the 17th century, the Dunbar family became joined through marriage to the Montgomerys of Co. Down (Hill 1869, 389–390).

336   DERRYGONNELLY: 212080 352400
CHURCH

In 1627 Sir John Dunbar built a church on his estate, the ruined remains of which stand just to the north of the village of Derrygonnelly. It is a relatively small and simple structure, rectangular in plan, orientated east-west, measuring 15.3m by 5.8m internally and with walls *c.* 1m thick, built from local sandstone rubble. The gables stand roughly to their original height of approximately 7m. The eastern gable contains a three-light window with ogee heads, and the western gable is surmounted by a belfry. The most striking feature of the church is its western entrance, where a semicircular arch possesses a moulded surround decorated with five-faced blocks. This is an Italian influence, and places the doorway of this otherwise modest church within the wider world of the European Renaissance. Above the doorway is an armorial plaque containing the coat-of-arms of Sir John Dunbar and his wife Katherine, bearing the year 1627.

FER 191:027

Lowry-Corry 1919, Table ii; *PSAMNI* 153; Waterman 1971

Fig. 4.32 View of Derrygonnelly Church with its attractive Renaissance-style doorway and armorial plaque above.

**337   DERRYGONNELLY: 211975 352090
      SETTLEMENT**

An area of historical and archaeological interest
lies within the town of Derrygonnelly, which began
its development in the 17th century, presumably as
the home of the nine British families documented
on the estate by Pynnar. There are no visible 17th-
century remains in the village.

FER 191:105
Hill 1877, 498

**338   DERRYGONNELLY: 211871 352475
      HOUSE AND BAWN**

The former site of the house of Sir John Dunbar,
which was recorded by the various 17th-century
surveys but since lost, has been re-discovered using
geophysical survey. When Bodley's survey was
conducted in 1613, a house had been built and a bawn
was in the early stages of construction. Pynnar found
the bawn complete and measuring 80ft by 45ft. The
1622 survey measured the bawn at 90ft by 42ft, with
three thatched and inhabitable flankers. Two houses
were described in the bawn in 1622: a single-storeyed
stone house – perhaps the dwelling described by
Bodley, and a two-and-a-half storey timber house.
At least one of the houses survived until the late 17th
century, although nothing remains above ground.

The location was discovered by geophysical
survey in 2005, undertaken in advance of a proposed
housing development. This revealed traces of a
rectangular bawn, with a large flanker at its south-
western corner, and various other internal features
that presumably relate to the buildings within.

FER 191:103
Hill 1877, 306 and 498–499; Trimble 1919, 316–317;
Hist. MSS Comm. 1947, 169; Ó Gallachair 1958, 310;
Waterman 1971; Johnston 1976, 182–183; Unpublished
geophysical survey notes in SMR file

339   DERRYGONNELLY: MILL   211900 352100

This is the approximate site of two water mills
noted by Pynnar. The author of the *Montgomery
Manuscripts*, who visited the site in 1696, stated that
one of the mills was for corn, the other a tucking
mill. No remains of either structure survive.

FER 191:105
Hill 1869, 389 and 1877, 498

Ardgort (Carrynroe)

There was apparently little progress on this estate,
which consisted of 2000 acres granted to Sir John
Hume in 1611, until visited by Bodley in 1613, who
noted a castle that was complete, a bawn that was in
the process of being built by Scottish workmen (Inv.
340), and the presence of 'above nine score head'
of cattle. Pynnar also referred to the castle, and a
village of twenty-four families (Inv. 341). When Sir
John died in 1639, the estate was inherited by his son,
Sir George Hume. Following the 1641 Rebellion,
it became more closely integrated with the other
proportions belonging to the family, Drumcose and
Moyglass, with the main seat now established at
Castle Hume in Drumcose. In the 18th century, the
lands were passed through marriage into the estate
of the earls of Ely (Hill 1877, 498).

**340   TULLY: CASTLE   212670 356640
      AND BAWN
      Tully Castle**

The well-preserved remains of a fortified house
and bawn built during the 1610s for Sir John Hume
are magnificently sited on the highest point of a
small peninsula overlooking Lough Erne. Pynnar
described the site as:

> …a Bawne of Lime and Stone, 100
> feet square and 14 feet high, having
> four Flankers for the Defence. There
> is also a fair strong Castle, 50 feet
> long and 21 feet broad.

During the 1641 Rebellion, its defences led to it
being used as a place of refuge for British settlers in
the region. Nonetheless, it was attacked and burnt
at Christmas 1641 by Rory Maguire. Eighty men,

women and children were massacred, prompting the site to be abandoned and never restored.

The castle is situated along the northern wall of the bawn. It is two storeys high, with attics, and is a typical T-plan house of Scottish style, having many parallels with Aughentaine Castle, Co Tyrone (Inv. 391) and Castle Balfour (Inv. 250). The main accommodation block is 14.6m by 4.6m internally, orientated east-west, and with a projection to the south that contains the entrance. The walls are of local limestone rubble with sandstone dressings. The ground floor vault appears to have been built using techniques that have been attributed to Irish masons. There are several gun loops on the ground and first floors. The remnants of the bawn survive to the south of the house.

FER 172:031

Hill 1877, 303, 494 and 499; Trimble 1919, 112 and 132; *PSAMNI* 148; Ó Gallachair 1958, 309; Waterman 1959b, 123–126; Johnston 1978, 369 and 1980a; Day and McWilliams 1992b, 75

**341   DRUMMENAGH BEG: 211320 355730
      SETTLEMENT
      Church Hill**

An area of historical and archaeological potential lies within the plantation settlement at Church Hill, although there are no upstanding 17th-century structures, and an archaeological evaluation carried out nearby in 2010 did not produce anything of significance. The fragmentary remains of a small, nearly square building, with sides measuring 5m in length, are probably a church or stone tower. The building is enclosed within a square area defined by a bank with an inner and outer ditch, though the outer ditch may be modern. The interior is divided into several areas by narrow, low banks.

Fig. 4.33 Front façade of Tully Castle.

FER 172:034 and FER 172:053
Hill 1877, 303, 494 and 499; Lowry-Corry 1919, 45–46; Davies 1941e, 140–141; Ó Gallachair 1958, 309; Sloan 2010

Enniskillen

The town of Enniskillen is situated on the River Erne, between the Upper and Lower loughs. This is a highly strategic position, not only for controlling the Co. Fermanagh region, but also as one of the main points of entry into Ulster from Connaught. From the early 14th century onwards, the region was dominated by the Maguire family, whose various rivalries with the O'Neills and the O'Donnells led to the building of several defensive structures (e.g. Inv. 345) and castles. The castle at Enniskillen (Inv. 343) is one such structure, originally built in the 15th century. The strategic importance of the locality resulted in focused efforts to build a plantation town there (Inv. 342), although initially other locations were considered, such as Lisgoole, situated upstream.

**342   ENNISKILLEN: 223200 344300
        SETTLEMENT**

The town of Enniskillen is possibly the best documented of all the plantation settlements in the county, but its growth in the 18th century has effectively destroyed all traces of its early 17th century origins, aside from the general position and layout of the town, along with the remains of an earthwork fortification (Inv. 345).

FER 211:083
Lewis 1837, I, 605–607; Dundas 1913, 7; Trimble 1919, 161–199; Dixon 1973, 5–6; Johnston 1976, 126–127; Day and McWilliams 1990d, 50–64

343   ENNISKILLEN: CASTLE   223150 344220

Enniskillen Castle was originally a keep within a small bawn that was built by the Maguires in the 15th century, a layout typical of Irish medieval tower houses. The castle was captured from the Maguires in 1594 by Captain John Dowdall (an event recorded on a pictorial map by John Thomas), though it was later besieged and recaptured. In 1602, it was damaged by Cuconnacht Maguire, thereby denying a military base to encroaching English armies. At the time of the Plantation therefore, the castle would have been in a highly ruinous state, as illustrated in a pictorial view of 1611. It was rebuilt between 1613 and 1619 by William Cole, who was appointed (in addition to the grant of his estate at Cornegrade) provost of the town and constable of the Royal Fort, and expressly tasked with the castle's repair. According to Carew, Cole re-built the keep, built a timber house beside it, extended or re-built the bawn to 26 feet in height, and added the Watergate Tower. The castle was attacked by Rory Maguire during the 1641 Rebellion, and besieged by the Jacobites in 1689, but withstood these attacks. The castle was being used as a constabulary depot by the 18th century, when efforts were made to repair the buildings and to build new fortifications on the western bank of the river. The site remained in military possession until 1950, and is now the Fermanagh County Museum.

The castle is situated on Castle Island in the River Erne, at the edge of the town. There are two plantation-period buildings, the keep and the Watergate Tower. The original configuration of the bawn does not survive, nor does Cole's house. The keep is a three-storey, rectangular building, with a pronounced base batter. The curtain wall has been enveloped within two ranges of Georgian barracks to the north and west, but remains freestanding to the east where it measures up to 6m in height. The Watergate Tower is a three-storey structure, with stepped battlements supported on square corbelling and is flanked by two corbelled, round turrets, roofed with conical stone caps. These features are typical of Scottish masonry and architectural traditions, and may well have been the work of the same individuals who created Monea Castle (Inv. 327) and Castle Balfour (Inv. 250).

Excavations within the castle grounds to the

Fig. 4.34 Enniskillen Castle was a Maguire Castle that was rebuilt by William Cole between 1613 and 1619. One of the new additions was the Watergate Tower, a three storey tower embellished with conical-roofed turrets that are corbelled out from the wall face.

east of the keep have revealed a ditch thought to be contemporary with the early 17th-century phase of building at the site. The ditch was essentially the enlargement of a natural stream bed, and further enhanced the defensive attributes of the site.

FER 211:039
Hill 1877, 481; Trimble 1919, 59–68, 192–193 and 271–274; *PSAMNI* 162; Jope 1951, 1953b and 1960; Johnston 1976, 159–160 and 1980a; Day and McWilliams 1990d, 50–51; Halpin 1990; Reeves-Smyth 2014, 335–340

344   ENNISKILLEN: **223780 343960**
         FORTIFICATION

A series of fortifications built by the Maguires are shown on a siege map of 1594, where a row of stakes – a salmon weir – connecting *Innis Ceithleann* to the mainland are depicted. Nothing visible remains of the fortifications, but it is possible that the stakes associated with the weir may lie within the riverine deposits.

FER 211:114
'Plat of the fort of Enniskillin, showing Captain Bingham's Camp', 1594 (NA MPF 1/80); Dunlop 1905, 328; Swift 1999, 47

345   ENNISKILLEN: **223168 343981**
EARTHWORK
The Sconce

This site is marked as a 'sconce' on all OS six-inch maps, apart from the 1st edition from 1835. It consists of an embankment along the River Erne, topped by a long, low mound. According to unpublished notes on file with the DfC:HED, in 1974, the eastern part of the embankment was truncated to make way for playing fields. The remains today consist of a bank of earth and stone 50m long, 2m high and 8m wide, running north-south.

FER 211:040

OS Revision Name Book 1857, 9; Trimble 1919, 61–62; *PSAMNI* 163; Rogers 1967b, 114

346   ENNISKILLEN: CHURCH   **223420 344250**
AND GRAVEYARD
Saint Macartin's Cathedral

Enniskillen Church was built around 1627. It was replaced in 1842 by Saint Macartin's Cathedral, a building in the gothic revivalist style, although the original 17th-century tower was left intact, with a further 4m of masonry added, and a spire 26m high put on top. The church is located on the higher of two hills on the island of Enniskillen, and a date stone above the main entrance to the church is inscribed with the year 1637. The interior eastern wall of the tower contains the remains of an earlier, possibly 17th-century entrance, although this was filled in and remodelled during the rebuilding work. Mounted on the western wall of the nave is a stone known as the 'Pokrich Stone', which bears the date 1628, and was originally in the graveyard to the north of the church, before being moved inside. The Cole family crypt, which may be an original 17th-century feature, lies beneath the cathedral, its long entrance passageway positioned on the north side of the exterior.

FER 211:086

Johnston 1976, 140 and 145; Day and McWilliams 1992b, 53–54

Fig. 4.35 1637 datestone above main entrance to Saint Macartin's Cathedral.

Other sites in Magheraboy

347   GARRISON: SETTLEMENT   **194200 351800**

The town of Garrison was the site of an ironworks founded by Sir John Hume shortly after 1611, which employed 100 men, and was destroyed in 1641. The town was not, however, situated on lands that were part of any grant, and there are no surviving 17th-century buildings or other features.

FER 189:010

McCracken 1957, 129; Johnston 1976, 128

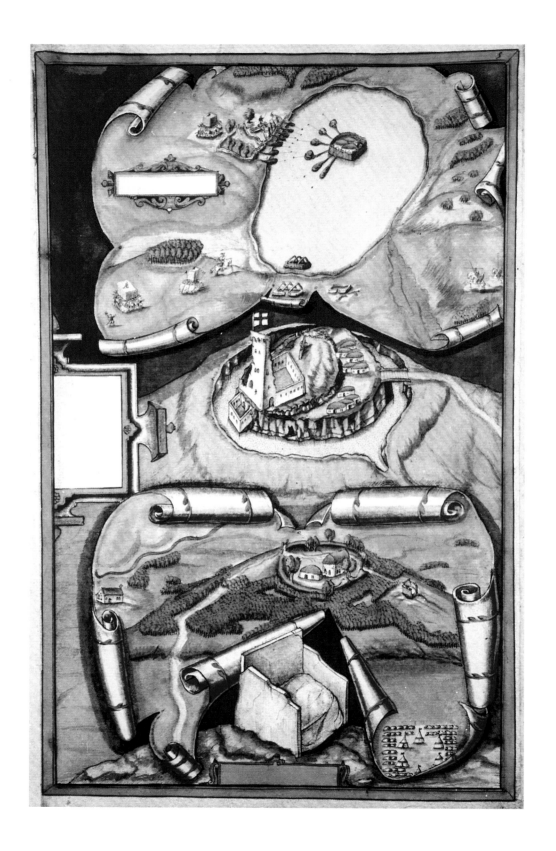

200

Chapter 5
County Tyrone

Introduction

Co. Tyrone was the centre of one the most powerful lordships in Gaelic Ireland, the earldom of Tyrone, with the O'Neills holding sway here since early medieval times. Following the Nine Years' War and the Flight of the Earls, the extensive estates of the earl of Tyrone were confiscated and apportioned to various English and Scottish landlords, as well as Gaelic Irish landlords who were considered deserving of a place in the new order. A sign of the new dispensation was a grant to Robert Lindsey, a Scottish undertaker, of the ancient inauguration site of the O'Neills at Tullaghoge – a large early medieval rath. Indeed, the chief castle of the earl at Dungannon was granted to Sir Arthur Chichester, the Lord Deputy of Ireland. Among the other new landowners were Sir George Hamilton whose estate was centred at Derrywoone, Sir Robert Newcomen in Newtownstewart, Sir Thomas Ridgeway in Augher, Sir Richard Wingfield in Benburb and Sir John Davies, who built not one but two castles – Castle Curlews and Castlederg. A number of native landowners were also granted lands, the most significant of whom was Turlough McArt O'Neill who was from Strabane originally, and who was allocated Castletown, just to the north of Omagh.

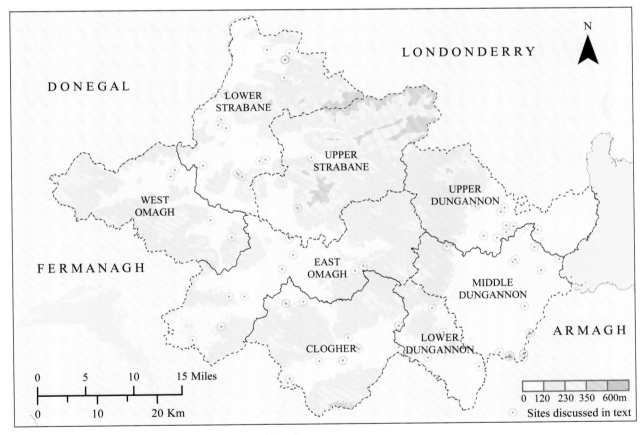

Fig. 5.1 Map of Co. Tyrone showing the baronies within the county.

The county has a number of fortified houses that survive from this period, their unique plans and overall appearance determined by the personal tastes of their owners. Castle Curlews possesses a bay window in each of its surviving exterior walls, while Derrywoone Castle is an L-plan house with a Scottish-style turret corbelled out from the building. Derrywoone was one of the sites excavated as part of the Ulster Scots Archaeological Project, the work revealing traces of the bawn that once would have protected the residence. Another fine example of élite architecture in the county is Newtownstewart Castle, the partial remains of which comprise a substantial building with crow-stepped gables and one surviving elaborate brick chimneystack. At Castlecaulfield are the ruins of a U-plan house with a gatehouse abutting onto it. Spur Royal Castle (otherwise known as Augher Fort) is a square tower with triangular bays that project from the middle of each side. Roughan Castle is also a square tower, though this time with round towers projecting from each corner. More militaristic in purpose is Mountjoy Castle built close to the western shore of Lough Neagh, and consisting of a central tower with large corner towers furnished with many gun loops.

Under the plantation scheme, new market towns and villages were established across the county, including Strabane, Newtownstewart, Fivemiletown and Augher, though nothing remains of the original houses erected at that time. Pre-existing church buildings were taken over by the settlers, with historical evidence suggesting the refurbishment of certain churches including Ballyclog Old Church in 1622, Clogher Cathedral in 1628 and Fintona Old Church after 1641. In terms of upstanding remains, Drumragh Church possesses a door decorated with moulding that may be 17th-century or earlier, while the ruins of Kildress Church, built in 1622, exhibit decorative window lights. One of the best-preserved plantation-period churches to be found in Ulster is St. Patrick's Church in Benburb. Still in use, this is a rectangular stone building, embellished with buttresses and lit by square-hooded, segmental-headed windows along the side walls and a large altar window decorated with tracery.

Barony of Strabane (Scottish undertakers)

Strabane and Dunnalong

James Hamilton, 1st earl of Abercorn, was granted two estates in the barony of Strabane in 1610. Hamilton was from a prominent family of Lowland Scottish Roman Catholic nobles and (like his namesake in Co. Down) had been a close ally of King James I. The 1st earl died in 1618 and was succeeded by his son, also called James. The lesser of the two estates, named 'Strabane' after the barony and its principal town (Inv. 349), was 1,000 acres in extent. Carew noted that several large timber houses had been built, together with a court, a brew house and 60 houses 'of fair coples' (Hill 1877, 527). Materials for building a stone castle had been prepared, and 120 cows had been imported (*ibid.*).

Pynnar recorded in 1619 that the earl's castle then stood complete, surrounded by a town of eighty houses, a school house, a church, and three water-powered corn mills (*ibid.* 527–528). By 1622, twenty new houses had been built along with a sessions house, and a market cross, 'with a strong Roome under it to keep prisoners in', but only one water mill (Treadwell 1964, 140). No archaeological traces of any of these early 17th-century structures have survived.

The earl of Abercorn's other allocation of land was 2,000 acres at Dunnalong, which was separated from the Strabane land holding by the Largie estate, owned by his brother, Sir George Hamilton. Pynnar recorded three or four 'good Houses built of Lime and Stone' (Hill 1877, 527–528), and by 1622 a castle (Inv. 348) had been constructed on the estate (Treadwell 1964, 141)

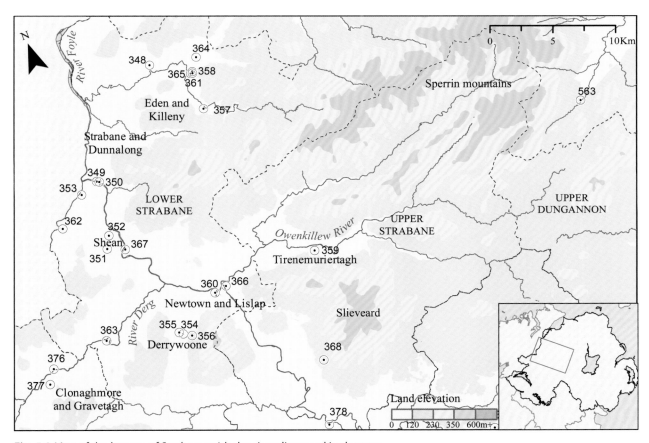

Fig. 5.2 Map of the barony of Strabane with the sites discussed in the text.

348 MOUNTCASTLE: CASTLE AND BAWN 241741 405157
Mount Castle

Mount Castle was built after the time of Pynnar's survey in 1619, but before 1622, as it was first described in the survey of that date. The surveyors described the building as

> . . . a good Castle of stone & lyme, 3 Stories high, but no body at this time dwelling in it; and about it a Bawne 54 foot long, 42 foot broad and 6 foot high, with two open Flanckers, but there is noe Gate to the Bawne

The castle had a relatively short period of use, as it already lay in ruins at the time of the Civil Survey of 1654, having been attacked in 1642. The remains are still visible, but are now located within a farm and are highly fragmentary, while the bawn, no longer standing, probably enclosed the entire plateau upon which the ruins stand. The remains consist of a fragment of walling some 4m high, topped by a fine, corbelled-out turret. This feature resembles the stairway at Derrywoone Castle, and is typical of Scottish architecture in the early 17th century. Running eastwards from the turret is a stone wall, which includes the remains of a chimney and a possible oven feature. According to local tradition, the lime mortar for the castle was mixed with cows' blood, rendering it particularly hard.

TYR 002:003

Hill 1877, 181, 288 and 529; Davies 1938a, 215–216; *PSAMNI* 214; Jope 1951, 43; Treadwell 1964, 141; Day and McWilliams 1990e, 92

349 STRABANE: SETTLEMENT 234500 397600

Strabane was a relatively large plantation town, and indeed had been a focus of settlement since early medieval times. Carew's survey stated that once the earl of Abercorn had taken possession, several large timber houses had been built, arranged around a courtyard that also included a 'great brew house'.

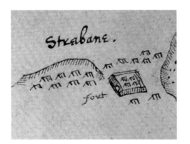

Fig. 5.3 Extract from the 1601 map by Robert Ashby of the Foyle Valley and Lough Swilly depicting a fort at Strabane.

It noted also that some twenty-eight timber-built houses had been erected in the town over the year preceding his 1611 survey, with a further thirty-two built before that time. Bodley's survey in 1613 described a prosperous town of merchants, tradesmen and cottagers, and a similar description was given by Pynnar in 1619, who added that a castle (see Inv. 350) and a stone-built school house had been erected, and that a church was being built, although work had paused since the death of the 1st earl in 1618. Each house in the town, which numbered fifty-three in 1619, was set within a garden plot. By the time of the 1622 survey, the settlement had grown to include 100 households, some of them living in stone-built houses. The church was apparently finished also, as was a market house, a session's house and dungeon, a water mill, and a bridge over the River Mourne.

There is no record of any archaeological discoveries relating to this period, perhaps because timber – which does not tend to survive well compared to stone or brick – was clearly the preferred building material there during the opening years of the Plantation. Furthermore, centuries of redevelopment would seem to have obliterated the early features.

TYR 005:024

Lewis 1837, II, 575–576; Hill 1877, 527–528; Camblin 1951, 20–21, 35, 50; Treadwell 1964, 140–154; Hunter 1982, 29; Robinson 1984, 208 and 221

350 STRABANE: CASTLE 234700 397500

The location of the earl of Abercorn's castle at Strabane is unknown. On a map of the Foyle valley drawn *c.* 1600, showing Docwra's fortifications in 'the Derrie', a 'fort' is depicted surrounded by the settlement 'Strabane'. A castle is shown on

Bodley's baronial map of 1609, near the confluence of the Mourne and Foyle rivers, which is probably a fortification erected by the O'Neills in the 15th or 16th centuries. It would seem likely this structure was re-used at the time of the Plantation and, if so, it was almost certainly expanded or re-edified, as Carew reported that the earl was 'preparing materials for building a fair castle and a bawn'. Pynnar described 'a very strong and fair Castle, but no bawne'. In 1641, Strabane was besieged and the castle was surrendered to Sir Phelim O'Neill, who was, in turn, driven out after only three days of occupation. Although the castle cannot be located, it is remembered by the street names 'Castle Place' and 'Castle Street'.

TYR 005:025 and TYR 005:019

Bodley Map of 'Parte of ye Baronie of Strabane', 1609 (NA MPF 1/48); 'Loch Swilly and the River Foyle', *c.* 1600 (NA MPF 1/335/1); Lewis 1837, II, 575; Hill 1877, 288–289 and 527–528; Simington 1937, 391; Treadwell 1964, 140; Hunter 1982, 29, 38

Shean

This estate, located to the south of Strabane on the Mourne River, originally belonged to Sir Thomas Boyd, who was granted 2,000 acres in 1610. Carew noted that Boyd had taken up residence on his estate and was engaged with the task of providing building materials (Hill 1877, 527). His occupation did not last long, however, as the estate was taken over by the earl of Abercorn at some point between 1611 and 1619, during which time a castle and bawn were built, and a settlement was established which, over the centuries, evolved into Sion Mills (*ibid.* 529).

351 SEEIN: CASTLE AND BAWN 233400 392125
In 1619, Pynnar described 'a large bawn with four flankers ... also a large strong castle begun and to be finished this summer', but the 1622 survey recorded only one flanker and no castle, and noted that the flanker was small and thatched, and served as the residence for the wife and servants of Mr Robert

Hamilton. The northern, eastern and western sides of a rectangular platform can be discerned here, perhaps indicating the remains of a bawn enclosure or garden terracing associated with 17th-century settlement.

TYR 009:014

Hill 1877, 527, 529; Treadwell 1964, 141

352 LIGGARTOWN: 233900 393100
SETTLEMENT
According to Pynnar, the estate of Shean contained a sizeable settlement of some 100 adult men and their families. Today, the site of the village is within Sion Mills, but there are no archaeological traces.

TYR 010:020

Hill 1877, 529

Largie (Cloghogenal)

The plantation estate of Largie comprised 2000 acres granted in 1610 to Sir George Hamilton, brother of the earl of Abercorn. According to Carew, Hamilton was resident by 1611, having built a bawn and timber house by that time. He brought with him Scottish settlers who had built timber houses, and had livestock – eighty cows and sixteen ponies or 'garrons' (Hill 1877, 527). Pynnar described a village of thirty coupled houses (Inv. 353), situated on a road at a 'convenient place', the word 'couple' meaning a cruck or roof timber that sprang from the ground or from a position in the house wall close to the ground. The 1622 survey referred to the construction of two houses within the bawn flankers, the bawn being the main residence of Sir George and his family when they were in Ireland (Treadwell 1964, 142).

353 CASTLETOWN: 233090 397020
SETTLEMENT
This is the former site of a bawn, a house, and village which, according to Pynnar, was inhabited by folk of 'British birth and descent' living in 'Irish coupled

houses'. This juxtaposition of Irish architecture and British settlers is noteworthy, as timber-framed buildings in English style were the norm in many other plantation settlements. The 1st edition OS six-inch map shows a rectangular hedged enclosure divided by a road, and a cluster of houses at Castletown. This location is now bounded by a modern housing development and the B85 road, with no visible 17th-century remains. An alternative location for the village described by Pynnar is Ballymagorry, to the north of Strabane (grid ref. 236600, 401000).

TYR 004:006

Hill 1877, 527 and 530; Treadwell 1964, 142; Roulston 2005, 181

Derrywoone

Also granted in 1610 to Sir George Hamilton was another estate consisting of 1,000 acres, and encompassing Lough Catherine and Island McHugh. Pynnar described both a bawn and castle (Inv. 354), and a village (Inv. 356) under construction in 1619, with building work still continuing at the time of the 1622 survey (Hill 1877, 530; Treadwell 1964, 142). The estate had a relatively stable population until the 1641 Rebellion, when apparently it was abandoned by the settlers (Robinson 1984, 221).

**354   BARONSCOURT: 236710 383560
      FORTIFIED HOUSE**
      Derrywoone Castle

Derrywoone Castle consists of the remains of a fortified house, situated on a natural rise on the eastern shore of Lough Catherine. Pynnar described a bawn with four flankers, two of which contained lodgings, but with no large house or 'castle' building existing. However, construction of the fortified house itself must have begun shortly thereafter,

Fig. 5.4 Derrywoone Castle is an L-shaped fortified house built by Sir George Hamilton during the years 1619–22.

as the 1622 survey described a 'fair stone howse, 4 stories high, which is almost finished ... the house takes up almost the full Bawne'. The Civil Survey of 1654 described the 'castle' as burned by insurgents, presumably in 1641 or shortly thereafter.

The three-storey house with attic is L-shaped, with the southern wing measuring approximately 15m by 7.5m externally, with the surviving portion of western wing (its gable end now mostly in ruins) measuring approximately 8m by 7.5m externally (see plan on page 223). The interior was well-lit and heated, with large rectangular windows and fireplaces evident on the various floors. A flanking tower survives at the north-eastern corner of the house. Although the building is much more

Fig. 5.5 The interior of Derrywoone Castle with large windows and fireplaces evident in the surviving walls.

domestic than defensive in character, the flanking tower contains gun loops. The building contains a fine example of a Scottish-style corbelled staircase, located at the re-entrant angle of the building, the inner corner of the 'L', above an entrance doorway.

Excavations in 2013 revealed traces of the bawn wall described by Pynnar. Its foundation courses consisted of an inner and outer face of rough, undressed stone, in-filled with rubble. Also exposed was cobbling in the interior of the bawn. A pit was discovered partly filled with lime mortar, demonstrating that building materials may have been prepared on site. Other features discovered under the cobbles may pre-date the construction of the plantation buildings.

TYR 017:034

Hill 1877, 291 and 530; Belmore 1903a, 48; Simington 1937, 385; *PSAMNI* 223; Jope 1951, 44; Treadwell 1964, 142; Rowan 1979, 135; F. Walsh *pers. comm.* 2014

355 BARONSCOURT: TOWER HOUSE AND BAWN   236460 383780
Island McHugh

Island McHugh is an early medieval *crannóg* on Lough Catherine with a long history of settlement, originally constructed over a natural island, from which archaeological finds stretch from Neolithic times to recent centuries. The tower house and bawn were probably built by the O'Neills in the 16th century and Davies, who excavated in 1937, was of the opinion that there was a 17th-century phase of occupation. He considered the tower house then to have been thatched (originally, it was slated) and occupied for a relatively short period, perhaps during the troubles of 1641 or later in the century. Various seasons of excavation in the 1930s and 1940s revealed many prehistoric, medieval and 16th-century artefacts, but information on activity during the Plantation and in subsequent decades remains elusive. A substantial portion of the tower house survives but is inaccessible.

TYR 017:033

Belmore 1903a, 37; *PSAMNI* 222–223; Davies 1946; Jope 1951, 44; Ivens *et al.* 1986, 99

Fig. 5.6 Island McHugh is an early medieval crannóg in Lough Catherine that continued in occupation into the 17th century.

356 BALLYRENAN: **237330 383190**
     SETTLEMENT

Pynnar's 1619 survey described a village associated with Derrywoone, as did the Inquisitions held in 1630. However, the settlement apparently did not survive the 1641 Rebellion, as the Civil Survey of 1654 records an estate laid entirely to waste.

TYR 017:073

Hill 1877, 530; Simington 1937, 385

Eden and Killeny

2,000 acres were granted in 1610 to Sir Claude Hamilton, whose brothers Sir George and the earl of Abercorn also held vast areas of neighbouring property (Hill 1877, 288–291). No progress was recorded by Carew, and Sir Claude was dead by the time Pynnar visited in 1619, at which point Sir George was in charge. Pynnar found a bawn and castle (Inv. 358) and six houses located close by (Hill 1877, 527 and 531). The development of the estate is documented differently by various historical accounts – it was described as deserted in 1622, whereas muster rolls record a relatively healthy population of forty-three adult males in 1630 (Treadwell 1964, 142; Robinson 1984, 221).

357 TIRKERNAGHAN: HOUSE   244541 400317
     Silver Brook House

Silver Brook House is an unusual survival of a 17th-century house, which was inhabited until the late 1950s. In all likelihood it was the residence of a freeholder on the Eden and Killeny estate, and two such freeholds were documented by Pynnar. The Civil Survey of 1654 indicates that the 160-acre townland of 'Teirkernovan' (Tirkernaghan) was held at that time by a Scottish settler, Hugh McKey, son of the original steward of the estate, Daniel McKey. The lands were sold shortly thereafter to Lt. John Leslie, whose family continued to occupy the house for many generations. It seems likely the house was built by McKey, its size befitting the steward of a large estate, although a date stone found beside the house, bearing the inscription 'I-L 1673', may represent the Latin initials of John Leslie, suggesting that the latter was responsible for the building of the house, or for its renovation at the very least.

Although currently enclosed by trees and buildings, the house would originally have had views eastwards over the nearby stream of Burn Dennet. The building, two-storeys in height – a third storey having been removed within living memory – is orientated approximately north-east to south-west, with a chimney stack projecting from each gable end. The walls are constructed from random rubble, and have been whitewashed. The most striking feature is the first-floor corner turret, which is supported on stone corbels, and appears to have been truncated with the removal of the third storey. Elsewhere, the fabric of the building has undergone extensive alteration, with sash windows inserted into the front and rear walls. Some blocked-up windows are visible in each of the walls, and smaller blocked-up features may originally have been gun loops. Blocked openings in the external north-eastern gable may indicate that there was once a cellar, now filled in. The façade has also been altered with a doorway inserted at first-floor level, and accessed via external concrete steps.

TYR 006:048

Hill 1877, 527 and 531; Simington 1937, 400

358 DUNNAMANAGH: CASTLE AND BAWN 244580 403380

Dunnamanagh Castle is an 18th-century ruin on the site of a bawn and castle built in or after 1613. It was described as 'both strong and beautiful' by Pynnar. Sir George Hamilton inherited this estate by 1619, and Pynnar noted a small village nearby. The castle was unoccupied at the time of the 1622 survey, and was destroyed during the 1641 Rebellion. After a century of more of abandonment, it was replaced with an 18th-century Gothic-style castle.

Part of the north-western perimeter may be a fragment of the original plantation bawn, but no other 17th-century features are visible.

TYR 003:004

Hill 1877, 292, 527 and 531; *OS Field Report* no. 14; Pringle 1935, 14; Rowan 1979, 271

Tirenemuriertagh

This estate of 1,500 acres was granted to James Haig in 1610, but there is no evidence that he ever came to inspect his proportion (Hill 1877, 292). In 1613 the lands passed to Sir William Stewart who, with financial assistance from the earl of Abercorn and Sir George Hamilton, developed the castle and bawn there (*ibid.* 531). Under its new ownership, the estate was renamed 'Monterlony', and the 1622 survey documented the construction of a bawn and castle, but recorded no other buildings. In 1629, ownership of the estate passed to Sir Henry Titchebourne who previously had leased a part of the estate (*ibid.*).

359 BELTRIM: CASTLE AND BAWN 248870 386360

The ruins of this bawn are incorporated within an enclosed 18th-century garden, on a level area to the east of the 18th-century house; to the north, the ground drops down to the Owenkillew River. The bawn was described by 1622 surveyors, who wrote

> …there is built by Sr George Hamilton a Bawne of lyme & stone, 42ft square 7ft high with noe flankers. There is within the Bawne the foundation of a castle 5ft high, but no gates to the Bawne nor any body dwelling there.

Sir George Hamilton's descendants remained in control of the part of the Tirenemuriertagh estate where the bawn stood, although Sir William Stewart and Sir Henry Titchbourne also held property elsewhere on the estate. It is not known why the buildings were never finished.

Elements of the bawn, incorporated into garden walls, survived the building of Beltrim Castle in the 18th century. The shell of one D-shaped flanker, its external side facing southwards, seems to be original, as does the wall that runs northwards from its eastern side.

TYR 018:047

Hill 1877, 292, 527 and 532; Simington 1937, 374; *Hist. MSS Comm.* 1947, 182; Treadwell 1964, 142–143; Rowan 1979, 311–312

Newtown and Lislap

2,000 acres were granted to James Clapham in 1610, on lands surrounding the residence of Sir Turlough Luineach O'Neill (Hill 1877, 289). Carew recorded a muster of settlers with their weapons, noting that no building had been embarked upon. Pynnar described the replacement of the O'Neill castle with Newtownstewart Castle (Inv. 360), along with the establishment of an associated town of fourteen houses, inhabited by English and Scottish settlers. A settlement of similar size was documented by the 1622 survey (Treadwell 1964, 143).

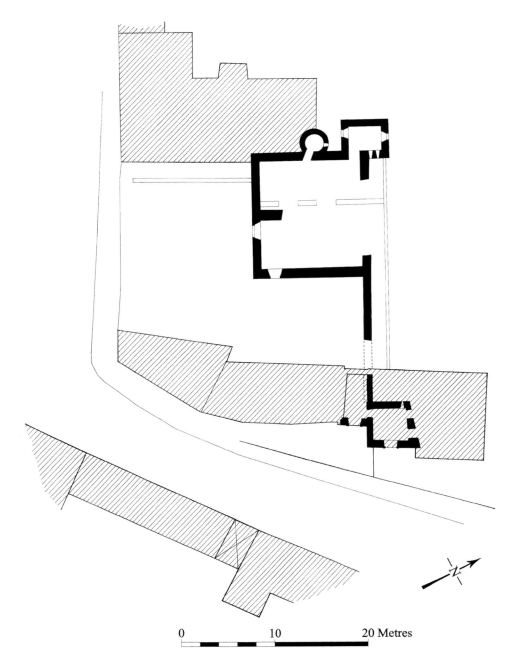

Newtownstewart Castle
Site plan showing newly discovered flanker

Fig. 5.7 Plan of Newtownstewart Castle, a fortified house and bawn with a bastion-shaped flanker enveloped within modern buildings.

360 NEWTOWNSTEWART: 240230 385820
CASTLE

The ruins of Newtownstewart Castle stand on a natural ridge above the floodplain of the River Strule. According to Pynnar, the castle and bawn were built on the site of an older castle by Sir Robert Newcomen, who briefly held the grant for this estate. By 1628 the castle was under the ownership of Sir William Stewart, who came into the estate through marriage. It was burned during the 1641 Rebellion, although this damage was evidently repaired, as James II is reputed to have spent two nights there in 1689, after which he personally ordered the destruction of the castle and the surrounding settlement.

Like many manor houses, the castle has only minor defensive features. The upstanding remains, approximately square in plan with each side 12.5m long, consist of three storeys and a basement. A circular tower, containing a stairs, projects from the

Fig. 5.9 The star-shaped brick chimney that crowns the central gable over the front façade of Newtownstewart Castle.

north-western wall of the building. A square block – a flanker measuring 3.5m internally – projects from the northern corner of the building. A single gun loop is apparent in the basement of this flanker, although two further gun loops and a blocked doorway were discovered here during archaeological excavations in 1999. Poorly-preserved clay flooring of 17th-century date was also found within the flanker during the course of these investigations. A substantial partition wall originally ran through the centre of the building, dividing it into two rectangular spaces on each floor. The unusual triple crow-stepped gables on the south-western wall are striking features, as is the star-shaped brick chimney that crowns the central gable. The north-western wall also survives to its original height of *c.* 14.5m. The walls are mostly built from stone rubble and lime mortar, with moulded sandstone

Fig. 5.8 Front façade of Newtownstewart Castle with its striking crow-stepped gables.

used for window and door dressings, and brick for the fire backings and chimney. These architectural details show a mixture of both English and Scottish masonry influences.

Excavations in 1999 also revealed a 7m length of bawn wall, running from the eastern corner of the castle. Burnt posts, one of which was dated by dendrochronology to 1616–17, were discovered *in situ* at a doorway in the eastern side of the building, matching the date of Newcomen's arrival. Traces of the eastern flanker of the bawn were discovered in 2007, enveloped within more recent buildings, 14m from the main castle.

TYR 017:047

Hill 1877, 280–290, 527 and 532–533; Belmore 1903a, 42–43; Moody 1938, 251; *PSAMNI*, 221; Meek and Jope 1958, 109–114; Treadwell 1964, 143; Day and McWilliams 1990e, 6–7; Ó Baoill 1999a and 2005; unpublished notes in the SMR file.

Ballymagoieth

1,000 acres were granted in 1610 to Sir John Drummond, and Carew noted that he had arrived in person, bringing with him a steward and three horses. Pynnar described a bawn of lime and stone with four flankers, and a timber house of cagework built within it. The exact location of the site is unknown, but presumably it was not far from the village of Donemana. Pynnar (Hill 1877, 534) also described a village (Inv. 361), with somewhat unhappy tenants:

> …they came and complained unto me, and said that for these many years they could never get anything from him [Drummond] but Promises'.

However, the estate was described as relatively prosperous in the 1622 survey, and Sir John and Lady Drummond were by then dwelling in a house of clay-and-stone within the bawn (Treadwell 1964, 143).

Fig. 5.10 The interior of Newtownstewart Castle, with partition wall to the left and doors allowing access into the stair turret on the right.

361   CREAGHAN GLEBE: **244750 403500**
     SETTLEMENT

Pynnar noted that Sir John Drummond had established a village a quarter of a mile from his bawn, containing ten houses and a water mill. This location correlates with the village of Donemana, but no obvious 17th-century features are visible there.

TYR 003:021

Hill 1877, 534

Sites on church-owned land in the barony of Strabane

Like many parts of Ulster, large swathes of Strabane were owned by the church in the early 17th century. These lands now contain (in addition to ruins of ancient churches themselves), the sites of various small manors leased to private individuals at the time of the Plantation, but not forming any part of 'official' plantation estates.

362   URNEY: HOUSE   230650 394900

In 1628, the glebe land for the parish of Urney was granted to Isaac Wood with the instruction to build 'a sufficient mansion of stone, thirty feet in length, twenty in height and eighteen in breadth'. This manor is not mentioned in the 1654 Civil Survey, but may lie on or near the location of the present-day Urney House.

> HB10/08/006
>
> Morrin 1863, 177; Simington 1937, 408

363   SCARVAGHERIN: CHURCH   230800 385130
AND GRAVEYARD

Local accounts regard this former church site as being founded by the Franciscan order around 1456. The partial remains of a church building are still visible, although only a short length of the northern wall survives. The church was contained within a parcel of 120 acres of abbey land in the parish of Ardstraw granted before 1654 to Sir Alexander Stewart, and may have been in use during plantation times, although this is not certain.

> TYR 016:044
>
> *PSAMNI* 220–221; Gwynn and Hadcock 1970, 274; Day and McWilliams 1990e, 9–10

364   BUNOWEN: CHURCH   245430 404520
AND GRAVEYARD

The ruins of a church and graveyard are located on the edge of a rise that drops south towards a stream known as Altinaghree Burn. According to the Civil

Fig. 5.11 The remains of Bunowen Church.

Survey of 1654, the 270 acres surrounding this church in the parish of Donoghkid (Donaghedy) were at that time leased by the Bishop of Derry to the Catholic Scottish planter Sir George Hamilton, who in turn had mortgaged the land to an Irishman, Patrick O'Devin.

The church appears to have been built on the platform of an earlier structure, although its date, or indeed that of the upstanding ruins, is not known. The church, measuring 19m east-west by 7.3m north-south, consists of the gable ends, which are in a fair state of preservation, and the remnants of the northern and southern side walls. The western gable-end appears to survive to its full height of approximately 7m, but the eastern gable is less well-preserved and is obscured by vegetation. A small window in the western gable is possibly of 17th-century date. The church is situated in a roughly rectangular graveyard with many 19th and 20th-century headstones evident, along with earlier examples which are lying flat or near buried.

> TYR 003:006
>
> Bodley Map of 'Parte of ye Baronie of Strabane', 1609 (NA MPF 1/48); *OS Field Report* no. 11; Reeves 1850, 70 and 73; Leslie 1937, 190–194; *PSAMNI* 214; Hamlin 2008, 380

365   CREAGHAN GLEBE: HOUSE   244720 403370

In 1628, glebe land for the parish of Donaghedy was granted to Robert Semphill with the instruction to build a 'sufficient mansion of stone, thirty feet in length, twenty in height and eighteen in breadth'. An 18th-century house, Earl's Gift Rectory (originally a glebe house for the nearby parish church), may be the site of Semphill's manor, although there are no 17th-century features or structures visible. A slightly raised earthen platform in woods adjacent to this location (grid ref. 244750, 403400) is another possible location.

HB10/09/002

Morrin 1863, 177

366   MOYLE GLEBE: HOUSE   241240 386040

In 1628, glebe land in the parish of Bodony was granted to Dr John Richardson with the instruction to build a house, although this was not accounted for in the 1654 Civil Survey. The glebe house here became known as 'Castle Moyle', and is shown on the 1st edition OS six-inch map, although it is not known whether there is a direct connection with any plantation-period development.

TYR 017:074

Morrin 1863, 176; Simington 1937, 407

367   CAMUS: CHURCH   234730 391600
AND GRAVEYARD

The remains of a church and graveyard in the parish of Camus, the history of which is obscure, are situated on See lands leased during the Plantation to Sir Claude Hamilton, the original grantee of Eden and Killiny. It may have been a medieval parish and, according to Hamlin, one 19th-century account claimed that it was destroyed during the 1641 Rebellion. The graveyard has been cut through by the construction of a now-disused railway line, and the church itself now stands alone, with the surrounding land having been ploughed up to the edges of its walls on three sides. The ruins, measuring 20m east-west by 6m north-south internally, consist of an eastern gable wall that survives to almost its full height. The northern and southern side walls are also present, although these appear to have been rebuilt at some point. The remainder of the graveyard survives further to the west, enclosed within a stone wall.

TYR 010:007

Reeves 1850, 131; Leslie 1937, 136–137; Davies 1941b, 44; *PSAMNI* 216; Hamlin 2008, 369

368   ERGANAGH GLEBE: HOUSE   246500 377750

This is the probable site for a house associated with glebe land for the parish of Cappagh. In 1628 these lands were granted to Jervis Walker with the instruction that he was to build: '... a sufficient mansion of stone...'. The OS six-inch maps reveal that the 19th-century rectory here replaced an earlier building, which may have been Walker's house, or a building associated with it. The surrounding area is now occupied by modern houses.

HB11/16/001

Morrin 1863, 176–177.

Barony of Omagh (English undertakers)

Finagh and Rarone

3,000 acres were granted in 1610–11 to George Tuchet, Lord Audley and his wife Elizabeth. The history of this huge estate is rather complex, as ownership changed several times, all without much development taking place in terms of building. When Lord Audley died in 1616 (by then elevated to the earldom of Castlehaven) the same estate was revalued at 11,500 acres. Bodley, Pynnar and the 1622 surveys all failed to record any structures as having been built there. Elizabeth's second husband Sir Pierce Crosby forfeited the estate in 1632 for not meeting the terms of the Plantation, although progress must have been made at some point as the Civil Survey of 1654 recorded the foundations of a bawn (Inv. 370), and the remains of Sixmilecross (Inv. 369), which had been established as a village on the estate, but was destroyed in 1641.

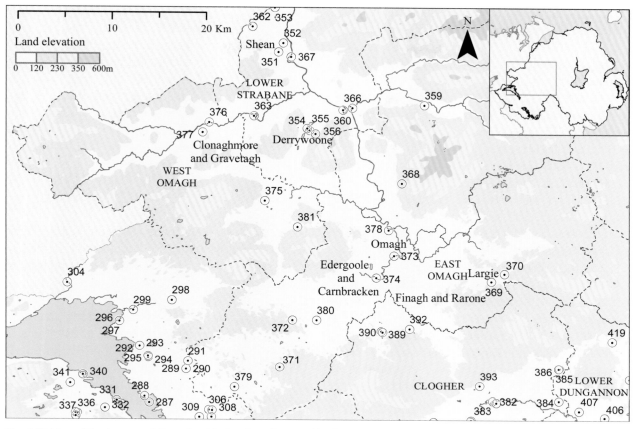

Fig. 5.12 Map of the barony of Omagh with the sites discussed in the text.

369   KILCAM: SETTLEMENT   256000 367000

Two houses, or one house and a mill, are marked on the Down Survey barony map of Omagh and labelled 'The 6 mile cross'. This is likely to be the village established in association with the bawn at Cloghfin or Bawnstown (Inv. 370). The village was founded in 1634, although it did not survive the 1641 Rebellion intact, as the 1654 Civil Survey stated that:

Fig. 5.13 Extract from the Down Survey barony map of Omagh depicting two houses labelled 'The 6 mile cross'.

ye River of Cooleigh [Cloghfin] wch had formerly a bridge over it, but now not any, there was a village formerly in the middle of it but now wast[e]

Surviving 17th-century remains or archaeological features have yet to be discovered.

TYR 044:059

Down Survey barony map of Omagh (TCD); Simington 1937, 330–332; McCusker 1982, 455–501

370   CLOGHFIN: BAWN   257380 367850

The bawn in the Finagh and Rarone estate was not recorded in any of the official surveys of the Ulster Plantation, but is mentioned in the Civil Survey of 1654, at which point it was described as a 'foundation', with the nearby village destroyed.

Presumably, it was constructed after 1622, perhaps in the 1630s, and damaged or demolished following the 1641 Rebellion.

The remains survived until the early 20th century as a short length of wall. Like several other sites in Cos Tyrone and Armagh, the bawn was constructed on an early medieval rath. However, the site has since been levelled, destroying all surface traces of both monuments.

TYR 044:028

OS Field Report no. 228; Simington 1937, 330–332

371 CASTLEMERVYN DEMESNE: 233531 357558 HOUSE AND BAWN
Trillick Castle

Trillick Castle is a fortified house, built by Captain James Mervyn between 1622 and 1630 on the southern slope of a small river valley. The ruins consist of the western gable end of a building, two storeys in height and topped by a tall chimney stack. The stack serves a fireplace and oven at ground-floor level (suggesting a kitchen), and a fireplace on the first-floor level. Fragments of the other walls exist; in the southern wall there is a window embrasure at ground-floor level, and in the northern wall some red brick, possibly the remains of a doorway. The exterior of the southern wall also has areas of surviving lime render. Although no remains survive of a bawn, if there was such an enclosure associated with the house, it is likely to be in or around the yard of the dairy farm to the south of the ruins. A geophysical survey carried out in 2008 did not detect any features from the plantation period.

TYR 049:002

Hill 1877, 535–537; Belmore 1903a, 56; M'Enery 1910, 58; Simington 1937; *Hist. MSS Comm.* 1947, 180; *PSAMNI* 246; McGranaghan and McHugh 2008

372 DROMORE: CHURCH AND 234900 362750 GRAVEYARD
Dromore Old Church

The substantial remains of a ruined church are situated on the edge of a rocky outcrop above the village of

Fig. 5.14 The western gable end of Trillick Castle crowned with a tall chimney stack that serves a fireplace and oven on the ground floor, as well as another fireplace on the first floor.

Dromore. Sixteenth-century records mention the church, and it is depicted on the Bodley map of 1609 on the edge of lands granted the following year to the Lord Audley. It was described as ruinous in the 1622 survey. When James Mervyn was granted these lands in 1622, the church may have been rebuilt, as it was subsequently burned during the 1641 Rebellion. It was not completely destroyed, however, as it was recorded as a roofed building on the Down Survey parish map of 'Drummoore and Kilskerry', drawn in the mid-1650s. The church was then rebuilt in the late 17th century, and was abandoned in 1846.

The ruins presumably date to the final, late 17th-century phase of building, although it is also probable that the foundations of the earlier church were re-used. The remains consist of a long nave, 20.4m east-west by 7.4m north-south externally, and a southern transept 7.0m square externally, with the eastern and western gable-ends surviving to their full height. There is an entrance in the western end of the northern wall, accessed via a narrow sunken path. The graveyard is enclosed by a stone wall, and contains memorial stones from the late 17th century onwards.

Excavations in 1991 uncovered burials within the church, and a grave slab dated 1674 for Elizabeth Mervyn, wife of Sir Henry Mervyn of Trillick, thus linking the church at Dromore with the estate centred upon Trillick Castle.

TYR 050:021

Down Survey parish map of Drummoore and Kilskerry (PRONI D597); Leslie 1929, 178; *PSAMNI* 246–247; Halpin 1991; Hamlin 2008, 383

373 DRUMRAGH (CALDWELL): 245680 369800 CHURCH AND GRAVEYARD
Drumragh Church

Drumragh Church is built on the site of a medieval parish church, and appears on the Bodley map of 1609. It is not entirely clear whether the lands that immediately surround the church were part of the Finagh and Rarone estate, or remained under

Fig. 5.15 Remains of Drumragh Church.

church control, as the Bishop of Derry leased nearly 1,000 acres to English planters from 1637 onwards.

The church, which is in a fair condition, although covered by vegetation, occupies a much higher position than the surrounding graveyard. The doorway incorporates pieces of a moulded surround which may be of 17th century date or earlier. The graveyard contains several early 18th-century memorial stones. There is no evidence for an enclosure.

TYR 043:036

Milligan 1903, 53–54; Leslie 1937, 212; *PSAMNI* 243; Gwynn and Hadcock 1970, 382; Day and McWilliams 1990e, 108; Hamlin 2008, 384

Brad

In 1610–11, Sir Marvin Tuchet, eldest son of Lord Audley, was granted 2,000 acres, though nothing was built according to the official surveys. Tuchet became the 2nd earl of Castlehaven on his father's death in 1616, although his life was beset with problems, culminating in his execution in London in 1631 for alleged sexual crimes (Herrup 1999, 99–115). The estate was transferred to Captain James Mervyn, along with those at Fentonagh, Edergoole and Carnbracken, at some time between 1620 and 1632 (Hill 1877, 536). There are no known archaeological sites of the plantation period on this proportion.

Fentonagh

Sir Ferdinand Tuchet, second son of Lord Audley, was granted 2,000 acres in 1610–11, forming an estate that should not be confused with one of the same name in the barony of Clogher. The 1622 survey recorded a castle with a bawn of lime and stone, within which William Hamilton, the provost of Strabane, was living. The bawn was 99ft long, 81ft broad and 9ft high, with three flankers, within one of which a minister and his family were living (Hill 1877, 536), but its location is not known.

Edergoole and Carnbracken

The plantation estate at Edergoole and Carnbracken has a complex history – Edward Blunt was granted 2,000 acres there in 1610–11. According to Pynnar, George Tuchet, the 1st earl of Castlehaven, had aborted an attempt to build a large house on the property, and instead finished one 'half so great', a three-storey house (Hill 1877, 536–537). The 1622 survey described a cross-shaped house on site, though only two storeys in height, surrounded by a stone-built bawn (Treadwell 1964, 144). The estate was then acquired by Sir Audley Mervyn, who was recorded as the owner of the manor house of Ballynahatty (Inv. 374) in the Civil Survey of 1654 (Simington 1937, 334).

374   BALLYNAHATTY: CASTLE AND BAWN   243800 367400

The *OS Memoirs* record the site of the castle of Sir Audley Mervyn as being located close to the village of Ballynahatty. Local tradition names a steep rise to the north-east of Ballynahatty Presbyterian Church as 'Castle Hill'. However, there are no surface indications of any structures in this location.

TYR 042:027

Hill 1877, 270 and 536; Simington 1937, 334; Treadwell 1964, 144; Day and McWilliams 1990e, 12

Clonaghmore and Gravetagh

A key figure in the Plantation of Ulster, Sir John Davies, was granted 2,000 acres in the barony of Omagh in 1610 (Hill 1877, 143, 271). On his estate he built two castles, Castle Curlews (Inv. 375) and Castlederg (Inv. 376), both of which were recorded by Pynnar (*ibid.* 537). There is however very little evidence that he ever took up permanent residence in either structure. The Down Survey recorded a third castle, Castlegore (Inv. 377), archaeological evidence of which has yet to be uncovered. Pynnar recorded sixteen families of British origin on the estate, the number of which had risen to twenty-four by 1622 (Robinson 1984, 220).

375   KIRLISH: FORTIFIED HOUSE AND BAWN   231960 375800
Castle Curlews

Castle Curlews is a fortified house situated on a ridge with excellent views over the surrounding country, and until recently, was heavily overgrown. The building is the more domestic in appearance of the two 'castles' built by Davies on his estate, the other being Castlederg Castle (Inv. 376). Built shortly after 1611 and occupied until at least 1654, it is now in ruins, having been damaged by stone robbing over the centuries.

The castle is two storeys in height, and the external walls are well preserved, apart from the western side which is represented only by an internal cross-wall structure, beyond which the rest of the building is lost beneath a mound of rubble. The building displays Renaissance influences, as the three surviving walls each contain a bay window, the best-preserved of which is in the south-eastern wall and only paralleled in Ulster at Dunluce Castle (Inv. 87). There are three surviving fireplaces set into the eastern, western and southern walls, along with gun loops at semi-basement level. Contrary to Pynnar's account of the site, there are traces of a flanker and bawn wall surrounding the castle.

Fig. 5.16 Castle Curlews, a 17th-century residence with the remains of a bay window.

A small-scale test excavation in 2007 did not locate any original occupation layers, but did reveal a significant depth of rubble in the interior of the castle.

TYR 033:009

OS Field Report no. 154; Hill 1877, 143, 271 and 537; Belmore 1903a, 53; *PSAMNI* 234; Jope 1960, 104; Waterman 1960, 89–96; Treadwell 1964, 144; McSparron 2007

376   CASTLEDERG: FORTIFIED   226050 384420
HOUSE AND BAWN
Castlederg Castle

The ruins of Castlederg Castle are situated on level ground overlooking a fording point across the River Derg. It was constructed by Sir John Davies (see Inv. 375 above) before 1619 on the site of an earlier castle. Early historical accounts indicate that this was a late medieval castle, probably built by the O'Neills, with ownership changing many times. Archaeological excavations have revealed a tower house, an enclosing ditch, and burials that all pre-date the Plantation. In the 1622 survey, the castle was described as 'a Bawne of stone and lyme, not finished, being 100 foot long, 80 foot broad and 5 foot high, with 3 open Flanckers of the same height with the Wall'.

The surviving remains consist of the northern wall of the bawn and two square flankers in the north-eastern and north-western corners of the same. While the remainder of the bawn only survives as foundations, there are indications that the south-eastern and south-western corners of the bawn were also provided with square flankers. The castle occupied the full length of the northern bawn wall, integrating the two flankers into its floor plan. The eastern gable of the building still survives, and, along with the two square corner turrets, indicates that the building had two floors. The southern façade of the building, which would have faced into the courtyard of the bawn, no longer survives. Access was gained via an entrance in the northern wall, leading into a north-south cross-passage that divided the ground floor into two rooms. The room to the west contains an oven in the northern wall, suggesting that this space served as a kitchen. Several gun loops are present in the walls of the house and flankers.

Archaeological excavations have shown that the castle was built upon the foundations of an earlier, 15th-century tower house and bawn, which was rebuilt and modified during the plantation period. It seems that the castle was added to the northern wall

Fig. 5.17 Aerial view of Castlederg Castle. The fortified house was built by Sir John Davies before 1619, at a fording point across the River Derg.

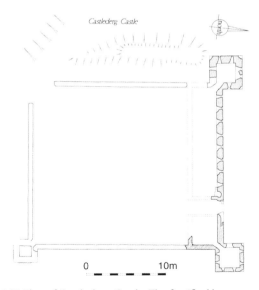

Fig. 5.18 Plan of Castlederg Castle. The fortified house occupied the full length of the northern bawn, integrating the two flankers into its floor plan (after Waterman 1960, Fig. 1).

of the bawn of the tower house, with the enclosing walls strengthened or rebuilt, and the flankers added.

TYR 016:016

Hill 1877, 271; Belmore 1903a, 53; Pringle 1935, 5; Simington 1937, 348; *PSAMNI* 219–292; *Hist. MSS Comm.* 1947, 180–181; Waterman 1960, 89–96; Treadwell 1964, 144; Newman 1991

377   CASTLEGORE: CASTLE   225360 383320

The site of a castle shown on the Down Survey barony map of Omagh is located on the lower slopes of Silver Hill on a prominent terrace, close to Sir John Davies' castle at Castlederg. The townland name 'Castlegore' suggests a castle, but there are no archaeological remains to indicate 17th-century activity here, aside from an inscribed stone in the gable-end of a farm building that reads 'Erected by Edward Edwards 1674'.

TYR 016:006

Down Survey barony map of Omagh (TCD)

Corporate town of Omagh

378   OMAGH: SETTLEMENT   245100 372600
AND FORT

The modern town centre of Omagh contains the site of an artillery fort, 'The Fort of the Omye', built by Edmund Leigh between 1605 and 1610, on lands adjacent to, and formerly owned by, the Franciscan Abbey of Omagh. In addition to the fort, Leigh was granted 330 acres of the surrounding lands. The early 17th-century town developed in the vicinity of the fort. A pictorial map of *c.* 1611 depicts the fort and town in great detail. The fort consisted of a walled enclosure with corner bastions carrying cannon, protected on one side by the River Strule, and on the other sides by a large ditch. A fine manor house and other ancillary buildings occupied the interior of the fort. The town itself consisted of a number of chimneyed houses arranged along a single street, along with a market cross, an inn and a mill house. An O'Neill castle lay in ruins on a rise on the eastern outskirts of the town, overlooking the meeting of

the Camowen and Drumragh tributary rivers. The fort later fell to Sir Phelim O'Neill in 1641, and was occupied and burned by Jacobite forces in 1689. The associated settlement grew very slowly; only twelve households were recorded in 1666. Both the fort and the friary ruins were demolished following a fire that almost completely destroyed the town in 1743.

The exact location of the fort is unknown but it seems to have been near Bell's Bridge, on rising ground on the southern bank of the Strule River. The 17th-century town occupied relatively level ground further to the south, although later development has since obliterated any 17th-century features. Various test excavations have been carried out in the vicinity since 2002, although none have uncovered archaeological remains from the 17th century.

TYR 035:016 and TYR 035:020

The Fort of Omaye [Omagh] in Ulster, c. 1611 (TCD MS 1209/34); Lewis 1837, II, 448–449; Hill 1877, 269 and 534–535; Simington 1937, 330 and 334; Camblin 1951, 56; Gwynn and Hadcock 1970, 273; Rowan 1979, 444–451; Robinson 1984, 161 and 211; Smyth 2006, pl. 2f

Sites on church-owned land in the barony of Omagh

379   DRUMSONNUS: HOUSE   228730 355310

The lands of the Bishop of Raphoe in the parish of Maghericrosse were leased to Andrew Hamilton in 1637. The Down Survey depicts a house in 'Drumsanes' built by Hamilton, which presumably became the site of the modern Drumsonnus House. No 17th-century remains are known to survive at the site above ground.

TYR 056:028

Down Survey parish map of Maghericross and Urney (PRONI D597); Simington 1937, 365

380   KILDRUM: CHURCH AND   237450 362760
GRAVEYARD

A church and graveyard were depicted on Bodley's 1609 map at this approximate location, and aerial photographs reveal that the site is enclosed by two or more concentric, oval earthworks – presumably medieval or earlier in origin. During plantation times, the surrounding lands in the parish of Dromore were leased from the Bishop of Dromore to Archibald Hamilton. The graveyard was used until 1712 and ploughed thereafter, and there are no surface traces of the church or graveyard, aside from a flattened area at the summit of a small glacial knoll called 'Church Hill'.

TYR 050:018

OS Field Report no. 259; Simington 1937, 363; Hamlin 2008, 383

**381 MAGHARENNY: CHURCH   235440 372930
AND GRAVEYARD**
Longfield Parish Church
This is the probable site of the medieval parish church of Longfield. At some point before 1654, the Bishop of Derry leased the surrounding lands, some 360 acres, to an English settler, Lt. Colonel Thomas Newburgh. The church was described as ruinous in 1622, but it may have been repaired during the 17th century or after, although historical sources are confused. It was probably in use until 1803 when a new parish church was built *c.* 500m to the north in the townland of Drumrawn. Its ruins were still upstanding as late as 1857, when the 2nd edition OS six-inch map depicted a rectangular building within an oval enclosure. Upstanding remains of the church do not survive, although there are faint traces of the enclosure in the form of a ploughed-out scarp just above ground level.

TYR 034:001

OS Field Report no. 159; Reeves 1850, 70 and 72; Leslie 1937, 246–248; Hamlin 1971, 82 and 2008, 390

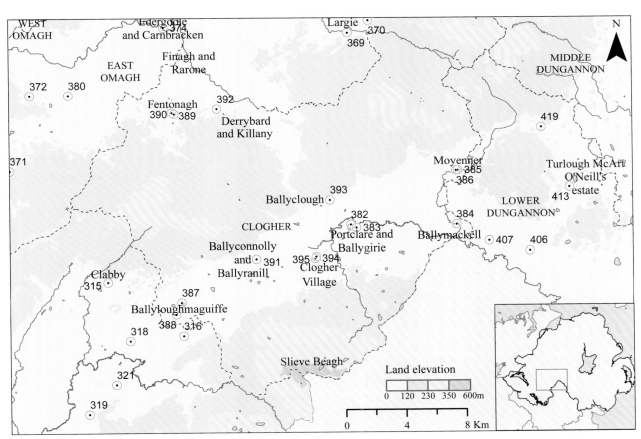

Fig. 5.19 Map of the barony of Clogher with the sites discussed in the text.

Derrywoone Castle (Inv. no. 354)

Derrywoone castle is situated in the Baronscourt estate, four miles to the south-west of Newtownstewart, in undulating wooded landscape. It overlooks Lough Catherine, which contains Island McHugh, a multi-period settlement, the history of which includes an O'Neill tower house that continued in occupation until the early 17th century. Derrywoone was acquired around 1612 by Sir George Hamilton of Greenlaw, a Scottish Catholic landowner. An inquiry into the general progress of the Ulster Plantation in 1619 does not mention a castle as having built here, but by 1622 another survey found that Hamilton had begun to build

> …a fair stone howse, 4 stories high, which is almost finished, and a Bawne of stone and lyme, 90 foot long, 70 foot broad and 14 foot high. The house takes up almost the full Bawne. As soon as it is finished, he [Hamilton] intends (as we are informed) to dwell there himself (Treadwell 1964, 142).

The castle is a fortified house which married defensive concerns with the need to provide comfortable surroundings for Sir George, his family and guests. The building is L-shaped in plan, with a western and southern wing, each of which is single-piled, and two bays in length. The house as a whole stands three-and-a-half storeys high, including the garret space at roof level. The walls are constructed of roughly coursed stone rubble bonded with a lime-based mortar, and the original external render still survives in places. The timber floors within the building were supported by wooden joists, the sockets of which are still evident today, and there was a simple fireplace on each floor. The gable end of the western wing only survives partially to third floor level, while the gable end of the southern wing still stands to its full height. The fireplaces in the southern gable are served by a large, rectilinear chimney embellished with quoin stones and a simple cornice.

At first-floor level, in the re-entrant angle between the two wings, is a corbelled stone turret which contained a stairwell that allowed access to the upper floors. Its appearance, with its carved curvilinear corbels, is directly influenced by the Scottish masonry tradition and can be paralleled at Castle Balfour, Co. Fermanagh (Inv. 250; Jope 1951, 32, and plates 3b and 3d). The turret overlooks the ground floor entrance, its empty embrasure indicating that a round-arched doorway, with a carved stone surround once stood here. A large circular flanker tower stands at the exterior north-eastern angle of the building where the two wings meet, protecting the approaches to the north and east with gun loops on the ground floor as the house was not enclosed by the bawn on this side.

The windows across the whole building are quite large (even in the north-eastern flanker), and are regularly spaced. It has been suggested that they were in fact half glass and half shutter, perhaps with iron grills to provide additional security. Such an arrangement can be seen in Scottish élite residences at the time. The first-floor windows are the largest, indicating that the most important chamber in the household – the great chamber – was located at this floor level. It was common for the most important rooms in such houses to be located at first-floor level, creating the Renaissance inspired ideal of the *piano nobile*, the 'noble floor' where the landlords such as Sir George would hold consort with his family and guests. The great chamber on the first floor was reached by a staircase, traces of which survive as stone steps incorporated into the eastern wall of the southern wing. However, to ascend to the rooms on the upper floors, such as the bed chambers or parlours, one would have to cross the great chamber and gain access via the spiral stairwell within the projecting turret. The more utilitarian rooms such as the kitchen, scullery, buttery and pantry were located on the ground floor, and at Derrywoone the kitchen is clearly indicated by the large fireplace located in the western gable end of the western wing. There is a blocked window in the north-western corner

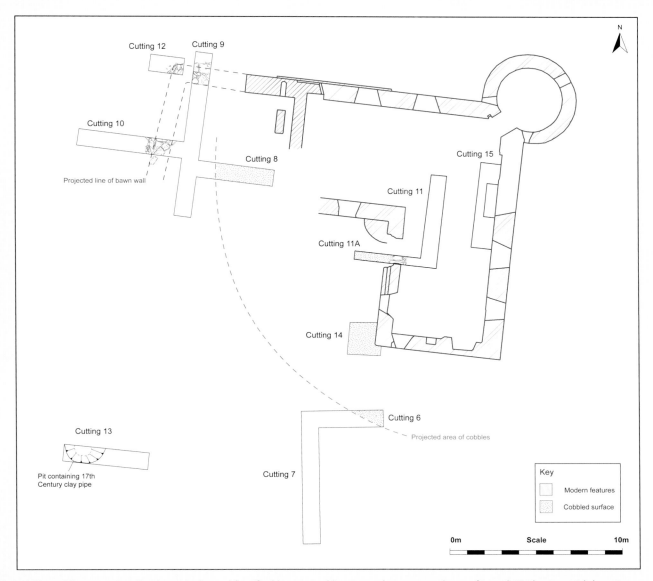

Cutting 12

Cutting 9

Cutting 10

Projected line of bawn wall

Cutting 8

Cutting 15

Cutting 11

Cutting 11A

Cutting 14

Cutting 6

Cutting 13

Projected area of cobbles

Pit containing 17th
Century clay pipe

Cutting 7

Key

Modern features

Cobbled surface

0m   Scale   10m

16 Plan of Derrywoone Castle, an L-shaped fortified house and bawn on the eastern shore of Lough Catherine with locations of excavation cuttings indicated.

of the kitchen through which food waste was probably thrown out, an interpretation given credence by a soil survey that indicated high phosphate readings in its vicinity. Derrywoone Castle obviously had internal partitions to create its various chambers, but no traces of these appear to have survived, either as plaster impressions in the walls, or as wall footings in the ground.

A key aim of the excavation carried out in 2013 was to explore the surroundings to identify potential dwellings or other structures associated with tenants on the estate. The documentary sources indicate that a number of families were settled within the precincts of the castle, though it was not possible to pinpoint the exact locations of their houses. Gradiometry and resistivity surveys were carried out, concentrating on a field to the south-east of the castle, as this was the only available green space in its immediate environs.

17 A turret containing a stairs projects from the re-entrant corner of Derrywoone Castle. The moulded corbelling supporting the turret is a Scottish-influenced architectural feature.

18 Archaeological excavation at Derrywoone Castle in 2013 revealed the foundation levels of the northern and western bawn walls. The walls defined an area 27.4m by 24.0m similar to that recorded in the 1622 survey (90ft by 79ft).

Some potential pits and ditches were identified, and five trench cuttings were opened, but these failed to yield any evidence of tenant housing or other associated features. However, the geophysical anomalies were found to include a backfilled water course and a pathway, both of which are depicted on the 1st edition of the OS six-inch map of the area (Walsh 2016a, 11).

At the castle itself, eleven cuttings were opened up to allow the extent and interior of the bawn to be traced. This was followed up by an investigation of the entrance area and internal ground floor of the fortified house. The foundation levels of the northern and western bawn walls were uncovered, along with the cobbled stone surface of the bawn interior. The walls defined an area (27.4m by 24m) similar to that recorded in the 1622 survey (90ft by 79ft). The foundation of the bawn wall (*c.* 1.5m in width) consisted of an inner and outer line of undressed, rough stone blocks, with an infill of smaller stones. Following the clearance of vegetation from the fortified house, a short section of the actual bawn wall, some 3m high and 1m thick, was found projecting from the north-western corner of the castle. The bawn enclosed a yard, partly covered by a cobbled stone surface, the stones of which were either placed flat or pitched upwards on their sides. Elsewhere, the yard surface consisted of redeposited subsoil clays, hardened by compaction, and small stones. After the castle was abandoned and fell into ruin, the bawn wall was robbed for building material, and rubble started to accrue within the area of the bawn (*ibid.* 17–19).

Excavation inside and outside the fortified house also showed that the formal approach to the ground floor entrance was paved by a cobbled stone surface. The threshold was comprised of large, flat stones, and was basically a continuation of the stone foundation of the building. Inside the house there were no surviving traces of the floor; there was no evidence for cobbling or timber floorboards, though it is most likely that

19 The excavation also revealed that parts of the interior of the bawn were covered by a cobbled stone surface including the approach to the ground floor entrance of the fortified house.

horizontal timbers originally supported floor boards before abandonment. These investigations did however prove that there was no cellar (*ibid.* 24).

The construction of the castle was clearly a conscious replacement of the pre-existing O'Neill lordly residence on nearby Island McHugh. The 1622 survey recorded that a number of British families resided on the estate, including two freeholders, ten leaseholders and six cottagers. The estate was badly damaged during the 1641 Rebellion, and the Civil Survey of 1654 recorded that the castle was in a ruinous state, having been burned by insurgents in the 1640s. Sir George Hamilton died *c.* 1653, and the estate passed to his son James, who died a few years later in 1658 without an heir. Following Restoration, Sir George of Dunnalong, a nephew of Sir George and also a Catholic, acquired Derrywoone in 1667. It has been suggested, however, that the fortified house was not rebuilt as the new landlord lived elsewhere (Roulston 2005, 172). After the death of Sir George in 1679, the estate passed to his Protestant grandson, Captain James Hamilton, who eventually attained the title of 6th earl of Abercorn in 1703 (*ibid.* 172).

Barony of Clogher (English undertakers)

Portclare and Ballygirie

Sir Thomas Ridgeway was granted 2,000 acres in 1610. Carew noted that he had brought twelve carpenters to Ulster, all employed in felling timber destined for the building of tenements (Inv. 383) and a water-mill (Hill 1877, 539). By 1613, a tower house and bawn had been constructed (Inv. 382), while Pynnar described the existence of the village of Augher, which contained fifteen houses. The surveys recorded a population undergoing rapid expansion, rising from eight in 1611 to sixty-five by 1613 (Robinson 1984, 220). In 1617 a licence was granted to Emmanuel Ley and Richard Waltham for the retailing of wine, along with the manufacture and sale of *aqua vitae* or distilled spirits (*Cal. Pat. Rolls Jas I*, 343). The estate was amalgamated with Ballymackell in 1622 following its purchase by Sir James Erskine.

382 CASTLEHILL DEMESNE: 256130 353810
TOWER HOUSE AND BAWN
Spur Royal Castle or Augher Fort

A tower house and bawn were erected by Sir Thomas Ridgeway between 1610 and 1613, and although Bodley described a tower with four storeys, all later surveys and the surviving remains indicate one of three storeys, with a crenellated parapet. An original and very fine doorway can be seen in the eastern wall, and uniquely amongst plantation houses, the building is star-shaped in plan, the square tower having triangular bays that project from the middle of each side. The resulting shape resembles the emblem on the reverse side of the 'spur royal', a Jacobean gold coin. One circular flanker from the bawn survives to the east of the tower.

The castle was unsuccessfully besieged by the forces of Sir Phelim O'Neill and Colonel Rory Maguire in November 1641, but was burnt by Lt. Colonel Thomas Lloyd in 1689, and dismantled thereafter by order of the Irish Parliament. It appears in a 1791 engraving by the antiquarian Francis Grose,

Fig. 5.20 Spur Royal Castle is a tower-house with triangular bays projecting from the middle of each side of the building. It was built by Sir Thomas Ridgeway between 1610 and 1613.

by which stage the bawn had mostly disappeared, although the surviving flanker was depicted with a conical roof. The site was redeveloped between 1827 and 1832, when parts of the old castle were restored and incorporated into a newly built two-storey mansion.

TYR 059:039

Grose 1791, pl. 100; Hill 1877, 53, 145, 264 and 539–540; Marshall 1896, 278; *PSAMNI*, 255; Day and McWilliams 1990e, 48–51

383 AUGHER TENEMENTS: 256500 353600
SETTLEMENT

The site of a village, established in association with Lord Ridgeway's estate at Portclare and Ballygirie.

According to Pynnar it included some fifteen houses, including two that were stone-built, the remainder being of 'Cage work and Couples'. It is unknown whether any archaeological remains of this settlement survive, given subsequent redevelopment in the town.

TYR 059:094

Morrin 1863, 558; Hill 1877, 540

Ballymackell

1,000 acres were granted in 1611 to George Ridgeway, brother of Sir Thomas Ridgeway, later the earl of Londonderry. Bodley recorded that lime had been burnt for the purposes of constructing the bawn (Inv. 384), and that stone had been quarried and 'drawn to the place 300 car load'. Timber had been cut for the construction of a wooden house but, when Pynnar visited in 1619, no such house was reported, and the 1622 survey recorded only the foundations of a house within the bawn. The estate however, as a settlement, was a success, with the population rising steadily between 1611 and 1619 (Robinson 1984, 220). It was renamed 'Thomas-Court' in honour of the earl of Londonderry, and sold to Sir James Erskine in 1622. Erskine also purchased the Portclare and Ballygirie estate, and in 1665 combined all of these lands into the manor of Portclare, which was later renamed 'Favour Royal Estate' (Hill 1877, 541).

384   LISMORE: BAWN   263144 353809
   Favour Royal Bawn

Favour Royal bawn was built in 1611, and in 1619 Pynnar described a 'Bawne of Lyme and Stone, 80ft square, having four Flankers, but no house in it', although subsequently the 1622 survey indicated that a house foundation had been dug. The ruins are located on level ground with good views to the north, east and west and across Ballygawley Water. They consist of a bawn, square in plan and measuring *c*. 24m x 24m, and four surviving circular flanker towers. The flankers are small

Fig. 5.21 Favour Royal Bawn in Lismore with one of the circular flankers visible in the background.

and appear to be purely defensive, not being large enough to accommodate living space. At ground-floor level there are five gun loops in each flanker. The structure is built of coursed, rough-dressed masonry and is preserved best on the south-eastern and south-western sides.

There are no visible remains inside the bawn, although the interior is slightly elevated, perhaps indicative of significant rubble within the bawn.

TYR 059:037

OS Field Report no. 302; Hill 1877, 266–267 and 540–541; Marshall 1930; *PSAMNI* 255; Treadwell 1964, 145; Robinson 1984

Moyenner

1,000 acres were granted to William Turvin in 1611, and by 1613 a large portion of the bawn (Inv. 385) had been constructed (*Hist. MSS Comm.* 1947, 180). The lands were sold to Sir Gerard Lowther in or around 1614, while the bawn was let to a Mr William Pringle who dwelt in a 'poor Cabbin', according to Pynnar (Hill 1877, 541–542). By 1622, William Grimes had possession of the estate and dwelt in a timber house with his family, at which time twenty-six cottagers were noted as being armed with 'pike and shot'.

385 BALLYGAWLEY: HOUSE AND BAWN — 263240 357490
Ballygawley Castle

This bawn was first documented by Bodley, who mentioned that parts of a wall, ten feet high, had been built. Pynnar recorded the presence of a complete bawn with two flankers, while the 1622 survey described the bawn, flankers and a timber house. Nineteenth-century accounts described the castle and bawn as still surviving.

The site is located on a terrace overlooking a steep slope to the north of the Ballygawley Water. An underground barrel vault was once visible, but this has since been covered over. Only two square flanking towers survive at the southern side of the castle site, although these are obscured by dense vegetation.

TYR 059:072

Mason 1819, 156; Lewis 1837, I, 135; Hill 1877, 267, 539–542; Marshall 1930, 76; *Hist. MSS Comm.* 1947, 180; Treadwell 1964, 145

386 BALLYGAWLEY: SETTLEMENT — 263130 357470

This is an area of historical and archaeological interest within the plantation village of Ballygawley. There are no visible remains of structures or features from the settlement, although archaeological remains may survive in those areas not yet impacted by development.

TYR 059:092

Mason 1819, 146–151 and 156–157; Lewis 1837, I, 135; Hill 1877, 267; Marshall 1930, 76; *Hist. MSS Comm.* 1947, 180; Treadwell 1964, 145

Ballyloughmaguiffe

Walter and Thomas Edney jointly received a grant of 1,500 acres in 1610, and by 1611, foundations had been laid for a house (Hill 1877, 539). Pynnar, who erroneously recorded Lord Burleigh as being in possession of the estate, recorded a bawn (Inv. 387) and the presence of nineteen families, most of whom had recently arrived, and were able to form

'60 Men with Arms' (*ibid.* 542; Robinson 1984, 220). The original patentees let much of the land to native Irish tenants, and eventually sold the estate to Sir Henry Titchbourne in 1629. At this point, the manor was renamed Blessingbourne, and a tannery was built soon after at Ballinelurgan with a weekly market every Saturday (Hill 1877, 542–543).

387 ANNAGH DEMENSE: HOUSE AND BAWN — 244870 348600
Blessingbourne Manor

According to Pynnar, a bawn with three flankers had been built at Loughmaguife [sic], within which were a 'castle' (presumably a stone-built structure), and a timber and clay house. The present house on the site dates to the 1870s, and its construction likely obliterated any earlier remains. The Blessingbourne demesne contains several earthworks, boundaries and enclosures, some of which could have a 17th-century origin.

HB13/01/003; TYR 064:027 and TYR 064:028

Hill 1877, 539 and 542

388 FIVEMILETOWN: SETTLEMENT — 244500 347800

The village of Fivemiletown is associated with the plantation estate at Ballyloughmaguiffe or Blessingbourne. Pynnar referenced five freeholders, ten lessees and

> Cottagers in Fee, 4. Each of these a House and Garden Plott, and greasing on the Commons for Cows and Garrons. Total, 19 Families, who, with their under Tenants, are able to make 60 Men with Arms.

There are no visible remains of the 17th-century settlement in the village today.

TYR 064:044

Hill 1877, 542

Fentonagh

2,000 acres were granted to Sir Francis Willoughby in 1610, which were then sold soon afterwards to John Leigh. By 1611, 200 trees had been felled and squared in preparation for building (Hill 1877, 539). Bodley noted the existence of part of a wall for a house of clay and stone, later described by Pynnar as a house and bawn (Inv. 389). Pynnar also noted that a few 'couples for the roof' had been assembled, and recorded a village containing eight houses, the location of which is not known (*ibid*. 543). Forty-one families were also recorded by Pynnar on the estate (*ibid*.).

389　CASTLETOWN: HOUSE　　244325 361529
###　　AND BAWN

This is the possible site of a bawn and house, described by Pynnar as having been built and lived in by John Leigh, who purchased the Fentonagh estate from the original grantee, Sir Francis Willoughby. The 1622 survey described the bawn as '93 ft square, with 3 flankers'. Although supposedly located on a hill known as 'Castleton Hill', the site cannot now be precisely located. There are no visible remains of the house or bawn on the west-facing slope, although on the summit there is a flat, rectangular field that could represent a construction platform. Some ruins are depicted on the 1st edition OS six-inch map at this point, and the *OS Memoirs* of 1835 identify these with the 17th-century bawn.

　TYR 051:052
　Hill 1877, 265, 539 and 543; *Hist. MSS Comm.* 1947, 180; Treadwell 1964, 146; Day and McWilliams 1993c, 83

390　CASTLETOWN: CHURCH　　244462 361441
###　　AND GRAVEYARD
Fintona Old Church

The ruins of a church built *c.* 1642, with later additions in two phases, comprise of a rectangular nave 24.8m by 8.8m externally, with stone walls that are on average 1m thick. Added later were a small 4m by 3m bell tower on the eastern end, and an extension to the south, which only survives as a stretch of wall foundation, 3m long. There are three doorways in the church building, one in the eastern wall and two in the northern wall. The floor of the nave contains a number of family grave plots, and there is a grave slab, bearing the year 1694, mounted on the northern wall. Local traditions state that the parish church for the Fentonagh estate was destroyed in 1641 and this church was built as its replacement, re-using stones from the earlier building. The church was described as still in use but in poor condition at the time of the first Ordnance Survey in the 1830s; on later editions of the six-inch map the building is captioned 'Church, in ruins'.

　TYR 051:035
　Ó Gallachair 1974, 2–10; Day and McWilliams 1990e, 83

Ballyconnolly and Ballyranill

2,000 acres were initially assigned in 1610–11 to Thomas Roache, but in 1613 were granted to Edward Kingswell. The estate was sold in 1616 to Sir William Stewart without any construction having taken place (Hill 1877, 544). Under its new landlord, progress on the estate was swift; Pynnar described a village already containing nine houses in 1619, with more being built (*ibid*.). The tenants, a total of twenty-two families in Pynnar's time, were capable of arming sixty-four men with 'sword, pike and caliver' (*ibid*.). Indeed, the population rose steadily on the estate between 1618 and 1622, and during this period a large castle, Aughentaine Castle, was built (Robinson 1984, 220; see also Inv. 391).

391　AGHINTAIN: FORTIFIED　　249850 351510
###　　HOUSE AND BAWN
Aughentaine Castle

A fortified house and bawn, built around 1619–20 by Sir William Stewart, was described by Pynnar as being under construction and 'now three Stories high, and when it is finished will be the fairest Castle in the whole precinct.' Inquisitions from 1628 described a bawn

Fig. 5.22 Aughentaine Castle is a fortified house built around 1619–20 by Sir William Stewart. The building was originally a three-storied T-plan house.

Fig. 5.23 A Scottish-style corbelled stair turret in the north-western corner of Aughentaine Castle.

…erected round about the castle and other buildinge, which is 12 foote in height and in circuit 780 foote.

The castle was destroyed by Sir Phelim O'Neill during the 1641 Rebellion and was never restored. It was originally a three-storied Scottish-style T-plan house, the main block being 17m by 7m externally with a 7m-wide northern wing extending from the main block by at least 5m. The ruins suffered a major collapse in 1935 and today consist of the western gable of the castle, standing 12m high but in poor condition, with a number of large cracks in the masonry. This gable contains three square-headed window openings, one on each floor, and is surmounted by a square chimney stack. There is some recently collapsed walling close to the distinctive corbelled stair turret in the north-western corner, which is similar in design to that at Derrywoone Castle (Inv. 354). Architectural features survive in the interior, consisting of fireplaces, windows and several gun loops. Nothing remains of the bawn.

TYR 058:012

Hill 1877, 268 and 544; Belmore 1903a, 63; Davies 1939, 72–82; *PSAMNI* 252; Skillen *et al.* 1940, 172; *Hist. MSS Comm.* 1947, 180; Treadwell 1964, 146; Day and McWilliams 1990e, 26 and 34

Derrybard and Killany

2,000 acres were granted to Sir Anthony Cope in 1611. The estate was retained by the Cope family, but they defaulted on the terms of the grant sometime before 1631 (Hill 1877, 545). Pynnar recorded a bawn of lime and stone with two open flankers and a small house within, 'all lying waste'. No inhabitants are recorded until *c*. 1630 when twenty-eight adult males were noted (Robinson 1984, 220).

392   DERRYBARD: BAWN   247300 361800
This is the former site of a small house owned by Sir Anthony Cope, and set within a bawn of clay and stone. Pynnar noted that as early as 1619 the house

was uncovered and lying waste, with the estate 'all inhabited with Irish'. A 19th-century manor is marked here on the 1st edition OS six-inch map, still existing as a ruined house surrounded by gardens, farm buildings and farmyard. Even the oldest of the farm buildings do not contain any remains or features of 17th-century date.

TYR 051:053

Hill 1877, 545

Ballyclough

In 1610–11, William Parsons, the Surveyor General of Ireland, was granted 1,000 acres upon which were built a bawn (see Inv. 393), a large stone house, and a small village comprising nine houses (Hill 1877, 539 and 545). Pynnar recorded fifteen families on the estate, most of whom lived in the village (*ibid.*). The population rose steadily between 1611 and 1619 (Robinson 1984, 220).

393   KNOCKMANY: BAWN   254750 355500
Cecil Manor

Pynnar noted that William Parsons built a bawn of lime and stone. Although its whereabouts are not known for certain, a likely location is the former 'Cecil Manor', built in the early 19th century and now destroyed, the grounds now making up Knockmany Forest Park.

TYR 059:093

Hill 1877, 539 and 545

Clogher

Clogher was one of twenty-five 'corporate towns' proposed in 1609 (Robinson 1984, 153–155). Such towns were self-governing and independent of plantation estates, although Clogher's fortunes were bolstered by investment by Sir Richard Wingfield, a servitor who was granted a plantation estate elsewhere, in Benburb (see Inv. 411). Clogher was not officially incorporated until 1629, when letters patent were issued for the establishment of a parliamentary borough, governed by a portreeve and twelve burgesses (Inv. 395).

394   CLOGHER: CATHEDRAL   253760 351560

The 17th-century cathedral of Clogher was built by Sir Richard Wingfield, but was completely replaced by the current building between 1740 and 1745. A free-standing stone, inscribed with the date 1628, lies inside the doorway, and commemorates the construction or refurbishment of the earlier building. The location of the 17th-century church was slightly to the north-west of the current church, at the centre of what is now a graveyard. No visible remains of the original building survive.

TYR 058:032

Crawford 1918; Davies 1938b, 227–230; *PSAMNI* 252–253; Roe 1960; Bailey 1963, 187–188; Gwynn and Hadcock 1970; Johnston 1972, 9–11; Day and McWilliams 1990e, 27–29; Hamlin 2008, 371–375

Fig. 5.24 A date stone, inscribed with the year 1628, lies inside the doorway of Clogher Cathedral, commemorating the construction or refurbishment of an earlier building on the site by Sir Richard Wingfield.

395 CLOGHER DEMESNE: **253820 351670** **Ocarragan**
**   SETTLEMENT**

This is an area of archaeological interest within the village of Clogher, where burgage plots, a prison, a school, a market and a mill were built according to plans laid out by Sir Richard Wingfield. No remains of the 17th-century settlement survive above ground.

  TYR 059:085

  Lewis 1837, I, 342; Robinson 1984, 153–158.

Barony of Mountjoy (Scottish undertakers)

The Barony of Mountjoy is an extinct barony comprising the modern Barony of Dungannon Upper, together with several townlands around Stewartstown, now part of the Barony of Dungannon Middle (see Figure 5.25).

Sir Robert Hepburn was granted 1,500 acres in 1610. Carew noted that the land had been planted with oats and barley, and that one hundred and forty cows and eight mares were kept. A stone house, to be four storeys in height, was being built and a 'good store of timber' had been felled in preparation. Carew noted the presence of seven households on the estate. Pynnar recorded a 'Bawne of Clay and Stone' with a 'small House within it'. There were also ten houses, inhabited by British families (Hill 1877, 547), but the location of the settlement is unknown. The bawn was recorded as in ruins by 1622 (Treadwell 1964, 147). According to the official surveys, the adult male population of the estate fluctuated between twenty and forty in the period 1611 to 1622 (Robinson 1984, 221).

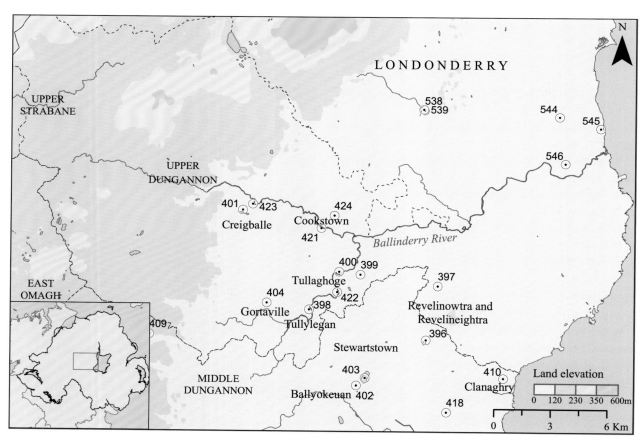

Fig. 5.25 Map of the barony of Mountjoy with the sites discussed in the text.

There are no known archaeological sites on the estate that date to plantation times.

Revelinowtra and Revelineightra

Andrew Stewart (Lord Ochiltree, later Baron Stewart) was granted 3,000 acres in 1610, and the following year Carew recorded that following his arrival in Ireland, he had built five timber houses 'within an old fort [rath], about which he is building a bawn' (Hill 1877, 546–548). This implies that one of the several raths in the vicinity was the focus of 17th-century development, and perhaps this was a deliberate choice of site – a powerful new Scottish landlord choosing to reside within an ancient 'Irish' site could barely have escaped comment at the time. According to Carew (*ibid.*), stone, brick and lime were prepared for the construction of a castle and Stewart had also brought twelve horses, fifty cows and 'three score young heifers landed at Island Magy [Magee]'. Bodley recorded that the house had been constructed to first-floor level (*Hist. MSS Comm.* 1947, 177). By the time of Pynnar's survey, not much more work had been carried out save thatching of the castle roof, along with British families living in what Pynnar termed 'poor Irish houses' (Hill 1877, 548). The population rose swiftly between 1618 and 1619, according to Robinson's (1984, 221) analysis, and a church was recorded on the estate by the 1622 survey (Inv. 397).

396   STEWARTSTOWN: CASTLE   285990 370770
AND SETTLEMENT
Castle Farm

According to Carew, Andrew Stewart had built several timber houses by 1611, and was in the process of building a bawn and preparing stone, brick and lime for a castle. The castle was still under construction in 1613, and finished by 1622, although the bawn was never completed. The location of Stewartstown Castle and bawn is currently unknown.

TYR 039:010

OS Field Report no. 208; Hill 1877, 286, 546 and 547–548; Simington 1937, 250; *Hist. MSS Comm.* 1947, 177; Treadwell 1964, 147–148

397   BALLYCLOG GLEBE: 286600 373690
CHURCH AND GRAVEYARD
Ballyclog Old Church

Bodley's map of 1609 depicts a church at Tagberkragh, probably a medieval parish church, the parish of Ballyclog being named after the bell of St. Patrick. The lands surrounding the church were included in the large grant of 'Revelinnowtra' and 'Revelinneightra' to Andrew Stewart in 1610, although the immediate surroundings may have been under freehold. Its history is somewhat obscure. It was described as under construction in the Regal Visitation of 1622, presumably as the replacement for, or the reconstruction, of an earlier building. In 1693, the church was recorded as being in good condition but the parish was very poor.

The remains comprise a near rectangular graveyard and a roofless, largely rebuilt, church building, with views to the south, west and east. The church is situated on a raised area within the graveyard and may occupy an earlier site. It is mostly built of sandstone rubble, with all the walls having a pronounced external batter at the base. It is rectangular in plan, measuring 13m east-west by

Fig. 5.26 View of Ballyclog Old Church.

233

6m north-south, with a bell tower and porch at the western end added later. Stone-carved windows in the north wall appear to be 17th-century in date. The interior of the church has been disturbed by burials and the construction of a stairway leading to a crypt. The building was extensively repaired in the 1960s, with many original details changed.

TYR 039:044

Bodley Map of 'Parte of ye Baronie of Donganon', 1609 (NA MPF 1/45/2); Leslie 1911, 128; Hamlin 2008, 367

Tullylegan

George Crawford was granted 1,000 acres in 1610, and Carew described how materials for building were being gathered, including the felling of timber (Hill 1877, 546). By 1619, when Pynnar visited, the estate was in the ownership of Captain Alexander Sanderson, and a bawn and house had been built (*ibid.* 548).

398   TULLYLAGAN: BAWN   279800 372400
Tullylagan Manor

Tullylagan Manor was built in 1828, at what is probably the former site of a bawn. Pynnar's survey mentioned a bawn with two flankers and

> ...a good house of lime and stone; himself [Cpt. Sanderson], with wife and family, dwell therein. About him are some houses inhabited with British.

At Tullylagan Manor today, there are no visible remains of any 17th-century structures. The 19th-century building, now a hotel, stands in landscaped grounds, the development of which would have obliterated any earlier features.

An alternative location for the bawn lies just to the south-east of Tullylagan Manor (grid ref. 279860 372250), where a wall partly encloses another 19th-century residence sited on an elevated position overlooking the Killymoon River. This wall is now

a rectangular garden feature, standing over 1.5m high and enclosing an area at least 50m across. It is best preserved along its northern length where square projections resembling bawn flankers are situated at the north-western and north-eastern corners. The eastern side of the enclosure is missing, presumably due to a roadway no longer visible but marked crossing this location on the 1st edition OS six-inch map.

HB09/05/019, TYR 038:048

Hill 1877, 548

Tullaghoge

1,000 acres were granted to Robert Lindsey, brother of Bernard Lindsey, in 1610 or 1611 (the patents do not survive – see Hill 1877, 288). The estate encompassed the ancient inauguration 'fort' of the O'Neill clan, albeit on O'Hagan lands. The occupation of a site of such national importance could be interpreted as a very deliberate act by the incoming planters. Carew noted the construction of a timber house and the presence of eight mares, eight cows with calves, five oxen, swine and a 'competent portion of arms' (Hill 1877, 546). Robert Lindsey was dead by the time of Pynnar's survey, which recorded that his widow was in possession of the estate and the timber house, which was now enclosed by a 'bawn' planted with hedging (*ibid.* 550). It is likely however that the ramparts of the ancient O'Neill fort were being passed off as a bawn in order to comply with the legal requirements. The 1622 survey recorded that the house in the old fort had been abandoned, with Mrs Lindsey then inhabiting a small thatched house at the foot of the hill (Treadwell 1964, 148).

399   TULLAGHOGE: HOUSE   282500 374300
AND BAWN
Tullaghoge Fort

Tullaghoge Fort is located on the summit of a prominent hill with a gradual approach from the west, and consists of the substantial earthwork remains of an early medieval rath associated with

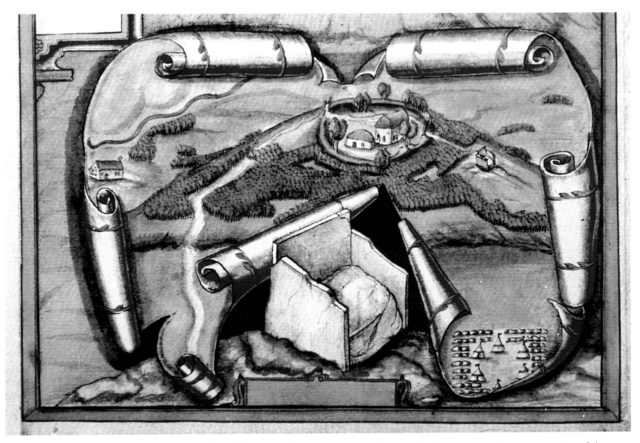

Fig. 5.27 While Tullaghoge Fort is located in O'Hagan territory, it was associated with the inauguration ceremonies of the O'Neills. Richard Bartlett's map of *c.* 1600 of the fort depicts two thatched buildings within, along with a stone inauguration seat outside.

the inauguration ceremonies of the O'Neills. Two thatched buildings are depicted within the rath on a Bartlett illustration drawn around 1600, although these pre-date the plantation grant to Lindsey. While Pynnar described the site as occupied by Mrs Lindsey and her family, the length of time spent there by the Lindseys was minimal, as the 1622 survey suggested that occupation shifted from the summit to the base of the hill, perhaps to where Loughry Manor was built a decade later (Inv. 400). Today, the site shows no trace of the 17th-century occupation.

TYR 038:016

Hill 1877, 546 and 550

Fig. 5.28 Aerial view of Tullaghoge Fort. This important inauguration site was occupied briefly by a Mrs Lindsey and her family following the plantation of the area.

400 LOUGHRY: FORTIFIED HOUSE   281370 374448

Loughry Manor

Loughry Manor was built in 1632 by Robert Lindsey, a descendant of the original plantation grantee. The house, destroyed during the 1641 Rebellion, was rebuilt in 1671, and the site was extensively redeveloped around 1800, and is now part of Loughry College.

    TYR 038:049

    Hill 1877, 546, 550

Creigballe

Bernard Lindsey was granted 1,000 acres in 1610 or 1611. By 1619 the estate was owned by Alexander Richardson, and a bawn containing a timber house had been built (Inv. 401). The population rose steadily between 1618 and 1622 (Robinson 1984, 221).

401 OAKLANDS: BAWN   276250 377800

A bawn of clay and stone, with lime-rendered walls and four flankers, was described by Pynnar. Drum Manor, the ruined house at the site of this former bawn, is a 19th-century mansion. There are no visible remains of the bawn, and given the heavily landscaped gardens and altered topography, any archaeological remains would be expected to be slight.

    HB09/04/007

    Hill 1877, 546 and 550

Ballyokeuan

1,000 acres were granted to Robert Stewart in 1610, and Carew recorded that building was underway, as timber had been felled and other materials were ready. The estate was later granted to Andrew Stewart who built a castle and bawn (Inv. 402). The population increased steadily between 1611 and 1630 (Robinson 1984, 221).

402 ROUGHAN: CASTLE   282317 368271

The remains of Roughan Castle are located on the summit of a hill that has panoramic views in all directions, including north-eastwards towards Roughan Lough. It was built in 1618 by Sir Andrew Stewart and later held by Sir Phelim O'Neill who, as a fugitive in 1653, was captured on the nearby *crannóg* (Inv. 403) that can be seen from the path leading to the castle.

The remains consist of a three-storey building with a central square block, flanked by round towers at each corner. The building is reminiscent of the gate-houses of medieval castles such as Carrickfergus, but in miniature – the central block measuring 9m across, with each corner tower projecting a further 3m. The castle was originally three-storeyed, with much of the masonry from the upper floor now missing. The two towers on the south-eastern side of the castle are connected at second-floor level by an arch with moulded corbels. The north-western wall of the main block contains fireplaces at first- and second-floor level. The rooms within the round towers are square in plan on the upper floors. The towers each have several gun loops at ground and

Fig. 5.29 The south-western side of Roughan Castle. This fortified house was built by Sir Andrew Stewart in 1618 and consists of a three-storey block with circular towers projecting from each corner.

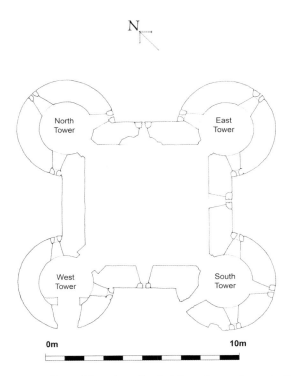

N

North
Tower

East
Tower

West
Tower

South
Tower

0m   10m

Fig. 5.30 Plan of Roughan Castle. There is a wall scar in the south-western side of the south tower where the bawn wall would have connected with the building (after Jope 1951, Fig. 4).

first-floor level, and there is an entrance in the western tower, originally round-headed, but now partially collapsed.

TYR 046:002

Hill 1877, 287, 546 and 550–551; Crone 1904, 95–96; Simington 1937, 251; *PSAMNI* 244–245; *Hist. MSS Comm.* 1947, 178; Jope 1951, 37; Treadwell 1964, 148–149; Robinson 1974, 270; Day and McWilliams 1993c, 55

403   ROUGHAN: CRANNÓG   282770 368680

This *crannóg* on Roughan Lough, like hundreds of similar sites in Ireland, was probably originally constructed during the 6th or 7th centuries as a high-status settlement or stronghold. The defensive nature of these artificial islands meant that they were reoccupied many times, especially by Gaelic forces in the 16th and 17th centuries. In 1602, the English cartographer Richard Bartlett

depicted a *crannóg* under attack which may have been Roughan Lough during Lord Mountjoy's successful assault on the forces of Hugh O'Neill, earl of Tyrone. In this image, the *crannóg* contains two thatched buildings and a timber structure of some kind; on the mainland, the English are shown positioned behind stockades and earthwork defences. The *crannóg* was used as a hideout by Sir Phelim O'Neill, who was arrested there in 1657 and later executed in Dublin for his leading role in the 1641 Rebellion. The site survives as a tree-covered island, impossible to access without a boat; all traces of the buildings and the other defences depicted by Bartlett have vanished.

TYR 046:001

PSAMNI 245; Hayes-McCoy 1964, 9–10, pl. V; O'Sullivan 1998

Gortaville

Robert Stewart received another 1,000 acre grant in this barony in 1610. Carew noted that he had brought with him tenants and cattle, and that timber had been felled, and materials were ready for construction. Pynnar recorded David Kennedy as the owner of the estate, implying that it was sold sometime between 1611 and 1619 (Hill 1877, 548–549), while also noting that there was a bawn enclosing a timber house (*ibid.*). The population rose steadily between 1618 and 1622, but by 1630 had already entered a phase of decline (Robinson 1984, 221).

404   ROCKDALE: BAWN   277546 372752

The site of David Kennedy's bawn at Gortaville (the modern spelling is Gortavilly) is occupied by an 18th- to 19th-century house and demesne. The bawn was described by Pynnar as being 80 feet square, built of lime and stone with three flankers, and enclosing a timber house. There is a ruined rubble stone wall, with its inner face lined with brick, enclosing a rectangular area. Although much of its fabric is probably a 19th-century garden wall, the exterior has two unusual rounded corners at the north-east and north-west that may represent the remains of the original bawn flankers.

HB09/05/015

Hill 1877, 547 and 551

Barony of Dungannon (servitors and Irish)

Dungannon

In January 1610, Sir Arthur Chichester, Lord Deputy of Ireland, was granted a rural estate encompassing 1140 acres, and an additional 500 acres for the town of Dungannon (Hill 1877, 315). Carew and Pynnar described his efforts to rebuild the ancient O'Neill castle in the town (Inv. 405), which by Pynnar's time in 1619 consisted of nine stone houses and twelve timber houses built of cagework and frames, all

still under construction, as well as three English houses. Pynnar added that whilst this work was underway, the townsfolk took temporary residence in small, presumably Irish-style, cabins (Hill 1877, 551–552). When the 1622 survey was made, the newly-constructed town was described in detail: the houses all had glazed windows and slated roofs, and each contained between five and fourteen rooms, and had stone chimneys. There was also a gaol, a session house and a church. Leadwork and turned wood were noted as part of the fabric of these buildings (Treadwell 1964, 149).

**405   DUNGANNON: CASTLE,   279900 362620
HOUSE AND BAWN**
Dungannon Castle
In 1610–11, Sir Arthur Chichester built a fort on the

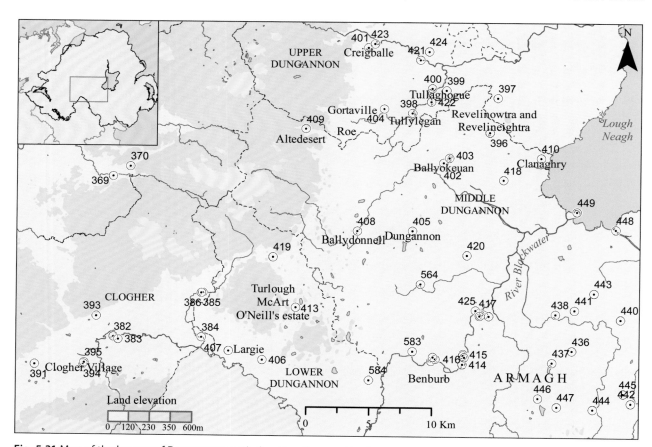

Fig. 5.31 Map of the barony of Dungannon with the sites discussed in the text.

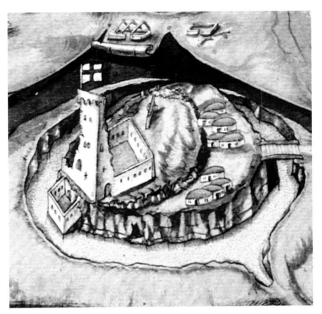

Fig. 5.32 Dungannon Castle was the chief residence of Hugh O'Neill, earl of Tyrone, and following the end of the Nine Years' War, it was depicted by Bartlett in *c.* 1600 as a tower house and bawn in a ruinous condition, surrounded by a large water-filled ditch.

Fig. 5.33 Excavations at Castle Hill revealed the demolished foundations of the O'Neill medieval tower house (to the right of the picture), and the walls and spear-shaped bastion from Sir Arthur Chichester's early 17th-century fortification (to the left of the picture).

site of a medieval castle belonging to the O'Neills on a prominent hill with panoramic views of the surrounding countryside. This earlier castle had been the chief residence of Hugh O'Neill, earl of Tyrone, and following the end of the Nine Years' War, it was depicted by Bartlett in *c.* 1600 as a tower house and bawn in a ruinous condition, surrounded by a large water-filled ditch. Pynnar described it as '120 feet square', with four flankers and enclosed by a counterscarped ditch (presumably the medieval ditch was re-used). The bawn was captured by the O'Neills during the 1641 Rebellion, and it was subsequently destroyed in 1646. A gentleman's residence was built on the site *c.* 1790, and two circular towers from this later building survive.

Although there are no visible remains of Chichester's bawn, the hill has been subject to archaeological investigation in recent years. Excavations in 2007, to the north-west of the castle, revealed the medieval ditch still open in Pynnar's time, and a well, the upper fills of which contained 17th-century pottery.

During a separate excavation campaign in the same year jointly carried out by Channel 4's Time Team, the Environment Heritage Service: Built Heritage and the Centre for Archaeological Fieldwork in Queen's University Belfast, the remains of a curtain wall and a spear-shaped bastion belonging to Chichester's early 17th-century fort were discovered at the summit of the hill. At some stage in the mid- or late 17th century, the fort was modified for the use of artillery, with the interiors of both the bastion and the medieval castle filled in with clay. The buildings and surrounding enclosure subsequently suffered episodes of stone robbing, presumably during the construction of a new residence in the late 18th century. In the late 20th century, the site was developed as a British army base, which included the construction of a helicopter landing pad on the summit.

TYR 054:017

Hill 1877, 315, 551 and 552; Belmore 1903a, 41; *PSAMNI* 249–250; Hayes-McCoy 1964, 8–10, pl. V; Treadwell 1964, 149; Day and McWilliams 1993c, 44; Salter 1993, 146; Chapple 2003; Bowen 2007b; Donnelly *et al.* 2007; Donnelly *et al.* 2008; Murray *et al.* 2010

Largie

2,000 acres were granted in 1610 to Lord Ridgeway who, according to Carew, the next year employed carpenters to build a timber hall. Pynnar described the construction of a lime and stone bawn on the estate in 1619, with three English households dwelling near it (Hill 1877, 551–553). However, the estate was not a success, with the 1622 survey indicating that the house no longer existed, and that the land was wholly occupied by the Irish (Treadwell 1964, 150).

406 ANNAGH: HOUSE 268000 352000

Nothing remains of 'Anacale House', which is depicted on the Down Survey maps of both barony and parish. Much of the area is now low-lying marshy ground. Within the wider area, a possible alternative location for the house is the site of a nearby 18th-century house and associated outbuildings (grid ref. 267888 351790).

TYR 060:050

Down Survey parish map of Aghalow, Carneteale and Killeshill (PRONI D597/4)

Fig. 5.34 Extract from the Down Survey parish map of Aghalow, Carneteale and Killeshill (c. 1656–58) illustrating 'Anacle House' in today's townland of Annagh.

407 RAVELLA: HOUSE 265300 352700
AND BAWN
Ravella Castle

Pynnar referred to a bawn with four flankers, and a timber house, now identified with 'Ravella Castle' at Aughnacloy, which by the end of the 17th century was occupied by the Moore family. The building was destroyed by the mid-19th century with no visible remains of the bawn or any other structure

surviving, though it has been suggested by Marshall that the castle was situated on the lower slopes of a hillside that faces north-eastwards. It is possible that an adjacent farmyard occupies the location of the bawn, as the ground surface there has been levelled at some point in the past to provide a rectangular platform that has traces of stone walls present around the perimeter.

TYR 060:051

Hill 1877, 551–553; Marshall 1925

Ballydonnell

A grant of 1,000 acres was made in early 1610 to Sir Toby Caulfield, who built the castle described below (Inv. 408). Pynnar also documented the construction of a stone bridge and a water mill nearby (Hill 1877, 553). The 1622 survey (Treadwell 1964, 150–151) described a flurry of building activity on the estate – cagework houses, orchards, gardens, fields, a dam or millpond being laid out, along with

> …a smale Village built containing 20 houses of English Fashion, inhabited by British, whereof most are Artificers & handycraftsmen.'

408 LISNAMONAGHAN: 275510 362590
HOUSE AND BAWN
Castle Caulfield

The substantial remains of an English-style house built in 1614 by Sir Toby Caulfield, first Baron Charlemont, stand on a rise on the site of an O'Donnell fort, with the Torrent River flowing immediately to the north-west. Pynnar described some on-going construction work within the castle.

The three-storey house was originally U-shaped in plan, but the south-western wing does not survive. Also present is a bawn wall and the remains of a gatehouse. The bawn once enclosed the level area to the north of the house, suggesting that the house was built later, outside the bawn. The house is not fortified, but the gatehouse with its engraved

Fig. 5.35 The remains of an English-style house built in 1614 by Sir Toby Caulfield, first Baron Charlemont, in the village of Castlecaulfield. To the left of the photo are the ruins of gate house and bawn. Unusually the house stood outside the bawn.

Fig. 5.36 The Caulfield coat-of-arms placed over the entrance of the gatehouse at Castle Caulfield.

Fig. 5.37 A mullion and transom dividing a window into four lights in Castle Caulfield.

Caulfield coat of arms contains gun loops and murder holes.

The house was captured, burned and partly demolished by Patrick Modder O'Donnelly during the 1641 Rebellion, but was later repaired, and reoccupied by the Caulfields into the 1660s.

TYR 054:001

Hill 1877, 316, 513 and 551; Belmore 1903a, 74; Simington 1937, 278; *PSAMNI* 249; *Hist. MSS Comm.* 1947, 178; Jope 1958, 101–107 and 1960, 97–123; Waterman 1960, 89–96; Treadwell 1964, 150–151; Rowan 1979, 175–176

Roe

Manor Roe was a grant of 1,000 acres made in 1610 to Sir Francis Roe, and Pynnar described a small house of brick and stone enclosed by a bank, ditch and hedge (Hill 1877, 316, 553). Although initially successful, this estate had seemingly lost all of its settlers by 1630 (Robinson 1984, 221), and archaeological evidence of it has not yet been discovered.

Altedesert

1,000 acres were granted to William Parsons at an unknown date, as the original patents have been lost (Hill 1877, 552), although it was probably made after 1611, as Parson's property was not mentioned by Carew. In 1619, Pynnar described a stone bawn (Inv. 409), which was apparently abandoned by 1622 (Treadwell 1964, 151), with no further development or settlement occurring on the estate.

**409   THE BONN: HOUSE   271330 371020
       AND BAWN**

A bawn and house here were described by Pynnar as comprised of 'Stone and Lyme, 70 feet square, with two Flankers, with a House within it'. The site, which was re-occupied in the mid-18th century and used as a farmyard, is located within drumlin countryside, with extensive views of the surrounding area.

Occupation of the house seems to have been short lived, as the site was referred to simply as a bawn by 1622, and it is possible that the English tenants had departed by then. No visible remains of the bawn survive.

Excavation and survey in 1980 revealed the base of a circular flanker with an external diameter of 4m, the wall of which was 75cm thick, situated on the edge of the more recent farmyard. Other archaeological traces of the plantation house and bawn were ephemeral, and it was not possible to establish whether the layout of the farmyard mirrored that of the original bawn.

TYR 037:001

Hill 1877, 553; Treadwell 1964, 151; Brannon 1984, 177–181

Clanaghry

A small grant of 480 acres was made in 1610 or 1611 to Sir Francis Ansley (Hill 1877, 554). According to Carew, Ansley constructed an earthen bawn, surrounded by a ditch, and had timber resources to build a substantial English house therein. Pynnar did not add any details, and in the 1622 survey it is stated that Ansley was not bound to build here (Treadwell 1964, 151). Plantation sites on this estate have not been positively identified, although Mountjoy Castle (Inv. 410) is situated on the estate.

**410   MAGHERALAMFIELD: 290110 368690
CASTLE**
Mountjoy Castle

The ruins of Mountjoy Castle are located on a low hill, with extensive views of Lough Neagh and the surrounding countryside. It was built as a military campaign fort by Lord Mountjoy in 1602, during the Nine Years' War, replacing an earlier O'Neill fortification nearby on the foreshore of Lough Neagh, which was depicted by Richard Bartlett *c.* 1600. The castle was under the command of Sir Frances Roe from 1602 into plantation times, although Roe was also granted his own estate

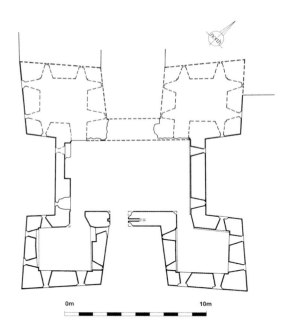

Fig. 5.38 Plan of Mountjoy Castle. The castle was built as a military campaign fort by Lord Mountjoy in 1602 during the Nine Years' War, and was under the command of Sir Frances Roe from 1602 into plantation times (after Jope 1960, Fig. 4).

nearby. It was described by Carew as

> ...a fair Castle of stone and brick, covered with slate and tile ... compassed about by a good strong rampier of Earth, well ditched and flanked with bulworks.

During the 1641 Rebellion, the castle was captured by Irish forces, then repossessed by Sir John Clotworthy in 1642, and partly burnt in 1643.

The remains consist of a central block with four angle bastions, although the north-western bastion has been partly demolished. The castle is a two-storey building of brick, built on stone foundations; with the outside walls of the lower storey faced with stone. The four bastions are provided with numerous gun loops, which allowed for all approaches to the castle to be covered by flanking fire. The entrance was in the eastern wall of the central block. The stairs to the first floor were probably in the central block,

Fig. 5.39 Mountjoy Castle, unusually for fortifications of the time, is largely built of brick, though the outside walls of the lower storey are faced with stone. The building was provided with four corner bastions and numerous gun opes.

Fig. 5.40 The interior of Mountjoy Castle with the main entrance to the right.

the upper levels being reached from a staircase in the south-eastern bastion. An archaeological test excavation to the north-west of the castle did not find anything of significance.

TYR 047:002

Lewis 1837, I, 374; Marshall 1924b; *PSAMNI* 246; Jope 1960, 97–123; Day and McWilliams 1993c, 31; Carver 2006

Benburb

2,000 acres were granted in 1610 to Sir Richard Wingfield (elevated to a peerage in 1618 as Viscount Powerscourt) a distinguished soldier who had held the office of Marshall of Ireland (Hill 1877, 316). Pynnar described a bawn and castle (Inv. 411), and a church (Inv. 412) being built. The population of the estate rose from thirty adult males in 1619 to forty-six by 1630 (Robinson 1984, 221).

| 411 | BENBURB: HOUSE AND BAWN | 281470 351990 |

Benburb Castle

The remains of a bawn built by Sir Richard Wingfield *c.* 1615 are dramatically situated on the edge of a ridge on the northern bank of the River Blackwater, with excellent views to the south, east and west. The site was a stronghold of Shane O'Neill, and is shown on pre-plantation maps. Wingfield's estate was described by Pynnar as including

> a Bawne of Lyme and Stone, 120 feet square, 14 feet high, with two Flankers, in which there is built in each a good House, three Stories high.

Records are confused over the history of the bawn, as it was never actually occupied by the Wingfield family. Local traditions state that Benburb Castle

Fig. 5.41 An aerial view of Benburb Castle (built by Sir Richard Wingfield *c.* 1615) shows a bawn dramatically situated on the edge of a ridge on the northern bank of the River Blackwater.

Fig. 5.42 As described by Nicholas Pynnar in 1618–19, the north-western tower of Benburb Castle is more like a tall house than an ordinary bawn flanker.

Fig. 5.43 View of square-hooded, multi-light window in St. Patrick's Church in Benburb.

was attacked in 1641, and abandoned thereafter, which is likely as the building is not mentioned in later taxation documents.

The entrance faces to the north, where higher ground in the direction of Benburb village obscures views. The bawn walls enclose an irregular rectangular area, measuring *c.* 40m by 34m, and stand at almost their full height of *c.* 5m. They have gun loops at frequent intervals, and are well-preserved, except on the south-west. As described by Pynnar, the towers at the north-western and north-eastern corners are large, contain fire places, and are much more like tall houses than ordinary bawn flankers. The north-western tower is the better preserved. At the south-eastern corner of the bawn is a circular tower with a spiral staircase, with steps down to a postern gate at the cliff edge. The late 18th-century house along the south-western side of the bawn is privately occupied.

TYR 061:002

Hardy 1834, 365–366; Hill 1877, 315–316, 551 and 554; Marshall 1924a, 10; *PSAMNI* 257; Davies 1941a, 31–34; Treadwell 1964, 151

412 BENBURB: CHURCH AND GRAVEYARD   281780 352140
St. Patrick's Church

St Patrick's Church, built by the Wingfield family, was described by Pynnar as 'ready to have the roof set up'. Although showing some later additions, it retains many of its original 17th-century features and is thus an excellent example of the gothic architectural style of the plantation period.

The church is located on the highest part of a polygonal enclosure, with land sloping to the south, west and east. It consists of a long, rectangular stone building, 32m by 12m externally, with an east-west orientation. The seven original side windows are square-hooded, and each is divided by transoms and mullions into six lights, the uppermost lights having segmental arched tops. The eastern window, also original, is a large pointed arch, divided into a number of segmental-headed lights with cusped tracery towards the top, above which is a small human head. The southern door in the nave is round-headed; its drip-mouldings having splayed terminals with carved *fleur-de-lis* motifs. A tower was added to the western end in 1837, and subsequently re-built in 1892. This later tower includes a doorway in its northern wall, comparable in appearance to the 17th-century doorway in the nave, with drip-

Fig. 5.44 View of altar window divided into a number of lights, with cusped tracery above, in the east wall of St. Patrick's Church in Benburb.

mouldings having splayed terminals with carved rosette motifs.

The surrounding polygonal graveyard is enclosed by a substantial stone wall. A possible original graveyard, of smaller extent, is defined by an oval-shaped platform around the church, extending immediately to the east of the church and sloping from the building to the south and south-west.

> TYR 061:025
> Leslie 1911, 181; Marshall 1924b; *PSAMNI* 257; Rowan 1979; Ó Conluain 1987, 50

Turlough McArt O'Neill's estate

Of the several O'Neills who were granted their own estates in Co. Tyrone during the Plantation, Turlough McArt O'Neill was allocated the largest proportion (4,000 acres), having been relocated from his own castle and lands near Strabane. His tenure was mentioned by Carew in 1611, although the grant was not formally made until 1614 (Hill 1877, 314). Bound by the same conditions as British settlers, O'Neill set about building a bawn, as described by Pynnar in 1619 (Inv. 413). In the 1622 survey, although the works were described as still unfinished, and much of the estate 'sold away', there was a fine coupled timber house on the estate, i.e. a house built using cruck roof timbers (Treadwell 1964, 151).

413   CASTLETOWN: HOUSE   270640 356310
       AND BAWN

According to Pynnar, O'Neill 'made a Piece of a Bawne, which is five feet high, and hath been so a long time', and his tenants all 'do plough after the Irish manner'. The possible remains of this bawn may be incorporated into a wall in the south-western gable of a ruined 19th-century house at Castletown. The wall fragment is approximately 3m long and 4.5m high, and is not bonded with the house walls. Furthermore, it is thicker than the other house walls and could, therefore, be the remains of a bawn wall or part of a square flanker tower.

> TYR 060:008
> Hill 1877, 316–317, 551–552 and 554; *PSAMNI* 255; Simington 1937

Other Irish estates in Dungannon

Within the barony of Dungannon, sixty estates were granted to Irish individuals, the largest of which is described above. The grants were made in 1613 or 1614, following years of correspondence on the matter between the Crown and government representatives in Ireland, most notably Sir Arthur Chichester. The majority of these estates were small, ranging from 60 to 120 acres, and there is no historical evidence of any construction having taken place. However some grants were larger, including 1,000 acres to Brian Crossagh O'Neill, and other grants, spanning the county border with Armagh, to Niall O'Neill (800 acres), Catherine Ní Neill (1600 acres), Brian O'Neill (370 acres) and Con Boy O'Neill (700 acres; see Hill 1877, 314–319; Robinson 1984, 199–200). There are no known archaeological sites on these lands that date to the time of the Plantation.

Military sites in Dungannon

414 TULLYDOWEY: ARTILLERY FORT 283950 351740

The earthwork remains of an English military artillery fort built in 1601, known as Mullin Fort, were recorded by Bartlett on his two maps of the Third Blackwater Fort and the Blackwater Valley. The fort, which has been planted with trees, is located close to the River Blackwater, and consists of a natural hill scarped to form a D-shaped platform, measuring 70m north-south by 60m east-west and 2m high, with commanding views over the surrounding area. There is some indication of a surrounding ditch along the northern side of the platform, and a possible entrance flanked with earthen banks along the south-western side.

TYR 062:001

OS Field Report no. 310; Hayes-McCoy 1964, 5–6, pl. III and 14–15, pl. VIII

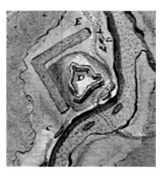

Fig. 5.45 An English military artillery fort built in 1601, known as Mullin Fort, was recorded by Richard Bartlett *c.* 1600 on his map of the Blackwater Valley.

415 DRUMDERG: ARTILLERY FORT 284010 352570

This is the site of a second Blackwater artillery fort, built by the Lord Deputy Burgh and defended against Hugh O'Neill, earl of Tyrone, from the winter of 1597 through to the following summer. Bartlett's map of the Blackwater Valley and a contemporary account indicate that it was roughly constructed, consisting of an earthen bank and ditch enclosing a rectangular space, on a high slope overlooking a fording point across the River Blackwater, at Portmore. There are no extant traces of this fort, with the site being occupied by farm buildings associated with nearby Portmore House, built in 1875. There is a direct line of sight with a third artillery fort built by O'Neill (Inv. 416).

TYR 062:007

Richard Bartlett 'A description of the valley of Blackwater showing fortified positions of Irish and English in the O'Neill wars, 1602' (NLI MS2656-8); Hayes-McCoy 1964, 14–15, pl. VIII

416 DRUMDERG: ARTILLERY FORT 283990 352430

A third Blackwater fort, also overlooking the ford at Portmore, was built by Hugh O'Neill shortly after 1595, but was probably partly demolished after it was captured by Lord Deputy Burgh in 1597. Bartlett's map of the Blackwater Valley indicates that this was only one of a number of minor earthworks known as sconces built by O'Neill, defending fording points across the Blackwater. A contemporary illustration shows the fort at Drumderg to have been quite substantial, being defended by a pair of circular bastions on its landward side, and described as '200 paces long & 40 paces with in the Bawne'. Aerial photographs show evidence for a large rounded bastion and traces of a rampart at this location, 185m to the north-west of Burgh's Fort (Inv. No. 415). From the ground, these remains are not clearly visible, and are only represented by a small rise in the field.

TYR 062:012

Richard Bartlett 'A description of the valley of Blackwater showing fortified positions of Irish and English in the O'Neill wars, 1602' (NLI MS2656-8); Falls 1950, 203–204; Jope 1960, 114, pl. xii; Hayes-McCoy 1964, 14–15, pl. VIII

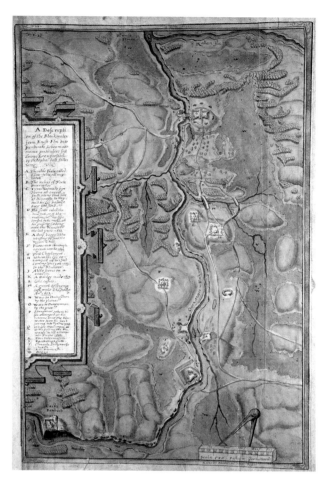

Fig. 5.47 Extract from Bartlett's map of Charlemont illustrating the sconce or small fortification covering the Tyrone bank of the River Blackwater.

TYR 062:014

Map of Charlemont, Co. Tyrone, by Thomas Phillips, 1685 (NLI MS2557/28); 'A description of the valley of Blackwater showing fortified positions of Irish and English in the O'Neill wars, 1602' (NLI MS2656-8); Hayes-McCoy 1964, 7, pl. IV

**418 CLOGHOG: ARTILLERY   287110 366830
      FORT AND ENCLOSURE**

This substantial earthwork, historically undocumented but in good condition, is a 17th-century star-shaped artillery fort that consists of a flat rectangular area enclosed on three sides by linear, flat-topped banks and partially infilled ditches. The banks are 2m high and the ditches 0.7m deep today, but they are likely to have been more substantial in the past. The enclosure measures some 26m by 16m, and is orientated north-east to south-west. Bastion flankers are located on the south-west and north-west, the north-western bastion currently forming part of a garden boundary.

TYR 047:023

Church sites in Dungannon

**419 KILLEESHIL: CHURCH   268800 360450
      AND GRAVEYARD**

Killeeshil Church is depicted on the Down Survey map of the parish (1656–58), its location now occupied by St Paul's Church and an associated graveyard. An earlier church enclosure, c. 70m in diameter, is only partly visible on the ground, but

Fig. 5.46 Bartlett recorded a number of forts on his c. 1600 map of the Blackwater Valley including three fortifications at Tullydowey (Mullin Fort) and Drumderg.

417 MOY: SCONCE   285240 355940

This is the site of an English military fortification shown on the 1602 illustration of Charlemont by Bartlett and on the 1685 map of the Charlemont and Moy fortifications by Phillips. This small fortification was built in 1602 to protect the Tyrone side of the bridge crossing the Blackwater at Charlemont. The fortification, also known as a sconce, was depicted by Bartlett as a square fort (approximately 20 yards square) defended by a ditch and a bank, further embellished with palisade defences. Inside were two thatched houses. No remains of the fortification have survived, although archaeological traces may still exist below-ground.

Fig. 5.49 The large altar window in the eastern wall of Derryloran Church, with its segmental-headed lights, topped with tracery.

is visible on aerial images. The current church is located on the lower, north-facing slope of a hillside with views to the north, north-east and north-west. It occupies the site of a much earlier church, for which the earliest reference is 1442. The church was noted as a ruin in 1701.

TYR 053:016

Down Survey parish map of Carneteale, Aghavow and Killishel (PRONI D597/4); Belmore 1904, 93; Leslie 1911, 332; Hamlin 2008, 388

420 LAGHEY: CHURCH AND GRAVEYARD   284250 360670

An inscription above the entrance to St. Andrew's Church claims that it was first built in 1620. The site of an earlier, undocumented, late medieval church may be marked by a raised, circular earthen platform (35m in diameter and *c.* 2m high), situated in the graveyard to the west of today's church. Bodley's map of 1609 depicted the medieval church as a roofless building with the name 'Leaghagh'. The platform contains the earliest grave markers in the graveyard, dating to the early 18th century.

TYR 055:001

Bodley Map of 'Parte of ye Baronie of Donganon', 1609 (NA MPF 1/45/2); *OS Field Report* no. 274; Hamlin 2008, 402

421 GLEBE (DERRYLORAN): CHURCH AND GRAVEYARD   280420 376800
Derryloran Church

This ruined church is situated on the south-western edge of Cookstown and, like many medieval church sites in this part of Ulster, is sited beside a stream, in this case the Ballinderry River. The church was built on the site of a pre-Norman parish church associated with St. Luran, which was recorded as being plundered in 1195. The survey of 1622 reports a church as '*almost finished*' in the locality; and the present ruins seems to be that of the 17th-century church, but incorporating medieval foundations. The large altar window in the eastern wall, with its segmental headed lights, topped with tracery, and the square-hooded windows in the south wall, tie in with an early 17th-century dating for this rebuilding. The western porch is an 18th-century addition, and the church was in use until 1822. Archaeological monitoring of groundworks at a development site *c.* 250m south-west of the church revealed no archaeological remains datable to the 17th century.

TYR 038:019

O.S. Field Report no. 193; Leslie 1911, 211–214; *PSAMNI*

239; Davies 1942, 8–11; Gwynn and Hadcock 1970, 379; Brannon 1986, 89–98; Bailie and Bowen 2007; Hamlin 2008, 378

422   DESERTCREAT: CHURCH AND GRAVEYARD   281280 373340
Desertcreat Church

Desertcreat Church, the parish church for Derryloran, is probably of medieval origin, the current rectangular building being of 18th- or 19th-century construction. It is situated on a slight ridge or platform within its graveyard, which may indicate that it was built on an earlier site. The lands surrounding the church, some 820 acres, were in 1620 granted by the See of Armagh to James Stewart, a Scottish planter. In 1622, it was noted that there was a rector resident and a 'church in building'. The Civil Survey mentions in 1654 'the old Chappell of Drumcha and the dwelling stone house of the fors'd James Stewart.'

TYR 038:022

Reeves 1850, 55; Leslie 1911, 220; Simington 1937, 290–291; Hamlin 2008, 378

423   KILDRESS UPPER: CHURCH AND GRAVEYARD   276770 378120

The ruins of Kildress Church are located on a small knoll with extensive views overlooking the Ballinderry River. It is a rectangular, gabled building, measuring 15m x 6m, orientated east-west. The building is rubble-built with carved quoins and window surrounds. It was built around 1622, probably on the site of a medieval parish church associated with St. Patrick, although the early history of the site is obscure. The present building was burnt in 1641 and later restored in 1698. Some of the windows were altered around 1800, and the eastern gable was probably reconstructed then, perhaps re-using tracery from before. The church fell into disuse in 1818. Original, 17th-century features are still visible however; the western wall contains an entrance with a flat-arched window above, now in a highly ruinous condition, while the fenestration

Fig. 5.50 Kildress Church was built around 1622, probably on the site of a medieval parish church associated with St. Patrick.

elsewhere is an assortment of square-headed and arched windows that would have ensured that the interior of the church was well lit. These windows are mostly incomplete; the best-preserved example (now blocked-up) is a flat-headed window in the western end of the southern wall, measuring 1.4m high and 0.7m wide.

TYR 029:019

Leslie 1911, 325; Young 1913; Pringle 1935, 11; *PSAMNI* 233; Davies 1941e, 144; Hamlin 2008, 388

Other sites in Dungannon

424   COOKSTOWN: SETTLEMENT   281100 377500
The plantation town of Cookstown was originally built on church land by Allan Cooke, and was then largely destroyed in 1641, although the Civil Survey

of 1654 described it as a small market town. The lands were eventually acquired by William Stewart of Killymoon Castle in 1750, who embarked upon the redevelopment of the town. No traces of the original village survive, apart from possible elements of the historic street layout. A mill race survives to the south, and it is possible that the focus of the village was originally on sloping ground, closer to the mill and river.

TYR 029:067

Lewis 1837, I, 395–396; Camblin 1951, 81–82; Robinson 1984, 163–164

425   MOY: SETTLEMENT   284980 356140

The site of a settlement on the west bank of the Blackwater is shown on Thomas Phillips' 1685 map of Charlemont and Moy. Today, this location is at the southern end of the Diamond in Moy, but no trace of the 17th-century settlement survives. It is possible that the original settlement influenced the existing town plan.

TYR 062:015

Map of Charlemont by Thomas Phillips, 1685 (NLI MS 2557/28)

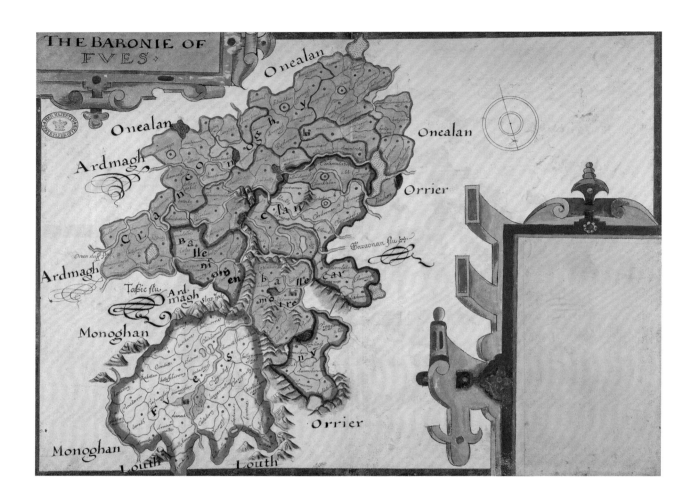

Chapter 6
County Armagh

Introduction

Until the advent of the Plantation, northern Co. Armagh was dominated by the O'Neills of Tyrone, with the O'Neills of the Fews and the O'Hanlons of Orior controlling much of the rest of the county. Armagh City was (and still is) the chief diocesan centre of Ireland, giving this area a strategic and cultural importance in the development of plantation settlement in Ulster. Many of the castles, manor houses, bawns and forts built or re-used in the county, however, do not survive. Indeed, twenty-three out of the thirty-three sites historically documented no longer have visible remains, but despite this attrition, there are still notable examples of early 17th-century architecture to be seen. Castleraw is a cruciform house that was erected by Sir Anthony Cope by 1622, its rather unusual plan having parallels elsewhere in Ireland and England. Later in date is Richhill – a Y-plan house decorated with Flemish gables at roof level – built by Major Edward Richardson c. 1670, which clearly illustrates the development of a country house that lacked the defensive elements of manor houses built the previous generation. There are also the fragmentary remains of a fortified house, supposedly built by the O'Connors or the O'Neills, on Derrywarragh Island in Lough Neagh (although it is also possible that Sir Toby Caulfield was responsible), illustrating that the Gaelic Irish élite were perhaps borrowing aspects of planter architecture. Here a brick chimney stack can be seen, although archaeological excavation would be required to elucidate more fully the ground plan of the building.

Armagh was of strategic significance with a number of fortifications built in the county during the late 16th and early 17th centuries. One of these was Moyry Castle located in the Gap of the North – an important ancient routeway linking Ulster with Leinster. This is a simple square tower built in 1601 as a campaign fort during the Nine Years' War under the direction of a Dutch engineer, working on behalf of Mountjoy's army. The English cartographer Richard Bartlett recorded a number of campaign forts on the River Blackwater during the Nine Years' War, including one erected on the Armagh side of the river by Walter Devereux, earl of Essex in 1575. It consisted of a large rectangular earthwork enclosure situated close to a wooden bridge over the river. Bartlett also portrayed Charlemont Fort, a square earthwork fort with bastions and a large

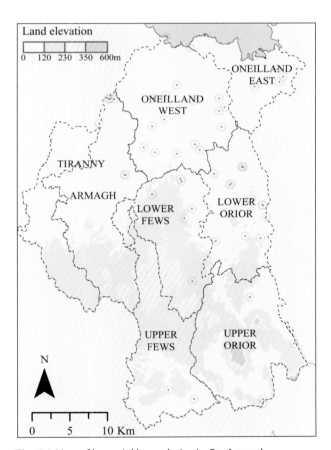

Fig. 6.1 Map of baronial boundaries in Co. Armagh.

outwork, which was later redeveloped in stone in the 1620s. Mountnorris was an early medieval rath re-used as a garrison fort, its earthworks embellished with a couple of bastioned outworks. Also of interest are the numerous English- and Irish-style houses depicted by Bartlett at Mountnorris and Charlemont housing the garrisons there. Other raths in the county, often referred to as 'Danish Forts', were used as bawns, as was the case at Brughas and Ballybrannan; the re-use of the earlier banks appears to have been an expedient measure by the settlers to build defensive strongholds with the minimum of effort and materials.

Armagh City was devastated during that war, with Bartlett recording a cathedral fortified by an English garrison surrounded by ruinous monastic buildings, and a few Irish-style houses still standing. The city did recover though, and by 1618 there were at least 120 households. As with the other counties, settlements arose under the patronage of landlords. Thus, Lurgan was founded by William and John Brownlow, and by 1619 was described as having forty-two houses, and paved streets, two water mills, and a wind mill. Originally associated with an O'Hanlon castle, Tandragee was re-established by Sir Oliver St. John, and by 1621 there were thirty-five English-style houses there, along with one water mill. By 1631, Portadown had a Saturday market and two fairs, on 1 November and Pentecost respectively. However, there are no known surviving buildings with a construction date earlier than the 18th century in Lurgan, Tandragee or Portadown, although street patterns may preserve the original layout of these settlements.

Barony of Oneilland (English undertakers)

Dowcoran and Ballynemony (Lurgan)

The lands around the town of Lurgan were two adjoining estates of 1,500 and 1,000 acres respectively. In 1610 these were allocated to John Brownlow and his son William, the latter becoming the owner of both upon the death of the father sometime between 1611 and 1619 (Hill 1877, 262 and 556). Carew in 1611 (*ibid.* 555) stated that both father and son had arrived in Ireland to manage affairs on their respective estates, but together they were

> ...dwelling in an Irish house. [They have] brought over six carpenters, one mason, a tailor and six workmen

> . . . Preparations to build two bawns.

John Brownlow built his bawn at Dowcoran in an oak-wood, naming the residence Brownlowe-Derry (*ibid.* 260). Pynnar in 1619 (*ibid.* 556–557) found there

> ...a very fair house of Stone and Brick, with good Lyme, and hath a Strong Bawne of Timber and Earth, with a Pallazado about it.

while at Ballynemony there was 'a strong Stone House within a good Island' – Oxford Island in Lough Neagh (Inv. 426) – although it is not clear whether William Brownlow ever lived there; it may have been erected to comply with plantation terms. Pynnar also recorded the first phase of what was to

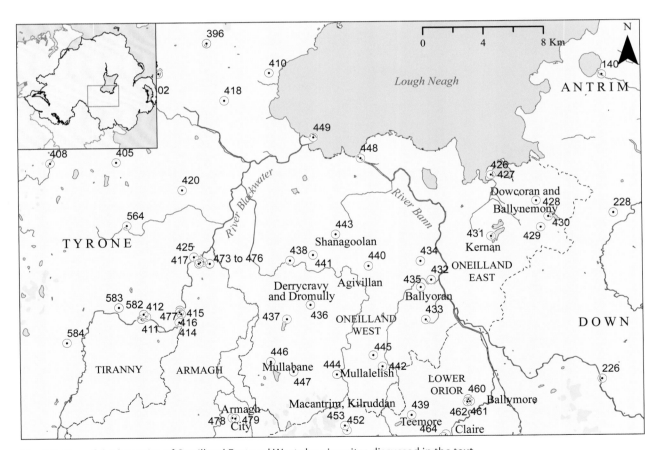

Fig. 6.2 Map of the baronies of Oneilland East and West showing sites discussed in the text.

become the town of Lurgan (*ibid.*; see Inv. 429). A similar report was made by the 1622 survey, which added that the Dowcoran bawn was now of lime and stone, and had one flanker, at the south-east, and that there were plans to add another diagonally opposite (Treadwell 1960, 128). Although attacked and expelled briefly in the 1640s, the Brownlow family stayed in the area and were central to the development of Lurgan in the 17th and 18th centuries, particularly the development of the linen industry, which was the economic mainstay of the town until the late 20th century (Clendinning 1969).

426   ANNALOIST: HOUSE   304730 361580

This is the likely site of the plantation house for the Ballynemoney proportion, built within the ruins of the old church (Inv. 427), and occupied by the Brownlows from *c.* 1611 until their move to Dougher in *c.* 1619 (Inv. 428). According to the 1622 survey, the house was, at that time, occupied by a freeholder, Wilfred Truman. Today there are no visible remains, although excavations at the church in 1968 revealed wall footings and other features that could indicate a house.

ARM 006:029

Clendinning 2005, 106–132

427   OXFORD ISLAND,   304730 361580
ANNALOIST: CHURCH
AND GRAVEYARD

The post-medieval church, which was built on a medieval site, was partly excavated during development work on Oxford Island in the 1960s, when a number of undated burials and wall foundations were unearthed, along with fragments of brick and glazed medieval pottery. The location is now an access road and car park in the Lough Neagh Discovery Centre.

ARM 006:011

Reeves 1847, 312–313; Atkinson 1925, 188–190; Collins n.d.

428   DOUGHER: HOUSE   307720 359790
AND BAWN
Woodville House

A house and bawn were built in 1619 at this general location by the Brownlow family. The 1622 survey described a

> ...howse of Castle of stone, and brick, lay'd with lime, 3 stories high . . . compassed with a strong Bawne of lyme, and stone, 159 foot long, 93 foot broad, and 15 foot in height, with a fair Flancker square to the South East; and he [Brownlow] is purposed to make another opposite.

A possible site for the bawn is located in the grounds of Woodville House, a 19th-century manor house. The appearance of some outbuildings on the site suggests the existence of an earlier house. However, an archaeological evaluation in 2007 found evidence for prehistoric and early medieval occupation of the site and nothing from the 17th century.

ARM 006:023

Hill 1877, 555–556; Treadwell 1960, 128; O'Regan 2007

429   LURGAN: SETTLEMENT   308000 358000

Lurgan was founded by William Brownlow around 1619. Inquisitions in 1629 stated that there was to be a market every Friday at 'Ballilurgan' and fairs on the feast-days of St. James and St. Martin, i.e. 1 May and 1 November. Pynnar stated the settlement had forty-two houses in 1619, inhabited by English, with paved streets, two water mills and a wind mill. The 1622 survey only accounted for forty houses and the windmill. The town was attacked and burnt in October 1641, with several of its occupants killed, but it was rebuilt, and flourished over the subsequent centuries. There are no known archaeological structures or features dating to the early 17th century in Lurgan.

ARM 006:024

Lewis 1837, I, 323; Hill 1877, 556–557; Fitzpatrick 1904; Treadwell 1960, 128

430   LURGAN: BAWN   308000 358000
Brownlow House

This is an alternative site for the bawn discussed above (Inv. 428). The Down Survey barony map of Oneilan depicts a castle at this location. The present house – now owned by the district council – was built by Brownlow's descendants in 1836, perhaps replacing an earlier building.

> HB14/24/018
> Down Survey barony map of Oneilan (PRONI D597)

Kernan

An estate of 1,000 acres was originally granted to a Mr James Matchett. According to Carew, Matchett's eldest son was resident and a bawn was under construction in 1611. By Pynnar's time, the estate had been sold to Sir Oliver St. John, Lord Viscount Grandison (Hill 1877, 557), who had

> …two Bawnes of Timber, and moated about, and made very strong. There is in each of these an English House of Cage work, and two English families dwelling in them.

An Inquisition in 1621 recorded that Grandison had also built twenty English houses and a water mill (Inv. 431; Paterson 1961, 119). The 1622 survey (Treadwell 1960, 129) stated, contrary to Pynnar's report, that there was only one bawn, with

> …a smale Timber howse thatched & compassed about with a Ditch, & a Quickset hedge. But we are informed his L[ordshi]p intends very shortly to build a stone howse & a Bawne upon it. In this house there now liveth two poor servents . . . There is also a Water Mill upon this Proporcon.

The population of the estate at that time consisted of nine or ten freeholders, fifteen leaseholders and eight Irish families. All above-ground traces of this plantation estate have now vanished.

431   BALTEAGH: WATER MILL   304700 357400

There are no visible remains at the approximate site of a mill, referred to by Inquisitions in 1621 as 'a water-mylle upon the river running through the land of Balteagh'.

> ARM 006:030
> Paterson 1961, 119

Ballyoran (Portadown)

An estate of 2000 acres on either side of the Upper Bann was granted in 1610 to William Powell – who immediately sold it – in lieu of back-pay for service in the King's Stables (Hill 1877, 261). The Carew survey (Hill 1877, 555) noted that the estate was in the possession of a Reverend Richard Roulston in 1611, and that one house was under construction. Bodley (*Hist. MSS Comm.* 1947, 78) recorded that Roulston had

> …set up a windmill and erected there 8 tenements, and hath the frames of 4 other ready to be erected. There are 100,000 bricks already burnt, and as many more ready for burning, with lime and other provisions lying in readiness for making of a brick house and bawn, whereof the foundation is laid.

Roulston, who was also the grantee of the Teemore estate, 9km to the west, suffered financial difficulties, which resulted in the sale of the estate to Richard Cope of Loughgall. He divided the estate into two parcels of 1,000 acres, keeping one and selling the other to Michael Obbyns (Paterson 1961, 120). Pynnar found the brick-built house complete, encompassed by 'a Bawne of Sodds, with a Pallazado upon it of Boards, ditched about' (Hill

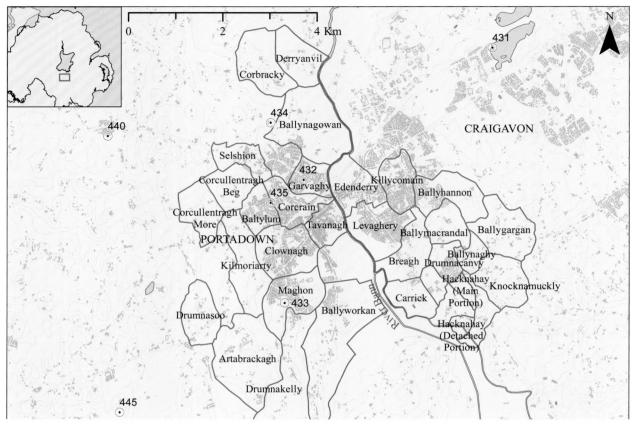

Fig. 6.3 Map of the proportion or plantation estate of Ballyoran.

1877, 558). The 1622 survey was consistent with his report, describing the bawn as '…but a yarde & Garden inclosed with a Pale' (Treadwell 1960, 129). These descriptions of the timber bawn suggest the possible re-use of an early medieval rath. Obbyns had to forfeit part of his estate to the Crown in order to settle debts; by 1626 the estate had been reduced to only 620 acres, although it remained in the possession of the Obbyns family until the 19th century (Hill 1877, 558; Paterson 1961, 120).

**432   WOODSIDE, GARVAGHY: 300700 354500
         HOUSE AND BAWN**

A wooden and earthen bawn was described by Pynnar and the 1622 survey (see above), and is marked on Taylor and Skinner's road map of 1777. It is, however, not indicated on the early OS maps,

so that the location remains imprecise. The area is now a residential housing estate, and there are no remains dateable to the 17th century above ground.

ARM 009:019

Lewis 1837, II, 462–463; Hill 1877, 174, 261–262 and 558; Treadwell 1960, 129

433   MAGHON: CASTLE   300300 351800

According to Paterson, an early 17th-century castle was the original seat of the Workman family. This was presumably a freehold on the Ballyoran estate until it was replaced by the present Mahon House in 1846–47, which lies immediately north of where the castle once stood. There are no visible remains.

ARM 009:020

Paterson 1961, 120

434 DRUMCREE: PARISH 300000 355750
CHURCH AND GRAVEYARD

This 19th-century parish church probably stands on the site of the medieval parish church. The 1609 Escheated Counties map of Oneilland West shows a roofless church in this location, although there is nothing now visible of this earlier building.

ARM 009:022

View of the Archbishopric of Armagh by Thomas Ashe, 1703 (PRONI T848/1); Leslie 1911, 266–267; Anon. 1927; Neill 2009, 577

435 PORTADOWN: 300000 354000
SETTLEMENT

Inquisitions in 1631 mention that 'Portedowne', as founded by Michael Obbyns, had a Saturday market and two fairs, on 1 November and at Pentecost. The layout of the plantation-period town is not known, and structures or features from the early 17th century have not been identified.

ARM 009:029

Lewis 1837, II, 462–463; Hill 1877, 558; Treadwell 1960, 129–130

Derrycravy and Dromully

These were two contiguous estates of 2,000 and 1,000 acres, situated between Loughgall and Charlemont. They were originally granted to Lord Saye and Seale, who never took possession (Hill 1877, 264). Carew's survey states that Sir Anthony Cope was the owner of both by 1611, and that the building of a castle, 'Castleraw', was underway (see Inv. 436; *ibid.* 555). Pynnar's survey states that there was an additional

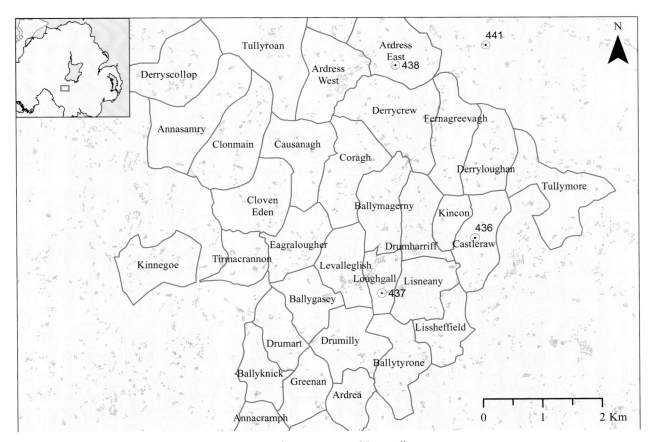

Fig. 6.4 Map of the proportion or plantation estate of Derrycravy and Dromully.

bawn with four flankers, with lodgings in one of them, along with two water mills, a windmill and fourteen timber houses (Inv. 437; *ibid.* 559). The 1622 survey clarifies that the bawn was situated in Dromully and occupied by William Pearson, Cope's steward, whereas the castle was in Derrycravy and occupied by Cope and his family (Treadwell 1960, 130).

436   CASTLERAW: CASTLE   292671 352851
AND ENCLOSURE

The ruined remains of a three-storied fortified house are located on the summit of a rounded drumlin with views in all directions. Carew recorded that it was under construction in 1611, writing

> They [Cope and his agents] have begun a fair castle of freestone, or other hard stone, 14 or 15 workmen, and 9 carpenters employed. Great part of the freestone for the coynes and windows are prepared 4 or 5 miles beyond Armagh.

while Bodley's survey recorded a disaster that befell the workers

> Cope had built a [f]air house of hewn stone wth clay, of great charge, wch being brought to perfection, a great part of it suddenly fell down, so it and whole must be demolished to ye ground, and newly raised with lime.

No such structure was mentioned by Pynnar in 1619, so presumably the rebuilding had not yet occurred. By the time of the 1622 survey, Castleraw had been rebuilt, and was described as a 'strong howse of lyme and stone'.

The ruins consist of the walls of a symmetrical, cruciform building, with only the parts of the northern wall of the western wing surviving to three storeys. Here there is a large opening caused by collapse, although a splayed window opening

Fig. 6.5 Fragmentary remains of Castleraw Castle.

survives at first-floor level. The remainder of the stonework is, at the time of writing, quite unstable, and much obscured by vegetation. The western and southern sides of the house only survive partially, reaching a maximum height of around 0.4m, or elsewhere as foundation courses. Much of the eastern side of the building is only traceable as footings, although the south-eastern corner is extant. The interior of the structure is at a lower level than the outside ground level.

The castle is surrounded by the fragmentary remains of what once was a large, near-square, earthwork enclosure defined by a bank and internal ditch, whose sides measure approximately 400m in length. The best-preserved remains of the enclosure are situated to the north and west. Its purpose is uncertain. Jope suggested that perhaps Cope was planning a defended settlement, since it is similar in scale and materials, for example, to the earthwork defences of Coleraine; though it has also been suggested that it might be a later deer park.

A ruined vernacular cottage immediately to the north-west of the castle dates to the early 19th century or earlier, and is likely to have been built partly from material taken from the ruins of Castleraw; it was demolished in the 1980s. Survey and excavation of the site in advance of this work did not reveal any 17th-century material, aside from brick, nor any trace of the original castle that fell shortly before Bodley's visit in 1613.

ARM 009:004

Hill 1877, 555; *PSAMNI* 1940, 63; *Hist. MSS Comm.* 1947, 174; Jope 1953a; Treadwell 1960, 130; Brannon 1983b; N. Brannon *pers. comm.* 2015

437 LOUGHGALL: SETTLEMENT 291100 351900
Pynnar's survey recorded that Cope '...hath built fourteen houses of timber, which are inhabited with English families'. This town is marked on the Down Survey map of the barony as 'Loggull towne'. This correlates with the position of Loughgall manor house, a late 18th or early 19th-century building, but there are no visible 17th-century remains. The walled garden at Loughgall was for many years thought to be the remains of the bawn at Dromully, as described by Pynnar, although small-scale excavations recorded in the SMR files determined that the enclosure was of 18th-century origin. Archaeological traces of a timber-framed building were uncovered (and subsequently preserved *in situ*) in nearby Levalleglish in 2003, with surface finds from the site indicating a late 17th-century date.

ARM 008:036

Down Survey barony map of Oneilan (PRONI D597); Hill 1877, 559; Dunlop 2003

438 ARDRESS: HOUSE 291350 355850
A house destroyed in 1641 was replaced by the earliest phase of the current Ardress House, which

Fig. 6.6 View of Ardress House.

dates to the *c.* 1660s. Of the earlier, plantation-period building, nothing remains, although the late 17th-century building is one of the few surviving examples of its kind in Ulster, despite many 18th- and 19th-century modifications. It is a two-storey, five-bay building with gable ends, owned by the National Trust and is open to the public.

HB15/02/048

Brett 1999, 82–84

Teemore

Also known as 'Semore', this was an estate of 1,000 acres granted to Rev. Richard Roulston. Carew stated that Roulston was living there in 1611, and had erected some English-style timber buildings (Paterson 1961, 122). Pynnar described a bawn (Inv. 439) and nine houses, all inhabited by English (Hill 1877, 560). Roulston mortgaged the estate to Sir Francis Annesley, who had come to own it entirely by the time of the 1622 survey, but by then the bawn was already 'soe decayed that it was of little defence' (Treadwell 1960, 130). In the 18th century, the estate was sold by Annesley's descendants to the Cope family (Paterson 1961, 122–123).

439 TEEMORE: BAWN 299300 345300
There are no visible remains anywhere in the townland of a bawn referred to by Pynnar as '...a Bawne of Sodds, with a Pallazado, and moated about, and a little House in it.', though its description suggests the re-use of an early medieval rath.

ARM 013:034

Hill 1877, 560

Agivillan and Brochus
An estate of 2000 acres was granted to John Heron who died in 1616, leaving the estate to his brothers Sir Edward Heron and William Heron (Hill 1877, 561). Pynnar found two small bawns, each surrounded by houses inhabited by English (*ibid.*). The estate was sold to Sir John Dillon in 1620, who was also the

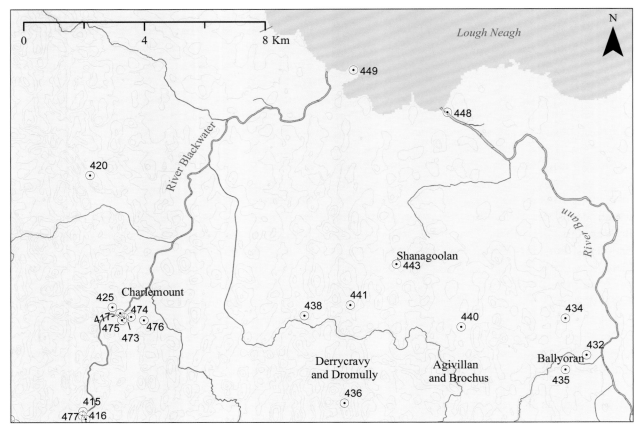

Fig. 6.7 Map of the distribution of sites and plantation estates between the Bann and Blackwater rivers.

owner of the neighbouring Mullabane estate (*ibid.*). The 1622 survey records only one timber house, roughcast with lime, occupied by Dillon and his family (Paterson 1961, 123). The estate was acquired by the Waldron family by 1630, and eventually merged during the 18th century with those of other propertied families in Ulster – the Copes and subsequently the Molyneuxes.

440   TIMAKEEL: BAWN   **296540 355460**

This is the possible site of one of the 'Two small Bawnes of Earth, with a Pallazado upon them, and a Ditch about them' recorded in Pynnar's survey. It is possible that the earthen bawn in this townland may be a re-used rath, corresponding to the 'Site of Fort' marked on the 2nd edition OS six-inch map at this location, and of which traces can still be seen in the

landscape. However, excavations around this area in 1999, 2002 and 2007 uncovered no 17th-century remains.

ARM 009:002

Hill 1877, 561; Large 2007

441   BRUGHAS: BAWN   **292870 356210**

This location is another possible site of one of the bawns referred to above (Inv. 440), or indeed both of them, as Pynnar's survey is unclear as to whether they adjoined each other or not. The 1st edition OS six-inch map shows a small circular enclosure, a rath which may have been re-used for a small palisaded earthen bawn. There are now no visible remains, and the area is occupied by recent farm buildings and an orchard. There is a local account of a mound in the immediate area, but this has since been destroyed.

ARM 005:007

Hill 1877, 561; Neill 2009, 348

442 BALLYBREAGH: HOUSE   297407 348627

At this site, which lies within the neighbouring Mullalelish estate, there are no visible remains of a house erected in *c*. 1620 by John Dillon, who acquired the Agivillan estate from the Heron family. Inquisitions for that year mention a mansion house measuring 60ft by 20ft in the townland of Ballenraye, which correlates with the modern townland of Ballybreagh. The only large house in this townland on the 1st edition OS six-inch map was at Wheat Field; it was demolished in the 1970s, and the area has been extensively landscaped since.

ARM 013:044

Hill 1877, 561

Shanagoolan

Also known as 'Kannagoolan', this was an estate of 1,500 acres granted to William Stanhawe. According to Carew (Hill 1877, 555), Stanhawe's son Stephen was overseer, but had done nothing. Pynnar, and the 1622 surveyors, also found nothing built. The ownership of the estate can, however, be traced at various points, and it remained under the ownership of Stanhawe's descendants until the turn of the 20th century (Paterson 1961, 126).

443 CLONTYLEW: HOUSE   294400 357600

Clontylew House is the possible site of a house, which was burnt by insurgents along with its ancillary buildings, according to the deposition of one Christian Stanhawe on 19 July, 1642. The house was probably built after 1628, as no buildings on the estate were mentioned in Pynnar's survey, or in the Inquisitions of 1628. The grounds have been landscaped, and there are no indications of earthworks that could be associated with an earlier structure.

ARM 005:010

Deposition of Christian Stanhawe, 1642 (TCD MS 836, ff 075r-076v, currently available via *http://www.1641.tcd.ie*); Hill 1877, 561

Mullalelish and Leggacorry

2,000 acres were granted to Francis Sacheverell (whose surname is spelled in different ways in the historical documents). Carew stated that he had '…brought over three masons, one carpenter, one smith, nine labourers, and two women; four horses and a cart' (Hill 1877, 555). Pynnar gave no details of buildings on the estate; the 1622 survey stated that in Legacorry there was a house and bawn (Inv. 444), and that in Mullalelish, another dwelling was under construction (Inv. 445; Treadwell 1960, 131). For some unknown reason, Leggacorry was leased in 1622 for a term of 21 years to Archibald Atcheson, who owned large estates in the Fews barony (Paterson 1961, 126). Sacheverell's granddaughter, Ann, inherited the estate in 1649, and married Edward Richardson in 1654; their descendants, based at Richhill, maintained ownership of the estate until the late 19th century (*ibid*. 128).

444 RICHHILL: HOUSE   294370 348100
AND BAWN
Richhill House

Richhill House (also known as 'Richhill Castle') was built in *c*. 1670 for Major Edward Richardson on a spur of high ground overlooking the village of Richill. It is a Y-plan house, with the front façade of the building flanked by projecting wings, and a centrally placed stairwell block to the rear. The main entrance and windows are arranged in a symmetrical manner, while the roofline is distinctive with its pedimented gables and dormer windows, and panelled chimneystacks. The 1622 survey recorded a previous house and bawn on the site, described as a

…dwelling house of stone and lyme,

covered with Thatch, and about it is a Bawne of Clay and Stone, rough-cast with lyme, 198 foot long, 19 foot broad [sic], 8 foot high, with 4 open Flanckers of the same height.

It is not known if any of the fabric of the earlier buildings were re-used in the construction of Richhill House, as the exterior walls have been rendered, obscuring details of the masonry.

HB15/15/001

Treadwell 1960, 131; Jope 1960, 118–120

445 ROWANTREES HILL, MULLADRY: BAWN AND SETTLEMENT   296800 349400

The house of Francis Sacheverell at Mulladry, in this approximate location, is mentioned in the 1641 Depositions as having been attacked and burned in 1641. The site at Rowantrees Hill was identified as an ancient castle at the time of the 1st edition OS six-inch map in 1835. The present farm buildings at this location do not show any 17th-century features.

ARM 009:010

Hill 1877, 260 and 262–263

Mullabane

An estate of 1,000 acres in the vicinity of Hockley, was granted to John Dillon. Carew reported that Dillon and his family were resident in 1611, and had brought twenty-two English families, cattle, horses and various workmen and servants, and had cut down many oak trees (Hill 1877, 555–556). Bodley stated that there was much building undertaken within a 'strong rath' (*Hist. MSS Comm.* 1947, 175). Pynnar and the 1622 surveyors found two villages totalling twenty-nine families, and a 'fair' but unfinished brick-built house, but no bawn (Hill 1877, 563–564; Treadwell 1960, 131–132). The estate was inherited in 1637 by Henry Dillon, grandson of the original grantee, who sold it in the 1650s after coming of age. (Paterson 1961, 128–129).

446 BALLYBRANNAN: RATH AND BAWN   290000 349000

The site of an early medieval rath, and perhaps also the location described by Bodley in 1613 as that of

> …certain small buildings within a strong rath . . . He [John Dillon] hath cast his clay for brick, and made other provisions ready for a stone house to be set in the said rath, which he purposeth to fortify and make defensible.

The rath survives as a low and level, semicircular earthwork platform, with sides sloping southwards from its southern edge. Along the northern side of the platform, nothing distinct survives, and there is no trace of any features indicative of post-medieval settlement.

ARM 012:085

Hist. MSS Comm. 1947, 175

447 HOCKLEY: SETTLEMENT   291500 348300

Pynnar recorded in 1619 that there was on the Mullabane estate '…a great Store of Tenants, the which have made two Villages, and dwell together.' One of these villages was Hockley, which today is comprised of 19th-century and more recent buildings, with nothing obvious surviving from the plantation-period village. It is not clear where the second village was located.

ARM 012:086

Hill 1877, 564–565; Paterson 1961, 128

Other sites in the Barony of Oneilland

448 DERRYINVER: BOAT TIMBER   296100 362800

An oak rib from a clinker-built boat (one where the longitudinal timbers overlap on their edges) was found in the 1990s among reeds in a marsh close to the mouth of the Upper Bann, the entrance to Lough Neagh. It was dated by dendrochronology to AD

1612 + 9 or later; as the sample did not contain any sapwood, it is impossible to state the upper limit for the felling date of the tree. The rib was fastened by trenails, wooden dowels or pegs, which swell when soaked and thereby hold the timber fast, a technique commonplace in the 17th-century.

ARM 002:009

D. Brown *pers. comm.* 1994 (archived in SMR files); McCarthy 2005, 66–69

449   DERRYWARRAGH ISLAND: 292990 364250
FORTIFIED HOUSE
AND ENCLOSURE
O'Connor's stronghold

The remains of a 17th-century fortified house stand near the north-eastern shore of Derrywarragh Island in Lough Neagh, at a strategic position close to the mouth of the River Blackwater and the border with County Tyrone. It is situated at the end of a ridge overlooking Lough Neagh, and possibly was built to monitor this part of the lough. The site is referred to as 'The O'Connor's Stronghold' in the *OS Memoirs* and maps, but locally it was known as O'Neill's Castle, at least in the early part of the 20th century. Between 1607 and 1628, the lands that surround the 'castle' were leased by Sir Toby Caulfield (see Inv. 408), raising the possibility that the house was constructed by Caulfield or one of his under tenants. The ruins consist of the eastern side of a fortified house, measuring approximately 5.5m by 4m and 10m in height. Three chimney flues can be seen in the masonry, which is topped by a brick chimney stack. There is much archaeological potential in the area surrounding the ruins; some 10m to the south of the house are the remains of a low bank-and-ditch earthwork that cuts off the end of the ridge, and is presumably associated with the building. Geophysical survey in the environs of the house in 2012 revealed the presence of buried features likely to be related to the house and its gardens.

ARM 002:001

PSAMNI 1940, 61; Day and McWilliams 1990a, 121; Donnelly *et al.* 2004; Mussen 2012

Barony of Fews Lower (Scottish)

Coolemalish

An estate of 1,000 acres was granted to Henry Acheson, who sold it to his brother Archibald. Carew (Hill 1877, 564–565) described the presence of people, cattle and horses on the estate, and that materials had been prepared for building. Pynnar found a bawn (Inv. 450) but nothing else, as did the 1622 survey; indeed in 1661 an Inquisition stated that the bawn was the only development on the estate (Hill 1877, 565; Paterson 1961, 129: see also Clancarny below).

450   CARRICKLANE: BAWN   295380 339270
Gosford Bawn

A bawn built by Henry Acheson was described by Pynnar as

> …a Bawne of Clay and Stone, being 120 feet long, and 80 feet broad, with four Flankers. In this Bawne there is

Fig. 6.8 View of remains of fortified house on Derrywarragh Island.

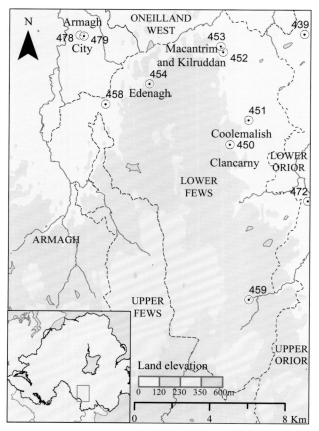

Fig. 6.9 Map of the barony of Fews Lower showing sites discussed in the text.

a House, the one half is Stone and Lyme, and the upper part is Timber.

In the 1950s, it was noted that the remains of unusually thick walls, perhaps bawn walls, were incorporated into the out-offices of a farm at this location. However, they have not since been located, nor is there any local knowledge of them.

ARM 017:041

Hill 1877, 565–566; Treadwell 1960, 132

451 GOSFORD: CASTLE 296350 340600
Gosford Castle

Gosford Castle is a 19th-century building, on the site of a structure built around 1675. This, in turn, replaced an earlier structure some 400m to the east

of the current building, which was destroyed in 1641, leaving no visible remains from the early 17th century.

ARM 017:010

Brett 1999, 91–9

Macantrim and Kilruddan

These were initially two adjoining, but distinct, estates of 1,000 acres each, granted to James Craig and William Lawders respectively. Carew's survey (Hill 1877, 564) stated that Craig had built a mill and some tenements at Macantrim, and had already harvested his crops of oats and barley. At Kilruddan, Lawders had built and repaired houses, prepared further building materials, and had ten families, three servants, eighteen horses and sixty cows (*ibid.*). Bodley found Scotsmen at Macantrim, but no further progress with respect to building (*Hist. MSS Comm.* 1947, 176). By the time of Pynnar's survey, both estates were under the ownership of John Hamilton. Pynnar (Hill 1877, 566–567) found a bawn on each estate, both of stone and clay and 60ft square and 12ft high. At Kilruddan, there was a house within the bawn (*ibid.*), now unlocated, while the bawn at Macantrim became known as Hamiltonsbawn (Inv. 452).

452 HAMILTONSBAWN: BAWN 295000 344300
A bawn was built here by John Hamilton at some point between 1613 and 1619, the uncertainty resulting from it not being mentioned in either of the earlier surveys by Carew and Bodley. Pynnar described a stone and clay bawn, 60 feet square and 12 feet high, with two flankers. The 1622 survey described a slightly larger structure measuring 90ft by 63ft, and '...within the Bawne there is a little old thatched house, wherein lyes a poore Scottish man. But there is no Gate to the Bawne'.

The site of this bawn is well known, as it was built upon several times during the 18th century. In 1729, Johnathan Swift composed a jovial poem 'Whether Hamilton's Bawn Should Be Turned Into A Barrack

Or Malt-House', describing a debate between Sir Arthur and Lady Acheson (of Gosford) regarding the fate of the building. Lewis, in 1837, described the site as '…the ruins of a castle, which, until recently, was regularly garrisoned'. Today, the site is a broad, flat platform next to the roadside, with no visible remains.

ARM 013:014

Lewis 1837, II, 2; Treadwell 1960, 132

453   HAMILTONSBAWN: 294866 344620
ARMORIAL STONE

An armorial stone from John Hamilton's bawn (Inv. 452 above) has been built into the gable wall of a disused public house on the corner of the Main Street and Mullaghbrack Road in Hamiltonsbawn. It is an elaborately carved piece, with a shield carrying the Hamilton family coat-of-arms. Motifs representing the family include a heart and three cinquefoils. On top of the shield is a partly damaged zoomorphic crest, from which sprouts elaborate mantling that surrounds both sides of the shield. The stone is 2.5m above ground level and measures *c.* 0.6m × 0.7m. There is no motto, inscription or date on the stone.

ARM 013:027

Fig. 6.10 View of the armorial stone at Hamiltonsbawn.

Edenagh Estate

This was an estate of 1,000 acres, originally granted to Claude Hamilton, but reduced to 500 acres following a dispute with the dean of Armagh over land ownership (Hill 1877, 567; Paterson 1961, 130). Most of the estate was sold to John Hamilton in 1617 (*ibid.*).

454   KILLEEN: BAWN   291090 342560
Killeen House

The bawn on the plantation estate of Edenagh, built by Claud Hamilton, was described as under-construction by Carew in 1611 and Bodley in 1613. Inquisitions in 1617 stated that there was a

> …bawne of lime and stone, being 80 foote square and 9 in height, with rounds and flankers at the corners therof in the townland of Killeni.

Apparently this townland was not included in the lands sold to John Hamilton in 1617, and its history after that date is obscure. It is possible that the bawn was located on land that later became the grounds of Killeen House, but there are no known remains at this location.

ARM 012:087

Hill 1877, 567

Clancarny Estate

An estate of 2000 acres originally granted to Sir James Douglas. Clancarny was purchased by Archibald Acheson, who also acquired the adjoining Coolemalish estate (Hill 1877, 568), thereby creating a large estate of 3,000 acres around Markethill and Gosford. Pynnar (*ibid.*) found a bawn with four flankers, and

> …a Castle begun, which is 80 feet in length, 22 feet wide, and is now two Stories high. There is near to this

Bawne seven Houses inhabited with British Tennants.

The house was also described by the 1622 surveyors (Treadwell 1960, 133) as

…part of lyme and stone, part of lyme and clay . . . Himself [Acheson] and his wife and Familie doe inhabit in the said howse.

There are no known visible archaeological remains on the Clancarny lands originally granted to Douglas. The estates of Coolemalish and Clancarny were passed down through many generations of the Acheson family; the earldom of Gosford was established for Acheson's descendants in the 19th century and the title is still current, although much of the land was sold in the 1950s to the Forestry Service (Paterson 1961, 132).

Sir Turlough McHenry O'Neill's Estate

455 CREGGAN BANE GLEBE: 293210 315910
CHURCH AND GRAVEYARD

An 18th- to 19th-century parish church stands on the site of a 15th- or 16th-century predecessor, shown on Bodley's map of 1609 as being roofed and with a tower. A map of the graveyard prepared in 1909 indicated that some ruins of a former 'chapel' stood to the south of the current church, but these are no longer visible. The site has significance as the

Fig. 6.11 Extract from Bodley's map of 1610 illustrating church at Creggan Bane Glebe.

burial place of the O'Neills of the Fews whose vault, which is likely to be of similar date to the original church, is located at the site.

ARM 031:020

Leslie 1911, 206–207; Ó Fiaich 1973, 6–8; Neill 2009, 503–504

456 GLASDRUMMAN: TOWER 296600 314680
HOUSE AND BAWN
Glassdrummond Castle

A tower house that was the stronghold of the O'Neills of the Fews was once sited upon a highly defensible cliff top position overlooking Glassdrumman Lough. It was probably constructed in the late 15th century, or perhaps as late as the mid-16th century, and was deliberately burnt by Sean O'Neill in 1642 on the approach of an English army. The Down Survey parish map of 1655 shows 'a fayre castle' at this location, indicating that it was rebuilt by then. From the early 18th century onwards, it was used as a source of building material for nearby houses and roads, and only fragmentary vestiges survived until recent decades. In the 1970s remnants of a castle wall were visible, but this too has since disappeared. There is nothing now above ground to mark the archaeological and historical significance of the site.

ARM 031:027

Down Survey parish map of Cregan (PRONI D597/4); Ó Fiaich 1973, 24–25; Neill 2009, 478–480

Captain Anthony Smith's Estate

In 1611, Carew reported that Captain Anthony Smith had

. . . drawn some families of British to dwell upon the lands thereunto adjoining, which is a good relief to passengers between Dundalk and the Newrye (Hill 1877, 565).

This small-scale 'plantation' was undertaken in the mountainous region known as 'The Gap of the North', a natural frontier and one of the most important ancient routeways into Ulster from the south.

457   MOYRY PASS: CASTLE   305760 314660
AND BAWN
Moyry Castle

The remains of a castle built in 1601 under the direction of a Dutch engineer, working on behalf of Mountjoy's army, overlooks the Moyry Pass in the Gap of the North. The castle, which was never occupied for long, was part of an estate awarded to Captain Anthony Smith, although there were disputes between Smith and Lord Moore, Viscount Drogheda, concerning the boundaries of their respective properties. Carew described it as

Fig. 6.12 Remains of a castle overlooking the Moyry Pass in the Gap of the North, built by Lord Deputy Mountjoy in 1601.

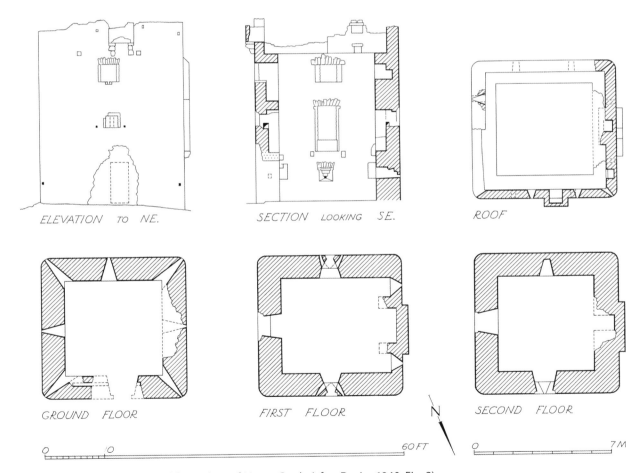

ELEVATION TO NE.   SECTION LOOKING SE.   ROOF

GROUND FLOOR   FIRST FLOOR   SECOND FLOOR

Fig. 6.13 Elevation, section and floor plans of Moyry Castle (after Davies 1940, Fig. 2).

...a pretty castle upon the park of the Moyrye . . . where Captain Anthony Smith is constable, and has a ward of 12 men.

The remains consist of a square three-storey tower of random rubble, with rounded corners. It is encompassed by fragments of a bawn wall, which stand up to 2.75m high.

ARM 032:005

Hill 1877, 565; Davies 1940; Hayes-McCoy 1964, 2, pl. I

Other sites in The Fews

458 KIRK HILL, BALLYMORAN: CHURCH, GRAVEYARD AND ENCLOSURE

288770 341440

This is the likely site of a church – probably the medieval parish church of Clonconchy – that was, according to Lewis, destroyed in 1641. An earthen bank 45m long, part of an irregular enclosure marked on the 1st edition OS six-inch map, is the only visible remnant. There was an extensive graveyard, which remained in use until the 19th century.

ARM 016:053

Lewis 1837, II, 286; Neill 2009, 495–496.

459 BALLINTEMPLE: CHURCH AND GRAVEYARD

296412 330769

Ballymoyer Old Church

A parish church with a roof and tower is depicted in 'Ballemoire' on the 1609 Bodley map of the Fews. This medieval church was replaced by another church, which according to tradition was built during the reign of Charles I (1625–1649), but not

finally completed until 1775. The remains of the later church consist of the roofless ruins of a rectangular building, measuring approximately 19m by 10m, orientated east-west, with walls of split stone rubble. There are two window openings in the side walls and one in the eastern gable. Unusually for a church, the upper portion of a chimney survives between the windows along the north wall. The graveyard is heavily used, containing rows of marker stones, and a scattering of memorial stones, the earliest dated 1713. The church was in use until 1833, when a replacement parish church was built immediately to the east.

ARM 021:030

View of the Archbishopric of Armagh by Thomas Ashe, 1703 (PRONI T848/1); Map of the 'Baronie of Fues' (NA MPF 1/60); Lewis 1837, I, 154–155; Leslie 1911, 139–140; *PSAMNI* 72; Gwynn and Hadcock 1970, 374 and 406; Neill 2009, 482–484.

Barony of Orior (Allocated to servitors and Natives)

Cornechino Estate

An estate of 500 acres was originally granted to Lord Audley, who passed it to his son-in-law Sir John Davies. He sold it soon after 1620 to Lord Grandison (see Inv. 460–462 below), but it seems that no development ever took place (Hill 1877, 569), and there are no known archaeological remains on the estate dating to the early 17th century. A further 2000 acres originally granted to Arte McBarron O'Neill also reverted to Lord Audley, and then passed to the second husband of his widow Elizabeth, Sir Piers Crosbie (Paterson 1961, 140).

Ballymore (Tandragee) Estate

An estate of 1,500 acres was granted to Sir Oliver St. John, who was elevated to the peerage around 1620, becoming Lord Viscount Grandison. The estate

Fig. 6.14 Extract from Bodley's map of 1609 illustrating the medieval church of Ballymoyer in Ballintemple.

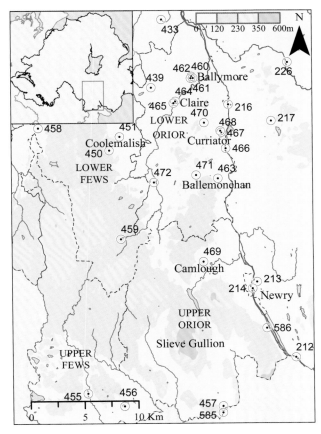

Fig. 6.15 Map of the baronies of Orior Upper and Lower, and Fews Upper showing sites discussed in the text.

was situated on former O'Hanlon territory around Tandragee, and Pynnar mentions a town (Inv. 461) but no bawn (Hill 1877, 570). In fact, Grandison re-edified the O'Hanlon stronghold (Inv. 462), and also erected a new church in the town by 1622 (Paterson 1961, 136).

460   BALLYMORE: CHURCH   303070 346360
Tandragee Church

A church built close to Tandragee Castle in the early 17th century was complete by the time of the 1622 survey, which described

> …a handsome Church, 60 foot in length, and 24 in breadth well furnished with Seates, Comunion Table, Capp, Font and a good Bell.

It was replaced in 1812 with the current building, and there is nothing visible of the old church, although an inscription on the baptismal font records its former existence. Remains of the old church were apparently uncovered during the 1812 rebuilding, and were said to have exhibited signs of a fire that the building suffered in 1641.

ARM 014:021

Treadwell 1960, 134; Tilson undated.

461   TANDRAGEE: SETTLEMENT   303200 346200

The origins of the village are medieval, originally associated with the O'Hanlon castle (Inv. 462), but the foundations of the present village are rooted in the plantation settlement of Ballymore founded by Sir Oliver St. John. The Inquisitions in 1621 recorded

> …a town thereunto adjoining [the castle], consisting of 35 English-lyke houses…also one water mylle upon the river Cowsher.

The 1622 survey noted twenty-seven houses. However, in the village today, there are no surviving buildings earlier than the 18th century.

ARM 014:022

Lewis 1837, II, 593–594; Hill 1877, 310, 569–570; Treadwell 1960, 134; Paterson 1961, 116.

462   BALLYMORE: CASTLE   303000 346180
Tandragee Castle

Tandragee Castle is a 19th-century structure, built on the site of an O'Hanlon stronghold dating from medieval times, rebuilt by Sir Oliver St. John, Lord Viscount Grandison, during the Plantation. The location (now that of a well-known potato crisp factory) occupies a commanding location above the town. The 1622 survey stated that

> …the Lord Grandizon hath built one castle of lyme and stone, 33 foot in Length and 29 foot broad, and 3 stories high, with an Addicon

of Building 66 foot in length and 20 foot broad, makeing it a stong and Comodious dwelling, being compassed about with a Bawe [sic] of lyme & stone, with a Flancker on the North side, 14 foot square, and a little Platforme adioyning to the house, on the Rock on the South side with Flanckers. There are in the same Bawne one Faucon and 2 Fauconnetts of Brasse [light cannon], mounted, and Armes within the Castle, Shott and Pike for 40 men.

This building was nonetheless attacked and burnt by the O'Hanlons in 1641. It was not rebuilt until the early 19th century, when Lewis recorded the work as under way. There are no visible remains of any fabric earlier than the 19th-century.

HB15/05/007

Lewis 1837, II, 593–594; Hill 1877, 310 and 569–570; Camblin 1951, 20 and 47; Treadwell 1960, 134; Paterson 1961, 116

Ballemonehan Estate

Also known as 'Drumbanagher', this was an estate of 1,000 acres granted to Sir Gerald Moore, Viscount Moore of Drogheda, one of the agents responsible for the 1603 Treaty of Mellifont that ended the Nine Years' War. Carew noted that Moore was providing timber for building, and Pynnar found a bawn (Inv. 463) inhabited only by an Irishman, who dwelt in one of the flanker towers (Hill 1877, 569–570). The same bawn, now under English occupancy, was recorded in 1622 (Treadwell 1960, 133–134)

463 KILLYBODAGH: HOUSE AND BAWN   305460 336540

This is the site of a house and bawn, built by Sir Gerald Moore. Pynnar described 'a Bawne of Lime and Stone, very near 100 feet square, with two

Flankers.' The 1622 survey added that one of the flankers contained

> ...a good strong house of stone, 20 foot square 3 stories high . . . The Gates of this Bawne are fitt to be made stronger.

Drumbanagher House, a ruined 18th- or 19th-century building, occupies the site and it seems unlikely that any early 17th-century remains survive.

ARM 022:020

Hill 1877, 570; Treadwell 1960, 133–134; Paterson 1961, 115

Claire Estate

This property of 2,000 acres was the amalgamation of two properties of 1,000 acres both granted in 1610; Tawnnavaltiny, to Sir John Bouchier, and Ballyclare, to Francis Cooke (Hill 1877 311–2; Paterson 1961, 137). The Bouchier family came to possess both before 1619. Carew mentioned that Sir John was providing building materials, while Pynnar and the 1622 surveyors found a bawn built by Sir John's younger brother Henry (Inv. 464), but no other buildings (Hill 1877, 569–571; Treadwell 1960, 134).

464 CLARE: CASTLE   301550 343980

Pynnar described a bawn of lime and stone built by Henry Bouchier, 100ft by 80ft and 14ft high, with two flankers and a stone house under construction. The structure was still unfinished at the time of the 1622 survey, which also stated that one of the two flankers was used as a dwelling house, and that two more flankers were planned for the bawn. The site was destroyed by fire in 1785, leaving no visible remains. The 1st edition OS six-inch map of 1835 shows Clare Castle in ruins, while the 2nd edition shows a quadrangular site and circular tower. A later folly, a stone and brick tower, stands close to the site, and immediately to the north is a range of

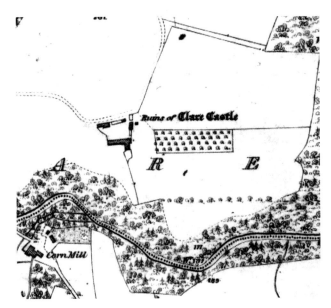

Fig. 6.16 Extract from 1st edition Ordnance Survey map (1835) depicting the ruins of Clare Castle.

farm buildings of similar scale to the historically documented dimensions of the bawn. These may have been built against the bawn when it was still standing.

ARM 013:020

Hill 1877, 570–571; Treadwell 1960, 134

465   DRUMINURE: MILL   301380 343800

It is possible that this 19th-century mill complex occupies the site of an earlier mill mentioned in the deposition of Elizabeth Roulston on 21 August, 1642, who stated that '…John Boomers wife fetcht forth of the Earle of Bathes mill & drowned in the river of the Cowsher…'.

ARM 013:045

Deposition of Elizabeth Roulston, 1642 (TCD MS 836, ff 068r-068v, currently available via http://www.1641.tcd.ie)

Curriator Estate

Also known as 'Brenoge', this was a small grant of 200 acres to Lieutenant Charles Poyntz, on lands bordering Co. Down, around the villages now known as Acton and Poyntz Pass (Hill 1877, 312). Carew (*ibid.*) stated that nothing had been built; only that building materials had been gathered. Pynnar's survey noted two bawns (see Inv. 466 and Inv. 467) but no other buildings. Poyntz, who was knighted for military service in 1636, married the sister-in-law of Sir Marmaduke Whitechurch, and the estate came to be greatly enlarged in size (Paterson 1961, 135). His granddaughter married Charles Stewart of Ballintoy, and their descendants held the estate until the early 19th century (*ibid.*).

466   LOUGHADIAN: BAWN   306200 339440

Lewis, writing in 1837, refers to the stump of a castle, said to have been built in 1647, probably on the site of the first bawn built by Poyntz, which was described by Pynnar as

> …80 feet square, the lower part whereof is of Stone and Clay, with a House in it; but he [Poyntz] not liking of the seat.

There are no visible remains at the site. The border between Down and Armagh has been slightly realigned since the 17th century, and this site now lies in Co. Down.

DOW 033:034

Lewis 1837, II, 432; Hill 1877, 569 and 571

467   BRANNOCK: BAWN   305800 340980

There are no visible remains at the site of a house and bawn built by Charles Poyntz and described by Pynnar as begun in 1619 to replace another bawn and house which Poyntz found inadequate. The 1622 survey described

> …a fair dwelling house of Brick… and hath an Orchard, Gardens, yardes, & Backsides, inclosed with a Ditch quicksett, besides a Bawne and Stable.

ARM 018:039
Hill 1877, 571; Treadwell 1960, 134

468   ACTON: VILLAGE   305710 341130

Poyntz built a small plantation village adjacent to his bawn (Inv. 467), named after his childhood home of Acton in Gloucestershire. The 1622 survey stated that eight English families were present in the village at that time. Although Acton has remained a population centre over the centuries, all traces of the 17th-century buildings have been lost.

ARM 018:043
Hill 1877, 571; Treadwell 1960, 134

Camlough Estate

1,000 acres were granted originally to Henry McShane O'Neill, who sold his reversion (the right to inherit the property) to Sir John Bouchier, who in turn sold the property to Sir Francis Blundell, after which it passed to Sir Toby Caulfield. Caulfield was in possession of the estate by the time of the 1622 survey, which was the first time that building work on the estate – in the form of a proposed bawn – was documented (Inv. 469; Paterson 1961, 139).

469   MAGHERIEHELIN: BAWN,   304050 328580
GRAVEYARD AND CHURCH
Convent of Mercy

The 1622 survey noted the intention of Lord Toby Caulfield (see Inv. 408 in Co. Tyrone) to build 'a Bawne & Castle, according to the Patterne of the Ld. Grandizons, at Ballymore' after he acquired the Camlough estate. Approximately 35m of the bawn wall survived until the 1960s, and has since been rebuilt and incorporated into a garden wall at the Covent of Mercy, near Bessbrook.

A map by Sir Josias Bodley in 1609 depicts a roofed church in 'Macheriehelin'; Reeves noted that this chapel stood next to the remains of Caulfield's bawn, and that the bawn in question was built from hewn stones taken from the ancient abbey of

Fig. 6.17 Extract from Bodley's map of 1609 depicting a church in Magheriehelin.

Killevey. Of the church nothing remains, although the reconstructed bawn wall delimits a burial ground, which presumably is also the site of the church.

ARM 026:020
Bodley Map of the 'Baronie of Orier', 1609 (NA MPF 1/59); Lewis 1837, I, 247; Leslie 1911, 156–157; Paterson 1948, 129; Treadwell 1960, 114; Neill 2009, 534–535.

Other sites in Orior Lower

470   SHANEGLISH: 304220 341910
ECCLESIASTICAL SITE

Place-name evidence suggests that there may have been an early ecclesiastical site within this townland, which was under church ownership in 1609. There is a local tradition of a graveyard at this site, which is located on the summit of a rounded hill. There are no visible remains or historical references to any church.

ARM 018:038
Glancy 1954, 87; Neill 2009, 543

471   LISNAGREE: EARTHWORK   303440 336870
Tyrone's Ditches

The origins of the linear ditches, described in documentary records and shown on all editions of the OS six-inch map, are debatable, but they were probably dug during the Nine Years' War. The association with the earl of Tyrone was noted in the *OS Memoirs*. Although the Co. Armagh Survey stated that there was no visible trace, a section of a substantial, curvilinear ditch survives. Its original extent is unknown but presumably it was much longer. The survival is a length of ditch some 50m long, 5–6m wide and 2m deep, situated between two

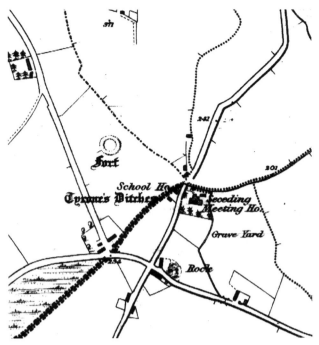

Fig. 6.18 Extract from 1st edition Ordnance Survey map (1835) depicting earthworks called 'Tyrone's Ditches' at Lisnagree.

roads and somewhat obscured by vegetation. There is no indication of an associated bank.

ARM 018:031

Lewis 1837, II, 472; Day and McWilliams 1990a, 10; Neill 2009, 153

**472   MOUNTNORRIS: 299520 336170
         SETTLEMENT AND FORTIFICATION**

A fort, constructed around 1600 within what was originally a bivallate rath, is illustrated on one of Bartlett's pictorial maps composed sometime after 1601, along with a sprawl of single-storey houses both inside and outside. Aside from the outer bank and ditch of the rath there are no visible remains. The extensive earthen outworks depicted by Bartlett have been tentatively identified with low topographical features in the surrounding fields, while the uneven interior of the rath perhaps reflects some of the houses. Nothing visible survives of the village.

ARM 021:001

Hayes-McCoy 1964, 3–4, pl. II; Neill 2009, 424–425

Barony of Armagh

Charlemont and the River Blackwater

**473   CHARLEMONT: 285380 355780
         ARTILLERY FORT
         Charlemont Fort**

Originally built by Lord Mountjoy in 1602 as a stronghold on the Blackwater, central to many other smaller fortifications on either side of the river, the fort saw many modifications during the 17th-century. The original fort, as depicted by Bartlett, was a square structure with half-bastions at each corner, along with additional outworks enclosing a village between it and the river. From 1603 and through the opening decades of the Plantation, it was under the command of Sir Toby Caulfield who

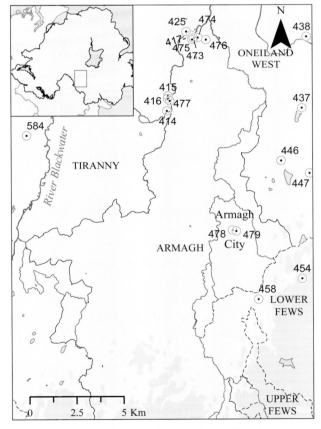

Fig. 6.19 Map of the barony of Armagh showing sites discussed in the text.

Fig. 6.20 Aerial view of Charlemont Fort, defended by a perimeter wall with corner bastions and outer defensive earthworks.

heavily reworked it in 1622. He built a house within the fort, rebuilt the bastions, and added a gatehouse and drawbridge to the southern side. Along with the adjoining town of Charlemont, the fort was seized by Irish forces under the command of Sir Phelim O'Neill in 1641. The occupation lasted nine years, during which another defensive ditch was dug around the town (see Inv. 474). The Irish garrison faced at least three attacks, all unsuccessful, in the 1640s – by Montgomery in 1642 and Monro in 1643 and 1645 – and during this time, further defences were added to the east of the fort. In July and August 1650, the fort was again besieged, this time by Coote's Parliamentarian army. Coote managed to force O'Neill to surrender the fort, but under terms favourable to O'Neill and at a huge cost – the loss of life was officially 50 men on the Parliamentarian side, but other estimates, based on contemporary accounts, suggest 500 to 800 fatalities.

The site is located at the end of a ridge overlooking the Blackwater River and close to Charlemont Bridge – a crossing that made the site so strategically important. An outer defensive earthwork of the fort survives as a bank *c.* 50cm to 2.0m high, somewhat truncated in places by recent developments. Inside this is a stone wall, obscured by vegetation in places, which preserves the outline of the fort.

ARM 004:001

Hayes-McCoy 1964, 7, pl. IV; Ó Tuat-Gáill 1911;

PSAMNI 61; Jope 1960, 101; Day and McWilliams 1990a, 80–81; O'Neill and Logue 2008

**474   CHARLEMONT: 285600 355810
EARTHWORK
Charlemont Fort, outer ditch**

The remains of a ditch and rampart around Charlemont, cast up by Phelim O'Neill's workers during 1641–42, are illustrated on the Thomas Phillips' map of 1685. This earthwork defence, almost 1300m in length, is retained by property boundaries in the village. The most visible surviving part of the earthwork is a bank some 50m long that runs north-south alongside the canal in a field to the east of Charlemont fort. It appears to survive no higher than *c.* 60cm, and is truncated at its southern end by a more recent field boundary.

ARM 004:011

Map of Charlemont by Thomas Phillips, 1685 (NLI MS 2557/28 and NLI MS 3137/37)

**475   CHARLEMONT: 285300 355700
SETTLEMENT**

The modern village of Charlemont has its origins in the early 17th century, when numerous English-style houses were erected surrounding the nearby fort, as depicted by Bartlett in 1602/03 and Thomas Phillips in 1685. Although no features survive above ground, the general layout still reflects its origins. Some low earthworks between the northern edge of the fort and the river are generally thought to be 17th-century in origin.

ARM 004:012

Richard Bartlett 'Plan of Charlemont Fort and bridge over the Blackwater', (NLI MS2656-4); Map of Charlemont by Thomas Phillips, 1685 (NLI MS2557/28 and NLI MS3137/37); Marshall 1924a

**476   ANNAGHMACMANUS: 286030 355695
FORTIFICATION**

No visible remains survive at the approximate site of fortifications constructed by Sir Phelim O'Neill

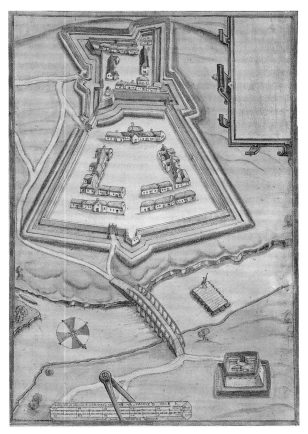

Fig. 6.21 Bartlett's map of Charlemont settlement *c.* 1602.

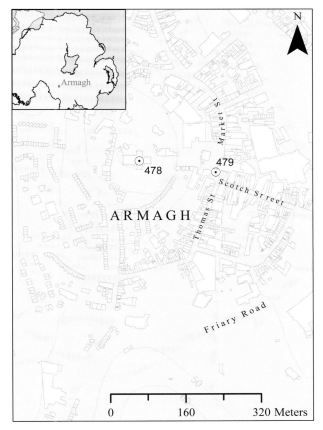

Fig. 6.22 Map of sites in Armagh City.

during the latter stages of the wars of 1641–1653, when this was an 'island' known as 'McKittrick's Island' in otherwise boggy ground.

ARM 004:013
Marshall 1924a

477 LISBOFIN: FORTIFICATION, 284100 352300 BRIDGE AND SETTLEMENT
Blackwater Fort

A map, 'The Plott of Black Water', dated 27 March 1587, shows a fortification in the style of a tower house, with earthen ramparts enclosing a number of houses, along with a village just outside. The fortification guarded a bridge crossing over the River Blackwater. The site, however, has long since been lost; the area is now a business park.

ARM 008:050
Blackwatertown 'The Plott of Black Water', 1587 (NA MPF 1/99)

Armagh City

Armagh has been the secular and spiritual centre of Ulster and is also traditionally the place where St Patrick began his ministry in Ireland in AD 445, and thus has been an important ecclesiastical centre from Early Christian times to the present day. The earliest church in the City, first documented in the late 7th century (Hamlin 2008, 222), was set within a rath-like earthen enclosure. The core of the Metropolitan Cathedral of St. Patrick dates to the 12th century, although the building has been restored many times since, including in 1660 to repair damage caused by an attack by Sir Phelim O'Neill in 1641 (for an overview, see Gallogly 1880). Archbishops during the Plantation were Henry Ussher (1595–1613: he was also a co-founder of Trinity College Dublin), Christopher Hampton (1613–1625), and James Ussher (1625–1656), a prolific scholar most famous for his computation in 1650 that dated the Creation to 4004 BC.

Since its foundation, the hill upon which the cathedral is situated was also the location of monastic and secular settlement (for an overview, see e.g. Camblin 1951, 5–8). Armagh was illustrated on a pictorial map, probably by Richard Bartlett around 1601, which depicted the cathedral, ruinous monastic buildings, and a few Irish-style houses (Hayes-McCoy 1964, 5–6, pl. III). Much of the land around the city was occupied by natives at the time of the Plantation (Glancy 1955, 115–117), and this situation remained unchanged until 1615, when Archbishop Hampton set his lands to various gentlemen, including Sir Edward Doddington (*ibid.*; see also Inv. 478).

**478   ARMAGH CITY: 287400 345200
SETTLEMENT
Armagh City Centre**

The first census in the city was conducted in 1618, when the town was found to consist of at least 120 households, with several cabins, stables, barns, kilns and shops. Nothing remains of these structures above ground, although foundations have been uncovered on several occasions during archaeological investigations in the city (see Inv. 479).

ARM 012:101

Glancy 1955; Lynn 1975–76 and 1988

**479   ARMAGH CITY: 287600 345150
SETTLEMENT
Market Street and Scotch Street excavations**

An excavation in Market Street in 1975 revealed a 17th-century occupation layer in an area that was formerly subject to waterlogging. Excavations in 1977, 1979 and 1980 in Scotch Street revealed the

Fig. 6.23 Excavations on Market Street in Armagh in 1975 revealed 17th-century features including cobbling.

presence of 17th-century pits and property divisions, although these features were not examined in detail at the time. Seventeenth-century documents show that Scotch Street is in an area known as *Na Ferta*, meaning 'graves' or 'burial monuments', but these date from the early medieval period. A site was found at 50–56 Scotch Street, with three phases of post-medieval activity overlaying early medieval burials and other medieval horizons. These were pits – interpreted as rubbish pits – and property boundaries. No trace of any of these archaeological features is visible on the ground.

ARM 012:089 and ARM 012:095–7

Lynn 1975–76 and 1988

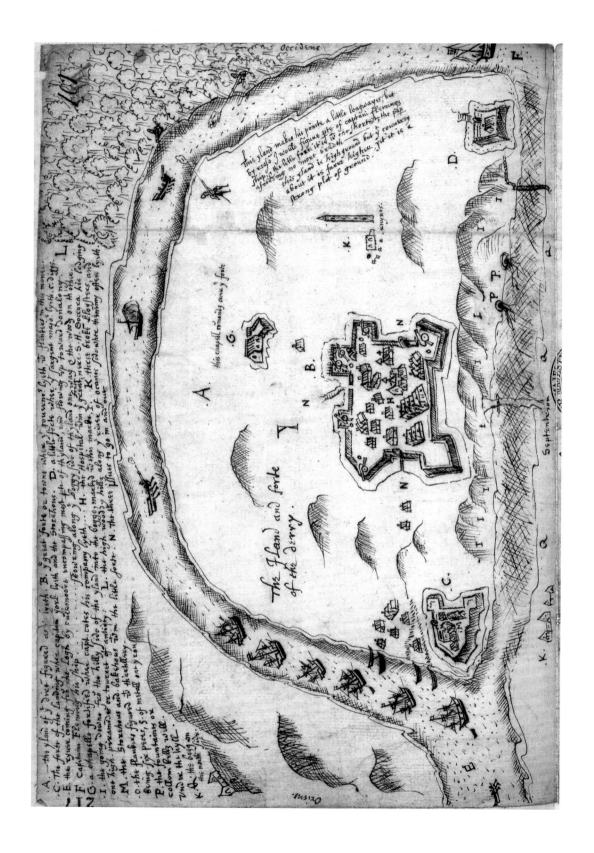

Chapter 7
County Londonderry

Introduction

The jewel in the Ulster Plantation was Co. Londonderry, which was previously known as the County of Coleraine until the City of London was 'encouraged' by the Crown to invest in new estates there. The territory fell originally under the O'Cahan lordship, along with the portion of the O'Neill lordship of Clandeboye that was west of the River Bann. Eleven (the Haberdashers soon pulled out pleading lack of funds) of the twelve London Great Companies and their affiliates (Curl 1986, 34–36) were chiefly involved: the Goldsmiths, Grocers, Fishmongers, Ironmongers, Mercers, Merchant Taylors, Clothworkers, Skinners, Vintners, Drapers and Salters. They came together under a representative company The Honourable The Irish Society (Curl 2000). As with plantation settlement elsewhere, the Companies were expected to build manor houses and bawns, encourage the development of market towns and villages, and promote agricultural and industrial development on their estates. Most of these settlements have continued to the present day, though less has survived of the individual buildings that were erected.

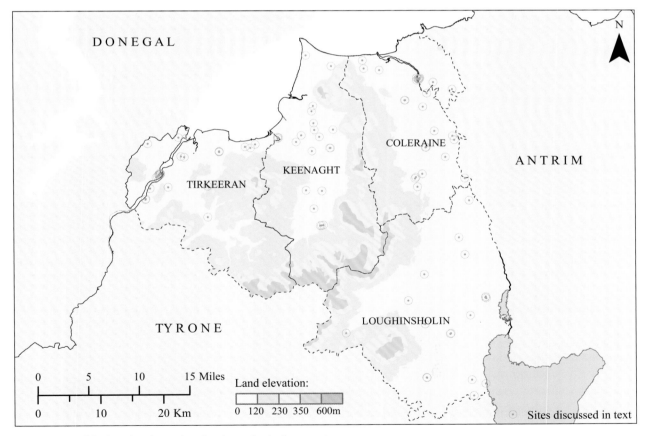

Fig. 7.1 Map of Co. Londonderry showing baronies in the county.

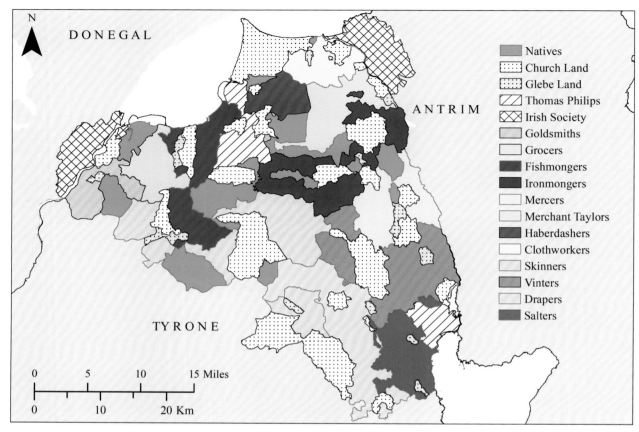

Fig. 7.2 Map of Co. Londonderry showing the different proportions granted to the London Companies in the county (re-drawn after Curl 2015).

The appearance and layout of the company settlements were recorded in 1622 by Thomas Raven, whose maps showed in great detail the various manor houses, bawns, parish churches and different types of housing that were occupied by the leaseholders and tenants on the various estates. The information on these maps tallies with surviving archaeological sites, such as the bawns at Ballykelly (the Fishmongers), Movanagher (the Mercers), Brackfield (the Skinners), Bellaghy (the Vintners) and Salterstown (the Salters). An exceptionally detailed drawing by Raven of the residence of Sir Edward Doddington at Dungiven (who leased the entire Skinner estate), along with a written description by Sir Thomas Phillips, compares closely with the upstanding remains of an Augustinian priory and tower house, and the excavated evidence of an English-style manor house located within the bawn.

Two towns were chosen by the government to secure the newly settled areas of the county – Coleraine and Derry. Coleraine at that stage was a pre-existing town of Anglo-Norman origin, but it was Derry – a Gaelic Irish ecclesiastical centre – that was destined to become the largest urban centre in the newly formed county, being renamed as Londonderry in honour of the London Companies to whom a charter was issued in 1613. The city was surrounded by an impressive wall that was built between 1613 and 1619 with angle bastions as platforms for artillery (e.g. Scott *et al.* 2008, 63–97; Scott 2011a), and which remains today as one of the most complete circuits in Europe. During the 1980s, archaeologists uncovered the cellars of several 17th-century houses in the city, the ground floors of which were plastered internally, and featured stone fireplaces, brick ovens and flagstone floors (Lacey 1981).

St. Columb's Cathedral is the most impressive church building erected in 17th-century Ulster in terms of scale and appearance, its perpendicular gothic style directly influenced by English church architecture (Curl 2000, 142–147). Indeed, it was the first post-reformation cathedral to be built in either Ireland or Britain. Smaller parish churches that were documented on Raven's maps of the different London Company Proportions: Ballykelly (the Fishmongers), Eglinton (the Grocers), Movanagher (the Mercers) and Dungiven (the Skinners), along with churches elsewhere such as Lissan, Maghera and Tamlaght O'Crilly, all point to an investment by the planter landlords and settlers keen to establish an enduring religious and cultural presence in the landscape.

The Londoners' Plantation

City of Londonderry

Derry, traditionally a sacred oak-grove upon a low hillside on the banks of the Foyle, was chosen as the site for a new town – the centrepiece of the involvement of the City of London in the plantation project, and an exemplar of all that the enterprise could bring to Ireland. The city is sited on what is virtually an island, nestled between the Foyle and the 'Bogside' – a palaeochannel that the river once cut through on a former course (Lacey 1990, 1–5). The wider landscape overlooks the city from much higher ground, which is its key defensive weakness. The settlement history of Derry is, however, long and complex; the area is particularly rich in Early Neolithic settlements for example, whose inhabitants were probably attracted there by the combination of fertile farmland, suitable building sites and materials, and the river itself, with its opportunities for communication and travel both inland and out to the sea (e.g. Thomas 2012, 1–2; Ó Baoill 2013, 1–35 and references therein). These

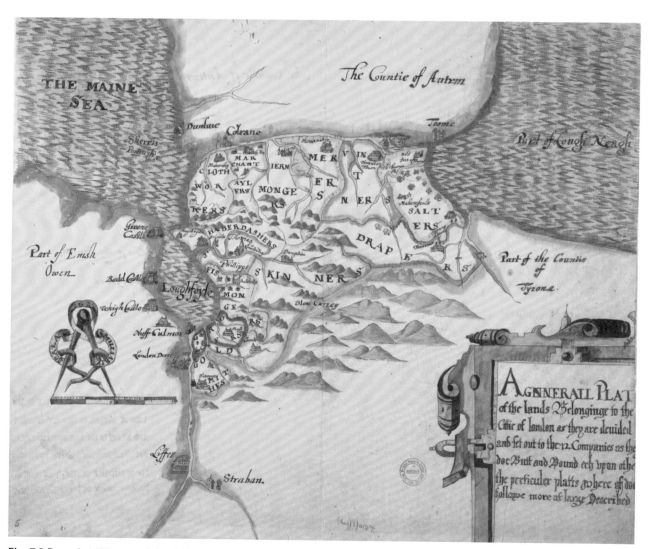

Fig. 7.3 Raven's 1622 map of the different proportions granted to the London Companies.

topographical attributes resulted in the site being of major importance in the early medieval period, with a monastery founded here by St Colum Cille (Columba) in AD 546, close to the borders of the secular lands of the two major dynasties of the Northern Uí Néills, the Cenél nEógain and Cenél Conaill (for an overview, see Ó Baoill 2013, 36–52). The ecclesiastical and secular settlement of Derry continued throughout the medieval period, although the region was always remote from the Anglo-Norman focus in the east of Ireland – instead Derry was a Gaelic centre, close to the power base of the O'Neill and O'Donnell lordships. By the 16th century, the English government had developed a close interest in Derry; some 700 English soldiers were based there during a successful campaign to quell an O'Neill revolt in 1566 (Lacey 1990, 68–70). A fire enveloped Derry the next year, probably destroying what remained of the medieval town, with a large explosion occurring at *Teampall Mór* (Inv. 486), then used as a magazine (ammunition store) (*ibid.*).

In 1600, the Annals of the Four Masters record events that heralded a major phase of redevelopment. Some 4,000 English soldiers and 200 cavalry had arrived at Culmore, and according to the Annals

> The English immediately commenced sinking ditches around themselves, and raising a strong mound of earth and a large rampart . . . After this they tore down the monastery and cathedral, and destroyed all the ecclesiastical edifices in the town, and erected houses and apartments of them. Henry Docwra was the name of the general who was over them. He was an illustrious Knight, of wisdom and prudence, a pillar of battle and conflict . . . The English . . . were seized with distemper and disease, on account of the narrowness of the place in which they were, and the heat of the summer season. (tr. O'Donovan 1848–1851, VI, 2193).

Docwra and his men had been sent to Derry as part of the English strategy devised by Lord Mountjoy to defeat Hugh O'Neill and bring to an end the Nine Years' War. Having fortified the 'Island of the Derrie', Docwra used it as a base to bring the area gradually under control (e.g. Scott 2011b) and, following the signing of the Treaty of Mellifont in 1603, which ended the war, he was appointed Governor. In 1606, he sold his interest to Sir George Paulett (whose daughters Elizabeth and Dorothy married prominent planters in the county – Sir Edward Doddington and Sir Thomas Phillips respectively), but in 1608 Derry was seized and destroyed by Sir Cahir O'Doherty, the last of the Gaelic lords still in the region following the Flight of the Earls in 1607. He was killed and his rebellion crushed by the army of Sir Arthur Chichester (Lacey 1990, 78–79).

Therefore, although in ruins, Derry's potential as a power-base for the government in north-western Ireland had been established. Plans for the Plantation of Ulster were under way, and Derry was marketed directly to the merchants of the City of London. A pamphlet (Hill 1877, 362) was prepared to entice the Londoners towards accepting the project as a profitable enterprise to invest in – in addition to abundant fishing and fowling,

> The harbour of Derry is very good . . . These coasts are ready for traffic with England and Scotland, and lie open and convenient for Spain and the Straits, and fittest and nearest to Newfoundland

An agreement between the Crown and the Great Companies was reached in 1610, with The Honourable The Irish Society formed in 1611 to represent the investors (Curl 2000); in 1613 the society was awarded the 'Charter of Londonderry' to undertake the building of a new, fortified town and work began immediately (see Ó Baoill 2013, 101–102). The historical documentation for the early development of the town is prodigious (for an overview, see Curl 1986). The town was never particularly populous; throughout the 17th century much of the townscape was open space, with the houses arranged along streets, each with a large garden (Thomas 2012, 3-4). The population rose slowly but steadily, especially in the 1620s; in 1622 there were only 171 'British' adult males in the city, but by 1628 there were 305 (Robinson 1984, 223). Unlike many British settlements, the town was not attacked in 1641, and indeed many settlers from the wider region flocked to the protection offered by its walls (Curl 2000, 151–152). In 1649, during the Confederate Wars, in an episode that challenges assumptions about traditional allegiances in Irish history, the Parliamentarian garrison in the town was attacked by a Royalist, Presbyterian army. It was besieged for twenty weeks before the besiegers were driven off by a force of Catholic soldiers under the command of Eoghan Roe O'Neill, acting on behalf of the Parliamentarians (Kelly 2001, 31–52). Later

in the century, the town was famously besieged by James II for 15 weeks in 1689, and there was much damage, but a period of rebuilding and expansion followed. In the 18th century, the city began expanding beyond the walls; the town became a centre of manufacturing, industry and international trade, even – briefly – eclipsing Belfast as the largest town in Ulster (Thomas 2012, 1–7).

480   LONDONDERRY: 243620 416730
CITY WALLS

In 1619, Pynnar described the newly-completed walls of 'London-Derry', noting that:

> The City of London-Derry is now compassed about with a very Strong Wall, excellently made and neatly

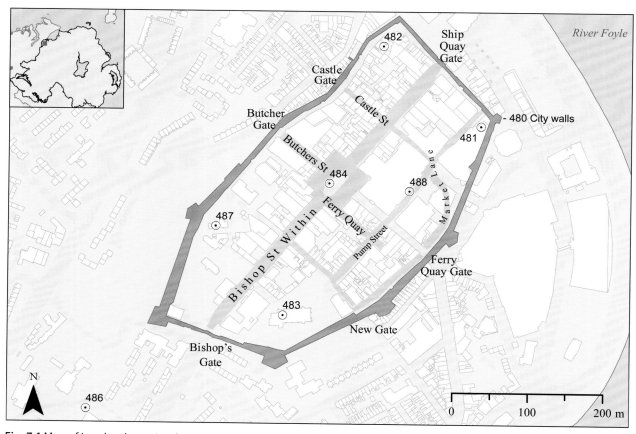

Fig. 7.4 Map of Londonderry city showing the individual sites discussed in text.

Fig. 7.5 Aerial view of the walled city of Londonderry, the street pattern reflecting the original 17th-century settlement.

wrought ; being all of good Lime and Stone ; the Circuit whereof is 283 Perches and 2/3, at 18 feet to the Perch ; besides the four gates which contain 84 feet : and in every Place of the Wall it is 24 feet high, and six feet thick. The gates are all battlemented, but to two of them there is no going up, so that they serve no great use ; neither have they made any Leaves for their Gates ; but make two Draw-Bridges serve for two of them, and two Portcullices for the other two. The Bullwarks are very large and good, being in number nine ; besides two half Bullwarks ; and for four of

them there may be four Cannons, or other great Pieces ; the rest are not all out so large, but wanteth very little. The Rampart within the City is 12 feet thick of Earth ; all things are very well and substantially done, saving there wanteth a House for the Soldiers to watch in, and a Centinell House for the Soldiers to stand in, in the Night, to defend them from the Weather, which is most extreme in these Parts.

The walls were commissioned by The Honourable The Irish Society, designed by Captain Thomas Raven and Sir Edward Doddington, and built between 1613 and 1619, with much of the construction supervised by Captain John Baker of Culmore Fort. The building works were undertaken by Peter Benson, a master bricklayer from London who had, by 1619, bought into the Plantation with the purchase of the Shragmirlar proportion in Donegal. The walls are still owned by The Honourable The Irish Society, and despite urban expansion and infrastructural development over the centuries, they remain intact and are among the most complete and best-preserved of any walled town in Europe.

The walls enclose an approximately rectangular area, 475m by 275m orientated north-east to south-west. For simplicity, most published descriptions of the walls and the historic town refer to the north-eastern wall as the 'north side' and re-orientate accordingly, which is the convention followed here. Their perimeter is 1.3km, and the walls stand 6m to 8m high and 4.5m to 9m in width. There were originally four gates: Shipquay Gate on the north side, Ferryquay Gate on the east side, Bishop Gate on the south side, and Butcher Gate on the west side. These gates still survive, though subject to much remedial works, and are joined by three additional gates - New Gate, Castle Gate and Magazine Gate. Eight bastions were originally built around the walls, of which five survive. A walk around the illuminated rampart walkway or terreplein reveals several features of military architecture, including gun loops, embrasures and sentry boxes. Twenty-

Fig. 7.6 The city walls of Derry~Londonderry overlooking the Bogside, with Royal Bastion in the background.

three cannon ranging in date from 1590 to *c.* 1780 are placed around the walls.

The foundations of Water Bastion, demolished around 1850, were uncovered during excavations in 1983. The wall was discovered to have an external batter and sandstone quoins at its corners.

LDY 014:033

Hill 1877, 386, 514–515 and 573–574; Moody 1939, 79–80, 150, 160, 171–172, 186, 196 and 254; *PSAMNI* 193 and pl. 44; Milligan 1948; Brannon 1986, 93–94; Lacey 1990, 92–96; Mitchell 1992, 14; Logue 1999a; Scott *et al.* 2008, 63–97; Scott 2011

481 LONDONDERRY: **243630 416740**
TOWN DITCH
Millennium Forum

Earthworks associated with the 17th-century town walls have been revealed by archaeological excavations in 1998 and 1999, which also uncovered a number of vaulted cellars. These may have been used for storage, or as a place of refuge, and were part of a network of similar underground structures that together constituted part of the town's original defences. The excavations also revealed the method of construction of the earthen rampart behind the city wall. The outer face of the wall was backed by 7m to 8m of clay, 2m to 3m high, comprised of material dug from the extra-mural town ditch. The ditch itself was partly excavated in 1978 at a site in Fountain Street, some 250m south-west of the Millennium Forum, where it was found to be 10m wide and 2m deep.

LDY 014:039

Logue 1999b; Ó Baoill 2013, 121–123

482 LONDONDERRY: **243500 416850**
TOWER HOUSE
O'Doherty's Castle; The Magazine

A tower house was built in the 15th or 16th century by the O'Dohertys to help maintain control over the harbour at Derry for the O'Donnell overlords. It was depicted on the early maps of Derry as a tower house inside a bastioned fort. In Carew's plan of Derry in

Fig. 7.7 Extract from Raven's 1622 map of Londonderry illustrating a tower house within the confines of the walled city. This castle was originally built by the O'Dohertys in the 15th or 16th century.

1611, it is marked as 'The little forte and Castle'. The building survived the construction of the adjacent city walls, and later into the 18th century when it was used as a magazine. The O'Doherty Tower Museum was built near this site in 1986, in the style of a medieval castle.

LDY 014:032

Sir Thomas Phillips' map and report, 1622-1841 Phillips MSS (PRONI T510); Moody 1938, 187; Davies and Swan 1939, 202; Milligan 1948, 7–8; Lacey 1990, 61–62; Day *et al.* 1996a, 98–99.

**483 LONDONDERRY: 243370 416480
CATHEDRAL
St Columb's Cathedral**

The Cathedral Church of St Columb occupies a prominent site within the walled city of Londonderry. It was built at a cost of £4,000 between 1628 and 1633, and is also the oldest surviving building within the city walls. The builder was William Parrott, and the works were supervised by Sir John Vaughan, as commemorated in an inscription in the western vestibule under the tower:

Fig. 7.8 St. Columb's Cathedral was built at a cost of £4000 between 1628 and 1633, and as such was the first post-reformation cathedral to be built in either Ireland or Britain.

if stones covld speake /
then london's prayse /
shovld sovnde who /
bvilt this chvrch and /
cittie from the grovnde /
vaughan aed

The building is in the Perpendicular Gothic style, a conservative choice, and was the last major application of that architectural idiom in Ireland until the Victorian Gothic Revival. Although somewhat modified over the centuries, much of the cathedral is original, and it remains the mother church of the diocese and an active place of worship in the city.

The cathedral consists of a six bay nave, lean-to aisles and a four-stage western tower, and its walls are of locally quarried stone with sandstone dressings. Originally there were circular towers located at the south-eastern and north-eastern corners of the main tower, as well as at the eastern corners of the church building. The former were subsequently removed, while the latter were retained when the cathedral was extended eastwards. The exterior walls of the nave and aisles are battlemented, so too are the circular corner towers towards the eastern end of the building, but these embellishments date from the early 19th century. The building became a significant military feature – a Parliamentarian citadel was built around the cathedral in the 1650s, incorporating part of its eastern wall, and this stood until the 1670s. An original timber spire was removed early in its history, and plans to rebuild it were disrupted by the 1689 siege, when its lead sheathing was reputedly made into pistol bullets and cannonballs, while the tower itself acted as an artillery platform. The tower was slightly heightened in 1778 when a new spire was added – then entirely rebuilt in 1802, with a replacement spire added around 1822. The interior of the cathedral was remodelled in the mid-19th century. The chancel was extended from the east of the building in 1887, although the original stonework from the east window was re-used during this work.

LDY 014:034

Moody 1939, 276–286; Lacey 1990, 99–101; Curl 2000, 142–148; Scott *et al.* 2008, 89–90; Ó Baoill 2013, 122, 127–135

Fig. 7.9 St. Columb's Cathedral dominated the 17th-century skyline of Londonderry as illustrated in Thomas Phillips' vista of the city in 1684–85.

484   LONDONDERRY: **243430 416660**
SETTLEMENT

Aside from St. Columb's Cathedral (Inv. 483), there are no upstanding buildings from the plantation period, although the overall layout of the city streets, as recorded by the early maps and surveys, has been maintained in today's street plan. Central to the space enclosed by the city walls is a town square, later termed 'The Diamond', in common with other plantation towns in Ulster. From this led four streets, now named after the original city gates that they connected: Shipquay Street (originally Silver Street) to the north, Ferryquay Street (originally Gracious Street) to the east, Bishop Street Within (originally Queene's Street) to the south, and Butcher Street (originally Shambles Street) to the west. Excavations

Fig. 7.10 Raven's map of the City of Londonderry in 1622 illustrating that the settlement was arranged around a town square, later known as 'The Diamond', from which ran four principal streets towards gates in the city walls.

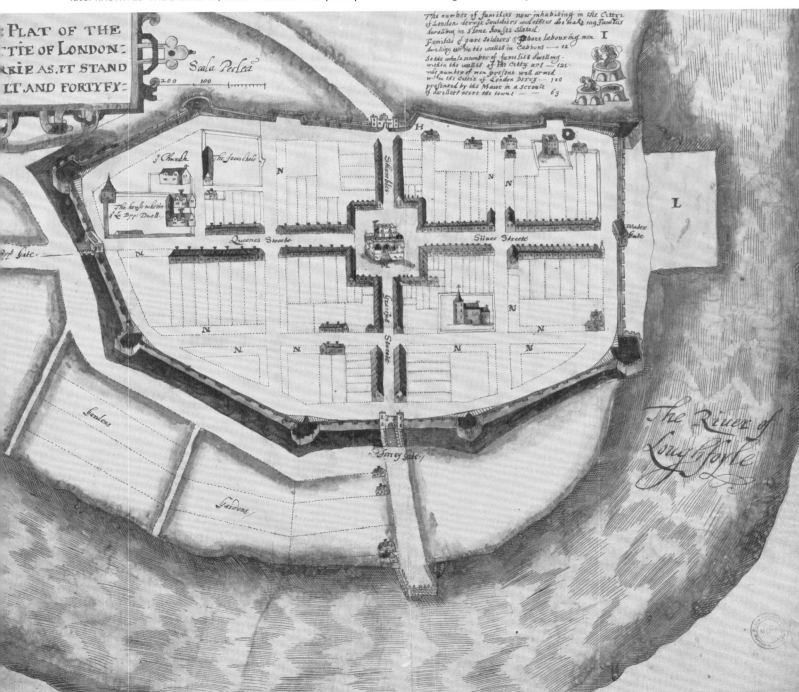

in 2014 at the Apprentice Boys' Museum in Magazine Street unearthed a ditch, house foundations, and clay tobacco pipes of early 17th-century date.

LDY 014:063

Camblin 1951; Lacey 1990; Ó Baoill 2013, 123–124; A. Gahan *pers. comm.* 2015

485   LONDONDERRY: 242916 416169
TOWER MILL
Lumen Christi College Tower Mill

The shell of a tower mill used as a Jacobite arsenal during the siege of 1689 stands in the grounds of Lumen Christi College (formerly St. Columb's College), on a strategic, elevated site known as 'Windmill Hill'. Its precise date of construction is

Fig. 7.12 The interior of the tower mill on 'Windmill Hill' with its brick-lined walling.

unknown, but it is presumed to be mid-17th century in date, thus making it one of the earliest examples in Ireland. The doorway at ground-floor level reveals a brick-lined chamber. In vertical section, its shape resembles a bullet, with the cellar walls tapering inwards at all sides towards a culvert at its base. There are no indications for a suspended floor within this chamber. The site was acquired by the Bishop of Derry, Frederick Augustus Hervey, in the late 18th century, and the structure was converted into a dovecote, with an icehouse built adjacent to it. The remains are in excellent condition, having recently been consolidated.

LDY 014:500

Dwyer 1893, 171–172; McCutcheon 1980, 231

Fig. 7.11 The remains of a mid-17th-century tower mill stand on 'Windmill Hill' in the grounds of Lumen Christi College. The windmill, illustrated on Phillips' vista of the city in 1684–5, was converted into a dovecote in the late 18th century, with an icehouse built beside it.

486   LONDONDERRY: CHURCH   243110 416350
Tempull Mór

This is a modern Roman Catholic church, built on the site of a medieval parish church whose foundations were pre-Norman. *Tempull Mór* became a cathedral in the mid-13th century, and was damaged during the Elizabethan wars. It is depicted as ruinous on many of the early 17th-century maps, though the date of its final destruction is, however, unknown. There are no visible remains of the earlier medieval church, but the site still remains a place of worship,

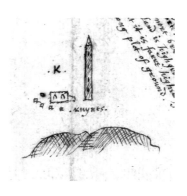

Fig. 7.13 Extract from Docwra's map of 'the Derrie' illustrating *Tempull Mór* (K), a cathedral that once stood in the area during the later medieval period. There are no visible remains of the cathedral, and the site is now occupied by St. Columba's Long Tower Church.

St. Columba's Long Tower Church occupying the site. This was the first Roman Catholic church built in the city after the Plantation, in 1784, its construction funded by Frederick Augustus Hervey, the Anglican 'Earl Bishop'.

LDY 014:025

Lacey 1990, 24–28, 36-40 and 50–52; Hamlin 2008, 267; Ó Baoill 2013, 76 and 170

487   LONDONDERRY: CHURCH   243280 416600
St Augustine's Church

Various sources suggest that this is where the monastic settlement in Derry was established by St Columba. The church, known as the *Dubh Regles*, became an Augustinian monastery sometime in the 14th century. Early 17th-century maps indicate a church at this location, and it is likely that the *Dubh Regles* was used for Protestant worship, first by Docwra's garrison, until the erection of St Columb's Cathedral, after which it became known as 'the little church'. The current building was constructed around 1868 and re-named St Augustine's. A test excavation at the site in 2013 recovered early

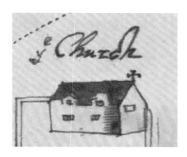

Fig. 7.14 Extract from Raven's 1622 map of Londonderry illustrating a church, known as the Dubh Regles, which had been an Augustinian monastery since the 14th century.

17th-century pottery from a 'graveyard' layer also containing human remains, and a 17th-century gunflint from the topsoil.

HB01/19/012

Ó Baoill 2013, 39, 58–59 and 124; McSparron 2013

488   LONDONDERRY: HOUSES   243536 416650
Linenhall Street Houses

Excavations in the 1980s revealed the cellars of some 17th-century houses, possibly built around 1630. They were constructed of stone with brick detail, and the interior walls were plastered and featured stone fireplaces and brick ovens. Flagstones covered the floors while ceramic tiles or slates were used to roof the houses. Interestingly, the walls of at least two of these houses were reflective of the modern property boundaries, and perhaps also of the 17th-century boundaries.

LDY 014:081

Lacey 1981; Ó Baoill 2013, 135–138

489   ELAGH MORE: CASTLE   241580 421650
Elagh Castle

The remains of an Irish castle of 14th-century or early 15th-century date are situated on the northern outskirts of the city. The site is also perhaps the early medieval royal site of the Uí Néill, 'Aileach' which pre-dates the famous Grianán of Aileach fort, 5km distant and visible from the castle. It occupies a prominent rocky outcrop and was an O'Doherty stronghold until 1600 when it was taken by troops under Sir Henry Docwra. From that point on it was occupied by an English garrison, although the O'Dohertys briefly reclaimed it in 1608. In 1621, the castle was leased to Peter Benson, the London bricklayer who had built the city walls of Londonderry, but by 1665 it had become derelict, and was abandoned. The fragmentary remains now visible consist of a double-towered gateway, with traces of a portcullis slot visible. Excavations in 2013 revealed archaeological evidence for the 17th-century garrison in the form of pottery sherds, but

Fig. 7.15 Elagh Castle is an O'Doherty castle of 14th-century or early 15th-century date that was occupied by an English garrison in 1600 and granted to Peter Benson in 1621.

no structural fabric is known to date from that time.

LDY 14A:003

Davies and Swan 1939, 178 and 202–204; *PSAMNI* 195; Day *et al.* 1996a, 98–100; Lacey 2006, 109–111; Ó Baoill 2013, 43, 77–79

Fort of Culmore

The Fort of Culmore is situated at the end of a peninsula that projects into the River Foyle, close to where it opens into the Lough, a position of high strategic importance, ideally located to monitor maritime traffic between the city and the Lough. Its military origins lie in the late medieval period when a fortification was erected there by the O'Dohertys. This came under Crown ownership in the 16th century and was refortified by Sir Henry Docwra immediately before his occupation of Derry (Ó Baoill 2013, 90). It was endowed with 300 acres to facilitate its maintenance (Hill 1877, 104). One of the conditions of the grant to the London companies was that they should keep a garrison there, and they spent £1100 re-building and garrisoning the fort between 1609 and 1629 (see Ó Baoill 2013, 91). By the time of Pynnar's survey (Hill 1877, 575), the fort, then under the command of Captain John Baker, was

...now finished and the Castle

built; all which is strong and neatly wrought; with Platforms for their Artillery; and this is the only key and strength of the River that goeth to the Derry.

490 CULMORE: EARTHWORKS 247652 422512
Culmore Fort

These are the remains of a large earthwork defensive line associated with Culmore Fort. There are no visible remains of the fort itself – the extant 'castle' at Culmore is a 19th-century blockhouse that replaced the earlier fortification, albeit in a form that probably closely resembled the earlier building. The earthwork consists of a bank and ditch that cut off the peninsula upon which Culmore Fort stood; its line marked on the 1st edition OS six-inch map by a tree belt. The date of the earthwork is uncertain; it could have originated during the late medieval, but is more likely to date to the conflicts of the 1640s or 1690s. It is possible that the earthwork was heightened or restored during the garrisoning of the fort by the London companies. The fort and earthwork are depicted in a detailed vista of Culmore Fort by Thomas Phillips in 1684–85. In this view the fort is surrounded by a bastioned curtain wall, with the earthwork further out, also possessing bastions.

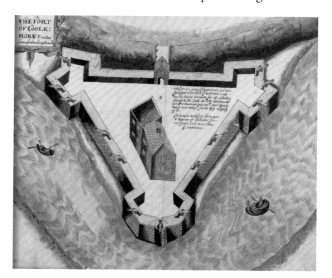

Fig. 7.16 Raven's 1622 map of Culmore Fort.

LDY 14A:001

'A prospect of Kilmore Fort and the River up to Londonderry' by Thomas Phillips, 1685, (NLI MS 2557/35 & NLI MS 3137/44); Davies and Swan 1939, 201–202; *PSAMNI* 194–195; Day and McWilliams 1995d, 43; N. Brannon *pers. comm.* 2015

491 CULMORE: CHURCH 246480 422660

A church, probably built for the Protestant garrison at Culmore, was destroyed in 1688, when the building was used as a headquarters and hospital by Jacobite forces. The site is now occupied by the Holy Trinity Church, built in 1876, and only the gables of the southern transept and the chancel of the original building survive, immediately to the east of the 19th-century building. The gable of the southern transept is approximately 6m in height, and measures 6.05m in length internally. The eastern gable of the chancel only survives to a height of 1m, and is 7.4m long. All of the walls are 80cm thick. The gable of the southern transept incorporates the remains of a large window opening, splayed internally along its jambs. There are fragments of render adhering to the internal wall of the transept.

LDY 14A:002

PSAMNI 194; Day and McWilliams 1995d, 64

Coleraine

Before the Plantation, settlement in the Coleraine area occurred on both banks of the River Bann, the western bank being the site of an early ecclesiastical centre, along with a castle (Inv. 526) and a church (Inv. 527), both later part of the Clothworkers' estate. The location is of key geographical importance in Ulster, as the Lower Bann connects Lough Neagh to the Atlantic, and hence much of Ulster to the wider world. The settlement became focused on the eastern bank, which was also the site of a medieval abbey (Inv. 493). Of the two major towns built by The Honourable The Irish Society, Coleraine's initial development occurred at a faster rate than Derry, and as such it became the first 'new' town in

Fig. 7.17 View of Culmore Church.

Ulster to be populated as a result of official policy. In September 1610, Sir John Davies, the Attorney-General and one of the architects of the Plantation, described (Hill 1877, 406)

> …so many workmen, so busy in their several places about their several tasks, as methought I saw Didoe's colony building of Carthage…

and proceeded to allude to Virgil's likening of Dido's workers to bees. Details of the works were provided in a report made in 1610 by John Rowley, an Irish Society agent, who described a terrace of twenty-six timber-framed houses in what is now called New Row (Robinson 1983, 129). A similar report by Carew a year later described (Hill 1877, 572) an earthen rampart six feet high, a mill-pond and mill-house containing three separate mills, one each for wheat, malt and a tucking mill, a pound (presumably for cattle) and a

> bridge or wharf made in the Bann, of 60 foot long, and 12 foot broad, of very strong oak timber, clasped together in the joints with bars and bolts of Iron, &c. &c.

A map of 1611 by Carew depicts the town as

under construction, with several rows of houses and a street layout that is partly recognisable today (Robinson 1983, 129), although it is perhaps more a record of what was intended, rather than what had been finished. Raw materials for the town could be readily supplied by river and there was local clay and rock, while lime was supplied for free by Sir Randall MacDonnell of Dunluce in return for the leasehold of a house in the town (Curl 1986, 44).

In 1616, a report by Commissioners indicated that not only was progress losing momentum, but that the weather was beginning to adversely affect the completed timber-framed buildings, and future buildings in the town should be made of stone (Moody 1939, 170). In 1619, Pynnar (Hill 1877, 576) gave a very negative account of progress, stating that few houses had been built, and that the earthwork defences

do begin to moulder away; for the Ramparts are so narrow that it is impossible they should stand, and

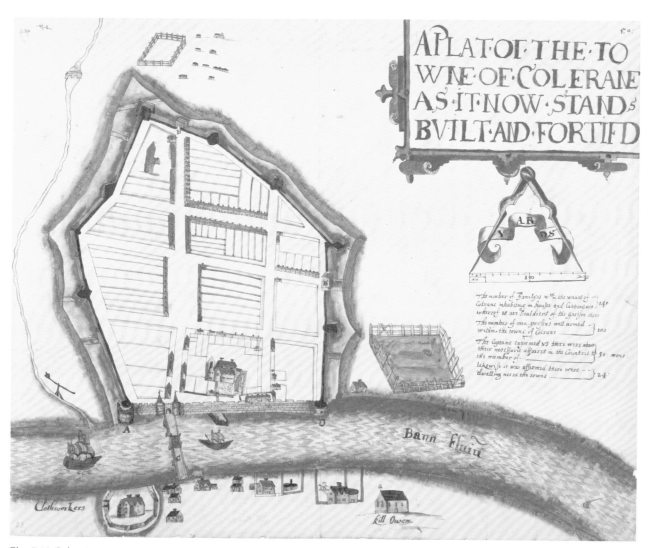

Fig. 7.18 Coleraine as it appeared in one of Raven's maps of 1622.

the Bullwarks so exceeding little that there cannot be placed any piece of Artillery, if occasion were.

Although few new developments were noted, the 1622 survey struck a more optimistic tone, recording eighteen stone houses and fifty-two of timber. By all accounts, therefore, the initial development at Coleraine was undertaken perhaps too hastily, but as the 17th century progressed there was gradual and sustained investment in the town. In 1642, it was besieged for six weeks by the Irish, until relieved by a Scots royalist army, which subsequently was defeated by parliamentarian forces (Gilbert 1879, 33). The town was re-developed after the wars (e.g. see Robinson and Brannon 1982), with The Irish Society maintaining control over the next two centuries, investing in and promoting it in the wider world.

492　COLERAINE: SETTLEMENT　284780 432410
The street plan of the plantation town of Coleraine consisted of streets laid out on an irregular grid – three orientated north-south and two approximately east-west, the northernmost of which intersects two north-south streets in a 'diamond' square market-place. This pattern can still be traced in the arrangement of streets surrounding The Diamond and the town hall. The houses of the new town, although ultimately proving unsatisfactory (see Inv. 493), were of an interesting, modular design that could be partly prefabricated (perhaps leading to the local legend that they were shipped from London). They took the form of very small 'tenements', sometimes combined to constitute a larger house. The town centre also contained various other sites listed below. A campaign of test excavation in the town in 1979 revealed the vestiges of a citadel (see Inv. 494), various late medieval features whose upper fills contained 17th-century pottery, and a very large cess pit (5–6m in diameter) of late 17th-century date.

LDY 007:091
Copy of Sir Thomas Phillips' report, *c.* 1717–*c.* 1722

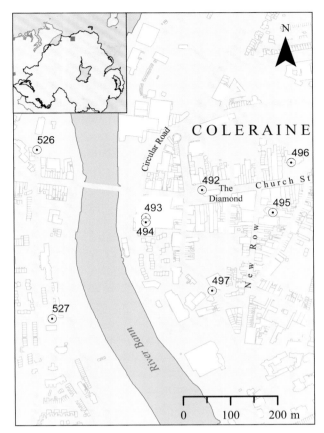

Fig. 7.19 Map of Coleraine showing the individual sites discussed in text.

Phillips MSS (PRONI T510/2); Moody 1939; Camblin 1951; Brannon 1977–79; Robinson 1983; Curl 1986, 44 and 52; Brannon 1988b

493　COLERAINE: HOUSES　284660 432350
**　　Cuile Raithin**
This is the site of a Dominican priory (founded in 1244) that survived into the early 17th century. During the Plantation, the priory buildings were used for a garrison (see Inv. 494), Sir Thomas Phillips' home and warehouses, before being demolished in the mid- to late 17th century. Earthwork vestiges of the priory survived until the 19th century, but have since been erased by development. Archaeological excavations in the late 1990s revealed the remains of some of the priory walls, and a large medieval

enclosure ditch now buried beneath a car park. The upper layers of the fill of the ditch contained 17th-century pottery. Also encountered was the corner of a post-medieval building and related features of unknown date. Extrapolating from the excavated features, it seems this building was a house with frontage onto Hanover Place, and was built upon an earlier wall that also shared this orientation, the earlier wall being, perhaps, a remnant from the plantation town.

LDY 007:019, LDY 007:098

Archdall 1786, 164; O'Laverty 1878–1887, IV, 165–171; Gwynn and Hadcock 1970, 223; McConway 1998 and 1999; Gahan 2003

494   COLERAINE: 284660 432340
FORTIFICATION
The Citadel

The site of a fortification, also on the site of the Dominican priory (see Inv. 493), is marked on a 1738 map as 'formerly the citadel'. Various Irish Society letters and records indicate that the citadel was built around 1625–1630, and demolished in 1670. Its presence in the town centre is perhaps attributable to the weakness of the outer defences of the town, with the citadel providing a place of refuge in case of attack. Nothing of this site is visible above the ground, but archaeological excavations retrieved 17th-century ceramics, and revealed traces of a wall some 2m thick, terminating in a north-eastern bastion. This wall was enclosed within a wide ditch that would have in effect created a moated site.

LDY 007:050

Mullin 1976; Brannon 1977–79, 1988b; McConway 1999

495   COLERAINE: HOUSE   284930 432360
New Row

One of the original timber-framed houses was erected in Coleraine in 1611, and its late 17th-century replacement survived until the 1980s. At least fifty-six such houses were built in Coleraine during the initial development of the town. However,

Fig. 7.20 Extract from Raven's 1622 map of Coleraine depicting the Dominican priory, later replaced by the Citadel.

the English construction method seemingly was not suited to the damp Irish climate, and the Commissioners' report of 1616 recorded that the weather was damaging the timber-framed houses, recommending that in the future, houses should be of stone only. In the late 17th century, the house at 10/12 New Row was replaced with a brick-built house with an oak timbered roof, which survived until the 1980s. A timber from the house has been dendrochronologically dated to 1674, implying that it was built that year or shortly thereafter. The roof frame contained butt purlins, along with mortice-and-tenon joints in the rafters at the ridge in lieu of a ridge beam, in the tradition of vernacular English carpentry that had, presumably, become established in Coleraine from the start of the Plantation. This roof structure was removed from the site, and re-erected on a building at the Ulster Folk Museum, where it can be viewed.

LDY 007:051

Robinson and Brannon 1982; Robinson 1983; Brannon 1988b

496   COLERAINE: CHURCH   284970 432470
St Patrick's Parish Church

In 1613–14, a medieval parish church, itself possibly on the site of an early monastery, was repaired and re-roofed to serve the needs of the town. It was subsequently replaced by the current building in the 1880s, and nothing of the earlier church can be seen, although medieval foundations were discovered in 1994 during archaeological excavations within the building, along with a series of burials, presumably from the same period. The church incorporates memorials to three individuals who were associated with the Ulster Plantation: Elizabeth, the first wife of Sir Edward Doddington, who was responsible for Dungiven and the Skinners' estate (the memorial celebrates the achievements of the man, and says little of his young wife, who died in 1610); Sir Tristram Beresford, who died in 1673, and was MP for the town and son of the Tristram who had a stake in many of the Londoners' estates; and John Rowley who died in 1617, agent to The Irish Society and the Drapers.

LDY 007:090

Reeves 1847, 75 and 247; O'Laverty 1878–1887, IV, 160–164; Gwynn and Hadcock 1970, 33; Curl 1986, 44–45, 51–52, 61, 91 and 108; Hamlin 2008, 266; N. Brannon *pers. comm.* 2015

497   COLERAINE: SETTLEMENT   284800 432190
Abbey Street, Coleraine

In 2001, an archaeological excavation in advance of building works was undertaken at Coleraine Baptist Church. In addition to various medieval finds, the work revealed evidence for 17th-century occupation in the form of gullies and a cess-pit.

LDY 007:095

Logue 2001

Goldsmiths

The Goldsmiths', in association with the Cordwainers, Painter-Stainers and Armourers, acquired 11,050 acres (Curl 1986, 69), and initially let their lands to a gentleman, John Freeman (Hill 1877, 576). The estate is situated on the eastern bank of the Foyle, opposite the Plantation town of Londonderry. The Goldsmiths' records indicate that Freeman was bound to build a castle and twelve houses, although due to various circumstances only six houses were built, along with the re-roofing of the parish church at Glendermot (Curl 1986, 279). Pynnar (Hill 1877, 576) noted a small village and a bawn and an incomplete castle, the bawn being 100

feet square with four flankers. This settlement is still known as New Buildings (Inv. 499), even though the original structures have long since been replaced. The location of the bawn is unknown, although a potential site is suggested in the *OS Memoirs* (Inv. 499). Pynnar also documented the presence of six freeholders, and twenty-four lessees on the estate. The estate also included a quarry, situated near New Buildings, from where the Londoners were able to acquire slate for roofing (Robinson and Brannon 1982, 174). The Goldsmiths sold their estate in the 18th century, but retained interest in the property in the form of reserve rent (Hill 1877, 576–577).

498   PREHEN: HOUSE AND   241920 414380
BAWN

The townland of Prehen was a freehold property on the Goldsmith's estate, and a map by Raven of their lands in 1619 depicts an unfortified, single-storey house close to the River Foyle, immediately to the south-west of the present Georgian mansion. On Raven's 1624 map, the house, still unfortified, was depicted as being somewhat further to the south than its actual location. The building was apparently destroyed during the 1641 Rebellion. The Civil Survey of 1654–56 records that the property was still owned by a freeholder, a Mr. John Elvin, at that stage.

Excavations at the site in 2006 failed to find any evidence of 17th-century occupation. However, a fragment of curving masonry, much like a bawn flanker, has been identified at the site incorporated within the walls of a later outbuilding. This discovery prompted a programme of geophysical survey and test excavation in 2013, which located the foundations of a circular flanker of a bawn with an external diameter of 5.5m and walls 70cm thick, with traces of render still adhering. This encompassed a separate, concentric inner ring of masonry of unknown function. Although finds of 18th- and 19th-century pottery were plentiful, the excavation was not able to clarify the date of the bawn structure, as the finds were not related to the construction phase of the walls. The Prehen

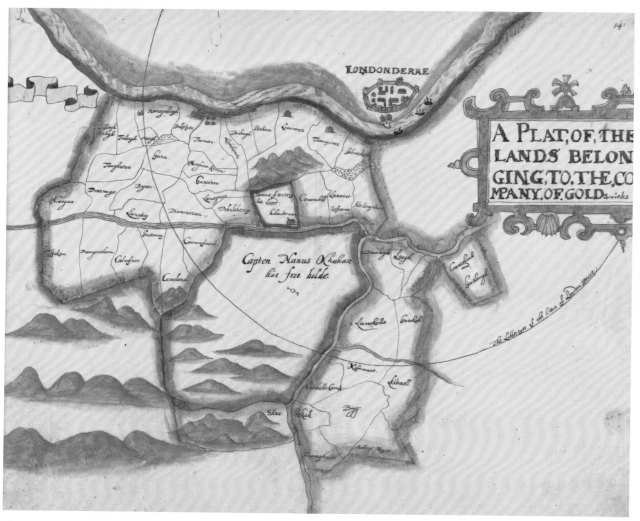

Fig. 7.21 One of Raven's 1622 maps of the Goldsmiths' estate situated on the eastern bank of the Foyle, opposite the Plantation town of Londonderry.

bawn therefore remains particularly enigmatic, as it was not depicted on any contemporary map nor described in any other historical source. It is possible that it post-dates the plantation period altogether, although on stylistic grounds this would be unusual.

LDY 014:083, HB01/04/001 A

Simington 1937, 225; McSparron and Mussen 2013

499   NEW BUILDINGS: HOUSE AND BAWN

The Goldsmiths' bawn, long disappeared, was described by Pynnar as '100 feet square, 16 feet high, with four flankers'. A detailed description was provided on Raven's 1622 map of the Goldsmiths' buildings, where the bawn is depicted as square, with flankers at three corners, one of which has a conical roof. A three-storey, three-bay manor house, U-shaped in plan and with two wings flanking either side of the front façade, occupied the fourth corner.

LDY 022:030

Hill 1877, 576–577

Fig. 7.22 Possible remains of a flanker associated with a previously unidentified bawn at Prehen.

500 NEW BUILDINGS: **241170 412580**
SETTLEMENT

At the village still known as 'New Buildings', Pynnar's survey described

> …six Houses of Stone, and six of Timber, very strong and well built, and seated in a very good and convenient place for the King's service.

Described by the 1622 survey, and depicted on Raven's 1622 map, it consisted of a street with six houses, seven small cabins, a water-mill, and the

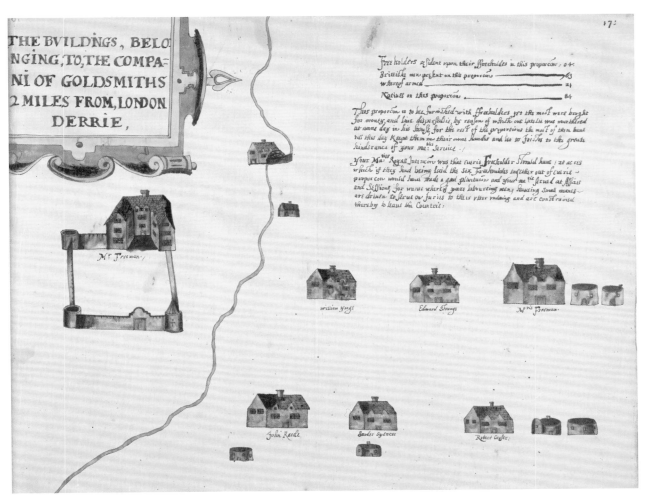

Fig. 7.23 One of Raven's maps of 1622 depicts the village at New Buildings established by the Goldsmiths, which consisted of a street with six houses, seven small cabins, a water-mill, and the bawn and castle.

bawn and castle. Taylor and Skinner's road map suggests that the village had changed little by 1777, and on it a few buildings are depicted on either side of the main road from Londonderry to Strabane. No structures or features from the early history of the village survive.

LDY 022:030

Copy of Sir Thomas Phillips' report, *c.* 1717–*c.* 1722 Phillips MSS (PRONI T510/2); Taylor and Skinner 1778, 37; Moody 1939, 163; Curl 1986, 279–283

501 PRIMITY: BAWN 241230 412670

The ruins of a second bawn or fortified dwelling in the New Buildings area were recorded in the *OS Memoirs* as once visible, but demolished by a farmer in 1799. The Civil Survey of 1654–56 records that the property was still in the ownership of the Goldsmiths at that stage. There are no visible remains.

LDY 022:025

Simington 1937, 223; Curl 1986, 282, pl. 201; Day and McWilliams 1995d, 49–50

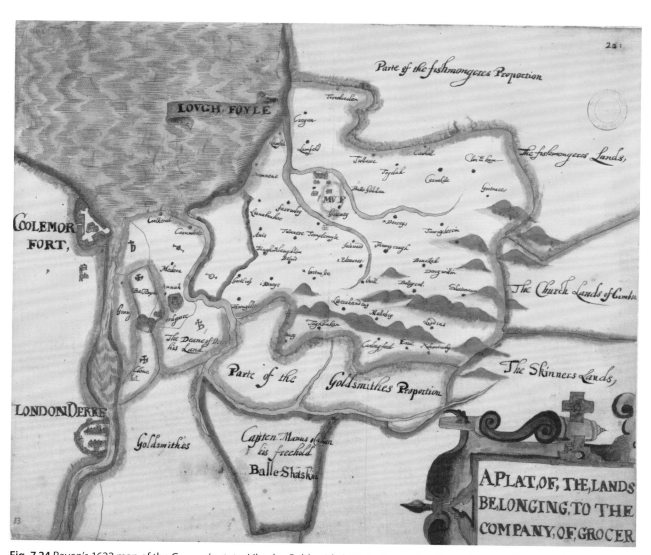

Fig. 7.24 Raven's 1622 map of the Grocers' estate. Like the Goldsmiths' estate, it was also situated close to Lough Foyle.

Grocers

The lands that comprise the Grocers' estate lie immediately to the east of those of the Goldsmiths to the south of Londonderry and Lough Foyle. The Grocers acquired 15,900 acres (Curl 1986, 69), and leased them to one Edward Rone who died before the Plantation got underway (Hill 1877, 577–578). It seems that the entire estate was let at quite a low rent, but that the cost of all building work, aside from the church (Inv. 504), was to be met by the tenants rather than the Company (Curl 1986, 156), and for 1617, Company records document nine stone houses and a mill (*ibid.*). Pynnar (Hill 1877, 577–588) recorded a degree of confusion and lack of management on the estate:

> Upon this proportion there is a Bawne in Building … By this Bawne there are built four Strong Houses of Lime and Stone, and well slated. There are four more that are built in other Places, somewhat further off. There are other Houses of Lime and Stone, that are upon the Land dispersed ; but they are built by the Tenants themselves ; and yet have no estates, and likely, as they tell me, to be removed, some of them having spent upon their building £100

The terms of the Plantation were eventually met due to the efforts of Rone's executors and of his brother-in-law, Robert Harrington, who was leased the property in 1619 (Curl 1986, 155). By 1622, buildings on the estate consisted of a church, a grist mill, the bawn and castle, sixteen stone houses and five timber houses (*ibid.* 157). The estate fell into ruin following the 1641 Rebellion and the Confederate Wars, and was temporarily confiscated from the Company (*ibid.*). The Civil Survey of 1654 revealed that by then much of the land was leased to Thomas Harrington, presumably the son of Robert, although there were several small freehold estates also, including significant holdings by Lt. Col. Tristram Beresford

(Simington 1937, 228–232). Beresford was the Grocers' agent, and he and their tenant, Harrington, held competing claims as to whom significant rent arrears were due. The Company sold the leasehold in the late 17th century, thereby raising funds, and released it to numerous individuals over the ensuing centuries, before finally selling it outright in the late 19th century (Curl 1986, 158–173).

502   MUFF: HOUSE AND BAWN   252940 420260
Glebe House

The site of a house is shown on the Raven map in the north-western corner of a bawn, Grocers' Hall, which was described by Pynnar as measuring 100 feet square, with four flankers. However, the depiction on Raven's map indicates only three flankers. The *OS Memoirs* state that the bawn 'was destroyed by the Company in the year [blank], together with some of the original houses erected at the Plantation', this being in the early 19th century, when the current rectory, Glebe House, was built. A small stream nearby is still known as the 'Castle Burn'. It is possible that some vestiges of the bawn

Fig. 7.25 Extract from one of Raven's 1622 maps showing house and bawn in the Grocers' village of Muff.

and house survive at the site, and a courtyard in the grounds of the rectory contains sections that are clearly of some antiquity, perhaps fragments of the bawn wall. A cellar in the rectory with a barrel-vaulted ceiling and a ground-floor window appears to pre-date the building.

LDY 015:008

Copy of Sir Thomas Phillips' report, *c. 1717–c. 1722* Phillips MSS (PRONI T510/2); Day and McWilliams 1995d, 96-100

503   EGLINTON: SETTLEMENT   252920 420315

The Grocers' village of Muff was founded in 1615 and, according to Raven's map, the houses were built along both sides of a street running westwards from the church (Inv. 504). Much of the area has since been redeveloped; there are no visible remains of the 17th-century village.

LDY 015:033

Copy of Sir Thomas Phillips' report, *c. 1717–c. 1722* Phillips MSS (PRONI T510/2)

504   EGLINTON: CHURCH   252951 420382

A church was built between 1619 and 1622 as part of the Grocers' village at Muff. It was not noted by Pynnar, but does appear on Raven's map where it is depicted as a rectangular hall with buttresses, a slated roof, and a large pointed-arched window with fine tracery. In 1622, the church was described as 'new built of stone and covered in slate, reading seat, and communion table, and many seats therein built by the parishioners'. The building became the parish church of Faughanvale in 1626, and remained in use until a replacement was built in 1826. The ruins consist of the eastern gable wall built of stone rubble, which stands to its full height and is supported by two buttresses. Traces of the lower courses of the other walls of the building are also visible, and include a possible entrance represented by a break in the southern wall. The large pointed arch in the gable, whose opening is dressed with red sandstone, tallies with Raven's illustration, though it has lost its tracery. There are

a number of grave plots within the church.

LDY 015:009

Copy of Sir Thomas Phillips' report, *c. 1717–c. 1722* Phillips MSS (PRONI T510/2); Curl 1986, 155 and 157

505   OGHILL: CASTLE   251058 414736

This is the site of a castle, of which there are no visible remains, built by a freeholder on the Grocers' estate, perhaps one of the houses referred to by Pynnar. The *OS Memoirs* state that a stone crucifix and other local stone landmarks were removed to build the castle, which upset the locals. The Civil Survey recorded a small, 60-acre estate held by Edward Lewis, an English gentleman and son of John Lewis, who had 'held and enjoyed' the freehold. The *OS Memoirs*, however, document the tradition surrounding the fate of Lewis, and his castle, slighted by locals upset by the new order:

> …the insulted peasantry thought it useless to remonstrate, but bound themselves by the most solemn oaths to take vengeance on the first opportunity. In process of time that opportunity was presented by the rebellion of 1641. The habitation of Lewis was attacked one autumnal morning by a large party, who destroyed many parts of it and killed the servants. He escaped himself by a back window, and secreted himself in a marsh near the bog where a scrag or covert of matted trees and brambles appeared to offer a secure shelter. However, owing to a heavy dew which lay on the grass, his enemies succeeded in tracing his footsteps to the scrag. Having drawn him out, they murdered him and thrust his body into a sheskin, or quagmire, which immediately closed over it, some even believed that he was forced in alive.

LDY 015:020

Simington 1937, 31; Day and McWilliams 1995d, 72–74 and 93

506   GRESTEEL MORE: **257100 421100**
SETTLEMENT

A cluster of houses was marked on the Down Survey map of this barony (Tirkeerin), to the north-west of Faughanvale Church in Killywool. The eastern edge of the modern village of Greysteel is the most likely

position that correlates with this point on the Down Survey map, but there are no visible remains.

LDY 15A:006

Down Survey barony map of Tirkeerin (PRONI D597/3)

Fishmongers

The Fishmongers Company and their affiliates were granted approximately 24,100 acres (Curl 1986,

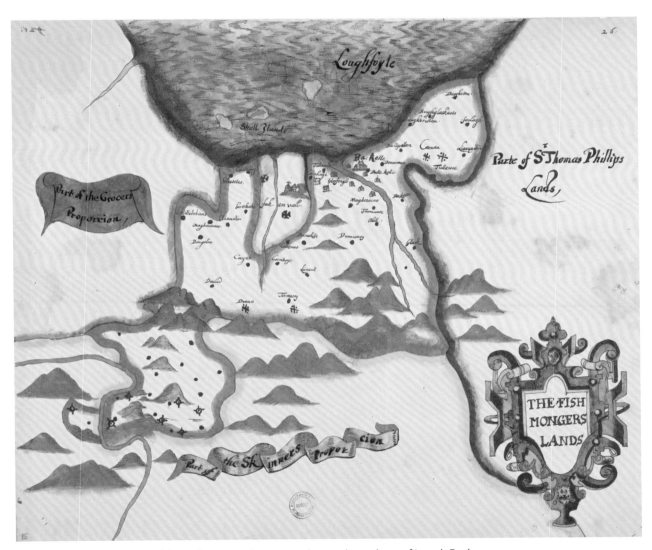

Fig. 7.26 Raven's 1622 map of the Fishmongers' estate on the southern shore of Lough Foyle.

69) of lands on the southern shore of Lough Foyle, immediately to the east of the Grocers' estate in the baronies of Tirkeeran and Keenaght, centred upon Ballykelly. The estate, known as the 'Manor of Walworth' or 'Ballykelly', was leased initially to James Higgins (Hill 1877, 578–579). Pynnar described a well-developed estate, with a bawn and castle (Inv. 507), three stone houses, twelve timber houses, a church, and a population of six freeholders and twenty-eight lessees (*ibid.*). Raven's map of the buildings at Ballykelly depicts a bawn, a church, several cottages or cabins and eleven 'English' houses, some of which have chimneys on their gables, which was unusual for the Planter settlements (cf. Curl 1986, 233). Entire thirds of the estate were sublet to various individuals, with much eventually being leased by a gentleman, one Christopher Freeman (*ibid.* 236). In the late 17th century, the estate was leased to the Hamilton and Beresford families, who remained in control until the 19th century, when the Company resumed ownership; the estate was sold around the turn of the 20th century (Curl 1986, 233–277).

507 BALLYKELLY: HOUSE AND BAWN   262420 422620

Walworth, or Ballykelly Bawn

These are the well-preserved remains of the Fishmongers' bawn, and also the former site of a fortified house, described by Pynnar as a 'Strong Bawne of Stone and Lime, 125 feet square, 12 feet high, with four Flankers, and a good House within it'. It is similarly described in the 1622 survey, although only three flankers are mentioned. According to local tradition, the bawn was attacked in 1641, and perhaps again in 1688. The bawn and three of the flankers survive remarkably intact, but the house has vanished. In the early 18th century, a single-storey house was built along the southern wall of the bawn, removing the south-western flanker. The bawn is approximately square, with each side measuring around 40m in length. The circular south-eastern flanker and the eastern bawn wall are intact and well-preserved; the flanker measures 3.6m in diameter

Fig. 7.27 The north-eastern flanker of the Fishmongers' bawn at Walworth or Ballykelly.

with walls 60cm thick. The diamond-shaped north-eastern flanker contains gun loops providing lines of defensive fire along the bawn walls. The same flanker has been used as a dove-cote, and various outbuildings have been built against the northern bawn wall, which also survives relatively intact. The north-western flanker, which has undergone at least two phases of restoration in the past, is a circular building, similar in size to the south-eastern flanker, and approached by sweeping steps on its eastern side. The western bawn wall is largely obscured by the later buildings, but parts of it can still be seen adjoining the north-western flanker. Extramural gardens may be of plantation origin.

LDY 009:007

Hill 1877, 578–579; Day *et al.* 1994b, 96, 99, 102

508 BALLYKELLY: SETTLEMENT   262275 422498

The plantation settlement of Ballykelly was located a short distance to the north-west of where the modern village is now sited. It is depicted on Raven's map as houses and cabins on either side of the Ballykelly river, which has been straightened over the course of recent centuries. It is now a greenfield site, and while there are no visible remains, there is considerable potential for archaeological remains to be preserved beneath the soil.

LDY 009:019

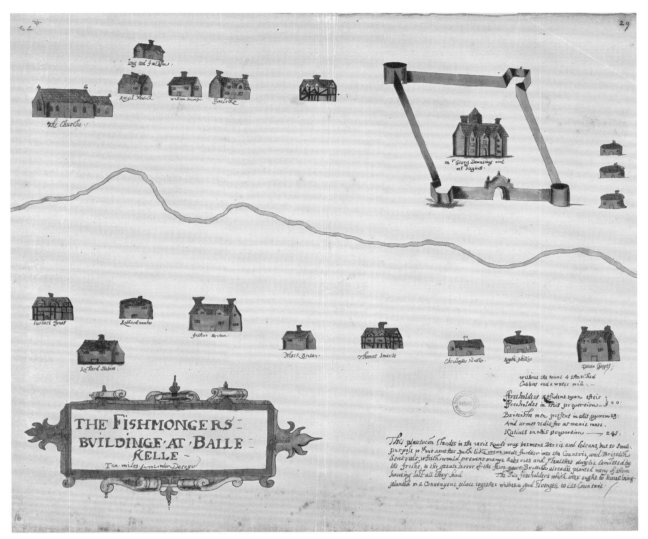

Fig. 7.28 Raven's 1622 map of the Fishmongers' village with houses and cabins on either side of the Ballykelly river. The manor, bawn and church are also illustrated. The plantation settlement was sited a short distance to the north-west of where the present-day village is located.

Copy of Sir Thomas Phillips' report, *c.* 1717–*c.* 1722 Phillips MSS (PRONI T510/2); Jope 1960, 108; Blades 1986

509 BALLYKELLY: CHURCH   **262250 422730**
AND GRAVEYARD
The Garrison Church

The Fishmongers' church at Ballykelly, which was illustrated on Raven's map at the opposite end of the settlement from the bawn, took the form of a five-bay nave, with an entrance on the southern wall, and a two-bay chancel. It was slighted in 1641 and 1689, but restored on both occasions. The chancel was re-built in the early 18th century by the Hamilton family (who leased part of the estate), and the church was used to house a family memorial. It was used for worship until 1795, when a replacement was built by Frederick Augustus Hervey, bishop of Derry, at Tamlaght Finlagan, although burials continued in

Fig. 7.29 The remains of the Garrison Church, where the nave and chancel are separated by a semi-circular archway.

the graveyard until the mid-19th century.

The ruins consist of a rectangular building, 20m by 8m externally, orientated east-west, the walls of which are of stone rubble with sandstone quoins. Both gables of the nave survive to near their full height of approximately 7m; the western gable contains a central window with splayed reveals. An opening in the wall of the eastern gable provided access to roof space created when a flat ceiling was added to the nave around 1719. The nave and chancel are separated by a semicircular archway in the eastern gable, the stone mouldings of which are particularly impressive for a building of otherwise modest scale.

LDY 009:002

Copy of Sir Thomas Phillips' report, *c.* 1717–*c.* 1722 Phillips MSS (PRONI T510/2); *PSAMNI* 190

**510   MULKEERAGH: CHURCH   265190 421920
AND GRAVEYARD
Tamlaght Finlagan Old Church**

This medieval church, now in ruins, was included in the Taxation of 1306. Its status during the plantation period is uncertain, although it is situated among the Fishmonger's lands. The current Tamlaght Finlagan parish church was built in the late 18th century.

The ruined remains of the old church consist of a rectangular building measuring 16.8m by 6.85m

internally, the walls of which are built of roughly-coursed stone slabs and are some 85cm thick. The eastern gable survives almost to its full height of 6m, with the other walls only preserved as low footings, somewhat obscured by vegetation. A rectangular projection from the northern wall, at the north-western corner of the building contains a curious small, near-circular chamber, the function of which is unclear, but may be the foundations of a tower. The church is set within a graveyard with numerous burials, and there are several graves also within the church building.

LDY 009:003

Gwynn and Hadcock 1970, 405; Curl 1986, 240; Hamlin 2008, 281

Ironmongers

The Ironmongers and their affiliates – the Brewers, Pewterers, Barber-Surgeons, Carpenters, Coopers and Scriveners – were granted some 19,450 acres (Curl 1986, 70) in the barony of Coleraine, on fertile lands at the confluence of several minor rivers and the Lower Bann. The company was reluctant to engage in the project, citing financial issues, although it eventually managed to make all the necessarily payments, even purchasing the shares of the Bowyers and Fletchers, who previously were associates of the Clothworkers (Curl 1986, 62). In 1614, the Company appointed an agent, George Canning, to run their estate (Hill 1877, 436). A series of letters between Canning and the Company revealed the challenges in building the castle, and also mentioned plans for a corn mill and various bridges (*ibid.* 438–442).

In time, a small settlement became established surrounding the bawn at Agivey (see Inv. 511). It would seem that there was much uncertainty on the estate surrounding the legal status of various freeholders and under-tenants, as well as the status of the extensive church lands. This uncertainty was not resolved until the estate was leased in 1630 to Paul Canning, presumably a relative of George Canning, (Hill 1877, 580). By that time, the estate

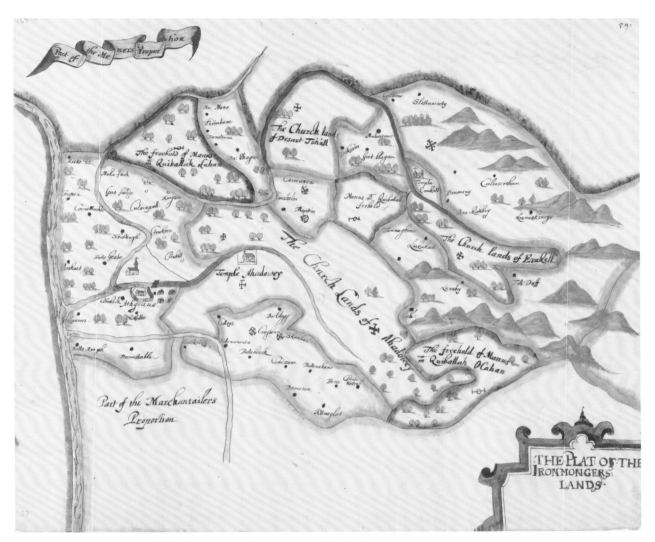

Fig. 7.30 Raven's 1622 map of the Ironmongers' estate, centred on Agivey.

had come to be known as the 'Manor of Lizard', and in the Great Parchment Book, the manor consisted of fourteen townlands, and included domestic and agricultural buildings, orchards, gardens and mills, and was licenced to operate a ferry on the Bann (*GPB*, folio L6v). It is not entirely clear from the various sources as to the significance of the bawn at Aghadowey (Inv. 513) which was either part of the estate or situated upon church lands encompassed by it. The estate lost its houses, churches, bridges, and the corn mill during the 1641 Rebellion, resulting in great financial loss for Canning (Hill 1877, 80).

That said, it remained leased to the Canning family until the 18th century, after which it was leased to a succession of other individuals (*ibid.*).

511   LISSAGHMORE: HOUSE,   290118 422884
BAWN, AND SETTLEMENT

The earliest record of the Ironmongers' settlement at Agivey is Pynnar's survey, which recorded that eight timber houses had been built and that a castle had been completed, although its bawn was incomplete along one side. The 1622 survey revealed that the

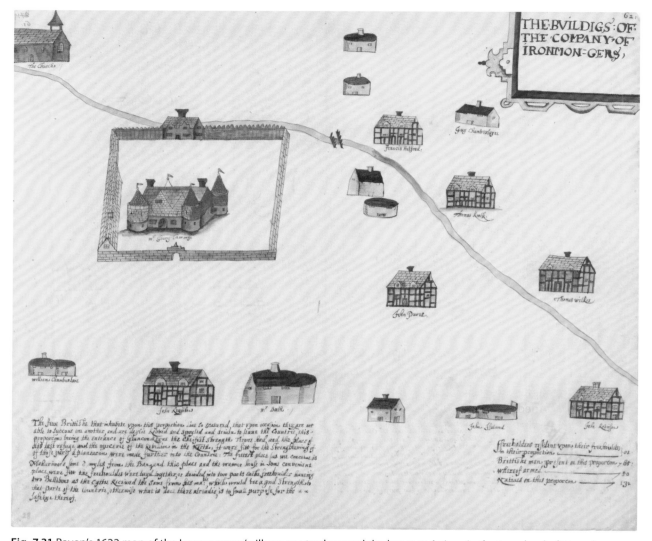

Fig. 7.31 Raven's 1622 map of the Ironmongers' village, centred around the bawn at Agivey in the townland of Lissaghmore.

missing side was now protected by a palisade. Inside the bawn were two manor houses – a free-standing, two-storey structure with a cellar, and another house, built against the bawn wall. The survey stated that the nearby village, 'Aghene', contained a church, a water-mill, six timber-framed houses and eight Irish-style cabins.

The main house within the bawn was described in the 1622 survey as having flanking towers at each corner – the arrangement also depicted on Raven's map, though the bawn itself was not provided with corner flankers. Virtually all trace of the village has disappeared, although the current pattern of public roads in the locality does follow the T-shaped distribution of houses and cabins that were depicted on Raven's map. The current Agivey House, immediately to the south-west of this location, is the likely site of the main house or castle. Its cellar is possibly of 17th-century date.

LDY 012:005

Hill 1877, 579–580; Jope 1960, 106–108; Blades 1980a, 47–51

**512 MULLAGHMORE: CHURCH 290400 422210
AND EARTHWORK**
Agivey Old Church

According to the *OS Memoirs*, a church was either built or re-edified at Agivey by George Canning, the Ironmongers' agent, or one of his immediate family. Sixth-century monastic origins have been claimed for the site, attributed to St. Guaire; it later became a Franciscan friary. The *OS Memoirs* state that the church was used from the Plantation until the mid-18th century, although services were only performed on alternative Sunday evenings.

The ruins consist of the lower wall footings of a rectangular building aligned east-west, measuring approximately 17m by 7.6m. The western wall is obscured beneath a mound of earth and stone. The eastern gable and parts of the northern wall are the best-preserved, standing up to a height of 2m, and the walls are 90cm thick. There was probably a tower and belfry at the western end, and a perforated stone found at the site and now in Garvagh Museum, may originally have been part of the first floor of the belfry, through which the bell-rope passed. The church is contained within a polygonal graveyard, in which most of the memorial stones date to the 18th and 19th centuries. There are two graves within the church, one of which is a brick-built crypt, perhaps the burial ground of the Canning family, as the *OS Memoirs* mention that the Cannings had 'a monument in the yard'.

According to the *OS Memoirs*, the church is also the site of a military entrenchment, dug around it during or just before the 1641 Rebellion, and local tradition holds that British forces altered the course of the nearby Agivey River for defensive purposes. Indeed, a palaeochannel is still visible, immediately to the south-east of the church.

LDY 012:003 (church) and LDY 012:012 (entrenchment)
PSAMNI 192; Gwynn and Haddock 1970, 372; Day and McWilliams 1993e, 27

**513 AGHADOWEY: TOWER 285800 420950
HOUSE AND BAWN**
Aghadowey Castle

The ruins of a bawn and tower house were visible until their demolition around 1970. The *OS Memoirs* record that the castle was enclosed by a square bawn with four flankers, and had been extended and adapted over the years for various generations of occupants, and that an orchard was planted within the bawn. At the site, the remains of a garden wall enclose some farm buildings, which could be a remnant of the orchard and therefore also the bawn. The wall appears to contain several possible openings, tentatively identified as gun loops, but no other architectural features are visible.

LDY 018:067
Day and McWilliams 1993e, 26–27

514 AGHADOWEY: CHURCH 285880 421000
When Aghadowey parish church was built in 1769, it replaced an earlier structure. The date of construction of the original church is unknown, but presumably it is of medieval origin. According to tradition, monastic settlements were founded by St. Guaire both here and at nearby Agivey. A church at Aghadowey is mentioned in passing in several of the documents related to the Ironmongers' estate. In 1622, the church was described as ruinous, but plans were instigated for its repair. There are several earthwork features in the immediate vicinity of the current church that may be the buried remains of earlier structures, although the area has not been surveyed in detail.

LDY 018:033
Reeves 1850, 74–75; Hamlin 2008, 255

515 INSHALEEN: MILL 285250 416600
A structure marked 'Ironmongers' on the Down Survey map of the barony of Coleraine, is depicted as a sprawling complex of roofless buildings. It lay just below the junction of the Agivey and Mettican rivers, possibly near the site of the modern Garvagh

Dungiven Priory (Inv. 531)

When archaeologists want to study sites such as the castles and churches included in this book, they have a number of investigative methods to hand. Excavation allows for the identification of buried walls, ditches and other features associated with settlement, along with the recovery of artefacts and food remains that were discarded by past occupants. The survey of upstanding buildings, whether reasonably or poorly preserved, can provide insights not only into architectural development, but also into how the built environment reflected cultural identity and social organisation. For sites occupied in the historic period, written accounts, illustrations and maps provide much valuable contextual information, particularly when sites are poorly preserved. Taken together, these different sources of information allow archaeologists to reconstruct with greater accuracy what existed in the past. An excellent example of this multi-disciplinary approach can be seen from a study in Dungiven, where the remains of a priory, a castle and a manor house were investigated using these different methods.

Dungiven was the centre of an estate owned by the Skinners, one of the London companies that were granted lands in the newly created county of Londonderry. It was a large estate, containing 49,000 acres of upland country in the southern margins of the county. Dungiven was originally acquired by Captain (later Sir) Edward Doddington in 1609, an army officer who was one of the group responsible for designing the walls around Londonderry (Scott 2011, 145–46). Though the lands were subsequently awarded to the Skinners' Livery Company, Doddington was retained as the company agent and continued to reside there (Curl 1986, 285–286).

20 Thomas Raven's 1622 map of the Skinners' settlement in Dungiven illustrates that Sir Edward Doddington had repaired the O'Cahan tower-house and the priory church there, as well as building an English-style house and bawn, and laying out a pleasure garden adjacent to the older castle.

An Augustinian priory already stood on the site, and was a religious foundation that once enjoyed the patronage of the O'Cahans, the Gaelic lords in the area. An early medieval monastery, supposedly founded here by St. Nechtán in the 6th century, continued in use over the centuries. The long nave of the church may date in part to the late 10th or early 11th centuries (*ibid.* 287). In the early 12th century, the monastery was refounded as an Augustinian priory, and continued in use through the medieval period. In the 13th century, a vaulted chancel supported by attractive ribbing and corbels typical of the period was added to the church. The arched window in the northern wall of the nave, with the remains of tracery, also dates to this refurbishment. The most striking feature of the church though, is the highly elaborate, carved-stone tomb in the chancel, traditionally ascribed to Cooey-na-Gall O'Cahan (who died in 1385), but whether erected at this time or in the following century has been debated (Hunt 1974, I, 130–132; McNeill 2001, 348–351). At some stage in the 15th or 16th centuries, a tower house was built against the western end of the priory church. At this time, it was not unknown for the residences of the clergy to be located at the western end of a church, and in many instances such accommodation was fortified in the manner of tower houses, an architectural form that was popular at the time.

When Doddington arrived, he refurbished the tower house and erected an English-style manor house, along with a bawn and a pleasure garden. The priory church now came to be re-used for Protestant services, with a new door and chancel arch inserted into the building. The site was included in surveys by Carew in 1611 and Pynnar in 1618–19, but the most detailed contemporary description of the priory church and castle was given by Sir Thomas Phillips in his 1622 survey (quoted in full in Brannon and Blades 1980, 91). This noted that 'the Old Castle of Dungiven' had been repaired and was protected by a round flanker, and now measured 27ft long by 22ft wide, was three storeys high, and covered by a slate roof. The survey stated that it was built against the 'old Abby Church', with dimensions of 50ft long by 27ft wide and 22ft high, the chancel being 25ft long by 24ft wide and 20ft high. The survey also referred to Doddington's new house as being built against one side of the tower house, 'a fair stone house' 46ft long by 21ft wide, and was two storeys high, with a slated roof. The house had a rear projecting block, a 'Returne of stone backward' that was 26ft long by 24ft wide, one-and-a-half storeys high, and covered with a slate roof (Brannon and Blades 1980, 91).

At the front of the manor house there were two small projecting blocks or porches. Extending from a corner was another new stone building (which was of timber in 1611), this time one storey in height, and measuring 100 feet in length, and again roofed with slate. This formed the southern side of a bawn, with the manor house forming the western side, and the church the northern. The eastern side was enclosed by

> …a wall of lyme and stone of 46 foot long, and 14 foot high, inclosing the former Bawne,
> being 76 foot long, and 46 foot broad (Brannon and Blades 1980, 91).

Given that only the nave and chancel of the church now remains, with a cemetery covering the rest of the site, Phillips' survey provided archaeologists with an opportunity to reconstruct the layout of the site as it would have existed in Doddington's time.

The cartographer, Thomas Raven, who accompanied Sir Thomas, also drew a plan of these buildings at Dungiven. Entitled 'The Skinners Buildinge at Dungevin', this was drawn from an easterly perspective and depicts the medieval priory church, the late-medieval tower house, along with the manor house and ancillary buildings that were erected by Doddington. Raven drew while standing on rising ground within the confines of the present-day cemetery, and it is still possible to compare his view with what remains today. His depiction of Dungiven Castle matches Phillips' written description, and also reveals the spatial layout of the complex, as well as the form and size of the buildings relative to each other. In addition, it illustrates formal gardens laid out to the rear of the house. This rich documentary and cartographic evidence, combined with the architectural and archaeological information, allows archaeologists to recreate the appearance of what the site would have looked like in the 1620s with a remarkable degree of accuracy.

On Raven's plan, the nave and chancel of the priory church are depicted with slate roofs, the chancel roof being slightly lower. The eastern gable end of the chancel is depicted with one large, arched window with tracery, something contradicted by the surviving remains where two simple lancet windows occupy the same position. Entry into the priory church was gained via a three-bay porch in the northern wall, with a round-arched doorway clearly evident on the plan. A tower house was built against the western gable-end

21 The ruins of Dungiven Priory stand within a cemetery. Raven drew his map while standing on the same spot and today it is still possible to compare his view of the buildings with what remains today.

of the church, and appears to have been a three-storey, oblong block with a square stair tower attached to its southeast corner, becoming circular above the adjoining nave roofline. The castle was lit by both narrow slit openings and cruciform loops, and rose to battlements, which were crenellated with stepped merlons, while a Scottish-style corbelled turret also formed part of the roofline defences (Jope 1951, 45). Inside the battlements was a slated roof, protruding from which was a brick chimney stack, comparable in design to those rising from the roof of the later manor house. Presumably the chimney stack was inserted into the tower house as part of Doddington's refurbishments.

The manor house was built against the southern wall of the tower house, and was a two-storey building, with an additional attic space as indicated by the presence of dormer windows. Each of the floors was lit by a pair of six-light windows, all similar in size. Entry to the manor house was gained via a porch placed to the side, close to where it abutted the tower house. A second porch was placed at the centre of the house – a single storey projection lit by a three-light window. Phillips' written description mentions this as the front return, '11 foot square'. The Raven plan does not depict the rear projecting block, a scullery, which was described in Phillips' account. Two brick chimney stacks rose from the slated roof of the manor house; their placement suggesting that there were fireplaces in both the centre and the southern gable end of the house.

A long, single-storey building, also roofed with slate, is depicted along the southern side of the bawn. At its western end a brick chimney stack protrudes from the roof, close to where the building abuts onto the manor house, while at its eastern gable end is a smaller, rectilinear building with a two-light window, and which possibly functioned as a flanker. The long building perhaps provided room for brewing, baking, washing and stabling – all of which were necessary for the running of a landed household in the early 17th century.

Excavations in 1982/83 (Brannon 1985) provided further insights into the manor house. The build-up of rubble from the collapse of the house had deterred generations of gravediggers from digging graves across the invisible threshold of the buried walls at this end of the cemetery. This had preserved the site of the house, and when the surviving walls were exposed, their internal faces were still covered with patches of white plaster rendering. The ground floor was divided into two rooms by a centrally placed chimney stack, now only marked by a spread of mortared stone. The floor of one of these rooms was covered with timber planks supported by joists. Access into the house was gained through a doorway placed directly in line with the chimney stack, along with a second front entrance, at the north-eastern corner of the manor house. Between the doorway and chimneystack was a small lobby through which the rooms could be accessed. The rear block was accessed internally via a door in the western wall and a short flight of sandstone steps. There was an additional doorway in the northern wall of the rear block that allowed access to a rear cobbled courtyard. The floor in this rear block was covered with regularly laid sandstone flags. A built-in drain was also visible in the north wall and this, along with the absence of a hearth, suggests that the ground floor of this rear block was used as a scullery where food storage and washing was carried out (*ibid.* 16).

22 Doddington also refurbished the priory church for Protestant services including the insertion of a new chancel arch between the altar and the main body of the church.

Most of the artefacts recovered derived from the furnishing and decoration of the house, and included decorated wall and floor tiles. Fragments of decorated ceiling plaster were also recovered from the area of the tower house, supporting the documentary evidence that it had been refurbished at this time. Handles, keys and locks for doors and furniture, along with hinges for doors and windows dating stylistically between *c.* 1620 and 1650 were also recovered. Domestic items were rather scarce, as refuse disposal by the occupants involved throwing material down a steep cliff into the River Roe just to the rear of the property. Buckles, the bone handle of a knife, a number of dressmakers pins and a fine brass candle trimmer/snuffer were the few finds that came closest to the personal possessions of the household (*ibid.* 17). It appears that by the later 17th century the castle had fallen out of use, while the priory church was replaced in 1711 by a parish church built a short distance away in Dungiven village (Curl 1986, 291).

sewage works, but there are no visible remains.

LDY 018:069

Down Survey barony map of Coleraine (PRONI D597/3)

516   GARVAGH: HOUSE   284251 416074

A house labelled 'Grangh' shown on the Down Survey map of the parish of 'Arragell' (Errigle) is likely to correspond to Garvagh House, a gentlemen's residence, the first incarnation of which was built in the early 17th century. Garvagh House was demolished in 1965 during the building of

Garvagh Primary School, and there are no visible remains.

LDY 018:070

Down Survey parish map of Desertoghill and Arragell (PRONI D597)

517   GARVAGH: SETTLEMENT   284100 415850

The village of Garvagh was rebuilt as a plantation town in the early 17th century. Aside from its general layout, nothing from that time remains upstanding.

LDY 018:071

Hill 1877, 387

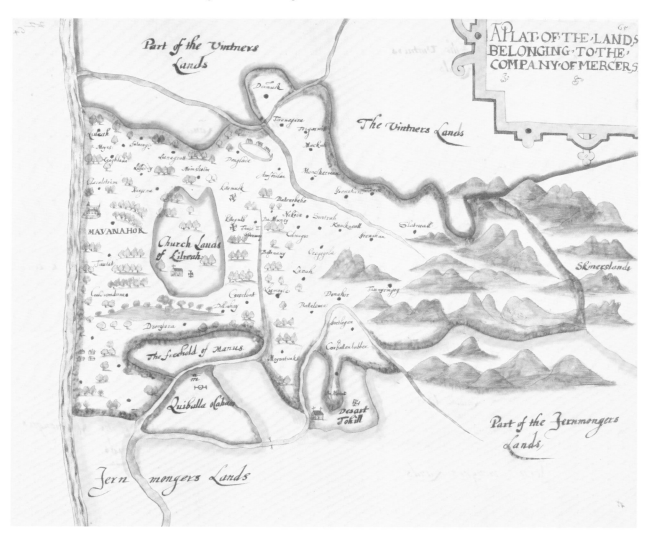

Fig. 7.32 Raven's 1622 map of the Mercers' estate, centred on Movanagher.

Mercers

The Mercers Company, with their affiliates the Masons, Innholders, Cooks and Broderers, acquired 21,600 acres (Curl 1986, 69). The estate, on lands to the south of the Ironmongers' estate, was situated by the Bann with its valuable eel and salmon fisheries at Movanagher and Portna, and encompassed large holdings of church land, along with native freeholds. Pynnar's survey (Hill 1877, 581–582) noted the dangers that these represented, stating

> there are in forty-six Townlands of this Proportion, that are set to the Irish of the Sept of Clandonells, which are the wickedest Men in all the Country.

Pynnar also recorded the presence of a castle and bawn and six timber houses, all of which were under the management of Richard Vernon (*ibid.*). Vernon, suspected of embezzlement, was replaced as agent in 1621 by Thomas Church, who had previously been a freeholder on the estate (Curl 1986, 127). The 1622 survey and Raven's maps describe a small village of four timber houses, eight cabins or cottages and a water mill, all near the bawn at Movanagher (*ibid.*). Most of these structures were, apparently, destroyed during the 1641 Rebellion. After the Confederate Wars, and until 1831, the estate was leased, in its entirety, to a succession of individuals. The company then resumed control of the estate until it was gradually liquidated over the course of the 20th century (Curl 1986 127–152).

518 MOVANAGHER: CASTLE, 292030 415890
BAWN AND SETTLEMENT

Movanagher was described in the 1622 survey as a manor house enclosed by a bawn wall, with three flankers, adjoined by a village and water-mill and occupied by English persons. The village was destroyed in 1641 and all traces of it, and the mill, have vanished, but the bawn is still extant and now encloses a farmyard, although its interior

Fig. 7.33 Excavations at Movanagher.

has been heavily modified over the years, and no original features remain. The site is located on a ridge overlooking the River Bann to the north with panoramic views all round. The ruins consist of a square bawn with walls approximately 20m long and 1.2m in thickness, orientated north-east to south-west, with a flanker at the western corner and traces of two others at the eastern and southern corners; the western flanker has a large tree encroaching upon its southern side, while the south-western wall contains gun loops.

Thomas Raven's 1622 map of Movanagher depicts a mixture of 'English' style timber framed houses and smaller 'Irish' style cabins in the village surrounding the bawn. Test excavations outside the bawn walls in 1980, at the presumed location of the village, uncovered a buried occupation layer containing glass and brick fragments, a 17th-century potsherd and a possible gunflint. A more recent programme of geophysical survey, testing and field-walking unearthed bricks, window glass and ceramics, presumably associated with one of the houses depicted by Raven. Subsequent excavation also revealed the remains of one of the Irish-style cabins depicted by Raven. This measured *c*. 6m by 4m, and was built of sod walling supported by a post-and-wattle core and yielded English and Irish ceramics of early 17th-century date.

LDY 019:003

Copy of Sir Thomas Phillips' report, *c*. 1717–*c*. 1722

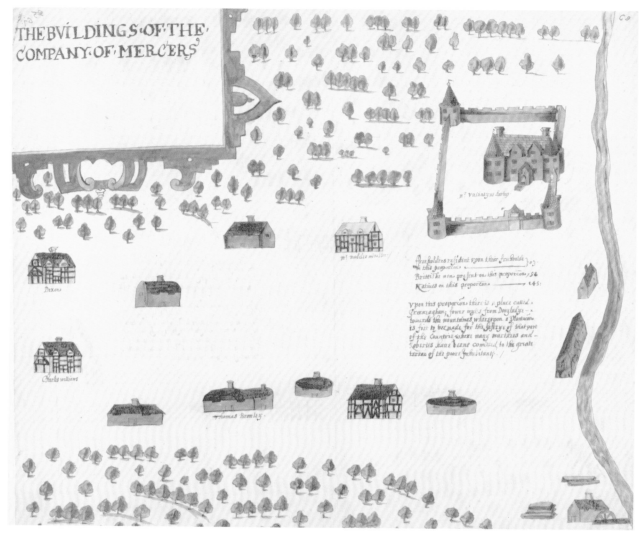

Fig. 7.34 Raven's 1622 map of the village established by the Mercers consisting of four timber-framed houses, eight cabins or cottages and a water mill, all near the bawn at Movanagher.

Phillips MSS (PRONI T510/2); *PSAMNI* 197; Jope 1960, 106, 114; Blades 1980b and 1986; Horning 2001 and 2007

**519   KILREA: CHURCH AND   292700 412290
        GRAVEYARD**
Kilrea Old Church
According to the 1622 Visitation Book, the medieval church at Kilrea was repaired by the Mercers. The ruins of the building still stand, and consist of the stone-rubble walls, 92cm thick, of a rectangular building with its long axis aligned east-west, and measuring 18.5m by 7.6m. There are three arched windows in the southern wall and a large arched window in the eastern gable. There appears to be a blocked-up window in the northern wall near its western end, and there is a small recess in the eastern end of the southern wall. Some handmade brick has been used in repairing the eastern gable window, and some other patches of the same wall. Surrounding the church is an earthwork enclosure,

consisting of a bank on the northern side, with an entrance to the north-west, a scarp sloping to the west of the church, and a wall to the south. Nearby excavations in 2006 revealed medieval features, but nothing from the plantation period.

LDY 027:003

Reeves 1850, 75; Downham and Reynell 1896, 254; Leslie 1937, 244; *PSAMNI* 202; Farrimond 2006; Hamlin 2008, 275

Merchant Taylors

The Merchant Taylors acquired 18,700 acres of land by the River Bann, to the south of Coleraine, and also surrounding church lands at Camus (Curl 1986, 69). The company was one of the more enthusiastic contributors to the project, and in addition to their own holding, were associates of the Clothworkers (*ibid.* 304). The early history of the estate is preserved in Company records, which state that the early building works were focussed on Macosquin; Raven's map of

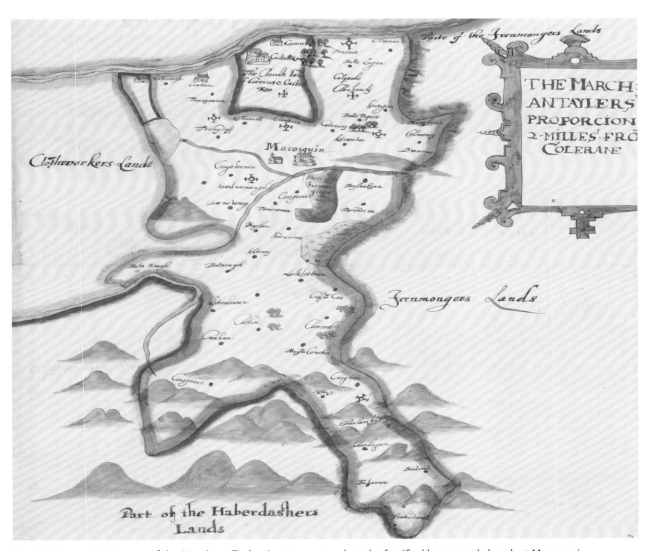

Fig. 7.35 Raven's 1622 map of the Merchant Taylors' estate, centred on the fortified house and church at Macosquin.

1616 depicts a castle, church and village of six houses (*ibid.* 304–307). Pynnar reported that the estate had been leased to a gentleman, Valentine Hartopp, and that a church, seven houses and a 'battlemented castle' were all complete, although the bawn of the castle was still under construction (Hill 1877, 582). The same structures at Macosquin were recorded by the 1622 survey, and on Raven's 1622 map of the settlement. Also illustrated on his more general map of the Company's proportion were Castle Roe, Camus church, and native freeholds in the vicinity. The Merchant Taylors' estate was plagued with financial troubles from its inception, a situation made worse through the enormous arrears that accumulated during the course of the 17th century. Eventually in 1729 the estate was sold (Curl 1986, 311–313).

520   MACOSQUIN: HOUSE,   282500 428800
BAWN AND SETTLEMENT

The village of Macosquin was built by the Merchant Taylors in 1615. The Raven map of 1622 shows a large house surrounded by a bawn wall, the church (Inv. 521) and seven houses. Nothing remains of these houses, and archaeological investigations in the area

Fig. 7.36 Extract from Raven's 1622 map of Macosquin, the village established by the Merchant Taylors, illustrating the fortified manor house inside an unfinished bawn with the corner flankers remaining to be built.

have not revealed any significant deposits. This is one of the few sites for which an accurate scaled site plan was drawn (*c.* 1615) with the village consisting of regular spaced houses measuring 32ft by 17ft, as well as a castle (50ft by 34ft) set within a bawn that was also divided into a designed pleasure garden, a stable yard, an inner court and an outer court. The bawn was protected by four corner flankers. Two lanes led from the main street to the Macosquin River.

LDY 007:045

Moody 1939, 307, pl. xii; Brannon 1983a, 93–99; Blades 1986, 259–261.

521   MACOSQUIN: CHURCH   282610 428820
AND GRAVEYARD
St Mary's Church

The Merchant Taylors built a parish church on the site of a 12th-century Cistercian monastery, known as the Abbey of the Virgin of the Clear Spring. The new church was built re-using the fabric of the earlier building, and it appears on detailed maps of the village in *c.* 1615 and 1622. According to the *OS Memoirs*, the abbey was destroyed by Cromwellian forces during the Confederate Wars. The present-day church, known as St. Mary's, though largely of 19th-century date, occupies the same area and has the same angled alignment to the road as did the abbey church depicted in the *c.* 1615 map of the Macosquin settlement. The monastic church appears to have been roofless at the time, though by 1622 Thomas Phillips was able to report that part of the medieval building was 'repaired and slated'. The church appears to incorporate earlier fabric with a small lancet window visible on the north side.

LDY 007:012

Jope 1951, 31–47; Brannon 1983a, 93; Curl 1986, 305, 308, 311; Moody 1939, 307, pl. xii

522   CASTLEROE: TOWER HOUSE   286040 429990
AND BAWN
Castle Roe

A medieval tower house and bawn were marked on Raven's maps of the Merchant Taylors' estate.

According to the archive of A. McL. May, Castle Roe was originally built by the O'Cahans in the late 13th century, and inhabited by a branch of the O'Neill family before the Plantation. The *OS Memoirs* state that unlike most property held by the London Companies, Castle Roe was not destroyed during the 1641 Rebellion on account of the hospitality extended to Irish troops by its housekeeper. The building was dismantled in the 18th century, its valuable oak roof sold and its building fabric used in other buildings. One wall remained standing up to the 1970s, when what remained of the site was destroyed during development work. Observations and records suggest that the castle consisted of a tower house located at the south-western corner of a bawn, with sides at least 30m in length.

LDY 007:021

May; Day and McWilliams 1995d, 109

Haberdashers

The Haberdashers' lands are situated to the south of Magilligan and east of the River Roe.

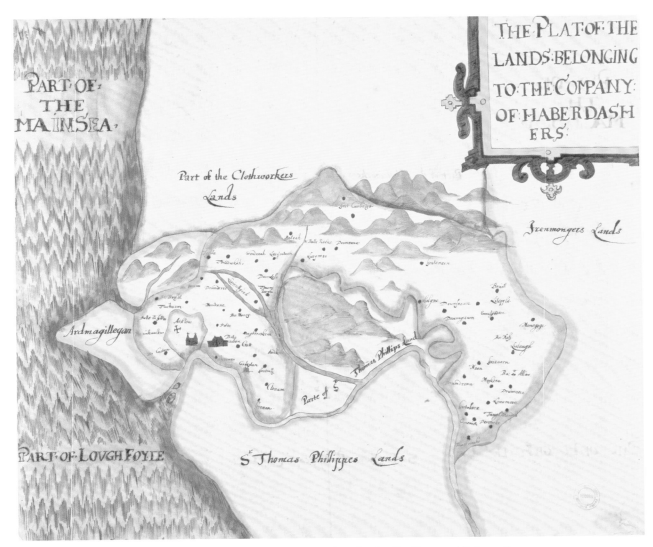

Fig. 7.37 Raven's 1622 map of the Haberdashers' estate, centred on the fortified house at Ballycastle.

The Haberdashers, in association with the Wax-Chandlers, Founders and Turners, were granted 23,100 acres, although nearly two-thirds of the required funds were contributed by two gentlemen, William Freeman and Adrian Moore. This resulted in much legal wrangling between the Company, their associates, these shareholders and Tristram Beresford, agent for the estate, and later joint proprietor (Curl 1986, 314–315). The estate was subsequently sold to the Beresford family in 1674 (*ibid.* 318). The estate was leased to Sir Robert

McClelland, the Laird Bombie, a Scottish planter who, in 1616, had already held, and sold, the Rosses estate in Co. Donegal (Hill 1877, 501 and 583). McClelland was relatively successful in attracting under-tenants from his ancestral lands in Galloway (Curl 1986, 315). Pynnar (Hill 1877, 583–584) reported a castle (Inv. 523)

…finished, being very strong and well wrought . . . There is no Bawn nor sign of any, nor any other kind

Fig. 7.38 Raven's 1622 map of the Haberdashers' estate centre at Ballycastle where a manor house, a bawn and a number of houses and cabins were located. One mile from the bawn was Artikelly, which had developed into another village where houses and cabins were laid out with clearly defined property boundaries.

of Building, more than slight Houses after the Irish manner.

By 1622, a bawn had been built around the castle, and was surrounded by a small settlement. One mile from the bawn was Artikelly (Inv. 524), which had been developed as a linear village of modest houses, each with its own garden plot.

523 BALLYCASTLE: HOUSE AND BAWN   267700 427000

The Raven map and the 1622 survey describe a castle or manor house enclosed by a bawn with four circular flankers, while nearby were three gabled houses and two Irish-style cottages. The castle was apparently destroyed during the 1690s, and there are no visible remains.

LDY 009:017
Curl 1986, 315–318

524 ARTIKELLY: SETTLEMENT   268000 425000

Raven's map of the Haberdashers' buildings depicts twenty-seven cottage-style thatched buildings, most of which are situated on either side of a single street. There are no visible remains of this village, which is now on a low ridge of ground in the vicinity of Aghanloo WWII airfield.

LDY 009:018
Hill 1877, 583–584; Curl 1986, 314–315

525 RATHFAD: CHURCH AND GRAVEYARD   267909 427891

The church at Rathfad was probably founded as early as the 6th century, but it is not known whether or not a medieval church was still standing when the Haberdashers acquired the surrounding lands. A church building, albeit in a ruinous state, was documented here by the 1622 survey. A new church was built in the late 17th century, replacing an earlier building. This was demolished in 1812; all that remains now at the site is a rectangular hollow in the ground, measuring 21m by 7m, orientated

east-west, at the centre of an oval graveyard.

LDY 005:001
Reeves 1850, 78 and 132; Leslie 1937, 89–93; Hamlin 2008, 255

Clothworkers

The Clothworkers, in association with the Merchant Taylors, Butchers, Brownbakers, Upholders, Bowers and Fletchers, acquired 13,450 acres (Curl 1986, 70). The estate lies on the western bank of the Lower Bann, across from Coleraine, and extends to the coastline at Downhill. The Clothworkers' investment in the project was almost beyond their means, and as a result, building on the estate was slow to proceed (*ibid.* 375–378). In 1618, the estate was leased to Sir Robert McClelland, who was also the tenant of the contiguous Haberdashers' estate (Hill 1877, 584). Pynnar's survey (*ibid.*) reported no progress, aside from works at the pre-existing Coleraine Castle (see Inv. 526). McClelland soon imported settlers from Scotland, and developed the village of Articlave which, like Artikelly on the Haberdashers' estate, was a linear village of modest dwellings that by 1622 also included a water-mill (Curl 1986, 380–381). From the late 17th century to the early 19th century, the estate was leased to the Jackson family, after which the company then resumed direct control for a period before selling in the 1870s.

526 WATERSIDE: CASTLE   284430 432500
Coleraine Castle

The medieval castle of Coleraine, situated near the western bank of the Bann, across from the plantation town (Inv. 492), was held by the O'Cahans, and was built upon an earlier monastic foundation. This was one of two castles in Coleraine – another stood on the eastern bank of the river – and both were garrisoned by the English in the late 16th century. The position of the castle on the west bank is indicated on the 1611 map of the town. Once the lands on the western bank had been allotted to the Clothworkers in 1617, the Company rebuilt the old castle. Pynnar (Hill

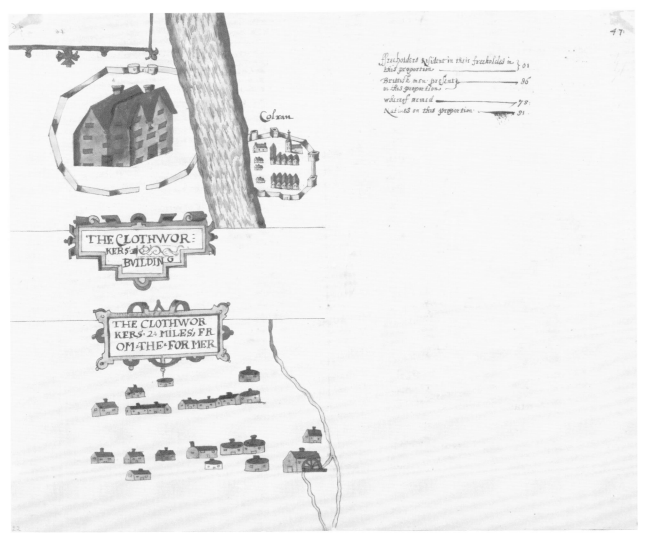

Fig. 7.39 Raven's 1622 map of the Clothworkers' manor house and bawn located on the west bank of the Bann across from the town of Coleraine. Two miles away, a village was established at Articlave consisting of houses and cabins arranged along a street. At one end of the village a mill and mill-race were located.

1877, 584) stated the castle was 'not as yet covered', and on the 1622 Raven picture map (although not on the version of Raven's Clothworkers' estate map also drawn in 1622 and shown in Fig. 7.39), the castle is described as 'voyd and unfinished', and depicts it in an irregular bawn. The castle was replaced in the 19th-century with a manor house, now also demolished.

LDY 007:018

Hill 1877, 584; McNeill 1983, 114–115; Curl 1986, 379–381

**527   CHURCHLAND: CHUCH   284460 432130
Killowen Parish Church**

The medieval parish church of Killowen was renovated in 1616, with further renovations made in 1690 and 1767. This church was succeeded by another building in 1830, though the position of the older building is marked on the 1st edition OS six-inch map. The remains of a brick-built structure lie in the grounds of the 1830 church. It rests on a basalt foundation, and is possibly a crypt or vault, or some

Fig. 7.40 Extract from Raven's 1622 map of the town of Coleraine illustrating Killowen Church on the west bank of the Bann within the Clothworkers' proportion.

other form of small building, now obscured by ivy. The precise dating of the structure is not known, but it is evidently much older than the adjacent mid-19th century church. Aside from this small structure, there are no other indications of earlier buildings.

LDY 007:097

Hill 1877, 584; Curl 1986, 375–378

528   ARTICLAVE: SETTLEMENT   278500 433800

The plantation settlement developed by Sir Robert McClelland is depicted on Raven's map of the Clothworkers' cottages closely sited around a wide street, and with a water mill. Archaeological monitoring of groundworks during development work in Articlave in 2009, did not uncover any features of interest.

LDY 007:046

Curl 1986, 380–381; Nicol 2009

529   DOWNHILL: CHURCH   275820 435410
AND GRAVEYARD
Dunboe Old Church

The ruins of a rectangular, post-medieval church, built of stone rubble and mortar, stand in a graveyard on the site of a medieval parish church. This older church was rebuilt or repaired by the Clothworkers in 1622. According to the A. McL. May archive in the SMR files, the 17th-century congregation was largely Presbyterian, and the Dunboe church was probably abandoned after a meeting house was built at Articlave in 1691. The site continued in use for burials, and includes a notable mausoleum of the

Bruce family of Downhill. The ruins consist of traces of a rectangular building, 18.0m by 6.5m internally, aligned east-west, containing and surrounded by numerous graves. The eastern gable wall survives to a height of 6m, but is otherwise featureless.

LDY 002:001

Lewis 1837, I, 567; Reeves 1850, 77, 83–84, 86; Leslie 1937, 213–214; *PSAMNI* 186; *May*; Hamlin 2008, 268–269

530   BIG GLEBE: FORTIFICATION   276030 434050

A star fort is marked on the Down Survey parish map of Dunbo, in a place then known as 'Tererinmore' which, in relation to the adjacent townlands, appears to correspond to the modern townland of Big Glebe. It is possible that the fort corresponds to a raised rath that was completely excavated there in the 1970s, although during the excavation, no substantial signs of post-medieval occupation were discovered.

LDY 002:003

Down Survey parish map of Dunbo (PRONI D597/3); Bratt and Lynn 1975–76

Fig. 7.41 A star fort is marked on the Down Survey parish map of Dunbo, in a place then known as 'Tererinmore', which appears to correspond to the present day townland of Big Glebe.

Skinners

The Skinners Company estate was the largest of the estates granted to the London companies. At 49,000 acres, it was a landlocked and mountainous expanse of land on the border with Co. Tyrone. Although largely unproductive, there were some valuable lands, especially in the vicinity of Dungiven (Curl 1986, 69–70 and 285). Coincidentally, the name Dungiven

Fig. 7.42 Raven's 1622 map of the Skinners' estate which was the largest proportion granted to any of the London companies. At 49,000 statute acres, it was a landlocked and mountainous expanse of land on the border with Co. Tyrone.

is derived from Dun Geimhin – 'fort of the hides or skins', and unrelated to the Skinners' Company, who like the others, were allocated their lands by lottery (McKay 2007, 64). The company leased the estate to Captain Edward Doddington, one of the designers of the walls of Londonderry and Constable of Dungiven Castle. Through his military endeavours, Doddington had previously become, briefly, the owner of the lands around Dungiven before they were granted to the Skinners (Curl 1986, 285–286).

Pynnar's survey recorded castles at Dungiven

(Inv. 531) and Crossalt (Inv. 534), both surrounded by villages of twelve houses each, along with a church (Hill 1877, 585). A memorial to Doddington's first wife Elizabeth (daughter of George Paulet, governor of Londonderry) in St. Patrick's Church, Coleraine (see Inv. 496) states in Latin that Doddington was the first in what was then the county of Coleraine to build in the 'Anglican' manner (Horning 2013a, 217). His second wife, Ann, a daughter of Tristram Beresford, inherited the lease of the estate after his death in 1618 (Hill 1877, 585; Moody 1939, 275), and

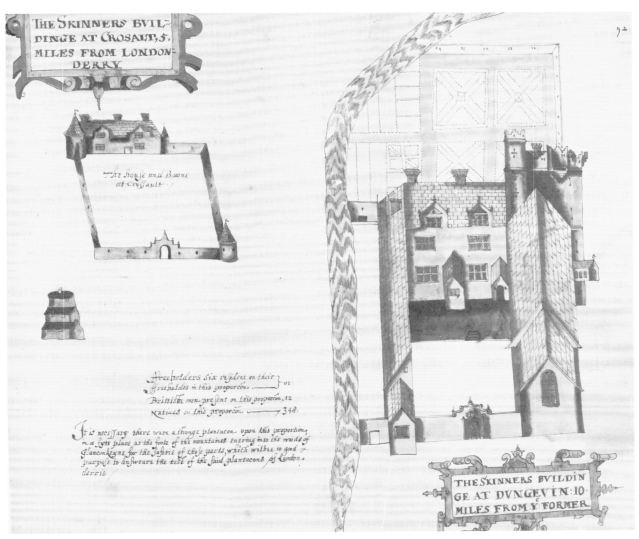

Fig. 7.43 Raven's 1622 map of the Skinners' estate where settlements were established at Dungiven and Crossalt. Dungiven was the site of a pre-Norman monastery, a medieval Augustinian priory and a 15th-century tower-house that was rebuilt by Edward Doddington for his personal use as a fortified manor house, with a church included in the complex of buildings.

the estate remained leased to individuals until the mid-19th century (Curl 1986, 285–303).

531   DUNGIVEN: PRIORY   269200 408260

Dungiven was the site of a pre-Norman monastery, a medieval Augustinian priory and a 15th-century tower house that was re-edified by Edward Doddington for his personal use as a fortified manor house, with a church included in the complex of buildings. The site was mentioned by Carew and Pynnar, but the most detailed contemporary description was given in Phillips' 1622 survey, which stated that

...the Old Castle of Dungiven, on a rock, upon the River of Roe, which is repaired, being in length 27 foot, in breadth 22 foot, 3 stories high, slated, having a round Flancker, toe w.ch is adioyning the old Abby Church, cont. in length 50 foot, in breadth 27 foot, and in height 22 foot slated, with a Chancell 25 foot long, and 24 foot broad, and 20 foot high; The walls of the said Church and Chancell, have been in part new builded, and the residue lately pointed with lyme, with a good new roof of Oake Timber slated; To the aforesaid Castle is added a fair stone house 46 foot long, 21 foot broad, and 2 stories high slated, with a Returne of stone backward, 26 foot long, 24 foot broad, a storie and a half high, slated, with a Returne forward 11 foot square. There is also another stone house newly builded of 100 foot long, one storie high, slated, which is one side of the Bawne, the said Church and Chancell making the other side, to which is builded a wall of lyme and stone of 46 foot long, and 14 foot high, inclosing the former Bawne, being 76 foot long, and 46 foot broad.

Raven's map of the buildings at Dungiven matches this description, and depicts formal gardens laid-out

Fig. 7.44 The remains of Dungiven Priory consist of a church, along with traces of a tower-house. The lower walls of the 17th-century manor house built adjacent to it were revealed during excavations in the 1980s, and can be seen in the foreground.

beside the house. The castle was captured in 1641 by Manus O'Cahan and probably damaged during his occupation, which lasted a year or less, but the complex ceased to be occupied in the 1670s. The church was used for services until *c.* 1710.

The surviving upstanding remains at Dungiven Priory consist of the church building and traces of the 15th-century tower house. The fabric of the church is mostly medieval, but includes 17th-century alterations in the form of the chancel arch and the northern door and porch. The most striking feature in the chancel is a highly elaborate carved stone tomb, traditionally that of Cooey-na-Gall O'Cahan (died 1385); albeit a late 15th-century date is suggested by the decorative stonework on the tomb. The tomb consists of an armed figure lying upon a stone chest, with six smaller gallowglass figures, all beneath an elaborate canopy of flamboyant tracery. Traces of the bawn wall survive; those of the 17th-century manor house were revealed during excavations at the site in the 1980s. The scale of the house, and the 1m-thick walls revealed during the excavation, match the 1622 description of a building measuring 14m by 7.3m.

LDY 031:015

Reeves 1850, 41–42; Brannon and Blades 1980; Brannon 1988d; McNeill 2001, 348–351

532 DUNGIVEN: SETTLEMENT   269500 408300

The plantation village of Dungiven was located near the priory, as noted in the 1622 survey, but there are no visible remains.

LDY 025:021

Day and McWilliams 1992c, 4–6.

533 DUNGIVEN: MILL   268980 408240

In the Civil Survey of 1654, the Skinners lands included 'Strangmore where upon the Castle and Abbey stands with a water mill'. A mill race is still evident downslope from the priory. A preliminary survey in the 1980s noted two derelict sandstone houses (now demolished) at this location, with local accounts describing water flowing through an opening at the base of one of the walls, thus suggesting a mill. Although dating to more recent centuries, these buildings perhaps replaced the 17th-century mill.

LDY 030:048

Simington 1937, 208; Day and McWilliams 1992c, 9

**534 BRACKFIELD: HOUSE 251090 409680
AND BAWN**

Originally known as 'Crossalt', the ruined remains of this bawn, built by Sir Edward Doddington, lie on the northern side of the Faughan river valley. Pynnar's survey mentions the bawn, twelve houses and a church nearby. Raven's map of the Skinners' buildings at Crossalt depicts only two small, gabled houses and an Irish-style cabin, at the north-eastern corner of the bawn. The bawn is well-preserved, having been used as a farmyard. The remains comprise a square enclosure, with sides measuring 20m externally, walls 75cm thick and an entrance facing north. A house some 18m long and 6m wide originally stood against the southern wall. There are two flankers, at the north-western and south-eastern corners; the north-western flanker surviving almost to roof height, with four gun loops. Only the stump of the south-eastern flanker remains. Two hearth recesses survive in the southern wall of the bawn,

Fig. 7.45 The well-preserved remains of the bawn built by the Skinners at Crossalt, now known as Brackfield.

and the eastern gable of the house can be traced in the east bawn wall. Excavations in 1983 uncovered only faint traces of the house and related features.

LDY 023:014

PSAMNI 200; *May*; Jope 1960, 108, 113; Blades 1986; Brannon 1990b

Vintners

The Vintners, in association with the Grocers and several other companies, acquired 32,600 acres of heavily wooded land beside the River Bann, to the north-west of Lough Beg (Curl 1986, 367–369). The estate, centred on Bellaghy, was leased to Baptist Jones, who was in charge of the early building works. Pynnar's survey recorded a bawn of brick and lime and 'a good Rampart, which is more than any of the rest have done' (Hill 1877, 586). There were also two houses in the bawn in Bellaghy, and ten more surrounding it, with a total population of seventy-six men (*ibid.*). Jones was apparently not good at paying his rent, and following his death in 1623, the Vintners' misfortune continued when their new agent, Henry Conway, who had married Jones' widow, also proved reluctant to settle debts (Curl 1986, 368). The estate was badly disrupted in 1641, and after the Confederate Wars it came into the possession of Sir John Clotworthy, Viscount Massereene, although the legality of his tenancy was disputed (Curl 1986, 372: see also Antrim castle, Inv. 130). The Company managed to regain control of the estate in the early 18th century, and sold it to its agent in 1739.

**535 OLD TOWN DEER PARK: 295340 396340
HOUSES AND BAWN**
Bellaghy Bawn

A bawn built in 1619 by Baptist Jones, and one of the best-known examples of such buildings in Ulster, was described in the 1622 survey as a

Manner house of lyme and brick
60 foot long, 27 foot broad, 2

Fig. 7.46 Raven's 1622 map of the Vintners' estate, centred on a fortified manor house in Bellaghy.

stories high, tyled, with a round flacnker, 30 foot broad 2 stories high batlemented, with a parapit and foot pace, leaded; and one house of brick opposite to the Former 54 foot long, 26 foot broad, one storie high with the like round Flancker; There is also a Brick Wall, 14 foot high coped with vent, and Crest, with a Rampier of earth 6 foot thick, faced with stone, which wall together with the said houses and Flanckers doe

make a court, or Bawne, 100 foot square paved, which Comands the Towne adjoyning thereunto, called Vintners Town…

The bawn and the houses were damaged and surrendered to insurgents during the 1641 Rebellion, but were repaired in 1643, and the site has remained in continuous use, with many other phases of building and landscaping having taken place over the centuries. Much of the original bawn walls survive, as does the south-eastern flanker and

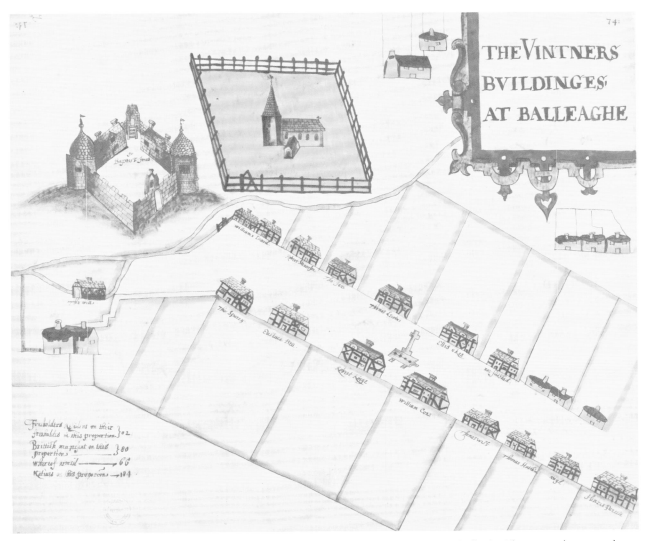

Fig. 7.47 Raven's 1622 map of the manor house and village established by the Vintners in Bellaghy. The manor house and bawn were built of brick, while the village for the most part consisted of timber-framed houses, along with a smaller number of Irish-style cabins. The market place was marked by a cross, and is where a stockade was also located.

the 'Rampier' described in 1622, which is a gun-platform excavated and restored in 1989. The bawn houses a museum, with exhibitions detailing the history of the building and housing archives of the locally-born poet, Seamus Heaney.

Excavations in 1989 located the stone foundations of the smaller of the two houses, and the north-western flanker. The house was a two-roomed structure with a central fireplace, with one of the rooms having a cobbled floor and probably served

as a kitchen. The flanker adjoined the house and, although the foundation courses survived, there were few finds associated with either structure as later activity at the site had obliterated any 17th-century occupation levels. During the excavation, the inner face of the western bawn wall was exposed for the first time in centuries, and was found to be in near-pristine condition with a fine example of English bond brickwork. The excavations also revealed that the stability of the (leaning) bawn wall

Fig. 7.48 Aerial view of Bellaghy village with the manor house and bawn still occupying one end of the main street as depicted on Raven's 1622 map.

Fig. 7.49 Excavations in 1989 revealed the smaller of the two houses depicted on Raven's 1622 map, along with the north-western flanker. The house was a two-roomed building with a central fireplace, with one of the rooms having a cobbled floor and probably served as a kitchen.

had been compromised by the fact that it was built, probably coincidentally, over the relatively loose fill of a rath ditch.

> LDY 037:003
> Copy of Sir Thomas Phillips' report, *c.* 1717–*c.* 1722 (PRONI T510/2); Jope 1960, 105–114; Curl 1986, 367–369; Brannon 1989a

Fig. 7.50 The south-eastern flanker of the manor house at Bellaghy with its brick walls exposed during building restoration.

**536   OLD TOWN DOWNING: 295185 396434
CHURCH**

Ballyscullion Parish Church, Bellaghy

Ballyscullion Parish Church was completed in 1794 on the site of an earlier church built by the Vintners in 1625. There are no remains of the earlier building.

> HB08/09/005
> Curl 1986, 372

**537   OLD TOWN DOWNING: 295270 396590
SETTLEMENT**

Bellaghy

The settlement created by the Vintners at Bellaghy also included 29 houses and a mill illustrated by Thomas Raven in 1622. There are no surface traces of the houses or mill.

> LDY 037:068
> Hill 1877, 586; Curl 1986, 367–369

Drapers

The Drapers Company acquired 38,000 acres of land in the south of Co. Londonderry, including large tracts of mountain and bog around Slieve Gallion (Curl 1986, 175). Between 1615 and 1619, the estate was trusted to an agent, John Rowley and his assistant (and later successor) Robert Russell, who

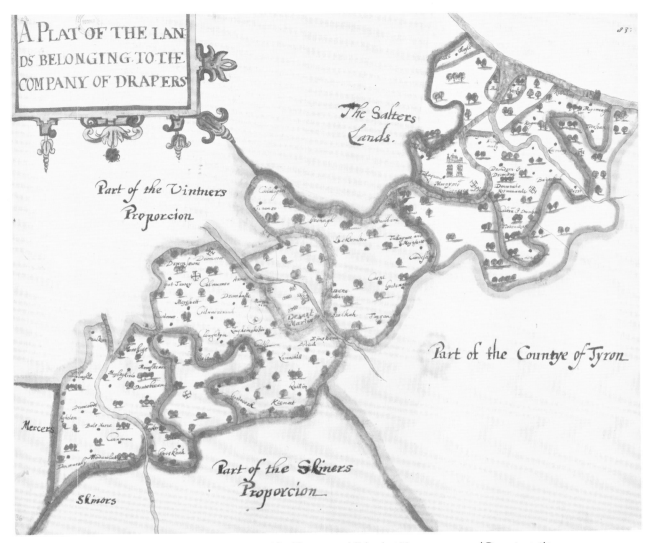

Fig. 7.51 Raven's 1622 map of the Drapers' estate with villages established at Moneymore and Desertmartin.

managed the construction of a castle and bawn, with a chapel within, and the village of Moneymore (*ibid.* 178). They installed a piped water system for the village, and charged high rents for the service. Russell also built and operated a large malt-house, and was reported often to pay his workers in beer, making Moneymore famous among natives and settlers alike for its drunken revelry, brawls and riots (*ibid.*). Pynnar was impressed by the six stone-built and six timber houses, the malt-house, a mill and the water supply, although the castle and bawn

remained unfinished (Hill 1877, 587). The Drapers also developed the village of Desertmartin, keeping the church there in good repair (Curl 1986, 186). From 1619 onwards, the estate was let, over brief intervals, to a series of leaseholders who proved unsatisfactory although development continued, so that by 1630, the village of Moneymore comprised twenty substantial houses and ten cottages (*ibid.*). The estate was attacked in 1641, and Moneymore razed. Its leaseholder by that time was Sir John Clotworthy, who unsuccessfully tried to purchase

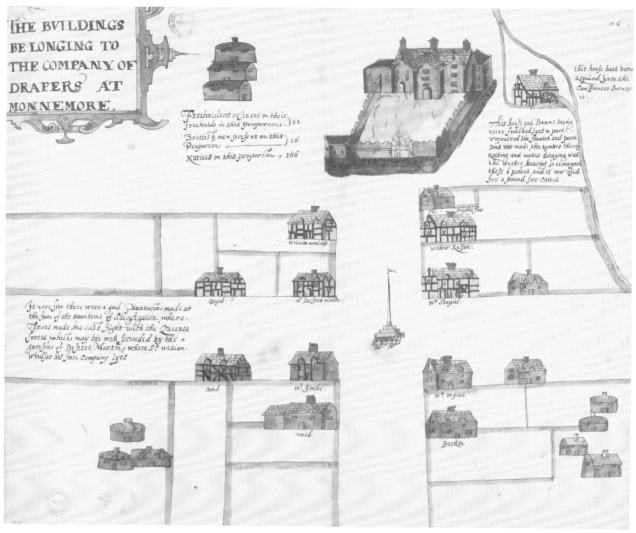

Fig. 7.52 Raven's 1622 map of the Drapers' village of Moneymore. The manor house is depicted as a three and a half storey building with gables, slate roof and brick chimneystacks. It was surrounded by a bawn with three corner flankers, two of which projected from the main house itself. The village was developed around a crossroads with stone-built houses, timber-framed houses and mud cabins.

the estate afterwards, but it was leased instead to his sister-in-law Mary and her husband Capt. Fitzgerald (Curl 1986, 186–231).

538 MONEYMORE: HOUSE AND BAWN 285830 383350

The Drapers' bawn at Moneymore on the Raven map of 1622 is occupied by the Orange Hall in

the town today, close to the summit of a hill, with commanding views of the townscape. On the 1622 map, the manor house is depicted as three stories in height with an attic. There was a projection in the front façade of the house which contained the main ground floor entrance. The roofline was gabled, with a number of chimneystacks evident, and the roofing appears to have been of slate. It was surrounded by a bawn with three corner flankers, two of which projected from the main house. According to an annotation on the map:

> This house and Bawne being neere finished, lyes in parte uncovered the flowers and particons not made, the tymber therof Rotting and walles decaying with the wether.

To the rear of the Orange Hall there is the remnant of the bawn wall, while traces of an extramural ditch have been recorded.

LDY 046:023

Copy of Sir Thomas Phillips' report, *c.* 1717–*c.* 1722 (PRONI T510/2); Blades 1986; Curl 1986, 175–178; N. Brannon *pers. comm.* 2015

539   MONEYMORE: SETTLEMENT 285800 383400
Raven's map of 1622 depicts a village at Moneymore centred upon a crossroads with a market cross in the middle, and comprised of timber-framed and stone houses and mud-walled cabins. At one end of the village lay the manor house and bawn, along with a mill house, but no remains of the original town survive above ground. A greenfield site on the outskirts of Moneymore was investigated archaeologically in 1989 in advance of a housing development, but no features earlier than the 18th century were found.

LDY 046:038

Hill 1877, 587; Moody 1939; Camblin 1951, 43–44; Curl 1986, 175–178; Brannon 1989b

540   CALMORE: CASTLE   282930 395990
Rowley's Castle
This is the site of a castle, although there are no reliable historical accounts of when it was built, or who was responsible for its construction. Local traditions suggest that it was built *c.* 1609, 'burnt' in 1689, and the ruins levelled in 1920. The *OS Memoirs* recorded it as standing in the mid-19th century, and suggested that it was a medieval building that later became the residence of one of the Rowley family,

but there are no visible remains. Local traditions also record that houses and outbuildings at Castle Hill are built of stone robbed from the castle in the 1900s.

LDY 036:017

Day and McWilliams 1995b, 68–69, 76–77 and 86–87

541   KNOCKNAGIN: CHURCH   285580 392130
Desertmartin Parish Church
Various earthen features are all that remain of a medieval church that was maintained by the Drapers when they came to take ownership of Desertmartin; indeed the building remained in use until the 1820s. The site has been used intensively for burials, and as a result the church now only survives as a rectangular hollow. A few structural wall stones are visible in the sides of the hollow, reaching a maximum height of three courses. The earliest visible memorial stone in the graveyard is dated 1708.

LDY 041:002

Reeves 1850, 83; Leslie 1937, I, 180–83; Gwynn and Hadcock 1970, 379; Hamlin 2008, 268; Curl 1986, 186

Salters

The Salters Company, in association with the Dyers, Cutlers, Saddlers, Joiners and Woolmen, acquired 23,250 acres of heavily wooded land surrounding Magherafelt and the north-western shore of Lough Neagh (Curl 1986, 320–321). The estate was managed on behalf of the Salters by Baptist Jones (see also the Vintners' estate) and leased to a succession of gentlemen farmers, initially one Hugh Sayer and, from 1627, Ralph Whistler (*ibid.*). Building on the estate had two foci, at Magherafelt, and at Salterstown on the shores of Lough Neagh. Pynnar's survey recorded a bawn and castle under construction at Magherafelt, along with seven houses 'of slight Cage-work, whereof five are inhabited with poor Men, the other two stand waste' (Hill 1877, 587–588). At Salterstown, there was a bawn and

> . . . a poor House within it of Cage-work . . . also 9 Houses of Cage-

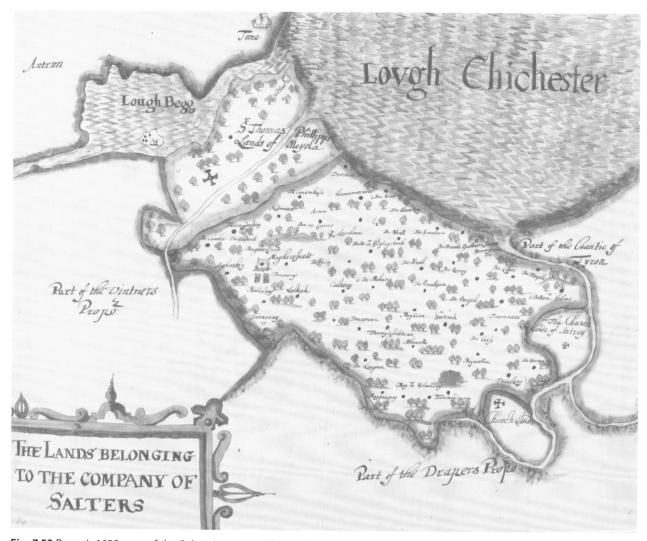

Fig. 7.53 Raven's 1622 map of the Salters' estate on the north-western shore of Lough Neagh. The Company established villages at Salterstown and Magherafelt.

work standing by the Bawn . . . also a Sawing Mill for Timber; but the Glass Houses are gone to decay, and utterly undone (*ibid.*).

Of these two villages, Salterstown was initially the larger, with the maps of Thomas Raven and the 1622 survey recording ten substantial timber-framed houses and four cottages at Salterstown, whereas Magherafelt had only eight complete houses (Curl 1986, 322–323). Both were destroyed in 1641, which

led to the temporary abandonment of Salterstown. Magherafelt was rebuilt, and although it was again plundered in 1688, it continued to grow over the centuries. The estate was leased until 1853, and after a period of direct control, was sold in 1897 (*ibid.* 323–348).

**542 MAGHERAFELT: CASTLE   289690 390590
AND BAWN**

In 1619, in what is now Magherafelt town centre,

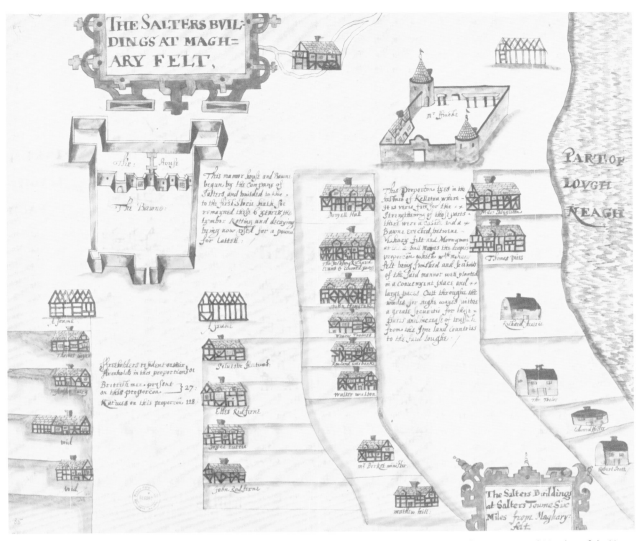

Fig. 7.54 Raven's 1622 map of the two settlements established by the Salters' Company at Salterstown and Magherafelt. Note that the house and bawn at the latter site still remained to be finished along with a couple of timber-framed houses. Given the copious amount of woodland in the locality, it is not surprising that most of the houses were built of timber.

Pynnar described a bawn

> 80 feet square . . . with two Flankers; and the Castle is now in building, being 60 feet long, and 20 feet wide.

Phillips' 1622 survey reported that work had halted, as the house was

> . . .builded to the first story hath soe remained theis 6 yeares, the timber rotting and decayinge, being nowe used for a pound for cattell.

The castle was attacked with cannon in 1641, and although the town of Magherafelt was rebuilt, it seems the castle was not, had it even been completed in the first place. The destruction of the castle was described in the *OS Memoirs*:

In lowering the Diamond or street of Magherafelt in 1799, 1811 and 1815, there was a large portion of the cellar walls of Magherafelt ancient castle raised. It stood south of the market house. The site is partly occupied by the street and partly by a range of dwelling houses.

There are now no visible remains of the castle or bawn.

LDY 042:022

Hill 1877, 587–588; Curl 1986, 321–323; Day and McWilliams 1990f, 81, 108 and 111

543 MAGHERAFELT: 289600 390500
SETTLEMENT

The early 17th-century town of Magherafelt was centred on 'The Diamond'. Although the town has inherited its general layout from the original, there are no known features or structures that survive from its founding.

LDY 042:031

Lewis 1837, II, 332–333; Camblin 1951, 43; Curl 1986, 321–323

544 BALLYNEILL BEG: 293000 383000
GLASSWORKS
Glass-House field

In 1611, William Robson, leased the patent to make glass on lands that were allocated by lottery to the Salters in 1613. Co-incidentally, Robson was a member of the Salters company. Presumably he was attracted by the abundant timber supplies in the region, as the lack of fuel in England was holding back the glass industry there. From around 1614, Salterstown was a significant centre of glass manufacturing and export although, perhaps due to patent problems, the business did not survive very long, and by 1619 the 'Glass Houses' were recorded by Pynnar as abandoned. Robson however became a warden of the Salters' company around this time, and his adopted son Ralph Whistler became

the Salters' main tenant from 1627. The field near Salterstown in which the site is located is still known locally as the 'Glass-House Field', but there are no visible traces of the works. The field is terraced to the south, but it is not known if this has any relation to the works.

LDY 047:027

Hill 1877, 587–588; Curl 1986, 320–323; Brannon 1998

545 BALLYMULTREA: HOUSE, 295180 382360
BAWN AND SETTLEMENT
Salters' Castle and Salterstown

The ruins of the Salters' manor house and bawn at Salterstown lie close to the shores of Lough Neagh. The bawn was complete at the time of Pynnar's survey and the house was finished soon after. Raven's 1622 map depicts a square bawn with an

Fig. 7.55 The southern gable of the manor house at Salterstown.

entrance facing south, a small house in the south-western corner and large circular flankers with conical roofs at the north-western and south-eastern corners. The bawn was captured and destroyed in 1641, and the walls have had a long history of re-use in agricultural buildings. The ruins match Raven's illustration approximately, although the house is much larger than depicted, a T-plan house occupying the entire western third of the bawn. Along with the ruins of the house, traces of the bawn and the flankers can be found, interspersed with more recent farm buildings. The bawn is orientated east-west, measuring 26m by 20.5m externally, the fragmentary remains of the house measuring 20.5m by 8.5m externally. The flankers were 8.5m in diameter. These walls, which are of rough-coursed stone rubble, contain many gun loops. The ruins of the house consist of the northern and southern gables, and a western projection. The southern gable is the better preserved, and indicates that it was a two-and-a-half storey building with flat-headed windows.

All traces above ground of the plantation village of Salterstown, which adjoined the castle, have vanished. However, geophysical survey and excavations in the late 1980s revealed house foundations and an occupation layer that produced numerous artefacts of 17th-century date, along with a well, dated to 1663 by dendrochronology, demonstrating that the site was reoccupied after the 1641 Rebellion.

LDY 049:001
Sir Thomas Phillips' map and report, 1622–1841 (PRONI T510); *PSAMNI* 213; Jope 1960, 105–114; Blades 1986; Miller 1991

**546   BALLINDERRY: CHURCH   293320 380420
AND GRAVEYARD**
Ballinderry Old Graveyard
A parish church and graveyard was located on glebe lands within the bounds of the Salters estate, near the county border with Tyrone. The site is of medieval origin, and was in use until the early 18th century, according to a memorial stone erected to a

rector and bearing the year 1707. The centre of the site contains a level area where the oval outline of a structure or earthwork measuring 15m by 4.5m can be traced; there are no other structural remains.

LDY 049:003
Leslie 1911, 124; Hamlin 2008, 256–257

Barony of Coleraine

Other sites in the barony of Coleraine

547   BOVAGH: HOUSE   288940 419370
On the Down Survey barony map of Coleraine, 'A house Ruinated' and orchard is marked at a position that correlates with the site of Bovagh House, built *c.* 1740. The Civil Survey of 1654 recorded that the townland of Bovagh was part of an estate of 1,000 acres belonging to Lt. Col. Tristram Beresford, which was situated among the parishes of Aghadowey, Kilrea, Errigal and Desertoghill and had come into Beresford family's ownership at some point before 1641. There are no 17th-century remains at the site although a number of late 19th-century farm buildings appear to have re-used handmade bricks (which may date to that earlier time) in their walls.

HB03/03/028
Down Survey barony map of Coleraine (PRONI D597/3); Simington 1937, 153

548   GLENLEARY: CASTLE   285400 427700
A castle was described in the *OS Memoirs* as '...surrounded by a square entrenchment having bastions of earth at the corners ... It was destroyed by the Irish in the rebellion of 1641'. The precise location is not known and there are no visible remains.

LDY 007:093
Day and McWilliams 1995d, 109–111

**549   BALLINDREEN SCOTCH: 290090 430660
CASTLE**
The site is described in the *OS Memoirs* as an ancient castle, 'the seat of the McKannery family

for centuries', which was razed to the ground in 1745. Stone from the castle was probably used for other buildings in the area, and there are now no visible remains.

LDY 008:013

Day and McWilliams 1993e, 50 and 57

550   TULLANS: MILL   287071 431784

A 17th-century mill was included in a lease of lands at Laccanreagh by a James Hamilton from the earl of Antrim, whose estates were located to the east of Coleraine. This stood probably on the site of a now derelict 19th-century mill building of random stone construction, the walls of which incorporate earlier fabric with large inclusions of handmade brick. The building is divided into sections, with a two-storey miller's house at the northern end, and the mill itself located at the south, along with a free-standing brick chimney. The window openings have red-brick surrounds that cut across former arched openings, suggesting at least one phase of rebuilding. Immediately to the south of the mill complex is a small stream that could have functioned as a mill-race.

LDY 007:105

Hill 1873, 439–440

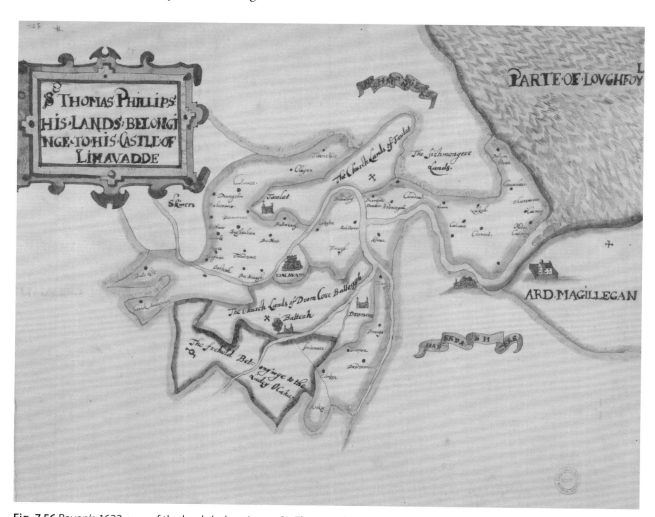

Fig. 7.56 Raven's 1622 map of the lands belonging to Sir Thomas Phillips who established his chief residence at Limavady.

Barony of Keenaght

Limavady and the estate of Sir Thomas Phillips

Sir Thomas Phillips was a soldier whose exploits during the Nine Years' War had won him lands in Ulster and much political influence over the project. One of the architects of the Londoners' involvement, he had held a freehold at Coleraine immediately before it was subsequently granted to the London companies. In 1610, to compensate for its surrender, Phillips was granted lands in Moyola in the Barony of Loughinsholin, near Toome, whose garrison he commanded, and some 13,100 acres near Limavady, the site of an O'Cahan castle (Curl 1986, 431). The developments that he undertook at Limavady were comparable to those of the London companies. He re-edified the O'Cahan castle, and enclosed it within a large bawn, and constructed mills, kilns, houses, formal gardens, orchards, and an inn (Hill 1877, 572; Curl 1986, 432–434).

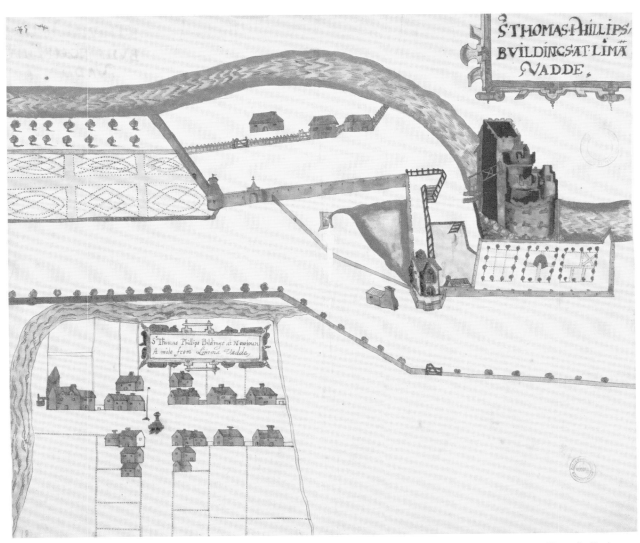

Fig. 7.57 Sir Thomas Phillips' development of Limavady was comparable to those of the London companies. He re-built the O'Cahan castle, and enclosed it within a large bawn, and constructed mills, kilns, houses, formal gardens, orchards, and an inn.

551 MONEYRANNEL: SETTLEMENT 266000 423000
Newtown-Limavady

This is the approximate location of the plantation settlement at Limavady, at the time called Newtown-Limavady. Before Sir Thomas Phillips received his grants, settlement in the area was associated with an O'Cahan castle, one mile upstream along the River Roe. By 1610, twenty-five English families had moved to the area following encouragement by Phillips. The settlement was named 'Newtown-Limavady', and was granted its charter in 1613. Raven's map of 'Newtown A mile from Limma Vadde' illustrates an inn, and some twenty houses and garden plots, arranged round a crossroads and a market cross, but of these there are no visible remains. In 1641–42 the castle was besieged for the entire winter by Irish forces, and although the garrison held out until relieved by parliamentary forces, the Irish returned, taking the castle and burning the town.

Limavady was rebuilt, but was damaged again in 1689 by the army of James II on its retreat from the Siege of Londonderry. Given the redevelopment that has occurred over the centuries since, there are now no visible remains of the early phases of building in the town. Archaeological investigations, made in advance of the construction of the Limavady Civic Centre, revealed a series of pits and linear features filled with soil and rubble, including bricks of probable 17th-century date. These features were interpreted as horticultural features and rubbish pits originally sited within a series of small garden plots in the 17th-century townscape.

LDY 009:016 and LDY 009:031
Lewis 1837, II, 439–440; Hill 1877, 572; Curl 1986, 432–434; Gahan and Long 2006

552 KILLANE: CASTLE 268120 423900

The *OS Memoirs* recorded a castle, said to have belonged to the O'Cahans. Aside from the local place names 'Castle River' and 'Castle Bridge', all other traces have vanished.

LDY 009:021
Day and McWilliams 1991c, 48 and 56–57

553 DEER PARK: CASTLE AND BAWN 267720 420390
O'Cahan's Castle

This castle, on a site known as 'O'Cahan's Rock', was located on a rocky shelf above the River Roe, with steep drops to the south, east and west, and was considered highly defensible. The original construction date is unknown, but is presumably later medieval. The castle, which was besieged in 1641–42 (see Inv. 551), became the main residence of the Phillips family from around 1611 until 1662, when they moved to 'New Hall' within the town of Limavady itself. According to the *OS Memoirs*, the walls could still be traced in the 1820s, but were subsequently destroyed. Mortar fragments and traces of a stone revetment at the northern end of the site were visible in 1941. The ditch surrounding the castle site is still visible. Archaeological testing in 2001 unearthed occupational debris and traces of a robbed-out medieval wall. Over the years, tree falls at the site have yielded material associated with the castle including decorative plasterwork of 17th-century date.

LDY 016:003
Copy of Sir Thomas Phillips' report, *c.* 1717–*c.* 1722 Phillips MSS (PRONI T510/2); Jope 1960, 109; Day and McWilliams 1991c, 57 and 76; Horning 2013a, 203–210 and 2013b

554 BOVALLY: MILL 268900 422750

A mill was marked on the Down Survey map of Drumcross parish between the townlands of Bovally and 'Drumount', the latter now called Drummond, on the Castle River which forms the

Fig. 7.58 Extract from the Down Survey parish map of 'Drumcross' (1656–58) which depicts a mill on the boundary between the townlands of Bovally and 'Drumount', the latter now called Drummond.

boundary between the two townlands. The Civil Survey confirms that these were See lands leased to the Phillips estate. Although nothing remains of the 17th-century mill, the ruins of an early 19th-century sawmill stand on the site.

LDY 010:052
Down Survey parish map of Drumcross and Baltiagh (PRONI D5927/2); Simington 1937, 213

555 GORTGARN: TOWER HOUSE   271100 423950
The Lady Whit's House

A crenellated tower house is designated 'The Lady Whits House Unforfeited' in the Down Survey parish map of Drumcross, located within 'The 3qr Gleab of Gortnegarne', which is now two adjoining townlands - Gortgran and Glebe. The Civil Survey indicates that these were See lands in the 17th century, but there is no historical identification of the 'Lady Whit' forthcoming. There are no visible remains.

LDY 010:053
Down Survey parish map of Drumcross and Baltiagh (PRONI D5927/2); Simington 1937, 213

Fig. 7.59 A tower-house is labelled as 'The Lady Whits House Unforfeited' in the Down Survey parish map of 'Drumcross' (1656–58), located somewhere within the present day townlands of Gortgran and Glebe.

Miscellaneous estates (Keenaght)

556 FLANDERS: CASTLE   268000 411000

A castle, the fragmentary remains of which were described in the *OS Memoirs*, supposedly was built here by Captain Arthur Carey in the 17th century, and was known locally as the 'Turret' or 'Round House'. The Civil Survey of 1654 states that the townlands of 'Derriarde' and 'Bellicarrigan' were held jointly by Tristram Beresford and a Major George Carey, while all other temporal lands in the Parish of 'Bovea' or 'Bovevagh' were, at that time, held by Beresford.

LDY 024:035
Day and McWilliams 1994, 15

557 BALLYMAGOLAND: HOUSE   266800 436250

There are no visible remains of a house marked on the Down Survey barony map of Keenaght on the approximate location of Magilligan Prison. According to the Civil Survey, the entire parish, then called 'Ardmagilligan', was comprised of See lands leased for sixty years in 1634 to an English gentleman, John Gage.

LDY 001:014
Down Survey barony map of Keenaght (PRONI D597/2); Simington 1937, 216–217.

Fig. 7.60 Part of the Down Survey barony map of Keenaght (1656–58) depicting a house in the general location of Magilligan Prison.

558 ARDMORE: CAUSEWAY   270560 420900

There are no visible remains of a causeway or road described in the *OS Memoirs* as connecting Balteagh church to a castle. In 1654, the four surrounding townlands and the site of the adjacent church (Inv. 559) were See lands, part of the large estate leased by Mrs Susanna Phillips.

LDY 017:050
Simington 1937, 214; Day and McWilliams 1991c, 28

Sites on church-owned land in the barony of Keenaght

559 ARDMORE: CHURCH   270690 420890
AND GRAVEYARD
Balteagh Old Church

According to local tradition, the site for the church at Balteagh was chosen by ravens that stole a plumb-line from a church being built at Killhoyle, and subsequently dropped it where the ruins of a medieval church, repaired or restored in the 17th century, now stand. The church, according to Reeves, was founded in the 15th century, and was mentioned in the Inquisitions in 1609. It was in use until the 1780s, although in 1777 it was severely damaged by a storm, and never properly repaired. A replacement parish church was built in the early 19th century across the road from the medieval church and graveyard. The remains consist of traces of the eastern and southern walls of a rectangular building, measuring 17m by 7m orientated east-west, with an outline of the rest of the building marked by a bank, cut in places by later burials. There is a gap in the southern wall, presumably the original entrance. The earliest memorial stone in the graveyard dates to 1764.

LDY 017:015

Reeves 1850, 132–133; Leslie 1937, 115–8; Hamlin 2008, 258

560   BOVEVAGH: CHURCH   266760 414010

The status of this medieval church and oratory – illustrated on the Down survey map of the 'Parish of Bouevy' – during the Plantation is not known, but its ruins still stand and the site would have been prominent throughout the period. The parish is situated between the Fishmongers' and Phillips' estates, and by the time of the Civil Survey in 1654 the lands were leased to Tristram Beresford. The ruins consist of a rectangular roofless building of mortared rubble, measuring 17m by 7.5m externally, with three small windows and an arched doorway in its western wall, and a larger window in the northern wall. The walls are approximately 1m thick. To the west of the church is a small oratory.

LDY 024:011

Down Survey parish map of Bouevy (PRONI D597); Simington 1937, 207; Hamlin 2008, 263

561   CRAIG: CHURCH AND GRAVEYARD   270840 434470
Skreen Church

Skreen is a medieval church and graveyard, and perhaps a *cillín*, used until the 18th century, but ruined by 1834. Reeves reported that in 1845 '… it was ploughed up, the foundations of the chapel cleared away and all the human remains found there were collected and buried in one pit'. The status of the church during the Plantation is not known; the surrounding lands were See lands not included in the grants to the London companies. The site is now a flat field; nothing remains above the surface.

LDY 002:002

Reeves 1850, 78; Hamlin 2008, 279

Barony of Loughinsholin

Thomas Dawson's estate

Thomas Phillips sold his interests in his lands near Toome, known as Moyola, in December 1622 to Thomas Dawson. The Civil Survey recorded that in 1654 Dawson was in the possession of an estate of 978 acres, centred upon 'Towne Arran Darneveagh' (Simington 1937, 170). This corresponds to the modern townland of Tamniaran, where the village of Castledawson, named after Dawson's descendants, is located.

562   TAMNIARAN: CASTLE   292815 393541
Castle Dawson

According to the *OS Memoirs*, this is the approximate site of Thomas Dawson's castle, but there is little other historical documentation of the site. The area was converted into a sports pitch in the 20th century, although it has now reverted back to farmland; it is likely that any archaeological remains have been erased.

LDY 042:007

Day and McWilliams 1992c, 44 and 93

Church sites in Loughinsholin

**563   MONEYCONEY: CHURCH   272990 390670
           AND GRAVEYARD
           Ballynascreen Church**

This early church site, traditionally associated with St. Columba, contains ruins, probably late medieval in date, consisting of a long, rectangular church building measuring 19m by 6m internally, with different phases of construction evident in the masonry; ascertaining the chronological development of the building is however hampered by a lack of dressed stones. The only fine stonework in the church is a miniature ribbed vault within a niche in the eastern wall. The church was described as uncovered in the 1622 Visitation Book, which added

> The Incumbent is Gilbert Sutton… not resident, but lyveth in another diocess, repayring sometimes to his Cure, wch in his absence (if any of his parishioners would come, as I suppose few or none doe) would be discharged (after a sort) by his Clerke, being an Irish scollar.

The church continued as a site of local importance, especially for burial, and there are several 18th-century memorial stones and a mortuary house for a Catholic priest, dated 1720.

LDY 040:003
Reeves 1850, 76 and 82–83; *PSAMNI* 210; Davies 1941c; Hamlin 2008, 257

**564   LISMULREVY: CHURCH   280558 358291
           Lissan Church**

Lissan is an undated post-medieval church with numerous 18th- and 19th-century additions, built on or near the site of an early medieval church. The building is shown on the first edition Ordnance Survey map of 1833, and was described in the *OS Memoirs* as 'a plain and very ancient structure'. The construction date is unknown but there is a date

of 1618 inscribed on the wall inside the doorway. The church, still in use, is a simple rectangular nave and chancel building measuring approximately 20m by 8m externally, with an entrance facing to the south, onto which has been added a porch, stair and vestry. The walls of the church, which exhibit a slight batter, are rendered with cement, thus obscuring details of the masonry. It is very well lit, with three windows with semicircular heads in the southern wall. The eastern gable of the nave contains a large, semicircular headed, three-light window, almost certainly dating to the 18th century, and which commemorates George Walker, the governor of Londonderry in 1689 and rector of the parish in 1688–90. The northern and western walls also contain large arched windows with semicircular heads.

LDY 046:001
Lewis 1837, II, 287; Leslie 1911, 348–350; Leslie 1948, 132–134; Rowan 1979, 362

**565   LARGANTOGHER: 285489 400251
           CHURCH
           Maghera Old Church**

The parish church at Maghera, originally of medieval date and recorded as being established by St. Lurach in the 6th century, was reputedly plundered by the Vikings in AD 832. The building, now in ruins, remained in use until 1819, and consists of a roofless, rectangular nave and chancel building measuring some 20m by 6m internally. The surviving masonry indicates that numerous repairs, insertions and other alterations were made to the building over the centuries. The earliest part of the church is the nave, which probably dates to the 10th century. The most significant later alteration is the belfry tower at the western end of the church, which was accessed by a door at first-floor level. Although the precise date of this addition is unknown, it is perhaps as late as the 18th century.

LDY 036:006
PSAMNI 209–210; *AMNI*, 113; Hamlin 2008, 275–278

566   DRUMNACANON: CHURCH   291060 406240
Tamlaght O'Crilly Parish Church

The ruined remains of a 17th-century church stand in Drumnacanon on what is generally thought to be the site of a medieval church. The 1622 visitation book stated

> The Church of Tawlaght O'Croyly hath good walls and a roofe of timber, but not covered . . . A gort or old glebe, 12 acres, belonging to ye parish, and of newe glebe one Towneland, a Tymber frame of building provided for it.

According to the Civil Survey, by 1654 the lands around the site were See lands leased to the heirs of Edward Rowley. A replacement church was built a short distance away in 1815, and the old church was deliberately demolished. The *OS Memoirs* state that two human skulls were found

> …in the heart of the east gable…One of them was of peculiar form being long and narrow and very convex at the forehead.

The ruins are obscured by dense vegetation which covers the low walls of a simple rectangular building measuring 17m by 7m internally, orientated east-west. The eastern gable is the best-preserved, and

Fig. 7.61 The ruined remains of Enagh parish church in Templetown.

contains an opening for an arched window. The interior is lower than the exterior due to burials around the church.

LDY 033:007

Reeves 1850, 53–54; Leslie 1937, I, 282–285; Simington 1937, 186; Hamlin 2008, 281; Day and McWilliams 1993a, 38

Barony of Tirkeeran

Church sites in Tirkeeran

567   TEMPLETOWN: CHURCH   246870 419550
AND GRAVEYARD
Enagh Church

The ruined remains of a church traditionally founded by St. Canice are located upon a slightly elevated ridge overlooking Lough Enagh and the site of Enagh Castle, an O'Cahan stronghold (Inv. 569). The ruins consist of the walls of a stone-built, rectangular church of medieval date, orientated east-west and measuring 24m by 5.5m, along with a south transept of later date and slightly finer construction, measuring 7m by 6m. Neither building phase is well-dated, however. The eastern gable contains a narrow lancet window at its centre, some 4m high, splayed internally and surrounded by sandstone moulding. The interior of the church features a significant number of burials. There are several 17th- and 18th-century memorial stones in the graveyard, but these are difficult to read due to heavy lichen growth. The ruins are in a good state of preservation having recently been consolidated.

LDY 014:015

Reeves 1850, 28–29; 1857, 19; Day *et al.* 1996a, 33–34, 46–47; Scott *et al.* 2011, 88–89

568   FAUGHANVALE: CHURCH   257923 420921
Faughanvale Old Church

A medieval church, thought to be on the site of an early monastery, was in ruins by the time of the 1622 Visitation. It sits within a walled graveyard which contains numerous uninscribed and undated stone grave markers that are tightly arranged in rows. The ruins consist of a rectangular church, orientated east-west, measuring 18.2 by 5.1m internally, with a porch in the northern wall. The two gable ends survive to near full height, and feature a fine transitional splayed window with sandstone mouldings in the eastern wall and a small, round-headed window in the western, which also features two buttresses.

LDY 015:024

Reeves 1850, 79; *PSAMNI* 195; Hamlin 2008, 273

Miscellaneous sites in Tirkeeran

569 TEMPLETOWN: 247370 419420
TOWER HOUSE
Enagh Castle

Green Island is a crannog in Lough Enagh, now attached to the mainland via a causeway built, according to local tradition, by heaping stones and earth upon the frozen surface of the lake during a cold winter. The crannog is the former site of 'Anagh' or Enagh Castle, an O'Cahan late medieval tower house, demolished in the 19th century. The tower house and the surrounding lands were ceded by Donnell O'Cahan to Sir Henry Docwra in 1602, who garrisoned it with some 100 soldiers. The stone foundations of the tower house were still visible when the *OS Memoirs* were written, but only a low mound remained when the site was archaeologically surveyed in 1941, and this is now overgrown with trees, although geophysical survey revealed the basic ground plan.

LDY 014:009

Davis 1941d; Day *et al.* 1996a, 48–49; Scott *et al.* 2011

570 LISAGHMORE, OR THE   244800 414600
TRENCH: BARRACKS

The *OS Memoirs* indicate that a 17th-century military entrenchment was made near the River Faughan. The memoirs also note that an 'old ruined barracks' was still standing in the 1830s. These features were apparently constructed by an English squadron during the 1640s and no visible traces remain. However, the entrenchment is remembered by two houses in the locality called 'The Trench'.

LDY 014:059

Day *et al.* 1996a, 49–50

571 COOLAGH: HOUSE   258700 421500

The townland of Coolagh is surrounded by the Fishmonger's lands, but the Civil Survey reveals that it was owned by the Bishop of Derry, and leased to Sir Thomas Staples of Lissan. On the Down Survey map of the barony a house is depicted at 'Coloagh' in Faughanvale. This site cannot now be located and there are no visible remains.

LDY 15A:007

Down Survey barony map of Tirkeeran (TCD); Simmington 1937, 242

Fig. 7.62 On the Down Survey map of the barony of Tirkeeran (1656–58) a house is depicted at 'Coloagh' in Faughanvale.

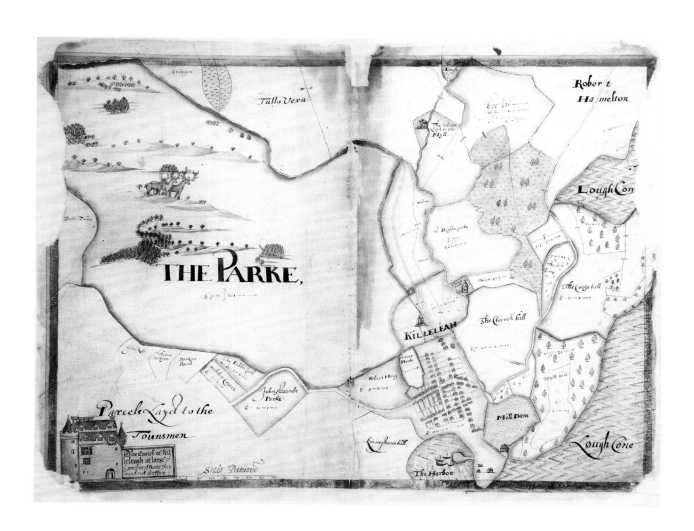

Chapter 8
Discussion and Conclusion

Introduction

This book has drawn together archaeological and historical evidence for settlement in Ulster in the first half of the 17th century. The landholding classes, whether Scottish and English landlords who were granted new estates in the Ulster Plantation, or the Gaelic Irish lords who survived the Nine Years' War, lived in tower houses and fortified houses. Many of these still remain today in varying degrees of preservation; some remained in use into modern times, while others were adapted and obscured by later additions. Many now stand as forlorn ruins, shorn of their roofs, floors and internal furnishings. Appraising their design and layout can provide insights into the organisation of early modern households, which were conceptualised around notions of class, ethnicity, religion and gender. The degree of movement and access allowed to individuals within these buildings very much depended on status or identity; a member of the landlord's family or one of their personal servants would have enjoyed greater freedom of movement than other servants, or tenants arriving to pay rents. What went on inside the tower houses and fortified houses was a reflection of society at large, and an understanding of how these buildings worked as living spaces allows the modern observer to appreciate this.

Scottish re-use of native tower houses

A number of older tower houses in eastern Ulster were re-occupied by Scots settlers, including Red Hall, Co. Antrim (Inv. 40), and Portaferry (Inv. 170) and Quintin (Inv. 172) on the Ards Peninsula in Co. Down. The tower houses in Ulster were part of the wider medieval building tradition in Ireland, and for the most part were little influenced by those constructed in Scotland. These buildings were built from the early 15th century (and possibly a little earlier) by the Gaelic Irish and Old English social élite, the aristocracy, the gentry, the clergy and merchants. Given their popularity, they could be found in both rural and urban contexts, a notable example of the latter being Carrickfergus, where a dozen tower houses lined the streets in the late 16th century. Given that most buildings in late medieval and early modern Ulster were made of timber or post-and-wattle, stone tower houses made a statement that advertised the wealth of their occupants. Mahee Castle (Inv. 178) and Narrow Water (Inv. 212) in Co. Down, for example, involved expenditures of £300 and £361 4s. 2d. respectively for their construction in the latter half of the 16th century, not insubstantial amounts of money that would have been beyond the reach of most people at the time (Loeber 2001, 272).

Tower houses were typically between four and five storeys high, their thick walls rising to battlements, with other defensive measures including machicolations, arrow slits and gun loops. Their doorways would have been protected by an iron grill known colloquially as a 'yett'. Going inside through the doorway, one was confronted by a 'murder hole' in the ceiling above. It must be remembered though that these were first and foremost élite residences, and not just simply fortified refuges. The various floors were divided into rooms or chambers, including the most important of all, the hall, where the castle's household would gather for meals and for more formal gatherings. The hall could be well furnished with attractively carved furniture, its walls covered with plasterwork, along with tapestries and wooden panelling. Sometimes the hall would not be located within the tower, but placed instead within a house built either close to or directly abutting against the side of the tower house. In the 16th century, Richard Stanihurst, an Old English writer from Dublin described these ancillary hall buildings as follows:

> Adjoining them [castles] are reasonably big and spacious palaces made of white clay and mud. They are not roofed with quarried slabs or slates, but with thatch. In the palace, they have their banquets but they prefer to sleep in the castle rather than in the palace because [sic] their enemies can easily apply torches to the roofs (quoted in McNeill 1997, 221).

As the tower house was the centre of a large country estate, various other buildings would also have been erected in its shadow, including the dairy, brew house, bake house, kitchen and stables, as well as lodgings for servants and workers. Typically, these were constructed of timber, post-and-wattle and mud, and hence have not survived the rigours of time. Along with the tower house, it was common for them to be situated within walled courtyards known as 'bawns'. The bawn could be built of either earth or stone, and was typically rectilinear in plan (circular examples were recorded, usually when the tower house re-occupied the site of an early medieval rath). The corners of rectilinear bawns were usually defended by small towers or turrets, also known as flankers, designed to provide cover along the walls, as well as the approaches to the castle. These flankers, either square, rectangular or circular in shape, were often provided with gun loops.

But there was more to tower houses than this. Their architecture could also act as a metaphor for claims of lordly power over the local community. As mentioned previously, the importance of the martial architecture is underlined in a Scottish courtier's advice to his son on the importance of retaining battlements on one's home, as failure to maintain such a feature would reduce the social standing of the family (McKean 2001, 57). Scottish settlers, like the MacDonnells of Co. Antrim, understood this when they appropriated older castles built by their Gaelic Irish and Scots predecessors. Re-use was not solely a matter of financial expediency, but emphasised that the new arrivals were taking on the mantle hitherto worn by the native lords and were now the new landowning élite. Consequently many tower houses continued to be occupied through the 17th century and beyond. For example, Portaferry Castle (Inv. 170) and Quintin Castle (Inv. 172), originally built by the local Old English Savage family, were refurbished by Sir James Montgomery between 1625 and 1650. Windows were widened, floors were re-inserted and new roofing was put in place, but their basic appearances remained unchanged.

Changing architectural tastes over the centuries though meant that a number of tower houses were integrated into larger country houses, obscuring their medieval form and layout. One example can be found at Red Hall (Inv. 40) in Co. Antrim, where William Edmonstone of Duntreath in Stirlingshire re-edified an existing tower house, adapting it to the needs of an early modern Scottish household. The tower house still survives under Georgian and Victorian accretions, with the thickness and batter of some walls hinting at its medieval origins. Inside, an oak staircase and roof timbers date to the early 17th century, while a wood-panelled chamber survives from the latter half of the century. This type of panelling is called wainscoting and was commonplace in élite houses of the Elizabethan and Jacobean eras.

The planners anticipated that the settlement of English and Lowland Scots in Ulster would bring about a social and cultural transformation that would finally undermine the recalcitrant Gaelic Irish lords. The new settlers would differ from the natives in their adherence to English common law, to Protestantism and in aspects of cultural behaviour including dress, language and building styles. Even so, native-built tower houses continued to remain an integral part of the built environment, with Scottish landlords, along with their English peers, choosing to reside in these older buildings, making use of a pre-existing settlement and communications infrastructure. Financial expediency and familiarity with tower houses in their homeland, along with concerns of promoting lineage, ensured that these buildings were to become part of the Ulster Scots archaeological legacy.

Scottish élite architecture in early 17th-century Ulster

While Scottish landlords did utilise pre-existing buildings on their estates, protracted warfare in previous decades had reduced the amount of suitable accommodation, meaning that many had to build anew. This was particularly the case in central and southern Ulster where the tradition of building tower houses was not as prevalent as elsewhere in Ireland; the Gaelic Irish lords in these regions having preferred timber houses and *crannógs*. In addition, the plantation scheme included provisions that obliged the grantees to build new defensible residences that would be surrounded by bawns. These fortified houses had a form and layout representing a novel architectural development in the Irish landscape. They contained more rooms than tower houses, and were better lit and heated. Such architecture advertised not only a change in the political dispensation for Ulster, but also a new lifestyle that was greater informed by more refined notions of polite disposition and genteel living. This was a period when the wealthy in Ireland and Britain came to be influenced by the ideals of the Renaissance, something which was to have an impact on their material culture, including the buildings that they constructed.

Jope and Waterman recognised Scottish influence in a number of early 17th-century élite buildings in Ulster. Jope (1951, 33) found ten extant buildings in Ulster that bore Scottish traits, along with another two that were known to have stood in the 19th century before their demolition. One of the lost examples was a Scottish style tower house, with a number of corbelled-out turrets and a crow-stepped gable that was built at Ballycastle, Co. Antrim (Inv. 71). Unfortunately this was demolished in the 1850s, but was still standing at the time of the first Ordnance Survey, when it was recorded. Besides these buildings, a number of other examples are now only known from 17th-century pictorial maps. Thomas Raven's map of Dungiven (Inv. 531) in 1622 features a corbelled turret projecting out from the battlements of the tower house there. The use of such turrets, whether roofed with conical caps or unroofed, and supported by moulded corbelled supports exemplify the influence of Scottish architecture in early modern Ireland.

Such turrets were well known in the Scottish Lowlands, though none have been found in the Western Isles or Highlands, highlighting the fact most Scots involved in the Ulster Plantation were Lowlanders. While nine buildings with these features were constructed by Scottish settlers in the first half of the 17th century, two were actually built before the start of the project, testifying to the longevity of contacts between this part of Ireland and Scotland. Intriguingly, a 19th-century view of a now demolished late 16th-century castle built by a Gaelic-Irish family, the Magennisses, in Newcastle, Co. Down (Inv. 218), shows a turreted building very much Scottish in appearance (*ibid.* 36). Also in the latter half of the 16th century, the gatehouse into the 'Upper Yard' of Dunluce Castle (Inv. 87) was rebuilt by the MacDonnells featuring two corner turrets in Scottish style, corbelled high up from the corners of the building. Here at Dunluce, the MacDonnells clearly followed the latest fashions in their homeland, creating an Italianate loggia or covered walkway which looks out of place on the windswept rocky coastline of north Antrim. The latter feature was clearly inspired by Renaissance ideals and compares well with examples at Crichton, near Edinburgh and St. Andrews (*ibid.* 38). This loggia was later blocked by the construction of an English-style manor house in the early 17th century, illustrating that architecture on the one site can reflect a mixture of Scottish, English and Irish influences.

While corbelled turrets projected out from the rooflines of fortified houses such as Kilwaughter Castle (Inv. 46) and Ballygally Castle (Inv. 53) in Co. Antrim, others were placed much lower down in the façades of their buildings, usually in the re-entrant angles between two wings of a building. Castle Balfour (Inv. 250), a fortified house with a T-shaped plan in Lisnaskea in Co. Fermanagh features a pair of corbelled stair turrets which rise from first-floor level in the north-western and south-eastern corners respectively of the main block. In Co. Tyrone, a fortified house at Aughentaine (Inv. 391) with a T-shaped plan, and another with a L-shaped plan at Derrywoone (Inv. 354) also feature corbelled stair turrets in their re-entrant angles.

Another feature of the Scottish architectural tradition is the use of crow-stepped gables to decorate the rooflines of buildings, such as at Newtownstewart, Co. Tyrone (Inv. 360) and the Old Customs House in Bangor, Co. Down (Inv. 149), where their owners were clearly demonstrating to all and sundry their cultural identity. However, this feature was also adopted by English and Irish families. John Dalway used crow-stepping for his bawn at Ballyhill (Inv. 35) near Carrickfergus, Co. Antrim, while further afield outside Ulster, the technique was used to decorate one of the gables of Ballymooney Castle, a fortified house in Co. Offaly built by Donell O'Carroll in *c.* 1622 (Lyttleton 2013a, 134, Fig. 6.20). It has been suggested that the moulded string-coursing still visible in the fragmentary ruins of Red Bay Castle, Co. Antrim, (Inv. 63) may also be the result of Scottish influences (Jope 1951, 38). As it happens, one James McDonald built this castle in 1561 for the English governor of Carrickfergus, Piers Crosby. Red Bay Castle was the scene of many skirmishes, but was restored by the MacDonnells in the early 17th century, and was still in a habitable condition when leased to John Stewart by the 2nd earl of Antrim in 1637.

One of the finest examples of Scottish architecture in Ulster is Monea Castle (Inv. 327) in Co. Fermanagh. This is a fortified house of oblong plan, three storeys high and built of roughly coursed limestone, but featuring sandstone door and window surrounds. The dressing on these surrounds is quite different from the usual dressed stonework seen in fortified houses elsewhere, and suggests the use of Scottish masons in its construction. The internal layout is quite different from fortified houses found in areas outside Scottish settlement, the ground floor comprising a series of vaulted chambers used as the kitchen, buttery and pantry. The principal chamber of the house, the hall or great chamber, was located immediately above on the first floor, with smaller, more private rooms to be found on the second floor, an arrangement that can be found in contemporary dwellings of the wealthy in Scotland. Projecting from the corners of the front façade are two circular towers, three storeys in height and, quite unusually, each crowned with a square-gabled attic storey, a feature which can be paralleled at Claypotts Castle in Dundee, Scotland.

Even though the plans and styles of fortified houses as a whole were innovative in an Irish context, details could be left in the hands of Gaelic Irish masons and which resulted in buildings, the designs of which were informed by new ideas but constructed with the masonry techniques of the older native tradition. Tully Castle (Inv. 340) in Co. Fermanagh was built between 1610 and 1618–19 for Sir John Hume, its T-shaped plan advertising the roots of its Scottish owner who hailed from Berwickshire. But Tully was built by Irish craftsmen and consequently differs from other Scottish fortified houses, with angle turrets at roof level being carried on smoothly splayed masonry and the stair turret being supported on a squinch, rather than either being carried on the moulded corbel courses that can be seen in other contemporary Scottish-style houses. Indeed, the barrel vault over the ground floor possesses tree-branch centring, similar in manner to the native use of wicker centring in late medieval and early modern Irish buildings (Johnston 1980a, 85; Waterman 1959b, 123). This idea of using projecting turrets spread into northern Connaught, with examples found in Parks Castle in Co. Leitrim and Rathlee Castle, Co. Sligo where the projecting turrets were again supported on smooth masonry rather than on moulded corbels. This technique was unknown in Scotland and appears to have been a local development of the corbelled turret style, illustrating how ideas on building techniques evolved as they spread beyond Scottish estates (Donnelly 2012, 45; Jope 1951, 33 and 45–46).

While the tradition of defensive building was still current in Scotland, in England (outside the Border counties) the defensive element in building had for long been visual rather than functional. English planters, faced with the need to build a fortified residence to comply with the conditions of plantation, had to improvise or to borrow ideas from their Scottish neighbours, or through employing native masons (Waterman 1961,

261). Castle Archdale (Inv. 292), a fortified house in Co. Fermanagh, while built on an English estate by 1615, bears traces of Scottish craftsmanship. The moulding around the bawn gateway is Scottish in origin, representing the earliest appearance of Scottish building methods in that county.

Scottish houses of the 'ordinary sort'

Unlike the fortified houses and castles occupied by wealthy landlords, little to no evidence survives of the homes erected by their tenants. The rigours of the Irish climate, combined with periodic rebellion and destruction, has meant that little remains of the houses and cabins that would have housed the bulk of the population, including the thousands of Scottish settlers who arrived in Ulster both before and after the Plantation. Even with excavation, most of these houses have proved elusive – building techniques such as mud-walling, portable cruck timbers to support roofs, and timber-framed construction all leave only ephemeral traces in the ground, and can be difficult to find even with archaeological excavation. The odd tantalising references can be found in historical sources, such as that to one William Lynne, a freeholder in the manor of Dunnalong in Co. Tyrone, who promised in 1614 to build within four years a 'good and sufficient house of stone and lime or stone and clay with windows and chimneys after the form of Scottish buildings' (Roulston 2005, 184). Even stone-built houses pre-dating 1650 have generally proved elusive. An example of surviving vernacular architecture from the first half of the 17th century may be found at Corry (Inv. 254) in Co. Fermanagh, where a mud-walled cabin still stands, its thatched roof supported by cruck trusses.

One of the exemplar sites investigated as part of the Ulster Scots Archaeological Project was Servants Hill (Inv. 153) on the outskirts of Bangor, Co. Down. The site was located on the lands of Sir James Hamilton in northern Co. Down and was among a number of settlements on the estate mapped in detail in 1625 by the English cartographer, Thomas Raven. A Scottish landowner, he had been encouraging the migration of settlers from Scotland, even before the advent of the Ulster Plantation, and by the mid-1620s this area of Co. Down had been well settled by Lowland Scots. Raven's map depicts a group of four houses that likely housed some of these settlers. They appear to have been thatched, mud-walled cabins, three of which are depicted with rounded corners. In appearance, they were little different from the cabins built by the Gaelic-Irish across Ulster, and illustrate the difficulty of assigning ethnic identity to particular architectural forms. Settlement was recorded elsewhere on the estate by Raven, including on one of the Copeland Islands (Inv. 156), Carrigullian (Inv. 186), New Comber (Inv. 247) and Groomsport (Inv. 150). Groomsport, on the shores of Belfast Lough, was depicted with a harbour and several rows of Irish-style cabins, even though the bulk of the population was Scottish in origin. It would seem that a dwelling from this period – a thatched and stone-built single-storey cottage of a simple, rectangular plan, with a central doorway and windows on each side – still survives on Cockle Row in the modern village.

While there has been some discussion of how differences in ethnic identities did or did not manifest themselves in buildings owned by the landed sort at the time, little archaeological and architectural work has contemplated how different and competing identities impacted upon the homes of the lower social orders. Horning (2001, 388) suggests that Irish housing and pottery were incorporated into the material culture of planters. Using the excavated evidence of a native vernacular style house in the plantation village of Movanagher, Co. Londonderry (Inv. 518), she has demonstrated that cultural change is seldom a one-way street, and that a blending of both native and settler cultures was necessitated by the needs of everyday living, resulting in a process of accommodation and adaptation on the part of the settlers (*ibid.* 385–96). Other contemporary villages in the same county, at Crossalt (Inv. 534) and Dungiven (Inv. 532), are a case in point with these settlements consisting entirely of Gaelic-style thatched dwellings (Blades 1986, 267). The process of adaptation was under way also in areas settled by the Scots. At Goodland (Inv. 69), which is on a coastal hilltop in northern Co. Antrim, lie the remains of 129 sub-rectilinear earthen huts overlooking Murlough Bay. Previous fieldwork on the site suggested that these huts represented a Gaelic Irish booleying settlement, but more recent geophysical survey, documentary research and some limited excavation has indicated that this was a Scottish Highland settlement associated with the MacDonnells, the structures at Goodland being paralleled by a contemporary house type in Scotland (Horning 2013a, 56–60).

Large numbers of Scottish settlers (both Catholic Highlanders and Protestant Lowlanders) settled in north Co. Antrim under the MacDonnells, and established other settlements in the region, including a town beside Dunluce Castle. Archaeological excavations in recent years have discovered extensive remains of this settlement (Inv. 88). Excavators were able to reveal cobbled streets, with evidence for stone-built and timber-framed houses lining their sides. These buildings were quite substantial, ranging in size from 30 to 85m^2, and were at least one-and-a-half storeys in height. The buildings included a merchant's house and a smithy, and many artefacts were found, including early 17th-century coins and a great variety of pottery, testimony to the daily lives of the townsfolk. At least forty houses were built here, along with a counting house, a courthouse and a gaol (Breen 2012). Another landowner who was encouraging Scottish settlement in eastern Ulster was Sir Hugh Montgomery, whose estate was centred on the town of Newtownards (Inv. 162) in Co. Down. By 1611, around one hundred houses had been built there, all inhabited by Scots. A market cross (Inv. 163) was erected at the eastern end of the High Street in 1636. It is a small octagonal sandstone structure, with a blocked doorway in its north-eastern side and a pyramidal stone roof.

Churches in Scottish-settled areas

Following the establishment of the Church of Ireland under the reign of Henry VIII, all religious buildings passed into the hands of a new, established Anglican Church with the monarch at its head. This was the time of the Reformation and Counter-Reformation, when continental Europe was rent apart by religious schism between Protestants and Catholics. Generally speaking, most people in Europe followed the religious convictions of their rulers and this was certainly the case for England and Scotland. But Ireland did not follow this pattern, with the bulk of the population instead, whether Gaelic Irish or Old English in origin, preferring to remain Catholic. Despite the rhetoric of government officials at the time who lauded religious reform, efforts to convert the population were hindered by lack of finances and suitably trained clergy, particularly those who could preach in Irish. Also, since the mid-16th century many of the church livings and finances had been passing into hands of landlords who were now reluctant to release them to the Church. Consequently, parishes were not properly supported and this impacted upon the investment and upkeep of church buildings. This situation was exacerbated by unstable political conditions in the decades previous to plantation which saw protracted warfare, land confiscations and economic hardship. Observers at the time decried the condition of the reformed church, and in 1596 the Munster planter and literary figure, Edmund Spenser, recommended in his *View of the present state of Ireland* (Fitzpatrick and O'Brien 1998, 111):

> Next care in religion is to build up and repair all the ruined churches, whereof the most part lie even with the ground, and some that have been lately repaired are so unhandsomely patched and thatched that men do even shun the places for the uncomeliness thereof. Therefore I would wish that there were order taken to have them built in some better form according to the Churches of England.

This situation was to continue unchanged into the 17th century. By 1615, for example, fewer than half of the Protestant churches in the country were in repair, while the representative of the Crown in Ireland, Lord

Deputy Thomas Wentworth, observed in 1634 that it was useless to introduce conformity with the liturgy used in England unless 'the decays of the material churches be repayred and an able clergy be provided' (*ibid.* 111–113; Gillespie 1995, 89; 1997, 22).

The churches in 17th-century Ulster were for the most part simple oblong, gable-ended structures, built of roughly coursed limestone and sandstone rubble. These contrasted unfavourably with the medieval parish churches in England and Western Europe, which were embellished with transepts, aisles, chapels and chantries, and were often built of ashlar fabric. This tendency towards simplicity appears to be typical of medieval Irish churches in general, with decorative embellishment confined solely to door and window openings. Despite the boom in the building of churches, during the 12th and 13th centuries, and again in the 15th, these were rarely elaborate. Recent research has found that the majority of churches that continued in use in post-1600 Ulster were of this undifferentiated plan (Roulston 2004, 206 and 208). Indeed in Scotland, many medieval parish churches were also rectangular in plan and lacked any further additions like a chancel (*ibid.* 209).

The relative simplicity of these churches, with ornamentation chiefly confined to pre-existing door and window openings, has meant that for most there are no surviving architectural features that are idiosyncratically Scottish. Layd Church (Inv. 61) in Co. Antrim would be typical; it is a relatively large medieval parish church, with a tower at its western end containing a vaulted floor. The eastern end of this building was extended at some stage in the late 17th century but nothing in its walls marks it as Scottish *per se*. However, the graveyard does preserve several 18th-century memorials to the MacDonnell family, and the church probably was a focus for religious observances among the settler community in the early 17th century. Another church in Templastragh, Co. Antrim (Inv. 78), has two graveyards associated with it, one of which is known as 'The Scotch Kirkyard', and according to *OS Memoirs*, the latter was chosen as a burial ground by Scottish settlers.

However, where church buildings enjoyed the patronage of landlords, there were more significant alterations or even rebuilding. The church at Dunluce, Co. Antrim (Inv. 89) was described as ruinous in 1622, though it was soon after reconstructed by Sir Randall MacDonnell, 1st earl of Antrim, a Roman Catholic, to serve the needs of the Scottish Protestants who inhabited the town that he established beside his castle. The ruins consist of a large, rectangular gable-end building, with an 18th-century entrance porch at its western end. There is a very large window in the eastern gable, which would have ensured that morning services were brightly illuminated. The earliest memorial in the graveyard is dated 1630 and marks the burial place of the offspring of Walter Kid, a Scottish merchant from Irvine, who lived in the town. Ballymoney Old Church (Inv. 96) in the same county was built in 1637, again by the earl of Antrim, drawing its congregation from Scottish Presbyterian settlers in the town. The remains consist of a stone building, along with a brick belfry tower added to it in the latter half of the 17th century. The graveyard contains several 17th-century memorial stones with the earliest being dated to 1610. At Donaghadee, Co. Down (Inv. 165), a parish church, unusually cruciform in plan, was built by Sir Hugh Montgomery in the 1620s on the site of an earlier church. At Derrygonnelly, Co. Fermanagh (Inv. 336), a simple rectangular church was built in 1627 by Sir John Dunbar, the local Scottish landlord there. Its most striking feature is its western entrance, a semicircular arch with a moulded surround decorated with five-faced blocks – an Italian influence – that framed the doorway of this church, and linked this otherwise modest building with the European Renaissance. Dunbar's patronage is marked by an armorial plaque placed above the entrance, containing his coat-of arms and those of his wife Katherine.

Conclusion

While the Scots played a prominent role in both 'official' and 'unofficial' schemes to establish settlers in the region, the Ulster Plantation also involved English and Gaelic Irish landlords as well as the London Companies. Within these estates, the landlords or their agents were obliged to erect fortified houses and create settlements within the vicinity of the same. Tenants resided in villages near or beside these fortified manor houses, while many also chose to live in separate homesteads dispersed across the estate. Mills were built to cater for increased agricultural production, while older churches were refurbished to cater for the tenants who were largely Protestant, though Scottish Highlanders of Catholic persuasion were also involved in settling the lands of the earl of Antrim in north Antrim. Our chief source of information on the types of buildings erected on these estates were the official surveys that were carried out periodically to review progress, beginning in 1611 and followed by others in 1613, 1618/19 and 1622. In addition, Thomas Raven's maps of the London Companies' settlements in Co. Londonderry in 1622 and the Hamilton estate in northern Co. Down in 1625 were of considerable assistance in identifying the spatial layout of settlements as well as the physical appearance of individual buildings. Bringing all this information together has allowed for the grouping of sites on the basis of the estate in which they were found, consisting of fortified houses and associated bawns, along with the villages and churches, as well as individual farmhouses.

Knowledge of such sites provides for a greater understanding of the political, cultural and social processes involved in the transformation of Ulster by plantation. The demise of the native lordships such as the O'Neills in Tyrone, the O'Cahans in Co. Londonderry and the Maguires in Co. Fermanagh, following the Nine Years' War, took place against a background of renewed colonialism, nascent capitalism, the Renaissance and the great religious schism rendered by the Reformation and Counter-Reformation. The physical appearance of the different building types used during the era of plantation – their form, layout and situation in the surrounding landscape – can tell us much about how people lived their daily lives. By studying these monuments it is possible to infer how households were organised, how people expressed their religious beliefs, and what sort of contacts they had with the outside world through travel and trade. This can allow for a better understanding of the lives of people at this time.

However, as can be seen in the gazetteer, there are varying levels of monument survival, with some better preserved than others. Archaeological sites can suffer the vicissitudes of war, rebellion, forfeiture of estates, economic dislocation and changing means of agricultural production. The 1st edition of the OS six-inch map series from *c.* 1830 offers a baseline on which to analyse the degradation of archaeological sites, the rate of which has accelerated due to more extensive and intensive agricultural practices. Comparisons with these early series of maps suggest that the proportion of monuments destroyed since first recorded is close to 30% in most Irish counties (O'Sullivan and Kennedy 1998, 90). While most of these were earthworks, typically raths, many masonry structures such as the tower houses and fortified houses included in this gazetteer have also fallen victim to modern agricultural practices.

There is a clear bias in survival and preservation towards sites associated with the landed elite in early modern Ulster. In general, non-élite settlement in Ireland is extremely difficult to study (certainly without excavation) due to poor rates of preservation and recognition. Archaeological fieldwork by Breen (2005 and 2012), Horning (2001, 2004 and 2013a), Klingelhöfer (1999 and 2000) and Lyttleton (2012 and 2013b) has sought to redress this imbalance with field survey, excavation and the interrogation of cartographic and documentary sources to elucidate the physical nature of the cabins and houses that would have housed most people. Seventeenth-century cartographic sources such as the Down Survey or the maps drawn by Thomas Raven clearly indicate that modest, ordinary homes were an integral part of the early modern built environment. Even though these structures are no longer standing, they have been included in the gazetteer, since their wall foundations and floors may still lie preserved beneath the sod waiting to be discovered some day. Rare examples of 17th-century vernacular architecture still survive upstanding at Ballyminstra, Co. Antrim (Inv. 108) and Corry, Co. Fermanagh (Inv. 254). These are houses, the roofs of which are supported by cruck trusses, a type of arched timber support which is characteristic of pre-1700 vernacular architecture.

The Ulster Scots Archaeological Project also involved the investigation of three sites – two fortified houses at Derrywoone, Co. Tyrone (Inv. 354) and Monea, Co. Fermanagh (Inv. 327), along with a greenfield site at Servants Hill (Inv. 153) on the outskirts of Bangor, Co. Down. While certain areas of Monea and Derrywoone Castle were investigated to answer questions of architectural interest, the principal aim of the fieldwork was to throw light upon the material culture of the ordinary people who once lived on these Scottish-owned estates. The potential locations of their housing in the vicinity of the fortified houses, and a group of four tenant houses in Servants Hill recorded on one of Raven's maps of the Hamilton estate were investigated. While a selection of artefacts including window fragments, iron nails, metal slag, ceramics, tobacco pipe fragments, musket balls, along with animal

Fig. 8.1 Nick Brannon gives a guided tour of Monea Castle.

bone were recovered, no structural evidence for any 17th-century house was found (even though a couple of Bronze Age houses were found at Servants Hill), underpinning the challenges faced in trying to locate and study non-elite settlement in this period of Ulster's history.

The investigations at Derrywoone, Monea and Servants Hill provided an opportunity for the project archaeologists to be involved in a programme of community outreach, school involvement and cross-community inclusion. This involved visits from both primary and secondary schools. Along with site tours and artefact displays, activities were arranged to familiarise visitors with the range of work carried out by archaeologists: surveying exercises using a theodolite, planning using tapes, trowelling, drawing buildings, washing artefacts and photography. There were also site visits from local community groups, while further publicity was generated by engaging with newspaper and television outlets. Members of *Claíomh*, a military 'living history' group were also involved, displaying period weaponry and armour, 17th-century blacksmithing and leather working. A blog was also posted to share the day-to-day events and findings of the excavations. This level of engagement with the whole community was invaluable in promoting awareness of the local archaeological heritage. Consequently, it is important to achieve the same level of awareness with a wider audience, informing people on the location and nature of plantation-period sites to be found in their midst. Whether Ulster Scots, Gaelic Irish or English, these represent a cultural and historical heritage, the continued survival of which in today's landscape is contingent on the support of the general public, and it is hoped that this book will go some way towards this achieving this.

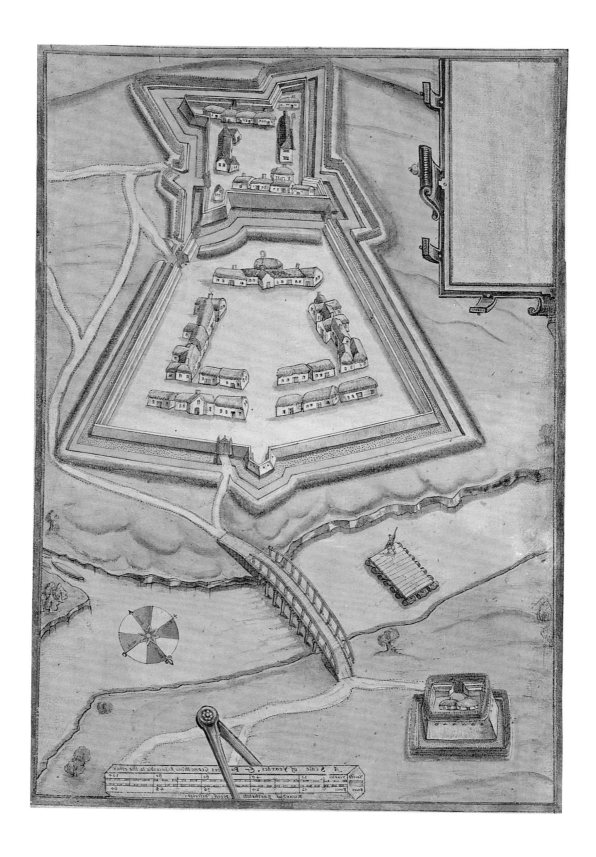

Appendix I
Battlefields (1600–1650) in Northern Ireland

Listed below are summary details of battles fought in the period 1600–1650 and recorded in the Northern Ireland Sites and Monuments Register. This covers the closing years of the Nine Years' War (1594–1603), the 1641 Rebellion, and the ensuing complex series of armed struggles known as the Irish Confederate Wars, which continued until 1653. These were rarely set-piece battles, and consequently they have left limited archaeological traces.

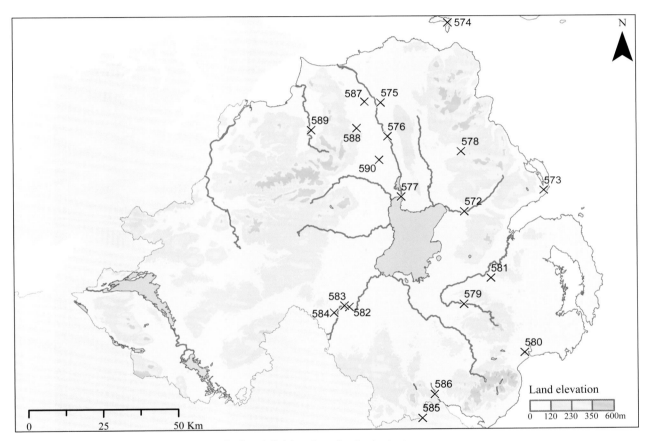

Fig. A1 Map of Northern Ireland showing the battlefields referred to in the text.

County Antrim

572 DUNADRY   320300 385200

A battle was fought here in 1649 between Royalist troops under a Col. Hamilton and Parliamentarian troops under Col. Owen O'Connolly. O'Connolly – noteworthy as a native Irish Protestant convert, and an informant to the Crown at the time of the 1641 Rebellion – was killed shortly after the defeat of his forces here.

ANT 050:185

O'Laverty 1878–1887, III, 229–230

573 WHITEHEAD   346900 392600

The *OS Memoirs* record a battle at this location in 1641 or 1642. Accounts disagree as to whether it was a pitched battle or a confrontation following an ambush.

ANT 047:067

Day and McWilliams 1991d, 65–66 and 75

574 GLEBE   315100 450850
Lag an Bhriste Mhóir

In 1642, the army of Sir Duncan Campbell, some 1600 men, attacked and defeated the local MacDonnell followers on Rathlin Island off the coast of Co. Antrim. The name *Lag an Bhriste Mhóir* translates as 'hollow of the great defeat', and the event is also remembered as the Campbell Massacre; it seems few were spared. Some accounts describe how the women were driven from their place of refuge on a nearby hill and over the cliffs at Roonivoolin.

ANT 001:084

O'Laverty 1878–1887, IV, 369–370 and 377; Forsythe and McConkey 2012, 451–452

575 BENDOORAGH   292600 423300

At this approximate location on 11 February, 1642, Irish and Highland Scots under Alisdair MacDonnell defeated Scots commanded by Col. Archibald Stewart.

ANT 017:061

O'Laverty 1878–1887, IV, 125 and 126

576 GORTEREGHY   294900 411600
The Battle of Portnaw

On 2 January, 1642, Irish and Highland troops under Alisdair MacDonnell fought and defeated Scottish troops commanded by Col. Archibald Stewart; the precise location is not known.

ANT 026:036

O'Laverty 1878–1887, IV, 79–80

577 TOOME   299200 390400

The precise location of the site of a battle fought on the 16 August, 1642, between Scottish troops under Major General Monroe and the Irish of Donnell Gimley O'Kane, is unknown.

ANT 042:024

Young 1895, 216

578 CREEVAMOY   319400 406300

The *OS Memoirs* record a battle between Irish insurgents and British settlers in 1641 at this approximate location.

ANT 033:098

Day *et al.* 1994c, 103

County Down

579 BALLENY   319900 353100

This is the approximate location of a battle fought in late September 1649 between Col. Robert Venables' Parliamentarian force and a regiment of Irish Confederate cavalry.

DOW 021:080

Young 1895, 71–72

580 DUNDRUM   340100 336400

O'Laverty recorded that at this location in Dundrum a battle was fought between Sir James Montgomery's garrison and Irish insurgent forces in 1642.

DOW 044:054

O'Laverty 1878–1887, I, 119 and 120

581 LISNASTREAN 329000 362200

In 1649, forces under Sir Charles Coote and Col. Robert Venables defeated royalist forces here.

> DOW 014:051
>
> O'Laverty 1878–1887, II, 224 and 245

County Tyrone

582 BENBURB 281600 352300

Battle of Benburb (1600)

On 16 July 1600, an inconclusive battle was fought between Hugh O'Neill, earl of Tyrone, and Lord Mountjoy. In 2008, archaeological surveying at the site in advance of development revealed no archaeological traces of the battle.

> TYR 061:041
>
> Marshall 1924b, 9; Falls 1950, 280; Gahan and Long 2008

583 BENBURB 279970 352770

Battle of Benburb (1646)

The second Battle of Benburb was fought on 5 June, 1646 over a 3km stretch of uneven terrain among the drumlins north of the River Blackwater. Here, Irish forces, under Owen Roe O'Neill, defeated General Robert Munroe's British forces, the first Irish victory in a formal pitched battle. Both O'Neill and Munroe were veterans of numerous continental military campaigns, and each had amassed a large army by 17th-century standards – some 6000 men on each side. Munroe's forces approached the battlefield from the west, marching along the northern bank of the Blackwater – they had crossed the river at Caledon. O'Neill's forces, similar in strength to the British, were camped along high ground, near Benburb Castle (Inv. 411). The main engagement occurred in Derrycreevy, between two small streams, although the fighting eventually spread towards Battleford Bridge.

At the centre of the main engagement, which was to the south of The Red House and on the southern slopes of a drumlin hillside, there are no visible archaeological remains of the battle, although lead shot has been occasionally found in the soils here. The location has extensive views, especially to the south and east. A smaller engagement also occurred before the main battle, to the west, in Ballaghkillgevill (Grid Ref 278200, 352200). Historical accounts mention the British soldiers who survived the rout, retreating towards Caledon, suffering terribly from exhaustion and many drowning in the Blackwater and at Tullygiven Lake.

> TYR 061:004
>
> Latimer 1896, 29–33; Hayes-McCoy 1969, 201–205

584 CAVANBOY (KILMORE) 276500 350400

A delaying action was fought in this valley on 5 June, 1646, between Major MacHugh Boy O'Neill's Irish forces and Viscount Montgomery's Scots cavalry, before the decisive engagement at Benburb.

> TYR067:010
>
> Hayes-McCoy 1969, 201

County Armagh

585 CARRICKBROAD 305740 314030

Battle of Moyry Pass

The Battle of Moyry Pass was fought between the Irish forces of Hugh O'Neill, earl of Tyrone and the English soldiers of Lord Mountjoy between 2 and 10 October 1600.

> ARM 032:019
>
> Falls 1950, 265; Bredin 1987, 69 and 70

586 FATHOM LOWER 309900 322200

On 14 October, 1600, in the aftermath of the Battle of Moyry Pass, the forces of Hugh O'Neill ambushed an English column led by Lord Deputy Mountjoy. The site is now in dense woodland, on the lower slopes of Anglesey Mountain, which forms part of the border with Co. Louth.

> ARM 029:042
>
> Bredin 1987, 69 and 70

County Londonderry

587   BALLINREES   **287200 423700**
The approximate location of a battle fought in the 1640s between Sir Phelim Roe O'Neill and an unknown opponent. The battle is mentioned in the *OS Memoirs* for the parish. There are no visible remains at the site, which is on the south side of the Macosquin river valley, less than 100m to the east of the river.

  LDY 011:051
  Day *et al.* 1995, 111

588   BALLYNAMEEN   **284500 414500**
  Battle of Garvagh at Ravelin's Hill
During this encounter, which probably took place in 1641, a loyalist force under Lt. Col. William Canning (son of George Canning, the Ironmongers' agent) was defeated by a detachment of Sir Phelim O'Neill's army. The site is close to the summit of Ravelin's Hill, with panoramic views. While the battle has left no trace in the landscape, lead shot has been found in ploughed fields in the locality.

  LDY 026:111
  Day and McWilliams 1994, 23

589   DRUMNEECHY   **269300 413900**
  AND GORTACLARE
This the approximate location recorded in the *OS Memoirs* of a battle fought in 1641 between English settlers and Irish insurgents. The exact position of the battlefield is not known, but the most likely site is close to the confluence of the Gelvin River and the River Roe, where an old ford is indicated on the OS maps.

  LDY 025:023
  Day and McWilliams 1994, 16 and 50

590   EDEN   **292000 403500**
The *OS Memoirs* record that a battle was fought and won at this location by the army of Sir Phelim Roe O'Neill, although who the opponents were is unknown. Nor it is known when the battle took place, but it was presumably fought following the outbreak of rebellion in October 1641, and before O'Neill entered hiding in 1650 (see Inv. 403).

  LDY 033:034
  Day and McWilliams 1993a, 94

Appendix II
Site Co-ordinates

Inv.	Townland	Irish Grid		6-figure grid ref.	ITM Grid		Decimal degrees (WGS84)		Postcode
		Eastings	Northings		Eastings	Northings	Latitude	Longitude	
1	Castle Place, Belfast	333900	374280	J339742	733889	874269	54.5989	−5.9279	BT1 5DF
2	Barrack Street, Belfast	333300	374270	J333742	733289	874259	54.599	−5.9372	BT12 4AJ
3	Pottinger's Entry, Belfast	334070	374380	J340743	734059	874369	54.5998	−5.9252	BT1 4DT
4	Waring Street, Belfast	334080	374550	J340745	734069	874539	54.6013	−5.925	BT1 2ED
5	Anne Street/Corn Market, Belfast	333900	374400	J339744	733889	874389	54.6	−5.9278	BT1 1QD
6	Belfast, Writer's Square	333830	374650	J338746	733819	874639	54.6023	−5.9288	BT1 1ER
7	Belfast, Talbot Street	333900	374680	J339746	733889	874669	54.6025	−5.9277	BT1 2HB
8	Belfast, Gordon Street	334110	374610	J341746	734099	874599	54.6018	−5.9245	BT1 3GA
9	Belfast, Queen Street	333590	374240	J335742	733579	874229	54.5986	−5.9327	BT1 6EA
10	Belfast, High Street	334140	374420	J341744	734129	874409	54.6001	−5.9241	BT1 2AG
11	Belfast, Stranmillis	333500	371300	J335713	733489	871289	54.5723	−5.9354	BT9 5DY
12	Malone	332579	370970	J325709	732568	870959	54.5696	−5.9498	BT9 6LE
13	Malone Upper	332170	369110	J321691	732159	869099	54.553	−5.957	BT9 5PB
14	Malone Upper	332780	369350	J327693	732769	869339	54.555	−5.9474	BT9 5GG
15	Mullaghglass	324790	368570	J247685	724780	868559	54.55	−6.0712	BT28 3SN
16	Slievenacloy	324530	370830	J245708	724520	870819	54.5703	−6.0743	BT28 3TE
17	Templepatrick	322800	385900	J228859	722790	885888	54.7061	−6.0947	BT39 0EJ
18	White House	335100	380820	J351808	735089	880808	54.6573	−5.9063	BT37 9UX
19	Monkstown	334530	385790	J345857	734519	885778	54.7021	−5.9129	BT37 0UG
20	Mallusk	329000	382000	J290820	728989	881988	54.6695	−6.0003	BT36 4WS
21	Carrickfergus	341430	387250	J414872	741418	887238	54.7133	−5.8052	BT38 7BG
22	Carrickfergus	341280	387420	J412874	741268	887408	54.7149	−5.8074	BT38 7AR
23	Carrickfergus	341500	387610	J415876	741488	887598	54.7165	−5.8039	BT38 7DW
24	Carrickfergus	341490	387550	J414875	741478	887538	54.716	−5.8041	BT38 7DQ
25	Corke Hill	341200	387420	J412874	741188	887408	54.7149	−5.8087	BT38 8AA
26	Carrickfergus	341184	387362	J411873	741172	887350	54.7144	−5.8089	BT38 7FB
27	Carrickfergus	341230	387380	J412873	741218	887368	54.7145	−5.8082	BT38 7FD
28	Carrickfergus	341200	387500	J412875	741188	887488	54.7156	−5.8086	BT38 8AD
29	Carrickfergus	341270	387560	J412875	741258	887548	54.7161	−5.8075	BT38 7AE
30	Carrickfergus	341360	387590	J413875	741348	887578	54.7164	−5.8061	BT38 7AG
31	Carrickfergus	341490	387460	J414874	741478	887448	54.7152	−5.8041	BT38 7AN
32	Dunrock, Middle Division	338480	389920	J384899	738469	889907	54.7381	−5.8497	BT38 9DL
33	Middle Division	339850	390120	J398901	739839	890107	54.7395	−5.8283	BT38 9DN
34	Middle Division	340450	390740	J404907	740438	890727	54.7449	−5.8187	BT38 9DG
35	Ballyhill	344270	391430	J442914	744258	891417	54.75	−5.7591	BT38 9BY
36	Dobbsland	344302	390723	J443907	744290	890710	54.7437	−5.7589	BT38 9BU
37	Crossmary	342890	391170	J428911	742878	891157	54.7481	−5.7806	BT38 9DA
38	Kilroot	344600	388600	J446886	744588	888587	54.7245	−5.7554	BT38 9BT
39	Kilroot	345000	389480	J450894	744988	889467	54.7323	−5.7487	BT38 9BS
40	Redhall	344990	394970	J449949	744978	894957	54.7816	−5.7461	BT38 9JL
41	Forthill	344831	393693	J448936	744819	893680	54.7702	−5.7492	BT38 9JH
42	Ballycarry	344800	393510	J448935	744788	893497	54.7686	−5.7498	BT38 9HN
43	White Head	347651	392022	J476920	747639	892009	54.7544	−5.7063	BT38 9QJ
44	Ballyprior More	345230	400860	D452008	745218	900846	54.8344	−5.7395	BT40 3TL
45	Portmuck	346125	402371	D461023	746113	902357	54.8477	−5.7248	BT40 3TP

Inv.	Townland	Irish Grid		6-figure grid ref.	ITM Grid		Decimal degrees (WGS84)		Postcode
		Eastings	Northings		Eastings	Northings	Latitude	Longitude	
46	Demense	335650	401500	D356015	735639	901486	54.8428	−5.8882	BT40 2TD
47	Ballyboley	338000	403800	D380038	737989	903786	54.8628	−5.8505	BT40 2WA
48	Curran And Drumaliss	341300	401600	D413016	741288	901586	54.8422	−5.8002	BT40 1AY
49	Inver	340050	402400	D400024	740039	902386	54.8497	−5.8193	BT40 3AB
50	Curran And Drumaliss	341000	402000	D410020	740988	901986	54.8459	−5.8047	BT40 1AX
51	Curran And Drumaliss	341240	401820	D412018	741228	901806	54.8442	−5.801	BT40 1AY
52	Town Parks of Larne	339500	402500	D395025	739489	902486	54.8508	−5.8278	BT40 2AB
53	Ballygally	337250	407810	D372078	737239	907796	54.8991	−5.8603	BT40 2QX
54	Carncastle	338150	408050	D381080	738139	908036	54.901	−5.8461	BT40 2QQ
55	Ballygalley	337300	407800	D373078	737289	907786	54.8989	−5.8595	BT40 2QX
56	Ballyruther	336000	409000	D360090	735989	908986	54.9101	−5.8792	BT40 2RA
57	Corkermain	336500	408400	D365084	736489	908386	54.9046	−5.8717	BT40 2QZ
58	Glenarm	330960	415090	D309150	730949	915075	54.9661	−5.9549	BT44 0AL
59	Glenarm Demesne	330750	414730	D307147	730739	914715	54.9629	−5.9584	BT44 0EE
60	Glenarm Demesne	331032	415333	D310153	731021	915318	54.9683	−5.9537	BT44 0AA
61	Moneyvart	324539	428930	D245289	724529	928914	55.092	−6.0491	BT44 0NQ
62	Layd	324438	429331	D244293	724428	929315	55.0956	−6.0505	BT44 0NH
63	Red Bay	324290	426170	D242261	724280	926154	55.0673	−6.0542	BT44 0SH
64	Turnarobert	307510	433140	D075331	707501	933123	55.1338	−6.3141	BT53 8RJ
65	Drumsonnus	307806	433246	D078332	707797	933229	55.1347	−6.3095	BT53 8RJ
66	Aghaleck And Corvally	312470	435700	D124357	712461	935683	55.1557	−6.2354	BT53 8SB
67	Cross	317950	442700	D179427	717940	942683	55.2173	−6.1465	BT54 6RD
68	Torr West	322750	440400	D227404	722740	940383	55.1954	−6.0722	BT54 6RQ
69	Goodland	319810	441300	D198413	719800	941283	55.2042	−6.1179	BT54 6RG
70	Town Parks, Ballycastle	311400	440700	D114407	711391	940683	55.2008	−6.2502	BT54 6DP
71	Town Parks, Ballycastle	311520	440610	D115406	711511	940593	55.2	−6.2484	BT54 6AP
72	Town Parks, Ballycastle	311380	441900	D113419	711371	941883	55.2116	−6.25	BT54 6LQ
73	Clare	310600	442100	D106421	710591	942083	55.2136	−6.2622	BT54 6LH
74	Bonamargy	312685	440867	D126408	712676	940850	55.202	−6.23	BT54 6PA
75	Tornaroan	314750	441850	D147418	714741	941833	55.2104	−6.1971	BT54 6QT
76	Ballintoy	303800	444800	D038448	703791	944782	55.2393	−6.368	BT54 6NA
77	Ballintoy Demesne	303890	444780	D038447	703881	944762	55.2391	−6.3666	BT54 6NA
78	Templastragh	300530	444280	D005442	700522	944262	55.2353	−6.4196	BT57 8TA
79	Currysheskin	299480	444250	C994442	699472	944232	55.2352	−6.4361	BT57 8SY
80	Currysheskin	299500	444200	C995442	699492	944182	55.2348	−6.4358	BT57 8SY
81	Clogher North	294100	440800	C941408	694092	940783	55.2053	−6.5218	BT57 8QD
82	Clogher North	294880	441450	C948414	694872	941433	55.211	−6.5093	BT57 8TG
83	Ballymoy	296900	443100	C969431	696892	943083	55.2254	−6.477	BT57 8PY
84	Bushfoot or Lissanduff	293500	442000	C935420	693492	941983	55.2162	−6.5308	BT57 8WB
85	Ballycarry	315600	451280	D156512	715591	951262	55.2948	−6.1799	BT54 6RS
86	Ballyconaghan	314400	451800	D144518	714391	951782	55.2998	−6.1986	BT54 6SB
87	Dunluce	290460	441370	C904413	690453	941353	55.2111	−6.5788	BT57 8UY
88	Dunluce	290410	441260	C904412	690403	941243	55.2101	−6.5796	BT57 8UY
89	Dunluce	290559	440959	C905409	690552	940942	55.2074	−6.5773	BT57 8UY
90	Ballymagarry	289450	440240	C894402	689443	940223	55.2011	−6.595	BT56 8NH
91	Beardiville	290120	437230	C901372	690113	937213	55.174	−6.5854	BT52 2LU
92	Ballyclogh	293000	437000	C930370	692992	936983	55.1714	−6.5403	BT57 8UD
93	Billy	295840	438240	C958382	695832	938223	55.182	−6.4953	BT57 8YJ
94	Glebe	296295	433762	C962337	696287	933745	55.1417	−6.4897	BT53 8AS
95	Benvardin	294710	433190	C947331	694702	933173	55.1368	−6.5148	BT53 8AF
96	Glebe	294940	425806	C949258	694932	925790	55.0705	−6.5136	BT53 6HY

Inv.	Townland	Irish Grid		6-figure grid ref.	ITM Grid		Decimal degrees (WGS84)		Postcode
		Eastings	Northings		Eastings	Northings	Latitude	Longitude	
97	Cross	291450	422700	C914227	691442	922684	55.0433	−6.5692	BT53 7PD
98	Kirkhill	297500	429240	C975292	697492	929224	55.1008	−6.4724	BT53 8HG
99	Kilraghts	301640	425830	D016258	701632	925814	55.0694	−6.4088	BT53 8NL
100	Castlequarter	306600	424370	D066243	706591	924354	55.0552	−6.3317	BT44 9JP
101	Castlequarter	306870	424130	D068241	706861	924114	55.053	−6.3276	BT44 9JP
102	Cloghgaldanagh	309540	414700	D095147	709531	914685	54.9678	−6.2894	BT44 9SF
103	Glebe	309380	414230	D093142	709371	914215	54.9636	−6.2921	BT44 9RF
104	Glebe	297470	412760	C974127	697462	912745	54.9528	−6.4785	BT44 8QT
105	Townparks of Ballymena	311270	402980	D112029	711261	902966	54.8621	−6.2669	BT43 7BJ
106	Galgorm	308180	402280	D081022	708171	902266	54.8565	−6.3153	BT42 1HL
107	Galgorm	308090	402380	D080023	708081	902366	54.8574	−6.3167	BT42 1HL
108	Ballyminstra	306550	400650	D065006	706541	900636	54.8422	−6.3413	BT42 2QF
109	Portglenone	298000	404000	C980040	697992	903986	54.8741	−6.4732	BT44 8BJ
110	Craigs	304340	408240	D043082	704331	908226	54.9109	−6.3729	BT42 1PE
111	Shane's Castle Park	311624	387979	J116879	711615	887967	54.7274	−6.2672	BT41 4NE
112	Shane's Castle Park	311610	388120	J116881	711601	888108	54.7286	−6.2673	BT41 4ND
113	Ballygrooby	308400	391900	J084919	708391	891887	54.7633	−6.3157	BT41 2PA
114	Caddy	308600	394750	J086947	708591	894737	54.7888	−6.3116	BT41 2PD
115	Portlee	303000	386000	J030860	702992	885988	54.7114	−6.4017	BT41 3LX
116	Carlane	301420	387180	J014871	701412	887168	54.7223	−6.4258	BT41 3NX
117	Staffordstown	303780	386690	J037866	703771	886678	54.7175	−6.3894	BT41 3LS
118	Toome	298945	390271	H989902	698937	890258	54.7506	−6.4631	BT41 3UG
119	Slaght	309600	398600	J096986	709591	898587	54.8232	−6.2946	BT42 2JW
120	Crebilly	314330	402740	D143027	714321	902726	54.8593	−6.2194	BT42 4DT
121	Connor	315000	397000	J150970	714991	896987	54.8076	−6.2112	BT42 3JZ
122	Broughshane	315130	406630	D151066	715121	906616	54.894	−6.2054	BT42 4DH
123	Eglish	313100	408700	D131087	713091	908686	54.9131	−6.2362	BT43 7JA
124	Toberdowney	331580	393620	J315936	731569	893607	54.7732	−5.955	BT39 9ZQ
125	Castletown	333070	393920	J330939	733059	893907	54.7755	−5.9318	BT39 9QF
126	Ballyeaston	328810	393380	J288933	728799	893367	54.7717	−5.9982	BT39 9SH
127	Ballyclare	328000	390000	J280900	727989	889987	54.7416	−6.0122	BT39 9FD
128	Drumadarragh	324600	393400	J246934	724590	893387	54.773	−6.0635	BT39 0TA
129	Kilbride	324760	391210	J247912	724750	891197	54.7533	−6.062	BT39 0SA
130	Townparks of Antrim and Balloo	314500	386730	J145867	714491	886718	54.7155	−6.2231	BT41 4DT
131	Townparks of Antrim	314950	386550	J149865	714941	886538	54.7138	−6.2161	BT41 4DE
132	Townparks of Antrim	314660	386740	J146867	714651	886728	54.7155	−6.2206	BT41 4DT
133	Muckamore	316780	385280	J167852	716770	885268	54.7019	−6.1883	BT41 4QA
134	Ballyginniff	311130	380920	J111809	711121	880908	54.6641	−6.2775	BT29 4RG
135	Dundesert	318300	377880	J183778	718290	877868	54.6351	−6.1677	BT29 4SH
136	Crookedstone	315150	382100	J151821	715141	882088	54.6738	−6.2148	BT29 4DX
137	Seacash	314500	379000	J145790	714491	878988	54.6461	−6.2261	BT29 4FB
138	Tullyrusk	321290	373350	J212733	721280	873339	54.5938	−6.1233	BT29 4HZ
139	Tullyrusk	321200	373620	J212736	721190	873609	54.5962	−6.1246	BT29 4HZ
140	Portmore	312150	368450	J121684	712141	868439	54.5519	−6.2665	BT28 2JT
141	Trummery	317439	362769	J174627	717429	862759	54.4997	−6.1871	BT67 0JN
142	Ballyellough	320450	366260	J204662	720440	866249	54.5303	−6.1392	BT28 2QX
143	Inisloughlin	318000	360500	J180605	717990	860490	54.4791	−6.1793	BT67 0HL
144	Lisnagarvy	326800	364200	J268642	726790	864190	54.5102	−6.042	BT28 1FJ
145	Lisnagarvy	326875	364310	J268643	726865	864300	54.5112	−6.0408	BT27 4XD
146	Lisnagarvy	326940	364330	J269643	726930	864320	54.5114	−6.0398	BT28 1XY

Inv.	Townland	Irish Grid		6-figure grid ref.	ITM Grid		Decimal degrees (WGS84)		Postcode
		Eastings	Northings		Eastings	Northings	Latitude	Longitude	
147	Bangor	350450	381190	J504811	750438	881178	54.6563	−5.6684	BT20 4BT
148	Bangor	350141	381146	J501811	750129	881134	54.656	−5.6733	BT20 4JE
149	Bangor	350577	382170	J505821	750565	882158	54.6651	−5.666	BT20 5EE
150	Groomsport	353684	383524	J536835	753671	883512	54.6763	−5.6171	BT19 6JP
151	Ballymaconnell	353950	380900	J539809	753937	880888	54.6526	−5.6144	BT19 6NE
152	Ballycroghan	352850	380050	J528800	752837	880038	54.6453	−5.6319	BT19 6UQ
153	Gransha	352900	378200	J529782	752887	878188	54.6287	−5.6321	BT19 7NZ
154	Ballysallagh Minor	346600	378700	J466787	746588	878688	54.6351	−5.7293	BT19 1UT
155	Conlig	350000	378150	J500781	749988	878138	54.6291	−5.677	BT23 7PS
156	Copeland Island	359160	383400	J591834	759147	883388	54.6735	−5.5324	BT21 0PH
157	Craigavad	342860	381590	J428815	742848	881578	54.6621	−5.7858	BT18 0BT
158	Ballyleidy	347250	379820	J472798	747238	879808	54.6449	−5.7187	BT19 1RJ
159	Holywood	339883	379263	J398792	739872	879251	54.642	−5.833	BT18 9AD
160	Holywood	340060	379380	J400793	740048	879368	54.643	−5.8302	BT18 9AT
161	Ballymenagh	340750	379500	J407795	740738	879488	54.6439	−5.8195	BT18 0LN
162	Newtownards	349230	373850	J492738	749218	873839	54.5908	−5.6911	BT23 7NY
163	Newtownards	349159	374031	J491740	749147	874020	54.5924	−5.6921	BT23 7JF
164	Donaghadee	359089	379843	J590798	759076	879831	54.6416	−5.5354	BT21 0AH
165	Donaghadee	358920	379870	J589798	758907	879858	54.6419	−5.538	BT21 0DB
166	Rosemount	358260	367850	J582678	758247	867839	54.5342	−5.5547	BT22 2NF
167	Greyabbey	358300	368140	J583681	758287	868129	54.5368	−5.5539	BT22 2NQ
168	Kirkistown	364454	358010	J644580	764440	858000	54.4439	−5.4646	BT22 1GB
169	Templecraney	359410	351100	J594511	759397	851091	54.3835	−5.546	BT22 1LT
170	Portaferry	359269	350850	J592508	759256	850841	54.3813	−5.5483	BT22 1PF
171	Ballyspurge	364277	355062	J642550	764264	855053	54.4175	−5.469	BT22 1QJ
172	Ballymarter	363170	350500	J631505	763157	850491	54.3769	−5.4885	BT22 1QA
173	Ballygalget	362500	354290	J625542	762487	854281	54.4111	−5.4967	BT22 1NF
174	Ardquin	358455	354500	J584545	758442	854491	54.4143	−5.5589	BT22 1PG
175	Castleboy	362520	355620	J625556	762507	855610	54.4231	−5.4957	BT22 1HW
176	Inishargy	360408	364724	J604647	760395	864714	54.5054	−5.5233	BT22 2RG
177	Newcastle	364702	353377	J647533	764688	853368	54.4022	−5.4633	BT22 1QQ
178	Mahee Island	352392	363951	J523639	752379	863941	54.501	−5.6473	BT23 6EP
179	Tullynakill	350136	364516	J501645	750124	864506	54.5067	−5.6818	BT23 6AF
180	Ballymartin	350800	363000	J508630	750788	862990	54.4929	−5.6724	BT23 6HR
181	Ballydorn	352458	362520	J524625	752445	862510	54.4881	−5.647	BT23 6QH
182	Ballymorran	352420	359860	J524598	752407	859850	54.4642	−5.649	BT23 6UD
183	Killinchy	350730	360850	J507608	750718	860840	54.4736	−5.6745	BT23 6PP
184	Balloo	348780	360880	J487608	748768	860870	54.4745	−5.7046	BT23 6RL
185	Balloo	350000	361000	J500610	749988	860990	54.4752	−5.6857	BT23 6PG
186	Carrigullian	350200	360100	J502601	750188	860090	54.4671	−5.6831	BT23 6TD
187	Ringhaddy	353840	358860	J538588	753827	858850	54.4548	−5.6276	BT23 6TU
188	Killyleagh	352350	352960	J523529	752337	852951	54.4023	−5.6536	BT30 9QA
189	Killyleagh	351950	351510	J519515	751938	851501	54.3894	−5.6605	BT30 9UE
190	Corporation	352400	351600	J524516	752387	851591	54.3901	−5.6535	BT30 9UE
191	Corporation	353000	352400	J530524	752987	852391	54.3971	−5.6439	BT30 9QX
192	Mullagh	351320	350620	J513506	751308	850611	54.3816	−5.6707	BT30 9TZ
193	Tullyveery	352039	353907	J520539	752027	853898	54.4109	−5.6579	BT30 9SQ
194	Tullymacnous	351200	354600	J512546	751188	854591	54.4174	−5.6705	BT30 9PW
195	Drumaghlis	342166	351183	J421511	742154	851174	54.3893	−5.8112	BT30 9JS
196	Ballylone Big	338200	351500	J382515	738189	851491	54.3932	−5.872	BT24 8SH
197	Strangford	358906	350023	J589500	758893	850014	54.374	−5.5543	BT30 7NG

Inv.	Townland	Irish Grid		6-figure grid ref.	ITM Grid		Decimal degrees (WGS84)		Postcode
		Eastings	Northings		Eastings	Northings	Latitude	Longitude	
198	Strangford	358862	349795	J588497	758849	849786	54.3719	−5.5551	BT30 7LL
199	Kilclief	359720	345750	J597457	759707	845741	54.3353	−5.5441	BT30 7NR
200	Castleward	357392	349850	J573498	757379	849841	54.3729	−5.5777	BT30 7LS
201	Castleward	357810	350580	J578505	757797	850571	54.3793	−5.5709	BT30 7LR
202	Walshestown	354529	349816	J545498	754516	849807	54.3734	−5.6217	BT30 7JX
203	Ardglass	355900	337220	J559372	755887	837212	54.26	−5.6072	BT30 7TR
204	Killough	353850	335800	J538358	753837	835792	54.2478	−5.6394	BT30 7QT
205	Bishops Court	355900	342400	J559424	755887	842392	54.3065	−5.6045	BT30 7EY
206	Downpatrick	348820	344350	J488443	748808	844341	54.3261	−5.7122	BT30 6BE
207	Downpatrick	348586	344631	J485446	748574	844622	54.3287	−5.7157	BT30 6EP
208	Quoile	349630	347010	J496470	749618	847001	54.3497	−5.6985	BT30 7JA
209	Ballydugan	346820	343030	J468430	746808	843022	54.3148	−5.7436	BT30 8HA
210	Dundrum	340475	336930	J404369	740463	836922	54.2618	−5.8439	BT33 0NF
211	Rostrevor	317000	318000	J170180	716990	817994	54.0977	−6.2113	BT34 3GJ
212	Narrow Water	312560	319390	J125193	712551	819384	54.1112	−6.2787	BT34 3LE
213	Newry	309020	326640	J090266	709011	826633	54.1771	−6.3302	BT34 2AH
214	Newry	308600	326000	J086260	708591	825993	54.1714	−6.3368	BT34 2EQ
215	Tullyconnaught	316230	344310	J162443	716220	844301	54.3342	−6.2129	BT32 5JN
216	Scarva	306470	343660	J064436	706461	843652	54.3305	−6.3632	BT63 6LZ
217	Loughbrickland	310448	342084	J104420	710439	842076	54.3155	−6.3026	BT32 3NQ
218	Murlough Upper	337630	331050	J376310	737619	831043	54.2098	−5.8902	BT33 0AB
219	Rathfriland	320127	333741	J201337	720117	833733	54.2384	−6.1573	BT34 5QR
220	Rathfriland	320000	333600	J200336	719990	833592	54.2371	−6.1593	BT34 5PU
221	Dromore	320093	353237	J200532	720083	853228	54.4134	−6.15	BT25 1AF
222	Dromore	320040	353350	J200533	720030	853341	54.4145	−6.1507	BT25 1AD
223	Grennan	317140	353190	J171531	717130	853181	54.4137	−6.1955	BT25 1LJ
224	Fedany	322290	347660	J222476	722280	847651	54.3628	−6.1184	BT32 3SB
225	Tullyrain	315100	347100	J151471	715091	847091	54.3595	−6.2292	BT32 4EG
226	Kilpike	311970	347690	J119476	711961	847681	54.3655	−6.2771	BT32 4NE
227	Hillsborough	324500	358600	J245586	724490	858590	54.4605	−6.0799	BT26 6SD
228	Ballymakeonan	312830	358950	J128589	712821	858940	54.4664	−6.2596	BT67 0AD
229	Ballymacarret	335040	374050	J350740	735029	874039	54.5966	−5.9104	BT5 4BL
230	Ballymacarret	336490	374430	J364744	736479	874419	54.5996	−5.8878	BT4 1FY
231	Ballymacarret	336110	373690	J361736	736099	873679	54.593	−5.894	BT5 4SH
232	Ballymacarret	335480	373520	J354735	735469	873509	54.5917	−5.9038	BT6 8HE
233	Ballymacarret	335050	373410	J350734	735039	873399	54.5908	−5.9105	BT6 8GG
234	Ballyhackamore	336800	373300	J368733	736789	873289	54.5894	−5.8835	BT5 5LF
235	Ballycloghan	338510	374590	J385745	738499	874579	54.6005	−5.8565	BT4 2AL
236	Knocknagoney	338950	376300	J389763	738939	876289	54.6157	−5.8488	BT4 2QD
237	Ballymaghan	338640	375680	J386756	738629	875669	54.6102	−5.8539	BT4 2HZ
238	Ballymaghan	338140	373300	J381733	738129	873289	54.589	−5.8628	BT5 6FN
239	Multyhogy	337300	373100	J373731	737289	873089	54.5874	−5.8759	BT5 6DT
240	Ballyrussell	342900	371600	J429716	742888	871589	54.5724	−5.79	BT16 1XD
241	Ballyoran	343160	373300	J431733	743148	873289	54.5876	−5.7852	BT16 1TB
242	Ballylisbredan	343070	372890	J430728	743058	872879	54.5839	−5.7868	BT16 2DY
243	Carrowreagh	342900	374150	J429741	742888	874139	54.5953	−5.7888	BT16 2PJ
244	Castlereagh	337550	371090	J375710	737539	871079	54.5693	−5.8729	BT6 9SA
245	Ballysallagh Major	345600	379200	J456792	745588	879188	54.6399	−5.7445	BT19 1UU
246	Hillhall	330031	364420	J300644	730020	864410	54.5114	−5.9921	BT27 5JQ
247	Cattogs	346690	368450	J466684	746678	868439	54.543	−5.733	BT23 5WW
248	Comber	345560	369740	J455697	745548	869729	54.5549	−5.7498	BT23 5EF

Inv.	Townland	Irish Grid		6-figure grid ref.	ITM Grid		Decimal degrees (WGS84)		Postcode
		Eastings	Northings		Eastings	Northings	Latitude	Longitude	
249	Castle Espie	348600	367270	J486672	748588	867259	54.5319	−5.7041	BT23 5WJ
250	Castle Balfour Demesne	236214	333670	H362336	636211	833662	54.2505	−7.4444	BT92 0GJ
251	Castle Balfour Demesne	236280	333990	H362339	636277	833982	54.2534	−7.4433	BT92 0LZ
252	Lisnaskea	236250	333650	H362336	636247	833642	54.2503	−7.4438	BT92 0GJ
253	Killycloghan	234100	320000	H341200	634097	819994	54.1278	−7.4783	BT92 9BQ
254	Corry	231702	321280	H317212	631699	821274	54.1395	−7.5149	BT92 9ES
255	Callow Hill	227750	326460	H277264	627748	826453	54.1863	−7.5749	BT92 9AH
256	Callow Hill	227700	326400	H277264	627698	826393	54.1857	−7.5757	BT92 9AH
257	Callow Hill	227940	326370	H279263	627938	826363	54.1855	−7.572	BT92 9AH
258	Crom	236450	323800	H364238	636447	823793	54.1618	−7.4419	BT92 8AR
259	Inishfendra	238034	323156	H380231	638031	823149	54.1559	−7.4178	BT92 8HS
260	Newtownbutler	241780	326100	H417261	641777	826093	54.1821	−7.36	BT92 8JU
261	Aghagay	241600	326100	H416261	641597	826093	54.1821	−7.3628	BT92 8FL
262	Sheeny	241100	326200	H411262	641097	826193	54.183	−7.3704	BT92 8AD
263	Manor Water House	237400	331100	H374311	637397	831093	54.2273	−7.4265	BT92 0BJ
264	Drummully	244270	320060	H442200	644266	820054	54.1276	−7.3228	BT92 8GX
265	Drumbrughas East	239400	324500	H394245	639397	824493	54.1679	−7.3967	BT92 8ES
266	Derrycorby	239000	326000	H390260	638997	825993	54.1814	−7.4026	BT92 8BQ
267	Doohat	238000	325000	H380250	637997	824993	54.1725	−7.418	BT92 8AB
268	Rathmoran	243570	331070	H435310	643566	831063	54.2266	−7.3319	BT92 7AS
269	Golan	243810	330290	H438302	643806	830283	54.2196	−7.3283	BT92 6AZ
270	Shannock	249400	329300	H494293	649396	829293	54.2102	−7.2428	BT92 6PA
271	Shannock	249400	329300	H494293	649396	829293	54.2102	−7.2428	BT92 6PA
272	Uttony	246660	327800	H466278	646656	827793	54.1969	−7.285	BT92 6HH
273	Magheraveely	246580	327710	H465277	646576	827703	54.1961	−7.2862	BT92 6NB
274	Lislea	248080	327170	H480271	648076	827163	54.1911	−7.2633	BT92 6JB
275	Drumrainy	247750	327250	H477272	647746	827243	54.1919	−7.2684	BT92 6LX
276	Aghavea	237300	338500	H373385	637297	838492	54.2938	−7.4271	BT94 4JP
277	Tattycam	243400	332000	H434320	643396	831993	54.235	−7.3343	BT92 5BT
278	Fargrim	244450	327180	H444271	644446	827173	54.1916	−7.319	BT92 6LB
279	Lisnashillida	243000	327100	H430271	642996	827093	54.191	−7.3412	BT92 8LD
280	Mullynagowan	243000	326500	H430265	642996	826493	54.1856	−7.3413	BT92 8LB
281	Agheraroosky East	244920	328250	H449282	644916	828243	54.2011	−7.3116	BT92 6DS
282	Clontivrin	248281	325751	H482257	648277	825744	54.1784	−7.2605	BT92 6FR
283	Lisgoole	224070	341730	H240417	624068	841722	54.3237	−7.63	BT92 2FR
284	Cavancarragh	207640	339670	H076396	607639	839662	54.3057	−7.8826	BT93 5DT
285	Tonyteige	225200	337700	H252377	625198	837692	54.2874	−7.613	BT92 2EG
286	Belcoo West	208220	338680	H082386	608219	838672	54.2967	−7.8737	BT93 5FJ
287	Horse Island	219700	353600	H197536	619698	853591	54.4305	−7.6964	BT94 1NY
288	Rossclare	219200	354300	H192543	619198	854291	54.4368	−7.7041	BT94 1SF
289	Castle Irvine Demesne	223600	357300	H236573	623598	857290	54.4636	−7.636	BT94 1EB
290	Castle Irvine Demesne	223600	357300	H236573	623598	857290	54.4636	−7.636	BT94 1EB
291	Townhill	223800	358200	H238582	623798	858190	54.4716	−7.6329	BT94 1GJ
292	Bunaninver	218660	359890	H186598	618658	859880	54.487	−7.712	BT94 1PX
293	Bunaninver	218660	359890	H186598	618658	859880	54.487	−7.712	BT94 1PX
294	Drumshane	219580	358610	H195586	619578	858600	54.4755	−7.6979	BT94 1AB
295	Drumshane	219570	358760	H195587	619568	858750	54.4768	−7.6981	BT94 1JW
296	Crevinish	216548	362623	H165626	616547	862613	54.5117	−7.7445	BT93 1RN
297	Crevinish	216555	362607	H165626	616554	862597	54.5115	−7.7444	BT93 1RN
298	Ederney	222100	364900	H221649	622098	864890	54.5319	−7.6586	BT93 0AR
299	Kesh	218000	363800	H180638	617999	863790	54.5222	−7.722	BT93 1SN

Inv.	Townland	Irish Grid		6-figure grid ref.	ITM Grid		Decimal degrees (WGS84)		Postcode
		Eastings	Northings		Eastings	Northings	Latitude	Longitude	
300	Rossbeg	201730	360480	H017604	601730	860470	54.4927	−7.9733	BT93 2AH
301	Belleek	194044	359070	G940590	594044	859060	54.48	−8.0919	BT93 3FX
302	Rossbeg	201340	360320	H013603	601340	860310	54.4912	−7.9793	BT93 2AH
303	Magherameenagh	197790	359210	G977592	597790	859200	54.4813	−8.0341	BT93 3ET
304	Pettigoe	211000	366800	H110668	610999	866789	54.5493	−7.83	BT93 8BD
305	Cornagrade	223200	344900	H232449	623198	844891	54.3522	−7.6432	BT74 6BP
306	Drummurray	226000	352800	H260528	625998	852791	54.423	−7.5994	BT94 2AJ
307	Drumkeen	226300	352020	H263520	626298	852011	54.416	−7.5948	BT94 2EA
308	Ballinamallard	226360	352760	H263527	626358	852751	54.4226	−7.5939	BT94 2FY
309	Salry	225000	352000	H250520	624998	851991	54.4159	−7.6149	BT94 2EW
310	Coolbuck	231500	342800	H315428	631497	842792	54.3329	−7.5157	BT94 5BJ
311	Belle Isle	228940	335530	H289355	628938	835522	54.2677	−7.5558	BT94 5HG
312	Castle Coole	225924	343310	H259433	625922	843302	54.3378	−7.6014	BT74 6FL
313	Castle Coole	225924	343310	H259433	625922	843302	54.3378	−7.6014	BT74 6FL
314	Agharainey	226000	344400	H260444	625998	844391	54.3475	−7.6001	BT74 6FR
315	Camgart	240000	350000	H400500	639997	849991	54.3969	−7.3841	BT75 0RQ
316	Aghavoory	244990	346320	H449463	644986	846311	54.3635	−7.3078	BT75 0NF
317	Maguiresbridge	234880	338480	H348384	634877	838472	54.2938	−7.4643	BT94 4LT
318	Rafintan	241440	345990	H414459	641437	845981	54.3608	−7.3625	BT75 0SS
319	Brookeborough	238700	341000	H387410	638697	840992	54.3162	−7.4053	BT94 4EZ
320	Stranafeley	238600	338700	H386387	638597	838692	54.2955	−7.4071	BT94 4HD
321	Drumhoy	240500	343000	H405430	640497	842992	54.334	−7.3773	BT94 4AZ
322	Stranafeley	238500	338250	H385382	638497	838242	54.2915	−7.4087	BT94 4FP
323	Gola	229650	338020	H296380	629648	838012	54.29	−7.5446	BT94 5ND
324	Portora	222210	345300	H222453	622208	845291	54.3558	−7.6584	BT74 4FJ
325	Portora	222200	345100	H222451	622198	845091	54.354	−7.6585	BT74 7EE
326	Portora	222200	345100	H222451	622198	845091	54.354	−7.6585	BT74 7EE
327	Castletown	216470	349370	H164493	616469	849361	54.3926	−7.7464	BT74 8EQ
328	Tullymargy	216300	347900	H163479	616299	847891	54.3794	−7.7491	BT74 8FR
329	Castletown	216000	349000	H160490	615999	848991	54.3893	−7.7537	BT74 8GF
330	Tullykelter	215520	348270	H155482	615519	848261	54.3827	−7.7611	BT74 8EF
331	Rosspoint or Cosbystown East	216260	353850	H162538	616259	853841	54.4329	−7.7494	BT93 7ES
332	Claragh	215000	353000	H150530	614999	852991	54.4253	−7.7689	BT93 7AX
333	Rossnafarsan	218220	351270	H182512	618219	851261	54.4096	−7.7194	BT93 7EJ
334	Dinnydoon	218000	346000	H180460	617999	845991	54.3623	−7.7231	BT74 8DU
335	Kilnaloo	219000	347000	H190470	618998	846991	54.3712	−7.7076	BT74 8BR
336	Derrygonnelly	212080	352400	H120524	612079	852391	54.4199	−7.8139	BT93 6BF
337	Derrygonnelly	211975	352090	H119520	611974	852081	54.4172	−7.8155	BT93 6HW
338	Derrygonnelly	211871	352475	H118524	611870	852466	54.4206	−7.8171	BT93 6JA
339	Derrygonnelly	211900	352100	H119521	611899	852091	54.4172	−7.8167	BT93 6HW
340	Tully	212670	356640	H126566	612669	856630	54.458	−7.8046	BT93 6HP
341	Drummenagh Beg	211320	355730	H113557	611319	855720	54.4499	−7.8255	BT93 6BR
342	Enniskillen	223200	344300	H232443	623198	844291	54.3468	−7.6432	BT74 7ES
343	Enniskillen	223150	344220	H231442	623148	844211	54.3461	−7.644	BT74 7HL
344	Enniskillen	223780	343960	H237439	623778	843951	54.3437	−7.6343	BT74 7BG
345	Enniskillen	223168	343981	H231439	623166	843972	54.3439	−7.6437	BT74 7HR
346	Enniskillen	223420	344250	H234442	623418	844241	54.3463	−7.6398	BT74 7DW
347	Garrison	194200	351800	G942518	594200	851791	54.4147	−8.0893	BT93 4ER
348	Mountcastle	241741	405157	C417051	641738	905143	54.8923	−7.3494	BT82 0LW
349	Strabane	234500	397600	H345976	634497	897587	54.825	−7.4632	BT82 8AX

Inv.	Townland	Irish Grid		6-figure grid ref.	ITM Grid		Decimal degrees (WGS84)		Postcode
		Eastings	Northings		Eastings	Northings	Latitude	Longitude	
350	Strabane	234700	397500	H347975	634697	897487	54.8241	−7.4601	BT82 8HJ
351	Seein	233400	392125	H334921	633397	892112	54.7759	−7.4809	BT82 9NL
352	Liggartown	233900	393100	H339931	633897	893087	54.7846	−7.473	BT82 9HW
353	Castletown	233000	397000	H330970	632997	896987	54.8197	−7.4866	BT82 9GP
354	Baronscourt	236710	383560	H367835	636707	883548	54.6987	−7.4306	BT78 4HB
355	Baronscourt	236460	383780	H364837	636457	883768	54.7007	−7.4344	BT78 4HD
356	Ballyrenan	237330	383190	H373831	637327	883178	54.6953	−7.421	BT78 4HB
357	Tirkernaghan	244541	400317	C445003	644537	900303	54.8486	−7.3065	BT82 0RB
358	Dunnamanagh	244580	403380	C445033	644576	903366	54.8761	−7.3054	BT82 0PA
359	Beltrim	248870	386360	H488863	648866	886348	54.7228	−7.2415	BT79 8PN
360	Newtownstewart	240230	385820	H402858	640227	885808	54.7187	−7.3756	BT78 4AS
361	Creaghan Glebe	244750	403500	C447035	644746	903486	54.8772	−7.3028	BT82 0PH
362	Urney	230650	394900	H306949	630647	894887	54.801	−7.5234	BT82 9RU
363	Scarvagherin	230800	385130	H308851	630797	885118	54.7132	−7.5221	BT82 9LS
364	Bunowen	245430	404520	C454045	645426	904506	54.8863	−7.292	BT82 0PJ
365	Creaghan Glebe	244720	403370	C447033	644716	903356	54.876	−7.3033	BT82 0PA
366	Moyle Glebe	241240	386040	H412860	641237	886028	54.7206	−7.3599	BT78 4JU
367	Camus	234730	391600	H347916	634727	891587	54.7711	−7.4603	BT82 8PE
368	Erganagh Glebe	246500	377750	H465777	646496	877738	54.6457	−7.2796	BT79 7SX
369	Kilcam	256000	367000	H560670	655995	866989	54.5482	−7.1345	BT79 0UB
370	Cloghfin	257380	367850	H573678	657375	867839	54.5556	−7.113	BT79 9NL
371	Castlemervyn Demesne	233531	357558	H335575	633528	857548	54.4653	−7.4828	BT78 3NZ
372	Dromore	234900	362750	H349627	634897	862740	54.5119	−7.4611	BT78 3JF
373	Drumragh (Caldwell)	245680	369800	H456698	645676	869789	54.5743	−7.2936	BT78 1PR
374	Ballynahatty	243800	367400	H438674	643796	867389	54.553	−7.323	BT78 1QN
375	Kirlish	231960	375800	H319758	631957	875789	54.6293	−7.5051	BT78 4QE
376	Castlederg	226050	384420	H260844	626048	884408	54.7071	−7.5958	BT81 7XH
377	Castlegore	225360	383320	H253833	625358	883308	54.6972	−7.6066	BT81 7RY
378	Omagh	245100	372600	H451726	645096	872589	54.5996	−7.3021	BT78 1ED
379	Drumsonnus	228730	355310	H287553	628728	855300	54.4454	−7.5571	BT78 3RN
380	Kildrum	237450	362760	H374627	637447	862750	54.5118	−7.4217	BT78 3HE
381	Magharenny	235440	372930	H354729	635437	872919	54.6033	−7.4515	BT78 4SW
382	Castlehill Demesne	256130	353810	H561538	656125	853801	54.4297	−7.135	BT77 0BE
383	Augher Tenements	256500	353600	H565536	656495	853591	54.4277	−7.1294	BT77 0EY
384	Lismore	263144	353809	H631538	663139	853800	54.4288	−7.0269	BT69 6BS
385	Ballygawley	263240	357490	H632574	663235	857480	54.4619	−7.0247	BT70 2EY
386	Ballygawley	263130	357470	H631574	663125	857460	54.4617	−7.0264	BT70 2HD
387	Annagh Demense	244870	348600	H448486	644866	848591	54.384	−7.3093	BT75 0QT
388	Fivemiletown	244500	347800	H445478	644496	847791	54.3768	−7.3151	BT75 0PB
389	Castletown	244325	361529	H443615	644321	861519	54.5002	−7.3158	BT78 2BU
390	Castletown	244462	361441	H444614	644458	861431	54.4994	−7.3137	BT78 2BR
391	Aghintain	249850	351510	H498515	649846	851501	54.4096	−7.2322	BT76 0UX
392	Derrybard	247300	361800	H473618	647296	861790	54.5023	−7.2698	BT78 2RB
393	Knockmany	254750	355500	H547555	654746	855490	54.445	−7.156	BT77 0DE
394	Clogher	253760	351560	H537515	653756	851551	54.4097	−7.1719	BT76 0AJ
395	Clogher Demesne	253820	351670	H538516	653816	851661	54.4107	−7.171	BT76 0AJ
396	Stewartstown	285990	370770	H859707	685983	870759	54.5778	−6.67	BT71 5JY
397	Ballyclog Glebe	286600	373690	H866736	686593	873679	54.6039	−6.6597	BT71 5LL
398	Tullylagan	279800	372400	H798724	679793	872389	54.5935	−6.7653	BT80 8UP
399	Tullaghoge	282500	374300	H825743	682493	874289	54.6101	−6.723	BT80 8UF
400	Loughry	281370	374448	H813744	681363	874437	54.6116	−6.7405	BT80 9AA

Inv.	Townland	Irish Grid		6-figure grid ref.	ITM Grid		Decimal degrees (WGS84)		Postcode
		Eastings	Northings		Eastings	Northings	Latitude	Longitude	
401	Oaklands	276250	377800	H762778	676244	877788	54.6425	−6.8188	BT80 9RT
402	Roughan	282317	368271	H823682	682310	868260	54.556	−6.7275	BT71 4HB
403	Roughan	282770	368680	H827686	682763	868669	54.5596	−6.7204	BT71 4EW
404	Rockdale	277546	372752	H775727	677540	872741	54.597	−6.8001	BT70 3JF
405	Dungannon	279900	362620	H799626	679893	862610	54.5056	−6.7664	BT70 1JP
406	Annagh	268000	352000	H680520	667994	851991	54.4119	−6.9525	BT69 6HY
407	Ravella	265300	352700	H653527	665295	852691	54.4186	−6.994	BT69 6BR
408	Lisnamonaghan	275510	362590	H755625	675504	862580	54.506	−6.8342	BT70 3NL
409	The Bonn	271330	371020	H713710	671324	871009	54.5823	−6.8967	BT70 3DT
410	Magheralamfield	290110	368690	H901686	690103	868679	54.5584	−6.607	BT71 5DY
411	Benburb	281470	351990	H814519	681463	851981	54.4099	−6.7451	BT71 7JZ
412	Benburb	281780	352140	H817521	681773	852131	54.4112	−6.7403	BT71 7LA
413	Castletown	270640	356310	H706563	670634	856300	54.4503	−6.9109	BT69 6EE
414	Tullydowey	283950	351740	H839517	683943	851731	54.4072	−6.707	BT71 7HR
415	Drumderg	284010	352570	H840525	684003	852561	54.4147	−6.7058	BT71 7HL
416	Drumderg	283990	352430	H839524	683983	852421	54.4134	−6.7062	BT71 7HL
417	Moy	285240	355940	H852559	685233	855930	54.4447	−6.6859	BT71 7TG
418	Cloghog	287110	366830	H871668	687103	866819	54.5422	−6.6539	BT71 5EQ
419	Killeeshil	268800	360450	H688604	668794	860440	54.4877	−6.9383	BT70 3AW
420	Laghey	284250	360670	H842606	684243	860660	54.4874	−6.6998	BT71 6RL
421	Glebe (Derryloran)	280420	376800	H804768	680413	876789	54.6329	−6.7545	BT80 9DH
422	Desertcreat	281280	373340	H812733	681273	873329	54.6017	−6.7422	BT80 8UH
423	Kildress Upper	276770	378120	H767781	676764	878108	54.6453	−6.8107	BT80 9RS
424	Cookstown	281100	377500	H811775	681093	877488	54.6391	−6.7438	BT80 8GZ
425	Moy	284980	356140	H849561	684973	856130	54.4466	−6.6899	BT71 7FA
426	Annaloist	304730	361580	J047615	704721	861570	54.4918	−6.3836	BT66 6NJ
427	Annaloist	304730	361580	J047615	704721	861570	54.4918	−6.3836	BT66 6NJ
428	Dougher	307720	359790	J077597	707711	859780	54.4751	−6.3381	BT66 6LY
429	Lurgan	308000	358000	J080580	707991	857990	54.4589	−6.3344	BT66 6RE
430	Lurgan	308510	358728	J085587	708501	858718	54.4653	−6.3263	BT67 9BJ
431	Balteagh	304700	357400	J047574	704691	857390	54.4542	−6.3855	BT64 1AZ
432	Garvaghy	300700	354500	J007545	700692	854491	54.429	−6.4482	BT62 1EG
433	Maghon	300300	351800	J003518	700292	851791	54.4048	−6.4552	BT62 3GH
434	Drumcree	300000	355750	J000557	699992	855740	54.4403	−6.4585	BT62 1PE
435	Ballyoran	300000	354000	J000540	699992	853991	54.4246	−6.4591	BT62 4BH
436	Castleraw	292671	352851	H926528	692663	852842	54.4157	−6.5724	BT61 8PT
437	Loughgall	291100	351900	H911519	691093	851891	54.4074	−6.5968	BT61 8JA
438	Ardress	291350	355850	H913558	691342	855840	54.4429	−6.5918	BT62 1SQ
439	Teemore	299300	345300	H993453	699292	845291	54.3466	−6.4728	BT62 2HN
440	Timakeel	296540	355460	H965554	696532	855450	54.4384	−6.5119	BT62 1WJ
441	Brughas	292870	356210	H928562	692862	856200	54.4458	−6.5682	BT62 1SE
442	Ballybreagh	297407	348627	H974486	697399	848618	54.3769	−6.5008	BT62 3TQ
443	Clontylew	294400	357600	H944576	694392	857590	54.458	−6.5442	BT62 1RE
444	Richhill	294370	348100	H943481	694362	848091	54.3727	−6.5477	BT61 9PR
445	Mulladry	296800	349400	H968494	696792	849391	54.3839	−6.5099	BT62 4HH
446	Ballybrannan	290000	349000	H900490	689993	848991	54.3816	−6.6147	BT61 8RL
447	Hockley	291500	348300	H915483	691492	848291	54.375	−6.5918	BT61 9HL
448	Derryinver	296100	362800	H961628	696092	862790	54.5044	−6.5163	BT66 6PQ
449	Derrywarragh Island	292990	364250	H929642	692982	864240	54.518	−6.5639	BT71 6BF
450	Carricklane	295380	339270	H953392	695372	839262	54.2932	−6.535	BT60 1SD
451	Gosford	296350	340600	H963406	696342	840592	54.305	−6.5197	BT60 1UG

Inv.	Townland	Irish Grid		6-figure grid ref.	ITM Grid		Decimal degrees (WGS84)		Postcode
		Eastings	Northings		Eastings	Northings	Latitude	Longitude	
452	Hamiltonsbawn	295000	344300	H950443	694992	844291	54.3385	−6.5392	BT60 1LX
453	Hamiltonsbawn	294866	344620	H948446	694858	844611	54.3414	−6.5412	BT60 1AW
454	Killeen	291090	342560	H910425	691083	842552	54.3236	−6.5999	BT60 1LE
455	Creggan Bane Glebe	293210	315910	H932159	693202	815904	54.0838	−6.5755	BT35 9DP
456	Glasdrumman	296600	314680	H966146	696592	814674	54.0721	−6.5241	BT35 9EA
457	Moyry Pass	305760	314660	J057146	705751	814654	54.0701	−6.3843	BT35 8JA
458	Ballymoran	288770	341440	H887414	688763	841432	54.3139	−6.6358	BT60 2AR
459	Ballintemple	296412	330769	H964307	696404	830762	54.2167	−6.5219	BT60 2JZ
460	Ballymore	303070	346360	J030463	703062	846351	54.3554	−6.4145	BT62 2AB
461	Tandragee	303200	346200	J032462	703192	846191	54.3539	−6.4125	BT62 2BW
462	Ballymore	303000	346180	J030461	702992	846171	54.3538	−6.4156	BT62 2AA
463	Killybodagh	305460	336540	J054365	705451	836532	54.2667	−6.3812	BT35 6SE
464	Clare	301550	343980	J015439	701542	843971	54.3343	−6.4387	BT62 2EX
465	Druminure	301380	343800	J013438	701372	843792	54.3327	−6.4413	BT62 2EX
466	Loughadian	306200	339440	J062394	706191	839432	54.2926	−6.3688	BT35 6SS
467	Brannock	305800	340980	J058409	705791	840972	54.3065	−6.3744	BT35 6TE
468	Acton	305710	341130	J057411	705701	841122	54.3079	−6.3757	BT35 6TE
469	Magheriehelin	304050	328580	J040285	704041	828573	54.1955	−6.4056	BT35 7AW
470	Shaneglish	304220	341910	J042419	704211	841902	54.3152	−6.3983	BT63 6LJ
471	Lisnagree	303440	336870	J034368	703431	836862	54.2701	−6.4121	BT35 6UG
472	Mountnorris	299520	336170	H995361	699512	836162	54.2646	−6.4725	BT60 2BX
473	Charlemont	285380	355780	H853557	685373	855770	54.4433	−6.6838	BT71 7SF
474	Charlemont	285600	355810	H856558	685593	855800	54.4435	−6.6804	BT71 7SE
475	Charlemont	285300	355700	H853557	685293	855690	54.4426	−6.6851	BT71 7SF
476	Annaghmacmanus	286030	355695	H860556	686023	855685	54.4424	−6.6738	BT71 6SN
477	Lisbofin	284100	352300	H841523	684093	852291	54.4122	−6.7045	BT71 7HL
478	Armagh	287437	345175	H874451	687430	845167	54.3477	−6.6552	BT61 7EE
479	Corporation	287600	345150	H876451	687593	845141	54.3474	−6.6527	BT61 7DJ
480	Londonderry	243620	416730	C436167	643616	916715	54.9961	−7.3184	BT48 6EB
481	Londonderry	243630	416740	C436167	643626	916725	54.9962	−7.3182	BT48 6AL
482	Londonderry	243500	416850	C435168	643496	916835	54.9972	−7.3202	BT48 6HH
483	Londonderry	243370	416480	C433164	643366	916465	54.9939	−7.3223	BT48 6PY
484	Londonderry	243430	416660	C434166	643426	916645	54.9955	−7.3213	BT48 6HP
485	Londonderry	242916	416169	C429161	642912	916154	54.9911	−7.3295	BT48 6UE
486	Londonderry	243110	416350	C431163	643106	916335	54.9927	−7.3264	BT48 6QQ
487	Londonderry	243280	416600	C432166	643276	916585	54.995	−7.3237	BT48 6PS
488	Londonderry	243536	416650	C435166	643532	916635	54.9954	−7.3197	BT48 6PE
489	Elagh More	241580	421650	C415216	641577	921634	55.0405	−7.3495	BT48 8LW
490	Culmore	247652	422512	C476225	647648	922496	55.0477	−7.2544	BT48 8JW
491	Culmore	246480	422660	C464226	646476	922644	55.0491	−7.2727	BT48 8JH
492	Coleraine	284780	432410	C847324	684773	932394	55.1316	−6.6707	BT52 1DN
493	Coleraine	284660	432350	C846323	684653	932334	55.1311	−6.6726	BT52 1DT
494	Coleraine	284660	432340	C846323	684653	932324	55.131	−6.6726	BT52 1DT
495	Coleraine	284930	432360	C849323	684923	932344	55.1312	−6.6683	BT52 1AA
496	Coleraine	284970	432470	C849324	684963	932454	55.1321	−6.6677	BT52 1AG
497	Coleraine	284800	432190	C848321	684793	932174	55.1297	−6.6704	BT52 1EX
498	Prehen	241920	414380	C419143	641917	914365	54.9752	−7.3453	BT47 2PE
499	New Buildings	241170	412580	C411125	641167	912565	54.959	−7.3572	BT47 2RL
500	New Buildings	241170	412580	C411125	641167	912565	54.959	−7.3572	BT47 2RL
501	Primity	241230	412670	C412126	641227	912655	54.9599	−7.3563	BT47 2QQ
502	Muff	252940	420260	C529202	652936	920245	55.0269	−7.1721	BT47 3AB

Inv.	Townland	Irish Grid		6-figure grid ref.	ITM Grid		Decimal degrees (WGS84)		Postcode
		Eastings	Northings		Eastings	Northings	Latitude	Longitude	
503	Eglinton	252920	420315	C529203	652916	920300	55.0274	−7.1724	BT47 3WA
504	Eglinton	252951	420382	C529203	652947	920367	55.028	−7.1719	BT47 3WA
505	Oghill	251058	414736	C510147	651054	914721	54.9775	−7.2025	BT47 3HX
506	Gresteel More	257100	421100	C571211	657095	921085	55.034	−7.1069	BT47 3YG
507	Ballykelly	262420	422620	C624226	662415	922604	55.047	−7.0233	BT49 9JU
508	Ballykelly	262275	422498	C622224	662270	922482	55.0459	−7.0256	BT49 9JU
509	Ballykelly	262250	422730	C622227	662245	922714	55.048	−7.026	BT49 9HU
510	Mulkeeragh	265190	421920	C651219	665185	921904	55.0404	−6.9802	BT49 9HW
511	Lissaghmore	290118	422884	C901228	690111	922868	55.0451	−6.59	BT51 4BX
512	Mullaghmore	290400	422210	C904222	690393	922194	55.039	−6.5858	BT51 4BY
513	Aghadowey	285800	420950	C858209	685793	920935	55.0285	−6.6581	BT51 4DW
514	Aghadowey	285880	421000	C858210	685873	920985	55.029	−6.6569	BT51 4DW
515	Inshaleen	285250	416600	C852166	685243	916585	54.9896	−6.668	BT51 5JE
516	Garvagh	284251	416074	C842160	684244	916059	54.985	−6.6838	BT51 5DY
517	Garvagh	284100	415850	C841158	684093	915835	54.983	−6.6862	BT51 5AF
518	Movanagher	292030	415890	C920158	692022	915875	54.982	−6.5624	BT53 7NT
519	Kilrea	292700	412290	C927122	692692	912275	54.9495	−6.5531	BT51 5AP
520	Macosquin	282500	428800	C825288	682493	928784	55.0996	−6.7075	BT51 4PN
521	Macosquin	282610	428820	C826288	682603	928804	55.0998	−6.7057	BT51 4PN
522	Castleroe	286040	429990	C860299	686033	929974	55.1097	−6.6516	BT51 3TR
523	Ballycastle	267700	427000	C677270	667694	926984	55.0857	−6.9397	BT49 0HT
524	Artikelly	268000	425000	C680250	667994	924984	55.0677	−6.9355	BT49 0JU
525	Rathfad	267909	427891	C679278	667903	927875	55.0936	−6.9362	BT49 0HY
526	Waterside	284430	432500	C844325	684423	932484	55.1325	−6.6761	BT51 3DR
527	Churchland	284460	432130	C844321	684453	932114	55.1292	−6.6758	BT51 3AL
528	Articlave	278500	433800	C785338	678494	933783	55.1452	−6.7687	BT51 4UP
529	Downhill	275820	435410	C758354	675814	935393	55.16	−6.8103	BT51 4SB
530	Big Glebe	276030	434050	C760340	676024	934033	55.1478	−6.8074	BT51 4SN
531	Dungiven	269200	408260	C692082	669194	908246	54.9171	−6.9207	BT47 4PF
532	Dungiven	269500	408300	C695083	669494	908286	54.9175	−6.9161	BT47 4PF
533	Dungiven	268980	408240	C689082	668974	908226	54.917	−6.9242	BT47 4UH
534	Brackfield	251090	409680	C510096	651086	909666	54.9321	−7.2029	BT47 3SW
535	Old Town Deer Park	295340	396340	H953963	695332	896327	54.8058	−6.5171	BT45 8LD
536	Old Town Downing	295185	396434	H951964	695177	896421	54.8067	−6.5195	BT45 8HT
537	Old Town Downing	295270	396590	H952965	695262	896577	54.808	−6.5181	BT45 8HT
538	Moneymore	285830	383350	H858833	685823	883338	54.6908	−6.6688	BT45 7PL
539	Moneymore	285800	383400	H858834	685793	883388	54.6913	−6.6693	BT45 7PD
540	Calmore	282930	395990	H829959	682923	895977	54.8049	−6.7102	BT45 5PX
541	Knocknagin	285580	392130	H855921	685573	892117	54.7697	−6.6701	BT45 5LW
542	Magherafelt	289690	390590	H896905	689683	890577	54.7552	−6.6068	BT45 6EE
543	Magherafelt	289600	390500	H896905	689593	890487	54.7544	−6.6082	BT45 6AB
544	Ballyneill Beg	293000	383000	H930830	692992	882988	54.6864	−6.5578	BT45 7TH
545	Ballymultrea	295180	382360	H951823	695172	882348	54.6803	−6.5242	BT45 6JH
546	Ballinderry	293320	380420	H933804	693312	880408	54.6632	−6.5536	BT80 0BU
547	Bovagh	288940	419370	C889193	688933	919355	55.0138	−6.6095	BT51 4AU
548	Glenleary	285400	427700	C854277	685393	927684	55.0892	−6.6624	BT51 3QY
549	Ballindreen Scotch	290090	430660	C900306	690083	930644	55.115	−6.588	BT52 2JU
550	Tullans	287071	431784	C870317	687064	931768	55.1256	−6.6349	BT52 2JB
551	Moneyrannel	266000	423000	C660230	665995	922984	55.05	−6.9673	BT49 9DN
552	Killane	268120	423900	C681239	668114	923884	55.0578	−6.9339	BT49 0TR
553	Deer Park	267720	420390	C677203	667714	920375	55.0263	−6.941	BT49 9NN

Inv.	Townland	Irish Grid		6-figure grid ref.	ITM Grid		Decimal degrees (WGS84)		Postcode
		Eastings	Northings		Eastings	Northings	Latitude	Longitude	
554	Drummond And Bovally	268900	422750	C689227	668894	922734	55.0473	−6.9219	BT49 0GF
555	Gortgarn	271100	423950	C711239	671094	923934	55.0578	−6.8872	BT49 0QW
556	Flanders	268000	411000	C680110	667994	910985	54.9419	−6.9388	BT47 4RQ
557	Ballymagoland	266800	436250	C668362	666795	936233	55.1689	−6.9516	BT49 0LR
558	Ardmore	270560	420900	C705209	670554	920885	55.0305	−6.8964	BT49 0NQ
559	Ardmore	270690	420890	C706208	670684	920875	55.0304	−6.8944	BT49 0NQ
560	Bovevagh	266760	414010	C667140	666755	913995	54.9691	−6.9575	BT47 4NP
561	Craig	270840	434470	C708344	670834	934453	55.1523	−6.8887	BT49 0LJ
562	Tamniaran	292815	393541	H928935	692807	893528	54.7811	−6.5573	BT45 8DD
563	Moneyconey	272990	390670	H729906	672984	890657	54.7586	−6.8661	BT45 7BS
564	Lismulrevy	280558	358291	H805582	680551	858281	54.4666	−6.7574	BT71 7ER
565	Largantogher	285489	400251	C854002	685482	900237	54.8427	−6.6691	BT46 5AZ
566	Drumnacanon	291060	406240	C910062	691053	906226	54.8955	−6.5806	BT46 5XF
567	Templetown	246870	419550	C468195	646866	919535	55.0212	−7.2671	BT47 6LN
568	Faughanvale	257923	420921	C579209	657918	920906	55.0323	−7.094	BT47 3DZ
569	Templetown	247370	419420	C473194	647366	919405	55.0199	−7.2593	BT47 6TQ
570	Lisaghmore, or The Trench	244800	414600	C448146	644796	914585	54.9769	−7.3003	BT47 2DH
571	Coolagh	258700	421500	C587215	658695	921484	55.0374	−7.0818	BT47 3XH
572	Dunadry	320300	385200	J203852	720290	885188	54.7004	−6.1337	BT41 2RY
573	Whitehead	346900	392600	J469926	746888	892587	54.7598	−5.7177	BT38 9TG
574	Glebe	315100	450850	D151508	715091	950832	55.2911	−6.188	BT54 6RS
575	Bendooragh	292600	423300	C926233	692592	923284	55.0484	−6.5511	BT53 7TE
576	Gortereghy	294900	411600	C949116	694892	911585	54.9429	−6.519	BT51 5SW
577	Toome	299200	390400	H992904	699192	890387	54.7517	−6.4591	BT41 3NJ
578	Creevamoy	319400	406300	D194063	719390	906286	54.8901	−6.139	BT42 4PP
579	Balleny	319900	353100	J199531	719890	853091	54.4123	−6.153	BT25 1FL
580	Dundrum	340100	336400	J401364	740088	836392	54.2572	−5.8499	BT33 0NZ
581	Lisnastrean	329000	362200	J290622	728989	862190	54.4917	−6.009	BT27 5PQ
582	Benburb	281600	352300	H816523	681593	852291	54.4126	−6.743	BT71 7JY
583	Benburb	279970	352770	H799527	679963	852761	54.4171	−6.768	BT71 7QF
584	Cavanboy (Kilmore)	276500	350400	H765504	676494	850391	54.3964	−6.8221	BT68 4XD
585	Carrickbroad	305740	314030	J057140	705731	814024	54.0645	−6.3848	BT35 8JQ
586	Fathom Lower	309900	322200	J099222	709891	822193	54.137	−6.3183	BT35 8NS
587	Ballinrees	287200	423700	C872237	687193	923684	55.053	−6.6354	BT51 3SR
588	Ballynameen	284500	414500	C845145	684493	914485	54.9708	−6.6804	BT51 5PL
589	Drumneechy and Gortaclare	269300	413900	C693139	669294	913885	54.9678	−6.9178	BT47 4RE
590	Eden	292000	403500	C920035	691992	903486	54.8707	−6.5668	BT44 8LP

Glossary

aisle, extension to church, usually running along either side of the nave, containing extra space for the congregation

alabaster, a fine-textured chalky stone, usually white in colour

antechamber, a room that serves as an entryway into a more important room

ashlar, dressed blocks of stone for building, laid in regular courses

balustrade, a row of balusters topped by a rail. Can be found running along the edge of balconies or stairways

barbican, a defensive structure such as a tower that protects the approach to a gateway or bridge

barrel vault, curved vault with semicircular profile. Typically found over the ground floors of tower houses

bartizan, stone turret that typically projects from a corner of a castle. Supported by corbels

base batter, lower portion of a castle wall that slopes outwards

bastion, projecting portion of castle wall for flanking defence, also known as a flanker. Can be rectangular, circular or angular in plan

bawn, walled courtyard of a tower house or a fortified house, commonly provided with gatehouse and corner flankers (word originates from Irish *bádhun* or cattle fort – an enclosure where cattle could be corralled)

bay, a division of the walls of a house. A house with a door and two windows on either side would be described as a five-bay structure

bay window, a window that protrudes from the façade of a building

belfry, a bell tower

buttery, a room within a castle in which beer and wine was stored, and prepared for serving

butt purlin, a horizontal roof timber that is tenoned into the side of a rafter

buttress, a block of masonry that supports a wall

cagework house, a timber-framed house

chancel, the eastern end of a church where the altar is located

charter, a legal document bequeathing a series of rights and privileges to a town

cinquefoil, see foil

couple, a pair of cruck trusses supporting a roof, see cruck truss

corbel, a stone that projects from a wall to carry floors, or other structures such as machicolation and turrets that project from the façade of a building

cornice, horizontal decorative moulding found along the top edge of a building or between the wall and ceiling of a room

counter-scarped ditch, in a rath or ringfort, where a ditch surrounding an internal bank is itself surrounded by a low external bank

crannóg, an artificial or artificially enhanced island dwelling constructed on a lake or marshy ground. Period of use spans from the early medieval period to the 17th century

crenellation, battlements or parapets of a castle punctuated with regular openings along the top of a wall

cross passage, a pair of exterior doors placed to the front and rear of a medieval house which created a passage that ran through the width of the building, separating the principal room, the hall, from more utilitarian rooms, namely the kitchen, buttery and pantry

crow-stepped gable, a gable, the profile of which is decorated with a stair-step arrangement of masonry

cruck truss, a curved timber roof support that rises from the ground to the ridge of a roof

curtain wall, a wall that encloses a castle

cusping, projecting points usually found in the upper portions of sculpted medieval windows

dendrochronology, scientific method of dating timber objects based on the analysis of tree rings

door surround, carved stone jambs and lintel around a doorway

dove-cote, structure designed to house pigeons

drip- or hood-moulding, moulding that projects externally from the top of a doorway or window

English bond brickwork, brick wall with alternating courses of the heads and sides (headers and stretchers) of the brick blocks exposed

entablature, upper part of a classical structure supported by columns

flanker, a tower, typically circular or rectilinear, placed at the corners of bawns or fortified houses to cover the perimeter

foil, a lobe shape found in decorative medieval stonework, commonly connected with other lobes to form quatrefoil (four-lobed) or a cinquefoil (five-lobed) shapes

folly, fanciful building typically built in country demesnes for scenic effect

free and common socage, a form of land tenure which involved payment of rent, but did not include feudal obligations

gargoyle, a roof spout typically found in later medieval churches, designed in the form of a grotesque human or animal figure

gazebo, a pavilion found in gardens that is roofed and open on all sides, and situated to command a view of the surroundings

Gothic, a later medieval architectural style with pointed arches, commonly seen in castles, churches and monasteries

great chamber, second most important room in a castle, by the early 17th century it had supplanted the hall as the most significant room

gun loop, opening for a gun or musket. Found within the walls of tower houses and fortified houses. Can also be found in the walls of bawns and flankers

hipped roof, a type of roof where all the sides slope down to the walls

hood-moulding, see drip-moulding

jamb, the vertical sides of a door or window opening

knight-service tenure, unpaid military service owed in return for grant of land during the Middle Ages. By early modern times, it was a form of tenure which was distinguished by heavier dues on tenants

lancet, a tall narrow window with a pointed arch, commonly seen on later medieval churches and monasteries

lintel, horizontal support (timber or stone) across the top of a window or doorway

loggia, a roofed open gallery set behind a row of columns or pillars, located on the side of a building

loop, small narrow window, typically found in castles

machicolation, stone structure projecting externally from the top of a castle. Supported by corbels

merlon, solid portion of crenellated parapet

mezzanine, an intermediate, ancillary floor space placed between two main floors of a building

mortice-and-tenon joint, a joint where two timbers are joined together by fitting a projecting piece on one timber into a slot of equal shape and size on the other

moulding, band of decorated stone, usually found around door and window openings

mullion, a vertical stone or timber dividing a window into separate lights

murder hole, an opening in a floor or vault above the entrance lobby of a tower house through which any attackers could be fired upon

nave, the main body of a church in which the congregation could gather for worship, stretching from the west wall to the chancel at the east end

newel, central pillar or post from which the steps of a spiral stairs project

palisade, timber fence used for fortification

pantry, a room for storing provisions and tableware

parlour, a room kept by family members in an early modern aristocratic household to dine and entertain in a more private setting

parterre, a symmetrical arrangement of flower beds and gravel paths found in early modern ornamental gardens. Beds were typically edged with low, tightly clipped hedging

pediment, a feature of classical architecture, a decorative gable placed above doorways and windows

piano nobile, the principle floor, usually the first floor, of a 17th-century country house, where the most important rooms were located

pilaster, a column-like projection attached to a wall

portcullis, gate of iron or wood which could be raised up and down in slots built into the jambs of a castle gateway

quoins, stones, usually carved as regular blocks, placed at the corners of buildings

rath, also known as a ringfort, is an early medieval settlement type consisting of a circular area enclosed by a bank and external ditch. Examples with two or more concentric banks and ditches are known

re-entrant corner, the inner angle of an L-shaped or T-shaped house where the two wings of the building meet

render, lime-based mortar covering used to protect the external surfaces of walls

rib vaulting, a type of vault supported by stone ornamental bands or ribbing

Romanesque, an architectural style influenced by Classical architecture, featuring round-headed arches, immediately pre-dating the Gothic style

round tower, freestanding belfry tower, dating to between the 10th and early 13th centuries, found on monastic sites

sconce, a small defensive earthwork, detached from a larger fortification

scullery, a small room where kitchen work such as preparing vegetables or washing dishes was done

segmental-headed window, top of window, the profile of which is the segment of a circle drawn from a point below

souterrain, an underground passage of early medieval date, typically built of stone

square-hooded window, window with square drip- or hood-moulding, see drip-moulding

squinch, masonry arch bridging an angle to support a stone structure in the same angle

string-coursing, narrow band of stone moulding running horizontally across the exterior of a building such as a fortified house, typically marking the floor levels within

tannery, place where animal skins are processed to produce leather

tracery, openwork of stone decorating the upper part of a window. Commonly seen in medieval churches

transept, extension projecting northwards or southwards from a church building, usually where the nave and chancel meet

Transitional, the term used to describe the style of architecture between Romanesque and Gothic

transom, a horizontal stone or timber dividing a window into separate lights

tucking mill, also known as a fulling mill, where newly-made woollen cloth was scoured of dirt and grease, as well as thickened.

vernacular architecture, a traditional building style based on local needs, materials and knowledge

wall-walk, walkway along the battlements or parapets of a castle

wicker-centring, frame used to support an arch under construction. In tower houses, it was common to use wicker mats to give shape to the arch. Once the mortar had dried and the arch had set in place, the centring was removed, leaving behind the impression of the wicker mats in the mortar

window surround, carved stone sill, jambs and lintel around a window

withdrawing chamber, a room to withdraw to, usually off from the great chamber in early 17th century residences

Bibliography

All internet sources cited are correct as of 31 August, 2016.

Cartographic Sources

A Survey of Col Mervyne Archdal's Estate, 1720 (PRONI D 605/1)

Richard Bartlett 'Plan of Charlemont Fort and bridge over the Blackwater', 1602. National Library of Ireland (MS2656-4)

Richard Bartlett 'Drawing of Dungannon Castle and the Stone Chair at Tullahogue, Co. Tyrone', 1602. National Library of Ireland (MS2656-5)

Richard Bartlett 'Drawing of Enish Loughan fort, Co. Antrim', 1602. National Library of Ireland (MS2656-6)

Richard Bartlett 'A description of the valley of Blackwater showing fortified positions of Irish and English in the O'Neill wars', 1602. National Library of Ireland (MS2656-8)

Bodley Maps of Escheated Counties of Ireland, 1609 (PRONI T1652)

Bodley Map of the 'Baronie of the Fues', 1609 (National Archives MPF 1/60)

Bodley Map of the 'Baronie of Orior', 1609 (National Archives MPF 1/59)

Derry National Archives (SP 63/207)

Down Survey barony map of Belfast, Co. Antrim (currently available via *http://www.downsurvey.tcd.ie*)

Down Survey barony map of Cary, Co. Antrim (currently available via *http://www.downsurvey.tcd.ie*)

Down Survey barony map of Dunluce, Co. Antrim (currently available via *http://www.downsurvey.tcd.ie*)

Down Survey barony map of Glenarm, Co. Antrim (currently available via *http://www.downsurvey.tcd.ie*)

Down Survey barony map of Massereene, Co. Antrim (currently available via *http://www.downsurvey.tcd.ie*)

Down Survey barony map of Toome, Co. Antrim (currently available via *http://www.downsurvey.tcd.ie*)

Down Survey county map of Antrim (currently available via *http://www.downsurvey.tcd.ie*)

Down Survey parish map of Billy, Co. Antrim (currently available via *http://www.downsurvey.tcd.ie*)

Down Survey parish map of Connor, Co. Antrim (currently available via *http://www.downsurvey.tcd.ie*)

Down Survey parish map of Drumaule and Magherochill, Co. Antrim (currently available via *http://www.downsurvey.tcd.ie*)

Down Survey parish map of Kilfaghtrim, Co. Antrim (currently available via *http://www.downsurvey.tcd.ie*)

Down Survey parish map of Larne, Co. Antrim (currently available via *http://www.downsurvey.tcd.ie*)

Down Survey barony map of Oneilan, Co. Armagh (currently available via *http://www.downsurvey.tcd.ie*)

Down Survey parish map of Cregan, Co. Armagh (currently available via *http://www.downsurvey.tcd.ie*)

Down Survey barony map of Iveagh, Co. Down (currently available via *http://www.downsurvey.tcd.ie*)

Down Survey barony map of Lecale, Co. Down (currently available via *http://www.downsurvey.tcd.ie*)

Down Survey parish map of Magheredril, Co. Down (currently available via *http://www.downsurvey.tcd.ie*)

Down Survey barony map of Clanawley, Co. Fermanagh (currently available via *http://www.downsurvey.tcd.ie*)

Down Survey barony map of Magherastephana, Co. Fermanagh (currently available via *http://www.downsurvey.tcd.ie*)

Down Survey county map of Fermanagh (currently available via *http://www.downsurvey.tcd.ie*)

Down Survey barony map of Coleraine, Co. Londonderry (currently available via *http://www.downsurvey.tcd.ie*)

Down Survey barony map of Keenaght, Co. Londonderry (currently available via *http://www.downsurvey.tcd.ie*)

Down Survey barony map of Tirkeerin, Co. Londonderry (currently available via *http://www.downsurvey.tcd.ie*)

Down Survey parish map of Bouevy, Co. Londonderry (currently available via *http://www.downsurvey.tcd.ie*)

Down Survey parish map of Desertoghill and Arragell, Co. Londonderry (currently available via *http://www.downsurvey.tcd.ie*)

Down Survey parish map of Drumcross and Baltiagh, Co. Londonderry (currently available via *http://www.downsurvey.tcd.ie*)

Down Survey parish map of Dunbo, Co. Londonderry (currently available via *http://www.downsurvey.tcd.ie*)

Down Survey barony map of Dungannon, Co. Tyrone (currently available via *http://www.downsurvey.tcd.ie*)

Down Survey barony map of Omagh, Co. Tyrone (currently available via *http://www.downsurvey.tcd.ie*)

Down Survey parish map of Carnetele, Aghavow and Killishel, Co. Tyrone (currently available via *http://www.downsurvey.tcd.ie*)

Down Survey parish map of Drummoore and Kilskerry, Co. Tyrone (currently available via *http://www.downsurvey.tcd.ie*)

Down Survey parish map of Maghericross and Urney, Co. Tyrone (currently available via *http://www.downsurvey.tcd.ie*)

Down Survey maps of parts of County Antrim, *c.* 1655 (PRONI D597/1)

Down Survey maps of parts of County Antrim, *c.* 1655 (PRONI D597/2)

Down Survey maps of the Counties of Donegal and Londonderry, *c.* 1655 (PRONI D597/3)

Down Survey maps of parts of the Counties of Down, Armagh and Tyrone, *c.* 1655 (PRONI D597/4)

County Fermanagh: Enniskillen 'Plat of the fort of Enniskillin, showing Captain Bingham's Camp', 1594 (National Archives MPF 1/80)

County Armagh: Blackwatertown 'The Plott of Black Water', 1587 (National Archives MPF 1/99)

Irish Historical Atlas (PRONI T2543/1)

Loch Swilly and the River Foyle. National Archives (MPF 1/335/1)

Map of the 'Baronie of Fues'. National Archives (MPF 1/60)

Map of the 'Baronie of Orier'. National Archives (MPF 1/59)

(Phillips MSS) Sir Thomas Phillips' map and report, 1622-1841 (PRONI T510)

(Phillips MSS) Copy of Sir Thomas Phillips' report which accompanied the surveys, *c*. 1717–*c*. 1722 (PRONI T510/2)

Report of the Plantation Commissioners, 1611 (PRONI T811/3)

The Fort of Omaye [Omagh] *in Ulster, c.* 1611 (TCD MS 1209/34)

The Ward Papers, 1691-*c*.1745 (PRONI D2092)

Thomas Phillips' Ground plan of Belfast, 1685 (PRONI T822)

Thomas Phillips' map of Charlemont, Co. Armagh, 1685 (NLI MS 2557/28)

Thomas Phillips' map of Charlemont, Co. Armagh, 1685 (NLI MS 3137/37)

Thomas Phillips' map of Belfast, 1685 (NLI MS 3137/41)

Thomas Raven's map of Clandeboye, 1625-1768 (PRONI T870)

Thomas Raven's map of Clandeboye Estate, 1625 (PRONI T870/1)

View of the Archbishopric of Armagh by Thomas Ashe, 1703 (PRONI T848/1)

★

Abraham, A.S.K. (1997) *An Archaeological Assessment and Works Programme for Shane's Castle, County Antrim*, Belfast (unpublished report in the archives of DfC:HED).

AMNI = Ministry of Finance (1963) *Ancient Monuments of Northern Ireland: Volume II Not in State Care*, Belfast (HMSO).

Anon. (1855) 'Antiquarian Notes and Queries', *Ulster Journal of Archaeology* (1st series) 3, 76–84.

Anon. (1860) 'Proceedings of the Scottish and English forces in the north of Ireland, A.D. 1642', *Ulster Journal of Archaeology* (1st series) 8, 77–87.

Anon. (1927) *Historical Sketch of Drumcree Parish*, Belfast (Witness Office).

Anon. (1941) 'Survey of Ancient Monuments: Additions and Corrections', *Ulster Journal of Archaeology* (3rd series) 4, 35–44.

Anon. (1944) 'Survey of Ancient Monuments: Third List of Additions and Corrections (Continued)', *Ulster Journal of Archaeology* (3rd series) 7, 117–121.

Anon. (1982) *A history of congregations in the Presbyterian Church in Ireland 1610–1982*, Belfast (Presbyterian Historical Society of Ireland).

Anon. (2009) *Guide to Historic Monuments of Northern Ireland in State Care*, Belfast (Graham & Heslip).

Archdall, M. (1786) *Monasticon Hibernicum or A History of the Abbies, Priories and other Religious Houses of Ireland*, London (G. G. J. and J. Robinson).

Arthur, D. (2009) *Ballymoney Old Church Graveyard*, Ballycastle (Impact Printing).

ASCD = Jope, E.M. ed. (1966) *An Archaeological Survey of County Down*, Belfast (HMSO).

Atkinson, E.D. (1925) *Dromore: An Ulster Diocese*, Dundalk (Dundalgan Press).

Bagenal, M., Hore, H.F. and Burghley (1854) 'Marshal Bagenal's Description of Ulster, Anno 1586', *Ulster Journal of Archaeology* (1st series) 2, 137–160.

Bailey, R.N. (1963) 'The Clogher Crucifixion: a Northumbrian parallel and its implication', *Journal of the Royal Society of Antiquaries of Ireland* 93(2), 187–188.

Bailie, W. and Bowen, P. (2007) 'Derryloran', *Excavations 2007*, 504, no. 1762 (also currently available via *http://www.excavations.ie*).

Bailie, W. and Ward, K. (2009) 'Lisnarick', *Excavations 2009*, 97–98, no. 373 (also currently available via *http://www.excavations.ie*).

Baillie, M.G.L (1974) 'A tree-ring chronology for the dating of Irish post-medieval timbers', *Ulster Folklife* 20, 1–23.

Bardon, J. (2012) *The Plantation of Ulster: The British Colonisation of the North of Ireland in the Seventeenth Century*, Dublin (Gill and MacMillan).

Beattie, K. (undated) *History of Ballymoney Old Church Graveyard*, (also currently available at *www.http://ballymoneygraveyard.com*)

Belmore, earl of (1895a) 'Monea Castle, County Fermanagh, and the Hamiltons', *Ulster Journal of Archaeology* (2nd series) 1(3), 195–208.

–   (1895b) 'Monea Castle, County Fermanagh, and the Hamiltons. With Some Notes on the Hume and Cathcart Families (concluded)', *Ulster Journal of Archaeology* (2nd series) 1(4), 256–277.

–   (1898) 'Gleanings for former Fermanagh articles. Corrections (continued)', *Ulster Journal of Archaeology* (2nd series) 4(3), 138–151.

–   (1903a) 'The Old Castles of County Tyrone', *Ulster Journal of Archaeology* (2nd series, special volume), 35–79.

–   (1903b) 'The Irish Historical Atlas', *Ulster Journal of Archaeology* (2nd series, special volume), 3–32.

–   (1904) 'Robert Vicars Dixon, D.D. (Archdeacon of Armagh), and the Parish of Cloghernie (continued)', *Ulster Journal of Archaeology* (2nd series) 10, 92–94.

Belshaw, R.R. (1896) 'Castle Robin', *Ulster Journal of Archaeology* (1st series) 2, 33–35.

Bell, J. (1897) 'Antiquarian notes on Ballymoney, Co. Antrim', *Ulster Journal of Archaeology* (2nd series) 3(3), 148–152.

Bence-Jones, M. (1978) *Burke's Guide to Country Houses, Volume 1: Ireland*, London (Burke's Peerage Ltd.).

Benn, G. (1877) *A History of the Town of Belfast*, London (Marcus Ward).

–   (1880) *A History of the Town of Belfast Volume 2: From 1799 Till 1810.* London (Marcus Ward).

Bigger, F.J. (1901) 'Arthur O'Neill, the Irish Harper', *Ulster Journal of Archaeology* (2nd series) 7(1), 1–7.

–   (1904) 'Sir Arthur Chichester, Lord Deputy of Ireland. With some notes on the Plantation of Ulster', *Ulster Journal of Archaeology* (2nd series) 10(1), 2 and 10(3), 1–12, 56–66 and 104–112.

–   (1905) 'Some historical notes about Dunluce and its builders', *Ulster Journal of Archaeology* (2nd series) 11(4), 154–162.

–   (1906) 'Some historical notes about Dunluce and its builders (Continued)', *Ulster Journal of Archaeology* (2nd series) 12(1), 22–35.

–   (1911a) 'The old barracks of Belfast', *Ulster Journal of Archaeology* (2nd series) 17, 74–78.

– (1911b) 'Hill Hall', *Ulster Journal of Archaeology* (2nd series) 17, 79.

Bigger, F.J. and Fennell, W.J. (1898) *Special Part of the Ulster Journal of Archaeology: The Ancient Franciscan Friary of* Bun-na-Margie, *Ballycastle, Co. Antrim*, Belfast (Marcus Ward and Co.).

– (1899) 'Teampull Lastrac, Dunseveric, Co. Antrim', *Ulster Journal of Archaeology* (2nd series) 5(2), 60–62.

– (1900) 'Dunluce Church, County Antrim', *Ulster Journal of Archaeology* (2nd series) 6(1), 4–6.

– (1908) 'The Round Church of Carrig-Fergus Castle', *Ulster Journal of Archaeology* (2nd series) 14(4), 182–189.

Blades, B.S. (1980a) ' "In the Manner of England": tenant housing in the Londonderry Plantation', *Ulster Folklife* 27, 39–56.

– (1980b) 'Movanagher, Co. Derry', *Excavations 1977–79*, 71, no. 22 (also currently available via *http://www.excavations.ie*).

– (1986) 'English Villages in the Londonderry Plantation', *Post-Medieval Archaeology* 20, 257–269.

Boston, C. K. (1910) *Scotch Irish Pioneers in Ulster and America*, Boston (Bacon and Brown).

Bowen, P. (2005) '10–16 Castle Place', *Excavations 2005*, 7–8, no. 15 (also currently available via *http://www.excavations.ie*).

– (2007a) '15 Belleek Road, Drumlyon', *Excavations 2007*, 142–143, no. 564 (also currently available via *http://www.excavations.ie*).

– (2007b) '2-4 Castle Hill, Dungannon', *Excavations 2007*, 505–506, no. 1769 (also currently available via *http://www.excavations.ie*).

Brannon, N.F. (1977–79) 'Coleraine, Derry', *Excavations 1977–79*, 70, no. 18 (also currently available via *http://www.excavations.ie*).

– (1980–4) 'Castle Street', *Excavations 1980–84*, 67, no. 7 (also currently available via *http://www.excavations.ie*).

– (1983a) 'Rescue excavations in Macosquin, County Londonderry', *Ulster Journal of Archaeology* (3rd series) 46, 93–100.

– (1983b) 'Two fortified houses at Castleraw, County Armagh', *Ulster Journal of Archaeology* (3rd series) 46, 165–166.

– (1984) 'Excavation at a farmyard in the Bonn townland, County Tyrone', *Ulster Journal of Archaeology* (3rd series) 47, 177–181.

– (1985) 'Archaeological excavations at Dungiven priory and bawn', *Benbradagh* 15, 15–18.

– (1986) 'Five excavations in Ulster, 1978–1984', *Ulster Journal of Archaeology* (3rd series) 49, 89–98.

– (1988a) 'Denvir's Hotel. Demesne of Down', *Excavations 1988*, 13–14, no. 12 (also currently available via *http://www.excavations.ie*).

– (1988b) 'Where history and archaeology unite', in eds A. Hamlin and CJ. Lynn 1988, 78–79.

– (1988c) 'In search of old Belfast', in eds A. Hamlin and C.J. Lynne 1988, 79–81.

– (1988d) 'A lost 17th-century house recovered', in eds A. Hamlin and C.J. Lynn 1988, 81–84.

– (1989a) 'Bellaghy Bawn, Bellaghy', *Excavations 1989*, 16–17, no. 15 (also currently available via *http://www.excavations.ie*).

– (1989b) 'Conyngham Street, Moneymore', *Excavations 1989*, 17, no. 17 (also currently available via *http://www.excavations.ie*)

– (1990a) 'Donegall Street, Belfast, Antrim', *Excavations 1990*, 11, no. 3 (also currently available via *http://www.excavations.ie*).

– (1990b) 'Excavations at Brackfield Bawn, County Londonderry', *Ulster Journal of Archaeology* (3rd series) 53, 8–14.

– (1998) 'A 1614–18 Londoners' glasshouse at Salterstown, Co. Derry?' *Archaeology Ireland* 12(2), 23.

– and Blades, B. S. (1980) 'Dungiven bawn re-edified', *Ulster Journal of Archaeology* (3rd series) 43, 91–96.

– and McSparron, C. (1997) 'Portora Castle, Enniskillen, Fermanagh', *Excavations 1997*, 63, no. 190 (also currently available via *http://www.excavations.ie*).

Bratt, A.D. and Lynn, C.J. (1975–76) 'Big Glebe, Derry', *Excavations 1975–76*, 27–28, no. 12 (also currently available via *http://www.excavations.ie*).

Bredin, A.E.C. (1987) *A History of the Irish Soldier*, Belfast (Century Books).

Breen, C. (2005) *The Gaelic Lordship of the O'Sullivan Beare*, Dublin (Four Courts Press).

– (2012) *Dunluce Castle: History and Archaeology*, Dublin (Four Courts Press).

Brett, C.E.B. (1971) *Historic Buildings in the Glens of Antrim*, Belfast (Ulster Architectural Heritage Society).

– (1996) *Buildings of County Antrim*, Belfast (Ulster Architectural Heritage Society).

– (1999) *The Buildings of Co. Armagh*, Belfast (Ulster Architectural Heritage Society).

Burns, J.F. (1984) 'Lisburn's castle and cathedral', *Lisburn Historical Society Journal* 5, 3–15.

Cal. Pat. Rolls Jas I= Commissioners on the Public Records of Ireland (1966) Calendar of the Irish patent rolls of James I, Dublin (Stationery Office for the Irish Manuscripts Commission).

Cal. SPI = Hamilton, H.C., Atkinson, E.G. and Mahaffy, R.P. eds (1860–1912) *Calendar of State Papers Relating to Ireland*, 24 vols, London (HMSO).

Camblin, G. (1951) *The Town in Ulster*, Belfast (Mullan & Son).

Campbell, A.A. and F.J.B. (1910) 'Miscellanea', *Ulster Journal of Archaeology* (2nd series) 16 (1/2), 93–96.

Canny, N. (1987) *From Reformation to Restoration: Ireland, 1534–1660*, Dublin (Helicon Limited).

– (1988) *Kingdom and colony, Ireland in the Atlantic world 1560–1800*, Baltimore and London (The John Hopkins University Press).

– (2001) *Making Ireland British, 1580–1650*, Oxford (Oxford University Press).

Carleton, T. (1976) 'Aspects of local history in Malone, Belfast', *Ulster Journal of Archaeology* (3rd series) 39, 62–67.

Carver, N. (2006) *Site 80m NW of 112 Mountjoy Road*, Belfast (unpublished report in the archives of DfC:HED), (also currently available via *http://www.qub.ac.uk/schools/ CentreforArchaeologicalFieldworkCAF*)

Case, H.J. (1953) 'The Neolithic site at Goodland, Co. Antrim', *Ulster Journal of Archaeology* (3rd series) 16, 24.

Chapple, R.M. (2003) 'Excavations at Castle Hill, Dungannon, Co. Tyrone', *Archaeology Ireland* 17(3), 24–29.

Clendinning, K. (1969) 'The Brownlow family and the rise of Lurgan. Review', *Journal of the Craigavon Historical Society* 1(1) (also currently available via *http://www.craigavonhistoricalsociety.org.uk/rev*).

– (2005) 'The Brownlow family & the development of the town of Lurgan in the 17th Century: Part II. William Brownlow & the formation of the manor of Brownlowsderry', *Seanchas Ardmhacha: The Journal of the Armagh Diocesan Historical Society*, 20(2), 106–132.

Collins, A.E.P. (n.d.) Unpublished notes in SMR file relating to excavations in 1968 at Annaloist Church, Northern Ireland Sites and Monuments Record (also currently available via *http://www.apps.ehsni.gov.uk/ambit/*).

Collis, M.H.H. (1896) 'Antrim parish church for three hundred years', *Ulster Journal of Archaeology* (2nd series) 3(1), 30–39.

– (1897) 'Antrim parish church for three hundred years continued', *Ulster Journal of Archaeology* (2nd series) 3(2), 90–98.

Conway, M. (1994) 'Antrim Castle gardens', *Excavations 1994*, 1–2, no. 1 (also currently available via *http://www.excavations.ie*).

Cordner, W.S. (1942) 'Some old wells in Antrim and Down. II', *Ulster Journal of Archaeology* (3rd series) 5, 90–95.

– Davies, O. and Davidson, R.C. (1947) 'Norman graveslabs', *Ulster Journal of Archaeology* (3rd series) 10, 70–72.

Crawford, H.S. (1912) 'A descriptive list of early cross-slabs and pillars', *Journal of the Royal Society of Antiquaries of Ireland* 2(3), 217–244.

– (1918) 'Supplementary list of early Irish crosses', *Journal of the Royal Society of Antiquaries of Ireland* 8(2), 174–179.

Crone, J.S. (1904) 'Ulster bibliography, Tyrone', *Ulster Journal of Archaeology* (2nd series) 2, 95–102.

Crookshank, R.R.G. (1899) 'Teampull Lastrac, Dunseveric, Co. Antrim', *Ulster Journal of Archaeology* 5 (4), 228.

Crothers, N. (1996) *Phoenix Gas Belfast Transmission Pipeline*, Belfast (unpublished report in the archives of DfC:HED).

– McQuillan, L. and Gahan, A. (2000) 'Rescue excavations at Templecorran, Ballycarry, County Antrim', *Ulster Journal of Archaeology* (3rd series) 59, 29–46.

Curl, J.S. (1986) *The Londonderry Plantation 1609–1641. The History, Architecture, and Planning of the Estates of the City of London and its Livery Companies in Ulster*, Chichester, Sussex (Phillimore & Co.).

– (2000) *The Honourable The Irish Society and the Plantation of Ulster, 1608–2000*, Chichester, Sussex (Phillimore & Co.).

– (2015) 'London's Derrie: the background to the building and financing of the walls', in B.G. Scott ed. 2015, 13–35.

D'Arcy, S.A. (1930) ' "Holed" stone at Cushendall, Co. Antrim', *Journal of the Royal Society of Antiquaries of Ireland* (6th series) 20(2), 192–193.

Davies, O. (1938a) 'Mountcastle', *Ulster Journal of Archaeology* (3rd series) 1, 215–216.

–   (1938b) 'Clogher crosses and other curved stones', *Ulster Journal of Archaeology* (3rd series) 1, 227–230.

–   (1939) 'Aughentaine Castle', *Ulster Journal of Archaeology* (3rd series) 2, 72–82.

–   (1940) 'Moiry Castle', *Report and Proceedings of the Belfast Natural History and Philosophical Society* (2nd series) 1(4), 31–38.

–   (1941a) 'The Castle of Benburb', *Ulster Journal of Archaeology* (3rd series) 4, 31–34.

–   (1941b) 'Finds near Newtownstewart', *Ulster Journal of Archaeology* (3rd series) 4, 44–48.

–   (1941c) 'Ballynascreen Church and legends', *Ulster Journal of Archaeology* (3rd series) 4, 57–63.

–   (1941d) 'Trial excavations at Lough Enagh', *Ulster Journal of Archaeology* (3rd series) 4, 88–101.

–   (1941e) in 'Survey of Ancient Monuments: additions' *Ulster Journal of Archaeology* (3rd series) 4, 139–144.

–   (1942) 'Derryloran Church', *Ulster Journal of Archaeology* (3rd series) 5, 8–11.

–   (1946) 'Excavation of a crannog at Deredis Upper, in Lough Inchin, Co. Cavan', *Journal of the Royal Society of Antiquaries of Ireland* 76(1), 19–34.

Davies, O. and Swan, H.P. (1939) 'The castle of Inishowen', *Ulster Journal of Archaeology* (3rd series) 2, 178–208.

Day, A. and McWilliams, P. eds (1990a) *Ordnance Survey Memoirs of Ireland Volume 1: Parishes of County Armagh I, 1835–8*, Belfast (Institute of Irish Studies in association with the Royal Irish Academy).

–   (1990b) *Ordnance Survey Memoirs of Ireland Volume 2: Parishes of County Antrim I, 1838–9, Ballymartin, Ballyrobert, Ballywalter, Carnmoney, Mallusk*, Belfast (Institute of Irish Studies in association with the Royal Irish Academy).

–   (1990c) *Ordnance Survey Memoirs of Ireland Volume 3: Parishes of County Down I, 1834–6, South Down*, Belfast (Institute of Irish Studies in association with the Royal Irish Academy).

–   (1990d) *Ordnance Survey Memoirs of Ireland Volume 4: Parishes of County Fermanagh I, 1834–5, Enniskillen and Upper Lough Erne*, Belfast (Institute of Irish Studies in association with the Royal Irish Academy).

–   (1990e) *Ordnance Survey Memoirs of Ireland Volume 5: Parishes of County Tyrone I, 1821, 1823, 1831–6, North, West and South Tyrone*, Belfast (Institute of Irish Studies in association with the Royal Irish Academy).

–   (1990f) *Ordnance Survey Memoirs of Ireland Volume 6: Parishes of County Londonderry I 1830, 1834, 1836, Arboe, Artrea, Ballinderry, Ballyscullion, Magherafelt and Termoneeny*, Belfast (Institute of Irish Studies in association with the Royal Irish Academy).

–   (1991a) *Ordnance Survey Memoirs of Ireland Volume 7: Parishes of County Down II, 1832–4, 1837, North Down and the Ards*, Belfast (Institute of Irish Studies in association with the Royal Irish Academy).

–   (1991b) *Ordnance Survey Memoirs of Ireland Volume 8: Parishes of County Antrim II, 1832–8, 1838–9, Lisburn and South Antrim*, Belfast (Institute of Irish Studies in association with the Royal Irish Academy).

–   (1991c) *Ordnance Survey Memoirs of Ireland Volume 9: Parishes of County Londonderry II 1833–5, Roe Valley Central*, Belfast (Institute of Irish Studies in association with the Royal Irish Academy).

–   (1991d) *Ordnance Survey Memoirs of Ireland Volume 10: Parishes of County Antrim III. 1833, 1835, 1839–40, Larne and Island Magee*, Belfast (Institute of Irish Studies in association with the Royal Irish Academy).

–   (1992a) *Ordnance Survey Memoirs of Ireland Volume 13: Parishes of County Antrim IV, 1830–38, Glens of Antrim*, Belfast (Institute of Irish Studies in association with the Royal Irish Academy).

–   (1992b) *Ordnance Survey Memoirs of Ireland Volume 14: Parishes of County Fermanagh II, 1834-5, Lower Lough Erne*, Belfast (Institute of Irish Studies in association with the Royal Irish Academy).

–   (1992c) *Ordnance Survey Memoirs of Ireland Volume 15: Parishes of County Londonderry IV 1824, 1833-5, Roe Valley Upper: Dungiven*, Belfast (Institute of Irish Studies in association with the Royal Irish Academy).

–   (1992d) *Ordnance Survey Memoirs of Ireland Volume 16: Parishes of County Antrim V, 1830-5, 1837-8, Giant's Causeway and Ballymoney*, Belfast (Institute of Irish Studies in association with the Royal Irish Academy).

–   (1992e) *Ordnance Survey Memoirs of Ireland Volume 17: Parishes of County Down IV, 1833-7, East Down and Lecale*, Belfast (Institute of Irish Studies in association with the Royal Irish Academy).

–   (1993a) *Ordnance Survey Memoirs of Ireland Volume 18: Parishes of County Londonderry V 1830, 1833, 1836-7, Maghera and Tamlaght O'Crilly*, Belfast (Institute of Irish Studies in association with the Royal Irish Academy).

–   (1993b) *Ordnance Survey Memoirs of Ireland Volume 19: Parishes of County Antrim VI, 1830, 1833, 1835-8, South-West Antrim*, Belfast (Institute of Irish Studies in association with the Royal Irish Academy).

–   (1993c) *Ordnance Survey Memoirs of Ireland Volume 20: Parishes of County Tyrone II 1825, 1833-5, 1840, Mid and East Tyrone*, Belfast (Institute of Irish Studies in association with the Royal Irish Academy).

–   (1993d) *Ordnance Survey Memoirs of Ireland Volume 21: Parishes of County Antrim VII, 1832-8, South Antrim*, Belfast (Institute of Irish Studies in association with the Royal Irish Academy).

–   (1993e) *Ordnance Survey Memoirs of Ireland Volume 22: Parishes of County Londonderry VI, 1831, 1833, 1835-6, North-East Londonderry*, Belfast (Institute of Irish Studies in association with the Royal Irish Academy).

–   (1994) *Ordnance Survey Memoirs of Ireland Volume 27: Parishes of County Londonderry VIII 1830, 1833-7, 1839, East Londonderry*, Belfast (Institute of Irish Studies in association with the Royal Irish Academy).

–   (1995a) *Ordnance Survey Memoirs of Ireland Volume 29: Parishes of County Antrim XI 1832-3, 1835-9, Antrim Town and Ballyclare*, Belfast (Institute of Irish Studies in association with the Royal Irish Academy).

–   (1995b) *Ordnance Survey Memoirs of Ireland Volume 31: Parishes of County Londonderry XI 1821, 1833, 1836-7: South Londonderry*, Belfast (Institute of Irish Studies in association with the Royal Irish Academy).

–   (1995c) *Ordnance Survey Memoirs of Ireland Volume 32: Parishes of County Antrim XII 1832-3, 1835-40: Ballynure and district*, Belfast (Institute of Irish Studies in association with the Royal Irish Academy).

– (1995d) *Ordnance Survey Memoirs of Ireland Volume 36: Parishes of County Londonderry XIV 1833–4, 1836, 1838: Faughanvale*, Belfast (Institute of Irish Studies in association with the Royal Irish Academy).

– (1996) *Ordnance Survey Memoirs of Ireland Volume 37: Parishes of County Antrim XIV 1832, 1839–40, Carrickfergus*, Belfast (Institute of Irish Studies in association with the Royal Irish Academy).

Day, A., McWilliams, P. and Dobson, N. eds (1993) *Ordnance Survey Memoirs of Ireland Volume 23: Parishes of County Antrim VIII 1831–5, 1837–8, Ballymena and West Antrim*, Belfast (Institute of Irish Studies in association with the Royal Irish Academy).

– (1994a) *Ordnance Survey Memoirs of Ireland Volume 24: Parishes of County Antrim IX, 1830-2, 1835, 1838-9, North Antrim Coast and Rathlin*, Belfast (Institute of Irish Studies in association with the Royal Irish Academy).

– (1994b) *Ordnance Survey Memoirs of Ireland Volume 25: Parishes of County Londonderry VII 1834–5, North-West Londonderry*, Belfast (Institute of Irish Studies in association with the Royal Irish Academy).

– (1994c) *Ordnance Survey Memoirs of Ireland Volume 26: Parishes of County Antrim X, 1830-1, 1833-5, 1839-40, East Antrim, Glynn, Inver, Kilroot and Templecorran*, Belfast (Institute of Irish Studies in association with the Royal Irish Academy).

Day, A., McWilliams, P. and English, L. eds (1995) *Ordnance Survey Memoirs of Ireland Volume 33: Parishes of County Londonderry XII: 1829-30, 1832, 1834-36, Coleraine and Mouth of the Bann*, Belfast (Institute of Irish Studies in association with the Royal Irish Academy).

– (1996a) *Ordnance Survey Memoirs of Ireland Volume 34: Parishes of County Londonderry XII 1831–8, Clondermot and the Waterside*, Belfast (Institute of Irish Studies in association with the Royal Irish Academy).

– (1996b) *Ordnance Survey Memoirs of Ireland Volume 35: Parishes of County Antrim XIII 1833, 1835, 1838: Temple Patrick and District*, Belfast (Institute of Irish Studies in association with the Royal Irish Academy).

Dempsey, J. (2004) 'Main Street, Newtownbutler', *Excavations 2004*, 160–161, no. 660 (also currently available via *http://www.excavations.ie*).

DEP = Downshire Estate Papers, 1803 (PRONI D.671/m4/31).

Dickson, J.M. (1901) 'The Agnews in County Antrim', *Ulster Journal of Archaeology* (2nd series) 7(4), 166–171.

Dixon, H. (1973) *The Buildings of Enniskillen*, Belfast (Ulster Architectural Heritage Society).

– (1975) *An Introduction to Ulster Architecture*, Belfast (1st edition, Ulster Architectural Heritage Society).

– (1977) *Historic Buildings, Groups of Buildings, Buildings of Architectural Importance in Donaghadee and Portpatrick*, Belfast (Ulster Architectural Heritage Society).

– (2008) *An Introduction to Ulster Architecture*, Belfast (2nd edition, Ulster Architectural Heritage Society).

Dobbs, R. (1683) *A Briefe Description of the County of Antrim, begun the 3rd of May 1683*, reproduced in G. Hill (1873), 376–389.

Donnelly, C. (2012) 'Landscape and architecture', in eds C. Foley and C. Donnelly 2012, 22-45.

–   Moore, P., and McGranaghan, C. (2004) 'O'Connor's Stronghold, Derrywarragh Island, Maghery, County Armagh', *Ulster Journal of Archaeology* (3rd series) 63, 123–129.

–   Murray, E. and Logue, P. (2007) 'Excavating with Time Team at Castle Hill, Dungannon, Co. Tyrone', *Archaeology Ireland* 21(4), 16 –19.

–   Murray, E. and McHugh, R. (2008) 'Dungannon Castle: its history, architecture and archaeology', *Dúiche Néill* 17, 11–24.

–   Ruffell, A., Ó Néill, J.J., McSparron, C. and McHugh, R. (2012) 'Investigations at Bruce's Castle', in W. Forsythe and R. McConkey 2012, 159–166.

Downham, G. and Reynell, W.A. (1896) 'The estate of the diocese of Derry. Part IV. The Deanery of Rathlowry', *Ulster Journal of Archaeology* (1st series) 2(4), 253–261.

Drew, T. (1872) *The Ancient Church of St Nicholas, Carrickfergus*, Belfast (W. Erskine Mayne).

Duffy, P., Edwards, D. and FitzPatrick, E. eds (2001) *Gaelic Ireland: Land, Lordship and Settlement, c.1250–c.1650*, Dublin (Four Courts Press).

Dundas, W.H. (1913) *Enniskillen Parish and Town*, Enniskillen (William Tempest).

Dunleath, Lady D., Rankin, P.J. and Rowan, A.J. (1970) *Downpatrick*, Belfast (Ulster Architectural Heritage Society).

Dunlop, C. (2003) 'Rectory Close, Loughgall, Armagh', *Excavations 2003*, 11–12, no. 30 (also currently available via *http://www.excavations.ie*).

–   (2005a) '9–15 Queen Street, Belfast', *Excavations 2005*, 8, no. 19 (also currently available via *http://www.excavations.ie*).

–   (2005b) 'Talbot Street, Belfast', *Excavations 2005*, 9, no. 21 (also currently available via *http://www.excavations.ie*).

–   (2010) *Carrickfergus Methodist Church, Albert Road, Carrickfergus, Co. Antrim*, Belfast (unpublished excavation report in the archives of DfC:HED).

–   and Dunlop, A. (2005) *Invasive site works at St. Patrick's Parish Church, Glenarm*, Belfast (unpublished excavation report in the archives of DfC:HED).

Dunlop, R. (1905) '16th-century maps of Ireland', *English Historical Review* 20, 309–337.

Dwyer, P. (1893) *The Siege of Derry in 1689*, London (Elliot Stock).

Ellis, S.G. (1985) *Tudor Ireland, Crown, Community and the Conflict of Cultures 1470–1603*, London and New York (Longman).

Erne, Earl of (1896) 'An account of some plantation castles on the estates of the earl of Erne in the County of Fermanagh', *Ulster Journal of Archaeology* (2nd series) 2, 73–85.

Evans, E.E. (1945) 'Field archaeology in the Ballycastle district', *Ulster Journal of Archaeology* (3rd series) 8, 14–32.

Falls, C. (1950) *Elizabeth's Irish Wars*, London (Methuen & Co.).

Farrimond, C.J. (2006) '22 Church Road, Kilrea, Derry', *Excavations 2006*, 92, no. 422 (also currently available via *http://www.excavations.ie*).

Fennell, W. (1900) 'Layde Cross', *Ulster Journal of Archaeology* (2nd series) 6(3), 183.

Fitzpatrick, E. and O'Brien, C. (1998) *The Medieval Churches of County Offaly*, Dublin (Government of Ireland).

Fitzpatrick, T. (1904) 'The sack of "The Lurgan" (a study)', *Ulster Journal of Archaeology* (2nd series) 10(4), 170–187.

Foley, C. and McHugh, R. (2014) *An Archaeological Survey of County Fermanagh, Volume 1, Part 1: The prehistoric period, Part 2: The Early Christian and medieval periods*, Belfast (NIEA).

–   and C. Donnelly eds (2012) *Parke's Castle, Co. Leitrim: Archaeology, History and Architecture*, Dublin (The Stationary Office).

Ford, A., McGuire, J. and Milne, K. eds (1995) *As By Law Established, the Church of Ireland Since the Reformation*, Dublin (The Lilliput Press).

Forsythe, W. and McConkey, R. (2012) *Rathlin Island: An Archaeological Survey of a Maritime Landscape*, Belfast (NIEA, Northern Ireland Archaeological Monographs 8).

Gahan, A. (2003) *Archaeological Assessment at Bishopsgate, Coleraine*, Belfast (unpublished excavation report in the archives of DfC:HED).

–   (2007) '7–11 Castle Lane', *Excavations 2007*, 4, no. 21 (also currently available via *http://www.excavations.ie*).

–   and Long, C. (2006) 'Limavady Civic Centre, Derry', *Excavations 2006*, 92–93, no. 425 (also currently available via *http://www.excavations.ie*).

–   and Long, C. (2008) *Benburb Waste Water Treatment Works*, Belfast (unpublished archaeological evaluation report in the archives of DfC:HED).

Gailey, A. (1984) *Rural Houses of the North of Ireland*, Edinburgh (John Donald).

Gallogy, J. (1880) *The History of St. Patrick's Cathedral, Armagh*, Dublin (Gill and Son: also currently available via *https://archive.org*)

Gaskell-Brown, C. and Brannon, N.F. (1978) 'The rath in Hillsborough Fort, County Down', *Ulster Journal of Archaeology* (3rd series) 41, 78–87.

G.B. (1857) 'Old Belfast', *Ulster Journal of Archaeology* (1st series) 5, 343–344.

GPB = The Great Parchment Book of The Honourable The Irish Society (1639), London Metropolitan Archives, LMA reference CLA/049/EM/02/018 (also currently available via *http://www.greatparchmentbook.org*).

G.H. (1859) 'Chiefs of the Antrim MacDonnells prior to Sorley Boy', *Ulster Journal of Archaeology* (1st series) 7, 247–259.

Gilbert Coll. Ms. 101 = *A collection of some of the murders and massacres committed on the Irish in Ireland since the 23rd of October 1641. With some observations and falsifications on a late printed abstract of murthers said to be committed by the Irish*, published by R. S., London, 1662. In the hand of Walter Harris, 18th century, Dublin (Dublin City Library).

Gilbert, J. T. (1879) *A Contemporary History of Affairs in Ireland, from 1641 to 1652*, Vol. I, Part I, Dublin (for the Irish Archaeological and Celtic Society; also currently available on Internet Archive via *www.http://archive.org*).

Gillespie, R. (1985) *Colonial Ulster, the Settlement of East Ulster 1600–1641*, Cork (Cork University Press).

–   (1995) 'The religion of Irish Protestants: a view from the laity, 1580–1700' in eds A. Ford *et al.* 1995, 89–99.

–   (1997) *Devoted People, Belief and Religion in Early Modern Ireland*, Manchester (Manchester University Press).

– (2006) *Seventeenth-Century Ireland, Making Ireland Modern*, Dublin (Gill & Macmillan; New Gill History of Ireland 3).

Girvan, W.D. (1972) *Historic Buildings, Groups of Buildings, Areas of Architectural Importance in North Antrim*, Belfast (Ulster Architectural Heritage Society).

– Oram, R. and Rowan, A.J. (1969) *List of Historic Buildings, Groups of Buildings and Areas of Architectural Importance in Antrim and Ballymena*, Belfast (Ulster Architectural Heritage Society).

Girvan, W.D.R. and Rowan, A.J. (1970) *The Historic Buildings in West Antrim*, Belfast (Ulster Architectural Heritage Society).

Glancy, M. (1954) 'The church lands of Co. Armagh', *Seanchas Ardmhacha: Journal of the Armagh Diocesan Historical Society,* 1(1), 67–100.

– (1955) 'The incidence of the Plantation on the City of Armagh', *Seanchas Ardmacha: Journal of the Armagh Diocesan Historical Society* 1(2), 115–160.

Graham, J. (1841) *Ireland Preserved; or, the Siege of Londonderry and Battle of Aughrim*, London (R. Groombridge).

Grainger, J. (1862) 'Results of excavations in High Street, Belfast' *Ulster Journal of Archaeology* (1st series) 9, 113–21.

Green, E.R.R. (1949) *The Lagan Valley, 1800–1850: A Local History of the Industrial Revolution*, London (Faber & Faber).

Grose, F. (1791) *Antiquities of Ireland*, London (Hooper).

Gwynn, A. and Hadcock, R.N. (1970) *Medieval Religious Houses: Ireland: with an appendix to early sites*, London (Longmans: reprinted 1988).

Halpin, E. (1990) 'Castle Barracks, Enniskillen', *Excavations 1990*, 32, no.53 (also currently available via *http://www.excavations.ie).*

– (1991) 'Dromore Old Church, Dromore', *Excavations 1991*, 44, no.121 (also currently available via *http://www.excavations.ie).*

Hamlin, A.E. (1971) 'Church sites in Langfield Parish, Co. Tyrone', *Ulster Journal of Archaeology* (3rd series) 34, 79–83.

– (1983) 'Collation seats in Irish Cistercian houses: Grey Abbey, County Down and Graiguenamanagh, County Kilkenny', *Medieval Archaeology* 27, 156–158.

– (2008) *The Archaeology of Early Christianity in the North of Ireland*, Oxford (British Archaeological Reports, British Series 460).

– and Lynn, C.J. eds (1988) *Pieces of the Past*, Belfast (HMSO).

Hardy, P.D. (1834) *The Dublin Penny Journal: Volume II*, Dublin (J.S. Folds).

Harris, W. (1744) *Ancient and Present State of Co. Down*, Dublin (E. Ershaw).

Hayes-McCoy, G.A. (1964) *Ulster and Other Irish Maps, c. 1600*, Dublin (The Stationery Office for the Irish Manuscripts Commission).

– (1969) *Irish Battles – A Military History of Ireland*, Belfast (Appletree Press).

Herrup, C.B. (1999) *A House in Gross Disorder: Sex, Law and the 2ⁿᵈ Earl of Castlehaven*, Oxford (Oxford University Press).

Heslip, R. (2012) 'The coin hoard from Ballyconaghan', in Forsythe and McConkey 2012, 176–179.

Hickey, H. (1985) *Images of Stone: Figure Sculpture of the Lough Erne Basin*, Belfast (Blackstaff Press).

Hill, G. (1865) *The Stewarts of Ballintoy, with Notices of Other Families in the District in the Seventeenth Century*, Coleraine (John McCombie: also currently available via *https://archive.org*)).

– (1869) *The Montgomery Manuscripts: 1603–1706*, Belfast (Archer & Sons: also currently available via *https://archive.org*)).

– (1873) *The MacDonnells of Antrim*, Belfast (Archer & Sons: also currently available via *https://archive.org*)).

– (1877) *An Historical Account of the Plantation in Ulster at the Commencement of the Seventeenth century, 1608–1620*, Belfast (McCaw, Stevenson & Orr: also currently available via *https://archive.org*)).

Hist. MSS Comm. 1947 = Historical Manuscripts Commission (1947) 'A survey carried out by Sir Josias Bodley', in *Report on the Manuscripts of the late Reginald Rawdon Hastings, Esq., of the Manor House, Ashby De la Zouche*, 159–192, London (HMSO).

Horning, A. J. (2001) 'Dwelling houses in the old Irish barbarous manner: archaeological evidence for Gaelic architecture in an Ulster plantation village', in eds P.J. Duffy *et al.* 2001, 375–396.

– (2004) 'Archaeological explorations of cultural identity and rural economy in the north of Ireland: Goodland, Co. Antrim', *International Journal of Historical Archaeology* 8(3), 199–215.

– (2007) 'On the banks of the Bann: the riverine economy of an Ulster Plantation village', *Historical Archaeology* 41(3), 94–114.

– (2013a) *Ireland in the Virginian Sea: Colonialism in the British Atlantic*, Chapel Hill, NC (UNC Press Books).

– (2013b) '*Leim an Mhadraigh*: exploring unwanted histories of the Atlantic world', in eds P. E. Pope and S. Lewis-Simpson 2013, 93–102.

– and Brannon, N.F. (2007) *Excavations at Goodland, April 2007*, Belfast (unpublished excavation report in the archives of DfC:HED).

Hunt, J. (1974) *Irish Medieval Figure Sculpture 1200–1600: a study of Irish tombs with notes on costume and armour*, 2 vols, Dublin (Irish Academic Press).

Hunter, R.J. (1982) 'The town of Strabane' in ed. R.J. Hunter 1982, 27 –39.

– ed. (1982) *The Plantation in Ulster in Strabane Barony, Co. Tyrone, c. 1600–41*, Derry (New University of Ulster).

– (2004) 'Hamilton, James, first Viscount Claneboye (*c*.1560–1644)', *Oxford Dictionary of National Biography*, Oxford (Oxford University Press), (also currently available via *http://www.oxforddnb.com*).

– (2012) *The Ulster Plantation in the Counties of Armagh and Cavan, 1608–41*, Belfast (Ulster Historical Foundation).

Hurl, D. (1996a) Unpublished notes in SMR file for Ballygally Castle, Co. Antrim, in Northern Ireland Sites and Monuments Record (currently available via *www.http://apps.ehsni.gov.uk/ambit/Default.aspx*).

– (1996b) 'The White House, Ballyspurge, Down', *Excavations 1996*, 15, no. 62 (also currently available via *http://www.excavations.ie*).

Inq. Ulst. = Hardiman, J. ed. (1829) *Inquisitionum in Officio Rotulorum Cancellariae Hiberniae*

Asservatorum Repertorium, 2 vols, Dublin (Commissioners of the Public Records of Ireland).

Ivens, R.J., Simpson, D.D.A. and Brown, D. (1986) 'Excavations at Island McHugh 1985: Interim Report', *Ulster Journal of Archaeology* (3rd series) 49, 99–103.

Johnston, D.N. (2003) 'Carncastle: a fortified islet on the north-east coast of Co. Antrim', in eds J.R. Kenyon and K. O'Conor 2003, 217–238.

Johnston, J.D. (1972) *Clogher Cathedral Graveyard*, Omagh (Graham and Sons).

– (1976) *The Plantation of County Fermanagh, 1610–41: an Archaeological and Historical Survey*, Belfast (unpublished MA thesis, The Queen's University of Belfast).

– (1978) 'Scotch settlement of County Fermanagh, 1610–1630', *Clogher Record*, 9(3), 367–373.

– (1980a) 'Settlement and architecture in County Fermanagh, 1610–1641', *Ulster Journal of Archaeology* (3rd series) 43, 79–89.

– (1980b) 'Settlement patterns in County Fermanagh, 1610–1660', *Clogher Record* 10(2), 199–214.

Jope, E.M. (1950) 'Excavations at Carrickfergus, 1949–50', *Ulster Journal of Archaeology* (3rd series) 13, 61–65.

– (1951) 'Scottish influences in the north of Ireland: castles with Scottish features, 1580–1640', *Ulster Journal of Archaeology* (3rd series) 14, 31–47.

– (1953a) 'Castleraw, near Loughgall, Co. Armagh', *Ulster Journal of Archaeology* (3rd series) 16, 63–67.

– (1953b) 'Enniskillen Water-Gate: a further note', *Ulster Journal of Archaeology* (3rd series) 16, 68.

– (1954) 'Mongavlin Castle, Co. Donegal', *Ulster Journal of Archaeology* (2nd series) 17, 169–172.

– (1956) 'Lissan Rectory, Kilwaughter Castle, and the buildings in the North of Ireland Designed by John Nash', *Ulster Journal of Archaeology* (3rd series) 19, 121–130.

– (1958a) 'Castlecaulfield, Co. Tyrone', *Ulster Journal of Archaeology* (3rd series) 21, 101–107.

– (1958b) 'Portora Castle, near Enniskillen', *Ulster Journal of Archaeology* (3rd series) 21, 107–108.

– (1960) 'Moyry, Charlemont, Castleraw and Richhill: fortification to architecture in the north of Ireland, 1570–1700', *Ulster Journal of Archaeology* (3rd series) 23, 97–123.

– ed. (1961) *Studies in Building History: Essays in Recognition of the Work of B.H. St. John O'Neil*, London (Odhams Press).

Kelly, W.P. (2001) 'The Forgotten Siege of Derry, March–August, 1649', in W.P. Kelly ed. 2001, 31–52.

– ed. (2001) *The Sieges of Derry*, Dublin (Four Courts Press).

Kelly, B., Roycroft, N. and Stanley, M. eds (2012), *Encounters Between Peoples*, Dublin (Archaeology and the National Roads Authority Monograph Series no. 9).

Kenyon, J.R. and O'Conor, K. eds (2003) *The Medieval Castle in Ireland and Wales*, Dublin (Four Courts Press).

Kilner, D. and Bailie, W. (2008) 'Crebilly, Ballymena', *Excavations 2008*, 6–7, no. 24 (also currently available via *http://www.excavations.ie*).

Kilner, D. and McClorey, V. (2009) 'Holy Trinity Church, Lisnaskea', *Excavations 2009*, 98, no. 374 (also currently available via *http://www.excavations.ie*).

Klingelhöfer, E. (1999) 'Elizabethan settlements: Mogeely Castle, Curraglass, and Carrigeen, Co. Cork (Part 1)', *Journal of the Cork Historical and Archaeological Society* 104, 97–110.

–   (2000) 'Elizabethan settlements: Mogeely Castle, Curraglass, and Carrigeen, Co. Cork (Part 2)', *Journal of the Cork Historical and Archaeological Society* 105, 155–174.

Knox, A. (1875) *A History of the County of Down from the Most Remote to the Present Day*, Dublin (Hodges, Foster and Company).

Kovacik, J. and Bowen, P. (2007) 'Willowfield Church, Belfast', *Excavations 2007*, 6, no. 31 (also currently available via *http://www.excavations.ie*).

Lacey, B. (1981) 'Two seventeenth-century houses in Linenhall St., Londonderry', *Ulster Folklife* 27, 57–62.

–   (1990) *Siege City: The Story of Derry and Londonderry*, Belfast (Blackstaff Press).

–   (2006) *Cenel Conaill and the Donegal Kingdoms AD500–800*, Dublin (Four Courts Press).

Large, S. (2007) *Proposed Housing Development at Scotch Street, Moy Road, Portadown, Phase 3*, Belfast (unpublished excavation report in the archives of DfC:HED).

Latimer, W.T. (1896) 'The Battle of Benburb', *Journal of the Royal Society of Antiquaries of Ireland* 6 (1), 29–33.

Lawlor, H.C. (1939a), 'Killyleagh Castle, Co. Down', *Ulster Journal of Archaeology* (3rd series) 2, 15–21.

–   (1939b) 'Mote and mote-and-bailey castles in de Courcy's Principality of Ulster (Continued)', *Ulster Journal of Archaeology* (3rd series) 2, 46–54.

Leslie, J.B. (1911) *Armagh Clergy and Parishes: being an account of the clergy of the Church of Ireland in the Diocese of Armagh, from the earliest period, with historical notices of the several parishes, churches & c.*, Dundalk (William Tempest).

–   (1929) *Clogher Clergy and Parishes*, Enniskillen (printed for the author at the offices of the *Fermanagh Times* by R.H. Ritchie).

–   (1937) *Clergy of Derry and Raphoe*, Enniskillen (J. B. Leslie).

–   (1948) *Supplement to Armagh Clergy and Parishes*, Dundalk (W. Tempest, Dundalgan Press).

Lewis, S. (1837) *A Topographical Dictionary of Ireland*, Vols I and II, London (S. Lewis & Co.).

Loeber, R. (1991) *The Geography and Practice of English Colonisation in Ireland from 1534 to 1609*, Athlone (The Group for the Study of Irish Historic Settlement).

–   (2001) 'An architectural history of Gaelic castles and settlements, 1370–1600', in eds P.J. Duffy *et al.* 2001, 271–314.

Logue, P. (1998) 'Castle Walls, Antrim', *Excavations 1998*, 1, no. 1 (also currently available via *http://www.excavations.ie*).

–   (1999a) 'Bishop's Street Without, Derry', *Excavations 1999*, 38, no. 128 (also currently available via *http://www.excavations.ie*).

–   (1999b) 'Millennium Theatre, Derry', *Excavations 1999*, 38, no. 129 (also currently available via *http://www.excavations.ie*).

–   (2001) 'Abbey Street, Coleraine', *Excavations 2001*, 58, no. 247 (also currently available via *http://www.excavations.ie*).

Lowry, T.K. ed. (1867) *The Hamilton Manuscripts containing an account of the settlement of the territories of the Upper Clandeboye, Great Ardes, and Dufferin, in the county of Down.* Belfast (Archer and Sons).

Lowry-Corry, D. (1919) 'Ancient church sites and graveyards in Co. Fermanagh', *Journal of the Royal Society of Antiquaries of Ireland* 9(1), 35–46.

Luckombe, P. (1788) *The Compleat Irish Traveller*, London (Printed for the Proprietors and Sold by the Booksellers).

Lynn, C.J. (1975–76) 'Armagh City, Market Street', *Excavations 1975–76*, 7, no. 6 (also currently available via *http://www.excavations.ie*).

– (1988) 'Excavations at 46–48 Scotch Street, Armagh', *Ulster Journal of Archaeology* (3rd series) 51, 69–84.

Lynn, W.H. (1905) 'Notes on the ruins of Dunluce Castle, County of Antrim, with explanation of a reconstructed plan of the earlier fortress', Ulster Journal of Archaeology (2nd series) 11(3), 97–107.

Lyttleton, J. (2012) 'Natives and newcomers: plantation-era archaeology on Irish road schemes', in eds B. Kelly *et al.* 2012, 77–92.

– (2013a) *The Jacobean Plantations in Seventeenth-Century Offaly: An Archaeology of a Changing World*, Dublin (Four Courts Press).

– (2013b) 'The Lords Baltimore in Ireland', in eds P. E. Pope and S. Lewis-Simpson 2013, 259–269.

– and O'Keeffe, T. eds (2005) *The Manor in Medieval and Early Modern Ireland*, Dublin (Four Courts Press).

MacDonald, P. (2002) *Mahee Island, County Down*, Belfast (unpublished report in the archives of DfC:HED), (also currently available via *http://www.qub.ac.uk/schools/ CentreforArchaeologicalFieldworkCAF*).

– (2006) 'Excavations within the Woolworths and Burton building, High Street, Belfast', *Ulster Journal of Archaeology* (3rd series) 65, 49–62.

– (2008) 'Inisloughlin', *Excavations 2008*, 9–12, no. 33 (also currently available via *http://www.excavations.ie*).

– (2009) *Blundel's House, Dundrum Castle, Co. Down*, Belfast (unpublished report in the archives of DfC:HED), (also currently available via *http://www.qub.ac.uk/schools/ CentreforArchaeologicalFieldworkCAF*).

– (2011) 'Excavations at Blundell's House, Dundrum Castle', *Lecale Review* 9, 55–59.

MacDonnell, H. (1992) 'A seventeenth-century inventory from Dunluce Castle', *Journal of the Royal Society of Antiquaries of Ireland* 122, 109–27.

MacHaffie, F. G. (1975) *The Short Sea Route, Portpatrick–Donaghadee, Stranraer–Larne, Cairnryan–Larne*, Prescot, Merseyside (T. Stephenson and Sons).

MacManus, C. (2006a) 'Brookeborough', *Excavations 2006*, 173–174, no. 714 (also currently available via *http://www.excavations.ie*).

– (2006b) 'Magheralin', *Excavations 2006*, 116, no. 539 (also currently available via *http://www.excavations.ie*).

Marshall, J.J. (1896) 'Clogher-na-righ', *Journal for the Royal Society of Antiquaries of Ireland* 6, 278.

– (1905) 'The dialect of Ulster (continued)', *Ulster Journal of Archaeology* (2nd series) 11(2), 64–70.

– (1924a) *History of Charlemont Fort and Borough and of Mountjoy Fort*, Dungannon (Tyrone Printing Company).

– (1924b) *Benburb: Its Battlefields and Histories: with an Account of Blackwater-Foot and Coney Island*, Dungannon (Tyrone Printing Company).

– (1925) *Annals of Aughnacloy*, Dungannon (Tyrone Printing Company).

– (1930) *Clochar na Righ: being a history of the town of and district of Clogher, in the county of Tyrone. Also some account of the parish of Errigal Keerogue, in the county of Tyrone, and the parish of Errigal Truagh, in the county of Monaghan*, Dungannon (Tyrone Printing Company).

Mason, W.S. (1819) *A Statistical Account, Or, Parochial Survey of Ireland: Drawn Up From The Communications of the Clergy, Vol. III*, Dublin (Faulkner Press).

May = A. McL. May archive (unpublished and undated manuscript in the archives of DfC:HED).

McAlister, G. and Gault, A. (2015) 'The MacQuillans and Dunluce Castle', *Archaeology Ireland* 29(1), 9–11.

McCarthy, M. (2005) *Ships' Fastenings: from Sewn Boat to Steamship*, College Station, Texas (Texas A and M University Press).

McConnell, C. (1999) *The Family Chichester and Carrickfergus*, Carrickfergus (Carrickfergus Borough Council).

McConway, C. (1998) 'Bishopsgate, Coleraine', *Excavations 1998*, 24, no. 94 (also currently available via *http://www.excavations.ie*).

– (1999) 'St. Mary's Dominican Friary, Hanover Place, Coleraine', *Excavations 1999*, 36–37, no. 125 (also currently available via *http://www.excavations.ie*).

– (2001) 'Gordon Street, Belfast', *Excavations 2001*, 1–2, no. 7 (also currently available via http://www.excavations.ie).

McCracken, E. (1957) 'Charcoal burning ironworks in seventeenth and eighteenth-century Ireland', *Ulster Journal of Archaeology* (3rd series) 20, 123–138.

McCusker, P.J. (1982) 'Ballentaken – Beragh in the 17th century', *Seanchas Ardmacha: Journal of the Armagh Diocesan Historical Society* 10(2), 455–501.

McCutcheon, W.A. (1980) *Industrial Archaeology of Northern Ireland*, London (HMSO).

M'Enery, M.J. (1910) 'Destruction of Castle Mervyn, County Tyrone', *Journal of the Royal Society of Antiquaries of Ireland* 40(1), 58.

McErlean, T. (1984) *The Historical Development of the Park at Castle Coole,* Vol. I. (unpublished report for the National Trust in archives of DfC:HED).

– McConkey, R. and Forsythe, W. (2002) *Strangford Lough: An Archaeological Survey of the Maritime Cultural Landscape*, Belfast (Environment and Heritage Service, Northern Ireland Archaeological Monographs 6).

McGranaghan, C. (2007) 'An architectural survey of Dalway's Bawn, Ballyhill, County Antrim', *Ulster Journal of Archaeology* (3rd series) 66, 139–149.

– and McHugh, R. (2008) *Trillick, Co. Tyrone*, Belfast (unpublished report in the archives of DfC:HED), (also currently available via *http://www.qub.ac.uk/schools/CentreforArchaeologicalFieldworkCAF*).

McKay, P. (2007) *A Dictionary of Ulster Place-Names*, 2nd edition, Belfast (*Cló Ollscoil na Banríona*).

McKean, C. (2001) *The Scottish Chateau: The Country House of Renaissance Scotland*, Stroud (Sutton).

McKenna, J.E. (1896) 'Lisgool Abbey, County Fermanagh, with notes on some Maguire chalices', *Ulster Journal of Archaeology* (2nd series) 3(1), 50–54.

– (1900) 'The Dominicans and Franciscans of Bally MacManus and its neighbourhood, etc.', Ulster Journal of Archaeology, (2nd series) 6(3), 133–141.

–　　　(1920) *Parochial Records Diocese of Clogher, Monaghan*, Enniskillen (Fermanagh Herald).

McKillop, F. (2000) *History of Larne and East Antrim*, Ballymena (Ulster Journals).

McMullen, S. (2007) 'Antrim Castle Gardens'. *Excavations 2007*, 1–2, no. 3 (also currently available via *www.http://www.excavations.ie*).

McNeill, T.E. (1975) 'Ulster mottes: a checklist', *Ulster Journal of Archaeology* (3rd series) 38, 49–56.

–　　　(1981) *Carrickfergus Castle, County Antrim*, Belfast (HMSO).

–　　　(1983) 'The stone castles of northern County Antrim', *Ulster Journal of Archaeology* (3rd series) 46, 101–128.

–　　　(1987) 'The castle of Castlereagh, Co. Down', *Ulster Journal of Archaeology* (3rd series) 50, 123–128.

–　　　(1997) *Castles in Ireland, Feudal Power in a Gaelic World*, London and New York (Routledge).

–　　　(2001) 'The archaeology of Gaelic lordship east and west of the Foyle', in eds P. J. Duffy *et al.* (2001), 346–356.

–　　　(2004) 'Excavations at Dunineany Castle, Co. Antrim', *Journal of the Society for Medieval Archaeology* 48, 167–200.

McSparron, C. (2007) *Castle Curlews, Co. Tyrone*, Belfast (unpublished report in the archives of DfC:HED), (also available via *http://www.qub.ac.uk/schools/CentreforArchaeologicalFieldworkCAF*).

–　　　(2013) *St Augustine's, Co. Londonderry*, Belfast (unpublished report in the archives of DfC:HED), (also currently available via *http://www.qub.ac.uk/schools/CentreforArchaeologicalFieldworkCAF*).

–　　　and Mussen, S. (2013) *Prehen, Co. Londonderry*, Belfast (unpublished report in the archives of DfC:HED), (also currently available via *http://www.qub.ac.uk/schools/CentreforArchaeologicalFieldworkCAF*).

Meek, H. and Jope, E.M. (1958) 'The castle at Newtownstewart, Co. Tyrone', *Ulster Journal of Archaeology* (3rd series) 21, 109–114.

Miller, O.G. (1991) *Archaeological Investigations at Salterstown, County Londonderry, Northern Ireland*, (unpublished Ph.D. thesis, University of Pennsylvania).

Milligan, C.D. (1948) *The Walls of Derry: Their Building, Defending and Preserving*, 2 vols, Londonderry 1948 and 1950 (W&G Baird, re-printed in one volume by Ulster Society Publications, Lurgan, 1996).

Milligan, S.F. (1903) 'Ancient ecclesiastical bells in Ulster', *Journal of the Royal Society of Antiquaries of Ireland* 33(1), 46–57.

Mitchell, B. (1992) *The Making of Derry: An Economic History*, Londonderry (Genealogy Centre).

Moody, T.W. (1938) 'Ulster Plantation papers', *Analecta Hibernica* 8, 179–298.

–　　　(1939) *The Londonderry Plantation, 1609–41, the City of London and the Plantation in Ulster*, Belfast (William Mullan & Son).

Morrin, J. (1863) *Calendar of the Patent and Close Rolls of Chancery in Ireland of the Reign of Charles the First*, Dublin (HMSO / Alexander Thom).

Morris, H. (1911) 'Some Antiquities of Rathlin', *Ulster Journal of Archaeology* (2nd series) 17, 39–46.

Muhr, K. (2014) 'The place-names of County Fermanagh', in C. Foley and R. McHugh 2014, Vol. I.1, 17–54.

Mullin, T.H. (1979) *Coleraine in Bygone Centuries*, Belfast (Century Services).

Murphy, E and Manchester, K. (2002) 'Evidence for leprosy in medieval Ireland', in eds C.A. Roberts *et al.* 2002, 193–199.

Murray, E., Donnelly, C. and Logue, P. (2010) 'Rediscovering the O'Neill tower house and Chichester's military fort at Castle Hill, Dungannon', in eds E. Murray and P. Logue 2010, 84–88.

– and Logue, P. eds (2010) *Battles, Boats and Bones: Archaeological Discoveries in Northern Ireland, 1987–2008*, Belfast, (TSO Ireland and Northern Ireland Environment Agency).

Murray, E.V. (2010) 'St. Nicholas' Church, Carrickfergus', *Excavations 2010*, 6, no. 24 (also currently available via *http://www.excavations.ie*).

– (2011) *Ballycarry south-west, Co. Antrim*, Belfast (unpublished report in the archives of DfC:HED).

Mussen, S. (2012) *The O'Connor's Stronghold, Co. Armagh*, Belfast (unpublished report in the archives of DfC:HED), (also currently available via *http://www.qub.ac.uk/schools/CentreforArchaeologicalFieldworkCAF*).

Neill, K. (2009) *An Archaeological Survey of County Armagh*, Belfast (Northern Ireland Environment Agency).

Newman, C. (1991) 'Castlederg Castle, Castlesessiagh, Tyrone', *Excavations 1991*, 43–44, no. 119 (also currently available via *http://www.excavations.ie*).

Nicol, S. (2009) 'St. Paul's Church, Articlave Lower, Derry', *Excavations 2009*, 44, no. 175 (also currently available via *http://www.excavations.ie*).

Ó Baoill, R (1991) 'Toome Castle', *Excavations 1991*, 4, no. 10 (also currently available via *http://www.excavations.ie*).

– (1993) 'Recent excavations in medieval Carrickfergus', *Carrick and District Hist. J.*, 7, 54–63.

– (1998) 'Further excavations in medieval Carrickfergus', *Carrick and District Hist. J.*, 9, 25–32.

– (1999a) 'Newtownstewart Castle, Newtownstewart', *Excavations 1999*, 291–292, no. 841 (also currently available via *http://www.excavations.ie*).

– (1999b) 'Gordon Street, Belfast', *Excavations 1999*, 1, no. 5 (also currently available via *http://www.excavations.ie*).

– (2003) *Carrickfergus, Co. Antrim excavations 1991–1995*, Belfast (unpublished report in the archives of DfC:HED).

– (2005) 'Excavations at Newtownstewart Castle, County Tyrone', *Ulster Journal of Archaeology* 64, 62–105.

– (2006) 'Excavations at Castle Gardens, Lisburn', *Lisburn Historical Society Journal* 10, 21–25.

– (2008) *Carrickfergus: The Story of the Castle and Walled Town*, Belfast (Northern Ireland Environment Agency).

– (2011a) *Archaeological excavations at Quoile Castle, Co. Down*, Belfast (unpublished report in the archives of DfC:HED).

– (2011b) *Hidden History Below Our Feet: The Archaeological Story of Belfast*, Belfast (Northern Ireland Environment Agency).

– (2011c) *Archaeological excavations at Carrickfergus Methodist Church*, Belfast (unpublished report in the archives of DfC:HED).

– (2013) *Island City: The Archaeology of Derry~Londonderry*, Belfast (Northern Ireland Environment Agency and Derry City Council).

– and Logue, P. (2005) 'Excavations at Gordon Street and Waring Street, Belfast'. *Ulster Journal of Archaeology* (3rd series) 64, 106–139.

Ó Conluain, P. (1987) 'Benburb and the Powerscourts', *Dúiche Neill*, 1(2), 50.

O'Donovan, J. ed. and trans. (1848–1851) *Annals of the Kingdom of Ireland by The Four Masters from the Earliest Period to the Year 1616*, 7 vols, Dublin (Hodges, Smith and Company).

O'Dowd, M. ed. (2000) *Calendar of State Papers. Ireland. Tudor Period 1571–1575*, Kew and Dublin (revised edition: Public Record Office and Irish Manuscripts Commission).

Ó Fiaich, T. (1973) 'The O'Neills of the Fews', *Seanchas Ardmhacha: Journal of the Armagh Diocesan Historical Society*, 7(1), 1–64.

Ó Gallachair, P.F. (1958) 'A Fermanagh survey', *Clogher Record* 2(2), 293–310.

– (1974) *Old Fintona: A History of the Catholic Parish of Donaghcavey in County Tyrone*, Monaghan (Cumann Seanchais Chlochair).

O'Keeffe, J. (2008) *The Archaeology of the Later Cultural Landscape in Northern Ireland: Developing Historic Landscape Investigation for the Management of the Archaeological Resource: A Case Study of the Ards, County Down*, Coleraine (unpublished Ph.D. thesis, The University of Ulster).

O'Laverty, J. (1878–1887) *An Historical Account of the Diocese of Down and Connor, Ancient and Modern*, 4 vols, Dublin (J. Duffy and Sons and M.H. Gill and Son).

O'Neill, J. and Logue, P. (2008) 'Charlemont Fort . . . a brief guide', *History Armagh, Summer 2008*, 32–35.

O'Regan, C. (2007) 'Woodville House, Dougher', *Excavations 2007*, 17–18, no. 78 (also currently available via *http://www.excavations.ie*).

Oram, D. and Robinson, P.S. (1986) 'Inishargy House', *Journal of the Upper Ards Historical Society* 10, 26–28.

OS Revision Name Book 1857 = Anon. (1857) *Revision Name Book of 1857 of Enniskillen*. Dublin: Ordnance Survey.

O'Sullivan, A. (1998) 'Crannogs in contested landscapes', *Archaeology Ireland* 12(2), 14–15.

O'Sullivan, M. and Kennedy, L. (1998) 'The survival of archaeological monuments: trends and attitudes', *Irish Geography* 31(2), 88–99.

Ó Tuat-Gáill, E. (1911) 'The fort of Charlemont in Tir-Eoighin, and some of its associations', *Ulster Journal of Archaeology* (2nd series) 17(1), 47–73.

Parkinson, E. (1927) *The City of Downe from its earliest days*, Belfast (W. E. Mayne).

Paterson, T.G.F. (1948) 'The cult of the well in County Armagh', *Ulster Journal of Archaeology* (3rd series) 11, 127–130.

– (1961) 'County Armagh in 1622: a plantation survey', Seanchas Ardmhacha: Journal of the Armagh Diocesan Historical Society 4(1), 103–140.

Perceval-Maxwell, M. (1973) *The Scottish Migration to Ulster in the Reign of James I*, London (Routledge & Kegan Paul).

Pinkerton, W. (1859) 'The "Pallace" of Carrickfergus', *Ulster Journal of Archaeology* (1st series) 7, 1–10.

Pococke, R. (1752) *Pococke's Tour in Ireland in 1752*, Dublin (reprinted in 2010, Kessinger Publishing, Whitefish, Montana).

Pollock, W.G. (1975) *Six Miles from Bangor: the Story of Donaghadee*, Belfast (Appletree Press).

Pope, P.E. with Lewis-Simpson, S. eds (2013) *Exploring Atlantic Transitions, Archaeologies of Transience and Permanence in New Found Lands*, Woodbridge, Suffolk (The Boydell Press; The Society for Post-Medieval Archaeology Monograph 8).

Porter, Rev. C. (1901) 'Ballygally Castle', *Ulster Journal of Archaeology* (2nd series) 7(2), 65–77.

Pringle, A. (1935) *County Tyrone Antiquities*, Belfast (published by the author).

Proudfoot, V.B., Wilson, B.C.S., Collins, A.E.P., Jope, M. and Balfour-Browne, F.L. (1962) 'Further excavations at Larrybane promontory fort, Co. Antrim', *Ulster Journal of Archaeology* (3rd series) 24–25, 91–115.

PSAMNI = Chart, D.A. ed. (1940) *A Preliminary Survey of the Ancient Monuments of Northern Ireland*, Belfast (HMSO).

Quinn, D.B. (1933) 'Anglo-Irish Ulster in the early sixteenth century', *Proceedings of the Belfast Natural History and Philosophical Society* 1932–1933, 66–64.

Rankin, P. (1979) *List of Historic Buildings, Groups of Buildings & Areas of Architectural Importance in Rathfriland & Hilltown*, Belfast (Ulster Architectural Heritage Society).

Reeves, W. (1847) *Ecclesiastical Antiquities of Down, Connor and Dromore*, Dublin (Hodges and Smith).

– (1850) *Acts of Archbishop Colton in His Metropolitical Visitation of the Diocese of Derry, AD 1397*, Dublin (Irish Archaeological Society).

Reeves-Smyth, T. (1991) 'Antrim Castle Gardens', *Excavations 1991*, 1, no. 1 (also currently available via *http://www.excavations.ie*).

– (2014) 'Lordship architecture in medieval County Fermanagh', in C. Foley and R. McHugh 2014, Vol I.2, 329–341.

Roberts, C.A., Lewis, M.E. and Manchester, K. eds (2002) *The Past and Present of Leprosy*, Oxford (Archaeopress, British Archaeological Reports, International Series 1054).

Robinson, P.S. (1974) *The Plantation of County Tyrone in the Seventeenth Century*, Belfast (unpublished Ph.D. thesis, The Queens University of Belfast).

– (1979) 'Vernacular housing in Ulster in the seventeenth century', *Ulster Folklife* 25, 1–28.

– (1982) 'Further cruck houses in South Antrim: problems of cultural-historical interpretation', *Journal of the Royal Society of Antiquaries of Ireland* 112, 101–111.

– (1983) 'Some late survivals of box-framed "plantation" houses in Coleraine, County Londonderry', *Ulster Journal of Archaeology* (3rd series) 46, 129–36.

– (1984) *The Plantation of Ulster: British Settlement in an Irish Landscape, 1600–1670*, Dublin (Gill and MacMillan).

– (1985) 'From thatch to slate: innovations in roof covering materials for traditional houses in Ulster', *Ulster Folklife* 31, 21–23.

– and Brannon, N.F. (1982) 'A seventeenth-century house in New Row, Coleraine', *Ulster Journal of Archaeology* (3rd series) 44–45, 173–178.

Roe, H. (1960) 'A stone cross at Clogher, Co. Tyrone', *Journal of the Royal Society of Antiquaries of Ireland* 90(2), 190–206.

Rogers, M. (1967a) 'Archaeological fragments from Fermanagh', *Clogher Record* 6(2), 396.

– (1967b) *Prospect of the Erne*, Enniskillen (Watergate Press).

Roulston, W. (2004) *The Provision, Building and Architecture of Anglican Churches in the North of Ireland, 1600–1700*, Belfast (unpublished PhD thesis, The Queen's University of Belfast).

– (2005) 'Seventeenth-century manors in the barony of Strabane', in eds J. Lyttleton and T. O'Keeffe 2005, 160–187.

Rowan, A. (1979) *The Buildings of Ireland: North West Ulster, the counties of Londonderry, Donegal, Fermanagh, and Tyrone*, Harmondsworth, Middlesex (Penguin).

Salter, M. (1993) *Castles and Stronghouses of Ireland*, Worcester (Folly Publications).

Savage-Armstrong, G.F. (1888) *The Ancient and Noble Family of the Savages of the Ards*, London (Marcus Ward & Co.).

Scott, B.G. (2011) 'Plans and economies: defending the Plantation city of Londonderry', *The Journal of Irish Archaeology* 10, 141–154.

– ed. (2015) *Walls 400: Studies to Mark the 400th Anniversary of the Founding of the Walls of Londonderry*, Derry~Londonderry (Guildhall Press).

– Brown, R.R., Leacock, A and Salter C.J. (2008) *The Great Guns like Thunder: the cannon from the City of Derry*, Derry~Londonderry (Guildhall Press).

– McHugh, R. and Hunter, R.J. (2011) 'The use of cannon against Enagh Castle, Co. Londonderry', *Ulster Journal of Archaeology* (3rd series) 70, 83–112.

Shirley, E.P. (1855) 'Catalogue of maps and plans relating to Ireland, in Her Majesty's State Paper Office, Whitehall, London', *Ulster Journal of Archaeology* (1st series) 3, 272–291.

Sidebotham, J.M. (1950) 'A settlement in Goodland townland, Co. Antrim', *Ulster Journal of Archaeology* (3rd series) 13, 44–53.

Simington, R.C. ed. (1937) *The Civil Survey, 1654–1656, Counties of Donegal, Londonderry and Tyrone*, vol. III, Dublin (Irish Manuscripts Commission).

Simon, B. (2009) *If Trees Could Talk: the Story of Woodlands around Belfast*, Belfast (Forest of Belfast).

Simpson, M.L. and Dickson, A. (1981) 'Excavations in Carrickfergus, Co. Antrim, 1972–1979. A summary report on the excavations directed by the late T.G. Delaney', *Medieval Archaeology* 25, 78–89.

Skillen, J., McClintock, H.F. and Mogey, J.M. (1940) 'Correspondence', *Ulster Journal of Archaeology* (3rd series) 3, 172.

Sloan, B. (2007) *Portaferry, Co. Down,* Belfast (unpublished report in the archives of DfC:HED), (also currently available via *http://www.qub.ac.uk/schools/CentreforArchaeologicalFieldworkCAF*).

– (2010) *Magheraveely, Co. Fermanagh*, Belfast (unpublished report in the archives of DfC:HED), (also currently available via *http://www.qub.ac.uk/schools/CentreforArchaeologicalFieldworkCAF*).

Smyth, J. Rev. (1939) 'The parish of Glenravel. With notes on some of its parish priests', *Down and Connor Historical Society Journal* 10, 6–35.

Smyth, W.J. (2006) *Map-making, Landscapes and Memory: A Geography of Colonial and Early Modern Ireland c.1530–1750*, Cork (Cork University Press).

Steele, W.B. (1937) *The Parish of Devenish, County Fermanagh: Materials for its History*, Enniskillen, (Fermanagh Times).

Stevenson, J. (1920) *Two Centuries of Life in Down 1600–1800*, Belfast (McCaw, Stevenson & Orr).

Swift, M. (1999) *Historical Maps of Ireland*, Edison, New Jersey (Chartwell).

Taylor, G. and Skinner, A. (1778) *Maps of the Roads of Ireland Surveyed 1777*, London (G. Terry).

Thomas, A. (2012) *Derry~Londonderry. Irish Historic Towns Atlas No. 15*, Dublin (Royal Irish Academy).

Tilson, R. (undated) *A Guide and Brief History of St Mark's Church, Ballymore Parish,* Armagh (published privately: extract available at *http://www.ballymore.armagh.anglican.org*).

Treadwell, V. (1960) 'The Survey of Armagh and Tyrone, 1622', *Ulster Journal of Archaeology* (3rd series) 23, 126–137.

– (1964) 'The Survey of Armagh and Tyrone, 1622 (continued)', *Ulster Journal of Archaeology* (3rd series) 27, 140–154.

Trimble, W.C. (1919) *The History of Enniskillen with Reference to Some Manors in Co. Fermanagh, and Other Local Subjects,* Enniskillen (William Trimble).

Vinycomb, J. (1892) 'Historical and descriptive account of the City of Belfast', *Journal of the Royal Society of Antiquities of Ireland* 22, 323–326.

Wakeman, W.F. (1884) 'Report on some Plantation castles of County Fermanagh', *Journal of the Royal Society of Antiquarians of Ireland* 16, 147–148.

Walsh, F. (2013) *Archaeological excavation at lands adjacent to Carnbane Industrial Estate, Newry, Co. Down, Carnmee and Lisduff townlands,* Belfast (unpublished report in the archives of DfC:HED).

– (2014) *Final report of excavation of Bronze Age settlement and site of Plantation houses, Ballymagee, Co. Down*, Belfast (unpublished report in the archives of DfC:HED).

– (2016a) *Final report for excavations at Derrywoone, Baronscourt, Co. Tyrone, Ulster Scots Archaeological Research Project,* Belfast (unpublished report in the archives of DfC:HED).

– (2016b) *Final report for excavations at Monea Castle, Co. Fermanagh, Ulster Scots Archaeological Research Project,* Belfast (unpublished report in the archives of DfC:HED).

Waterman, D.M. (1951) 'Excavations at Dundrum Castle', *Ulster Journal of Archaeology* (3rd series) 14, 15–29.

– (1952) 'Excavations at the entrance to Carrickfergus Castle, 1950', *Ulster Journal of Archaeology* (3rd series) 15, 103–118.

– (1958) 'A note on medieval pottery from Nendrum and Grey Abbey, Co. Down', *Ulster Journal of Archaeology* (3rd series) 21, 67–73.

– (1959a) 'Castle Archdale, Co. Fermanagh', *Ulster Journal of Archaeology* (3rd series) 22, 119–123.

– (1959b) 'Tully Castle, Co. Fermanagh', *Ulster Journal of Archaeology* (3rd series) 22, 123–126.

– (1959c) 'Tullykelter Castle, Co. Fermanagh', *Ulster Journal of Archaeology* (3rd series) 22, 127–129.

– (1960) 'Sir John Davies and his Ulster buildings: Castlederg and Castle Curlews, Co. Tyrone', *Ulster Journal of Archaeology* (3rd series) 23, 89–96.

– (1961) 'Some Irish seventeenth-century houses and their architectural ancestry', in ed. E.M. Jope 1961, 251–274.

– (1962) *A guide to Narrow Water Castle, County Down,* Belfast (HMSO).

– (1964) 'The water supply of Dundrum Castle, Co. Down', *Ulster Journal of Archaeology* (3rd series) 27, 136–139.

– (1967a) 'A note on Strangford Castle, County Down', *Ulster Journal of Archaeology* (3rd series) 30, 83–86.

– (1967b) 'Agheeghter Castle, Co. Fermanagh', *Ulster Journal of Archaeology* (3rd series) 30, 87–88.

– (1968) 'Castle Balfour, Lisnaskea, Co. Fermanagh', *Ulster Journal of Archaeology* (3rd series) 31, 71–76.

–   (1969) 'Callowhill Church, Co. Fermanagh', *Ulster Journal of Archaeology* (3rd series) 32, 113.

–   (1971) 'Derrygonnelly Church, Co. Fermanagh', *Ulster Journal of Archaeology* (3rd series) 34, 110–12.

–   and Morton, W.R.M. (1958) 'A note on Dundrum Castle', *Ulster Journal of Archaeology* (3rd series) 21, 63–66.

Wauchope, G.M. (1929) *The Ulster Branch of The Family of Wauchope, Wauhope, Wahab, Waughop, Etc.* London (Marshall).

Williams, B.B. (1985) 'An earthwork in Slievenacloy townland, County Antrim', *Ulster Journal of Archaeology* (3rd series) 48, 149–152.

Wilson, A.M. (1991) 'Lords of Downpatrick 1512–1617', *Lecale Miscellany* 9, 59–65.

Young, R.M. (1895) *Historical Notices of Old Belfast and Its Vicinity*, Belfast (Marcus Ward).

–   (1913) *Historical Notes on the Parish of Kildress*, Cookstown (printed at the Mid-Ulster Printing Works).

Illustration Credits

Chapter Dividers (in order of appearance)

Down Survey barony map of Clanawley, Co. Fermanagh. Courtesy of Trinity College Dublin

Richard Bartlett 'Drawing of Enish Loughan fort, Co. Antrim', 1602. This image is reproduced courtesy of the National Library of Ireland (MS2656-6)

Crown Copyright. DfC-HED

Monea Castle. IAC Archaeology.

Richard Bartlett 'Drawing of Dungannon Castle and the Stone Chair at Tullahogue, Co. Tyrone', 1602. This image is reproduced courtesy of the National Library of Ireland (MS2656-5)

Map of the 'Baronie of Fues'. Courtesy of the National Archives (NA MPF 1/60)

Derry. Courtesy of the National Archives (SP 63/207)

Thomas Raven map of Clandeboye Estate (PRONI T870/1). Courtesy of Ards and North Down Borough Council

Richard Bartlett 'Plan of Charlemont Fort and bridge over the Blackwater', 1602. This image is reproduced courtesy of the National Library of Ireland (MS2656-4)

1. Introduction

1.1 AECOM/IAC Archaeology

1.2 Rowan McLaughlin, based upon Land & Property Services data with the permission of the Controller of Her Majesty's Stationery Office, © Crown copyright and database rights MOU 204

1.3 Thomas Raven map of Clandeboye Estate (PRONI T870/1). Courtesy of Ards and North Down Borough Council

2. Antrim

2.1 Rowan McLaughlin, based upon Land & Property Services data with the permission of the Controller of Her Majesty's Stationery Office, © Crown copyright and database rights MOU 204

2.2 Rowan McLaughlin, based upon Land & Property Services data with the permission of the Controller of Her Majesty's Stationery Office, © Crown copyright and database rights MOU 204

2.3 Rowan McLaughlin, based upon Land & Property Services data with the permission of the Controller of Her Majesty's Stationery Office, © Crown copyright and database rights MOU 204

2.4 Thomas Phillip's 1685 map of Belfast. Courtesy of the British Library Board (Maps.K.Top.51.37)

2.5 Crown Copyright. DfC-HED

2.6 Courtesy of Northern Archaeological Consultancy

2.7 Rowan McLaughlin, based upon Land & Property Services data with the permission of the Controller of Her Majesty's Stationery Office, © Crown copyright and database rights MOU 204

2.8 Down Survey barony map of Belfast. Courtesy of Trinity College Dublin.

2.9 Crown Copyright. DfC-HED

2.10 AECOM/IAC Archaeology

2.11 Rowan McLaughlin, based upon Land & Property Services data with the permission of the Controller of Her Majesty's Stationery Office, © Crown copyright and database rights MOU 204

2.12 Crown Copyright. DfC-HED

2.13 Rowan McLaughlin, based upon Land & Property Services data with the permission of the Controller of Her Majesty's Stationery Office, © Crown copyright and database rights MOU 204

2.14 Crown Copyright. DfC-HED

2.15 Crown Copyright. DfC-HED

2.16 Crown Copyright. DfC-HED

2.17 Crown Copyright. DfC-HED

2.18 Crown Copyright. DfC-HED

2.19 Crown Copyright. DfC-HED

2.20 Crown Copyright. DfC-HED

2.21 Rowan McLaughlin

2.22 Crown Copyright. DfC-HED

2.23 Crown Copyright. DfC-HED

2.24 Crown Copyright. DfC-HED

2.26 Crown Copyright. DfC-HED

2.27 Down Survey barony map of Belfast. Courtesy of Trinity College Dublin

2.28 Rowan McLaughlin, based upon Land & Property Services data with the permission of the Controller of Her Majesty's Stationery Office, © Crown copyright and database rights MOU 204

2.29 Crown Copyright. DfC-HED

2.30 AECOM/IAC Archaeology

2.31 Paul Logue

2.32 Rowan McLaughlin, based upon Land & Property Services data with the permission of the Controller of Her Majesty's Stationery Office, © Crown copyright and database rights MOU 204

2.33 Rowan McLaughlin, based upon Land & Property Services data with the permission of the Controller of Her Majesty's Stationery Office, © Crown copyright and database rights MOU 204

2.34 Crown Copyright. DfC-HED

2.35 Crown Copyright. DfC-HED

2.36 Crown Copyright. DfC-HED

2.37 Crown Copyright. DfC-HED

2.38 Rowan McLaughlin, based upon Land & Property Services data with the permission of the Controller of Her Majesty's Stationery Office, © Crown copyright and database rights MOU 204

2.39 AECOM/IAC Archaeology

2.40 Rowan McLaughlin, based upon Land & Property Services data with the permission of the Controller of Her Majesty's Stationery Office, © Crown copyright and database rights MOU 204

2.41 Down Survey parish map of Kilfaghtrim. Deputy Keeper of the Records, Public Record Office of Northern Ireland (PRONI D597/2)

2.42 Rowan McLaughlin, based upon Land & Property Services data with the permission of the Controller of Her Majesty's Stationery Office, © Crown copyright and database rights MOU 204

2.43 Rowan McLaughlin

2.44 Rowan McLaughlin, based upon Land & Property Services data with the permission of the Controller of Her Majesty's Stationery Office, © Crown copyright and database rights MOU 204

2.45 Crown Copyright. DfC-HED

2.46 Rowan McLaughlin, based upon Land & Property Services data with the permission of the Controller of Her Majesty's Stationery Office, © Crown copyright and database rights MOU 204

2.47 Rowan McLaughlin, based upon Land & Property Services data with the permission of the Controller of Her Majesty's Stationery Office, © Crown copyright and database rights MOU 204

2.48 Rowan McLaughlin, based upon Land & Property Services data with the permission of the Controller of Her Majesty's Stationery Office, © Crown copyright and database rights MOU 204

2.49 Crown Copyright. DfC-HED

2.50 Crown Copyright. DfC-HED

2.51 Crown Copyright. DfC-HED

2.52 Crown Copyright. DfC-HED

2.53 Courtesy of Centre for Archaeological Fieldwork QUB

2.54 Crown Copyright. DfC-HED

2.55 Crown Copyright. DfC-HED

2.56 AECOM/IAC Archaeology

2.57 AECOM/IAC Archaeology

2.58 Rowan McLaughlin, based upon Land & Property Services data with the permission of the Controller of Her Majesty's Stationery Office, © Crown copyright and database rights MOU 204

2.59 Rowan McLaughlin

2.60 Rowan McLaughlin, based upon Land & Property Services data with the permission of the Controller of Her Majesty's Stationery Office, © Crown copyright and database rights MOU 204

2.61 Rowan McLaughlin

2.62 Rowan McLaughlin, based upon Land & Property Services data with the permission of the Controller of Her Majesty's Stationery Office, © Crown copyright and database rights MOU 204

2.63 Dublin Penny Journal

2.64 Crown Copyright. DfC-HED

2.65 Crown Copyright. DfC-HED

2.66 James Lyttleton

2.67 Crown Copyright. DfC-HED

2.68 Crown Copyright. DfC-HED

2.69 AECOM/IAC Archaeology

2.70 Crown Copyright. DfC-HED

2.71 Rowan McLaughlin, based upon Land & Property Services data with the permission of the Controller of Her Majesty's Stationery Office, © Crown copyright and database rights MOU 204

2.72 AECOM/IAC Archaeology

2.73 Down Survey parish map of Connor. Deputy Keeper of the Records, Public Record Office of Northern Ireland (PRONI D/597)

2.74 AECOM/IAC Archaeology

2.75 AECOM/IAC Archaeology

2.76 Rowan McLaughlin, based upon Land & Property Services data with the permission of the Controller of Her Majesty's Stationery Office, © Crown copyright and database rights MOU 204

2.77 Crown Copyright. DfC-HED

2.78 Rowan McLaughlin, based upon Land & Property Services data with the permission of the Controller of Her Majesty's Stationery Office, © Crown copyright and database rights MOU 204

2.79 Richard Bartlett 'Drawing of Enish Loughan fort, Co. Antrim', 1602. This image is reproduced courtesy of the National Library of Ireland (MS2656-6)

2.80 Crown Copyright. DfC-HED

2.81 Crown Copyright. DfC-HED

Ballygally Exemplar Figures
1-3 Crown Copyright. DfC-HED

Dunluce
4, 6, 7 Crown Copyright. DfC-HED

3. Down

3.1 Rowan McLaughlin, based upon Land & Property Services data with the permission of the Controller of Her Majesty's Stationery Office, © Crown copyright and database rights MOU 204
3.2 Rowan McLaughlin, based upon Land & Property Services data with the permission of the Controller of Her Majesty's Stationery Office, © Crown copyright and database rights MOU 204
3.3 Rowan McLaughlin, based upon Land & Property Services data with the permission of the Controller of Her Majesty's Stationery Office, © Crown copyright and database rights MOU 204
3.4 Thomas Raven map of Clandeboye Estate (PRONI T870/1). Courtesy of Ards and North Down Borough Council
3.5 Thomas Raven map of Clandeboye Estate (PRONI T870/1). Courtesy of Ards and North Down Borough Council
3.6 Crown Copyright. DfC-HED
3.7 Crown Copyright. DfC-HED
3.8 Thomas Raven map of Clandeboye Estate (PRONI T870/1). Courtesy of Ards and North Down Borough Council
3.9 AECOM/IAC Archaeology
3.10 Thomas Raven map of Clandeboye Estate (PRONI T870/1). Courtesy of Ards and North Down Borough Council
3.11 Thomas Raven map of Clandeboye Estate (PRONI T870/1). Courtesy of Ards and North Down Borough Council
3.12 Thomas Raven map of Clandeboye Estate (PRONI T870/1). Courtesy of Ards and North Down Borough Council
3.13 Thomas Raven map of Clandeboye Estate (PRONI T870/1). Courtesy of Ards and North Down Borough Council
3.14 Crown Copyright. DfC-HED
3.15 Crown Copyright. DfC-HED
3.16 Crown Copyright. DfC-HED
3.17 AECOM/IAC Archaeology
3.18 Crown Copyright. DfC-HED
3.19 Rowan McLaughlin, based upon Land & Property Services data with the permission of the Controller of Her Majesty's Stationery Office, © Crown copyright and database rights MOU 2043.20 Crown Copyright. DfC-HED
3.20 Crown copyright. DfC-HED
3.21 Crown Copyright. DfC-HED
3.22 Crown Copyright. DfC-HED
3.23 Crown Copyright. DfC-HED
3.24 Crown Copyright. DfC-HED

3.25 Rowan McLaughlin, based upon Land & Property Services data with the permission of the Controller of Her Majesty's Stationery Office, © Crown copyright and database rights MOU 204

3.26 Crown Copyright. DfC-HED

3.27 Crown Copyright. DfC-HED

3.28 Crown Copyright. DfC-HED

3.29 Rowan McLaughlin, based upon Land & Property Services data with the permission of the Controller of Her Majesty's Stationery Office, © Crown copyright and database rights MOU 204

3.30 Rowan McLaughlin, based upon Land & Property Services data with the permission of the Controller of Her Majesty's Stationery Office, © Crown copyright and database rights MOU 204

3.31 Crown Copyright. DfC-HED

3.32 Rowan McLaughlin

3.33 Thomas Raven map of Clandeboye Estate (PRONI T870/1). Courtesy of Ards and North Down Borough Council

3.34 Crown Copyright. DfC-HED

3.35 Crown Copyright. DfC-HED

3.36 Thomas Raven map of Clandeboye Estate (PRONI T870/1). Courtesy of Ards and North Down Borough Council

3.37 Crown Copyright. DfC-HED

3.38 Crown Copyright. DfC-HED

3.39 Rowan McLaughlin, based upon Land & Property Services data with the permission of the Controller of Her Majesty's Stationery Office, © Crown copyright and database rights MOU 204

3.40 Crown Copyright. DfC-HED

3.41 Thomas Raven map of Clandeboye Estate (PRONI T870/1). Courtesy of Ards and North Down Borough Council

3.42 Crown Copyright. DfC-HED

3.43 Rowan McLaughlin, based upon Land & Property Services data with the permission of the Controller of Her Majesty's Stationery Office, © Crown copyright and database rights MOU 204

3.44 Crown Copyright. DfC-HED

3.45 Crown Copyright. DfC-HED

3.46 Crown Copyright. DfC-HED

3.47 Crown Copyright. DfC-HED

3.48 Crown Copyright. DfC-HED

3.49 Crown Copyright. DfC-HED

3.50 Crown Copyright. DfC-HED

3.51 Down Survey barony map of Lecale. Courtesy of Trinity College Dublin.

3.52 Down Survey barony map of Lecale. Courtesy of Trinity College Dublin.

3.53 Rowan McLaughlin, based upon Land & Property Services data with the permission of the Controller of Her Majesty's Stationery Office, © Crown copyright and database rights MOU 204

3.54 Crown Copyright. DfC-HED

3.55 Crown Copyright. DfC-HED

3.56 Crown Copyright. DfC-HED

3.57 Crown Copyright. DfC-HED

3.58 Rowan McLaughlin, based upon Land & Property Services data with the permission of the Controller of Her Majesty's Stationery Office, © Crown copyright and database rights MOU 204

3.59 Crown Copyright. DfC-HED

3.60 Crown Copyright. DfC-HED

3.61 Crown Copyright. DfC-HED

3.62 Rowan McLaughlin

3.63 Rowan McLaughlin, based upon Land & Property Services data with the permission of the Controller of Her Majesty's Stationery Office, © Crown copyright and database rights MOU 204

3.64 Crown Copyright. DfC-HED

3.65 Crown Copyright. DfC-HED

3.66 Crown Copyright. DfC-HED

3.67 Crown Copyright. DfC-HED

3.68 Rowan McLaughlin, based upon Land & Property Services data with the permission of the Controller of Her Majesty's Stationery Office, © Crown copyright and database rights MOU 204

Servants Hill Exemplar Figures

8 Thomas Raven map of Clandeboye Estate (PRONI T870/1). Courtesy of Ards and North Down Borough Council

9-11 IAC Archaeology

4. Fermanagh

4.1 Rowan McLaughlin, based upon Land & Property Services data with the permission of the Controller of Her Majesty's Stationery Office, © Crown copyright and database rights MOU 204

4.2 Rowan McLaughlin, based upon Land & Property Services data with the permission of the Controller of Her Majesty's Stationery Office, © Crown copyright and database rights MOU 2044.3 Crown Copyright. DfC-HED

4.3 Crown Copyright. DfC-HED

4.4 Crown Copyright. DfC-HED

4.5 Crown Copyright. DfC-HED

4.6 AECOM/IAC Archaeology

4.7 Crown Copyright. DfC-HED

4.8 Crown Copyright. DfC-HED

4.9 Crown Copyright. DfC-HED

4.10 AECOM/IAC Archaeology

4.11 Rowan McLaughlin, based upon Land & Property Services data with the permission of the Controller of Her Majesty's Stationery Office, © Crown copyright and database rights MOU 204

4.12 Rowan McLaughlin, based upon Land & Property Services data with the permission of the Controller of Her Majesty's Stationery Office, © Crown copyright and database rights MOU 204

4.13 Rowan McLaughlin, based upon Land & Property Services data with the permission of the Controller of Her Majesty's Stationery Office, © Crown copyright and database rights MOU 204

4.14 AECOM/IAC Archaeology

4.15 Down Survey barony map of Clanawley. Courtesy of Trinity College Dublin.

4.16 Rowan McLaughlin, based upon Land & Property Services data with the permission of the Controller of Her Majesty's Stationery Office, © Crown copyright and database rights MOU 204

4.17 Crown Copyright. DfC-HED

4.18 Crown Copyright. DfC-HED

4.19 AECOM/IAC Archaeology

4.20 Crown Copyright. DfC-HED

4.21 Crown Copyright. DfC-HED

4.22 Rowan McLaughlin, based upon Land & Property Services data with the permission of the Controller of Her Majesty's Stationery Office, © Crown copyright and database rights MOU 204

4.23 Rowan McLaughlin, based upon Land & Property Services data with the permission of the Controller of Her Majesty's Stationery Office, © Crown copyright and database rights MOU 204

2.24 Rowan McLaughlin, based upon Land & Property Services data with the permission of the Controller of Her Majesty's Stationery Office, © Crown copyright and database rights MOU 204

4.25 Crown Copyright. DfC-HED

4.26 Crown Copyright. DfC-HED

4.27 Courtesy of Gavin Donaghy

4.28 IAC Archaeology

4.29 Crown Copyright. DfC-HED

4.30 Crown Copyright. DfC-HED

4.31 Crown Copyright. DfC-HED

4.32 Crown Copyright. DfC-HED

4.33 Crown Copyright. DfC-HED

4.34 Crown Copyright. DfC-HED

4.35 AECOM/IAC Archaeology

Monea Castle Exemplar

12-15 IAC Archaeology

5. Tyrone

5.1 Rowan McLaughlin, based upon Land & Property Services data with the permission of the Controller of Her Majesty's Stationery Office, © Crown copyright and database rights MOU 204

5.2 Rowan McLaughlin, based upon Land & Property Services data with the permission of the Controller of Her Majesty's Stationery Office, © Crown copyright and database rights MOU 204

5.3 Loch Swilly and the River Foyle (National Archives MPF 1/335/1)

5.4 IAC Archaeology

5.5 IAC Archaeology

5.6 Reproduced from Land & Property Services data with the permission of the Controller of Her Majesty's Stationery Office, © Crown copyright and database rights MOU 204

5.7 – 5.10 Crown Copyright. DfC-HED

5.11 AECOM/IAC Archaeology

5.12 Rowan McLaughlin, based upon Land & Property Services data with the permission of the Controller of Her Majesty's Stationery Office, © Crown copyright and database rights MOU 204

5.13 Down Survey barony map of Omagh. Courtesy of Trinity College Dublin.

5.14 Crown Copyright. DfC-HED

5.15 AECOM/IAC Archaeology

5.16 Crown Copyright. DfC-HED

5.17 Crown Copyright. DfC-HED

5.18 Crown Copyright. DfC-HED

5.19 Rowan McLaughlin, based upon Land & Property Services data with the permission of the Controller of Her Majesty's Stationery Office, © Crown copyright and database rights MOU 204

5.20 Augher Castle. Courtesy of Buildings of Ireland Collection/Alistair Rowan, Irish Architectural Archive

5.21 Crown Copyright. DfC-HED

5.22 Crown Copyright. DfC-HED

5.23 Crown Copyright. DfC-HED

5.24 AECOM/IAC Archaeology

5.25 Rowan McLaughlin, based upon Land & Property Services data with the permission of the Controller of Her Majesty's Stationery Office, © Crown copyright and database rights MOU 204

5.26 AECOM/IAC Archaeology

5.27 Richard Bartlett 'Drawing of Dungannon Castle and the Stone Chair at Tullahogue, Co. Tyrone, 1602. This image is reproduced courtesy of the National Library of Ireland (MS2656-5)

5.28 Crown Copyright. DfC-HED

5.29 Crown Copyright. DfC-HED

5.30 Crown Copyright. DfC-HED

5.31 Rowan McLaughlin, based upon Land & Property Services data with the permission of the Controller of Her Majesty's Stationery Office, © Crown copyright and database rights MOU 204

5.32 Richard Bartlett 'Drawing of Dungannon Castle and the Stone Chair at Tullahogue, Co. Tyrone, 1602. This image is reproduced courtesy of the National Library of Ireland (MS2656-5)

5.33 Courtesy of Centre for Archaeological Fieldwork, QUB.

5.34 Down Survey parish map of Aghalow, Carneteale and Killeshill. Courtesy of Deputy Keeper of the Records, PRONI D/597/4

5.35 – 5.42 Crown Copyright. DfC-HED

5.43 AECOM/IAC Archaeology

5.44 AECOM/IAC Archaeology

5.45 – 5.46 Richard Bartlett 'A description of the valley of Blackwater showing fortified positions of Irish and English in the O'Neill wars, 1602'. Courtesy of National Library of Ireland (MS2656-8)

5.47 Richard Bartlett 'Plan of Charlemont Fort and bridge over the Blackwater'. This image is reproduced courtesy of the National Library of Ireland (MS2656-4)

5.48 Down Survey parish map of Carnetele, Aghavow and Killishel. Courtesy of Deputy Keeper of the Records, PRONI D/597/4

5.49 AECOM/IAC Archaeology

5.50 AECOM/IAC Archaeology

Derrywoone Exemplar Site

16-19 IAC Archaeology

6. Armagh

6.1 Rowan McLaughlin, based upon Land & Property Services data with the permission of the Controller of Her Majesty's Stationery Office, © Crown copyright and database rights MOU 204

6.2 Rowan McLaughlin, based upon Land & Property Services data with the permission of the Controller of Her Majesty's Stationery Office, © Crown copyright and database rights MOU 204

6.3 Rowan McLaughlin, based upon Land & Property Services data with the permission of the Controller of Her Majesty's Stationery Office, © Crown copyright and database rights MOU 204

6.4 Rowan McLaughlin, based upon Land & Property Services data with the permission of the Controller of Her Majesty's Stationery Office, © Crown copyright and database rights MOU 204

6.5 Crown Copyright. DfC-HED

6.6 Crown Copyright. DfC-HED

6.7 Rowan McLaughlin, based upon Land & Property Services data with the permission of the Controller of Her Majesty's Stationery Office, © Crown copyright and database rights MOU 204

6.8 Crown Copyright. DfC-HED

6.9 Rowan McLaughlin, based upon Land & Property Services data with the permission of the Controller of Her Majesty's Stationery Office, © Crown copyright and database rights MOU 204

6.10 AECOM/IAC Archaeology

6.11 Map of the 'Baronie of Fues' (National Archives MPF 1/60)

6.12 Crown Copyright. DfC-HED

6.13 Crown Copyright. DfC-HED

6.14 Map of the 'Baronie of Fues' (National Archives MPF 1/60)

6.15 Rowan McLaughlin, based upon Land & Property Services data with the permission of the Controller of Her Majesty's Stationery Office, © Crown copyright and database rights MOU 204

6.16 Rowan McLaughlin, based upon Land & Property Services data with the permission of the Controller of Her Majesty's Stationery Office, © Crown copyright and database rights MOU 204

6.17 Map of the 'Baronie of Orier' (National Archives MPF 1/59)

6.18 Rowan McLaughlin, based upon Land & Property Services data with the permission of the Controller of Her Majesty's Stationery Office, © Crown copyright and database rights MOU 204

6.19 Rowan McLaughlin, based upon Land & Property Services data with the permission of the Controller of Her Majesty's Stationery Office, © Crown copyright and database rights MOU 204

6.20 Crown Copyright. DfC-HED

6.21 Richard Bartlett 'Plan of Charlemont Fort and bridge over the Blackwater'. This image is reproduced courtesy of the National Library of Ireland (MS2656-4)

6.22 Rowan McLaughlin, based upon Land & Property Services data with the permission of the Controller of Her Majesty's Stationery Office, © Crown copyright and database rights MOU 204

6.23 Crown Copyright. DfC-HED

7. Londonderry

7.1 Rowan McLaughlin, based upon Land & Property Services data with the permission of the Controller of Her Majesty's Stationery Office, © Crown copyright and database rights MOU 204

7.2 Rowan McLaughlin, based upon Land & Property Services data with the permission of the Controller of Her Majesty's Stationery Office, © Crown copyright and database rights MOU 204

7.3 Courtesy of Deputy Keeper of the Records (PRONI T510/1)

7.4 Rowan McLaughlin, based upon Land & Property Services data with the permission of the Controller of Her Majesty's Stationery Office, © Crown copyright and database rights MOU 204

7.5 Crown Copyright. DfC-HED

7.6 Crown Copyright. DfC-HED

7.7 Courtesy of Deputy Keeper of the Records (PRONI T510/1)

7.8 Crown Copyright. DfC-HED

7.9 Phillip's painting of Derry. Courtesy of The British Library Board (Maps.K.Top.54.33.a)

7.10 Courtesy of Deputy Keeper of the Records (PRONI T510/1)

7.11 Crown Copyright. DfC-HED

7.12 Crown Copyright. DfC-HED

7.13 Derry. Courtesy of the National Archives (SP 63/207)

7.14 Courtesy of Deputy Keeper of the Records (PRONI T510/1)

7.15 Crown Copyright. DfC-HED

7.16 Courtesy of Deputy Keeper of the Records (PRONI T510/1)

7.17 AECOM/IAC Archaeology

7.18 Courtesy of Deputy Keeper of the Records (PRONI T510/1)

7.19 Rowan McLaughlin, based upon Land & Property Services data with the permission of the Controller of Her Majesty's Stationery Office, © Crown copyright and database rights MOU 204

7.20 Courtesy of Deputy Keeper of the Records (PRONI T510/1)

7.21 Courtesy of Deputy Keeper of the Records (PRONI T510/1)

7.22 Crown Copyright. DfC-HED

7.23 Courtesy of Deputy Keeper of the Records (PRONI T510/1)

7.24 Courtesy of Deputy Keeper of the Records (PRONI T510/1)

7.25 Courtesy of Deputy Keeper of the Records (PRONI T510/1)

7.26 Courtesy of Deputy Keeper of the Records (PRONI T510/1)

7.27 Crown Copyright. DfC-HED

7.28 Courtesy of Deputy Keeper of the Records (PRONI T510/1)

7.29 Crown Copyright. DfC-HED

7.30 Courtesy of Deputy Keeper of the Records (PRONI T510/1)

7.31 Courtesy of Deputy Keeper of the Records (PRONI T510/1)

7.32 Courtesy of Deputy Keeper of the Records (PRONI T510/1)

7.33 Crown Copyright. DfC-HED

7.34 Courtesy of Deputy Keeper of the Records (PRONI T510/1)

7.35 Courtesy of Deputy Keeper of the Records (PRONI T510/1)

7.36 Courtesy of Deputy Keeper of the Records (PRONI T510/1)

7.37 Courtesy of Deputy Keeper of the Records (PRONI T510/1)

7.38 Courtesy of Deputy Keeper of the Records (PRONI T510/1)

7.39 Courtesy of Deputy Keeper of the Records (PRONI T510/1)

7.40 Courtesy of Deputy Keeper of the Records (PRONI T510/1)

7.41 Down Survey parish map of Dunbo. Courtesy of Deputy Keeper of the Records (PRONI D597/3)

7.42 Courtesy of Deputy Keeper of the Records (PRONI T510/1)

7.43 Courtesy of Deputy Keeper of the Records (PRONI T510/1)

7.44 Crown Copyright. DfC-HED

7.45 Crown Copyright. DfC-HED

7.46 Courtesy of Deputy Keeper of the Records (PRONI T510/1)

7.47 Courtesy of Deputy Keeper of the Records (PRONI T510/1)

7.48 Crown Copyright. DfC-HED

7.49 Crown Copyright. DfC-HED

7.50 Crown Copyright. DfC-HED

7.51 Courtesy of Deputy Keeper of the Records (PRONI T510/1)

7.52 Courtesy of Deputy Keeper of the Records (PRONI T510/1)

7.53 Courtesy of Deputy Keeper of the Records (PRONI T510/1)

7.54 Courtesy of Deputy Keeper of the Records (PRONI T510/1)

7.55 Crown Copyright. DfC-HED

7.56 Courtesy of Deputy Keeper of the Records (PRONI T510/1)

7.57 Courtesy of Deputy Keeper of the Records (PRONI T510/1)

7.58 Down Survey parish map of Drumcross and Baltiagh. Courtesy of Deputy Keeper of the Records (PRONI D5927/2)

7.59 Down Survey parish map of Drumcross and Baltiagh. Courtesy of Deputy Keeper of the Records (PRONI D5927/2)

7.60 Down Survey Barony map of Keenaght. Courtesy of Deputy Keeper of the Records (PRONI D597/2)

7.61 Crown Copyright. DfC-HED

7.62 Down Survey Barony map of Tirkeeran. Courtesy of Deputy Keeper of the Records (PRONI D597/3)

Dungiven Priory Exemplar

20 Courtesy of Deputy Keeper of the Records (PRONI T510/1)

21 Crown Copyright. DfC-HED

22 AECOM/IAC Archaeology

8. Discussion & Conclusion

8.1 IAC Archaeology

Index

Note: reference in *italics* denotes a Figure